SUB, *199*
TEST, *201*
VERR (286), *292*
VERW (286), *292*
WAIT, *293*
XCHG, *112*
XLAT or XLATB, *113*
XOR, *203*

TASM Directives

%BIN, *453*
%CONDS, *454*
%CREF, *455*
%CREFALL, *456*
%CREFREF, *456*
%CREFUREF, *456*
%CTLS, *456*
%DEPTH, *458*
%LINUM, *465*
%LIST, *465*
%MACS, *466*
%NEWPAGE, *468*
%NOCONDS, *469*
%NOCREF, *469*
%NOCTLS, *469*
%NOINCL, *469*
%NOLIST, *470*
%NOMACS, *470*
%NOSYMS, *470*
%NOTRUNC, *470*
%OUT, *471*
%PAGESIZE, *476*
%PCNT, *477*
%POPLCTL, *477*
%PUSHLCTL, *478*
%SUBTTL, *480*
%SYMS, *480*
%TABSIZE, *481*
%TEXT, *481*
%TITLE, *483*
%TRUNC, *483*
.186, *447*
.286, *447*
.286P, *448*
.287, *449*
.386, *449*
.386P, *450*
.387, *451*
.8086, *452*
.8087, *452*
.ALPHA, *311*
.CODE, *314*
.CONST, *317*
.CREF, *455*
.DATA, *315*
.DATA?, *315*
.ERR, *459*
.ERR1, *459*
.ERR2, *459*
.ERRB, *459*
.ERRDEF, *459*
.ERRDIF or .ERRDIFI, *459*
.ERRE, *459*
.ERRIDN or .ERRIDNI, *459*
.ERRNB, *459*

.ERRNDEF, *459*
.ERRNZ, *459*
.FARDATA, *318*
.FARDATA?, *318*
.LALL, *463*
.LFCOND, *464*
.LIST, *466*
.MODEL, *320*
.RADIX, *368*
.SALL, *479*
.SEQ, *311*
.SFCOND, *479*
.STACK, *322*
.TFCOND, *482*
.XALL, *485*
.XCREF, *485*
.XLIST, *485*
=, *378*
ALIGN, *344*
ARG, *407*
ASSUME, *312*
CATSTR, *345*
CODESEG, *314*
COMM, *108*
COMMENT, *440*
CONST, *317*
DATASEG, *315*
DB, *346*
DD, *347*
DF, *347*
DISPLAY, *457*
DOSSEG, *316*
DQ, *348*
DT, *347*
DW, *349*
ELSE, *410*
ELSEIF, *411*
ELSEIF1, *411*
ELSEIF2, *411*
ELSEIFB, *411*
ELSEIFDEF, *411*
ELSEIFDIF, *411*
ELSEIFDIFI, *411*
ELSEIFE, *411*
ELSEIFIDN, *411*
ELSEIFIDNI, *411*
ELSEIFNB, *411*
ELSEIFNDEF, *411*
EMUL, *458*
END, *317*
ENDIF, *412*
ENDM, *413*
ENDP, *414*
ENDS, *350*
EQU, *378*
ERR, *459*
ERRIF, *459*
ERRIF1, *459*
ERRIF2, *459*
ERRIFB, *459*
ERRIFDEF, *459*
ERRIFDIF, *459*
ERRIFDIFI, *459*
ERRIFE, *459*
ERRIFIDN, *459*
ERRIFIDNI, *459*
ERRIFNB, *459*
ERRIFNDEF, *459*

GROUP, *319*
IF, *420*
IF1, *420*
IF2, *420*
IFB, *420*
IFDEF, *420*
IFDIF or IFDIFI, *420*
IFE, *420*
IFIDN or IFIDNI, *420*
IFNB, *420*
IFNDEF, *420*
INCLUDE, *422*
INCLUDELIB, *423*
INSTR, *356*
IRP, *423*
IRPC, *424*
JUMPS, *462*
LABEL, *356*
LOCAL, *425*
LOCALS, *426*
MACRO, *427*
MASM, *466*
MASM51, *466*
MODEL, *320*
MULTERRS, *467*
NAME, *468*
NOEMUL, *469*
NOJUMPS, *462*
NOLOCALS, *426*
NOMASM, *466*
NOMASM51, *466*
NOMULTERRS, *470*
NOWARN, *471*
ORG, *364*
P186, *472*
P286, *472*
P286N, *472*
P287, *472*
P386, *472*
P386N, *473*
P387, *473*
P8086, *473*
P8087, *473*
PAGE, *475*
PNO87, *473*
PROC, *428*
PUBLIC, *430*
PURGE, *431*
QUIRKS, *478*
RADIX, *368*
RECORD, *369*
REPT, *431*
SEGMENT, *321*
SIZESTR, *373*
STACK, *322*
STRUC, *375*
SUBSTR, *377*
SUBTTL, *480*
TITLE, *483*
UDATASEG, *323*
UFARDATA, *323*
UNION, *380*
WARN, *484*

The Waite Group's
Turbo Assembler®
Bible

Gary Syck

SAMS

A Division of Macmillan Computer Publishing

11711 North College, Carmel, Indiana 46032 USA

For My Father

FIRST EDITION
FIRST PRINTING—1991

International Standard Book Number: 0-672-22716-9
Library of Congress Catalog Card Number: 90-62944

From The Waite Group
Development Editors: *Mitchell Waite and Scott Calamar*
Editorial Director: *Scott Calamar*
Managing Editor: *Karen Marcus*
Assistant Editor: *Joel Fugazzotto*
Content Editor: *James Stockford*
Technical Reviewer: *Christopher Hill*

From SAMS
Publishing Director: *Richard K. Swadley*
Product Manager: *Joseph B. Wikert*
Acquisitions Editor: *Richard K. Swadley*
Development Editor: *Dan Derrick*
Production Editor: *Rich Limacher*
Cover Design: *Glenn Santner*
Illustrator: *Don Clemons, T. R. Emrick*
Compositor: *Douglas and Gayle*
Production Assistance: *Scott Boucher, Brad Chinn, Denny Hager, Tami Hughes, Lisa Naddy, Dennis Sheehan, Louise Shinault, Bruce Steed, Christine Young*

Indexers: *Hilary Adams*

Printed in the United States of America

Contents

Preface

Acknowledgments

About the Author

Introduction

I. Programming MS-DOS Systems   1

1   Overview of the MS-DOS Operating System   3

2   Introduction to Using Turbo Assembler   21

3   Introduction to the Turbo Debugger   51

II. Processor Instructions   63

4   Data Movement Instructions   65

5   Arithmetic, Logic, and Bit-Shift Instructions 115

6   Procedures, Loops, and Jumps   205

7   Processor Control and Protected Mode Operation 245

III. TASM Directives and Operators

295

8 Segment Declaration   297

9 Data Definition and Storage Allocation   325

10 Macros, Procedures, and Tools for Modular Programs   385

11 Code Generation, Error Handling, and Listings   433

IV. Techniques

487

12 Writing Assembly Modules for High Level Languages   489

13 Using System Resources   511

14 Accessing and Controlling the Hardware   543

15 Video Control: Text and Graphics   565

V. Appendixes

599

A TASM and TLink Command-Line Options   601

B Debugger Commands   605

C BIOS and DOS Interrupts and Functions   611

D ASCII Conversions   681

Preface

Every year compilers for high level languages get a little smarter. The code they produce gets smaller and faster. But despite all their progress, programmers can still squeeze a bit more efficiency from a program by turning to assembly language. Other reasons for using assembly language are: to access hardware, to extend languages that do not provide a way to access MS-DOS or BIOS, or just for the fun of it.

Just as the compilers are getting better at generating efficient object code, assemblers are getting better at providing high level concepts like modular programming and abstract data types. With these new features, using assembly language is no more difficult than using any other computer language.

Whether you need only an occasional assembly routine or you intend to write everything in assembly language, this book gives you the knowledge required to use Turbo Assembler with confidence. The provided examples show you how to use assembly language in order to solve real problems in the MS-DOS environment. The quick start tutorials at the beginning of the book illustrate just how easy it is to get started with assembly language. After that, the in-depth tutorials cover all other aspects of the assembler.

Because assembly language is often used to interface directly with BIOS, MS-DOS, and your hardware, the last four chapters are dedicated to showing you how these things work. The examples come from actual programs so that you can see some practical uses for assembly language.

This book is designed to be used by programmers at all experience levels. If you are just starting out with assembler, reading through the tutorials in order and working the examples will ensure that you grasp all the key ideas of assembly language. Programmers who know a little bit about this language should read through parts two and three to find out about the commands available in Turbo Assembler. For the more experienced programmer, the reference pages at the end of each chapter (in Parts II and III) provide a quick way to get information on any given instruction or directive.

The Waite Group hopes that you are pleased with the convenience and utility of this book. If you have questions or suggestions, or if you would like to contribute to a future revision, please feel free to contact us at 100 Shoreline Highway, Building A, Suite 285, Mill Valley, California 94941, U.S.A.

Acknowledgments

From the author:

I would like to acknowledge several of the people who have made significant contributions to this book. First I would like to thank the people of The Waite Group who kept me on track through this project, specifically Scott Calamar, James Stockford, and Chris Hill. Many others have also made contributions: Harry Letize and Dick Balaska who taught me assembly language, Steve Hope who showed me how to get inside MS-DOS computers, and of course my wife Kathy who put up with many evenings of neglect while I worked on this book.

Gary Syck

From The Waite Group:

Special thanks to author Gary Syck for his hard and diligent work on this book, and for being one of the most professional and accommodating authors The Waite Group has worked with. Thanks to Nan Borreson of Borland International for timely betas and product support assistance. Thanks to Richard Swadley for being a supportive and good-natured "anchor" in a sea of changes. We appreciate the hard work and programming expertise of Chris Hill in reviewing the manuscript for technical accuracy. Thanks to Jim Stockford for "returning to the scene of the crime" and editing the content of this Bible. Thanks to Joel Fugazzotto for his ongoing support and assistance, and to Ruth Myers for enduring the never-ending rigors of copying and shipping. And finally, thanks to Mitchell Waite for his inspiration, advice, and life wisdom.

Scott Calamar

Trademarks

All terms mentioned in this book that are known to be trademarks or service marks are listed below. In addition, terms suspected of being trademarks or service marks have been appropriately capitalized. SAMS cannot attest to the accuracy of this information. Use of a term in this book should not be regarded as affecting the validity of any trademark or service mark.

ANSI is a registered trademark of American National Standards Institute.

IBM is a registered trademark and IBM PC, IBM XT, and PS/2 are trademarks of International Business Machines Corporation.

Intel, Intel 8088, 8086, 80186, 80286, 80386, 8087, 80287, and 80387 are registered trademarks of Intel Corporation.

Lotus and 1-2-3 are registered trademarks of Lotus Development Corporation.

Microsoft and MS-DOS are registered trademarks and Codeview is a trademark of Microsoft Corporation.

Turbo Assembler and Turbo Debugger are registered trademarks of Borland International, Inc.

About the Author

Gary Syck works as a computer programmer in the Puget Sound area. He has been programming using a variety of systems since 1980. Most of these programs have been written in assembly language, C, and Pascal. He is currently working on data communications programs for the IBM PC, but he's also interested in databases and graphics programming.

Introduction

The Waite Group's Turbo Assembler Bible is made up of four major parts. The first part describes the MS-DOS operating system and introduces Turbo Assembler and Turbo Debugger. The second and third parts contain descriptions of the instructions and directives used by Turbo Assembler. The chapters in these parts include both an in-depth tutorial and a quick reference guide for all of the assembler directives and processor instructions. The last part shows how to use assembly language programs to control various parts of the computer.

PART I: PROGRAMMING MS-DOS SYSTEMS

This part gives some background on programming MS-DOS systems, and how to use Turbo Assembler to write programs and Turbo Debugger to debug programs.

Chapter 1: Overview of the MS-DOS Operating System

This chapter shows you how an MS-DOS system is organized. It includes information about the 80x86 family of microprocessors, MS-DOS functions, ROM BIOS, and the memory map.

Chapter 2: Introduction to Using Turbo Assembler

This chapter is a quick tour through the instructions and directives that make up an assembly language program. Here you learn how to write, assemble, link, and run simple assembly language programs. The basic concepts from this chapter give you the background required to follow the examples used throughout the rest of the book.

Chapter 3: Introduction to the Turbo Debugger

This chapter is a hands-on description of how to use Turbo Debugger. It takes you through a sample debugging session that uses many of the features of Turbo Debugger to find the problem in a program example.

**PART II:
PROCESSOR
INSTRUCTIONS**

Part II shows all the instructions used by the 8088 through 80386 processors. The instructions are grouped into four chapters by categories.

Chapter 4: Data Movement Instructions

The instructions in this chapter are used to move data between memory and the registers of the 80x86 processors. This chapter includes information on the many ways of addressing memory, the stack, and the powerful string instructions.

Chapter 5: Arithmetic, Logic, and Bit-Shift Instructions

This chapter teaches you the instructions used to manipulate data. It describes the instructions for the mathematical operations (adding, subtracting, multiplying, and dividing); logical operations (and, or, not, exclusive or); and bit-shift operations.

Chapter 6: Procedures, Loops, and Jumps

The instructions in this chapter are used to transfer control from one area of a program to another. There are several examples of how to use these instructions to emulate the flow of control constructs used in high level language, such as *while* and *for* loops, *if-then-else* decisions, and functions.

Chapter 7: Processor Control and Protected Mode Operation

This chapter describes the flags and special instructions used to control the microprocessor. Many of the instructions described here deal with the protected mode that is used in 80286 and 80386 processors. A brief example of how to switch in and out of protected mode on the 80386 is also included.

**PART III:
TASM DIRECTIVES
AND OPERATORS**

This part contains the tutorials and reference pages for the directives and operators used in Turbo Assembler programs. You learn how to manipulate segments, store data, create modular programs, and use the advanced conditional assembly capabilities of Turbo Assembler.

Chapter 8: Segment Declaration

This chapter describes the directives used to declare and use segments. Not only do you learn about the powerful, but complex, traditional segment declarations; but you also see how to use the new simplified segment declarations.

Chapter 9: Data Definition and Storage Allocation

This chapter leads you from the simple storage allocation directives, such as DB and DW, through more complex memory structures. These directives enable you to use abstract data items, such as those found in high level languages like C and Pascal.

Chapter 10: Macros, Procedures, and Tools for Modular Programs

Modular programming makes it easier to write and maintain large programs. This chapter describes the directives used in Turbo Assembler to implement modular programs. The trade-offs between macros and procedures are discussed, as well as the generation of function libraries.

Chapter 11: Code Generation, Error Handling, and Listings

In this chapter you learn how to make different configurations of your program from a single source file by using conditional assembly directives. You also see how to modify the way certain instructions (such as those for the floating point) are assembled. The last part of this chapter shows you how to control what kind of information is in the listing file and how it is formatted.

PART IV:
TECHNIQUES

This part shows you how to use the skills gained in the previous parts in order to create useful assembly language programs. These chapters teach you how to add assembly language routines to high level languages, how to use the resources provided by BIOS and MS-DOS, and how to use your hardware directly. The last chapter ties this all together in several routines in order to handle the various video systems available for IBM PCs and compatibles.

Chapter 12: Writing Assembly Modules for High Level Languages

Many programmers prefer to write most of a program in a high level language, and use assembler for parts of the program that require optimum performance or special hardware interfaces. This chapter shows you how to make function calls, pass parameters, and share data between high level languages and assembly routines. An example is provided that shows you how to convert a routine from C to assembly language in order to increase performance.

Chapter 13: Using System Resources

This chapter teaches how to use BIOS and MS-DOS to find out what resources are available and how they may be used. You learn how best to use memory, printers, the keyboard, and serial ports.

Chapter 14: Accessing and Controlling the Hardware

This chapter continues the discussion of resources begun in the previous chapter. It takes the discussion to another (even more basic) level by describing how to interface directly with the hardware associated with an IBM PC or compatible computer. The examples show you how to access the keyboard and serial ports directly.

Chapter 15: Video Control: Text and Graphics

This chapter goes into detail on how to use the video cards commonly used in IBM PCs and compatibles. The CGA, EGA, and VGA cards are fully explained through the use of examples that exploit their capabilities.

**CHAPTER
ORGANIZATION**

Chapters 4 through 11 begin with a tutorial section that fully describes the commands related to that chapter. The tutorial defines all the terms and concepts necessary to understand the commands presented. Each command is compared and contrasted to similar commands, so that you are able to choose the best command for every situation in your programs. The tutorial sections also contain program examples that show you how these commands can be used.

After each tutorial and following a summary, these chapters contain reference entries for each command described in the chapter. Each reference entry provides a structured guide to the purpose, syntax, usage, and appropriate examples of the command. Figures I-1 and I-2 illustrate the format of these reference pages.

To make this book more useful as a reference guide, the inside front and back covers contain "locator tables." These tables enable you to find any particular reference entry (listed alphabetically under all appropriate categories) and the page on which it appears.

Expanded name of the instruction

A bullet appears if the instruction is available in the 8088/8086, 80286, and 80386 processors

Mnemonic for the instruction

Short description of where instruction is used

Syntax showing mnemonic and operands

Describes how the flags are affected

Special notes about the instruction indicating allowable combinations of operands and typical use of the instruction

Related instructions and how they are related

Shows encoding of instruction and timing for each addressing mode. Timing is shown in number of clock cycles needed to execute the instruction. Here are the symbols used:

88 = 8088, 86 = 8086, 286 = 80286 in real mode, 386 = 80386 in real mode.

(w) = Clock cycles for word operands in 8088

A - in the timing information denotes range not a subtraction

n = number of repetitions or bit shifts, (noj) = no jump taken

EA = Time required to compute the effective address. Depends on the addressing mode as follows:

Mode	Sample Operand Formats	Clock Cycles
Base or Index	[bx],[bp],[si],[di]	5
Displacement	label	6
Base + Index	[bx + si], [bp + di]	7
	[bx + di], [bp + si]	8
Base or Index + disp	[bp + 6], array [si]	9
Base + Index + disp	[bx + si + 2], [bp + di + 4]	11
	[bx + di + 6], [bp + si + 2]	12
Segment Override	ds:[bp + 10]	Add 2 extra clock cycles

One or more examples illustrating how the instruction is used

---

Pop Data Off of the Stack   88/86   286   386
▲   ▲   ▲

POP

PURPOSE To get a word or double word (80386 only) from the top of the stack, and then adjust the stack pointer.

SYNTAX pop   reg/mem   *Pop the data into a 16-bit register or memory location.*

FLAGS The flags are unaffected by this instruction.

COMMENTS The stack is used to store temporary values and the return addresses of functions. Except in protected mode there is no checking to see if the stack has overflowed or underflowed. The programmer must be certain that there is enough room in the stack for the program.

SEE ALSO
POPA, POPF   *Other pop instructions*
PUSH, PUSHA, PUSHF   *To put data on the stack*

TIMING

Addressing	Encoding	Example		88/86	286	386
reg	01011reg	pop	ax	12/8	5	4
mem	10001111	pop	data	25/17+EA	5	5
	mod,000,r/m displacement					
segreg	000,sreg,111	pop	es	12/8	5	7
80386 segreg	00001111	pop	fs	-	-	7
	10,sreg,001					

EXAMPLE The stack is often used to save a register, so that the register can be used for something else. This is important when using the special purpose registers.

```
; This routine moves a string from Source to Dest.
; The size of the string is in the first byte of the string.
; The CX, SI, DI, and ES registers are saved on the stack
; and then POPped off after the move.

SafeCpy   PROC
          push cx                    ; Save cx
          push si                    ; Save si
          push di                    ; Save di
          push es                    ; Save es
          mov  si,offset Source
          mov  di,offset Dest
          push ds                    ; Copy the DS register
          pop  es                    ; into the ES register
          mov  cl,[si]               ; Get the length
          xor  ch,ch
          cld                        ; Set direction to forward
          rep  movsb                 ; Copy the string
          pop  es                    ; Restore es The registers are
                                     ; restored in the opposite
                                     ; order from when they were
                                     ; saved.
```

Figure I-1. *Format of reference entry for 80x86 instructions.*

Name of directive	
Short description of where directive is used	
Syntax showing operands, if any	
Special notes about the directive explaining where it is particularly useful and why	
Related directives and how they are related	
An example illustrating how the directive is used	

ALIGN

PURPOSE To move the location counter to the next boundary address.

SYNTAX ALIGN boundary *The boundary must be a power of two (2, 4, 8, etc.).*

COMMENTS The different processors in the 80x86 family can get better performance by aligning data to boundaries that match the data bus size of the chip. Some high level languages align data on specific boundaries. The ALIGN directive can make the data compatible.

SEE ALSO EVEN *Align to even-numbered addresses*

EXAMPLE
```
          .MODEL   SMALL
          .DATA
data1     DB    1      ; Unaligned data
          ALIGN   4      ; Typical alignment on 80386 for
                         ; performance
data2     DW    ?      ; Aligned data
```

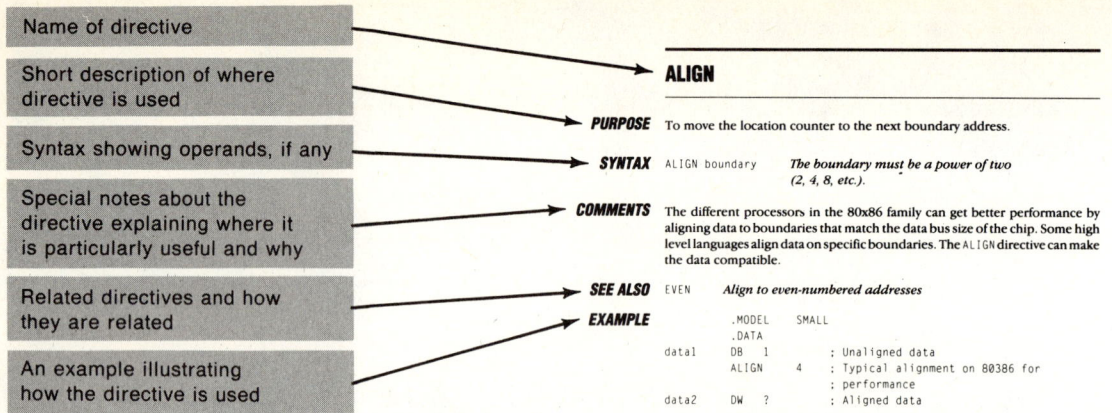

Figure I-2. *Format of reference entry for Turbo Assembler directives.*

I

Programming MS-DOS Systems

► Overview of the MS-DOS Operating System,

► Introduction to Using Turbo Assembler,

► Introduction to the Turbo Debugger,

Chapter *1* *Overview of the MS-DOS Operating System*

The first step in writing a computer program is to understand the environment in which the program runs. The type of processor, memory, peripherals, and operating system affect how to design and code your program. You would not design a large graphical interface for a system lacking the processing power or memory to handle it. A simple text-based interface is much more appropriate for this kind of system.

The basic environment for Turbo Assembler programs is an IBM PC-compatible computer running the MS-DOS operating system. You should be familiar with this environment and the possible variations before diving into a Turbo Assembler programming project. This chapter shows you what the MS-DOS environment is all about and how your programs interact with it.

If you have programmed MS-DOS computers in high level languages, you may be familiar with some of the information presented here. Now you must become familiar with it from the point of view of an assembly language programmer. In many cases this means looking at details of the environment that you never considered when using a high level language, such as C or Pascal.

Every program in the system must interact with MS-DOS in some way. In the simplest case, MS-DOS loads the program. In other cases it manages memory and peripherals for the program. The first part of this chapter shows you how the MS-DOS operating system works and how your programs interact with it.

Another aspect of the MS-DOS system that is fundamental to the way programs work is the 80x86 processor. Each instruction in an assembly language program represents an 80x86 instruction. Therefore, you need to understand the 80x86 in order to write assembly language programs for it. The first part of this chapter describes the 80x86 processor architecture.

The 80x86 Processor Family

All MS-DOS computers are built around one of the CPUs in the Intel Corporation 80x86 family. All of the newer chips in this family are compatible with older chips in the family. You can write programs for any MS-DOS computer by using only instructions for the oldest (8088) CPU. Most MS-DOS programs ignore the new instructions of the newer processors. The main advantage of using a newer processor with MS-DOS is that each new chip is faster than the last.

Another feature of the newer processors is the ability to use more memory. The 8088 and 8086 can address up to a megabyte (1,048,576 bytes) of memory. The 80286 can address up to 16 megabytes of memory, and the 80386 can address up to 4 gigabytes (4,294,967,296 bytes). Unfortunately, MS-DOS is not designed to use all of this memory. You need to write software that accesses this memory without using MS-DOS or install an expanded memory driver to access the memory. The advantage of the expanded memory driver is that it provides an allocation scheme, as does MS-DOS, for main memory. This prevents multiple programs that use expanded memory from interfering with each other.

Segmented Memory

Programs for the 80x86 family use memory in a series of overlapping 64K segments. Any reference to a memory location must include the address of the segment being used along with the offset of the data in the segment. The processor uses four segment registers to hold segment addresses for various types of operations. The Code Segment (CS) register is the segment used for instructions. The Data Segment (DS) register is where data comes from. The Stack Segment (SS) register gives the location of the stack. The last segment is the Extra Segment (ES). It is used as an auxiliary data segment. The common notation for referring to an 80x86 address is to give the segment, followed by a colon (:), then the offset. For example, the data at segment 40h and offset 12h is written as 40:12. Note that hexadecimal numbers are assumed when dealing with addresses. You can also specify an address with registers. For the data at offset 24h in the segment indicated by the DS register, write DS:24.

Figure 1-1 illustrates the segment concept. Note that each segment begins on a 16-byte boundary. This lets the CPU put a 20-bit address (enough for 1 megabyte of memory) in a 16-bit register. The CPU assumes that the lower four bits of the segment address are 0. When the CPU needs to get an instruction or a data item, it adds the 16-bit segment offset to the 20-bit segment address to get the actual address to use.

When an MS-DOS program starts the registers, CS, ES, and SS are ready for use. The program must set the DS register to point to the data area for the program. Programs that use more than 64K of data will have to change the values of the DS and ES registers as required to access the data being used.

Physical Memory

65620
65604
65588
65572
65556

Segment 3 { Segment 2 {

92
76
80
64
48
32
16
0

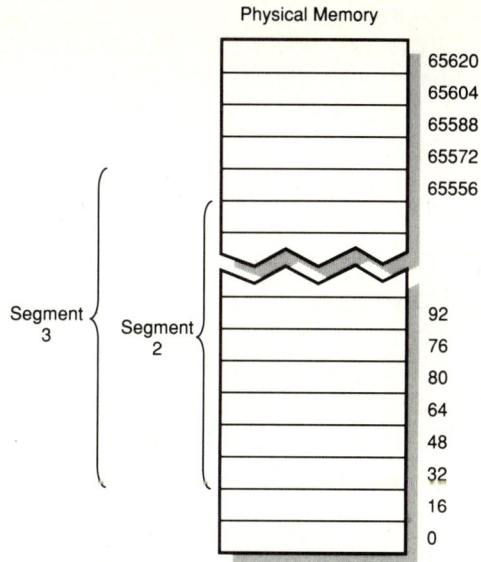

Figure 1-1. *Memory segmentation.*

Registers

There are nine 16-bit registers. Eight of these can be used in mathematical or data movement instructions. The ninth is the Instruction Pointer (IP). It is used to determine the location of the next instruction to execute. There are special instructions that change the contents of the IP register.

The eight 16-bit registers are not exactly general purpose registers. Although any one of them can be used as a data register, each has some special purpose in some instructions. Table 1-1 summarizes the uses of each register.

There are also eight 8-bit registers. These registers are actually the high and low bytes of the AX, BX, CX, and DX registers. The 8-bit registers use the same first letter as the corresponding 16-bit register with an H (high byte) or an L (low byte) in place of the X. For example, the AX register is divided into the AH and AL registers.

The last register is the flags register. This register contains flags that tell things about the last arithmetic operation, the state of interrupts, and whether string operations move backwards or forwards through memory. Figure 1-2 shows the meaning of the bits in the flags register. There are several instructions for setting and clearing flags and testing the value of certain flags. Table 1-2 summarizes these instructions.

Table 1-1. *Register Usage*

Register	Use
AX	Accumulator. Some instructions (such as multiply and divide) can use only this register.
BX	Base index register. Used in data address calculations.
CX	Loop and repetition counter.
DX	Extended accumulator and data. Used in 32-bit operations.
SI	Source Index. Used in string operations.
DI	Destination Index. Used in string operations.
SP	The Stack Pointer.
BP	Base Pointer. Used in data address calculations.
CS	Code Segment. The number of the segment used for code.
DS	Data Segment. The number of the segment used for data.
ES	Extra Segment. The number of the auxiliary data segment.
SS	Stack Segment. The number of the segment used for the stack.

Table 1-2. *Flag Manipulation Instructions*

Mnemonic	Description
CLC	Clear the carry flag
CLD	Clear the direction flag
CLI	Clear the interrupts enabled flag
CMC	Complement the carry flag
LAHF	Copy the low byte of the flags register to AH
POPF	Put the word from the top of the stack into the flags register
PUSHF	Put the flags register onto the top of the stack
SAHF	Copy AH into the low byte of the flags register
STC	Set the carry flag
STD	Set the direction flag
STI	Set the interrupts enabled flag

15	14	13	12	11	10	9	8	7	6	5	4	3	2	1	0
				OF	DF	IF	TF	SF	ZF		AF		PF		CF

Unused

String
Direction

Overflow

Enable
Interrupts

Trap Sign Zero

Auxiliary
Carry

Parity

Carry

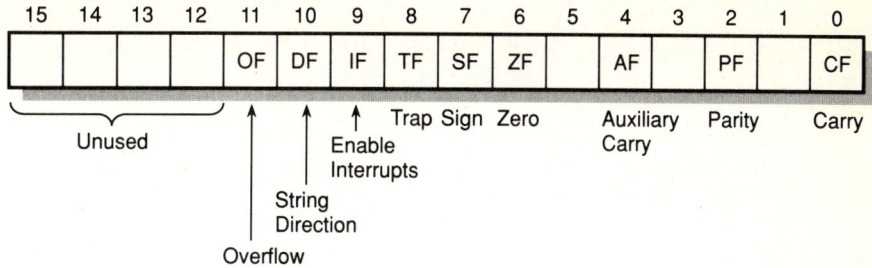

Figure 1-2. *The flags register.*

The Stack

The stack is vital to the proper execution of subroutines, including calls to MS-DOS functions. When a program calls a subroutine, it pushes the address of the instruction following the call on the stack. When the subroutine is done, it pops the address off of the stack and resumes executing at that point. Another use for the stack is to temporarily. save the contents of a register while the register is used for something else. For example, if a program needs to loop through a series of instructions a number of times, it must use the CX register. If the CX register holds some important piece of data, then the program should push it on the stack while the loop runs and then pop it off when the loop finishes. Some programs use the stack to pass from one procedure to another.

All stack operations use memory pointed to by the stack segment register (SS). The stack pointer (SP) register is the offset into this segment of the last data pushed on the stack. When a program pushes data on the stack, the CPU decrements the SP register by two and stores the data at the new location pointed to by SS:SP. To pop the data, the CPU reads the data at SS:SP, then increments the SP register by two. Notice that all stack operations use 16-bit values. Thus the SP register always moves two bytes at a time.

The stack is often the source of bugs in programs. If you push several registers on the stack, you must pop them off in the reverse order. Failure to use the correct order results in data being restored to the wrong register. Another common error is to pop too many or too few items off of the stack and then try to return from a subroutine. This results in the CPU trying to execute code at the wrong location, with disastrous results. At best, the program will crash; at worst, it can jump to the routine to format your hard disk.

You can use the stack to move data from one register to another. For example, no instructions exist to move the data in a segment register to another segment register. You can use the stack to overcome this problem with the following code:

```
    .
    .
    .
push ds          ; Save the DS register on the stack
pop  es          ; Put the value in the ES register
    .
    .
    .
```

Programs can move the stack by modifying the SS and SP registers. When moving the stack, be careful not to use it until you have changed both the SS and SP registers. Despite careful programming you could still have a problem if an interrupt occurs in the middle of the stack change code. To prevent this problem, the CPU ignores interrupts for one instruction following any change to the SS register. If the next instruction loads the SP register, then you should have no trouble with interrupts:

```
mov  ax, SEG NewStackSeg   ; Get the new segment for the
                           ; stack into AX
mov  ss, ax                ; Load the stack segment
                           ; register
mov  sp, 1024              ; Set the stack pointer. This
                           ; instruction cannot be
                           ; interrupted due to the
                           ; preceding change of the SS
                           ; register
```

Interrupts

Hardware devices in the computer use interrupts to get the CPU's attention. For example, when you press a key, the circuits that control the keyboard generate an interrupt so that the CPU knows it must read the keyboard data. When an interrupt occurs, the CPU finishes the instruction currently executing. It then pushes first the flags, then CS, then IP, and finally jumps to the interrupt handler for the specific interrupt. When the interrupt handler is done, it executes an IRET instruction, which pops IP, CS, and the flags from the stack so that execution resumes at the instruction following the interrupted instruction.

The CPU knows where to go by looking up the address in the interrupt vector table. This table begins at location 0:0 and extends up to location 40:0. Each entry is four bytes long and contains the offset and segment of the interrupt handler. For example, pressing or releasing a key generates interrupt number 9. The ninth entry in the interrupt vector table begins at location 0:24h (9 * 4). The first word at this location is the offset of the address of the routine to use, and the second word is the segment of the routine.

Your program can change the address of any interrupt, but you must be careful that the interrupt being changed does not occur while it is being changed. The easiest way is to let MS-DOS do the change. Function 25h sets an interrupt vector, and function 35h reads the current interrupt location. (See Chapter 14 for more information on using interrupts.)

MS-DOS

MS-DOS is a single-tasking microcomputer operating system designed for use on 80x86-based computers. Most of the computers that run MS-DOS are compatible with the IBM PC. This is not a requirement; many MS-DOS systems have little more in common with the IBM PC than the type of processor used.

MS-DOS handles many of the details of using an 80x86-based computer system. You can rely on MS-DOS to properly load your program, manage memory, keep track of disk files, send data to peripherals, and do many other things as well. Without this help, even a simple programming project would be too much. Imagine how difficult writing a database application would be if MS-DOS did not handle files for you.

The Parts of MS-DOS

MS-DOS is divided into several subsystems. Figure 1-3 is a memory map of an MS-DOS system. Note that there are four major parts of MS-DOS. The part that most people see is the command processor. The command processor is a program called COMMAND.COM that MS-DOS uses to get commands from users. It prints the MS-DOS prompt, gets input from the user, and—if the input is a valid command—executes the command. The command processor also executes batch files, in which case the input comes from a file instead of a user.

THE FILE SYSTEM One of the jobs of the file system routines is to control the way files are arranged on the disk. Figure 1-4 shows the layout of an MS-DOS disk. A disk is divided into a number of clusters which are made up of a number of sectors which are, in turn, made up of bytes of data. Each cluster on the disk can be one of five types of data. The first type is the configuration/boot data. This type of data is always in the first cluster on the disk. Whenever the computer is powered up or reset, a program in the BIOS ROM reads the configuration information and the boot program into memory. Then it jumps to the boot program, which reads the rest of MS-DOS into memory.

```
┌─────────────────────────┐
│         ROM BIOS        │
│                         │  FE00:0
├─────────────────────────┤
│        ROM BASIC        │
│      (IBM PC Only)      │  F600:0
├─────────────────────────┤
│       I/O Adapter       │
│        ROM Space        │
├─────────────────────────┤
│      Fixed Disk ROM     │  C800:0
├─────────────────────────┤
│        Video BIOS       │
│                         │  C000:0
├─────────────────────────┤
│      CGA Video Buffer   │
│                         │  B800:0
├─────────────────────────┤
│  Monochrome Text Buffer │  B000:0
├─────────────────────────┤
│         EGA/VGA         │
│      Graphics Buffer    │
│                         │  A000:0
├─────────────────────────┤
│  Transient COMMAND.COM  │
└─────────────────────────┘  } Program
                                Memory
┌─────────────────────────┐
│  Resident COMMAND.COM   │
├─────────────────────────┤
│      Device Drivers     │
├─────────────────────────┤
│    File Control Blocks  │
├─────────────────────────┤
│         MS-DOS          │
│                         │  60:0
├─────────────────────────┤
│     MS-DOS Data Area    │  50:0
├─────────────────────────┤
│      BIOS Data Area     │  40:0
├─────────────────────────┤
│     Interrupt Vectors   │  0:0
└─────────────────────────┘
```

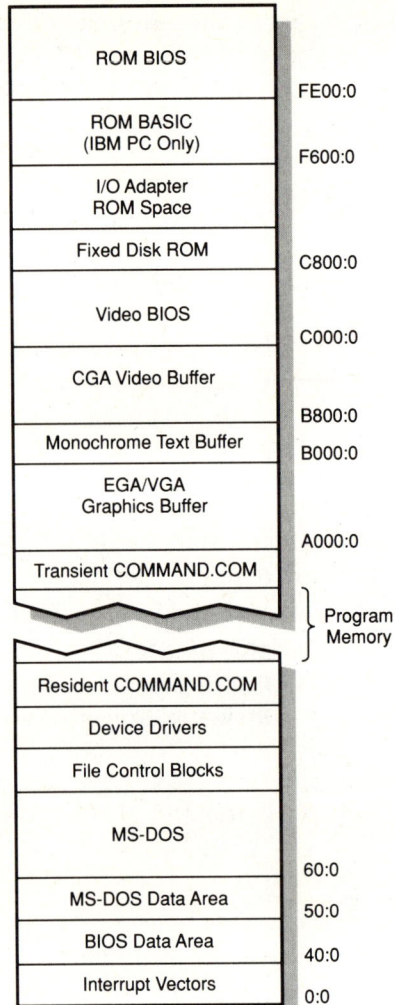

Figure 1-3. *DOS memory map.*

The next type of cluster is FAT information. The FAT (or File Allocation Table) contains an entry for each cluster on the disk. When combined with information from the directories, the FAT tells what files or directories are in each cluster.

The third type of cluster contains directory information. Each directory is a database of information about files and subdirectories. Figure 1-5 shows the format of the directory and how the FAT tells where the files are.

The files themselves are the fourth kind of cluster found on MS-DOS disks. Notice that a cluster can belong to only one file. If the file is smaller than the cluster, the remaining space is wasted. If your disk has a large number of very small files, it is possible to run out of clusters but still have a large amount of unused disk space. If you are in this situation, you should consider running a utility that reformats your disk with smaller clusters.

The fifth type of cluster is the unallocated space. These clusters are available to the file system when it needs to create or expand a file or directory. The FAT indicates that a cluster is unallocated by having a 0 in the entry for that cluster. When MS-DOS deletes or shortens a file, it modifies the FAT to indicate that the freed clusters are now available. The data that was in the file is still on the disk. If the clusters have not been assigned to another file and the clusters in the erased file were contiguous, a file unerase utility can restore the file simply by restoring its directory and FAT entries.

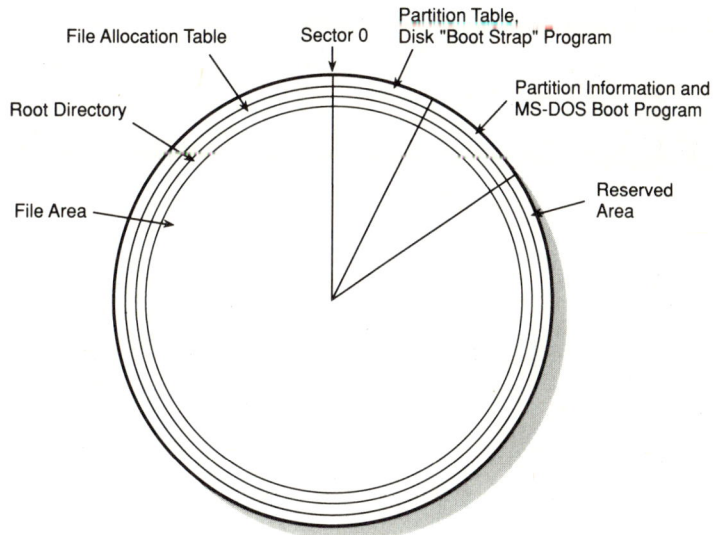

Figure 1-4. *The layout of a DOS disk.*

DEVICE DRIVERS   When the file system needs to read or write the disk, it calls a *device driver*. Device drivers let MS-DOS make use of different kinds of disk drives and other peripherals. From the point of view of MS-DOS, each device driver looks the same. MS-DOS can send a command to the device driver, such as "read sector 12," and the device driver does whatever is necessary to read sector 12 on its device.

Entries are 12 or 16 bits.
Each entry stands for a cluster.

Directory		FAT	
Byte 0	File Name	-16	⎫
		-14	⎬ Reserved clusters
		-15	
		-16	⎭
		0	⎫
		0	⎬ Unused clusters
		0	⎭
8	Extension		⎬ Clusters for other files
11	Attributes	Next Cluster #	
12	Reserved	0	Unused cluster
		-9	Bad cluster
			⎬ Clusters for other files
		Next Cluster #	
		Next Cluster #	
		-1	⎬ Last cluster in file
22	Last Changed Time		
24	Last Changed Date		
26	Starting Cluster Number		
28	File Size		
32			

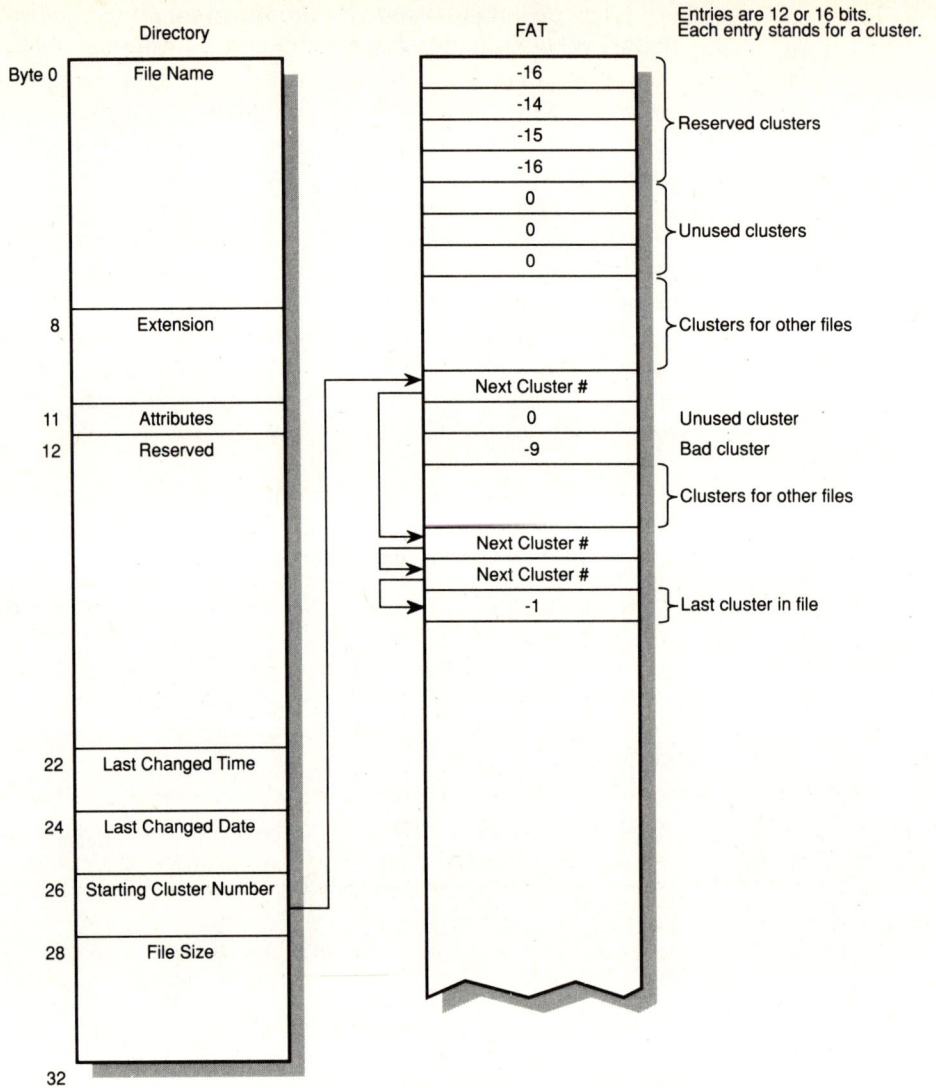

Figure 1-5. *Format of directories and the FAT.*

Several device drivers, such as those for the screen and the keyboard, are built into MS-DOS; but they can be replaced or more of them can be added by editing the CONFIG.SYS file. This must be in the root directory of the boot drive. A typical CONFIG.SYS file might contain these commands:

```
FILES = 20
BUFFERS = 20
DEVICE = ANSI.SYS
```

MS-DOS reads the CONFIG.SYS file during the boot process. In the preceding example, it would read the first line and set the maximum number of open files to 20. The second line tells MS-DOS to make 20 buffers for reading and writing files. The last line says to load a device driver named ANSI.SYS. The ANSI.SYS device driver replaces the built-in device driver for reading the keyboard and writing to the screen.

You should check your CONFIG.SYS file to see that it has at least 20 files, 20 buffers, and that it loads the ANSI.SYS driver. The first two settings are required for running Turbo Assembler, and the ANSI.SYS device driver is used by some of the sample programs in this book.

PROGRAM INTERFACE

The last part of MS-DOS is the program interface. This is the part that you need to know well, if you want to put MS-DOS to work in your programs. In order for MS-DOS to respond to a command, the program must give control to MS-DOS. This is done through a command called a *software interrupt*. The software interrupt works like a hardware interrupt; but, instead of being activated by an external event, it is activated by a software instruction. This is a way for one routine to give control to another and get control back when the second routine is done. The 80x86 allows up to 256 different interrupts, the first 16 of which are dedicated to hardware events. MS-DOS uses five of the remaining interrupts for programs to send it commands. Table 1-3 shows these MS-DOS interrupts.

Table 1-3. *MS-DOS Interrupts*

Interrupt	Description
20h	Terminate program (obsolete)
21h	General DOS Services
25h	Absolute disk read
26h	Absolute disk write
27h	Terminate and stay resident (obsolete)

MS-DOS can do much more than five things. The General DOS Services interrupt (21h) is the entry point for over 75 different functions. Programs can select which function to run by putting the function number in the AH register. MS-DOS looks at this register to see what function to run, and it looks at some of the other registers to get data for the function. (See Appendix C for a list of the MS-DOS functions.)

MS-DOS and Programs

When you type the name of a program at the MS-DOS prompt, you begin a chain of events that results in the program being executed. The first step in the chain is to find the program on the disk. Programs are stored in files on the disk. Each file has a unique name that identifies it. The name consists of four parts: drive letter, path name, file name, and extension. You can run the program simply by entering the file name and letting MS-DOS fill in the other parts of the name. There are three possible extensions for a file that MS-DOS can run. The .EXE and .COM extensions are files that contain 80x86 code, and .BAT files are batch files that can be executed by the command processor. MS-DOS tries each of these extensions in each directory that it searches to find the program. The first directory that MS-DOS looks at is the current directory. This is the directory whose files you see when you type DIR at the MS-DOS prompt. If the file is not in the current directory, then MS-DOS searches each directory specified in the PATH environment variable. (To see the names of the directories, type the command PATH at the MS-DOS prompt.) If the file is not in any of these directories, MS-DOS prints the message, "Bad command or filename."

If MS-DOS does find the file, the next step is to allocate some memory for the program to use. MS-DOS actually allocates two areas of memory for the program: one is for a copy of the environment variables, and the other is for the program itself. The environment variables contain data that was set up with the PROMPT, PATH, and SET commands. Many programs use these variables for configuration information.

Programs with the .EXE extension contain two numbers that determine the amount of memory MS-DOS allocates for the program. These numbers are set up by the linker or by special utility programs. One number tells MS-DOS the minimum amount of memory that the program needs. If the system does not have enough memory, MS-DOS prints "Insufficient memory" and returns control to the command processor. Otherwise it looks at the other variable to determine the maximum amount of memory that the program needs. If this value is zero, or larger than the available memory, MS-DOS allocates all available memory to the program. Once the program is loaded, it can use MS-DOS functions to modify the memory allocations.

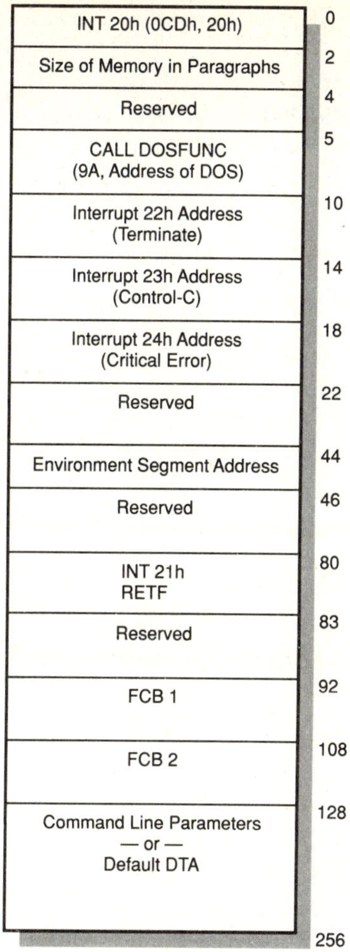

INT 20h (0CDh, 20h)	0
Size of Memory in Paragraphs	2
Reserved	4
CALL DOSFUNC (9A, Address of DOS)	5
Interrupt 22h Address (Terminate)	10
Interrupt 23h Address (Control-C)	14
Interrupt 24h Address (Critical Error)	18
Reserved	22
Environment Segment Address	44
Reserved	46
INT 21h RETF	80
Reserved	83
FCB 1	92
FCB 2	108
Command Line Parameters — or — Default DTA	128
	256

Figure 1-6. *Format of the PSP.*

The next step in running the program is to create a Program Segment Prefix (PSP). This is a block of memory that contains information about the program being loaded. Figure 1-6 shows the format of the PSP. One of the most common uses of the PSP is to get information that was on the command line and the values of the environment variables.

Now MS-DOS is ready to load the program into memory. When the program was linked, the linker had no way of knowing where in memory MS-DOS would put the program. To handle this problem, the linker puts information in .EXE files to tell the loader what locations in the program contain references to segment addresses. The program loader uses this information to "fix up" the segment references. Note that offsets are relative to some segment, so they do not need to be fixed up.

After fixing up the locations in the program, MS-DOS initializes some of the registers. It sets the stack segment (SS) and stack pointer (SP) registers to point to the end of the stack segment. The extra segment (ES) and data segment registers point to the PSP. The last registers to set up are the code segment (CS) and instruction pointer (IP) registers. Loading these registers causes the CPU to begin executing the program.

MS-DOS and Memory

MS-DOS manages memory. Before it runs a program, it allocates two memory areas for the program to use. It also provides functions for allocating memory, freeing memory, and changing the size of a previously allocated memory area. Most applications have MS-DOS allocate all available memory to the program when it starts up. This is fine if the program does not try to run any other programs while it is loaded. On the other hand, if the program *does* run other programs (say, to use FORMAT to format a data disk) it must free up enough memory for the other programs to run. This can be done by changing the size of the program memory area to become just large enough to contain the program. The following example shows how to do it:

```
        .MODEL SMALL
        .CODE
Start PROC
        mov   bx, ss            ; Get the location of the
                               ; stack segment (The last
                               ; segment in the program)
        mov   ax, cs            ; Get the location of the code
                               ; segment (The first segment
                               ; in the program)
        sub   bx, ax            ; Subtract the starting
                               ; location from the ending
                               ; location to get the size of
                               ; the program. (now in BX)
        add   bx, 1024/16       ; Add in the size of the stack
                               ; segment in 16-byte
                               ; paragraphs
        mov   ah, 4Ah           ; Put re-size memory area
                               ; command in AH
        int   21h              ; The location of the block is
                               ; already in ES, so call MS-DOS
        mov   ah, 4Ch           ; Put MS-DOS exit program
                               ; command in AH
        int   21h              ; Call MS-DOS
Start ENDP
        .STACK 1024
END Start
```

The first three lines of this example tell the assembler about the program that follows. (See Chapter 2 for more information about the format of assembler programs.) To calculate the size of the program, the program instructions use the facts that the code segment is at the beginning of the program and the stack segment is at the end of the program. MS-DOS expects the size to be the number of 16-byte paragraphs required. This is convenient because that is the way the segment registers are set up. MS-DOS also expects the ES register to contain the address of the memory segment to resize. This is also convenient because MS-DOS sets ES to this location before starting the program.

Some programs allocate memory only when they need it, and free it when they don't. For example, a program that reads a data file needs a place to put the data while it finds the information it needs. Once it has the required information, the buffer is no longer required and can be freed. When you are allocating and freeing memory, be careful that your program does not cause memory fragmentation. If the free memory areas are not next to each other, your program may not be able to allocate new memory areas because there is no single area large enough. Figure 1-7 illustrates this problem.

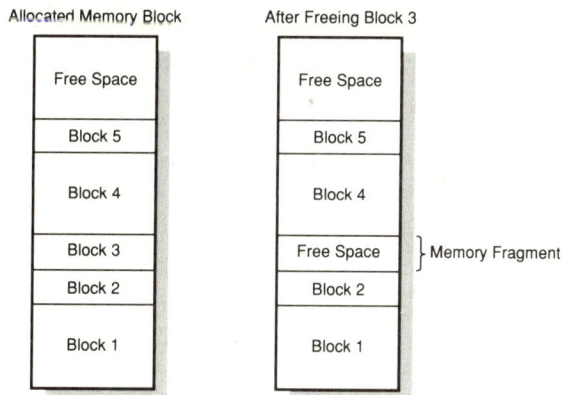

Allocated Memory Block	After Freeing Block 3	
Free Space	Free Space	
Block 5	Block 5	
Block 4	Block 4	
Block 3	Free Space	} Memory Fragment
Block 2	Block 2	
Block 1	Block 1	

Figure 1-7. *Memory fragmentation.*

The solution to memory fragmentation is to allocate as few blocks as possible. Programs that use the MS-DOS memory allocations often limit themselves to one memory block. When the program needs more data, the program expands the block. When it needs less data, it decreases the block size. This technique prevents memory fragmentation by never leaving a freed block between two allocated blocks.

MS-DOS and Peripherals

MS-DOS handles peripherals. Without MS-DOS each program would need specialized code for each peripheral that it might use. MS-DOS provides a uniform interface to all peripherals in the computer.

MS-DOS divides peripherals into two types. One is block type devices, such as disk drives that have directories and files. The other type is character devices, such as printers and terminals that send and receive data one byte at a time. When a program sends a command to a character device, MS-DOS routes it to the device driver for that peripheral. For block devices the commands must go through the file system code that makes the appropriate device driver calls.

Each device has a name that programs use to tell MS-DOS what device to use. For block devices all names are a single letter of the alphabet. To read or write data on a block device, a program must indicate which block device to use and the name of the file on that device. Character devices have names that can be up to eight letters long. To read or write a character device, simply give MS-DOS the name of the device.

To avoid having to pass device or file names to MS-DOS for every operation, MS-DOS uses the OPEN FILE function (number 3Dh) to associate the file or device with a file handle. The program can use the file handle in all future references to the file. When the program is done with the file or device, it tells MS-DOS by calling the CLOSE FILE function (number 3Eh). (See Chapter 13 for more information on using files.)

MS-DOS has several built-in devices that can be used from programs. Table 1-4 shows some of these devices. You can add other devices or replace the existing ones by adding *DEVICE* statements to the CONFIG.SYS file.

Table 1-4. *MS-DOS Built-In Devices*

Device	Description
CON:	The keyboard and CRT
AUX:	The auxiliary I/O device. Usually equal to COM1:
PRN:	The standard printer device. Usually LPT1:
COM1:	The first serial port
COM2:	The second serial port
LPT1:	The first parallel port
LPT2:	The second parallel port

In addition to being able to access devices through the file functions, certain devices have special functions in MS-DOS. For example, there are eight functions that work with the keyboard and CRT. There are three more for using the serial (functions 3 and 4) and printer ports (function 5). The keyboard functions allow programs to get keystrokes one at a time or as a string (function 0Ah). When getting single keys, a program can specify whether the keys should be echoed on the screen (function 1) or not (function 7 or 8). One other function lets the program check whether a key has been pressed (function 0Bh). Function 0Ch lets a program clear out the type-ahead buffer before reading the keyboard. To send data to the screen, the program can choose to send one character at a time (function 2) or a string of characters (function 9). The eighth console function (function 6) can read or write the console device, depending on the state of the DL register.

Summary

The environment in which a program runs is important to the program designer. Different operating systems and CPUs require different approaches to writing programs. Turbo Assembler programs are designed to work with the MS-DOS operating system. MS-DOS provides many useful functions for use by programs. It has an easy-to-use interface that lets programs use files and I/O devices. It also keeps track of what memory locations the programs are using. This keeps programs from interfering with each other.

All MS-DOS programs use CPUs from the 80x86 family. Turbo Assembler provides instructions that match the powerful instruction set of this family. These instructions provide ways to manipulate data in memory and registers. There are also instructions for setting up and using a stack. The stack can be used to save registers while they are being used for something else. The stack also makes sure that subroutines return to the correct location.

MS-DOS uses software interrupts to receive commands from programs. The software interrupt is similar to a subroutine call, except that it does not use an explicit subroutine address. Instead, it uses an interrupt number. The CPU uses the interrupt number to look up the subroutine address from a table in low memory.

2 Introduction to Using Turbo Assembler

Turbo Assembler comes with all of the programs that you need to make assembly language source files into working programs. The only other program that you need is a text editor to prepare your source files. This chapter guides you through the steps of creating a source file and using the assembler. The first part of the chapter shows how to run the various programs to assemble and link a program. You learn how to use the various programs required to make a working program. You also learn about the MAKE utility to help with programs that have several source files.

The next part of the chapter describes how the assembler works. It shows how the assembler looks at the directives and instructions in your source code. Following that, there is a section on assembler directives. These are the commands that you use to tell the assembler what to do. A few directives are presented in this part as examples.

The last section is an introduction to processor instructions. These are the instructions that the 80x86 executes in the final program. There are several examples that show how to use some of the instructions and explain the addressing modes of the 80x86.

Installing Turbo Assembler

Before you begin, be sure that you have installed all of the utilities that come with Turbo Assembler. The easiest way to do this is to use the *install* program that is on the Turbo Assembler diskette. This program puts all of the required files into a subdirectory. The default subdirectory is \TASM, but you can tell the install program to put the files anywhere on the hard disk. After the install program is finished, check the PATH variable by typing PATH at the MS-DOS prompt. One of the directories in the list should be the \TASM directory (or whatever directory you are using). That directory should contain several files including TASM.EXE, TLINK.EXE, and MAKE.EXE. This chapter explains the use of these and other utilities.

You can in fact copy the files, but the install program is easier and also unpacks the example and utility files. You should also run the install program on the Turbo Debugger and Turbo Profiler diskettes. These files are not required for writing assembly language programs, but they can be useful. Chapter 3 shows you how to use Turbo Debugger to find bugs in Turbo Assembler programs.

Turbo Assembler comes with a number of examples of assembly language programs. These are a good place to look when you want to learn how certain features of the assembler can be used. If you did not use the install program, or asked it not to unpack sample programs, you may find that these files have a .ZIP extension. This indicates that they are a compressed archive containing one or more files. You can use the UNZIP utility provided to convert these files into assembly language sources. You should create a separate directory for each example that you would like to examine. Then copy the .ZIP file to that directory and type UNZIP filename. This extracts the files for the example and places them in the directory. Now you can use your editor to examine or change the examples.

The one program that is not included with Turbo Assembler is a text editor. Fortunately, there are many high quality text editors available for MS-DOS computers. Be sure that the PATH variable includes the directory that contains the text editor. Typically your system will have a path statement in the AUTOEXEC.BAT file in the root directory of the boot drive, so that the path is set automatically whenever you boot the computer. If, for example, you put the Turbo Assembler programs in C:\TASM, the editor in C:\EDIT, and your MS-DOS utilities in C:\DOS; you could use this path statement:

```
PATH C:\TASM;C:\EDIT;C:\DOS
```

Creating a Source File

The best way to see how Turbo Assembler works is to create an actual program. The following program prints the message "My First Assembler Program" on the screen. This example is used because it illustrates several concepts that are discussed in this chapter.

Listing 2-1. *A Simple Assembly Language Program*

```
; FIRST.ASM    A simple assembly language program
        .MODEL    SMALL           ; Tell the assembler to use
                                  ; the small memory model
Prnstr  EQU  9                    ; Make a symbol PRNSTR that
                                  ; stands for the number 9
Exitprg EQU  4Ch                  ; Make a symbol EXITPRG that
                                  ; stands for the number 4Ch
        .DATA
; The next line puts a string in memory at Mesg. The 0Dh and 0Ah
; at the end are carriage return and line feed. The dollar sign
; is used by MS-DOS to mark the end of the string

Mesg    DB   "My First Assembler Program", 0Dh, 0Ah, '$'


        .CODE
Start   PROC                      ; The beginning of a procedure
                                  ; named Start

        mov   ax, SEG DGROUP      ; Get the segment address of
        mov   ds, ax              ; the data area
        mov   dx, OFFSET Mesg     ; Get the address of the
                                  ; string and put it in DX
        mov   ah, Prnstr          ; Put the MS-DOS print string
                                  ; command in AH
        int   21h                 ; Call MS-DOS with print
                                  ; command in AH
        mov   ah, Exitprg         ; Put MS-DOS exit program
                                  ; command in AH
        int   21h                 ; Call MS-DOS with the exit
                                  ; program command
Start   ENDP                      ; The end of the Start
                                  ; procedure
        .STACK    512             ; Make an area for the stack
                                  ; that is 512 bytes long
        END  Start                ; Mark the end of the program
                                  ; and tell MS-DOS to begin the
                                  ; program at Start
```

As you enter this program, notice the format of a typical assembly language program. The first character in the first line is a semicolon (;). This indicates that the rest of the text on the line is a comment. Comments are intended to explain what the program is doing. The assembler ignores them.

An assembly language program is aligned in three columns. The first column contains labels and symbols, which help make programs easier to understand. Labels mark locations of text or data in the program. For example, in Listing 2-1 the label Mesg marks the location of the string "My First Assembler Program." The line mov dx, OFFSET Mesg gets the offset for the symbol Mesg and copies it into DX. This is much easier than keeping track of the offsets of each of the locations and putting the value in the code.

Symbols are names used in the program to stand for constants. For example, Listing 2-1 uses the symbols Prnstr and Exitprg to stand for the numbers 9 and 4Ch. Whenever Prnstr occurs in the program, the assembler substitutes the number 9; and for Exitprg the assembler uses 4Ch. The reason for using symbols to replace numbers is to make the program easier to read. If you see the number 9 in a program, you do not know if it is an MS-DOS command, an ASCII character, or a number. On the other hand, the symbol Prnstr not only indicates that this is an MS-DOS command, but it also gives a clue as to which one. In this book all symbols and labels are in mixed upper- and lowercase to distinguish them from directives and program instructions.

The second column contains assembler directives or program instructions. Assembler directives are special commands that tell the assembler what to do. An example of a directive is the EQU command used to define symbols. This command does not generate any code. It tells the assembler what to do when it finds the symbol in the program. In this book all assembler directives are in upper case to distinguish them from program instructions.

Program instructions are what the assembler turns into the code that makes up the program. Each program instruction corresponds to a single 80x86 instruction. For example, the first instruction in this program is MOV. The assembler looks at this instruction and puts the code 0B8h into the object file.

The third column contains *operands*. This is the data that is used by the directive or program instruction. Each directive or instruction has its own type and number of arguments. The MOV instruction at the beginning of the program copies data between its two arguments: ax, SEG DGROUP. The first one is the location into which to copy the data (called the *destination operand*), and the second is the data to copy (called the *source operand*).

If you type all 37 lines of this program into a file, you begin to see why all programs are not written in assembly language. A comparable program can be written in BASIC, C, or PASCAL in about 5 lines. After you assemble and link the program, however, you can see one reason for using assembly language. The executable file is only 557 bytes long: 45 bytes are for the program itself and the rest is for the stack. It is difficult to achieve this level of compactness with a high–level language.

Making an Executable File from the Source Code

There are two steps to convert a source file into an executable file. The first is to assemble the source file into an object file, and the command to do this is:

```
tasm first
```

If everything goes well, you should see something like:

```
Turbo Assembler  Version 2.0  Copyright  1988, 1990 Borland
International

Assembling file:     first.ASM
Error messages:      None
Warning messages:    None
Passes:              1
Remaining memory:    260K
```

If there is an error in the file, there will be one or more error or warning messages. These messages indicate the line in which the error occurs. Check the indicated line against the listing above. It is possible to mistype something and cause an error on another line. For example, if you misspell EXITPRG at the beginning of the program, the error shows up at the end of the `Start` procedure where EXITPRG is used.

There is one step left to make a working program. This step is called *linking*. The term "linking" refers to the fact that this step lets you link several object files into a single program. In this case there is only one object file, but it must be linked anyway. This is done to simplify the design of the assembler, so that it always creates a linkable object file and lets the linker turn it into a working program. The command to do this is:

```
tlink first
```

The linker will respond by printing:

```
Turbo Link  Version 3.0  Copyright  1987, 1990 Borland
International
```

When the linker is finished, it will have created the file FIRST.EXE. The rest of this section gives more information on the assembler and linker.

The Assembler

Many programs can be assembled by simply giving the name of the file to assemble on the command line, as was done in the last section. In some cases, you may want to give the assembler special instructions about how the file should be handled. There are two types of instructions that you can give the assembler from the command line. The first type is command line switches to tell the assembler what options to use. The second type tells the assembler what files to assemble.

COMMAND LINE SWITCHES

You can give the assembler several instructions by entering switches with the TASM command. Table 2-1 shows the switches that can be used with the TASM command.

After experimenting with these switches, you may find one or two that you would like to use all the time. For example, if you are writing routines that you want to link with routines from a high level language, you should use the /ml switch to make case-sensitive labels and symbols. To avoid typing switches every time you want to assemble a file, you can put the switches in a configuration file. The name of the configuration file for Turbo Assembler is TASM.CFG. This file should be in the same directory as the Turbo Assembler exccutable files. When you start the assembler, it looks for this file to get the switches to use before assembling any source files. A typical TASM.CFG file looks like this:

```
/iC:\TASM\INCLUDE
/ml
/zi
```

The first switch in this file tells the assembler to look in the directory C:\TASM\INCLUDE for "include files." These files usually contain definitions for symbols and macros (see Chapter 10) that are used in several source files. Some programmers make one or more standard include files for things that they use in most programs. It is convenient to have all the include files in one place and use the /i switch to tell the assembler where they are.

The second switch tells the assembler to make all symbols case sensitive. Without this option the symbols `ThisSym` and `THISSYM` would be the same symbol. This switch is required for linking assembly language routines with certain high level language programs (see Chapter 12).

The last switch tells the assembler to include debugging information in the object file. This is required if you want to use the Turbo Debugger to debug the program. The information includes the names of all labels and symbols, and the line number of each instruction.

FILE NAMES

You can tell Turbo Assembler what file names to use by specifying the names on the command line. The first file name is the name of the source file. This can be any valid MS-DOS text file. If you do not specify an extension, TASM uses .ASM. You can even use wild cards to assemble more than one file at a time:

```
tasm s*
```

This command assembles all files that start with "s" and have an .ASM extension in the current directory.

Table 2-1. *Switches for the TASM Command*

Option	Description
/a	Sort segments in alphabetical order
/c	Generate cross-reference listing
/dSYMBOL[=VAL]	Define a symbol as 0 or VAL
/e	Use emulated floating point instructions
/h,/?	Show a list of options
/iPATH	Get include files from PATH
/jDIRECTIVE	Execute DIRECTIVE before assembling
/khNUMBER	Set the hash table size to NUMBER
/ksNUMBER	Set string pool size to NUMBER
/l	Generate normal listing
/la	Generate expanded listing
/ml	Make all symbols case sensitive
/mNUMBER	Use NUMBER passes to resolve forward references
/mu	Make all symbols case insensitive
/mvNUMBER	Set maximum length for symbols
/mx	Make global symbols case sensitive
/n	Do not include symbol tables in listings
/p	Check for code segment overrides in protected mode
/q	Do not included unneeded records in the OBJ file
/s	Do not sort segments
/r	Use real floating point instructions
/t	Do not print anything if the assembly was successful
/w[−]WARNING	Disable warning type WARNING
/w+WARNING	Allow warning type WARNING
/w0	Do not print warning messages
/w1,/w2	Print warnings
/x	Include false conditionals in the listing
/zi	Include full debugging information
/zd	Include line number information for debugging

Another way to assemble several files is to separate the file names with semicolons. You can include different options with each of the names:

```
tasm /c source1; /ic:\tasm\include source2
```

There are three types of output file that TASM can create. The first type is the object file. This file contains the code and data that the linker will use to make the program. The next file type is the listing file. This is a text file showing the source code and the object code that the assembler generates. The last type of file is the cross-reference listing. This is also a text file that lists all the labels and symbols, and where they are used. The default names for these files are made from the name of the source file. The object file uses the .OBJ extension, the listing file uses the .LST extension, and the cross-reference file uses the .CRF extension. If you want to use different names for these files, you can put them on the command line separated by commas. For example, you may want to assemble several different versions of the same source (see conditional assembly in Chapters 10 and 11) into different object and listing files. You can do this with the following commands:

```
tasm /dVersion=1 /l /c PROG.ASM,PROG1.OBJ,PROG1.LST,PROG1.CRF
tasm /dVersion=2 /l /c PROG.ASM,PROG2.OBJ,PROG2.LST,PROG2.CRF
tasm /dVersion=3 /l /c PROG.ASM,PROG3.OBJ,PROG3.LST,PROG3.CRF
```

This example makes three different versions of the program PROG.ASM. The first switch tells the assembler to define the symbol Version with a different value for each version of the program. The /l switch tells the assembler to generate a listing file, and the /c switch tells it to generate a cross-reference file.

The Linker

The object files created by the assembler contain the code and data from the source file. They also contain any global symbol names that are to be shared among several modules. The linker's job is to take the information in the object file and make it into an executable file that can be used by the MS-DOS program loader.

The command line for the linker lists all of the files that need to be linked to create a source file. The names can be separated by spaces or by plus signs:

```
tlink first second third
```

or

```
tlink first+second+third
```

Each of the files named contains parts of the program to be created. Chapter 10 describes the directives that your programs can use to tell the linker how these parts fit together.

LINKER SWITCHES   There are several switches that you can use when running the linker. Table 2-2 shows these switches.

Table 2-2.   *Switches for the Linker*

Option	Description
/c	Do case sensitive match on symbol names
/d	Generate a warning for duplicate symbols in libraries
/i	Initialize all segments
/l	Include debugging information in the executable file
/m	Include public symbols in the map file
/n	Do not use the default libraries
/s	Include a list of segments in the map file
/x	Do not create a map file

Most programs do not require any of these switches to be set. One exception is for programs that include object files from high level languages. Many high level languages use case sensitive symbol names. Not only do you have to assemble files with the /ml switch, but you must also use the /c switch when linking.

Turbo Debugger requires that the debugging information able to be put in the object files with the /zi assembler switch must be in the executable file. The /l switch tells the linker to do this.

If the program has only one source file, you can use the listing file generated by the assembler to see where the pieces of the program are. With multiple files this is not so easy. Each listing file is written as if it is the only file in the program. You need some way of getting the global picture of how all the modules are laid out. The linker provides this information in the form of a map file.

If you do not use the /m, /s, or /x options, the linker makes a map file that includes the names and locations of all the segments and the starting address for the program. The /m option makes the linker add in all public symbols. These are the symbols that can be shared among modules. The /s option tells the linker to put more information about segments into the map file. If you do not want to make a map file, use the /x option. This may speed up the linking process on systems that have slow disk drives.

The linker gets the name for the executable file and the map file from the name of the first object file in the list. It uses .EXE as the extension for executables and .MAP for map files. If these names are not what you want, you can give the names to use separated by commas:

```
tlink first second third,myprog,mapfile
```

This command links the files FIRST.OBJ, SECOND.OBJ, and THIRD.OBJ into an executable file named MYPROG.EXE. It also makes a map file named MAPFILE.MAP.

There is one more type of file that you can use with the linker called *object libraries*. These files contain several object modules that have commonly used routines. If you are linking to high level languages, you probably need to link in one or more object libraries. For example, to link an assembly language routine named ASMSTUFF to a Turbo C program named CPROG, use this command:

```
tlink /c /m C0S CPROG ASMSTUFF,CPROG,CMAP,CS EMU
```

The /c switch tells the linker to use case sensitive symbol names. The /m switch tells the linker to generate a map file. The first three file names (C0S, CPROG, and ASMSTUFF) are the object files to link. The C0S file is a start-up module required by Turbo C programs. The file name to use for the executable file (CPROG) appears after the first comma. The next name is the name of the map file (CMAP). The last two names are the library files for the C run-time library (CS) and the floating point emulator (EMU). You also use a similar command line for linking Assembler routines with other high level languages.

**LINKER
RESPONSE
FILES**
As a program grows and more modules get added, the link command line gets longer and longer. To save having to type a long command line every time, you can put the link instructions into a file. The file looks just like the command line except that you can use carriage returns instead of commas. To use the file, just put the name of the file on the command line preceded by an "at" sign (@). This command gets the files to link and the linker options from a file named LINKFILE.LNK:

```
tlink @linkfile.lnk
```

Using the MAKE Utility

It is difficult to manage large programs that have many modules without special tools. Every time you make a change, you must reassemble all of the changed files and then relink the object files. If the change is to a variable used by many different modules, you have to be sure that all affected modules get reassembled. One way to solve this problem is to make an MS-DOS batch file that reassembles all the modules and then links them. The problem with this technique is the time it takes.

The MAKE.EXE program helps manage large programs by comparing the date and time of the source files to the date and time of the object files. When the source file is newer than the object file, MAKE runs the assembler on the source file. MAKE.EXE uses a file of commands, that you create, to determine what to do with which files.

The make file depends on the date and time information in order for files to have accurate information. You should use the MS-DOS commands DATE and TIME to be sure that they are correct before editing your source files or running the make file. The MS-DOS DIR command can be used to check the date and time information for the file. If it is not correct, you can use the TOUCH.EXE utility to set the date and time of the file to the current date and time.

The following example is a make command file that makes a program called BIG.EXE from the sources FIRST.ASM, SECOND.ASM, and THIRD.ASM. This file can be created with the same text editor used for program sources. The default name for make files is MAKEFILE.

```
big.exe: first.obj second.obj third.obj
      tlink first second third,big

first.obj: first.asm
   tasm first

second.obj: second.asm
   tasm second

third.obj: third.asm
   tasm third
```

To use this make file use this command:

```
make
```

If BIG.EXE is up-to-date, then the make utility will do nothing. The interesting part happens when we change one of the source files. Suppose that the SECOND.ASM file has been updated. The make utility begins by reading the first line of the make file. The first file on this line is the file to make (called the target file). The files after the colon are the source files for this target file. The make utility looks at each of the source files to see if the target file must be updated. The first file to check is FIRST.OBJ. The make utility looks through the rest of the make file to see if this file is a target file in any of the other make instructions. In this case there is:

```
first.obj: first.asm
```

In this instruction, FIRST.OBJ is the target and FIRST.ASM is the source. Since there are no make instructions with FIRST.ASM as the target, the make utility gets the date and time for FIRST.ASM and compares it to the date and time for FIRST.OBJ. In this case the object file is newer than the source file, so no action is taken. The make utility can now go back to the first line and compare the date and time of FIRST.OBJ to the date and time of BIG.EXE. Once again the file is newer than the dependency, so no action is taken.

The make utility does a similar operation for each dependency in the current make instruction. When the make utility gets to the rule for SECOND.OBJ, it sees that it has to make the file. To do this it reads the line following the make instruction:

```
tasm second
```

The make utility passes this line to MS-DOS to assemble the file. The process of assembling the file changes the date and time of the file. This is the date and time that the make utility uses to compare with the date and time of BIG.EXE. Since SECOND.OBJ was just updated, it is newer than BIG.EXE. But before acting on this information, the make utility has to check the rest of the dependencies. In this case THIRD.OBJ does not need to be updated. The make file can now execute the line:

```
tlink first second third, big
```

This completes the make operation and leaves you with an updated program.

There are several other types of commands that you can put in a make file. Any line that begins with a number sign (#) is a comment. The comments in this make file describe some of the features you can use in make files:

```
# This make file makes a program called FANCY.EXE
# the next line tells the make utility to assemble any
# dependency with an .ASM extension.
.asm.obj:
    tasm $*
# The $* represents the file name without an extension.
# The next line is a macro named OBJS. The reference $(OBJS) will
# be replaced with the text from this line.
OBJS=first.obj second.obj third.obj

# See if any of the object files or the link file are newer than
# the program file
fancy.exe: $(OBJS) fancy.lnk
    tlink @fancy.lnk

# Check the sources. There is no need to tell the make utility
# what to do because of the rule for .asm files above.
first.obj: first.asm

second.obj: second.asm

third.obj: third.asm
```

```
# If the make file is newer than the link file, make a new link
# file.
fancy.lnk: makefile
        echo $(OBJS) > fancy.lnk
        echo fancy.exe >> fancy.lnk
```

How the Assembler Works

The basic task for Turbo Assembler is to convert an assembly language source
file into an object file. To accomplish this task, the assembler performs several
types of operations. The assembler begins by reading lines from the source file
and parsing them for commands. When the command found is an assembler
directive, the assembler modifies its operation according to the directive. In
Listing 2-1 the very first line is:

```
.MODEL SMALL
```

This is an assembler directive telling the assembler that the default size
for all label addresses is 16 bits and that functions use NEAR calls and returns.
Another interesting directive is:

```
.DATA
```

This directive tells the assembler to put the code or data that follows into
a segment named _DATA. In the final program, this code or data can be
accessed by putting the segment address of _DATA into a segment register. All
code or data in the program must be in some segment. While the assembler can
make sure that the code or data for a segment is in that segment, it is up to the
programmer to make sure that the address of the segment is in the segment
register being used.

Turbo Assembler keeps a location counter for each segment. Each
command that results in code or data being placed in the segment will advance
the location counter to point to the next available location. When the
assembler comes to a label, it puts the label into its symbol table along with the
value of the location counter. When the assembler sees the label used later, it
outputs the location of the symbol. Figure 2-1 shows the contents of the data
segment and the symbol table after assembling the instructions in the _DATA
segment.

When the assembler gets to the .CODE directive, it stops putting data into
the _DATA segment and begins placing it in the _TEXT segment. The first
directive in the _TEXT segment is:

```
Start    PROC
```

This directive tells the assembler that the following instructions are part of a procedure named Start. The effect of this directive is not felt until the procedure returns to the calling procedure. There are two kinds of return instructions in the 80x86 instruction set, called NEAR and FAR. NEAR procedures are all in the same code segment, while FAR procedures can be in different segments. In this case, the fact that the procedure does not declare itself as NEAR or FAR means to use the default—which comes from the MODEL directive at the beginning of the program. The SMALL model implies that the default procedure type is NEAR.

The first instruction in the Start procedure is:

```
mov    ax, SEG DGROUP
```

The second operand gets the segment address of a label called DGROUP. This label is a structure called a *group*. Groups are collections of segments that can be treated like a single segment. (See Chapter 8 for more information on groups.) In this case, the _DATA segment is combined with the STACK segment.

All of the statements in the _TEXT segment are labels or assembly language instructions. The assembler puts the labels into a symbol file and converts the instructions to codes that can be executed by the 80x86 processor.

This works fine until the assembler comes to a line like this:

```
call   PrnStr
```

In this case, the assembler cannot find the symbol PrnStr in the symbol table because it has not been defined yet. The assembler solves this problem by putting PrnStr in the symbol table and indicating that there is an unresolved reference to this symbol. Instead of putting the location of the symbol in the output code, the assembler puts two zero bytes. If the argument to the .MODEL directive is LARGE, indicating that the default procedure type is FAR, the assembler would output four zero bytes (the space required for a FAR label).

One problem with this technique has to do with JMP instructions (JuMP to a location). For each JMP instruction, the assembler must decide between a FAR, NEAR, or SHORT JMP. The number of bytes required for these statements are 4, 2, and 1, respectively. If the label is not in the symbol table, the assembler cannot decide which one to use. It solves the problem by outputting four NOP (No OPeration) instructions. When it finds the symbol, it can overwrite one or more of the NOPs with the address of the label.

To prevent the assembler from outputting NOPs after every JMP instruction, you can tell it what kind of label to expect. To force the assembler to use a SHORT JMP, use an instruction like this:

```
jmp    SHORT dest
```

Offset   Symbol

0	'M' Mesg
	'y'
	' '
	'F'
	'i'
	'r'
	's'
	't'
	' '
	'A'
	's'
	's'
	'e'
	'm'
	'b'
	'l'
	'e'
	'r'
	' '
	'P'
	'r'
	'o'
	'g'
	'r'
	'a'
	'm'
	0Dh
	0Ah
	'$'
29	0 SpcCnt
	0

Symbol Table

Name	Offset	Type
Mesg	0	BYTE
SpcCnt	29	WORD

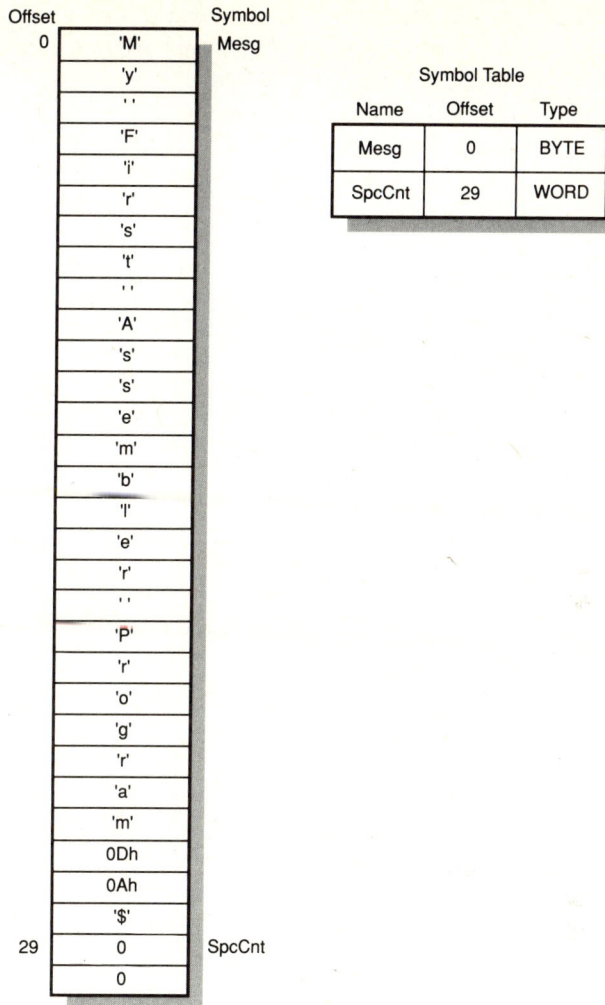

Figure 2-1. *Data segment and the symbol table.*

Another way to avoid the problems of forward references is to tell the assembler to use more than one pass. Each pass gives the assembler more information about the actual location of forward references. By default, the assembler makes only one pass through the program. You set a larger number of passes with the /mNUMBER command line option. The number of passes required properly to resolve all forward references depends on a variety of factors. Most programs can be done in less than five passes.

The last program directive in Listing 2-1 is the END directive. This directive tells the assembler that there are no more commands in the source file. It can also tell the assembler what label to use for the starting address of the program. In this case the END directive tells the assembler that the Start procedure is the place to begin executing this program. The assembler puts a code in the object file that is eventually passed to MS-DOS to indicate the segment and offset of the Start procedure.

Directives

Table 2-3 lists the directives that Turbo Assembler recognizes. The directives fall into four categories: segment control, symbols and expressions, macros and procedures, and conditional assembly and processor control. The table shows the directives in each of these categories along with a chapter reference where more information can be found.

Table 2-3. *Turbo Assembler Directives*

Segment Directives (Chapter 8)

.ALPHA, ASSUME, .CODE, CODESEG, .CONST, CONST, .DATA, DATASEG, .DATA?, DOSSEG, .FARDATA, FARDATA, .FARDATA?, GROUP, .MODEL, MODEL, SEGMENT, .STACK, STACK, UDATASEG, UFARDATA

Symbols and Expressions (Chapter 9)

$, @code, @CodeSize, @CPU, @curseg, @data, @DataSize, ??date, @fardata, @fardata?, @FileName, ??filename, @Model, @Startup, ??time, ??version, @WordSize, (), *, +, -, ., /, :, [], AND, ALIGN, BYTE, BYTE PTR, CATSTR, .CONST, CONST, CODEPTR, .CREF, DATAPTR, DB, DD, DF, DP, DQ, DT, DUP, DWORD, DWORD PTR, EQ, EQU, EVEN, EVENDATA, EXTRN, FAR, FAR PTR, FWORD, FWORD PTR, GE, GLOBAL, GT, HIGH, INSTR, LARGE, LE, LENGTH, LOW, LT, MASK, MOD, NE, NEAR, NEAR PTR, NOT, OFFSET, OR, ORG, PTR, PWORD, PWORD PTR, QWORD, QWORD PTR, RECORD, SEG, SHL, SHORT, SHR, SIZE, SIZESTR, SMALL, SUBSTR, SYMTYPE, TBYTE, TBYTE PTR, THIS, .TYPE, TYPE, UNION, UNKNOWN, WIDTH, WORD, WORD PTR, XOR

Macros and Procedures (Chapter 10)

ARG, ENDM, ENDP, EXITM, IRP, IRPC, LOCAL, LOCALS, MACRO, PROC, REPT, USES

.186, .286, .286C, .286P, .287, .386, .386C, .386P, .387, .8086, .8087, ELSE, ELSEIF, EMUL, END, ENDIF, .ERR, ERR, .ERR1, .ERR2, .ERRDEF, .ERRDIF, .ERRDIFI. .ERRE, .ERRIDN, .ERRIDNI, ERRIF, ERRIF1, ERRIF2, ERRIFB, ERRIFDEF, ERRIFDIF, ERRDIFI, ERRIFE, ERRIFIDN, ERRIFDNI, ERRIFNB, ERRIFNDEF, .ERRNB, .ERRNDEF, .ERRNZ, JUMPS, IF, IF1, IF2, IFB, IFDEF, IFDIF, IFDIFI, IFE, IFIDN, IFIDNI, IFNB, IFNDEF, INCLUDE, INCLULDELIB, MASM, MASM51, MULTERRS, NOEMUL, NOJUMPS, NOLOCALS, MOMASM51, NOSMART, ORG, P186, P286, P286N, P286P, P287, P386, P386N, P386P, P387, P8086, P8087, PNO87, QUIRKS, SMART

MASM and IDEAL Mode

Turbo Assembler is designed to be compatible with Microsoft's MASM Assembler versions 4.0 and 5.1. This means that Turbo Assembler can compile programs written for MASM. If compatibility with MASM is not important, you can switch the assembler to IDEAL mode. Using IDEAL mode has some advantages, such as assembling up to 30% faster. The other advantages include a more consistent syntax for directives and better handling of complex data types. To use IDEAL mode you must include the IDEAL directive in the program. You can also invoke IDEAL mode from the command line with the /jideal option. Chapter 11 contains complete descriptions of both MASM and IDEAL modes.

The descriptions of directives in this book include both the MASM and IDEAL mode versions of the directive. One thing you may have noticed in the list of directives is that there are many directives that only differ by a period (.) at the beginning of the directive. These directives do the same thing in MASM mode. The directives without the period exist because in IDEAL mode a directive cannot begin with a period.

Segments

Turbo Assembler handles the segmented architecture of the 80x86 chips by requiring that all code and data be in named *segments*. The named segments can be used to give the assembler clues about what values are in the segment registers, so that it knows where to start counting when it computes the offset of a symbol. For example, if a symbol is defined at the beginning of a segment named _DATA, then the assembler knows that the offset for that symbol is 0. On the other hand, if the assembler knows that the segment register being used contains the address of a segment that is 32 bytes less than the address of _DATA, the assembler knows to add 32 to the offset for the symbol. Turbo Assembler has a number of directives for controlling how segments are laid out, and to tell the assembler what value to expect in each of the segment registers. These directives are covered in Chapter 8.

The example program in Listing 2-1 uses several directives to put code and data in different segments. The directives used (`.DATA`, `.CODE`, and `.STACK`) are called the simplified segment directives. They declare the predefined segments _DATA, _TEXT, and STACK. Programs that use other segments, or must be compatible with older versions of MASM, can use the `SEGMENT` directive. This directive lets you create a segment with any name you like. The `SEGMENT` directive requires more information about the segment. You must tell the assembler how the segment will be combined with other segments and how it will be placed in memory. A SEGMENT statement that does the same thing as the .DATA statement looks like this:

```
_DATA     SEGMENT   WORD, PUBLIC, 'DATA'
```

Other requirements for using the segment directive include the `ENDS` and `ASSUME` directives. The `ENDS` directive marks the end of the segment. The `ASSUME` tells the assembler what segment address it can expect to find in a given segment register. This is important when several segments have been combined into a group. If the segment register contains the address of the group, the assembler must use a different offset than if the segment register contains the address of a segment. Figure 2-2 shows how this works. If the example at the beginning of the chapter did not use simplified segment directives, it would require an `ASSUME` directive such as:

```
ASSUME   CS:_TEXT, DS:DGROUP, ES:NOTHING, SS:STACK
```

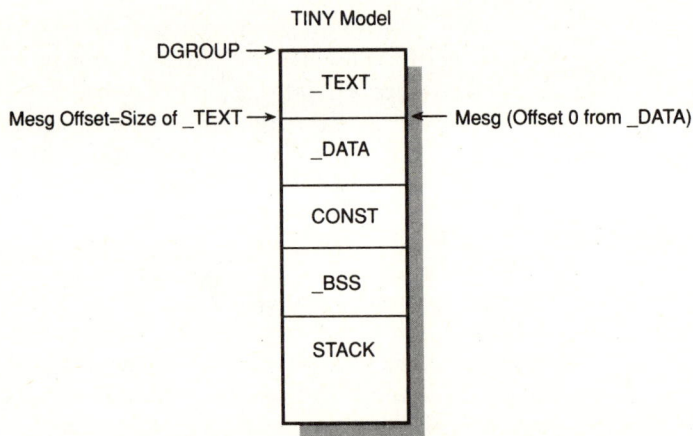

Figure 2-2. *Different offsets for segments and groups.*

Most programs can be written using the simplified segment directives. The segment names have been chosen so that they match segments used in high level languages. This makes it easier to combine assembly language routines into high level language programs.

Symbols and Expressions

Turbo Assembler provides a large number of directives for manipulating symbols. In the simplest case, the assembler replaces symbols with the string or number that goes with the symbol. For example, a program that reads records from a file might have a symbol that tells how many bytes there are in a record, and another that tells the size of the memory buffer:

```
RecSize   EQU   22             ; Set the size of a record
BuffSize  EQU   1024
```

You can use the RecSize symbol to tell you how many bytes to copy from the buffer. The BuffSize symbol can be used when you define the buffer to set aside the correct number of bytes. At some point your program may need to know how many records will fit in the buffer. You could define another symbol with the value 46, or you could have the assembler figure it out for you. This statement puts the number of records in a buffer into the CX register:

```
mov  cx, BUFFSIZE/RECSIZE
```

It is important to realize that the assembler evaluates this expression while assembling the program. If you want to include a value from memory or a register in an expression, you will have to use program instructions to do it. For example, the expression in this statement is not allowed:

```
mov   ax, RECSIZE * bx   ; Can't use registers in
                         ; expressions
```

You should use the following code:

```
mov   ax, RECSIZE       ; Put RECSIZE in AX
mul   bx                ; Multiply ax times bx and put
                        ; the result in ax
```

Macros and Procedures

The next example is a function to print a string and then get an input string from the user:

Listing 2-2.   *Procedure Calls*

```
; File   Macexam.ASM
        .MODEL      SMALL
Prnstr  EQU  9                       ; MS-DOS print string function
Inpstr  EQU  0Ah                     ; MS-DOS input string function
Exitprg EQU  4Ch                     ; MS-DOS exit program function
        .DATA
Prmpt   DB   "Enter string: $"       ; Prompt string
InputStr DB  40                       ; Number of characters to get
        DB   ?                       ; The number of characters
                                     ; typed (set after call to
                                     ; GetStr)

        DB   40 DUP('$')             ; Space for the input string

        .CODE
Start   PROC
        mov  ax, SEG DGROUP          ; Get the data segment
        mov  ds, ax                  ; put it in the DS register
        mov  dx, OFFSET Prmpt        ; Put the offset of the data
                                     ; to print
        call PrntStr                 ; Print the string
        mov  dx, OFFSET InputStr     ; Get the address of the data
                                     ; required by GetStr
        call GetStr                  ; Get input from the user
        mov  dx, OFFSET InputStr     ; Get the address of the
                                     ; inputted data
        call PrntStr
        mov  ah, Exitprg
        int  21h
Start   ENDP

; Procedure to print a string
PrntStr PROC
        mov  ah, Prnstr              ; Put MS-DOS command in AH
        int  21h                     ; Call MS-DOS
        ret                          ; Return to the instruction
                                     ; following the call
PrntStr ENDP

; Procedure to get an input string
GetStr  PROC
        mov  ah, Inpstr              ; Put MS-DOS command in AH
        int  21h                     ; Call MS-DOS
        ret                          ; Return to the instruction
```

```
                                    ; following the call
GetStr    ENDP

          .STACK     512
END       Start
```

The beginning of the program uses the same kind of set-up information as was used in Listing 2-1. The data section of the program sets up two variables. The first one is Prmpt. This is the string that will be printed. The next variable is InStr. This variable comes in three parts. The first part is a byte that contains the amount of memory available in the third part. The second part is a byte that will be set to the number of characters typed. The last part is space to store the string that the user types. This InStr variable is in the format expected by the MS-DOS get-a-string function.

The code portion of the program contains three procedures. The first procedure begins by loading the DS register with the segment address of DGROUP. The next step is to put the offset for Prmpt into the DX register. Then the program calls the procedure PrntStr. This procedure uses the MS-DOS print string function to print the string, and then returns control to the instruction following the CALL instruction. In this case the next instruction puts the offset of the variable InStr into the DX register. After that, the program calls the function GetStr in order to use the MS-DOS get-input function to get a string. The last step is to print out the input string.

The Start procedure could have been written with the instructions to print a string and get input in place of the calls to the PrntStr and GetStr procedures. This would have meant that the code for PrntStr would occur twice in the program, using more memory. The advantage of *not* using procedures is the performance gain from *not* having to execute the call and ret instructions.

Macros let you use code that occurs several times in the program without having to type the code every time you need it, and without the performance penalty of procedures. A macro that does what PrntStr does looks like this:

```
PrntStr   MACRO
          mov  ah, Prnstr          ; Put MS-DOS print string
                                    ; command in AH
          int  21h                 ; Call MS-DOS
PrntStr   ENDM
```

When the assembler sees the symbol PrntStr in the program, it replaces the symbol with the instructions in this macro.

Conditional Assembly

Conditional assembly allows you to write source code that can be used to generate different versions of a program by simply changing a few symbols. You can use conditional assembly to make several versions of the example program at the beginning of this chapter. For example, you might have different versions of the program to work on 80- or 40-column screens.

In the example program two lines above the `NextLp:` label, there is a statement that checks to see if the next line will be too large for the screen. For an 80-column screen, the line will be too large when CX is 51 or larger. For a 40-column screen, the line will be too large when CX is 11 or larger. The following conditional assembler code will check for 51 if the symbol `SCREEN80` is defined or 11 if `SCREEN40` is defined:

```
          .
          .
          .
ifdef     SCREEN80
          cmp  cx, 51
elseifdef SCREEN40
          cmp  cx, 11
else
          display   "No Screen size selected"
          err
endif
          .
          .
          .
```

As the assembler is going through the source, it is looking for conditional assembly directives. The first one in this example (`ifdef SCREEN80`) checks to see if the symbol `SCREEN80` has been defined. If it has, the assembler assembles the instructions between that directive and the `elseifdef` directive. At this point the assembler does not carry out or assemble any instructions until it sees the `endif` directive. If the `SCREEN80` symbol has not been defined, then the assembler will skip the instructions between the first `ifdef` and the `elseifdef` directives.

If the `SCREEN40` symbol has been defined, then the assembler carries out the instructions from the `elseifdef` directive to the `else` directive. If `SCREEN40` is not defined, then the assembler executes the instructions in the final `else` clause. The first instruction tells the assembler to display an error message on the screen. The second tells the assembler that there has been an error. This will print the line number on the screen and cause the assembler not to generate an object file.

To use this new program, you must have some way to define `SCREEN80` or `SCREEN40`. You can do it in the source file with the `EQU` statement (just like any other symbol), or you can do it on the command line when you assemble the program. The /d option lets you define symbols that will be used in the program. For example, to define `SCREEN80` use:

```
tasm /dSCREEN80 first
```

Instructions

In between the directives in a Turbo Assembler program are the program instructions. The assembler will convert these instructions into codes that can be understood by the 80x86 processor. In Listing 2-1 at the beginning of this chapter, the first two instructions are:

```
mov   ax, SEG DGROUP
mov   ds, ax
```

The assembler converts these instructions into:

```
B8 00 00 8E D8
```

Each program instruction in the source is a single machine instruction. Machine instructions use from 1 to 3 bytes of memory plus storage for any operands. Table 2-4 shows the instructions that Turbo Assembler understands. The table divides the instructions into four categories with a cross-reference to the chapter containing more information for each category.

Table 2-4.   *80x86 Instruction Set*

Data Movement Instructions (Chapter 4)

IN, INS(286), LDS, LEA, LES, LFS(386), LGS(386), LODS, LSS(386), MOV, MOVS, MOVSX(386), MOVZX(386), OUT, OUTS(286), POP, POPA(286), POPF, PUSH, PUSHA(286), PUSHF, REP, REPE, REPZ, REPNE, REPNZ, SETA(386), SETNBE(386), SETAE(386), SETNB(386), SETB(386), SETNAE(386), SETBE(386), SETNA(386), SETC(386), SETE(386), SETZ(386), SETG(386), SETNLE(386), SETGE(386), SETNL(386), SETL(386), SETNGE(386), SETLE(386), SETNG(386), SETNC(386), SETNE(386), SETNZ(386), SETNO(386), SETNP(386), SETPO(386), SETNS(386), SETO(386), SETP(386), SETPE(386), SETS(386), STOS, XCHG, XLAT, XLATB

Arithmetic, Logic and Bit-Shift Instructions (Chapter 5)

AAA, AAD, AAM, AAS, ADC, ADD, AND, BSF(386), BSR(386), BT(386), BTC(386), BTR(386), BTS(386), CBW, CDQ(386), CMP, CMPS, CWD, CWDE(386), DAA, DAS, DEC, DIV, IDIV, IMUL, INC, MUL, NEG, NOT, OR, RCL, RCR, ROL, ROR, SAL, SAR, SBB, SCAS, SHL, SHLD(386), SHRD(386), SUB, TEST, XOR

Procedures, Loops, and Jumps (Chapter 6)

BOUND(286), CALL, ENTER(386), ESC, HLT, INT, INTO, IRET, JA, JAE, JB, JBE, JC, JCXZ, JE, JECXZ(386), JG, JGE, JL, JLE, JMP, JNA, JNAE, JNB, JNBE, JNC, JNE, JNG, JNGE, JNL, JNLE, JNO, JNP, JNS, JNZ, JP, JPE, JPO, JS, JZ, LEAVE(386), LOCK, LOOP, LOOPE, LOOPZ, LOOPNE, LOOPNZ, NOP, RET, RETF, RETN

Table 2-4. *Continued*

Processor Control (Chapter 7)

ARPL(286), CLC, CLD, CLI, CLTS(286), CMC, ESC, HLT, LAHF, LAR(286), LGDT(286), LIDT(286), LLDT(286), LMSW(286), LOCK, LSL(286), LTR(286), SAHF, SGDT(286), SIDT(286), SLDT(286), SMSW(286), STC, STD, STI, STR(286), VERR(286), VERW(286), WAIT

Moving Data

The 80x86 has several instructions for moving data. The MOV instruction moves data between two registers or between a register and memory. When the assembler sees a MOV instruction and both of the operands are registers, it outputs the code for a register move. When one of the operands references memory, the assembler determines the addressing mode and outputs the appropriate codes.

Several of the data movement instructions are designed to work with more than one memory location. These instructions are called string instructions because they work on strings of data.

ADDRESSING
MODES

There are nine different ways of specifying the address of memory data on the 80286 and older CPUs. The 80386 has three additional modes. These different ways are called *addressing modes* and are summarized in Table 2-5.

Table 2-5. *80x86 Addressing Modes*

Name	Explanation
Implied	Several instructions (CBW, MUL, LAHF...) only work with certain registers. Most often the register is the 8- or 16-bit accumulator (AL or AX).
	cbw ; Convert the byte in AL to a ; word in AX
Immediate	The data is in the byte or word following the instruction. This mode can only be used to load a register.
	mov ax, 1234h ; Copy 1234h to the AX ; register

Name	Explanation
Direct	The data is at the address following the instruction. mov ax, Symbol ; Copy the data at Symbol into AX
Indexed	The data is at the address in the SI or DI registers. mov [si], ax ; Copy the contents of AX to ; the memory location in SI.
Base	The data is at the address in the BX or BP registers. Using the BP register implies that the segment register is SS. mov ax, [bx] ; Copy the data at the memory ; location in BX to AX

Direct indexed	The address for the data is the sum of the SI o DI register and the byte or word following the instruction.
	
	mov ax, [si+4] ; Add 4 to SI to get the
	    ; address of the data and copy
	    ; it to AX

Direct base	The address for the data is the sum of the BX or BP register and the byte or word following the instruction. Using the BP register implies that the segment register is SS. mov [bp-2], ax ; Copy AX to the word at BP-2

Base indexed	The address of the data is the sum of the SI or DI register and the BX or BP register. Using the BP register implies that the segment register is SS.
	
	mov ax, [bx+di] ; Add BX and DI to get the
	    ; address of the data to copy
	    ; to AX

Table 2-5. *Continued*

Name	Explanation
Direct base indexed	The address of the data is the sum of the SI or DI register, the BX or BP register, and the byte or word following the instruction. Using the BP register implies that the segment register is SS.

```
mov  ax, [bp+si+2]        ; Add BP, SI, and 2 to get the
                          ; address of the data to copy
                          ; to AX
```

Name	Explanation
Direct scaled index	The address of the data is the sum of a specified register times a scaling factor (2, 4, 8) and the byte, word, or double word following the instruction. (80386 only)

```
mov  [ebx*2+Table], ax   ; Copy ax to the word at
                               ; the sum of the offset
                               ; of Table to the
                               ; contents of the EBX
                               ; register times 2
```

Name	Explanation
Base scaled index	The address of the data is the sum of a specified base register and another register times a scaling factor (2, 4, 8). (80386 only)

```
mov  eax, [ebx+ecx*4]      ; Copy the data at the
                           ; sum of EBX and ECX
                           ; times 4 to EAX
```

Name	Explanation
Direct base scaled index	The address of the data is the sum of a specified base register, another register times a scaling factor (2, 4, 8), and the byte, word, or double word following the instruction. (80386 only)

```
mov  [ecx+ebx*8+4], cx     ; Copy CX to the word at
                           ; the sum of ECX, EBX*8,
                           ; and 4
```

The *implied addressing* mode requires no operands, as the instruction only works with specific registers. Instructions that use implied addressing include CBW (Convert Byte to Word) and CWD (Convert Word to Double). These instructions only work with the AH and AX registers (CBW) or the AX and DX registers (CWD).

Immediate addressing means that the data to load into the register follows the instruction. This is the only addressing mode in which data can be loaded but not stored. One interesting aspect of the immediate mode is that you can use an 8-bit value to set a 16-bit register. Turbo Assembler takes care of this feature for you. When it sees an instruction with immediate data, it checks to see if the number is small enough to fit in eight bits (–128 to 127). If the number is small enough, it uses the 8-bit form of the instruction.

The next addressing mode is *direct addressing*. In this mode the two bytes following the instruction are the offset portion of the address of the data to use. By default, the segment portion of the address comes from the DS register. You can tell the assembler that you want to override the default segment register by including the segment name in the instruction:

```
mov   es:Storage, ax          ; Use the ES register for the
                              ; address of the data.
```

The 80x86 includes two index registers called SI and DI. When these registers contain a data address offset, they can be used to access that memory location. This addressing mode is called *indexed addressing*. The value of this addressing mode lies in dealing with arrays of data. To get at an item in an array, you must compute the address of the item and use the computed address when accessing the data. For example, to get the third item in an array of words starting at the symbol IArray, you can use this code:

```
mov   si, 3                   ; Get the item number
shl   si, 1                   ; Shifting 1 bit left is like
                              ; multiplying by two (the size of
                              ; an item in the table)
add   si, OFFSET IArray
                              ; Add in the address of the first
                              ; item
mov   ax, [si]                ; Get the data
```

The BX and BP registers can be used in the same way as the SI and DI registers for accessing memory. This addressing mode is called *base mode*. The difference is that *index mode* is slightly faster than base mode. Another difference is that when using the BP register in base mode, the default segment register is the SS (stack segment) not DS.

In the indexed mode example, the offset of the first item in the array had to be added to SI before it could be used. The indexed direct addressing mode could be used here to avoid this step. This mode takes the address following the instruction and adds it to the index register to get the address of the data. Using indexed direct addressing, the example becomes:

```
mov  si, 3                  ; Get the item number
shl  si, 1                  ; Shifting 1 bit left is like
                            ; multiplying by two (the size of
                            ; an item in the table)
mov  ax,[IArray+si]         ; Get the data
```

The BX and BP registers can be used in the same way. This is called *base direct addressing*. The other combinations that you can use are *base indexed*, in which you add a base register to an index register to get the address, and *direct base indexed*. This last mode combines a direct offset with a base register and an index register.

For programs that will run on an 80386, you can use any data register as an index register and scale the index by 2, 4, or 8 in computing the address. This would reduce the example code to two lines:

```
mov  si, 3                  ; Get the item number
mov  ax, [IArray+si*2]      ; Get the data from the array
```

Note that no matter what the addressing mode is, one of the operands must be a register. If you want to move data from one memory location to another, you must put the data in a register first. The only exception to this rule is that you can move immediate data to a memory location without first using a register.

Summary

Writing a program is an iterative process. The first step is to edit the source file, then assemble it, then link the object file, and after that test the program. The results of this testing indicate what changes you need to make, so you go back to the beginning and do it all again.

Turbo Assembler comes with the tools for assembling and linking the program. These tools have been designed to be as easy to use as possible. In the simplest case, you need only list the files to assemble or link on the command line. There are also several options for each of these utilities. You can see a list of the options by typing the program name followed by /h.

In addition to the assembler and linker, there is also the MAKE utility. This is a program that can help to assure that all the changed files get reassembled and linked into the program. It works by comparing the last update data and time of the source with the data and time of the object file. If the source is newer, then it is reassembled.

There are two kinds of commands that make up an assembly language source. The first type, assembler directives, give instructions to the assembler itself. These instructions do not generate any code, but they can affect the code that is generated. For example, a conditional assembly directive does not itself create any code, but it does determine if the code in the conditional block will or will not be included in the program.

The rest of the source is made up of program instructions. The assembler converts these instructions into the codes that the 80x86 processor can run. Assembly language is a close analog of machine language. Each program instruction stands for a single machine instruction. This gives you control over exactly what the processor is doing as it runs your program. There are no wasted instructions—unless you put them there.

Chapter *3* *Introduction to the Turbo Debugger*

Into everyone's programs a few bugs must crawl. The problem may come from a bad design, not knowing how an instruction works, side effects from other routines, or simply by making a mistake. One way to get these bugs out of your program is to inspect the source code to make sure that it does what you mean for it to do. This technique is prone to the same sources of error as writing the code in the first place. Another way to remove program bugs is to add code to print out the values of variables and registers. This not only gives you the values of the data, but, by seeing what prints and what doesn't, you can tell what code is running or not running. The problem with this is that the added code may change the behavior of the program.

Fortunately there is an alternative: *debugging* software. This is a program that lets you run portions of your program while you examine the state of registers and memory. There are several programs like this available for debugging Turbo Assembler programs. This chapter shows you how to use Turbo Debugger to debug Turbo Assembler programs.

You can see how to use Turbo Debugger to examine a sample program that has a bug in it. This shows you many of the features available in Turbo Debugger.

Using Turbo Debugger

Turbo Debugger lets you step through the instructions in your program while you examine the source code, the CPU registers, and memory. The debugger automatically places the part of the source file that goes with the code you are running on the screen. You can step through the program one instruction at a time, or you can set break points at various locations in the program and let the program run until it gets to a break point.

Turbo Debugger also includes many extra commands that make debugging easier. At first, the number of commands is quite intimidating. To make things easier, these commands are organized into pull-down menus. To find out what a particular command does, you can use the built-in help system. With a little guidance and some experimenting, you can become quite comfortable with Turbo Debugger.

Preparing To Use Turbo Debugger

The symbol names and line number information that Turbo Debugger requires is not part of a normal MS-DOS program. You must put it there by telling the assembler and the linker that you want it. The command line option for Turbo Assembler is /zi, and for TLINK it is /v. To assemble and link a program called MISTAKE.ASM for use with Turbo Debugger, use these instructions:

```
tasm /zi mistake
tlink /v mistake
```

These instructions put data at the end of the executable file that tell the debugger the names of symbols and the locations of source lines. If you do not include this information, Turbo Debugger does not show any source information. You can use Turbo Debugger in this way, but many of the useful features of the debugger won't be available.

The next step is to start the debugger. There are three versions of Turbo Debugger to choose from, depending on what type of CPU you have available. The standard version runs on all IBM-PC compatible machines. If you have an 80286 or 80386, you can use the *protected mode* versions of Turbo Debugger (TD286 and TD386). Protected mode offers several hardware debugging features of which Turbo Debugger can take advantage. All three of these debuggers use the same commands and displays; if you know one, you know them all. The command to start debugging a program, called MISTAKE.EXE with the standard debugger, is:

```
td mistake
```

The Turbo Debugger Screen

When Turbo Debugger comes up, you see a screen similar to Figure 3-1. The line at the top of the screen is the main menu. The line at the bottom shows what some of the function keys do. These two lines will help you find all the available commands. The large window just below the menu is the Module window. This window shows the source being executed. Notice that this window has a double line around it, which means that this is the current window and any keyboard input will be directed to it.

Below the Module window is the Watches window. You can put symbols in this window so that you can watch them. This window has a single line around it, indicating that it is not the current window. To make it the current window, you need to know the window number. This is the number in the upper right corner of the window. When you press the ALT key and the window number on the numeric keypad, the window becomes the current window.

As you use the debugger, you will change the number and locations of windows on the main screen. Each window shows different kinds of information about the program being debugged. Using a mouse can make keeping all of the windows properly organized much easier. If you do not have a mouse, you can use commands from the Window menu to move windows around.

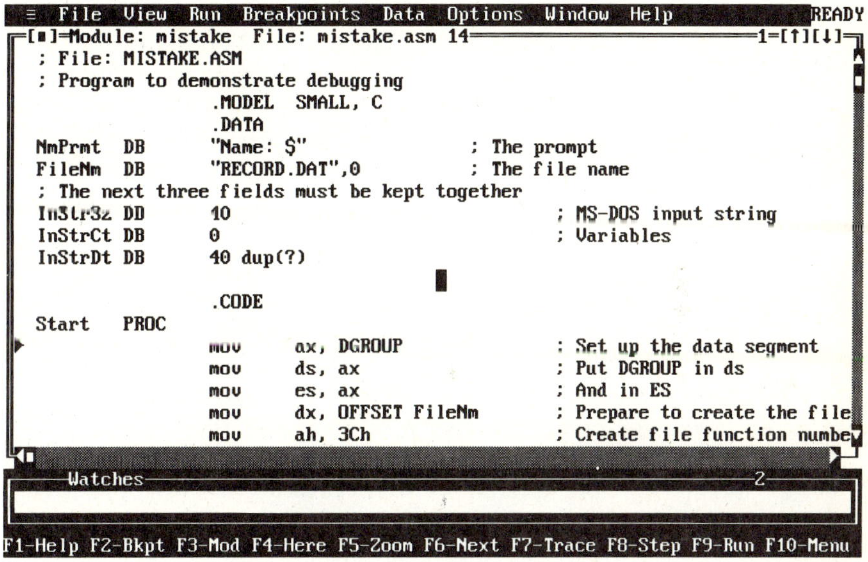

```
≡  File  View  Run  Breakpoints  Data  Options  Window  Help          READY
┌[■]=Module: mistake  File: mistake.asm 14═══════════════════1=[↑][↓]┐
│ ; File: MISTAKE.ASM                                                  █
│ ; Program to demonstrate debugging                                   │
│                 .MODEL  SMALL, C                                     │
│                 .DATA                                                │
│ NmPrmt  DB      "Name: $"              ; The prompt                  │
│ FileNm  DB      "RECORD.DAT",0         ; The file name               │
│ ; The next three fields must be kept together                       │
│ InStr3z DD      10                          ; MS-DOS input string    │
│ InStrCt DB      0                           ; Variables              │
│ InStrDt DB      40 dup(?)                                            │
│                                        █                             │
│                 .CODE                                                │
│ Start   PROC                                                         │
│▶                mov     ax, DGROUP           ; Set up the data segment│
│                 mov     ds, ax               ; Put DGROUP in ds      │
│                 mov     es, ax               ; And in ES             │
│                 mov     dx, OFFSET FileNm    ; Prepare to create the file│
│                 mov     ah, 3Ch              ; Create file function numbe▼│
│◄■                                                                  ■►│
├──Watches─────────────────────────────────────────────────────2──────┤
│                                                                      │
└──────────────────────────────────────────────────────────────────────┘
F1-Help F2-Bkpt F3-Mod F4-Here F5-Zoom F6-Next F7-Trace F8-Step F9-Run F10-Menu
```

Figure 3-1. *The initial Turbo Debugger screen.*

Entering Commands

Turbo Debugger does not use a command line for entering commands as DEBUG does. In addition to the menus and function keys, you can enter commands in specific windows. For example, pressing return in the Watches window will let you edit the expression under the cursor. Some menu functions have special *hot keys* like ALT-X for Quit. Pressing the hot key is the same as selecting the menu option. Menu options that have hot keys show such keys in the menu.

Any time you are not sure about a command, you can ask for help by pressing F1. The help screen that you see is related to the command or window that contains the cursor. This feature is very helpful when you are learning the program. You can look for a command that seems interesting, and then ask the program to explain it to you.

FUNCTION KEYS Many of the commonly used functions can be accessed with function keys. For example, to trace an instruction you can use the F7 key. There are menu options for most of the function key actions, but you may find it easier to use these keys than to work your way through the menus. The actions for each of the function keys are displayed at the bottom of the screen. To get help with these keys, you need to find the corresponding menu option, put the cursor on it, and press F1.

Pressing and holding the ALT key reveals more function keys. This feature adds a few more functions to the list of commonly used functions. As with the plain function keys, there are menu options for each of these commands. You will find that these commands do not get used as much as the plain function keys, but they are useful enough to take a look at.

The third group of function keys is a bit different from the other two. First of all, it does not use the function keys at all. If you press and hold the CTRL key, you see a list of functions. To access the functions in this list, you use the first letter of the function name instead of a function key. The list will be different, depending on the current window. For example, while the Module window is current there are commands like *Module* to change the program being debugged. When the Watches window is current, there are commands like *Edit* that let you change the contents of the Watches window.

The control key functions are called *local menus*. You can see these menus in a different format by pressing ALT-F10 or the right mouse button. When you bring up the menu this way, you can place the cursor over a menu option and press F1 to get help with that command.

TOP LEVEL MENUS The easiest way to use the main menu is by means of a mouse. All that you need to do is put the mouse cursor over the menu item you are interested in, and then press the left button. If you do not have a mouse, you can still use the menus. Pressing the F10 key puts a cursor on the menu bar. At this point pressing the left and right arrow keys moves the cursor from one menu to the next. When the cursor is on the menu you want, press return to pull it down. Now the up and down arrow keys move the cursor between the menu options, and return executes the option.

Knowing what types of commands to expect in each menu can help you find a particular command quickly. Table 3-1 shows what each menu is about. While you are running the debugger, you can use the F1 key to get information on each of the menus.

Table 3-1. *The Main Menu in Turbo Debugger*

System	Update the screen
File	Select the program to debug
View	Add windows to the screen
Run	Execute instructions
Breakpoints	Set break conditions
Data	Edit and display data
Options	Set Turbo Debugger options
Window	Move, resize, and close windows
Help	Provide information about the debugger

Debugging an Example

The next example is a program that is supposed to print a prompt, get the user's response, write it to a file, and exit. It does the first three things correctly, but instead of exiting it loops back to the question.

Listing 3-1. *A Program with an Error*

```
; File: MISTAKE.ASM
; Program to demonstrate debugging
          .MODEL    SMALL, C
          .DATA
NmPrmt    DB    "Name: $"              ; The prompt
FileNm    DB    "RECORD.DAT",0         ; The file name
; The next three fields must be kept together
InStrSz   DB    40                     ; MS-DOS input string
InStrCt   DB    0                      ; Variables
InStrDt   DB    40 dup(?)
CREATFILE EQU   3Ch
WRTDATA   EQU   40h
CLOSEFILE EQU   3Eh
PROGEXIT  EQU   4Ch
PRNTSTR   EQU   9h
GETSTR    EQU   0Ah
CHAROUT   EQU   2h
LF        EQU   0Ah

CR        EQU   0Dh
```

```
              .CODE
Start         PROC
              mov   ax, DGROUP            ; Set up the data segment
              mov   ds, ax                ; Put DGROUP in ds
              mov   es, ax                ; And in ES
              mov   dx, OFFSET FileNm     ; Prepare to create the file
              mov   ah, CREATFILE         ; Create file function number
              sub   cx, cx                ; Create a normal file
              int   21h                   ; Call MS-DOS
              mov   bx, ax                ; Copy the file handle to BX
              call  GetData               ; Call function to get inputs
              mov   ah, WRTDATA           ; Write data function number
              mov   dx, OFFSET InStrDt    ; Get the address of the data
              mov   ch, 0                 ; The size of the data
              mov   cl, InStrCt           ;
              int   21h                   ; Call MS-DOS
              mov   ah, CLOSEFILE         ; Close file function number
              int   21h                   ; Call MS-DOS
              mov   ah, PROGEXIT          ; Exit program function
              int   21h                   ; Call MS-DOS


Start         ENDP
; Prompt the user and get the data
GetData       PROC
              push  bx                    ; Save the BX register (the
                                          ; file handle)
              mov   dx, OFFSET NmPrmt     ; Get the address of the
                                          ; prompt
              mov   ah, PRNTSTR           ; MS-DOS print string function
              int   21h                   ; Call MS-DOS
              mov   dx, OFFSET InStrSz    ; Get the address of the input
                                          ; variables
              mov   ah, GETSTR            ; MS-DOS get string function
              int   21h                   ; Call MS-DOS
              mov   ah, CHAROUT           ; Character output function
              mov   dl, CR                ; Carriage return
              int   21h                   ; Call MS-DOS
              mov   dl, LF                ; Line feed
              int   21h                   ; Call MS-DOS
              ret                         ; Return to calling routine
GetData       ENDP
              .STACK   512
END  Start
```

The data section of this program sets up the five variables used in this program. The first variable (NmPrmt) is the string to use as a prompt for the user. The next variable (FileNm) is the name of the file for the data. The next three variables (InStrSz, InStrCt, InStrDt) define the data required by the MS-DOS get-the-string function.

The code section contains two procedures. The first procedure (Start) sets up the DS register, opens the file, calls the GetData procedure, writes the data, closes the file, and exits to MS-DOS. The GetData procedure uses MS-DOS functions to print the prompt, get the user's response, and print a carriage return and line feed. When it is finished, it returns to the calling routine.

When this program is assembled, linked, and run, it keeps asking for the user's name, and eventually hangs. To exit the program, you must press the CTRL-C key. This is not the way the program is supposed to work. It is time to use Turbo Debugger to find out what is going wrong.

First, be sure that you have assembled and linked the sample file with the debugging options (/zi and /v). Then start the debugger with the example program. The screen should look like the one shown in Figure 3-1.

Now you can use the F7 key to trace the program one instruction at a time. This key executes the current instruction and moves the triangle to the next instruction. What is missing is any indication of what the instruction did. For most assembly language programs you would at least like to see the registers. The View menu controls what is displayed, so look there for a command. The command that looks like it should do the job is called *Registers*. When you select this command, you see a window that shows the contents of the registers (see Figure 3-2). You should use the mouse or the Windows menu to move this menu over to the side and reduce the size of the Module window. This lets you see the registers as you trace through the rest of the program.

The left side of the Registers window shows the 13 CPU registers used by 80x86 processors. The right side of the Registers window shows the state of the 8 CPU flags. The initials used in the window stand for: Carry, Zero, Sign, Overflow, Parity, Auxiliary carry, Interrupts enabled, and Direction.

As you trace through the program, you can watch the values in the registers change. When you get to the call GetData line, you have two ways to go. The first way is to continue to trace instructions. Tracing a call moves the current instruction triangle to the routine called, and makes sure that the function is in the source code window. The other option is to let the processor execute the entire function and return control to the debugger after the function returns. This is called *stepping* in Turbo Debugger, and it happens when you press the F8 key. If you do this with the example program, it continues to ask for a name until you press the CTRL-C key. From this information it would appear that the problem is in the GetData process.

Unfortunately, it is too late to see what caused the problem. You need to start over from the beginning of the program. The command to do this is in the Run menu under Program Reset. This command puts everything back to the way it was when the debugger was started.

```
 ≡  File  View  Run  Breakpoints  Data  Options  Window  Help          READY
   ┌─Module: mistake  File: mistake.asm 14─────────────────────1──────────┐
   │ ; File: MISTAKE.ASM                                                   │
   │ ; Program to demonstrate debugging                                    │
   │               .MODEL   SMALL, C                                       │
   │               .DATA                                                   │
   │ NmPrmt  DB        "Name: $"              ; The prompt                 │
   │ FileNm  ┌─[■]═Reg═3═[↓]─┐T",0            ; The file name              │
   │ ; The ne│ ax 0000     │c=0│st be kept together                       │
   │ InStrSz  │ bx 0000     │z=0│                    ; MS-DOS input string │
   │ InStrCt  │ cx 0000     │s=0│                    ; Variables           │
   │ InStrDt  │ dx▐0000     │o=0│                                          │
   │          │ si 0000     │p=0│                                          │
   │          │ di 0000     │a=0│                                          │
   │ Start    │ bp 0000     │i=1│                                          │
   │►         │ sp 01FE     │d=0│, DGROUP          ; Set up the data segment│
   │          │ ds 6781     │   │, ax             ; Put DGROUP in ds        │
   │          │ es 6781     │   │, ax             ; And in ES              │
   │          │ ss 679A     │   │, OFFSET FileNm  ; Prepare to create the file│
   │          │ cs 6791     │   │, 3Ch            ; Create file function numbe│
   │          │ ip 0000     │   │                                          │
   └─Watch────└─────────────┴───┘──────────────────────────────2──────────┘
   ┌──────────────────────────────────────────────────────────────────────┐
   │                                                                        │
   └────────────────────────────────────────────────────────────────────────┘
 F1-Help F2-Bkpt F3-Mod F4-Here F5-Zoom F6-Next F7-Trace F8-Step F9-Run F10-Menu
```

Figure 3-2. *The Registers window.*

Instead of tracing to the beginning of the GetData routine, you can use the F4 (Go To Cursor) command. Before using this command, use the arrow keys to move the cursor to the first line in the GetData function. When the cursor is in position, press the F4 key. The debugger then lets the processor execute instructions until it gets to the line indicated by the cursor. When the debugger gets control back, you should see the current instruction triangle at the same line as the cursor.

The first instruction to trace is push bx. You can see from the Registers window that the value in BX is 5. That looks OK, so you go on to the next instruction. This is mov dx, OFFSET NmPrmt. After tracing the instruction, the Registers window shows that DX has a value in it—but that does not tell you much. You can use the Watches window to see what is in the memory pointed to by DX. First, press ALT-2 to make the Watches window active. Then, press CTRL-W to add a new watch string to the window. Figure 3-3 shows the window that comes up for inputting a watch string. The string [BYTE PTR DX],s tells the debugger to show the string at the location in the DX register. When you enter this string, you see it in the Watches window along with the string Name: $RECORD.DAT. The reason that the debugger shows RECORD.DAT in this string is that it uses a zero byte to tell where the end of the string is. If you look at the source for the data section, you see that the first zero following the name prompt is at the end of the file name.

```
  ≡  File  View  Run  Breakpoints  Data  Options  Window  Help          PROMPT
 ┌[■]=Module: mistake   File: mistake.asm 40════════1=[↑][↓]═╗══Reg─3─────
                                         ; f▲       ax 0005   c=0
           mov      dx, OFFSET NmPrmt     ; Get the a  bx 0005   z=1
                                         ; p       cx 0000   s=0
           mov      ah, 9                ; MS-DOS pr  dx 0000   o=0
 ┌[■]=Enter expression to watch══════════   ; C       si 0000   p=1
 │                                    StrSz ; Get the a  di 0000   a=0
 │ [BYTE PTR DX],s                            ; v       bp 0000   i=1
 │                                          ; MS-DOS ge  sp 01FA   d=0
 │ ██OK██   Cancel ■    Help ■               ; C       ds 6796
 └────────────────────────────────────       ; Character  es 6796
                                         ; Carriage  ss 679A
           int      21h                  ; C       cs 6791
           mov      dl, 0Ah            ▌; Line feed  ip 002E
           int      21h                  ; C
           ret                           ; R
 GetData ENDP
               .STACK  512
 END      Start
◄■                                                                     ►
   ─Watches──────────────────────────────────────────────────2─
 │
 Enter item prompted for in dialog title
```

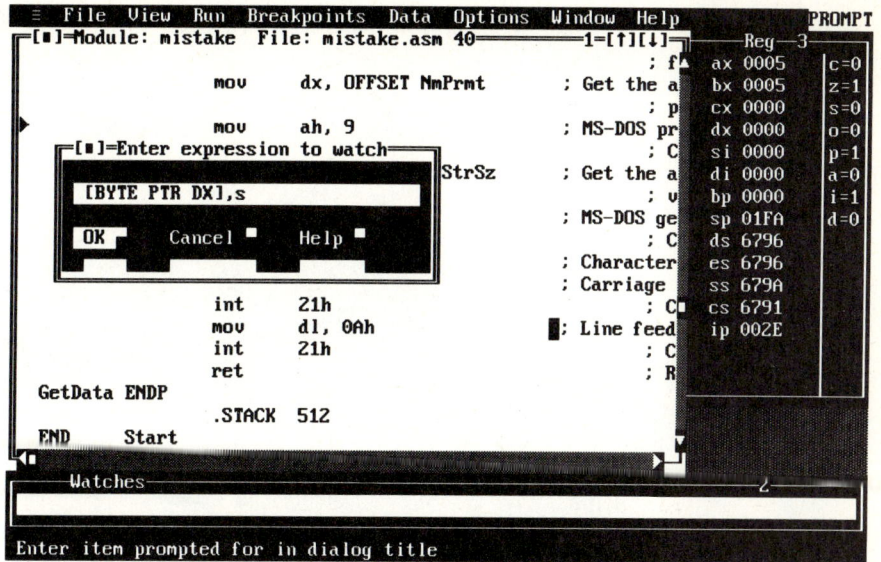

Figure 3-3. *The Watches window input box.*

MS-DOS prints the right thing because it uses the dollar sign ($) to mark the end of the string. You can verify this by tracing past the `int 21h` instruction and then looking at the user screen. The command to do this is ALT-F5. The debugger switches to the user screen and stays there until you press a key. You should see the string `Name:` along the left edge of the screen.

After pressing a key to return to the debugging screen, use the F7 key to continue tracing. When you get to the next `int 21h` and press F7 or F8, note that the debugger automatically switches to the user screen. It does this because it recognizes that the MS-DOS call requires user input. After you input the string, the debugger regains control so you can continue debugging.

Now use the F7 or F8 key to execute up to the return instruction. You know from the symptoms that the `GetData` does not return, so you need to find some explanation for why the return instruction does not work. One thing to do is to check the number on the top of the stack. This should be the return address for the function. You can use the Dump window to examine the contents of any memory location such as the top of the stack. The command to bring up the dump screen is called Dump, and it can be found in the View menu. Selecting this command brings up the window shown in Figure 3-4.

```
 ≡  File  View  Run  Breakpoints  Data  Options  Window  Help          READY
 ┌──Module: mistake  File: mistake.asm 51──────────1────┐  ┌─Reg─3──────┐
 │ GetData PROC                                         │  │ ax 020A   c=0│
 │            push    bx                      ; S       │  │ bx 0005   z=1│
 │                                            ; f       │  │ cx 0000   s=0│
 │            mov     dx, OFFSET NmPrmt       ; Get the a  │ dx 000A   o=0│
 │                                            ; p       │  │ si 0000   p=1│
 │            mov     ah, 9                   ; MS-DOS pr │ di 0000   a=0│
 │            int     21h                     ; C       │  │ bp 0000   i=1│
 │            mov     dx, OFFSET InStrSz       ; Get the a │ sp 01FA   d=0│
 │    ┌─[■]=Dump══════════════════════4=[↑][↓]┐ ; v      │  │ ds 6796     │
 │    │ ss:01FA 05 00 15 00 00 00 FB 52 ♠ § ♫ ⌐R ▲OS ge │  │ es 6796     │
 │    │ ss:0202 09 02 48 00 00 00 09 00 ○⌂H  ○   ■ ; C  │  │ ss 679A     │
 │    │ ss:020A 21 00 00 00 07 00 00 00 !      ·  acter  │  │ cs 6791     │
 │    │ ss:0212 01 00 00 00 00 00 1F 00 ☺    ▼  ▼iage    │  │ ip 0043     │
 │    └◄■                                     ┘ ; C      │  │             │
 │            mov     dl, 0Ah                 ; Line feed │  │             │
 │            int     21h                     ; C       │  │             │
 │►           ret                             ; R       │  │           ▓ │
 │ GetData ENDP                                         │  │             │
 └─Watches─────────────────────────────────────────────2──────────────┘
  [BYTE PTR DX],s              "ORD.DAT"
 Ctrl: G-Goto S-Search N-Next C-Change F-Follow P-Previous D-Display B-Block
```

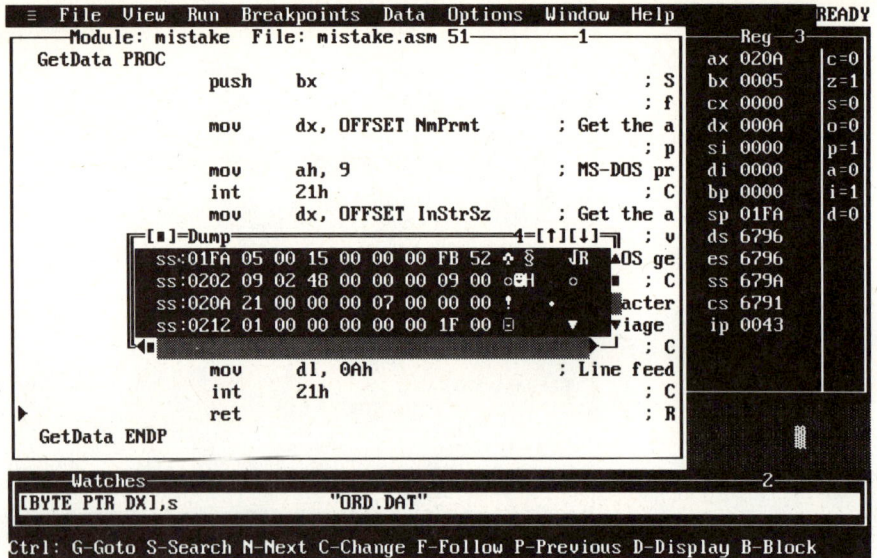

Figure 3-4. *The Dump window.*

The first thing you want to do with this window is to set the starting address to the top of the stack. The command to tell the Dump window what memory to display is CTRL-G. This brings up a window for entering the starting address. You can enter the address as a segment and an offset like `1234:0002`, or you can use an expression just as you would in an assembler program. The expression `ss:sp` is the location at the top of the stack. After entering this expression, the first value is 05.

To find out what is at offset 5 in the code segment (the location that the return instruction goes to), you can use the CPU window. The command to bring up the CPU window is in the View menu. Figure 3-5 shows the CPU window. The upper left corner of this window shows the code in memory. Use the arrow keys to move this code around until you see offset 5.

The instruction at offset 5 is `mov  es, ax`. This is not the instruction following the call to `GetData` (`mov  ah,  40h`). So now you need to find out what has "messed up" the stack. Pressing ALT-1 puts the Module window containing the source on top of the other windows so you can look at the source. Use the arrow keys to put the `GetData` function on the screen and look for instructions that affect the stack. The first instruction in the `GetData` function is `push  bx`. This instruction pushes the BX register onto the stack, so that it can be restored when the function returns. If you look at the rest of the function, you see that there is no `pop  bx` instruction to restore BX. That is the problem. Use ALT-X to exit the debugger, and use your text editor to add a POP instruction to the end of the GetData function, just before the RET instruction. Recompile and relink the program and you're done.

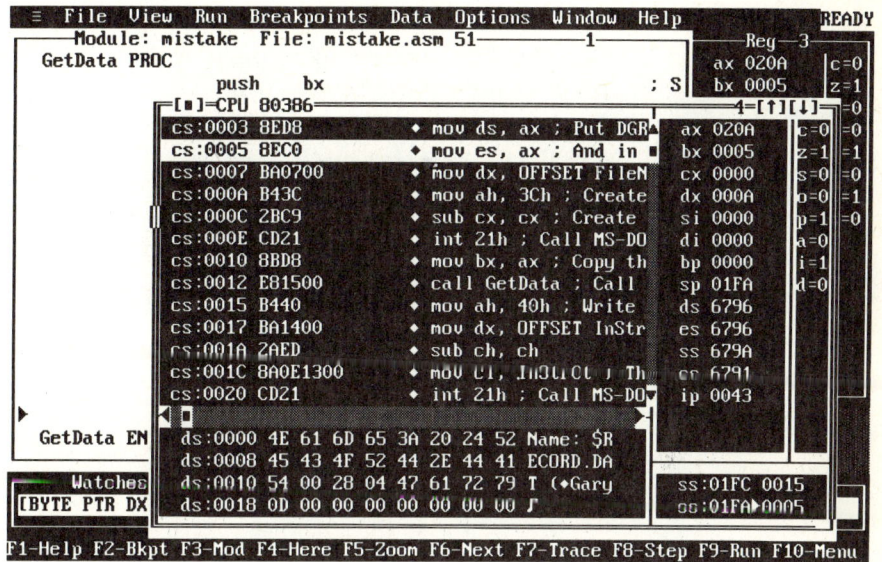

```
≡ File  View  Run  Breakpoints  Data  Options  Window  Help        READY
┌─Module: mistake   File: mistake.asm 51─────1───────┌──Reg─3─┐
│ GetData PROC                                        │ ax 020A│c=0
│              push    bx                        ; S  │ bx 0005│z=1
│    ┌─[■]─CPU 80386────────────────────────────────4─[↑][↓]─┐=0
│    │ cs:0003 8ED8          ◆ mov ds, ax ; Put DGR▲ ax 020A│c=0│=0
│    │ cs:0005 8EC0          ◆ mov es, ax ; And in ■ bx 0005│z=1│=1
│    │ cs:0007 BA0700        ◆ mov dx, OFFSET FileN  cx 0000│s=0│=0
│    │ cs:000A B43C          ◆ mov ah, 3Ch ; Create  dx 000A│o=0│=1
│    │ cs:000C 2BC9          ◆ sub cx, cx ; Create   si 0000│p=1│=0
│    │ cs:000E CD21          ◆ int 21h ; Call MS-DO   di 0000│a=0│
│    │ cs:0010 8BD8          ◆ mov bx, ax ; Copy th   bp 0000│i=1│
│    │ cs:0012 E81500        ◆ call GetData ; Call    sp 01FA│d=0│
│    │ cs:0015 B440          ◆ mov ah, 40h ; Write    ds 6796│
│    │ cs:0017 BA1400        ◆ mov dx, OFFSET InStr   es 6796│
│    │ cs:001A 2AED          ◆ sub ch, ch             ss 679A│
│    │ cs:001C 8A0E1300      ◆ mov cl, InStrl ; Th    cs 6791│
│ ▶  │ cs:0020 CD21          ◆ int 21h ; Call MS-DO▼  ip 0043│
│    └◄─□─────────────────────────────────────────▶┘
│ GetData EN │ ds:0000 4E 61 6D 65 3A 20 24 52 Name: $R │
│            │ ds:0008 45 43 4F 52 44 2E 44 41 ECORD.DA │
┌─Watches┐   │ ds:0010 54 00 28 04 47 61 72 79 T (◆Gary │ ss:01FC 0015
│[BYTE PTR DX│ ds:0018 0D 00 00 00 00 00 00 00 ♪        │ ss:01FA▶0005
└───────────────────────────────────────────────────────────────────┘
F1-Help F2-Bkpt F3-Mod F4-Here F5-Zoom F6-Next F7-Trace F8-Step F9-Run F10-Menu
```

Figure 3-5. *The CPU window.*

Summary

Turbo Debugger is a powerful tool for looking into the way a program works. Not only is it useful for finding bugs in programs that you are writing, but you can also use it to find out how someone else's program works. Rather than poring over every line of a strange program, you can let Turbo Debugger run portions of the program to see what each portion does.

The main feature of Turbo Debugger is the ability to see your source code while you are debugging. Instead of trying to decipher the binary numbers that make up the program, you can look at your source code, complete with symbols and comments. In addition, when you tell Turbo Debugger to do something, you don't need to know the address of the code or data—just the symbol name.

Turbo Debugger also gives you a number of ways to look at memory. You can see memory as a list of hexadecimal values, as in the Dump window, or you can look at it as a string or an integer or a character with the Watches window. This lets you look at data in a way that makes immediate sense. For example, if you are looking for a variable with 100 in it, you would like to see 100 and not 64 00.

Finally, Turbo Debugger has a number of commands to control whatever program portions you want to run. You can step through the instructions one at a time, run up to a certain point in the program, or run a loop a certain number of times. These commands let you skip over parts of the program in which you are not interested and instead go directly to the code you want to see. As your programs grow in size, this will save on debugging time and leave you with more time to write actual programs.

II

Processor Instructions

► Data Movement Instructions,

► Arithmetic, Logic, and Bit-Shift Instructions,

► Procedures, Loops, and Jumps,

► Processor Control and Protected Mode Operation,

Chapter 4 Data Movement Instructions

One of the most important things that the 80x86 processor does is to move data from one location to another. Many of the 80x86 instructions and MS-DOS functions require data to be in specific registers. Typically, this data will come from memory variables. The first section in this chapter shows how to move data from memory to registers and back again.

Many functions need temporary variables to hold data. If the function needs only a few temporary variables, you can put them in registers. The problem with this concerns what to do when there are more temporary variables than registers. Another problem concerns what to do when the function calls another function that also uses the registers for temporary variables. The second section in this chapter shows how to use the stack for storing temporary variables.

An important source of data is the I/O ports. This is how the 80x86 sends and receives data and commands from other parts of the computer. The keyboard, screen, parallel and serial ports all rely on the I/O instructions described in the next section of this chapter.

The last section deals with reading and writing blocks of data. The Intel Corporation documentation refers to these instructions as string instructions. There is no reason to restrict the use of these instructions to strings. They can be used any time you want to with data arrays.

Moving Data

The MOV (MOVe data) instruction copies data from one location to another. The format of the instruction is:

```
mov   destination, source
```

Both destination and source can be registers, or one of them can be a memory location, or the source can be an immediate value. You cannot use the move instruction to copy data from one memory location to another. For example, if you use the AX register to calculate the number of times a loop should run you will have to move the result to the CX register for use with the LOOP instruction.

The MOV instruction can be used to load or store the contents of a segment register. When segment registers are involved you cannot use the immediate addressing mode. Another interesting thing about loading segment registers has to do with the stack segment and interrupts. Look at the following code fragment:

```
mov   ss, seg newstack
mov   sp, offset stackpoint
```

If an interrupt comes along between these two instructions, it will try to push the flags and the return address on newstack; but the stack pointer will be pointing to some unknown location. The 80x86 processor handles this by disabling interrupts until after whatever instruction follows a MOV to the stack segment. You may have problems with this feature if you are using a very early version of the 8088, or 8086 chips. If your program might need to run on one of these older processors, you should surround these instructions with CLI (CLear Interrupt flag) and STI (SeT Interrupt flag) instructions.

Addressing Modes

The 80x86 instruction set includes twelve ways to copy data values to or from a register. These different ways are known as addressing modes, because they involve ways to calculate the address of the data in memory. This address is known as the effective address (EA) for the instruction. Table 4-1 summarizes the addressing modes available.

Table 4-1. *80x86 Addressing Modes*

Name	Explanation
Implied	Several instructions (CBW, MUL, LAHF...) only work with certain registers. Most often the register is the 8 or 16 bit accumulator (AX or AL).
`cbw`	`; Convert the byte in AL to a` `; word in AX`
Immediate	The data is in the byte or word following the instruction. This mode can only be used to load a register.
`mov   ax, 1234h`	`; Copy 1234h to the AX` `; register`

Name	Explanation
Direct	The data is at the address following the instruction.

```
mov    ax, Symbol  ; Copy the data at Symbol into
                   ; AX
```

Indexed	The data is at the address in the SI or DI registers.

```
mov    [si], ax    ; Copy the contents of AX to
                   ; the memory location in SI.
```

Base	The data is at the address in the BX or BP registers. Using the BP register implies that the segment register is SS.

```
mov    ax, [bx]    ; Copy the data at the memory
                   ; location in BX to AX
```

Direct indexed	The address for the data is the sum of the SI or DI register and the byte or word following the instruction.

```
mov    ax, [si+4]  ; Add 4 to SI to get the
                   ; address of the data and copy
                   ; it to AX
```

Direct base	The address for the data is the sum of the BX or BP register and the byte or word following the instruction. Using the BP register implies that the segment register is SS.

```
mov    [bp-2], ax  ; Copy AX to the word at BP-2
```

Base indexed	The address of the data is the sum of the SI or DI register and the BX or BP register. Using the BP register implies that the segment register is SS.

```
mov    ax, [bx+di] ; Add BX and DI to get the
                   ; address of the data to copy
                   ; to AX
```

Direct base indexed	The address of the data is the sum of the SI or DI register, the BX or BP register, and the byte or word following the instruction. Using the BP register implies that the segment register is SS.

```
mov    ax, [bp+si+2]   ; Add BP, SI, and 2 to get the
                       ; address of the data to copy
                       ; to AX
```

Table 4-1. *Continued*

Name	Explanation
Direct scaled index	The address of the data is the sum of a specified register times a scaling factor (2, 4, 8) and the byte, word, or double word following the instruction. (80386 only)

```
mov   [ebx*2+Table], ax  ; Copy ax to the word at
                         ; the sum of the offset
                         ; of Table to the
                         ; contents of the EBX
                         ; register times 2
```

Name	Explanation
Base scaled index	The address of the data is the sum of a specified base register and another register times a scaling factor (2, 4, 8). (80386 only)

```
mov   eax, [ebx+ecx*4]   ; Copy the data at the
                         ; sum of EBX and ECX
                         ; times 4 to EAX
```

Name	Explanation
Direct base scaled indexed	The address of the data is the sum of a specified base register, another register times a scaling factor (2, 4, 8), and the byte, word, or double word following the instruction. (80386 only)

```
mov   [ecx+ebx*8+4], cx  ; Copy CX to the word at
                         ; the sum of ECX, EBX*8,
                         ; and 4
```

Putting the Effective Address in a Register

As the addressing mode becomes more complex, the amount of time required to get a piece of data increases. If you are going to access the data item several times, it would be better to add up all the values used to make the address and access the data with the result. The LEA (Load Effective Address) instruction does just that. The format is:

```
lea   register, memory
```

The next example adds the word in a table at SI+BX to the next 4 words in the table. It takes 184 clock cycles.

```
        xor   ax,ax                   ; clear ax
        mov   cx,4
aloop:
        add   ax,table[si+bx]         ; add in a number
        inc   bx                      ; go to the next word
        inc   bx
        loop aloop                    ; loop cx times
```

Using LEA reduces the number of clock cycles to 173:

```
        xor   ax,ax
        mov   cx,4
        lea   di, table[si+bx]        ; put the address in DI
aloop:
        add   ax,[di]
        inc   di
        inc   di
        loop aloop
```

Segment Overrides

In each of the addressing modes, the effective address is the offset into the default segment. For indexed modes that use the BP register, the default segment is the stack segment (SS); all other modes use the data segment (DS). Other segments can be used with these modes by using a segment override prefix. To use the extra segment with the direct mode, for example, use this format:

```
    mov   ax,es:data
```

Segment overrides are common in programs that have several data segments, such as large, huge, or compact model programs. These programs usually put commonly used data items in the segment indicated by the DS register and move the ES register to whatever other segment is currently being used.

Each segment override adds two cycles to the time to calculate the effective address. This is not a problem for programs that use a small number of segment overrides. For routines that use many segment overrides, you may want to consider putting the segment being used into the DS register. For example:

```
    push ds             ; Save the current data segment
    mov  ax, ExtraSeg   ; Get the address of the segment
```

```
        mov  ds, ax             ; Put the segment in DS
           .                     ; Use the data in ExtraSeg
           .
           .

        pop  ds                 ; restore the original data segment
```

Loading Far Pointers

Turbo Assembler keeps track of the segment and offset of each label in the
program. For data that is in the segment indicated by the DS register, the
program only uses the offset portion of the address. This is called a *near
pointer*. When the data is in another segment, the program must load a
segment register before accessing the data. The segment and offset together is
called a *far pointer*.

Some routines save pointers in memory to be used later in the program.
If the program uses far pointers, the code might look like this:

```
            .DATA
FarDataOffset  DW    OFFSET DataItem      ; Store the offset
FarDataSegment DW    SEG DataItem         ; Store the segment
            .CODE
              .

              .

              .
            mov  bx, FarDataOffset
            mov  es, FarDataSegment
              .

              .

              .
```

An easier way is to use the load far pointer instructions. For example, the
LES (Load far pointer into ES) can be used to code the previous example like
this:

```
            .DATA
FarDataPtr      DD   DataItem            ; Store offset and segment
            .CODE
              .

              .

              .
            les  bx, FarDataPtr
              .

              .

              .
```

In this case the double word at `FarDataPtr` is read into the BX and ES registers. Note that, unless you use a segment override, `FarDataPtr` must be in the current data segment. To change the data segment, you could use the LDS instruction (Load far pointer into DS). This instruction puts the data into the destination register and the DS register.

The 80386 has two more segment registers and three more Load Far Pointer instructions. The new registers are FS and GS. The new instructions are LFS (Load far pointer into FS), LGS (Load far pointer into GS), and LSS (Load far pointer into SS).

Exchanging Values

There are times when you would like to swap two values. For example, when sorting a list of data, you must swap values to get the list in the correct order. To do this with the MOV instruction requires four instructions and two extra registers.

```
mov   ax,Data1      ; Save the data
mov   bx,Data2      ; in registers
mov   Data1,bx      ; Restore the data
mov   Data2,ax      ; in the opposite order
```

To shorten the code in this situation we can use the XCHG (eXCHanGe data) instruction. The format for this instruction is:

```
XCHG reg/mem,mem/reg
```

In this instruction, `reg/mem` is a register or memory location. As with other instructions, if you use a memory operand, the other operand must be a register.

With the XCHG instruction the example above becomes:

```
mov   ax,Data1      ; Get 1 operand in ax
xchg  ax,Data2      ; Exchange it with the other
                    ; operand
mov   Data1,ax      ; Store the new ax in the first
                    ; operand
```

Loading the Accumulator from a Table Lookup

There is more than one way to encode the characters used by the computer. MS-DOS computers use ASCII codes, while other systems may use EBCDIC, BAUDOT, or some other scheme. The XLAT (transLATe data) instruction can be used to help convert from one system to another by doing a table lookup. To use the XLAT instruction, the BX register must point to a table of values. The AL register is used to indicate what table entry to use. After the instruction, AL will contain this entry.

There is a code size verses execution time trade-off with this instruction. The same table can be used with an indexed addressing mode of the MOV instruction to get the same result in less than half the time. On the other hand, using the MOV instruction will use twice the number of bytes of memory.

The next example assumes there is a table of bytes that represent the EBCDIC encoding for characters. The table is arranged in the order of the ASCII character set. The routine is called with an ASCII character in AL, and returns with the EBCDIC value in AL.

```
mov  bx, offset ASC2EBC      ; Get the address of the
                             ; conversion table
xlat                         ; Do the lookup
```

Moving Small Data to Large Registers on the 80386

When using the large registers on the 80386, you need some way to load the 32-bit registers. One way is to load them from 32-bit memory locations. This can be inconvenient if you already have the data in one of the 16-bit registers. You would need to use something like the following code.

```
       .DATA
dblspace  dd   1 dup(?)           ; Make space for a 32-bit
                                  ; value
       .CODE
       mov  word ptr dblspace, ax ; Save register in big
                                  ; space
       mov  word ptr dblspace+2,0 ; Clear the high word
       mov  eax,dblspace          ; Load the 32-bit
                                  ; register
```

The 80386 saves you this effort by providing the MOVZX (MOVe with Zero eXtend). This instruction uses an 8- or 16-bit memory or register source operand and a 16- or 32-bit register destination operand. The code above can be reduced to:

```
movzx eax,ax
```

The problem of moving small data to large registers is even worse for signed values. You would have to check the sign bit of the small register, and store 0 or 0ffffh in the high word depending on the sign. Instead you can use MOVSX (MOVe with Sign eXtend). This instruction uses the same operands as the MOVZX instruction, but it checks the sign bit of the source and extends it into the high byte or word of the destination.

Using the Flags To Set a Byte to One

One of the many new instructions that are included in the 80386 instruction set is the SET (SET conditionally) instruction. This instruction looks at the flags and, if a certain condition is set, it sets a byte specified by the operand to 1. There are 18 conditions that can be set. Table 4-2 shows them all.

Table 4-2. *The 80386 SET Instruction*
Unsigned Arithmetic Tests

Mnemonic	Description
SETB/SETNAE	If Below/Not Above or Equal (CF=1)
SETAE/SETNB	If Above or Equal/Not Below (CF=0)
SETBE/SETNA	If Below or Equal/Not Above (CF=1 ZF=1)
SETA/SETNBE	If Above/Not Below or Equal (CF=0 and ZF=0)

Signed Arithmetic Tests

Mnemonic	Description
SETL/SETNGE	If Less/Not Greater or Equal (SF<>OF)
SETGE/SETNL	If Greater or Equal/Not Less (SF=OF)
SETLE/SETNG	If Less or Equal/Not Greater (ZF=1 or SF<>OF)
SETG/SETNLE	If Greater/Not Less or Equal (ZF=0 or SF=OF)

Equality Tests

Mnemonic	Description
SETE/SETZ	If Equal/Zero (ZF=1)
SETNE/SETNZ	If Not Equal/Not Zero (ZF=0)

Sign Flag Tests

Mnemonic	Description
SETS	If Sign is negative (SF=1)
SETNS	If Sign is positive (SF=0)

Carry Flag Tests

Mnemonic	Description
SETC	If Carry flag set
SETNC	if Carry flag not set

Table 4-2. *Continued*

Mnemonic	Description
	Overflow Flag Tests
SETO	If Overflow flag set
SETNO	If Overflow flag cleared
	Parity Flag Tests
SETP/SETPE	If Parity/Parity Even (PF=1)
SETNP/SETPO	If Not Parity/Parity Odd (PF=0)

The SET instructions can be used after a compare or arithmetic operation to set a flag byte that might be used later in the program. You could use this instruction to count the number of times a certain condition comes up. For example, this routine reads a list of 20 numbers and counts how many of them are over 21:

```
        mov   cx, 20              ; Twenty numbers
        sub   dx,dx               ; Set DX to 0
        sub   ah,ah               ; Set AH to 0
        mov   bx,offset table
aloop:
        cmp   word ptr [bx],21    ; Compare to 21
        seta  al                  ; if above al = 1
        add   dx,ax               ; Add to the count
        loop  aloop               ; Do it CX times
```

The Stack

The stack is an area of memory used to store data and function return addresses. You can use the stack to store the state of the flags and registers, to pass values to functions, or to store local data for a function. The stack grows to accommodate more data, and shrinks when the data is no longer required. To make this work, the stack operates on a Last-In-First-Out (LIFO) principle. The last word (all stack items are words) saved is the first word recovered.

The stack works by using a special register called the *stack pointer*. To store data on the stack, the processor decrements the stack pointer by two (the size of a word), and then it stores the data at the memory location in SS : SP. This operation is called *pushing*. To get the data back, the word at SS : SP is read, and then the SP is incremented by two. This is called *popping*.

Pushing and Popping Data

The PUSH and POP instructions work as complements. In other words, if you use a PUSH instruction, you should generally use a POP instruction somewhere later in the program. Failing to keep the stack balanced is a common error in assembly language programs.

The PUSH (PUSH data) instruction is used to push data on the stack. The format of the instruction is:

```
PUSH reg/mem/immediate
```

The register is one of the 16-bit registers or a segment register. The memory value is also a 16-bit value. To push immediate values requires a 80286 or 80386. The 80386 can also push 32-bit registers and memory values.

The POP (POP data) instruction uses the same format to undo the work of the PUSH instruction. These instructions are handy for temporarily saving the contents of a register while the register is used for something else. For example, the following code fragment uses the CX register to control two loops. The LOOP instruction only works with the CX register. The CX value used in the outer loop must be saved while the inner loop is running.

```
        sub  ax, ax       ; Set AX to 0
        mov  cx, 20       ; Run the outer loop 20 times
outer:
        push cx           ; Save the cx register
        mov  cx, 15       ; Run the inner loop 15 times
inner:
        inc  ax
        loop inner        ; Decrement CX and loop while not 0
        pop  cx           ; Get the outer CX back
        loop outer        ; Decrement the out CX and loop
                          ; AX is 300 ( 20 * 15 )
```

When a subroutine is going to be called from many different places, it is a good idea to push the registers that the routine uses, and pop them when the function is done. This makes sure that the calling routine does not lose data by having registers scrambled by the subroutine.

If a routine uses all of the registers, it would have to push all of the registers. The code for this uses 8 bytes and takes 24 clock cycles. On a 80286 or 80386, you can push all the data registers with a single instruction. The PUSHA (PUSH All) instruction pushes all of the 16-bit registers, and the PUSHAD (PUSH All Double) instruction pushes all of the 32-bit registers. To pop all of the data registers, use the POPA (POP All) and POPAD (POP All Double) instructions. These instructions do not affect the segment registers.

The final kind of push/pop gets and puts the flags. This is the same register that is used in the LAHF and SAHF instructions. To push the flags, use the PUSHF (PUSH Flags) instruction. On the 80386 the flag register is 32 bits long. To push the 32-bit flag register, use PUSHFD (PUSH Flags Double). To get the flags back, use POPF (POP Flags) and POPFD (POPFlags Double).

Moving Data on the Stack

The base addressing and direct base addressing modes that use the BP register use the stack segment to get data. This can be used to release the memory used by local variables when the subroutine returns. The area of the stack used for function data is called a *stack frame*. The example below shows how to set up, use, and release local data space for three words.

```
push bp                   ; Save the old BP
mov   bp,sp               ; Make BP point to the top of
                          ; the stack
sub   sp,6                ; Make room for 3 words
mov   word ptr [bp-2],1   ; Put 1 in the first variable
mov   word ptr [bp-4],2   ; Put 2 in the second
mov   word ptr [bp-6],3   ; Put 3 in the third
                          ; Do the rest of the routine
  .

  .
mov   sp,bp               ; Get rid of the local data
pop   bp                  ; Get the old BP back
ret                       ; Go back to the calling
                          ; routine
```

Stack frames are important in modular programs. They provide a way for one function to pass data to another, and a place for the routine to store temporary variables without affecting memory used by other routines. To pass data to a function, the calling routine pushes the data on the stack, and then calls the function. The function accesses the data in the same way that it gets local data. When the function is done, it moves the stack pointer to the original position, so that the memory can be used by the next function.

Figure 4-1 shows the stack with several stack frames on it. Note that to access passed values, you must add a displacement to BP; and for local variables, you subtract the displacement.

```
                                              High Addresses


          ┌──────────────────┐
          │   Argument 1     │  ←─BP+6
          ├──────────────────┤
          │   Argument 2     │  ←─BP+4
          ├──────────────────┤
          │  Return Address  │
          ├──────────────────┤
          │     Old BP       │  ←─BP
          ├──────────────────┤
          │ First local (WORD) │ ←─BP-2
          ├──────────────────┤
          │ Second local (DWORD) │ ←─BP-6
          └──────────────────┘

                                              Low Address
```

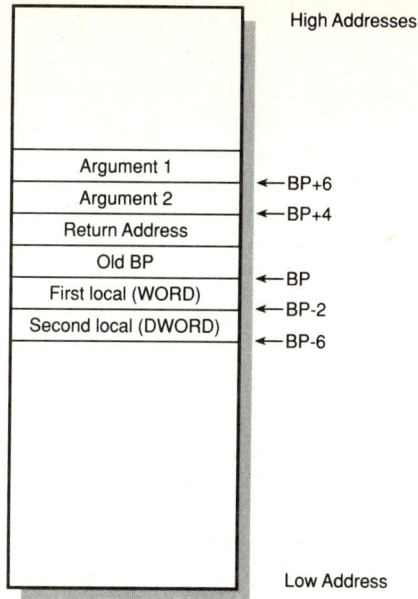

Figure 4-1. *Local variables on the stack.*

String Operations

With the previous commands, data can be moved one byte, word, or double
word at a time. This is not always the way the data comes. It would be useful
to be able to do a MOV on any size block of data.

The 80x86 has several instructions for operating on a block of data in
memory. These instructions are called *string operations*, even though they do
not always operate on strings.

The string operations work by using the SI and DI index registers. In
general, SI points to a location in the data segment for the source array, and
DI points to a location in the extra segment for the destination array. Any
segment override used will only affect the source segment.

After a string instruction operates on the data, it adjusts the index
register. The amount of the adjustment is related to the size of the data used.
For byte operations the index registers are adjusted by one, for words by two,
and for double words by four. The direction flag determines whether the index
is increased or decreased. When the direction flag is cleared, the size of the
operands is added to the index registers. Otherwise, the size is subtracted from
the index registers.

Moving Data from the Source Array to the Destination

The MOVS (MOVe String) instruction will copy the byte, word, or double word (80386 only) from the location in DS:SI to the location in ES:DI. There are four formats that can be used with this instruction. The first format tells what size to use by specifying operands. This format also lets you use a segment override on the source:

```
MOVS dest, [seg:]source
```

For this instruction dest and source are defined to be the size you want to use. Despite the use of operands, this instruction actually uses implied addressing. The operands tell the assembler if the data should be moved a byte, word, or a double word (80386 only) at a time.

Another way to specify the size is to append a B (Byte), W (Word), D (Double word) to the instruction.

The fact that the index registers get updated means that this instruction can be used several times in a row to copy the whole array. The following code fragment uses this feature to copy 20 bytes from Str1 to Str2.

```
       cld                      ; Set direction to forward
       mov   si,OFFSET Str1     ; Get the address of Str1 in SI
       mov   di,OFFSET Str2     ; Get the address of Str2 in DI
       push ds                  ; Copy the DS register
       pop  es                  ; into the ES register
       mov   cx, 20             ; Set the number of bytes
mloop:
       movsb                    ; Move a byte
       loop mloop               ; Do it 20 times
```

The REP Prefix

In the previous example, the loop command was used to make a very efficient loop to move the string. Using the REP (REPeat) prefix could make it even more efficient. The REP prefix can be used with certain instructions to repeat the instruction the number in the CX register times. In the string copy example, the loop could be replaced by the following command:

```
rep movsb
```

The repeat prefix has improved with age. On the 8088 and 8086, it was faster to use the loop instruction and it took the same number of bytes. With the 80286 and 80386, the size has stayed the same but the time to execute has been trimmed. Another problem that affects all but the 80386 processor is that if the repeated instruction uses a segment override, and an interrupt occurs during the repeated instruction, unpredictable results could occur. You should consider the kinds of machine your program will run on before deciding to use the REP prefix with a segment override.

Loading and Storing with Strings

Sometimes a program needs to do more than just copy a string. Perhaps the data in a string must have a value added, or a particular number is at the end of the string. In this case you need to be able to do the two steps of moving (Load and Store) as separate instructions. The instructions for loading and storing elements of a string are LODS (LOaD String) and STOS (STOre String). The formats are very much like those for the MOVS instruction except that, when an operand is used to tell the size, only one is required:

```
LODS [seg:]source
```

In this case the size of the data at source is used. The segment override is optional. Note that by using two instructions instead of MOVS, you can use a segment override on both operands.

Both LODS and STOS move the data to or from the accumulator. For 8-bit operations it is AL, for 16-bit operations it is AX, and for 32-bit operations (80386 only) it is EAX.

One use of the LODS and STOS instructions is to change all of the letters in a string to upper case as it is copied. In this example the string at Str1 is converted to upper case as it is copied to Str2:

```
        cld                     ; Set direction to forward
        mov   si, OFFSET Str1   ; Get the addresses of
        mov   di, OFFSET Str2   ; the strings
        push  ds                ; Copy the DS register
        pop   es                ; to the ES register
Uloop:
        lodsb                   ; Get a byte
        or    al,al             ; Set the flags
        jz    Done
        cmp   al,'a'            ; Check for lower case
        jb    NotLow            ; if < 'a' it is not
        cmp   al,'z'
        ja    NotLow            ; if > 'z' it is not
        sub   al, 20h           ; Change to upper case
NotLow:
        stosb                   ; Store the byte
        jmp   Uloop
Done:
```

The STOS instruction can be used with the REP prefix to set a range of memory to a particular value. In the next example, the 18-byte block of data at Spaces is set to 20h (ASCII value of a space character). Note that STOSW is used to store two bytes at once. This speeds things up considerably by reducing the number of times the loop needs to run.

```
cld                     ; Set the direction to forward
mov   di, OFFSET Spaces ; Get the address of Spaces
mov   ax, 2020h         ; Put 2 spaces in AX
mov   cx, 9             ; Put half the number of bytes
                        ; to store in CX
rep stosw               ; Store the bytes two at a
                        ; time
```

Checking Array Boundaries

When a routine is handed an address, good programming practice requires the routine to check that the address is within the boundaries of the array. Failure to do so could result in the routine changing memory that it was not meant to change. This often results in a problem later in the program. This type of bug is one of the most difficult to find.

With the 8088 and 8086, checking if a number is within the correct limits can be done with compare and conditional jump instructions as in the following example:

```
cmp   si, Lowlimit   ; Check the pointer against the
                     ; lower limit
jb    Outbounds      ; If it is below, go to the error
                     ; routine
cmp   si, Upperlim   ; Check against the upper limit
ja    Outbounds      ; Jump if too high
.                    ; Do the routine with the good
.                    ; address
.
Outbounds:           ; Do some kind of error report
```

The 80286 and 80386 have made this operation somewhat simpler. The BOUND (check array BOUNDs) instruction will do both compares in a single instruction. The format of the instruction is:

```
BOUND register, boundaries
```

For this instruction, register is a register containing the address to check, and boundaries is a pointer to a location in memory that contains the lower and upper boundaries. The difficult part of using this instruction comes from the way that it reports an address out of bounds. Instead of setting flags, the result of an out-of-bounds address is to generate an interrupt 5. This can be used if the program has some generic action that should be performed whenever there is an out-of-bounds pointer taken by the program.

In MS-DOS, interrupt 5 is normally used to print the contents of the screen on the printer. You can use the MS-DOS functions 25h and 35h to save the old interrupt 5 vector and replace it with the address of a routine in your program. If you do this, the print screen key will call you routine instead of printing the screen. Because of this, the BOUND instruction is not recommended for use in MS-DOS systems.

Input and Output Operations

When you use an I/O instruction, the processor sends a signal indicating that the next access is for I/O — not memory. Next, it puts a number on the address bus that indicates what port to use, and reads or writes data on the data bus. On IBM PC compatible systems, many of these ports are defined for specific uses. For example, the ports used to access the parallel and serial ports are usually the same for all compatibles. Other ports are defined only for a particular make and model of computer. The ports used to access the real-time clock registers are different on different systems. You should consult the documentation for your computer before using I/O instructions.

The I/O Instructions

The instructions for using these ports are IN (INput) and OUT (OUTput). There are two formats used with I/O instructions. For ports number 0 to 255 (0FFh), the first format uses an immediate value to specify the port to use.

```
in    acc, port
out   port, acc
```

For this instruction, acc is one of the accumulator registers (AL or AX), and port is an 8-bit number that tells what port to use. For the ports greater than 255, use this format:

```
in    acc, dx
out   dx, acc
```

The acc is an accumulator register (AL or AX), as in the previous example. Instead of getting the port from an immediate value, the port number is in the DX register.

Because the I/O instructions deal with the outside world, special consideration should be made for timing. The IN instruction tells you what is at the port at the time that the instruction is executed. It is possible that the port does not contain valid information at this time. Different devices will use different techniques to let the program know when the data is valid.

One way to signal that the data is ready is to put a zero at the port until the data is ready. You can use this technique for any port that does not use 0 as a valid data value. In this case a loop can be used that reads the port until data shows up:

```
iloop:
    in    al,123h     ; Read the port
    or    al,al        ; Set the flags
    jz    iloop        ; Loop if the data is 0
```

A similar technique is to leave the high bit at the port off until the data is ready. In this case you can use the same loop as before, but change the Jump if zero (JZ) instruction to Jump if not sign (JNS).

Another technique commonly used is to use a status port to tell when the data at the data port is ready. In this case the program loops on the status port until the status byte says there is data ready. Then the data port is read.

Some devices use an index register to make different data available at a data port. For example, some real-time clock chips have several registers that can all be accessed through the same port. First, the program must tell the real-time clock chip what register to use. Then the data port can be read or written. Often chips that use this kind of system need some time between setting the index register and reading or writing the data port. The most common way to perform this delay is with a JMP $+2 instruction. The following example shows how to read register 10h of a real-time clock chip:

```
    mov   al,10h       ; Set up the register to use
    out   70h,al       ; Send the register # to the index
                       ; port
    jmp   $+2          ; Jump to the next instruction
    jmp   $+2          ; Do it again. This wastes time
                       ; while the port is settling down
    in    al,71h       ; Read the data port
```

Input and Output on the 80386

In addition to being able to use 32-bit registers with the I/O instructions, the 80386 also has two special string input instructions and the ability to prevent low priority programs from using the I/O instructions.

The string instructions are INS (INput String) and OUTS (OUTput String). They use a format similar to other string instructions:

```
INS [es:]dest, DX
    INSB                For bytes
    INSW                For words
    INSD                For double words
```

The first format uses a memory location to specify the size of the data to use. Only the size of the operand is used. The data always comes from DS:SI for outputting, and to ES:DI for inputting. These instructions can be used with the REP prefix to send or receive a series or data elements.

There are not many cases where you can send or receive a series of data without some kind of control over the data rate. For this reason you should be careful when using string I/O with the REP prefix. On the other hand, it can be very convenient to have an instruction that combines the steps of reading a data port and storing the data in memory.

Using an IN instruction to check a status register, and an INS instruction to get and store the data can be very efficient. This example shows such a technique:

```
        mov   di, OFFSET buffer  ; Get the address of the
                                 ; buffer
        push  ds                 ; Save the ds register
        pop   es                 ; in the es register
        mov   cx,22              ; Set loop counter to number
                                 ; of bytes to read
rloop:
        mov   dx,123h            ; Load the status port number
sloop:
        in    al,dx              ; Read the status port
        test  al,status          ; Check the status bit
        jz    sloop              ; Keep checking
        mov   dx,331h            ; Move to the data port
        insb                     ; Read and save the data
        loop  rloop              ; Do it all again
```

Summary

Data must be moved into registers before it can undergo any operation. Data must also be in the correct register for certain operations.

Memory data can be and is divided into segments. Some of the segments, such as the code, data, and stack segments, are used to store specific kinds of data. Different addressing modes allow the data to be located in several useful ways.

String instructions can be used to operate on blocks of data. In some cases, by using the REP prefix you can operate on a block of data with a single instruction.

Data can also be read and written to the outside world by using I/O instructions. These instructions are used to manipulate the hardware controlled by your computer.

IN

IN

PURPOSE To read data from an input port.

SYNTAX

IN   accum, immed   *Put data from port at immed in the accumulator.* immed *can be 0 to 255.*

IN   accum, dx   *Put data from the port indicated by the DX register in the accumulator. DX can be 0 to 65535.*

FLAGS The flags are unaffected by this instruction.

COMMENTS In order to use this instruction, you must know about the hardware being used. For example, some devices use different port numbers on different computers. You should also be aware of any protocol used by the device to ensure that the data for the port is valid.

SEE ALSO

OUT   *To output data*

INS/OUTS   *For I/O with strings*

TIMING

Addressing	Encoding	Example	88/86	286	386
immed	1110010w port	in ax,3f8h	14/10	5	12
DX	1110110w	in al,dx	12/8	5	13

EXAMPLE Write a routine to see if the serial port has a character ready then read the character.

```
     mov  dx,3f8h      ; Get the COM1 port status register
sloop:
     in   al,dx        ; Get the status byte
     test al,40h       ; Check the character in status
     jz   sloop
     add  dx,          ; Move to the COM1 data port

     in   al,dx
```

INS/INSB/INSW/INSD

PURPOSE
To receive a series of data elements from a port address and save them in successive memory locations pointed to by the ES and DI registers.

SYNTAX
INS   [es:]dest,dx   *Get data from the port indicated by DX. The dest operand is used to get the data size only.*

INSB   *Get a byte.*
INSW   *Get a word.*
INS   *Get a double word (80386 only).*

FLAGS
The flags are unaffected by this instruction.

COMMENTS
The INS instruction reads data from the port indicated by the DX register. The data read goes into memory at the location pointed to by ES:DI. After the data is read, the DI register is adjusted according to the size of the data read and the state of the direction flag. This instruction can be used with the REP prefix.

SEE ALSO
IN, OUT   *Input and output commands*
OUTS   *Output a string*

TIMING

Addressing	Encoding	Example		88/86	286	386
implied	0110110w	insw	-	5	15	

EXAMPLE
Write a routine to read a byte from the port at 123h, 20 times.

```
mov  dx,123h     ; Set up the port
mov  cx,20h      ; Set up the count for repeating
rep  insb
```

Load Far Pointer to DS

LDS

Load data segment and offset.

PURPOSE   To load a far pointer into the DS and offset register.

SYNTAX   LDS   reg,memory   *Memory contains a far pointer that is loaded into the segment and the register named.*

FLAGS   The flag registers are unaffected by these instructions.

COMMENTS   The load far pointer instructions simplify the use of far pointers in assembly language programs. Instead of using two instructions to load the segment and offset register you can do the operation in a single instruction.

   When using this instruction on the 80386 you must know if the segment uses 32-bit offsets or 16-bit offsets. If the segment uses 32-bit offsets, then the register for the offset must be 32 bits.

SEE ALSO   LES, LFS, LGS, LSS   *Load far pointers to other segment registers*

TIMING

Addressing	Encoding		Example		88/86	286	386
Implied DS	11000101 mod,reg,r/m		LDS	bx,fpoint	24/16+EA	7	7
Implied ES	11000100 mod,reg,r/m		LES	di,fpoint	24/16+EA	7	7
Implied FS	00001111 10110100 mod,reg,r/m		LFS	edi,fpoint	-	-	7
Implied GS	00001111 10110101 mod,reg,r/m		LGS	dx,fpoint	-	-	7
Implied SS	00001111 10110010 mod,reg,r/m		LSS	bp,fpoint	-	-	7

EXAMPLE Write a routine to copy the string pointed to by FarPoint1 to the string pointed to by FarPoint2.

```
        .MODEL LARGE
        .DATA                   ; The data segment
FarPoint1 DD    String1
FarPoint2 DD    String2
        .FARDATA                ; Another data segment
String1   DB    "This is the source string",0
String2   DB    40 dup(?) ; Space for the new string
        .CODE                   ; The code segment
StrCpy  PROC
    cld                         ; Set the direction to forward
    push ds                     ; Save the current data segment
    les  di,FarPoint2           ; Get the destination pointer
    lds  si,FarPoint1           ; Get the source pointer. Note that
                                ; this was done second. That is
                                ; because the pointers may not be
                                ; in the same segment as the string
                                ; pointed to by FarPoint1. The
                                ; segment for FarPoint1 will
                                ; overwrite whatever is in DS
cloop:
    lodsb                       ; Read a byte from the source
    stosb                       ; Save it in the destination
    cmp  al,0                   ; Check for the end of the string
    jnz  cloop
    pop  ds
    ret

StrCpy  ENDP
```

Load Far Pointer to the ES Register   88/86   286   386
                                                     ▲   ▲   ▲

LES

Load extra segment and offset.
See LDS.

Load Far Pointer to the FS Register   88/86   286   386
                                                                    ▲

LFS

Load FS and offset.
See LDS.

Load Far Pointer to the GS Register   88/86   286   386
                                                                    ▲

LGS

Load GS and offset.
See LDS.

Load Far Pointer to the SS Register   88/86   286   386
                                                                    ▲

LSS

Load stack segment and offset.
See LDS.

Load Effective Address   88/86   286   386
                                                     ▲   ▲   ▲

LEA

PURPOSE   To calculate an effective address and put the result in a register.

SYNTAX LEA reg, memory *Memory is one of the addressing modes that generates an effective address.*

FLAGS The flags are unaffected by this instruction.

COMMENTS This instruction can be used to save time when using the more complex addressing modes. It lets you calculate a complex address and then use the result in a less complex addressing mode.

SEE ALSO MOV *Move data between a register and a memory location*

TIMING

Addressing	Encoding	Example		88/86	286	386
reg,mem	10001101	lea	bx,[si+bx+4]	2+EA	3	2
	mod,reg,r/m					

EXAMPLE This routine adds the 20 words at Table[SI+BX].

```
            .MODEL    SMALL
            .DATA                   ; The data segment
Table       DW    100 dup(?)        ; The table of data
            .CODE                   ; The code segment
; Enter with SI and BX set up for the part of the table to use
AddEm       PROC
            lea   bx,Table[si+bx]   ; Get the address of the first
                                    ; word into bx
            xor   ax,ax             ; Clear ax
            mov   cx,20             ; Set count to 20
aloop:
            add   ax,[bx]           ; Add the word at bx
            inc   bx                ; Move bx to the next word
            inc   bx
            loop aloop
            ret                     ; Return with the sum in AX
AddEm       ENDP
```

LODS

LODS

PURPOSE   To load a byte, word, or double word into the accumulator.

SYNTAX

LODS	[seg:]src	*Src is used to specify the size of the data to load. Seg is an optional segment override.*
LODSB		*Load bytes.*
LODSW		*Load words.*
LODSD		*Load double words.*

FLAGS   The flags are unaffected by this instruction.

COMMENTS   The data loaded comes from the memory pointer to by DS:SI (unless a segment override is used). Each time the LODS instruction is used, the SI register will be adjusted according to the size of the data and the state of the direction flag.

     Although this instruction may be used with the repeat prefix, this is uncommon because it does not make sense repeatedly to load the accumulator with different values.

SEE ALSO

STOS	*Store data to a string*
MOVSB	*Move data from one string to another*

TIMING

Addressing	Encoding	Example	88/86	286	386
implied	1010110w	lodsb	16/12	5	5

EXAMPLE   Write a routine to "XOR" the 512 bytes in Buffer together. This calculation is often used to CheckSum a block of data.

```
          .MODEL   SMALL
          .DATA
Buffer    DB   512 dup(0)        ; Space for data
          .CODE
CheckSum  PROC
          cld                    ; Set direction to forward
          mov  si, offset Buffer ; Get the address of Buffer
          mov  cx,512            ; Put the buffer size in CX
          xor  bl,bl
```

```
xloop:
          lodsb                    ; Get a byte
          xor   bl,al              ; Xor in the data
          loop xloop               ; Do it 512 times
          ret                      ; Return with the checksum in
                                   ; AX
CheckSum   ENDP
```

Move Data   88/86   286   386
                                                          ▲   ▲   ▲

MOV

PURPOSE   To copy a data value in a register or memory location.

SYNTAX

MOV	reg,reg	*Move from a register to a register.*
MOV	mem,reg	*Move from a register to memory.*
MOV	reg,mem	*Move from memory to a register.*
M O V	reg,immed	*Move an immediate value to a register.*
M O V	mem,immed	*Move an immediate value to memory.*
MOV	reg,seg	*Move from a segment register to a 16-bit register.*
MOV	mem,seg	*Move from a segment register to memory.*
MOV	seg,reg	*Move from a 16-bit register to a segment register.*
MOV	seg,mem	*Move from memory to a segment register.*
MOV	reg,spcl	*Move from a 80386 control, debug, or test register to a 32-bit register.*
MOV	spcl,reg	*Move from a 32-bit register to a 80386 control, debug or test register.*

FLAGS   The flags are unaffected by this instruction.

COMMENTS   This instruction simply copies the data in one location to another. Be sure that both operands are the same size.

In order to prevent stack corruption during an interrupt, the interrupts are turned off for one instruction following a move into the SS register. This feature does not work on some of the older versions of the 8088 and 8086.

SEE ALSO   MOVSX, MOVZX   *Move from 16-bit to 32-bit registers*

MOV

Addressing	Encoding	Example	88/86	286	386
reg,reg	1000101w 11,reg,r/m	mov ax,bx	2	2	2
mem,reg	1000101w mod,reg,r/m displacement	mov temp,dx	13/9+EA	3	2
reg,mem	1000100w mod,reg,r/m displacement	mov ax,value	12/8+EA	5	4
reg,immed	1100011w mod,000,r/m data	mov bx,4	4	2	2
mem,immed	1100011w mod,000,r/m displacement data	mov data,21	14/10+EA	3	2
mem,accum	1010001w displacement	mov value,ax	14/10	3	2
accum,mem	1010000w displacement	mov ax,value	14/10	5	4
segreg,reg	10001110 mod,sreg,r/m	mov ds,ax	2	2	2
segreg,mem	10001110 mod,sreg,r/m displacement	mov es,extra	12/8+EA	5	5
reg,segreg mod,sreg,r/m	10001100	mov ax,ss	2	2	2
mem,segreg	10001100 mod,sreg,r/m displacement	mov extra,ds	13/9+EA	3	2
reg,cntlreg	00001111 00100000 11, creg,r/m	mov eax,cr0	-	-	6
cntlreg,reg	00001111 00100010 11, creg,r/m	mov cr5,ebx	- CR0=10,CR2=4,CR3=5		
reg,debugreg	00001111 00100001 11, dreg,r/m	mov edx,dr3	- DR0-3=22,DR6-7=14		

Addressing	Encoding	Example	88/86	286	386
debugreg,reg	00001111 00100011 11, dreg,r/m	mov dr4,eax	- DR0-3=22,DR6-7=16		
reg,testreg	00001111 00100100	mov ecx,tr4 11,treg,r/m	-	-	12
testreg,reg	00001111 00100110	mov tr3,eax 11,treg,r/m	-	-	12

EXAMPLE Most of the examples in this book use the move instruction in one way or another. Here is one more.

These routines save and restore the AX, BX, CX, and DX registers.

```
        .MODEL SMALL
        .DATA
RegBuf  DW   4 dup(?)            ; Space for 4 registers

        .CODE
SaveRegs PROC
        mov  [RegBuf+0], ax      ; Save AX
        mov  [RegBuf+2], bx      ; Save BX
        mov  [RegBuf+4], cx      ; Save CX
        mov  [RegBuf+6], dx      ; Save DX
        ret
SaveRegs ENDP

RestRegs PROC
        mov  ax, [RegBuf+0]      ; Restore AX
        mov  bx, [RegBuf+2]      ; Restore BX
        mov  cx, [RegBuf+4]      ; Restore CX
        mov  dx, [RegBuf+6]      ; Restore DX
        ret
RestRegs ENDP
```

Move String Data	88/86	286	386
	▲	▲	▲

MOVS

PURPOSE To copy data pointed to by DS:SI to ES:DI, then update the pointer registers.

MOVS

SYNTAX MOVS [es:]dest,[seg:]src   *The destination and source are used to determine the data size.*
This format allows a segment override on the source.

MOVSB   *Move bytes.*
MOVSW   *Move words.*

MOVSD   *Move double words.*

FLAGS The flags are unaffected by this instruction.

COMMENTS After the data is moved, the index registers are updated based on the size of the data used and the state of the direction flag. For bytes, the index registers move one; for words, two; and for double words, four. If the direction flag is set, then the index registers are decremented; otherwise, they are incremented.

The REP prefix can be used with this instruction to move a block of data with one instruction. Set the CX register to the number of items to move, before using the REP prefix.

SEE ALSO REP   *The repeat prefix*
LODS *Load data from a string*
STOS *Store data to a string*

TIMING

Addressing	Encoding	Example	88/86	286	386
implied	1010010w	movsw	26/18	5	7

EXAMPLE Reading data from the disk in 8192-byte blocks is more efficient than reading a large number of smaller records. This routine shows how to copy a record from this block.

```
          .MODEL    SMALL
          .DATA
Buffer    DB   8192 dup(?)          ; The disk data buffer
FileHand  DW   ?                    ; The file handle

          .CODE
; Enter with the record number in AX, record size in CX and the
; offset to copy the record to in DI. The file must be open and
; the handle in FileHand
GetRec    PROC
          mul  cx                   ; Get the offset of the record
                                    ; in the file in DX and AX
          push ax                   ; Save the low word of the
                                    ; file offset
          push cx                   ; Save the record size
```

```
            and   ax, 0E000h          ; Round to lower 8K boundary
            mov   cx, dx              ; Put the high word in CX for
                                      ; MS-DOS
            mov   dx, ax              ; Put the low word in DX
            mov   ax, 4200h           ; MS-DOS lseek function
            mov   bx, FileHand        ; Get the file handle
            int   21h                 ; Call MS-DOS
ReadLp:
            mov   dx, OFFSET Buffer   ; Place for the data
            mov   cx, 8192            ; The number of bytes to read
            mov   ah, 3Fh             ; Read file function
            int   21h                 ; Call MS-DOS
            pop   cx                  ; Get the record size back
            pop   ax                  ; Get the low word of the
                                      ; offset
            and   ax, 1FFFh           ; Get the offset into the
                                      ; buffer
            mov   si, OFFSET Buffer   ; Point at the buffer
            add   si, ax              ; Add in the offset
            add   ax, cx              ; Calculate the end of the
                                      ; record
            cmp   ax, 8192            ; See if the record wraps
            ja    skip1               ; if not skip this
            sub   ax, ax              ; Set ax to 0
            jmp   SHORT skip2
skip1:
            sub   ax, 8192            ; See how many bytes left over
            sub   cx, ax              ; See how many bytes in this
                                      ; block
skip2:
            cld                       ; Set the direction to forward
            rep   movsb               ; Copy the record
            or    ax, ax              ; Set flags from AX
            jz    done                ; If no more bytes we're done
            push  cx                  ; Push a 0 for the next buffer
                                      ; offset
            push  ax                  ; Push the number of bytes
                                      ; left
            jmp   ReadLp              ; Read the next block
done:
            ret
GetRec      ENDP
```

MOVSX

MOVSX

PURPOSE   To move data from a signed 8- or 16-bit register to a signed 16- or 32-bit register.

SYNTAX

MOVSX	reg,reg	*Move from register to register.*
MOVSX	reg,mem	*Move from memory to register.*

FLAGS   The flags are unaffected by this instruction.

COMMENTS   This instruction is useful for sign-extending small values into larger registers. It is more versatile than using the CBW and related instructions because it can be used with any of the registers, while CBW is limited to the AL and AX registers.

SEE ALSO

CBW, CWD, CDQ, CWDE	*Sign extend instructions*
MOVZX	*Moves and zero extends values*

TIMING

Addressing	Encoding	Example	88/86	286	386
reg,reg	00001111	movsx eax,cx	-	-	3
	1011111w mod,reg,r/m				
reg,mem	00001111	movsx ax,signb	-	-	6
	1011111w mod,reg,r/m displacement				

EXAMPLE   This example sums the numbers in a table and puts the result in AX. All of the entries in the table are between [-]128 and 127. To save memory, the table contains bytes and the MOVSX instruction is used to make them into words. If the numbers are between 0 and 255, you can use the MOVSZ instruction in place of the MOVSX instruction.

```
        .MODEL    SMALL
        .386                    ; Allow 80386 instructions
        .DATA
Table   DB  128 dup(?)
        .CODE
SumUp   PROC
        mov  cx, 128            ; The size of the table
        sub  ax, ax             ; Start AX at 0
        mov  si, OFFSET Table   ; Get the offset of the first
                                ; item
```

```
SLoop:
            movsx bx, BYTE PTR [si]  ; Get a byte and sign-extend
            add   ax, bx             ; Add the word to the total
            loop SLoop               ; Loop CX times
            ret
SumUp       ENDP
```

Move and Zero Extend   88/86   286   386
                                                                            ▲

MOVZX

PURPOSE
To move unsigned data from an 8- or 16-bit value to a 16- or 32-bit register, setting the upper bits to 0.

SYNTAX

MOVZX	rcg,reg	*Move and extend from one register to another.*
MOVZX	reg,mem	*Move and extend from memory to a register.*

FLAGS
The flags are unaffected by this instruction.

COMMENTS
This instruction is used to get data from the smaller registers to larger ones. Without it you would have to set the upper portion of a word to zero yourself. Since there is no way to access the separate words in the 32-bit register, zero-extending into them would be very difficult without this instruction.

SEE ALSO
MOVSX   *Move signed values to larger registers*

TIMING

Addressing	Encoding	Example	88/86	286	386
reg,reg	00001111	movzx ax,bl	-	-	3
	1011011w mod,rcg,r/m				
reg,mem	00001111	movzx ecx,count		-	6
	1011011w mod,reg,r/m				

EXAMPLE
See MOVSX.

OUT

OUT

PURPOSE   To output a byte, word, or double word from the accumulator to an I/O port.

SYNTAX
OUT	port,acc	*Send the data in the accumulator (AL, AX, or EAX) to the port specified.*
OUT	dx,accum	*Send the data in the accumulator to the port in the DX register.*

FLAGS   The flags are unaffected by this instruction.

COMMENTS   The ports used are dependent on the type of computer being used. Check with your computer's documentation before writing programs that directly access the hardware.

In protected mode this instruction will generate a general protection fault if it is used while the current privilege level is less than the I/O privilege level.

SEE ALSO
OUTS	*Output strings*
IN, INS	*Input instructions*

TIMING

Addressing	Encoding	Example	88/86	286	386
immed,accum	1110011w	out 20h,al	14/10	3	10
dx,accum	1110111w	out dx,ax	12/8	3	11

EXAMPLE   The real-time clock chip in many PC compatibles has some registers that can be used by the programmer. To use a register, you must set an index port to the register number you would like to use.

```
; This code saves the upper and lower nibbles in the bl register
; to registers 10h, and 11h on the RTC chip. The index port is at
; 70h and the data port is at 71h.
        mov   al,10h        ; The first RTC register to use
        out   70h,al        ; Set the index port
        mov   al,bl         ; Get the data
        and   al,0fh        ; Mask the low nibble
        out   71h,al        ; Send the data
        mov   al,11h        ; The second RTC register to use
```

```
out    70h,al
mov    al,bl
shr    al,1              ; Move the high nibble to the
shr    al,1              ; low nibble
shr    al,1
shr    al,1
out    71h,al            ; Send it
```

Output a String   88/86   286   386
                                                               ▲   ▲

OUTS

PURPOSE To output a byte from the memory indicated by DS:SI, then update the index register.

SYNTAX OUTS dx,[seg:]src   *Use src to indicate the size of the data. Seg is an optional segment override.*

OUTSB   *Output a byte.*
OUTSW   *Output a word.*
OUTSD   *Output a double word.*

FLAGS The flags are unaffected by this instruction.

COMMENTS This instruction uses the index register SI to get the data to be output. After the data is sent, SI is updated according to the size of the data used and the state of the direction flag.

The REP prefix can be used with this instruction to send a string of data with one instruction. There are very few devices that can use the stream of data that is produced. Check your documentation carefully before using this form.

SEE ALSO OUT   *Output from the accumulator*
IN, INS *Input instructions*

TIMING

Addressing	Encoding	Example	88/86	286	386
implied	0110111w	OUTSB	-	5	14

OUTS

EXAMPLE   The OUTS instruction can be used to send a string of bytes to the serial port. Before each byte is sent, your code must check the UART status register to see if the UART is ready to send another byte.

```
; Send the string of bytes at SerialData to the serial port.
; The first byte of the string contains the number of bytes
; in the string.
; Check the status byte at 3f9 before sending the data to
; the output port at 3f8.
SendStr PROC
        cld                 ; Set the direction to forward
        mov  si,OFFSET SerialData
        lodsb               ; Get the length of the string
        mov  cl,al          ; Put it in the count register
        xor  ch,ch
Sloop:
        mov  dx,3f9         ; Set to the status port
Tloop:
        in   al,dx          ; Get the status byte
        test al,8           ; Test the ready to send flag
        jz   Tloop          ; If not ready keep testing
        dec  dx             ; Set DX to the Data port
        outsb               ; Otherwise, send the data
        loop Sloop          ; Do the next byte
        ret
SendStr ENDP
```

Pop Data Off of the Stack   88/86   286   386
                                                               ▲   ▲   ▲

POP

PURPOSE   To get a word or double word (80386 only) from the top of the stack, and then adjust the stack pointer.

SYNTAX   pop   reg/mem   *Pop the data into a 16-bit register or memory location.*

FLAGS   The flags are unaffected by this instruction.

COMMENTS The stack is used to store temporary values and the return addresses of functions. Except in protected mode there is no checking to see if the stack has overflowed or underflowed. The programmer must be certain that there is enough room in the stack for the program.

SEE ALSO

| POPA, POPF | *Other pop instructions* |
| PUSH, PUSHA, PUSHF | *To put data on the stack* |

TIMING

Addressing	Encoding	Example	88/86	286	386
reg	01011reg	pop ax	12/8	5	4
mem	10001111	pop data	25/17+EA	5	5
	mod,000,r/m displacement				
segreg	000,sreg,111	pop es	12/8	5	7
80386 segreg	00001111	pop fs	-		7
	10,sreg,001				

EXAMPLE The stack is often used to save a register, so that the register can be used for something else. This is important when using the special purpose registers.

```
; This routine moves a string from Source to Dest.
; The size of the string is in the first byte of the string.
; The CX, SI, DI, and ES registers are saved on the stack
; and then POPped off after the move.

SafeCpy    PROC
           push cx              ; Save cx
           push si              ; Save si
           push di              ; Save di
           push es              ; Save es
           mov  si,offset Source
           mov  di,offset Dest
           push ds              ; Copy the DS register
           pop  es              ; into the ES register
           mov  cl,[si]         ; Get the length
           xor  ch,ch
           cld                  ; Set dircction to forward
           rep  movsb           ; Copy the string
           pop  es              ; Restore es The registers are
                                ; restored in the opposite
                                ; order from when they were
                                ; saved.
```

POP

```
          pop  di          ; Restore di
          pop  si          ; Restore si
          pop  cx          ; Restore cx
          ret
SafeCpy   ENDP
```

Pop All Registers   88/86   286   386
                                                                    ▲   ▲

POPA, POPAD

PURPOSE   To pop DI, SI, BP, SP, BX, DX, CX, AX in one instruction.

SYNTAX   POPA   *Pops 16-bit registers.*
             POPAD   *Pops 32-bit registers (80386 only).*

FLAGS   The flags are unaffected by this instruction.

COMMENTS   This instruction can save time and memory when all of the registers need to be saved.

   Note that although the SP register is on the stack, the value is not put into the SP register by this instruction. Instead, it is discarded.

SEE ALSO   PUSHA   *Pushes all the registers on the stack*
               POP, POPF   *Other pop instructions*
               PUSH, PUSHF *Other push instructions*

TIMING

Addressing	Encoding	Example	88/86	286	386
implied	01100001	popa	-	19	24

EXAMPLE   Routines like the MS-DOS functions, that use many or all of the registers and don't know about the routines that call them, must save all of the registers to prevent interfering with the calling program. The PUSHA and POPA instructions make this a very simple operation.

```
; The beginning and the end of a routine called by an
; Interrupt that must save all the registers
```

```
Routine:
        pusha           ; Save all
          .
          .
          .
        popa            ; Restore all
        iret            ; Return to calling routine
```

Pop the Flags Register   88/86   286   386
                                                      ▲   ▲   ▲

POPF/POPFD

PURPOSE   To pop the top value off of the stack and put it in the flags register.

SYNTAX   POPF   *Pop a 16-bit value.*
               POPFD   *Pop a 32-bit value.*

FLAGS   The flags are set to the values found on the stack.

COMMENTS   The flags are organized into a word according to the following format:

Flag	Bit position
Carry flag	0
Parity flag	2
Auxiliary carry	4
Zero flag	6
Sign flag	7
Trap flag	8
Interrupt flag	9
Direction flag	10
Overflow flag	11

SEE ALSO   PUSHF, PUSHFD   *To push the flags register*
               POP, POPA, POPAD   *Other pop instructions*
               PUSH, PUSHA, PUSHAD   *Other push instructions*

POPF/POPFD

TIMING

Addressing	Encoding		Example	88/86	286	386
implied	10011101	popf		12/8	5	5

EXAMPLE The PUSHF/POPF instructions can be used to save the results of a compare until later in the program.

```
; Compare the AX register to 21. Do some calculations that
; require the AX register and change the flags (Multiplying
; for example). Then Add 15 to the AX register if the
; original was less than 21

        cmp  ax,21
        pushf            ; Save the result of the compare
        .                ; Do other processing
        .
        .
        popf             ; Get the flags back
        jge  skip        ; Don't add if over 21
        add  ax,15

skip:
```

Push Data on the Stack   88/86   286   386
                                                              ▲   ▲   ▲

PUSH

PURPOSE To move the stack pointer and copy the data to the stack at the new location.

SYNTAX
PUSH	reg/mem	*Push a 16-bit register or memory value on the stack.*
PUSH	immed	*Push an immediate value on the stack.*

FLAGS The flags are unaffected by this instruction.

COMMENTS The stack is used to store temporary values and the return addresses for function calls. Except in protected mode, there is no checking for overflow or underflow of the stack. The programmer should be sure that there is enough space on the stack before using stack operations.

On the 8088 and 8086, a PUSH SP instruction will decrement the SP and push that value. The 80286 and 80386 push the value that was in SP before the decrement.

SEE ALSO POP   *Pop data off of the stack*
PUSHF, PUSHFD, PUSHA, PUSHAD *Other push instructions*
POPF, POPFD, POPA, POPAD   *Other pop instructions*

TIMING

Addressing	Encoding	Example	88/86	286	386
reg	01010reg	push ax	15/11	3	2
mem	11111111	push data	24/16+EA	5	5
	mod,110,r/m displacement				
segreg	00,sreg,110	push es	14/10	3	2
80386 segreg	00001111	push gs	-	-	2
	10,sreg,000				
immediate	011010s0	push 12	-	3	2

EXAMPLE One way to copy a segment register is to push the segment to copy from, and pop the segment to copy to. The advantage here is that the copying can be done without using another register or a special memory location.

```
; Copy the DS register to the ES register using the stack
    .
    .
    .
push ds    ; Save the contents of the DS register on the
           ; stack.
pop  es    ; Restore into the ES register. Now ES = DS
    .
    .
    .
```

Push All Registers   88/86   286   386
                                                                  ▲   ▲

PUSHA/PUSHAD

PURPOSE To push the contents of AX, CX, DX, BX, SP, BP, SI, and DI, with a single instruction.

PUSHA/PUSHAD

SYNTAX PUSHA   *Push all 16-bit registers.*
PUSHAD   *Push all 32-bit registers.*

FLAGS The flags are unaffected by this instruction.

COMMENTS Routines, like the MS-DOS functions that use many or all of the registers and do not have any control over the calling routine, can use this instruction to protect all of the registers from becoming scrambled.

SEE ALSO POPA, POPAD   *Pop all of the registers*
PUSH, PUSHF, PUSHFD   *Other push instructions*
POP, POPF, POPFD   *Other pop instructions*

TIMING

Addressing	Encoding	Example	88/86	286	386
implied	01100000	pusha	-	17	18

EXAMPLE After all the registers have been pushed, they can be referenced by setting the BP register equal to the SP register and using the base + displacement addressing mode. When the POPA instruction restores the registers, the new values will be used.

```
; This routine saves all of the registers on the stack
; Then the location corresponding to the AX register is
; set to one. When the routine exits, the AX register
; becomes one.

    pusha                       ; Save all of the registers
    mov   bp,sp                 ; Set bp = sp
    mov   word ptr [bp+14], 1   ; Set stack for AX to 1
    .                           ; Do further processing
    .
    .
    popa                        ; Restore all the registers.
    ret                         ; Return to calling routine
```

Push the Flags

PUSHF/PUSHFD

PURPOSE   To put the flag register on the stack.

SYNTAX   PUSHF
PUSHFD

FLAGS   The flags are unaffected by this instruction.

COMMENTS   On the 80386 there are two new flags (Resume Flag and Virtual 8086 Mode Flag). To accommodate them the flag register was extended to 32 bits. You must use the PUSHFD instruction if you want these flags preserved. Otherwise you can use the PUSHF instruction to save all of the other flags.

SEE ALSO   POPF, POPFD   *To get the flags off of the stack*
PUSH,   PUSHA,PUSHAD   *Other push instructions*
POP, POPA, POPAD   *Other pop instructions*

TIMING

Addressing	Encoding	Example	88/86	286	386
implied	10011100	pushf	14/10	3	4

EXAMPLE   One use of the PUSHF instruction is to simulate an interrupt. An interrupt pushes the flags on the stack, and then pushes CS and IP and goes to the interrupt service routine. Some programs intercept interrupts, call the original interrupt function, and then do their own processing. To call an interrupt function, you must push the flags first. A PUSHF followed by a CALL is the same as an interrupt.

```
; This routine intercepts interrupts caused by pressing keys
; The original Interrupt routine address is stored at
; OldKeys

NewKey    PROC    FAR
          pushf                        ; Out the flags on the stack
                                       ; to simulate
                                       ; an Interrupt
```

PUSHF/PUSHFD

```
call DWORD cs:[OldKeys]   ; Call the function whose
                          ; Address is at OldKeys
     .                    ; Do more processing
     .
     .
     iret                 ; Return from the Interrupt
```

Repeat String   88/86   286   386
                                                               ▲   ▲   ▲

REP

PURPOSE To decrement the CX register and repeat the following instruction until `CX=0`.

SYNTAX `REP   instruction`

FLAGS The flags are unaffected by this instruction.

COMMENTS The repeat prefix can be used with the MOVS and STOS instructions. It can be used with the LODS instruction, but it does not make much sense to load the accumulator from a string of values.

With the 80286 and 80386, the REP prefix can also be used with the INS and OUTS instructions.

SEE ALSO `REPNE,REPE` *Repeat while CX and the zero flag*

Addressing	Encoding	Example	88/86	286	386
rep MOVS	11110010 1010010w	rep movsb	9+25/17n	5+4n	8+4n
rep STOS	11110010 1010101w	rep stosw	9+14/10n	4+3n	8+4n
rep INS	11110010 0110110w	rep insb	-	5+4n	13+6n
rep OUTS	11110010	rep outsb	-	5+4n	12+5n

EXAMPLE See the example for MOVSB.

Set a Byte Conditionally   88/86   286   386
                                                                          ▲

SET Condition

PURPOSE To set various flags and combinations of flags; and set the specified register or memory location to 1, if the condition is true; or 0, if it is not true.

SYNTAX

SETAE	reg/mem	*Set the register or memory if CF=0.*
SETNB	reg/mem	*Set the register or memory if CF=0.*
SETBE	reg/mem	*Set the register or memory if CF=1 or ZF=1.*
SETNA	reg/mem	*Set the register or memory if CF=1 or ZF=1.*
SETA	reg/mem	*Set the register or memory if CF=0 and ZF=0.*
SETNBE	reg/mem	*Set the register or memory if CF=0 and ZF=0.*
SETE	reg/mem	*Set the register or memory if ZF=1.*
SETZ	reg/mem	*Set the register or memory if ZF=1.*
SETNE	reg/mem	*Set the register or memory if ZF=0.*
SETNZ	reg/mem	*Set the register or memory if ZF=0.*
SETL	reg/mem	*Set the register or memory if SF<>OF.*
SETNGE	reg/mem	*Set the register or memory if SF<>OF.*
SETGE	reg/mem	*Set the register or memory if SF=OF.*
SETNL	reg/mem	*Set the register or memory if SF=OF.*
SETLE	reg/mem	*Set the register or memory if ZF=1 or SF<>OF.*
SETNG	reg/mem	*Set the register or memory if ZF=1 or SF<>OF.*
SETG	reg/mem	*Set the register or memory if ZF=0 or SF=OF.*
SETNLE	reg/mem	*Set the register or memory if ZF=0 or SF=OF.*
SETS	reg/mem	*Set the register or memory if SF=1.*
SETNS	reg/mem	*Set the register or memory if SF=0.*
SETC	reg/mem	*Set the register or memory if CF=1.*
SETNC	reg/mem	*Set the register or memory if CF=0.*
SETO	reg/mem	*Set the register or memory if OF=1.*
SETNO	reg/mem	*Set the register or memory if OF=0.*
SETP	reg/mem	*Set the register or memory if PF=1.*
SETPE	reg/mem	*Set the register or memory if PF=1.*
SETNP	reg/mem	*Set the register or memory if PF=0.*
SETPO	reg/mem	*Set the register or memory if PF=0.*

SET Condition

FLAGS   The flags are unaffected by this instruction.

COMMENTS   This instruction is similar to the conditional jump instructions. Instead of jumping or not, based in the condition, the set instruction sets the operand to 1, if the condition is true; or 0, if not.

The SET instructions make it easier to make complex conditional expressions. For example, to see if the value in AX is between two values, the conditional expression is:

```
AX > LowLimit AND AX < HighLimit
```

There are two ways to evaluate this expression. One is to do the first compare (AX > LowLimit). Then, if it is true, do the second compare. This works well for simple expressions but it can get messy for more complex ones. With the SET instruction you can set a flag byte with the results of each compare, and then and the flags together for the final result.

SEE ALSO   JCondition   *Jump on the same conditions used here*

TIMING

Addressing	Encoding	Example		88/86	286	386
reg	00001111 1001cond mod,000,r/m	setb	al	-	-	4
mem	00001111 1001cond mod,000,r/m	setc	flag	-	-	5

Note: See table 4-2 for the possible conditions

EXAMPLE   This routine checks to see if AX is between the memory variables LowLimit and HighLimit. It returns a 1 in AX if true, and 0 if not.

```
          .MODEL    SMALL
          .DATA
LowLimit  DW    ?
HighLimit DW    ?
Flag1     DB    ?         ; Set to 1 when AX > LowLimit
Flag2     DB    ?         ; Set to 1 when AX < HighLimit
          .CODE
```

```
LimTest    PROC
           cmp  ax, LowLimit     ; Compare AX to LowLimit
           seta Flag1            ; Set Flag1 if above
           cmp  ax, HighLimit    ; Compare AX to HighLimit
           setb Flag2            ; Set Flag2 if below
           mov  ax, Flag1        ; Put the first result in AX
           and  ax, Flag2        ; Logical AND with result two
           ret                   ; Return with the final result in
                                 ; AX
LimTest    ENDP
```

Store to a String   88/86   286   386
                                                          ▲   ▲   ▲

STOS

PURPOSE To store the accumulator in memory at the location in the ES and DI registers. After saving the data, STOS adjusts DI to point to the next item.

SYNTAX STOS [es:]dest   *The size of dest determines the size of the data. The actual address must be in ES:DI.*

STOSB   *Store bytes.*
STOSW   *Store words.*
STOSD   *Store double words.*

FLAGS The flags are unaffected by this instruction.

COMMENTS The STOS instruction can be used with the REP prefix. This is useful when you want to set a block of memory to some known value.

SEE ALSO CLD, STD   *Controls the direction flag*
LODS   *Load from a string*

TIMING

Addressing	Encoding	Example	88/86	286	386
implied	1010101w	stosb	15/11	3	4

STOS

EXAMPLE   The STOS instruction can be used to clear a block of memory to a known value. When setting a range of bytes, there is a performance gain from setting two bytes at a time.

```
; Store 20 0's at DataBlk. To save time 10 words of 0's
; are saved instead of 20 bytes of 0's

Set0      PROC
          cld                   ; Set the direction to forward
          mov  di, OFFSET DataBlk
          mov  ax, SEG DataBlk
          mov  es, ax
          xor  ax, ax           ; ax = 0
          mov  cx, 10           ; The number of words to save
          rep  stosw            ; Save 0's
          ret
Set0      ENDP
```

Exchange Data Values   88/86   286   386
                                                          ▲   ▲   ▲

XCHG

PURPOSE   To swap the data in the source and destination operands.

SYNTAX   XCHG   *reg/mem, mem/reg*

FLAGS   The flags are unaffected by this instruction.

COMMENTS   The XCHG instruction does the work of three MOV instructions and a temporary register. For example, to swap the AX and BX registers with move instructions, you would code:

```
          mov  cx, ax    ; Put AX in a temp register
          mov  ax, bx    ; Copy BX to AX
          mov  bx, cx    ; Copy the temp value (AX) to BX
```

SEE ALSO   MOV   *To copy data*
                XLAT   *Translate by table look up*

XCHG

TIMING

Addressing	Encoding	Example		88/86	286	386
reg, reg	1000011w 11,reg,r/m	xchg	cx, si	4	3	3
mem, reg	1000011w mod,reg,r/m displacement	xchg Numb, dx		17+EA	5	5
accum, reg	10010reg	xchg ax, bx		3	3	3

EXAMPLE   The 80x86 processor stores data in memory with the least significant byte first. Other processors, such as the 68000, store data with the most significant byte first. This example shows how to use the XCHG instruction to convert an area of integers from one format to another. Note that running this function a second time on the same array will restore it to its original state.

```
        .MODEL     SMALL
        .CODE
; Flip the words in the array at DS:SI. The number of words is in
; CX
FlipEm  PROC
        mov  ax, WORD PTR [si]    ; Get the word
        xchg ah, al
        mov  WORD PTR [si], ax    ; Save the flipped word
        inc  si                   ; Move SI to the next word
        inc  si
        loop FlipEm               ; Do it CX times
        ret
FlipEm  ENDP
```

Translate Data

	88/86	286	386
	▲	▲	▲

XLAT/XLATB

PURPOSE   To return the value from a table at DS:BX using the AL register as an index.

XLAT/XLATB

SYNTAX   XLAT [[seg:]memory]   *Only the segment override is used. The location of the table is in ES:BX.*

XLATB [[seg:]mem]   *This is a synonym for XLAT.*

FLAGS   The flags are unaffected by this instruction.

COMMENTS   This instruction is useful in translating from one encoding scheme to another.

TIMING

Addressing	Encoding	Example	88/86	286	386
implied	11010111	xlat	11	5	5

EXAMPLE   The XLAT instruction can be used to encrypt data with a simple substitution code. Use a table with all of the ASCII character set in it. Then scramble the table. This table can now be used to make the substitutions.

```
; Use the scrambled table at CodeTable to encode a character
; The character to encode is in AL.
          .DATA
; The encoded table
CodeTable  DB    061, 010, 107, 114, 021, 110, 097, 066
           DB    009, 002, 098, 123, 068, 119, 023, 109
           DB    065, 025, 081, 050, 005, 077, 091, 070
           DB    018, 063, 027, 054, 029, 085, 031, 115
           DB    033, 112, 024, 015, 090, 038, 039, 040
           DB    041, 127, 043, 044, 045, 111, 047, 080
           DB    113, 020, 051, 124, 053, 028, 055, 056
           DB    057, 120, 059, 017, 001, 062, 026, 106
           DB    060, 008, 125, 013, 069, 035, 071, 072
           DB    121, 074, 075, 076, 022, 078, 079, 048
           DB    019, 082, 083, 099, 030, 086, 128, 088
           DB    089, 037, 036, 092, 093, 094, 095, 096
           DB    007, 011, 084, 100, 101, 102, 103, 104
           DB    105, 064, 003, 108, 016, 006, 046, 034
           DB    049, 004, 032, 126, 117, 118, 014, 058
           DB    073, 012, 123, 052, 067, 116, 042, 087

Encrypt    PROC
           mov   bx, OFFSET CodeTable     ; BX points to the table
           xlat                           ; Convert AL
           ret
Encrypt    ENDP
```

Chapter 5 Arithmetic, Logic, and Bit-Shift Instructions

Arithmetic is used to evaluate equations, figure offsets for arrays, count items, adjust the stack frame, and much more. The 80x86 processors provide instructions for adding, subtracting, incrementing, decrementing, multiplying, and dividing. These instructions can use numbers that are stored in several different formats, such as signed, unsigned, and binary coded decimal. The first section in this chapter shows how the arithmetic instructions work.

Programs use logical and bit-shift instructions to evaluate logical expressions, manipulate bit flags, and to simulate certain arithmetic operations. Many of these operations are not directly available in high level languages. This can cause a beginning assembly language programmer to overlook such instructions. The second section of this chapter shows you how to use these instructions to save memory and increase performance in your programs.

Arithmetic Operations

The 80x86 processor can use 8-, 16-, or 32-bit numbers that are in registers or memory. The general format for arithmetic instructions is similar to this:

```
add     mem/reg,reg/mem/immediate
```

For this instruction mem/reg is a register or memory location, and reg/mem/immediate is a register, a memory location, or an immediate data value. The first operand is called the *destination operand*. This is not only one of the numbers to use, but it also indicates the place to put the result. The second operand provides the other number to use and is called the *source operand*. Each of the two operands must be the same size. You cannot add an 8-bit number to a 16-bit number. Only one of the operands can be a memory value.

If the destination operand is a memory value, the source operand must be a register or an immediate value. If the source operand is a memory value, the destination must be a register.

Displaying Numbers

Before you can output a number to the screen or printer, you must convert it to a string of ASCII characters. When you get a number from a user, it will be a string of characters. These characters must be converted to numbers that the processor can use before any arithmetic operations can be performed. The next example shows how to get a number from the user, convert it to a binary number, convert the number back to a string, and print it on-screen. It is divided into two functions (GetNumb and PrntNumb), so that you can use them when experimenting with the arithmetic instructions.

```
; Get and print numbers
          .MODEL    SMALL
          .DATA
Prompt    DB   0Dh, 0Ah, ">>$"
TmpSize   DB   20
TmpCnt    DB   ?
TmpStr    DB   20 dup(?)

          .CODE
; This function tests the get and put functions
FuncTest  PROC
          mov  ax, SEG DGROUP   ; Get the data segment
          mov  ds, ax           ; put it in DS
          mov  es, ax           ; and in ES
          call GetNumb          ; Get a number from the user
          call PrntNumb         ; Print the number
          mov  ah, 4Ch          ; MS-DOS exit function
          int  21h              ; Call MS-DOS
FuncTest  ENDP

; Get a number from the user and put it in AX
GetNumb   PROC
          mov  dx, OFFSET Prompt ; The location of the prompt
                                 ; string
          mov  ah, 9            ; MS-DOS print string
          int  21h
          mov  dx, OFFSET TmpSize ; The address of the input
                                  ; buffer
          mov  ah, 0Ah          ; MS-DOS input function
          int  21h
          sub  ax, ax           ; Set AX to 0
```

```
            sub   cx, cx                 ; Set CX to 0
            sub   bx, bx                 ; Set BX to 0
            mov   cl, TmpCnt             ; Get the number of characters
            mov   si, OFFSET TmpStr      ; The location of the string
            mov   di, 10                 ; The digit multiplier
ConvLp:
            mul   di                     ; Multiply ax times ten
            mov   bl, BYTE PTR [si]      ; Get the next character
            inc   si                     ; Go to next char
            and   bl, 0Fh                ; Convert to a digit
            add   ax, bx                 ; Add the digit
            loop  ConvLp                 ; Do it for each
            push  ax                     ; character
            mov   dl, 0Dh                ; Print CR
            mov   ah, 2
            int   21h
            mov   dl, 0Ah                ; Print LF
            mov   ah, 2
            int   21h
            pop   ax
            ret
GetNumb     ENDP

; Print the number in AX on the screen
PrntNumb    PROC
            mov   di, 10                 ; The digit divisor
            sub   cx, cx                 ; Put zero in CX
PrntLp:
            sub   dx, dx                 ; Set DX to 0
            div   di                     ; Divide the number by ten
            push  dx                     ; put the remainder on the
                                         ; stack
            inc   cx
            or    ax, ax                 ; Any more?
            jnz   PrntLp
            cld
            mov   di, OFFSET TmpStr      ; The location of the string
StrLp:
            pop   ax
            add   al, '0'                ; Make it an ASCII digit
            stosb                        ; Save the digit
SK1:
            loop  StrLp
PNDone:
            mov   al, '$'                ; Terminate the string
```

```
            stosb
            mov   dx, OFFSET TmpStr
            mov   ah, 9
            int   21h
            ret
PrntNumb    ENDP

            .STACK    1024
END         FuncTest
```

The GetNumb routine uses two of the MS-DOS functions that are introduced in Chapter 1 to display the prompt and get a line of input from the user. After the MS-DOS calls, the line is in memory at TmpStr.

The rest of the routine converts the string into a number. The procedure for this is to get a character from the string, convert it to a numeric digit, multiply the previous digits by 10, and add in the current digit. Figure 5-1 shows this process in detail.

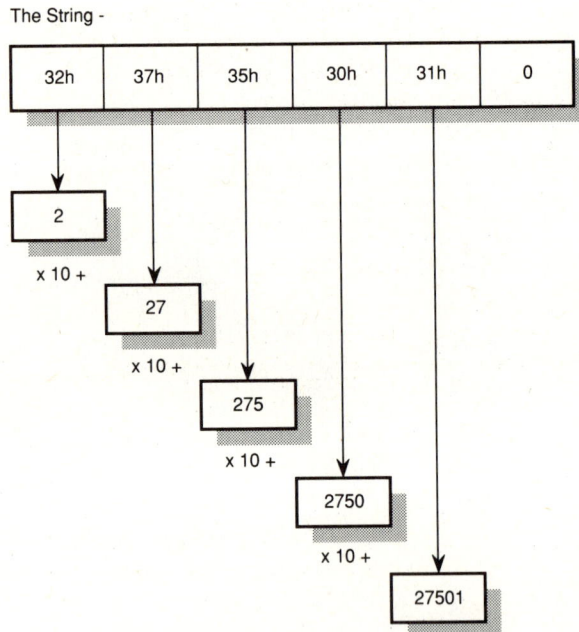

The String -

| 32h | 37h | 35h | 30h | 31h | 0 |

2

x 10 +

27

x 10 +

275

x 10 +

2750

x 10 +

27501

Figure 5-1. *Converting a string to an integer.*

The PrntNumb routine undoes the work of the GetNumb routine. Instead of repeated multiplication, this routine uses repeated division to find the digits. Each time the number is divided by ten, the remainder is another digit to be printed. Unfortunately, the digits produced in this manner are backwards. That is, the least significant digit is first, and the most significant digit is last.

PrntNumb uses the stack to reverse the digits. As it finds each digit, it pushes it on the stack. When there are no more digits, the digits are popped off the stack. Because the last item pushed is the first item popped, this will reverse the order.

Some of the examples presented in this chapter utilize these routines to demonstrate how to use various instructions. To use the examples, simply substitute the example routine for the FuncTest routine.

Addition

The ADD (ADDition) instruction adds the two operands together and puts the result in the destination operand. If the two numbers add up to a value that is too large for the size of the destination operand, the carry flag is set. The ADC (ADd with Carry) instruction adds the operands, and then adds in the carry bit. You can use this to add numbers that are larger than a word. This example shows how you can add two 32-bit numbers:

```
; The first 32-bit number is 12345678h
        mov   ax, 5678h      ; The low word of the first number
        mov   dx, 1234h      ; The high word of the first number
; Add 87654321h to AX and DX
        add   ax, 4321h      ; Add the low bytes to get 9999h in
                             ; AX and clear the carry
        adc   bx, 8765h      ; Add the high bytes and add in the
                             ; carry bit to get 9999h in AX
```

Subtraction

The two subtraction instructions are SUB (SUBtract) and SBB (SuBtract with Borrow). They use the same format as the ADD commands. The SUB instruction subtracts the source operand from the destination operand and puts the result in the destination operand. The carry flag is used to indicate that a borrow is required. When the value in the source operand is larger than the value in the destination, the carry is set.

The SBB instruction uses the carry flag as a borrow flag in the calculation. First, it subtracts the operands as the SUB instruction does. Then, if the carry is set (indicating a borrow) it subtracts one from the result. The following example shows how this works when subtracting 32-bit values.

```
            mov   ax, 0       ; Low word of the first number
            mov   dx, 500h    ; High word of the first number
            sub   ax, 89h     ; Subtract the low word giving 0FF77h in
                              ; AX and setting the carry flag
            sbb   dx, 488h    ; Subtract the high bytes to get 78h
                              ; then subtract the carry bit to get 77h
                              ; in dx
```

Incrementing and Decrementing

Adding and subtracting can be used to count items or to control the number of times that a loop should run. In these cases you may add one to a counter or subtract one from a loop variable. Using the add instruction to add one would take from two to six bytes and use at least four cycles. The 80x86 processor provides the INC (INCrement) instruction to add more efficiently by one. The format of this instruction is:

```
inc   reg/mem
```

For this instruction, reg/mem is a register or memory location. When this instruction is used on registers, it only takes one byte and executes in three clock cycles.

Subtracting by one can be done with the DEC (DECrement) instruction. It uses the same format as the INC instruction and can provide a similar savings.

The INC and DEC instructions are often used to count things or to keep track of how many times a loop should run. This next example uses these instructions and the GetNumb and PrntNumb routines to get a number, calculate the number of one (1) bits in the number, and display the result.

```
TestFunc PROC
            mov   ax, SEG DGROUP
            mov   ds, ax
            mov   es, ax
            call  GetNumb           ; Get a number
            mov   cx, 16            ; The number of times to
                                    ; run the loop
            sub   bx, bx            ; Set the BX to zero
BitLp:
            shl   ax, 1             ; Move the bits to the left,
                                    ; putting the high bit in the
                                    ; carry
            jnc   SkCnt             ; If no carry don't count
            inc   bx                ; otherwise count it
SkCnt:
            loop BitLp              ; Keep looping until 0
```

```
            mov   ax, bx              ; Put the count in AX for
                                      ; printing
            call  PrntNumb
            mov   ah, 4Ch
            int   21h
TestFunc  ENDP
```

Comparing Numbers

Much of what a program does is determined by comparing values. A routine
might want to count all the numbers in a table which are over a certain value.
Loops can run until a certain value is reached. A command processor knows
what the command is by comparing each command to commands in a table.

The CMP (CoMPare) instruction in the 80x86 processor works by doing
a subtract operation to set the flags, but it does not save the result of the
subtraction. The values in the source and destination operands remain
unchanged. The format of the CMP instruction is the same as for the SUB
instruction. If you think of the *compare* as a subtraction, you can remember
how the flags will be set. If the numbers are the same, subtracting gives 0—so
the zero flag is set. If the first number is less than the second number,
subtracting requires a borrow—so the carry flag is set. If the destination is
larger than the source operand, then neither the zero nor the carry flag is set.

This example compares the number in the AL register to 21. If the number
is equal to 21, it puts a 0 in AL. If it is above 21, it puts a one in AL; and if it is
below 21, AL gets a –1.

```
            cmp   al, 21
            jb    less              ; Jump if al is less than 21
            ja    greater           ; Jump if al is greater than 21
            xor   al, al            ; otherwise it must be equal
            jmp   short done        ; All done
less:
            mov   al, -1            ; Save -1 for less than 21
            jmp   short done
greater:
            mov   al, 1             ; Save one for greater than 21
done:
```

Multiplying and Dividing

There are some special considerations to be made when multiplying or dividing.
This comes from the fact that the result of a *multiply* can be up to twice the size
of the operands. For division, this means that a dividend can be twice the size of
the divisor and quotient. The 80x86 needs special rules about where the extra bits go.

MULTIPLICATION

There are two multiplication instructions: MUL (MULtiply) and IMUL (Integer MULtiply). The format of both instructions is:

```
mul   reg/mem        ; Unsigned multiply
imul  reg/mem        ; Signed multiply
```

For these instructions, `reg/mem` is a register or memory location. Notice that there is only one operand. This is because the MUL and IMUL instructions use an implied destination operand. If the register or memory location is an 8-bit value, then the implied operand is AL and the result goes into AX. If the operand is a 16-bit value, then the implied operand is AX and the result goes into `DX:AX`. With the 80386 you could specify a 32-bit operand, in which case the implied operand is EAX and the result goes into `EDX:EAX`.

80386 MULTIPLICATION

In addition to being able to multiply 32-bit numbers into 64-bit results, the 80386 has more choices for operands with the `imul` instruction. The extra formats are:

```
imul      reg,immediate
imul      reg1,reg/memory,immediate
imul      reg/mem1,mem/reg2
```

In the first format, the `reg` is a 16- or 32-bit register that is used as one of the operands, as well as the place for the result. The immediate value is the other operand, and it is also the same size as the register. If the result is larger than the register used, the carry and overflow bits are set and only the lower part of the result is saved. Your program should consider this an error because there is no way to know the value of the bits that are lost.

The second format multiplies `reg/memory` times `immediate` and puts the result in `reg1`. The same rules are used that apply to the first format about overflowing `reg1`.

The last format will multiply any 16- or 32-bit register or memory location by any 16- or 32-bit register or memory location. Both operands must be the same size and only one of them can be a memory location. Once again, if the result is too large to fit into the destination operand, the carry and overflow flags are set and the high bits are lost.

DIVISION

Division also uses implied operands. The two instructions are DIV (DIVide) and IDIV (Integer DIVide). Both instructions have one operand that can be either a register or memory value. The operand can be 8 or 16 bits, or with an 80386 it can be 32 bits. After the *divide*, the low half of the implied operand contains the quotient, and the high half contains the remainder. If the operand is 8 bits, then the implied dividend is AX, the quotient goes into AL, and the remainder goes into AH. For 16-bit operands, the implied operand is the 32-bit value in DX and AX, and the quotient goes into AX with the remainder in DX. On the 80386 a 32-bit operand uses EDX:EAX for the dividend, the result goes into EAX, and the remainder goes into EDX.

Always be sure to check for legal values before doing a divide. Dividing by zero or doing a divide that overflows the quotient register will cause an interrupt that may crash your program.

Multiplying and dividing are most often used to evaluate mathematical expressions. In the following example, we find the approximate circumference of a circle. The radius of the circle comes from the GetNumb function. For the sake of integer math, this routine uses the fraction 22/7 as an approximation for *pi*. First it multiplies by 22 and then divides by 7. The result is printed by the PrntNumb function.

```
TestFunc  PROC
          mov   ax, SEG DGROUP
          mov   ds, ax
          mov   es, ax
          call  GetNumb          ; Get the radius from the user
          mov   bx,22            ; We must use a memory location or
                                 ; register unless this is for an
                                 ; 80386
          mul   bx               ; Multiply the radius times 22. The
                                 ; result goes into DX:AX which is
                                 ; just where we want it for the
                                 ; upcoming divide instruction
          mov   bx, 7            ; Get ready to divide
          cmp   dx, bx           ; Make sure the result will fit
          jge   error            ; if dx >= 7 don't divide
          div   bx               ; The circumference is in AX
                                 ; DX contains the fractional part
          push  dx
          call  PrntNumb         ; Print the whole number part
          mov   dl, ' '          ; Get ready to print a space
          mov   ah, 2            ; MS-DOS print char function
          int   21h              ; Call MS-DOS
          pop   ax               ; Get the factional part
          call  PrntNumb
          mov   dl, '/'          ; Get ready to print a '/'
          mov   ah, 2
          int   21h
          mov   dl, '7'
          mov   ah, 2
          int   21h
error:
          mov   ah, 4Ch
          int   21h
```

Signed Arithmetic

When you start subtracting numbers, you must consider the possibility of negative numbers. When subtracting a large number from a smaller number, you can reverse the order and change the sign of the result. For example, to subtract 52 from 45, subtract 45 from 52 to get 7, and then change the sign to show –7. Let's look at how this works with binary numbers:

```
 52 = 00110100
-45 = 00101101
  7 = 00000111
```

If we do it in the original order we get:

```
 45 = 00101101
-52 = 00110100
- 7 = 11111001
```

The binary number 11111001 is called the *twos complement* of 7. This is the way that the 80x86 processor represents negative numbers. If you subtract 1 from 11111001, you get 11111000, which is -8. You can keep decrementing right down to -128; and from there you go back to 11111111, or 127. Using signed arithmetic means to consider all of the numbers that have the high bit set to be negative numbers. Thus, with 8 bits, the numbers from -128 (1000000) to 127 (01111111) can be represented. For 16-bit numbers, the range is from -32,768 to 32,767. For 32-bit numbers, like those used on the 80386, the range is from -2,147,483,648 to 2,147,483,647.

Changing Signs

The NEG (NEGate) instruction uses twos complementing to convert a negative number to a positive number or a positive number to a negative number. The format of the instruction is:

```
neg  reg/mem
```

For this instruction, reg/mem is any register or memory location. For most numbers this instruction sets the carry flag. If the number is zero, the carry is not set. If the number is the maximum possible negative number (-128 for eight bits and -32,768 for 16-bit numbers), the number is not changed and the overflow and carry flags get set. This is because there is no way to represent 128 with a signed 8-bit number, or 32,768 with a signed 16-bit number.

The NEG instruction is useful when printing signed numbers. If the number is negative, the minus sign can be printed and the number can be complemented with the NEG instruction before being set to an integer printing routine. To change the `PrntNumb` function to handle negative numbers, add this code to the beginning of the function:

```
        or    ax, ax              ; Set the flags
        jns   Positive            ; If no sign skip the next
                                  ; few lines
        push  ax                  ; Save AX
        mov   dl, '-'             ; Put a minus sign in DL
        mov   ah, 2               ; MS-DOS print char routine
        int   21h                 ; Call MS-DOS
        pop   ax                  ; Get AX back
        neg   ax                  ; Make it positive
Positive:                         ; Continue as before
```

Sign Extending

When you convert an unsigned value from an 8-bit to a 16-bit number, all you need to do is put a 0 in the high byte and copy the 8-bit value into the low byte. With signed values the procedure is a bit more complicated. For negative numbers, the high byte must be set to 0ffh for the 16-bit number to be the same as the 8-bit number. For example, the 8-bit code for –1 is 11111111, and the 16-bit code is 1111111111111111. In general, to make a signed number longer, you must copy the sign bit into each bit you add. This is called *sign extending* the number. The 80x86 processors provide several instructions for converting from one byte to two-byte and to four-byte signed numbers. The 80386 also has an instruction to convert four-byte signed numbers to eight-byte signed numbers.

To convert a one-byte signed number to a two-byte signed number, first put the number in the AL register. Then issue a CBW (Convert Byte to Word) instruction. The resulting two-byte signed number will be in the in the AX register. To continue sign extending to a four-byte signed number, leave it in AX and use the CWD (Convert Word to Double) instruction. The result will go into the DX and AX registers.

On the 80386 you can use the CWDE (Convert Word to Double Extended), in which case the result goes into the EAX register. This is useful if you want to continue the sign extension out to 8 bytes, because the 80386 has a CDQ (Convert Double to Quad) instruction that converts the 32-bit value in EAX to a 64-bit value in EDX and EAX.

Suppose you subtracted two 8-bit values and then wanted to use the `PrntNumb` function to display it. You can use the CBW instruction to convert the signed number in AL to a signed number in AX like this:

```
mov   al, 45
sub   al, 50        ; Subtract the 8-bit numbers
cbw                 ; Sign-extend the result
call  PrntNumb
```

Signed Multiplication and Division

The MUL instruction is used to multiply unsigned values. It does not do anything special to deal with the sign bit. If you want to multiply signed numbers, you could make the values positive with the NEG instruction and multiply them; but an easier solution is to use the IMUL instruction. If the result of the multiply is negative, the IMUL instruction sign extends the result into DX for 16-bit operations and into AH for 8-bit operations.

For division you should use the IDIV instruction when dealing with signed numbers.

Status Flags

In addition to putting the result in the destination operand, arithmetic instructions change the status flags. You have seen how the carry flag is used in adding or subtracting as a carry or borrow bit. Several other flags get set after arithmetic operations to let you know something about the result.

The zero flag is set whenever the result of an add, subtract, increment, or decrement is zero. Zero results are often interesting after decrementing to indicate that a loop is finished.

The sign flag is set if an add, subtract, increment, or decrement results in a number with the high bit on. The sign of the result is important to many mathematical formulas.

The overflow flag tells when a result is out of the range of signed numbers for the operand size being used. For example, if an 8-bit signed subtraction results in a number less than –128, there is no way to represent it in 8 bits. What is worse is that the byte would contain a result that would look like a positive number. Addition can result in a number greater than 127. The result here would look like a negative number. In either case the overflow bit would be set to tell us that we overflowed the range available, as in this example:

```
 21   00010101
115   01110011
137   10001000   (–118  and overflow set)
```

Two other bits get set by the add, subtract, increment, and decrement instructions. They are the parity flag and the auxiliary carry flag. These flags are left over from older Intel Corporation processors and are not used much in modern programs. You may run into an algorithm that uses them sometimes, so you should at least be aware of them and how they work. The parity flag is set when an odd number of bits in the result are on. This is often used when there is some question about the correctness of the data. If the parity bit is not what is expected then the data is likely to be bad. This kind of check is often part of data communications software.

The auxiliary carry is set when there is a carry out of bit 3 of an 8-bit number, or out of bit 3 or bit 7 of a 16-bit number. This flag can be used when adding Binary Coded Decimal (BCD) numbers to fix results that overflow:

```
47        01000111     (BCD format)
29        00101001     (BCD format)
76        01110000     (70 (BCD) with Auxiliary carry set)
```

Arithmetic with Binary Code Decimal (BCD) Numbers

There are several ways to represent numbers in a computer. The previous examples use binary encoding, each bit representing a binary digit. Another popular way to represent numbers is Binary Coded Decimal (BCD). BCD uses four bits to represent a decimal digit. Two of these digits fit into a byte.

The 80x86 processors have several instructions that use *Unpacked BCD* numbers. An Unpacked BCD number has only one digit in a byte. This can be a convenient format because the numbers used can be quickly converted to their ASCII equivalents by adding 30h to each digit.

The normal arithmetic instructions can be used on packed or unpacked BCD numbers, but some adjustments need to be made in some cases. This example shows what can happen when you add two BCD numbers:

```
 26 (BCD) = 00100110
+18 (BCD) = 00011000
 3E         00111110
```

Since *E* is not a valid decimal digit, some adjustment needs to be made. The DAA (Decimal Adjust Accumulator) instruction is used to fix a BCD number after an addition. It will fix the BCD number in AL. In the previous example, it would change 3E into 44. This instruction only works after an ADD or ADC instruction. To see why, look at what happens when we add 26 to 18 and then do a DAA:

```
 26 (BCD) = 00100110
+18 (BCD) = 00011000
 44         00111111    (3F)


do DAA:    01000100
```

In this case there is an overflow out of the lower four bits, so a different adjustment needs to be made. The overflow sets the auxiliary carry during the ADD, so the DAA instruction can make the correct adjustment.

With subtraction you need to make different adjustments. In this case, use the DAS instruction instead of the DAA instruction.

There are also instructions for adjusting unpacked BCD numbers. They are AAA (ASCII Adjust after Addition) and AAS (ASCII Adjust after Subtraction). They work just like their packed BCD counterparts, except the lower digit is in AL and the upper digit is in AH.

There are so many things that can happen when multiplying or dividing that the best procedure is to convert the BCD number to a binary number before operating on it, and convert it back afterwards. The AAD (ASCII Adjust for Division) instruction converts an unpacked BCD number in AH and AL into a binary number in AX. The AAM (ASCII Adjust for Multiplication) instruction takes the binary number in AL and makes an unpacked BCD number in AH and AL. Your program must ensure that the number in AL is less than 100 before issuing the AAM instruction.

BCD numbers are often used because they can easily be converted from or to the ASCII digits used in I/O. The following example reads two digits from the string at Inbuf, then adds 17 to the number, and finally saves the result in Outbuf:

```
mov   bx, OFFSET Inbuf   ; Get the address of
                         ; Inbuf
mov   ah, [bx]           ; Read the first digit
inc   bx                 ; Move to the next char
mov   al, [bx]           ; Read the second digit
and   ax, 0f0fh          ; Mask out the unused
                         ; bits
add   ax, 0107h          ; Add the unpacked BCD
                         ; version of 17
aaa                      ; Make adjustments
or    ax, 3030h          ; Convert back to ASCII
```

```
mov    bx, OFFSET Outbuf      ; Get the address of
                              ; Outbuf
mov    [bx], ah               ; Save the high digit
inc    bx                     ; Move to the next digit
mov    [bx], al               ; Save the low digit
```

Making a Simple Calculator

The main purpose of the arithmetic instructions is do arithmetic. Let's look at how they can be used to make a simple four-function calculator.

This calculator is a Reverse Polish Notation (RPN) machine. When a number is entered, it gets pushed on the stack. When a command is entered, the top two stack values are popped and evaluated. The result is displayed and pushed onto the stack.

The commands are "A" for addition, "S" for subtraction, "M" for multiplication, "D" for division, "P" to pop the top value off the stack, "C" to clear the stack completely, and "Q" to quit.

```
           .MODEL SMALL
           .DATA
Inpbuf     DB    10,0,10 dup(?)
Outbuf     DB    5 dup(?),0dh,0ah,"$"
Calcstk    DW    50 dup(?)
Stkptr     DW    0
Minus      DB    0
Prompt     DB    "INPUT> $"
Stkerrmsg  DB    "Stack empty error",0dh,0ah,"$"
Ovrerrmsg  DB    "Overflow",0dh,0ah,"$"
Cmderrmsg  DB    "Invalid input",0dh,0ah,"$"

           .CODE
Calculate PROC
           mov    ax, SEG DGROUP       ; Get the data segment
           mov    ds, ax               ; Put it in DS
           mov    es, ax               ; and in ES
Cmdlp:
           mov    ah, 9                ; MS-DOS display string
           mov    dx, OFFSET Prompt
           int    21h                  ; Call MS-DOS
           mov    ah, 0ah              ; MS-DOS buffered keyboard
                                       ; read
```

```
                mov   dx, OFFSET Inpbuf
                int   21h                           ; Call MS-DOS
                mov   dl, 0Ah
                mov   ah, 2
                int   21h
                mov   dl, 0Dh
                mov   ah, 2
                int   21h
                cmp   Inpbuf+2,'A'                   ; Check for add command
                jnz   NotAdd
                call  PopStack
                jc    Cmdlp                          ; If error don't add
                add   Calcstk[bx], ax                ; Change the value on the top
                                                     ; of the stack
                call  PrinTop                        ; Print the value
                jmp   Cmdlp
        NotAdd:
                cmp   Inpbuf+2,'S'                   ; Check for subtract command
                jnz   NotSub
                call  PopStack
                jc    Cmdlp
                sub   Calcstk[bx], ax
                call  PrinTop
                jmp   Cmdlp
        NotSub:
                cmp   Inpbuf+2,'M'                   ; Check for multiply command
                jnz   NotMul
                call  PopStack
                jc    Cmdlp
                imul  Calcstk[bx]
                jnc   MulOK
        Overflow:
                mov   ah, 9
                mov   dx, OFFSET Ovrerrmsg
                int   21h
                jmp   Cmdlp
        MulOK:
                mov   Calcstk[bx], ax                ; Save the result on the stack
                call  PrinTop
                jmp   Cmdlp
        NotMul:
                cmp   Inpbuf+2, 'D'                  ; Check for divide command
                jnz   NotDiv
                call  PopStack
```

```
        jc   Cmdlp
        mov  cx, ax
        mov  ax, Calcstk[bx]
        cmp  ax, 0
        je   Overflow
        cwd                          ; Sign-extend into DX
        idiv cx
        mov  Calcstk[bx], ax
        call PrinTop
        jmp  Cmdlp
NotDiv:
        cmp  Inpbuf+2, 'P'           ; Check for pop command
        jnz  NotPop
        call PopStack
        jmp  Cmdlp
NotPop:
        cmp  Inpbuf+2, 'C'           ; Check for clear
        jne  NotClr
        mov  Stkptr, 0               ; Set the stack pointer to 0
        jmp  Cmdlp
NotClr:
        cmp  Inpbuf+2, 'Q'
        jne  NotQuit
        mov  ah, 4Ch                 ; MS-DOS exit command
        int  21h                     ; Call MS-DOS
NotQuit:
        mov  bx, offset Inpbuf+2
        mov  Minus,0
        sub  ax, ax                  ; ax will hold the number
        cmp  BYTE PTR Inpbuf[bx], '-' ; Check for minus sign
        jnz  NotMinus
        mov  Minus,1
        inc  bx
NotMinus:
        cmp  BYTE PTR Inpbuf[bx], 0dh ; Check for the end
        je   Endnum
        cmp  BYTE PTR Inpbuf[bx], '0' ; Check for numbers
        jb   Cmderr
        cmp  BYTE PTR Inpbuf[bx], '9'
        ja   Cmderr
        shl  ax, 1                   ; Old number times two
        mov  cx, ax
        shl  ax, 1
```

```
            shl   ax, 1               ; Old times 8
            add   ax, cx              ; + old times 2 = old times 10
            mov   cl, BYTE PTR [bx]   ; Get the next digit
            and   cx, 0fh             ; Mask just the digit
            add   ax, cx              ; Add it in
            inc   bx
            jmp   NotMinus            ; Get more digits
Endnum:
            cmp   Minus, 0            ; Check the minus sign
            je    Positive
            neg   ax                  ; Negate if minus
Positive:
            mov   bx, Stkptr          ; Get the stack pointer
            mov   Calcstk[bx], ax     ; Save the number
            inc   bx
            inc   bx
            mov   Stkptr, bx          ; Advance the stack pointer
            jmp   Cmdlp
Cmderr:
            mov   ah, 9
            mov   dx, OFFSET Cmderrmsg
            int   21h
            jmp   Cmdlp

Calculate ENDP

PrinTop   PROC
            mov   ax, Calcstk[bx]     ; Get the number off the top
            or    ax, ax              ; Set the flags
            jns   pos2
            mov   ah, 5               ; DOS print char
            mov   dl, '-'             ; Print a minus sign
            int   21h
            neg   ax
pos2:
            mov   cl, 5               ; The maximum number of digits
            mov   bx, 10              ; Set up the divisor
            mov   di, OFFSET outbuf+4
MakeDigit:
            cmp   ax, 0
            je    Endprn
            cwd                       ; Sign-extend into dx
            div   bx
            or    dl, 30h             ; Make the digit ASCII
            mov   byte ptr [di], dl
```

```
                dec  di
                loop MakeDigit
Endprn:
                cmp  cl, 5                          ; If not digits saved
                jne  ep1
                mov  byte ptr [di],0                ; save a 0
                dec  cl
ep1:
                mov  ah, 9                          ; Print a string
                mov  dx, OFFSET Outbuf
                xor  ch, ch
                add  dx, cx                         ; Adjust for the unsaved
                                                    ; digits
                int  21h
                ret

PrintTop   ENDP

PopStack   PROC                                     ; Pop the top of the stack
                                                    ; into AX. Make BX point to
                                                    ; the new top of the stack
                mov  bx, Stkptr                     ; Get the stack pointer
                cmp  bx,0                            ; Check for the bottom of the
                                                    ; stack
                je   Stkerr
                dec  bx                             ; Move back one word
                dec  bx
                mov  Stkptr, bx                     ; Move the stack pointer
                mov  ax, Calcstk[bx]                ; Get the first operand
                jz   stkerr                         ; Jump if stack err
                dec  bx                             ; Line up on the new top of
                                                    ; the stack
                dec  bx
                clc                                 ; Says no error
                ret
stkerr:
                mov  ah, 9                          ; MS-DOS display function
                mov  dx, OFFSET Stkerrmsg
                int  21h
                stc                                 ; Indicate an error
                ret
PopStack   ENDP
                .STACK    1024
END
```

The first part of this program puts the segment address for DGROUP in the DS and ES registers. The ES register must be set up to make the string move instructions work properly. The instructions following `Cmdlp` are the main loop for the program. The first thing that the loop does is print a prompt and get a line of input from the user.

The line of input is stored at `Inpbuf+2`. The character at the beginning of the line is the command to be carried out. The program compares this character with a command character and, if the character does not match, it skips to the comparison for the next command. If the character is an A, S, M, or D (Add, Subtract, Multiply, or Divide), then the program pops an operand off of the stack and combines it with the next operand on the stack. The P (Pop) command pops one number off of the stack. The C (Clear) command pops all of the numbers off of the stack. The Q (Quit) command calls MS-DOS to exit the program.

If the first character of the line is not a command, then the program checks if it is a number. The code following the label `NotQuit` is responsible for this. If the first character is a minus sign, then it sets a flag indicating that this is a negative number. The algorithm for converting the number from a string to a binary number is the same as was used in `GetNumb` earlier in this chapter. The last step is to push the number onto the stack and return to the top of the loop.

Several of the commands call the function `PopStk` to get a number from the top of the stack. Note that this stack is the memory at `Calcstk` and not the stack used for the PUSH and POP instructions. This routine gets the stack offset from a variable named `Stkptr` and puts it in the BX register. The `PopStk` routine checks to see if this pointer is not zero to make sure that there is data on the stack. Next, it decrements the pointer so that it is below the word on top of the stack. Then it reads the word from the stack and decrements BX, so that it points to the next word on the stack. This is important because the arithmetic commands use this location as the destination operand, so that the result is on top of the stack.

The other routine used by the commands is `PrinTop`. This routine is just like `PrntNumb`, except that the number comes from the word on the top of the stack instead of the AX register.

Logic Instructions

Not all data manipulation is arithmetic. Data can be combined logically to solve Boolean expressions. Individual bits or groups of bits can be set or tested. Even some arithmetic operations can be done more efficiently by directly manipulating bits. The 80x86 processor has instructions for the logical operations and, inclusive or, exclusive or, and not. There is also an instruction to test individual bits or groups of bits.

Logical AND

The Logical AND performs a Boolean AND operation for each bit in the two operands. The format of the AND instruction is:

```
and      mem/reg,reg/mem/immediate
```

For this instruction, mem/reg is a memory location or register. The second operand can be a register, memory location, or an immediate value. Both operands must be the same size. If one is a memory location the other must be a register.

The two operands are compared bit by bit. Where the bit is one in both operands there will be a one in the result. All other combinations put a zero in the result for that bit. Lets look at what happens when the AND instruction operates on two values:

```
    10011011
and 10110101
    10010001
```

Notice that the only bit that are on in the result are the ones that were on in both operands.

You can use the AND instruction to mask out bits that will not be used in subsequent operations. For example the difference between lower case ASCII characters and upper case ASCII characters is that lower case characters have bit number 5 set to 1. If you make a mask that has all of the bits on except bit number 5, then AND the mask with an ASCII letter, the operation will guarantee that the letter is upper case. The code to do this looks like this:

```
mov  al, 'a'        ; Put 'a' (61h) in AL
and  al,11011111b   ; Make bit 5 a 0 giving 'A' (41h)
```

Logical Inclusive OR

The Inclusive OR uses the same format as the AND instruction. The difference is in the way the result is determined. When a bit is "Inclusive-ORed" with another bit, the result is a one if either of the bits is a one. The OR operation looks like this:

```
    10011011
or  10110101
    10111111
```

Here a bit is on in the result if it was on in either of the operands.

The OR instruction can be used to turn bits on in a byte. In the ASCII example above we could change the mask and use the OR instruction to turn on bit 5 and the letter becomes lower case:

```
mov  al, 'A'
or   al,00100000b    ; Make bit 5 a 1
```

Logical Exclusive OR

The Exclusive OR also uses the same format as the AND instruction. The difference between the XOR (eXclusive OR) instruction and the OR instruction is the result of combining two on bits. The XOR instruction puts a 0 in the result if both bits are on, instead of a one as the OR instruction does. Here is what happens when we "Exclusive-OR" the sample bytes:

```
     10011011
xor  10110101
     00101110
```

The XOR operation only turns on bits that are on in only one of the operands. One interesting effect of this operation is that a bit that is "Exclusive-ORed" with one will flip to the opposite state. You can use this with flags that must be toggled on and off.

The XOR instruction can be used to encrypt data. The advantage of encrypting with the XOR instruction is that if you "Exclusive-OR" the result with the same mask, you will get back the original value. This example "Exclusive-ORs" each byte of the string at Secret with 55h. The first time it is applied, the string will be encrypted; the second time, it will be decrypted.

```
Scrmble   PROC
          mov  bx, OFFSET Secret   ; Get the address of the
                                   ; string
Loop:
          cmp  [bx], 0             ; Check for the end of
                                   ; the string
          je   Done                ; if end jump to done
          xor  [bx], 55h           ; Encrypt the byte
```

```
                    inc   bx                      ; Move to the next byte
                    jmp   SHORT Loop              ; and loop
        Done:
                    ret
        Scrmble   ENDP
```

Look at what happens if you copy the string "Coded message" to `Secret`. The first letter is *C* (43h). After being "Exclusive-ORed" with 55h, it becomes control-V (16h). The function then increments BX to change at the next character in the string. When the byte at BX is 0, there are no more characters and the function exits with the string scrambled.

Logical NOT

The Logical NOT inverts the bits in the single operand. The format of the Logical NOT is:

```
not       reg/memory
```

For this instruction, `reg/memory` is a register or memory location. The bits in the operand will be flipped like in this example:

```
not 10011011
    01100100
```

In graphics programs letters that will get put on the screen are stored in arrays of pixels called bitmaps. Each bit in the bitmap represents a pixel on the screen. Normally each one (1) bit is a pixel that is `on`. When the cursor is on top of a letter, the bits in the bitmap are inverted so that the character is in *inverse video*. This example routine uses the not instruction to reverse the bits in an eight-byte bit map stored at letter.

```
                mov   bx, Offset Letter    ; Get the address of the
                                           ; bitmap
                mov   cx,8                 ; Set up to count 8 bytes
        Floop:
                not   BYTE PTR [bx]        ; Invert the bits of a
                                           ; byte. Note that we have
                                           ; to tell the assembler
                                           ; the size of the data to
                                           ; be inverted.
                inc   bx                   ; Move to the next byte
                loop Floop                 ; Do another one
```

Here is a sample bitmap for the letter *A*:

```
; Before inverting
Letter    DB    00010000b
          DB    01101100b
          DB    11000110b
          DB    11111110b
          DB    11000110b
          DB    11000110b
          DB    00000000b

; After inverting
Letter    DB    11101111b
          DB    10010011b
          DB    00111001b
          DB    00000001b
          DB    00111001b
          DB    00111001b
          DB    11111111b
```

Testing Bits

With the logical operations you can use the TEST instruction in a way similar to using the CMP instruction with arithmetic. The TEST instruction works just like the AND instruction except that it does not put the result into the destination operand. Instead it only sets that flags as if it were an AND instruction.

You can use the TEST instruction test the state of specific bits. For example, to determine if an ASCII letter is upper or lower case, you can TEST the character with a mask that has bit 5 on. This example sets the zero flag if the character in AL is upper case:

```
test al,00100000b    ; check the state of bit 5
```

Bit-Shift Instructions

There are many ways to encode data in a computer. Numbers can be binary, binary coded decimal (BCD), or even as a string of ASCII characters. Characters can be ASCII or BAUDOT or encrypted in some way. Each of these formats encodes bits in a byte in a unique manner. This variety means that the computer must often convert between the different formats. To make the conversions, the computer needs bit-shifting instructions to move bits around. Bit-shifting can be used to multiply by powers of two, to count bits, or to move bits that are used as flags.

Bit-shifting simply moves all to the bits in a byte or word to the right or left. Figure 5-2 shows what happens when a byte is shifted.

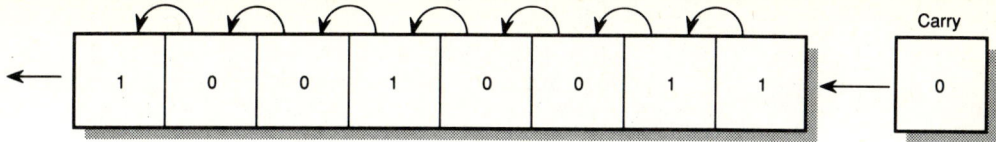

Figure 5-2. *Shifting a byte.*

One bit leaves the byte, all of the other bits move over one and some new bit moves into the other end. The difference between the various bit-shift instructions is what happens to the bit that leaves and the bit that moves into the other end. Certain algorithms exploit the way these end bits are moved.

Rotation

Rotation is when the bit that leaves one end of a byte becomes the bit that moves in. There are four rotation instructions in TASM. They are, ROR (ROtate Right), ROL (ROtate Left), RCR (Rotate through Carry Right), and RCL (Rotate through Carry Left). The ROR and ROL instructions rotate the data and copy the end bit into the carry flag. There are three formats used by the rotate and shift instructions. They are:

```
rol   mem/reg, 1          ; Rotate 1 place
rol   mem/reg, cl         ; Rotate the number of places
                          ; indicated by the value in CL
rol   mem/reg, immed      ; Rotate the number of places
                          ; indicated by the immediate
                          ; value (80286 and 80386 only)
```

For this instruction, mem/reg is any 8- or 16-bit memory location or register. Figure 5-3 shows the effect of rotating a byte one bit left.

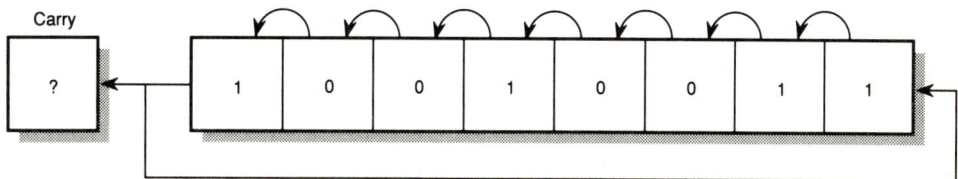

Figure 5-3. *Rotating left.*

After the ROL instruction in this example, the carry flag is set, showing that the bit that shifted out was a one, and the result is 00100111b. The ROR instruction does the same thing but the bits get shifted to the right giving 11001001b in the result and the carry flag set.

The RCL and RCR instructions rotate through the carry flag. This is a subtle, but important, difference from the ROL and ROR instructions. See figure 5-4 for what happens with RCL.

Now the result is 00100110b, and the carry is set. Instead of the high bit moving directly to the low bit, the carry moves into the low bit and the high bit moves into the carry. Think of this as having a 17-bit value instead of a 16-bit one, or a 9-bit value instead of an 8-bit one. Rotating through the carry is useful when you need to move bits out of one byte and into another.

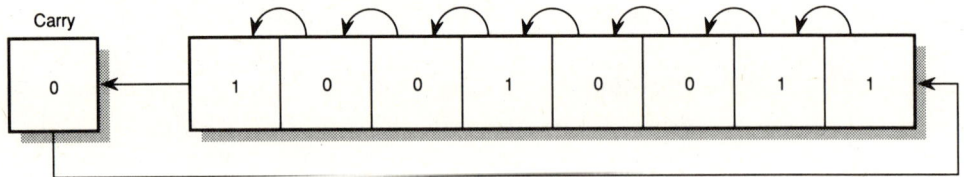

Figure 5-4. *Rotating left through the carry.*

The next example shows how to shift the 32-bit value in AX and DX one bit to the right:

```
shr   dx, 1          ; Shift the high word first
rcr   ax, 1          ; Rotate the carry from the high
                     ; word into the low word.
```

Shifting

The shift instructions move the data left or right but no bits wrap around and enter back into the register. There are four TASM instructions for shifting. They are, SAL (Shift Arithmetic Left), SAR (Shift Arithmetic Right), SHL (SHift Left), and SHR (SHift Right). The SAL, and SHL instructions move the bits to the left. The most significant bit moves into the carry and a 0 is shifted into the least significant bit. These instructions are actually the same. The assembler generates the same op code for both of them.

The SHR instruction is similar to the SAL and SHL instructions except that it moves the bit the other direction. That leaves it to the carry and moves a zero into the new bit. The SAR instruction is different. Instead of shifting a 0 into the high bit (like the SHR instruction does) it leaves this bit unchanged. The reason for this has to do with the fact that shifting the bits to the right is the same as dividing by two. Because the high bit is the sign bit shifting a one into this bit might change the sign of the result. Leaving this bit alone maintains the sign bit so that the result of the shift is correct.

The shift instructions are commonly used in mathematical computations. Think of how you multiply by ten. You simply shift the digits to the left and add a 0 to the end. For example to multiply 4 times ten add a zero to the end to get 40. This is what the shift instructions do, in the 80x86 except they do it in base 2. Therefore, shifting left one bit is the same as multiplying by two, shifting two bits multiplies by four, etc. Division works the same way in the other direction. Shifting right is the same as dividing by two.

A common use for this kind of shifty multiplying is in table lookups. When a program calls a DOS function it uses a function number in the AH register to let DOS know what function to run. DOS uses the function number to find the address of the function in its function table. Since each function address uses two bytes in the table, the function number must be multiplied by two before it can be used to access the table. This program uses a function number in the AH register to call a function in a table called FuncTab.

```
xor   bx,bx          ; Clear the bx register
mov   bl,ah          ; Put the function number in bx
shl   bx,1           ; Multiply by 2 (table entry size)
mov   bx,FuncTab[bx] ; Get the address from FuncTab
call  bx             ; Call it
```

A series of shifts and adds can be used to multiply a value by any constant. This works because any number can be expressed as the sum of several powers of two. For example, 12 can be thought of as the sum of eight (2^3) and four (2^2). So to multiply by twelve we could multiply by eight and by four then add the two results together. The following example uses this to multiply the value in the AX register by 12:

```
shl   ax,1    ; ax = the number * 2
shl   ax,1    ; ax = the number * 4
mov   bx,ax   ; bx = the number * 4
shl   ax,1    ; ax = the number * 8
add   ax,bx   ; Add them together for the number
              ; * 12
```

If AX contains 30 at the beginning of this routine the first shift makes it 60. The next shift doubles AX again for 120. The MOV instruction puts this value (AX * 4) into the BX register. The next shift doubles AX again so it becomes 240. The last instruction adds the two values together to get 360.

With an 8088 or 8086 the MUL instruction would take between 82 and 89 cycles to do the same thing that this code does in 12. There are some limitations, this code only multiplies by 12 and only for integers less than 65536/12.

NORMALIZING SEGMENTED POINTERS USING SHIFTS

Due to the 16-bit segmented architecture of the 80x86 processors, data must be addressed by a pair of registers. Because the segments overlap, there can be more than one way to address a single memory location. For example, 000A:1234 is the same as 012D:0004. This can make it difficult to compare pointers. One way around this problem is to use normalized pointers. A normalized pointer has the closest possible segment value in the segment register and the smallest possible value in the offset register. Using shift instructions is an easy way to normalize pointers. The following example normalizes the pointer in ES:BX.

```
; Enter with the segment in ES and the offset in BX
        mov   ax, bx      ; Save the offset
        shr   bx, 1       ; Divide by 2
        shr   bx, 1       ; Divide by 4
        shr   bx, 1       ; Divide by 8
        shr   bx, 1       ; Divide by 16
        mov   cx, es      ; Get the segment
        add   cx, bx      ; Add offset divided by 16
        mov   es, cx      ; Put it back
        and   ax, 0fh     ; Mask off the portion that went
                          ; into the segment
        mov   bx, ax
```

So if ES:BX is 000A:1234, the offset is shifted right to give 123. Then it is added to the segment to get 012D. The last step is to mask the original offset to leave only the lowest four bits. The result is that es:bx becomes 012D:0004.

ITERATING BIT-SHIFTS

In the previous examples data rotated or shifted one bit at a time. The 80X86 processors also can rotate or shift data more than one bit at a time. With the 80286 or 80386 processors simply change the value following the comma to the number of iterations desired. For example to swap the lower four bits with the upper four bits of the AL register use this instruction:

```
rol     al,4
```

For the 8088 and 8086 processors the cl register must be used for multiple rotations. To get the same result as the above example use the following code:

```
mov     cl,4
rol     al,cl
```

There are some performance issues that must be considered before using these forms of the instruction. The same result can be had by putting several one bit shifts in a row. The previous example would be coded:

```
rol     al,1
rol     al,1
rol     al,1
rol     al,1
```

This will use more memory, but in many cases it will run faster due to the slower micro code used for iterated shifts in the 8088 and 8086 processors. There are many factors that determine when using separate shifts will run faster. As a rule of thumb, when shifting less than six bits, separate shifts will run faster.

DOUBLE PRECISION SHIFTS ON THE 80386

The 80386 processor has two more shift instructions. They are SHLD (SHift Left Double precision) and SHRD (SHift Right Double precision). The format for these instructions is:

```
SHLD    reg/mem,reg/mem,count
```

For this instruction, reg/mem is a register or a memory value, and count is either an 8-bit number (0-256) or the CL register. These instructions shift bits from the second operand into the first operand. The third operand tells how many bits to shift. The operands can be 16- or 32-bit values. They must both be the same size, and only one of them can be a memory value.

Squeezing Out Unused Bits with the Shift Instructions

Bit-shift instructions are useful in reformatting data. One useful format change would be to squeeze the unused eighth bits out of a string of ASCII characters. (ASCII only uses seven bits, so one bit in each byte is wasted.) Squeezing is useful because a squeezed string uses 12.5% less space than an unsqueezed string.

To squeeze a string, this program reads a byte from a source string then shifts the bits out of the byte. The high bit is thrown away and the rest are shifted into a destination byte. When the source byte is all shifted a new byte is read. When the destination byte is full, it is written to the destination string. The program stops when the byte read from the source is a zero. Figure 5-5 shows how this program works.

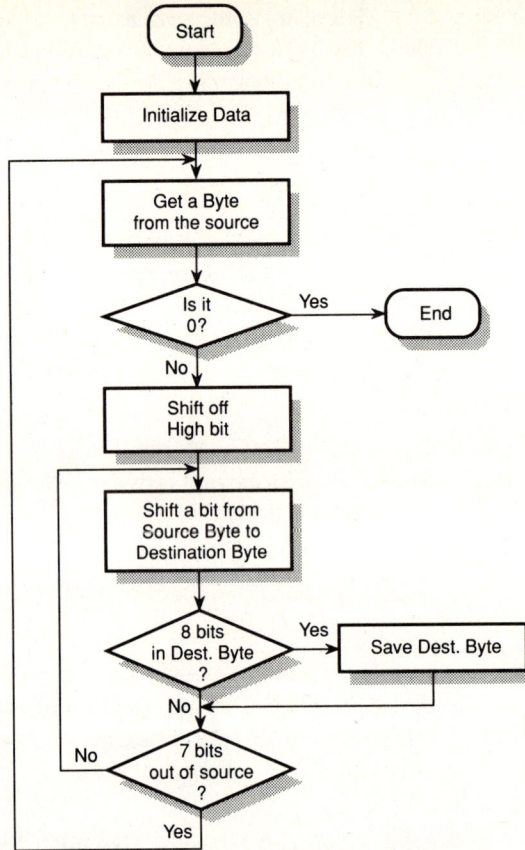

Figure 5-5. *Bit squeezing algorithm.*

```
        .MODEL    SMALL
        .DATA
Source  DB   80 dup(?)          ; Space for the source
Dest    DB   70 dup(?)          ; Space for the
                                ; destination string

        .CODE
Squeeze PROC
        mov  ax, SEG DGROUP
        mov  ds, ax
        mov  es, ax
        cld                     ; Set the direction flag
                                ; to forward
        mov  si, OFFSET Source  ; Get the address of the
                                ; source string
        mov  di, OFFSET Dest    ; Get the address of the
```

```
                                   ; destination
          push ds                  ; Copy data segment to
          pop  es                  ; extra segment
          mov  dh, 8               ; Number of bits to copy
NxtChar:
          mov  dl, 7               ; The number of bits in
                                   ; the destination byte

          lodsb                    ; Get a letter
          or   al, al              ; Set flags
          jz   Done                ; Exit on a zero
          shl  al, 1               ; Get rid of the high bit
NxtBit:
          shl  al, 1               ; Get a bit in the carry
          rcl  ah, 1               ; Put a bit in the dest
                                   ; byte
          dec  dh                  ; Count bits saved
          jnz  ChkSrc              ; Jump if more bits needed
          xchg ah, al              ; Otherwise put AH in the
                                   ; destination string

          stosb
          xchg ah, al
          mov  dh, 8               ; Reset the counter
ChkSrc:
          dec  dl                  ; Count the source bits
          jz   NxtChar             ; Get more bits
          jmp  short nxtbit        ; Keep shifting
Done:
          shl  ah, 1               ; Shift 0's into the last
                                   ; byte
          dec  dh
          jnz  Done
          xchg ah, al
          stosb                    ; Save the last byte
          xchg ah, al
          stosb                    ; Save the 0
          mov  ah, 4Ch
          int  21h
Squeeze   ENDP
          .STACK   1024
          END
```

Summary

The 80x86 processors provide many instructions for manipulating data: arithmetic instructions for manipulating numbers, logic instructions for manipulating flags and masks, and shift instructions for moving bits around. The purpose of the arithmetic instructions is obvious. They are used to calculate numerical values.

The use of the logic instructions is somewhat less familiar. The most common uses of these instructions is to mask portions of bytes or words and to manipulate flags. When using logic instructions to manipulate flags, remember that to clear a flag you should "AND" the bit with 0; to set the flag, "OR" it with 1; and to toggle the flag, "Exclusive-OR" it with 1.

In using the logical instructions to mask a portion of a byte or word, you might leave the bits in an inconvenient location. For example, if the information you want is in the high four bits of a byte, masking it still leaves the number in the high bits. To use the bits, you can use the bit-shift instructions to move the bits to where they can be used.

Another use of the bit-shift instructions is to multiply and divide numbers by constants. This is most efficient when the constant is a power of two, such as 2, 4, 8, 16, etc. By using the shift instructions, instead of the MUL or DIV instructions, you can improve the performance of your program.

ASCII Adjust after Addition　　　　　　　　　　　　　88/86　　286　　386
　　　　　　　　　　　　　　　　　　　　　　　　　　　　　▲　　　▲　　　▲

AAA

PURPOSE　The AAA instruction is used to fix up any overflows after adding two unpacked Binary Coded Decimal numbers.

SYNTAX　AAA

FLAGS

Overflow	Unpredictable result
Sign	Unpredictable result
Zero	Unpredictable result
Parity	Unpredictable result
Carry	Set if the digit in AL was greater than 9
Aux. carry	Set if the carry is set

The carry and auxiliary carry are set if the digit in AL is greater than 9. Otherwise they are reset.

The sign flag, overflow flag, zero flag, and parity flag get set to unpredictable values.

COMMENTS　Using unpacked BCD math can be convenient because it is so close to the ASCII codes required for I/O. When two BCD numbers are added, it is possible for the result to be an invalid BCD number. This instruction fixes the result.

SEE ALSO

AAS	*Adjust after subtraction*
DAA, DAS	*Adjust packed BCD numbers*
AAD, AAM	*Convert between binary and BCD numbers*

TIMING

Addressing	Encoding	Example	86/88	286	386
implied	00110111	aaa	8	3	4

EXAMPLE　Add the contents of the BX register to the value at BcdNum. Then store the result in BcdNum. All values are unpacked BCD.

```
            .DATA
BcdNum      DW   45h

            .CODE
            mov  bx, 27h
            mov  ax, BcdNum      ; Get the number in ax
```

```
add   ax, bx         ; AX = 6Ch
aaa                  ; Adjusted AX = 72h
mov   BcdNum,ax      ; Put the result back
```

ASCII Adjust for Division   88/86   286   386
                                                           ▲   ▲   ▲

AAD

PURPOSE   The AAD instruction converts the unpacked BCD number in AH and AL to a binary number in AX.

SYNTAX   AAD

FLAGS   Overflow   Unpredictable result
                Sign   Matches the sign bit of the result
                Zero   Set if the result is zero
                Parity   Set if there are an even number of bits in the result
                Carry   Unpredictable result
                Aux. carry   Unpredictable result

COMMENTS   Unpacked BCD is a very inefficient way to store numbers. A two-byte unpacked BCD value can range from 0 to 99, where the same two bytes can range from 0 to 65535 with binary encoding. Because of this and the fact that BCD arithmetic takes extra steps, most programs will convert numbers to binary. This instruction is useful for making the conversion.

SEE ALSO   AAM   *To convert binary to unpacked BCD*
                AAA, AAS   *For doing arithmetic on unpacked BCD numbers*

TIMING

Addressing	Encoding	Example	88/86	286	386
implied	11010101	AAD	60	14	19
	00001010				

EXAMPLE   This routine takes the ASCII digits at BcdNum, converts it to binary, and then stores the result in BinNum.

```
        .DATA
BcdNum  DB    "43"              ; The number to convert
```

```
BinNum    DW    ?                    ; Space for the result

          .CODE
          mov  ax, BcdNum            ; Get the number
          and  ax, 0F0Fh            ; Convert to unpacked BCD (0403h)
          aad                        ; Convert to binary
          mov  BinNum,ax            ; Save the result
```

ASCII Adjust for Multiplication   88/86   286   386
                                                        ▲   ▲   ▲

AAM

PURPOSE To convert a binary number to unpacked BCD.

SYNTAX AAM

FLAGS
Overflow	Unpredictable result
Sign	Matches the sign bit of the result
Zero	Set if the result is zero
Parity	Set if there are an even number of bits in the result
Carry	Unpredictable result
Aux. carry	Unpredictable result

COMMENTS This instruction is an easy way to prepare numbers that are less than 100 for output.

SEE ALSO
AAD	*To convert unpacked BCD to binary*
AAA, AAS	*To do arithmetic with unpacked BCD numbers*

TIMING

Addressing	Encoding	Example	88/86	286	386
implied	11000101	AAM	83	16	17
	00001010				

EXAMPLE Use the DOS `putchar` function to print the number at `BinNum`. Assume that the number is less than 100.

```
          .DATA
BinNum    DW   37
          .CODE
```

AAM

```
mov    ax, BinNum      ; Get the number
aam                    ; Convert it (AX = 0307h)
mov    bx, ax          ; Save the bcd number
mov    dl, bh          ; Get the high digit (03h)
add    dl, '0'         ; Make it ASCII
mov    ah,2            ; Function number for putchar
int    21h            ; Call MS-DOS
mov    dl,bl          ; Get the low digit (07h)
add    dl, '0'
int    21h            ; AH is still 2
```

ASCII Adjust after Subtraction   88/86   286   386
                                                                  ▲   ▲   ▲

AAS

SYNTAX   AAS

FLAGS

Overflow	Unpredictable result
Sign	Unpredictableresult
Zero	Unpredictable result
Parity	Unpredictable result
Carry	Set if the digit in AL was greater than 9
Aux. carry	Matches the Carry flag

COMMENTS   Using unpacked BCD math can be convenient because it is so close to the ASCII codes required for I/O. When two BCD numbers are subtracted, it is possible for the result to be an invalid BCD number. This instruction will fix the result.

SEE ALSO

AAA	*Adjust after addition*
DAA, DAS	*Adjust packed BCD numbers*
AAD, AAM	*Convert between binary and BCD numbers*

TIMING

Addressing	Encoding	Example	86/88	286	386
implied	00111111	AAS	8	3	4

EXAMPLE   Subtract the contents of the BX register from the value at BcdNum. Then store the result in BcdNum. All values are unpacked BCD.

```
    mov   ax, BcdNum      ; Get the number in AX
    sub   ax, bx
    aas                   ; The AX register always gets
                          ; adjusted
    mov   BcdNum, ax      ; Put the result back
```

If the value in the BX register is 0502h and the number at BcdNum is 0107h, the subtraction gives 03FBh. The AAS instruction adjusts this number to 0305h, the correct unpacked BCD result.

Add with Carry   88/86   286   386
                                                              ▲   ▲   ▲

ADC

PURPOSE   To add two numbers and the carry flag. It is most often used when adding multi-word values to include any carry out of the lower words.

SYNTAX   ADC reg, reg   *Add two registers.*
                ADC reg, memory   *Add memory to a register.*
                ADC memory,reg   *Add a register to memory*
                ADC reg, immediate   *Add an immediate value to a register.*
                ADC memory,immediate   *Add an immediate value to memory.*

FLAGS   Sign   Matches the sign bit of the result
                Zero   Set if the result is zero
                Parity   Set if there are an even number of on bits in the result
                Overflow   Set if the result overflows a signed value
                Carry   Set if the low bit of the operand was set
                Aux. carry   Set if there was a carry out of bit 3 or, if using 16-bit numbers out of bit 7

COMMENTS   This instruction is used after some other instruction that may have set the carry. Most often it is used to add the most significant word after the least significant word has been added.

SEE ALSO   ADD   *To add without the carry*
                STC, CLC   *To set and reset the carry flag*

ADC

TIMING

Addressing	Encoding	Example	88/86	286	386
reg/reg	0001000w 11,reg,r/m	adc ax,bx	3	2	2
mem/reg	0001000w mod,reg,r/m displacement	adc num,ax	24/16+EA	7	7
reg/mem	0001001w mod,reg,r/m displacement	adc ax,num	13/9+EA	7	6
reg/immed	100000sw mod,010,r/m data	adc bx,4	4	3	2
mem/immed	100000sw mod,010,r/m displacement data	adc num,5	23/17+EA	7	7
acc,immed	0001010w data	adc al,4	4	3	2

EXAMPLE   Add the 64-bit number at BigNum to the 32-bit number at SmallNum.

```
          .DATA
SmallNum  DD   12345678h

BigNum    DQ   4122323112312344h

          .CODE
          mov  ax, WORD PTR SmallNum      ; Get the low word of
                                          ; SmallNum (5678h)
          add  WORD PTR BigNum, ax        ; Add to BigNum (79BCh)
          mov  ax, WORD PTR SmallNum+2    ; Get the next word
                                          ; (1234h)
          adc  WORD PTR BigNum+2, ax      ; Add to BigNum with the
                                          ; carry (2465h)
          adc  word ptr BigNum+4, 0       ; Add in the last carry
          adc  word ptr BigNum+6, 0       ; BigNum =
                                          ; 41223231246579BCh
```

ADD

ADD

PURPOSE To add two numbers.

SYNTAX

ADD reg, reg	*Add two registers.*
ADD reg, memory	*Add memory to a register.*
ADD memory,reg	*Add a register to memory.*
ADD reg, immediate	*Add an immediate value to a register.*
ADD memory,immediate	*Add an immediate value to memory.*

FLAGS

Sign	Matches the sign bit of the result
Zero	Set if the result is zero
Parity	Set if there are an even number of on bits in the result
Overflow	Set if the result overflows a signed value
Carry	Set if the low bit of the operand was set
Aux. carry	Set if there was a carry out of bit 3 or, if using 16-bit numbers out of bit 7

COMMENTS This instruction simply adds two numbers together. If the result is too big to fit in the operand used, the carry flag is set. See the ADC to see one way to make use of the carry flag after this instruction.

SEE ALSO ADC *To add with the carry*

TIMING

Addressing	Encoding	Example	88/86	286	386
reg/reg	0000000w 11,reg,r/m	add ax,bx	3	2	2
mem/reg	0000000w mod,reg,r/m displacement	add num,ax	24/16+EA	7	7
reg/mem	0000001w mod,reg,r/m displacement	add ax,num	13/9+EA	7	6
reg/immed	100000sw mod,000,r/m data	add bx,4	4	3	2

ADD

Addressing	Encoding	Example	88/86	286	386
mem/immed	100000sw mod,000,r/m displacement data	add num,5	23/17+EA	7	7
acc,immed	0001010w data	add al,4	4	3	2

EXAMPLE   See the example for ADC.

Logical AND   88/86   286   386
                                                                         ▲   ▲   ▲

AND

PURPOSE   To perform a bit-wise Logical AND on the operands.

SYNTAX
AND reg,reg	*And two registers.*
AND reg,mem	*And a register with a memory value.*
AND mem,reg	*And a memory value with a register.*
AND reg,immed	*And a register with an immediate value.*
AND mem,immed	*And a memory value with an immediate value.*

FLAGS
Sign	Matches the sign flag of the result
Zero	Set if the result is zero
Parity	Set if there are an even number of on bits in the result
Overflow	Cleared
Carry	Cleared
Aux. carry	Unpredictable result

COMMENTS   This instruction is often used to mask off unwanted bits. "ANDing" a value with a mask will leave only the bits that are set to one in the mask. All other bits get set to 0.

SEE ALSO   OR, XOR, NOT   *Other logical instructions*

	Addressing	Encoding	Example	88/86	286	386
TIMING	reg/reg	0010000w 11,reg,r/m	and ax,bx	3	2	2
	mem/reg	0010000w mod,reg,r/m displacement	and num,ax	24/16+EA	7	7
	reg/mem	0010001w mod,reg,r/m displacement	and ax,num	13/9+EA	7	6
	reg/immed	100000sw mod,100,r/m data	and bx,4	4	3	2
	mem/immed	100000sw mod,100,r/m displacement data	and num,5	23/17+EA	7	7
	acc,immed	0010010w data	and al,4	4	3	2

EXAMPLE This function gets the keyboard shift status from BIOS. It masks off the bits that describe the *insert* state, *caps lock* state, *num lock* state, and *scroll lock* state. If the *caps lock* state was active, it sets the left shift key bit.

```
GetShift  PROC
          mov  ah, 2        ; Get shift status
          int  16h          ; Call BIOS keyboard routines
          test al, 40h      ; See if caps lock active
          jz   GS1          ; Jump if no caps lock
          or   al, 2        ; Set the left shift key bit
GS1:
          and  al, 0Fh      ; Leave only the low four bits
          ret
GetShift  ENDP
```

BSF, BSR

BSF, BSR

PURPOSE   To scan the bits of the source operand to find the first set bit. The position of the bit goes into the destination register.

SYNTAX   BSF reg, reg/mem   *Search from Least Significant Bit forward.*
BSR reg, reg/mem   *Search from Most Significant Bit rearward.*

FLAGS   The zero flag is set if any set bits are found; otherwise, it is cleared.

COMMENTS   The number returned by both of these instructions is the bit position number. Bit positions start counting at 0 with the least significant bit.

SEE ALSO   BT, BTC, BTR, BTS   *Bit test operations*

TIMING

Addressing	Encoding	Example	88/86	286	386
BSF					
reg, reg	00001111 10111100 mod,reg,r/m	BSF ecx, eax			10 + 3n
reg, mem	00001111 10111100 mod,reg,r/m displacement	BSF ecx, mask			10 + 3n
BSR					
reg, reg	00001111 10111101	BSR cx, ax mod,reg,r/m			10 + 3n
reg, mem	00001111 10111101 mod,reg,r/m displacement	BSR ecx, mask			10 + 3n

EXAMPLE A floating point number is stored in two parts. The first part is the *mantissa*, and the second part is the location of the binary point. A binary floating point number is said to be normalized if it has been adjusted so that the first bit is a one (1). Since the first bit is known to be a one, it does not need to be stored.

This example uses the BSR instruction to find out how much the mantissa must be shifted.

```
          .MODEL SMALL
          .386                    ; Allow 80386 instructions
          .DATA
FloatNumb DW    100               ; The mantissa
FloatExp  DB    0                 ; The binary point

          .CODE
Normalize PROC
          bsr  ax, FloatNumb      ; Get the position of the
                                  ; highest 1 bit
          sub  FloatExp, al       ; Adjust the binary point
          mov  cl, 16             ; The number of bits in a word
          sub  cl, al             ; Calculate the number of bits
                                  ; to shift
          shl  FloatNumb, cl      ; Shift the mantissa
          ret
Normalize ENDP
```

Bit Test, Bit Test and Complement,   88/86   286   386
Bit Test and Reset, Bit Test and Set   ▲

BT, BTC, BTR, BTS

PURPOSE To copy the bit specified by the source register from the destination register to the carry bit. The BTC instruction also complements the bit, the BTR resets (clears) it, and the BTS sets the bit.

SYNTAX
```
BT   reg/mem, reg/immed
BTC  reg/mem, reg/immed
BTR  reg/mem, reg/immed
BTS  reg/mem, reg/immed
```

COMMENTS These instructions are useful for determining the status of a specific bit. You can use the JC and JNC instructions to take action based on the state of the bit.

BT, BTC, BTR, BTS

SEE ALSO BSF, BSR *Scan for a bit*
JC, JNC *Jump based on the state of the carry flag*

TIMING

Addressing	Encoding	Example	88/86	286	386
BT					
reg, reg	00001111 10100011 mod,reg,r/m	BT ecx, eax			3
mem, reg	00001111 10100011 mod,reg,r/m displacement	BT Bit, ax			12
reg, immed	00001111 mod,100,r/m data	BT ax, 5			3
mem, immed	00001111 mod,100,r/m displacement	BT Bit, 10			8
BTC, BTR, BTS					
reg, reg	00001111 10bbb011 mod,reg,r/m	BTC ecx, eax			6
mem, reg	00001111 10bbb011 mod,reg,r/m displacement	BTR Bit, ax			13
reg, immed	00001111 mod,bbb,r/m data	BTC ax, 5h			6
mem, immed	00001111 mod,bbb,r/m displacement	BTS Bits, 6			8

bbb = 111 for BTC, 110 for BTR, and 101 for BTS

EXAMPLE In word processor programs, each keypress sets off a series of functions. The alphanumeric keys need to update the file and the screen, the cursor movement keys need to update the screen, etc. This example shows how you can use a word to hold flags for which functions must be run:

```
            .MODEL    SMALL
EXTRN       GetKey:PROC             ; These functions are in
EXTRN       UpdateFile:PROC         ; a different module
EXTRN       UpdataScrn:PROC
EXTRN       AutoSave:PROC
GETKEYFLG EQU  1
MAXFLAG   EQU  4

            .DATA
FuncFlags DW   0
FuncLst   DW   GetKey, UpdateFile, UpdateScrn, AutoSave
NextFlag  DW   0

            .CODE
MainLoop  PROC
            mov  ah, 1              ; See if a key is pressed
            int  16h
            jnz  NoKey              ; Skip the next stuff if no
                                    ; key pressed
            or   FuncFlags, GETKEYFLG; Set the flag to get a key
            mov  NextFlag, 0        ; And start at the first flag
NoKey:
            mov  bx, NextFlag
            bt   FuncFlags, bx      ; Test the flag
            jnc  NoFunc             ; If not set don't do the
                                    ; function
            shl  bx, 1             ; Times 2 for words
            add  bx, OFFSET FuncLst ; Add in the beginning of the
                                    ; table
            call WORD PTR [bx]      ; Call the function
NoFunc:
            inc  NextFlag           ; Go to the next bit
            cmp  NextFlag, MAXFLAG  ; See if we are done
            jl   MainLoop           ; If more flags loop
            mov  NextFlag, 0        ; Otherwise go to the first
                                    ; bit
            jmp  MainLoop           ; And go wait for a key
MainLoop  ENDP
```

Convert Byte to Word   88/86   286   386
                                                            ▲   ▲   ▲

CBW

PURPOSE   To sign-extend the byte in AL into the word in AX.

SYNTAX   CBW

FLAGS   The flags are unaffected by this instruction.

COMMENTS When doing signed arithmetic on different sized values, the sign bit must be considered before making a value larger. This instruction does that for you.

SEE ALSO CDQ, CWD, CWDE   *Other sign-extending instructions*

TIMING

Addressing	Encoding	Example	88/86	286	386
implied	10011000*	CBW	2	2	3

* On the 386, the CBW and the CWDE use the same encoding. When in 16-bit mode, the CWDE is preceded by the operand size byte (66h). In 32-bit mode, CBW is preceded by the operand size byte.

EXAMPLE   The CBW instruction can be used to get the absolute value of a signed number. See the example for CWD, and substitute CBW for CWD. Use the AL and AH registers instead of the AX and DX registers.

Convert Double to Quad   88/86   286   386
                                                                         ▲

CDQ

PURPOSE   To convert a signed double word number into a signed quad (4) word value.

SYNTAX   CDQ

FLAGS   The flags are unaffected by this instruction.

COMMENTS This instruction is often used to make a signed number 64 bits long, in order to use it as the dividend in a signed 32-bit divide.

SEE ALSO CBW, CWD, CWDE   *Other sign-extending instructions*

TIMING

Addressing	Encoding	Example	386
implied	10011001*	CDQ	2

* The CDQ and the CWD instructions use the same encoding. In 16-bit mode, the CDQ instruction is preceded by the operand size byte (66h). In 32-bit mode, the CWD instruction is preceded by the operand size byte.

EXAMPLE Use 32-bit signed division to divide the number at NumOne by the number at NumTwo. **Store the result at** NumOne.

```
        .MODEL    SMALL
        .DATA
NumOne  DD    12345h
NumTwo  DD    45h

        .CODE
        mov   eax, NumOne   ; Load the extended AX register
        cdq                 ; Extend it into EDX (EDX = 0 and
                            ; EAX = 1234Fh)
        idiv  NumTwo        ; Divide EDX:EAX by NumTwo (45h)
        mov   NumOne, eax   ; Save the result (438h)
```

CoMPare two operands   88/86   286   386
                                                            ▲   ▲   ▲

CMP

PURPOSE To compare two numbers and set the flags to indicate greater than, less than, or equal to.

SYNTAX
CMP reg,reg	*Compare two registers.*
CMP reg,mem	*Compare a register to a memory value.*
CMP mem,reg	*Compare a memory value to a register.*
CMP reg,immed	*Compare a register to an immediate value.*
CMP mem,immed	*Compare a memory value to an immediate value.*

CMP

FLAGS

Sign	Matches the sign bit of the result
Zero	Set if the result is zero
Parity	Set if there are an even number of on bits in the result
Overflow	Set if the result does not fit in a signed operand
Carry	Set if the destination operand is less than the source operand
Aux. carry	Set if there is a borrow into bit 3 or, with 16-bit operands, into bit 7

Note that the actual result of the subtraction is not stored in the destination operand. The flags are set as if the subtraction had occurred.

COMMENTS

Think of this as a subtraction that does not save the result. This will make it easier to remember how the flags will be set for various conditions.

The `Jcondition` instructions often follow a compare to do something with the results.

SEE ALSO

SUB	*The subtract instruction*
Jcondition	*These instructions use the results of a compare*

TIMING

Addressing	Encoding	Example	88/86	286	386
reg/reg	0011100w 211,reg,r/m	cmp ax,bx	3	2	
reg/mem	0011101w mod,reg,r/m displacement	cmp ax,limit	13/9+EA	7	5
mem/reg	0011100w mod,reg,r/m displacement	cmp limit,bl	13/9+EA	6	6
reg,immed	100000sw mod,111,r/m data	cmp dx,5	4	3	3
mem,immed	100000sw mod,111,r/m displacement data	cmp value,6	14/10+EA	6	5
acc,immed	0011110w data	cmp ax,55	4	3	2

EXAMPLE This routine reads a list of unsigned numbers at NumList. For every number greater than 14, add one (1) to the CX register. Stop when the number equals 14.

```
                mov   bx, OFFSET NumList  ; Get the address of the list
TSLoop:
                cmp   WORD PTR [bx], 14   ; Compare the data to 14
                je    Done                ; Exit if equal
                cmc                       ; Make carry one for numbers >
                                          ; 14
                adc   cx, 0               ; Add the carry to CX
                jmp   TSLoop
Done:
```

Compare String   88/80   200   300
                                                       ▲   ▲   ▲

CMPS, CMPSB, CMPSW

PURPOSE To compare the byte or word at DS:SI to the byte or word at ES:DI. If the direction flag is cleared, the index registers are incremented after this instruction. Otherwise, they are decremented.

SYNTAX
CMPS [seg:]operand,operand
CMPSB
CMPSW

FLAGS

Sign	Matches the sign bit of the result
Zero	Set if the result is zero
Parity	Set if there are an even number of on bits in the result
Overflow	Set if the result does not fit in a signed operand
Carry	Set if the destination operand is less than the source operand
Aux. carry	Set if there is a borrow into bit 3 or, with 16-bit operands, into bit 7

Note that the actual result of the subtraction is not stored in the destination operand. The flags are set as if the subtraction had occurred.

COMMENTS The operands used with the CMPS instruction are only used to tell the assembler whether to use bytes or words, and to do a segment override for the source operand.

   You can use this instruction with the REPE or REPNE prefixes to compare blocks of data.

5—Arithmetic, Logic, and Bit-Shift Instructions   **163**

CMPS, CMPSB, CMPSW

SEE ALSO   LODS, LODSB, LODSW   *String Load*
MOVS, MOVSB, MOVSW   *String Move*
SCAS, SCASB, SCASW   *String Scan*
STOS, STOSB, STOSW   *String Store*
REP, REPNZ, REPZ   *Repeat prefix*

TIMING

Addressing	Encoding	Example	88/86	286	386
implied	1010011w	CMPSB	22	8	3

EXAMPLE   This example shows how to use this instruction to make a string compare function:

```
        .CODE
; The strings are at DS:SI and ES:DI they both end with a zero
; byte. The routine returns with the carry cleared if the strings
; match.
StrCmp  PROC
        cld
        sub  al, al
        sub  cx, cx              ; Set the count to 0
        repne scansb             ; Find the zero
        add  si, cx              ; Put SI back to the beginning
                                 ; of the string.
        neg  cx                  ; Make CX equal the number of
                                 ; bytes in the string
        repe cmpsb               ; Compare the strings
        clc                      ; Clear the carry
        jcxz Match
        stc                      ; Set the carry
Match:
        ret                      ; and exit
StrCmp  ENDP
```

Convert Word to Double   88/86   286   386
                                                                      ▲   ▲   ▲

CWD

PURPOSE   To extend the sign of the value of AX into the DX register.

SYNTAX CWD

FLAGS The flags are unaffected by this instruction.

COMMENTS This instruction is often used to prepare a sign 16-bit value to be the dividend in sign 16-bit division.

SEE ALSO CBW, CDQ, CWDE   *Other sign-extending instructions*

TIMING

Addressing	Encoding	Example	88/86	286	386
implied	10011001*	CWD	5	2	2

* On the 386, the CWD and the CDQ instructions use the same encoding. In 16-bit mode, the CDQ is preceded by the operand size byte (66h). In 32-bit mode, the CWD is preceded by the operand size byte.

EXAMPLE The CWD instruction can be used to get the absolute value of a number. This works because the CWD instruction puts –1 (0FFFFh) in DX if the number is negative, and 0 in DX if it is positive. "Exclusive-ORing" the number with DX will toggle all the bits in the number, if the number is negative; and leave it alone, if it is positive. This makes the negative number positive.

The only thing left is to compensate for the fact that negative numbers begin at –1, while positive numbers begin at 0. Adding one (1) to the number, if it is negative, does the trick. Since adding one is the same as subtracting minus one (–1)—and there is a minus one in DX—you can use the SUB instruction to finish the job.

The following routine uses this programming trick to get the absolute value of the number in AX.

```
cwd              ; Sign-extend AX into DX
xor  ax, dx      ; Invert ax if it was negative
sub  ax, dx      ; Add one if it was negative
```

Convert Word to Double Extended   88/86   286   386
                                                         ▲   ▲   ▲

CWDE

PURPOSE To convert a signed 16-bit value into a signed 32-bit value, and put the result in the EAX register.

CWDE

SYNTAX   CWDE

FLAGS   The flags are unaffected by this instruction.

COMMENTS   This instruction is the same as the CWD instruction, except that the result goes into the EAX register. This is useful when converting from 16-bit to 32-bit operations on the 80386.

SEE ALSO   CBW, CDQ, CWD   *Other sign-extending instructions.*

TIMING

Addressing	Encoding	Example	386
implied	10011000*	CWDE	3

* The CWDE instruction and the CBW instruction use the same encoding. In 16-bit mode, the CWDE instruction is preceded by the operand size byte (66h). In 32-bit mode, the CBW instruction is preceded by the operand size byte.

EXAMPLE   This code fragment reads a signed 16-bit number from SmallNum, and then gets it into the EAX register as a signed value.

```
         .DATA
SmallNum DW   8451h

         .CODE
         mov  ax, SmallNum    ; Get the value for AX (8451h)
         cwde                 ; Convert it and move it into
                              ; EAX (0FFFF8451h)
```

Decimal Adjust after Addition	88/86	286	386
	▲	▲	▲

DAA

PURPOSE   To adjust the result of an addition between two packed BCD numbers.

SYNTAX   DAA

FLAGS   Sign   Matches the sign bit of the result
           Zero   Set if the result is zero
           Parity   Set if there are an even number of on bits in the result

Overflow	Unpredictable result
Carry	Set if the result is greater than 99h
Aux. carry	Set if the result is greater than 99h

COMMENTS This instruction uses the auxiliary carry that was set by the previous addition to decide how to convert the number. Therefore, it can only be used after an add instruction, or if you set the auxiliary carry to the desired state.

Because you can tell from the flags if there is an overflow, it is possible to add long strings of binary numbers.

SEE ALSO

DAS	*Adjust after subtraction*
AAA, AAS	*Adjust unpacked BCD*
AAD, AAM	*Convert between binary and unpacked BCD*
ADD, ADC	*Add instructions*

TIMING

Addressing	Encoding	Example	88/86	286	386
implied	00100111	DAA	4	3	4

EXAMPLE Add the packed BCD number at `NumOne` to the packed BCD number at `NumTwo`. Afterwards, store the result at `NumOne`.

```
        .DATA
NumOne  DB   47h
NumTwo  DB   27h

        .CODE
        mov  al, NumOne      ; Get the first number (47h)
        add  al, NumTwo      ; Add them (6Eh)
        daa                  ; Adjust the result (74h)
        mov  NumOne, al
```

Decimal Adjust after Subtraction   88/86   286   386
                                                        ▲   ▲   ▲

DAS

PURPOSE To adjust the result of a subtraction between two packed BCD numbers.

SYNTAX DAS

DAS

FLAGS

Sign	Matches the sign bit of the result
Zero	Set if the result is zero
Parity	Set if there are an even number of on bits in the result
Overflow	Unpredictable result
Carry	Set if the result is greater than 99h
Aux. carry	Set if the result is greater than 99h

COMMENTS This instruction makes it possible to subtract packed BCD numbers without having to convert to binary first. Since it uses the state of the auxiliary carry flag to do the adjustment, it should only be used after a subtract instruction.

SEE ALSO

DAA	*Adjust after addition*
AAA, AAS	*Adjust unpacked BCD numbers*
SUB, SBB	*The subtraction instructions*

TIMING

Addressing	Encoding	Example	88/86	286	386
implied	00101111	DAS	4	3	4

EXAMPLE This routine subtracts the number at NumTwo from the number at NumOne. Afterwards, it puts the result in NumOne.

```
        .DATA
NumOne  DB    24h
NumTwo  DB     7h

        .CODE
        mov  al, NumOne    ; Get the number (24h)
        sub  al, NumTwo    ; Subtract (1Dh)
        das                ; Adjust the result (17h)
        mov  NumOne, al    ; Save the result
```

Decrement   88/86 286 386
                                                            ▲   ▲   ▲

DEC

PURPOSE To subtract one from a number.

SYNTAX

DEC reg	*Decrement a register.*
DEC memory	*Decrement a memory value.*

FLAGS

Sign	Matches the sign bit of the result
Zero	Set if the result is zero
Parity	Set if there are an even number of on bits in the result
Overflow	Set if the result is out of the range for signed values
Aux. carry	Set if there was a borrow out of bit 3 or, if using 16-bit operands, out of bit 7

COMMENTS   The decrement instruction is an easy way to subtract one (1) from a number quickly. Whenever you need to count down to an event or reduce a number by one, this instruction will save time and memory.

The only case where you need to use the subinstruction for subtracting by one is where you are interested in the state of the borrow (carry) flag after the subtraction. The decrement instruction does not affect the borrow (carry) flag.

SEE ALSO

INC	*Adds one to a number*
SUB	*The subtract instruction*

TIMING

Addressing	Encoding	Example	88/86	286	386
reg8	11111110 11001,r/m	DEC al	3	2	2
mem	1111111w mod,001,r/m	DEC counter displacement	23/15+EA	7	6
reg16/32*	01001reg	DEC ax	3	2	2

* Only the 80386 can use the 32-bit version.

EXAMPLE   This routine reads I/O port 3F8h and decrements the BX register every time the byte read is 0Dh. When the BX register is 0, it exits.

```
SDLoop:
        in   al, 3F8h      ; Get the byte from the COM1
                           ; data port
        cmp  al,0Dh        ; See if it is 0DH
        jne  SDLoop        ; if not loop
        dec  bx            ; Decrement BX
        jnz  SDLoop        ; loop until BX is zero
```

DIV

DIV

PURPOSE   To divide one unsigned number by another.

SYNTAX   DIV reg   *Divide by a register.*
DIV mem   *Divide by a memory value.*

FLAGS   The overflow flag, sign flag, zero flag, auxiliary carry, parity flag, and the carry flag are set to unpredictable values.

COMMENTS   The DIV instruction uses an implied register for the dividend. When dividing by 8-bit values, the register is AX. When dividing by 16-bit values, the registers are DX and AX. On the 80386 there may be a 32-bit operand. In this case the registers are EDX and EAX.

     If the divisor is a power of two (2, 4, 8, etc.), you should consider using shift instructions for dividing. The shift instructions will run much faster than the DIV instruction, especially on 8088 or 8086 processors.

     Dividing by zero or getting a result that will not fit in the destination operand will cause an interrupt. If the interrupt is not handled properly, it could crash the program. It is good practice always to check the values being used for this possibility. The easiest test is to compare the divisor with the high word or byte of the dividend. If the divisor is smaller than the high half of the dividend, the divisor is either zero or the result will overflow.

SEE ALSO   IDIV   *Divide signed numbers*
IMUL   *Multiply instructions*
SHR, SAR   *Shift right instructions*

TIMING

Addressing	Encoding	Example	88/86	286	386
reg8	11110110 mod,110,r/m	DIV bl	80-90	14	14
reg16	11110111 mod,110,r/m	DIV bx	144-162	22	22
reg32	11110111 mod,110,r/m	DIV ebx	-	-	38
mem8	11110110 mod,110,r/m	DIV bval	86-96+EA	17	17

Addressing	Encoding	Example	88/86	286	386
mem16	11110111 mod,110,r/m	DIV wval	150-176+EA	25	25
mem32	11110111	DIV dval	-	-	41

EXAMPLE This routine divides the value at BigNum by the number in BX, and saves the result in SmallNum.

```
        .DATA
BigNum  DD   214561h
SmallNum DW  ?

        .CODE
        mov  bx, 50h
        mov  ax, BigNum      ; Get the low word (4561h)
        mov  dx, BigNum+2    ; Get the high word (21h)
        cmp  dx, bx          ; Check for possible divide
                             ; problems
        jge  err             ; if DX is >= to the divisor it
                             ; will divide overflow
        div  bx              ; Divide (AX = 6A77h DX = 31h)
        mov  SmallNum, ax    ; Save the result
        .
        .
        .
err:
```

Integer Divide   88/86   286   386
                                                               ▲   ▲   ▲

IDIV

PURPOSE To divide signed integer values.

SYNTAX IDIV   reg   *Divide by a register.*
IDIV   mem   *Divide by a memory value.*

FLAGS The overflow flag, sign flag, zero flag, auxiliary carry, parity and carry flags are all set to unpredictable values.

IDIV

COMMENTS This instruction takes care of dividing by negative numbers. Since the dividend is always twice as wide as the quotient and divisor, the programmer must be careful properly to sign-extend when using this instruction.

When dividing by a power of 2 (2, 4, 8, etc.), you should consider the SAR instruction. The SAR instruction will copy the sign bit as it shifts to preserve the proper sign. It will almost always run faster than the IDIV instruction, especially on 8088 or 8086 processors.

Dividing by zero or getting a result that does not fit into the destination register will cause an interrupt. If the interrupt routine is not coded properly, it could crash your program. It is good practice to check the numbers to be divided to make sure they will work.

SEE ALSO

DIV	*Unsigned divide instruction*
MUL, IMUL	*Multiplication instructions*
SAR, SHR	*Right shift instructions*

TIMING

Addressing	Encoding	Example	88/86	286	386
reg8	11110110 mod,111,r/m	IDIV cl	101-112	17	19
reg16	11110111 mod,111,r/m	IDIV cx	165-184	25	27
reg32	11110111 mod,111,r/m	IDIV ecx	-	-	43
mem8	11110110 mod,111,r/m displacement	IDIV bval	107-118+EA	20	22
mem16	11110111 mod,111,r/m displacement	IDIV wval	171-194+EA	28	30
mem32	11110111 mod,111,r/m displacement	IDIV dval	-	-	46

EXAMPLE See the example for CBW.

IMUL

IMUL

PURPOSE   To multiply two signed integer values together.

SYNTAX

IMUL	reg	*Multiply by a register.*
IMUL	mem	*Multiply by a memory value.*

For the 80386 only:

IMUL	reg,immed	*Multiply a register by an immediate value.*
IMUL	reg1,reg2,immed	*Multiply reg2 by an immediate value then put the result in reg1.*
IMUL	reg,mem,immed	*Multiply a memory value by an immediate value, then put the result in a register.*
IMUL	reg1,reg2	*Multiply two registers.*
IMUL	reg,mem	*Multiply a register by a memory value.*

FLAGS

Sign	Unpredictable result
Zero	Unpredictable result
Parity	Unpredictable result
Carry	Set if result is larger than the operands
Overflow	Set if result is larger than the operands
Aux. carry	Unpredictable result

COMMENTS   The multiply instruction uses an implied multiplier and product register. For 8-bit multiplies, the multiplier comes from the AL register and the product goes into AX. For 16-bit multiplies, the multiplier comes from AX and the product goes into DX and AX. On the 80386, using 32-bit numbers uses the EAX register and puts the result in the EDX and EAX registers.

     The 80386 also uses some other addressing modes. They allow registers or memory to be multiplied by each other or by an immediate value. The thing to remember with these modes is that the product is saved in the same-sized register as the multipliers. This means that if the product is too large, bits will be lost. In this case the carry and overflow flags will be set.

SEE ALSO

MUL	*The unsigned multiply instruction*
DIV, IDIV	*The divide instructions*
SHL, SAL	*Left shift instructions*

IMUL

Addressing	Encoding	Example	88/86	286	386
reg8	11110110 mod,101,r/m	IMUL dl	80-98	13	9-14
reg16	11110111 mod,101,r/m	IMUL bx	128-154	12	9-22
reg32	11110111	IMUL ecx	-	-	9-38
mem8	11110110 mod,101,r/m displacement	IMUL bval	86-104+EA	16	12-17
mem16	11110111 mod,101,r/m displacement	IMUL wval	134-164+EA	24	12-25
mem32	11110111 mod,101,r/m displacement	IMUL dval	-	-	12-41
reg,immed	011010s1 mod,reg,r/m data	IMUL cx,4	-	21	9-38
reg,reg,immed	011010s1 mod,reg,r/m data	IMUL cx,ax,5	-	21	9-38
reg,mem,immed	001010s1 mod,reg,r/m displacement data	IMUL cx,wval,7	-	24	12-41
reg,reg	00001111 10101111 mod,reg,r/m	IMUL cx,ax	-	-	9-38
reg,mem or mem,reg	00001111 10101111 mod,reg,r/m displacement	IMUL ax,wval	-	-	12-41

EXAMPLE   This routine multiplies the number at NumOne by the number at NumTwo. If the result is too large for NumOne, it stores a zero. Otherwise, it stores the result.

```
            .DATA
NumOne      DW   1234h
NumTwo      DW   21h

            .CODE
            mov  ax, NumOne
            imul NumTwo        ; AX = 58B4h, DX = 25h, carry set
            jnc  SaveIt        ; If carry not set there was
                               ; no sign extension

            xor  ax, ax
SaveIt:
            mov  NumOne, ax
```

Increment   88/86   286   386
                                                     ▲   ▲   ▲

INC

PURPOSE   To add one to a number.

SYNTAX   INC   reg   *Increment a register.*
              INC   mem   *Increment a memory value.*

FLAGS   Sign   Matches the sign bit of the resullt
             Zero   Set if the result is zero
             Parity   Set if there are an even number of on bits in the result
             Overflow   Set if the operand was 127 (8-bit operations) or 32767 (16-bit operations)
             Aux. carry   Set if there was a carry out of bit 3 or, for 16-bit operations, out of bit 7

COMMENTS   The increment instruction provides an easy way to add one to a number. It can save memory and time over using an add instruction.

SEE ALSO   DEC   *The decrement instruction*
                ADD   *The addition instruction*

INC

TIMING

Addressing	Encoding	Example	88/86	286	386
reg8	11111110 11000,r/m	inc cl	3	2	2
reg16	01000reg	inc ax	3	2	2
reg32	01000reg	inc edx	-	-	2
mem	1111111w mod,000,r/m displacement	inc count	23/15+EA	7	6

EXAMPLE The following writes a routine to count all the words in a list. The word at the end of the list is 0.

```
        sub   cx, cx          ; Put 0 in CX, this will be the
                              ; count
        mov   bx, OFFSET List
WCLoop:
        cmp   [bx], 0          ; Check the value
        je    Done
        inc   cx              ; Increment the count
        inc   bx              ; Increment bx to point
        inc   bx              ; to the next word
        jmp   SHORT WCLoop     ; Do it again
Done:
        ret
```

Multiply

	88/86	286	386
	▲	▲	▲

MUL

PURPOSE To multiply two unsigned numbers together.

SYNTAX
MUL   reg   *Multiply by a register.*
MUL   mem   *Multiply by a memory value.*

FLAGS The overflow flag and the carry flag are set if the result is larger than the multipliers.

The sign flag, zero flag, auxiliary carry, and parity flag are set to unpredictable values.

COMMENTS The MUL instruction uses an implied operand for a multiplier and for the product. For 8-bit operations, the implied multiplier is AL. The product goes into AX. If AH is not zero, then the carry and overflow flags will be set. With 16-bit operations, the multiplier is AX. The product goes into DX and AX. If DX is not 0, then the carry and overflow flags are set. On the 80386 you can do 32-bit multiplies. The implied multiplier is EAX and the result goes into EAX and EDX. If EDX is not zero, the carry and overflow flags will be set.

SEE ALSO

IMUL	Signed multiply
SHL, SAL	Arithmetic shift instructions

TIMING

Addressing	Encoding	Example	88/86	286	386
reg8	11110110 mod,100,r/m	MUL cl	70-77	13	9-14
reg16	11110111 mod,100,r/m	MUL dx	118-113	21	9-22
reg32	11110111 mod,100,r/m	MUL ebx	-	-	9-38
mem8	11110110 mod,100,r/m displacement	MUL bval	76-83+EA	16	12-17
mem16	11110110 mod,100,r/m displacement	MUL wval	124-39+EA	24	12-25
mem32	11110110 mod,100,r/m displacement	MUL dval	-	-	12-41

EXAMPLE To find the number of bytes in an array, you can multiply the number of items in the array times the size of each item. The routine to do this is made simple by the MUL instruction

MUL

```
mov  ax, RecCnt       ; Get the number of records
mov  bx, RecSize      ; Get the size of a record
mul  bx
mov  ArraySize, ax    ; Save the low word
mov  ArraySize+2,dx   ; Save the high word
```

Negate   88/86   286   386
                                                        ▲   ▲   ▲

NEG

PURPOSE To change the sign of a signed number.

SYNTAX NEG   reg   *Change the sign of a register.*
            NEG   mem   *Change the sign of a memory value.*

FLAGS
Sign	Matches the sign of the result
Zero	Set if the result is zero
Parity	Set if there are an even number of bits in the result
Carry	Set if the result is not zero
Overflow	Set if all of the bits are on

COMMENTS The NEG instruction works by twos, complementing the number. The procedure for twos complementing is to invert all the bits, and then add to the result.

SEE ALSO NOT   *The Logical NOT instruction*

TIMING

Addressing	Encoding	Example	88/86	286	386
reg8	11110110 11,011,r/m	NEG al	3	2	2
reg16	11110111 11,011,r/m	NEG cx	3	2	2
reg32	11110111 11,011,r/m	NEG eax	-	-	2
mem8	11110110 mod,011,r/m displacement	NEG bval	24/16+EA	7	6

Addressing	Encoding	Example	88/86	286	386
mem16	11110111 mod,011,r/m displacement	NEG wval	24/16+EA	7	6
mem32	11110111 mod,011,r/m displacement	NEG dval	-	-	6

EXAMPLE   This function changes the word at SignNum to the absolute value of that word.

```
        mov   ax, SignNum
        neg   ax
        js    Done        ; Check the sign flag
        mov   SignNum, ax ; Save the result
Done:
        ret
```

If the number at SignNum is –45, the neg instruction changes it to 45. The JS instruction jumps if the sign is set. Otherwise the number is positive, so it should be saved at SignNum.

For a more efficient way to get the absolute value of a number, see the CWD instruction.

Logical NOT   88/86   286   386
                                                                               ▲   ▲   ▲

NOT

PURPOSE   To invert each of the bits in a binary number.

SYNTAX   NOT   reg   *Invert a register.*
              NOT   mem   *Invert a memory value.*

FLAGS   The flags are unaffected by this instruction.

COMMENTS   The Logical NOT is an important part of Boolean expressions. A common use of this instruction is to invert mask bytes used in Logical AND and OR operations.

NOT

SEE ALSO AND, OR, XOR *Other Boolean operations*

TIMING

Addressing	Encoding	Example	88/86	286	386
reg8	11110110 11010,r/m	NOT al	3	2	2
reg16	11110111 11010,r/m	NOT ax	3	2	2
reg32	11110111 11010,r/m	NOT eax	-	-	2
mem8	11110110 mod,010,r/m displacement	NOT bval	24/16+EA	7	6
mem16	11110111 mod,010,r/m displacement	NOT wval	24/16+EA	7	6
mem32	11110111 mod,010,r/m displacement	NOT dval	-	-	6

EXAMPLE This routine masks a bit out of the byte in AL. The bit is set in the byte at Mask.

```
         .DATA
Mask     DB    00010000b

         .CODE
         mov   bl, Mask   ; Get the bit
         not   bl         ; Invert the mask (11101111b)
         and   al, bl     ; Turn off the bit
```

Inclusive OR   88/86   286   386
                                                                    ▲   ▲   ▲

OR

PURPOSE To "Logical-OR" the bits in two binary numbers.

SYNTAX
OR	reg1,reg2	*OR two registers.*
OR	reg,mem	*OR a register with memory value.*
OR	mem,reg	*OR a memory value with a register.*
OR	reg,immed	*OR a register with an immediate value.*
OR	mem,immed	*OR a memory value with an immediate value.*

FLAGS The overflow flag and the carry flag are set to 0.
The auxiliary carry is set to some unpredictable value.
The sign flag, zero flag, and parity flag are set according to the result.

COMMENTS The Inclusive OR is commonly used to set bits in a byte.

SEE ALSO NOT, AND, XOR *Other logical operators*

TIMING

Addressing	Encoding	Example	88/86	286	386
reg,reg	0000100w 11,reg,r/m	OR ax,bx	3	2	2
mem,reg	0000100w mod,reg,r/m displacement	OR flags,cx	24/16+EA	7	7
reg,mem	0000101w mod,reg,r/m displacement	OR bx,mask	24/16+EA	7	7
reg,immed	100000sw mod,001,r/m data	OR bl,0fh	4	3	2
mem,immed	100000sw mod,001,r/m displacement data	OR flags,3	17 or 25+EA	7	7
acc,immed	0000110w mod,reg,r/m data	OR al,4	4	3	2

EXAMPLE See the example for AND.

RCL

RCL

PURPOSE   Use RCL to rotate bits to the left, and to move the high bit into the carry flag and the old carry into the low bit.

SYNTAX

| RCL | reg/mem, cl | *Rotate a register or memory value cl bits left.* |
| RCL | reg/mem, immed | *Rotate a register or memory value an immediate value number of bits 1 for 8088, 8086 0-31 for 80286, 80386.* |

FLAGS   The overflow flag is set when a single bit rotation changes the sign. The carry flag is set to the value of the high bit before the rotation.

COMMENTS   The RCL instruction moves all the bits in the operand to the left. The high bit in the operand gets copied into the carry flag, and the carry gets shifted into the low bit position. When the second operand is a one, the data is shifted one bit. When the second operand is `cl`, the data is rotated the number in `cl` times. For 80286 and 80386 processors, the second argument can be an 8-bit number (0 to 31) indicating the number of rotations desired.

SEE ALSO

| ROL, ROR, RCR | *Different rotate instructions* |
| SHL, SHR, SAL, SAR | *Shift instructions* |

TIMING

Addressing	Encoding	Examples	88/86	286	386
reg,1	1101000w 11010,r/m	rcl bx,1	2	2	9
mem	1101000w mod,010,r/m	rcl value,1	23/15+EA	7	7
reg,cl	1101001w 11010,r/m	rcl bx,cl	8+4n	5+n	9
mem,cl	1101001w mod,010,r/m	rcl value,cl	28/20+EA+4n	8n	10

Addressing	Encoding	Examples	88/86	286	386
reg,immed	1100000w	rcl bx,4	-	5+n	10
	11010,r/m				
mem,immed	1100000w	rcl value,10	-	8+n	9
	mod,010,r/m				

EXAMPLE This example shows how to use the RCL instruction when shifting a 32-bit value:

```
    .
    .
    .
shl  ax, 1              ; Shift the low word, put the
                       ; high bit in the carry
rcl  dx, 1             ; Rotate the high word
    .
    .
    .
```

Rotate through Carry Right   88/86   286   386
                                               ▲   ▲   ▲

RCR

PURPOSE Use RCR to rotate bits to the right, and to move the low bit into the carry flag and the carry into the high bit.

SYNTAX
```
RCR    reg/mem, cl
RCR    reg/mem, immed
```
Rotate a register or memory value cl bits right.
Rotate a register or memory value an immediate value number of bits
1 for 8088, 8086
0-31 for 80286, 80386.

FLAGS The overflow flag is set when a single bit rotation changes the sign.
The carry flag is set to the value of the high bit before the rotation.

COMMENTS The RCR instruction moves all the bits in the operand to the right. The low bit in the operand gets copied into the carry flag, and the carry gets shifted into the high bit position. When the second operand is a one, the data is shifted one

RCR

bit. When the second operand is `cl`, the data is rotated the number in `cl` times. For 80286 and 80386 processors, the second argument can be an 8-bit number (0 to 31) indicating the number of rotations desired.

SEE ALSO   RCL, ROR, ROL   *Different rotate instructions*
SHL, SHR, SAL, SAR   *Shift instructions*

TIMING

Addressing	Encoding	Examples	88/86	286	386
reg	1101000w 11011,r/m	rcr bx,1	2	2	3
mem	1101000w mod,011,r/m displacement	rcr value,1	23/15+EA	7	7
reg,cl	1101001w 11,011,r/m	rcr bx,cl	8+4n	5+n	3
mem,cl	1101001w mod,011,r/m displacement	rcr value,cl	28/20+EA+4n	8n	7
reg,immed	1100000w 11011,r/m data	rcr bx,4	-	5+n	3
mem,immed	1100000w mod,011,r/m data	rcr value,10	-	8+n	3

EXAMPLE   This example shows how to use the RCL instruction when shifting a 32-bit value:

```
        .
        .
        .
        shr   ax, 1          ; Shift the low word, put the
                             ; low bit in the carry
        rcr   dx, 1          ; Rotate the high word
        .
        .
        .
```

Rotate Left 88/86 286 386
▲ ▲ ▲

ROL

PURPOSE Use ROL to rotate bits to the left, and move the high bit into the carry flag and into the low bit.

SYNTAX
```
ROL   reg/mem, cl
ROL   reg/mem, immed
```
Rotate a register or memory value cl bits left.
Rotate a register or memory value an immediate value number of bits
1 for 8088, 8086
0-31 for 80286, 80386.

FLAGS The overflow flag is set when a single bit rotation changes the sign.
The carry flag is set to the value of the high bit before the rotation.

COMMENTS The ROL instruction moves all of the bits in the operand to the left. The high bit in the operand gets copied into the carry flag and shifted into the low bit position. When the second operand is a one, the data is shifted one bit. When the second operand is cl, the data is rotated the number in cl times. For 80286 and 80386 processors, the second argument can be an 8-bit number (0 to 31) indicating the number of rotations desired.

SEE ALSO
RCL, ROR, RCR   *Different rotate instructions*
SHL, SHR, SAL, SAR *Shift instructions*

TIMING

Addressing	Encoding	Examples	88/86	286	386
reg	1101000w 11000r/m	rol bx,1	2	2	3
mem	1101000w mod000r/m	rol value,1	23/15+EA	7	7
reg,cl	1101001w 11000r/m	rol bx,cl	8+4n	5+n	3
mem,cl	1101001w mod000r/m	rol value,cl	28/20+EA+4n	8n	7
reg,immed	1100000w 11000r/m	rol bx,4	-	5+n	3

ROL

Addressing	Encoding	Examples	88/86	286	386
mem,immed	1100000w mod000r/m	rol value,10	-	8+n	3

EXAMPLE This function converts a BCD number to two ASCII characters. The input value is in AL, and the output is in AX.

```
            .
            .
            .
            mov  al, 34h    ; Put a BCD number in AL
            call BCD2ASCII  ; Convert it
            .
            .
            .

BCD2ASCII PROC
            mov  ah, al     ; Put the number in the high byte
            rol  ah, 1      ; Swap the nibbles
            rol  ah, 1
            rol  ah, 1
            rol  ah, 1      ; AX = 4334h
            and  ax, 0f0fh  ; Mask off the high bits in each byte
                            ; AX = 0304h
            or   ax, 3030h  ; Make them ASCII AX = 3334h
            ret
BCD2ASCII ENDP
```

Rotate Right   88/86   286   386
                                                                    ▲   ▲   ▲

ROR

PURPOSE Use ROR to rotate bits to the right, and move the low bit into the carry flag and into the high bit.

SYNTAX
```
ROR    reg/mem, cl
ROR    reg/mem, immed
```
Rotate a register or memory value cl bits left.
Rotate a register or memory value an immediate value number of bits
1 for 8088, 8086
0-31 for 80286, 80386.

FLAGS
The overflow flag is set when a single bit rotation changes the sign.
The carry flag is set to the value of the high bit before the rotation.

COMMENTS
The ROR instruction moves all of the bits in the operand to the right. The low bit in the operand gets copied into the carry flag, and the carry gets shifted into the high bit position. When the second operand is a one, the data is shifted one bit. When the second operand is cl, the data is rotated the number in cl times. For 80286 and 80386 processors, the second argument can be an 8-bit number (0 to 31) indicating the number of rotations desired.

SEE ALSO
```
RCL, ROL, RCR
SHL, SHR, SAL, SAR
```
Different rotate instructions
Shift instructions

TIMING

Addressing	Encoding	Examples	88/86	286	386
reg	1101000w 11000,r/m	ror bx,1	2	2	3
mem	1101000w mod,000,r/m displacement	ror value,1	23/15+EA	7	7
reg,cl	1101001w 11000,r/m	ror bx,cl	8+4n	5+n	3
mem,cl	1101001w mod,000,r/m displacement	ror value,cl	28/20+EA+4n	8n	7
reg,immed	1100000w 11000,r/m	ror bx,4	-	5+n	3
mem,immed	1100000w mod,000,r/m	ror valuc,10	-	8+n	3

EXAMPLE
This function converts a BCD number to two ASCII characters. The input value is in AL, and the output is in AX.

ROR

```
                .
                .
                .

        mov   al, 34h     ; Put a BCD number in AL
        call  BCD2ASCII   ; Convert it
                .
                .
                .

BCD2ASCII PROC
        mov   ah, al      ; Put the number in the high byte
        ror   ah, 1       ; Swap the nibbles
        ror   ah, 1
        ror   ah, 1
        ror   ah, 1       ; AX = 4334h
        and   ax, 0f0fh   ; Mask off the high bits in each byte
                          ; AX = 0304h
        or    ax, 3030h   ; Make them ASCII AX = 3334h
        ret
BCD2ASCII ENDP
```

Shift Arithmetic Left   88/86   286   386
                                                             ▲   ▲   ▲

SAL

PURPOSE Use SAL to shift bits to the left. This is the same as multiplying by two.

SYNTAX
```
SAL  reg/mem, cl
SAR  reg/mem, immed
```
Shift a register or memory value CL bits left.
Shift a register or memory value an immediate value bits left
1 for 8088, 8086
0-31 for 80286, 80386.

FLAGS
Overflow   Set if the sign bit changes
Sign   Matches the sign bit of the result
Zero   Set if the result is zero
Parity   Set if there are an even number of bits in the result
Carry   Set if the low bit of the operand was set
Aux. carry   Unpredictable

COMMENTS The SAL instruction can be used to improve performance over the MUL instruction when the program needs to do multiplication by some power of two. This instruction is identical to the SHL instruction. The assembler recognizes both names for consistency.

SEE ALSO
SHL,SHR,SAR   *Different shift instructions*
RCL,RCR,ROR,ROL   *Rotate instructions*
MUL

TIMING

Addressing	Encoding	Examples	88/86	286	386
reg,1	1101100w 11100,r/m	sal bx,1	2	2	3
mem,1	1101100w mod,100,r/m displacement	sal value,1	23/15+EA	7	7
reg,cl	1101001w 11100,r/m	sal bx,cl	8+4n	5+n	3
mem,cl	1101001w mod,100,r/m displacement	sal value,cl	28/20+EA+4n	8n	7
reg,immed	1100000w 11100,r/m data	sal bx,4	-	5+n	3
mem,immed	1100000w mod,100,r/m data	sal value,10	-	8+n	3

EXAMPLE This routine multiplies a signed 32-bit number in DX,AX by 4. This could be done with a MUL command; but for 8088 and 8086 processors, this is much faster.

```
mov   dx, 41h      ; Put 41h in the high word
mov   ax, 1234h    ; Put 1234h in the low word
sal   ax,1         ; Multiply by 2 for 2468h
rcl   dx,1         ; Rotate will get the carry from
                   ; the previous shift 0082h
sal   ax,1         ; Do it again to multiply by 4
rcl   dx,1         ; dx = 0104h ax = 48D0h
```

SAR

SAR

PURPOSE Use SAR to shift bits to the right. This is the same as dividing by two. Because this instruction leaves the sign bit unchanged, it can be used to divide signed values.

SYNTAX
SAR   reg/mem,cl   *Shift a register or memory value cl bits right.*
SAR   reg/mem,immed   *Shift a register or memory value an*
                       immediate value bits right
                       1 for 8088, 8086
                       0-31 for 80286, 80386.

FLAGS
Overflow	Set if the sign bit changes
Sign	Matches the sign bit of the result
Zero	Set if the result is zero
Parity	Set if there are an even number of bits in the result
Carry	Set if the low bit of the operand was set
Aux. carry	Unpredictable

COMMENTS The SAR instruction can be used to improve performance over the integer divide (IDIV) instruction, when the program needs to do division by some power of two. The best use of this instruction is in evaluating equations that use signed values. It should not be used in unsigned calculations where the sign bit is not used.

SEE ALSO
SHL,SHR,SAL   *Different shift instructions*
RCL,RCR,ROR,ROL   *Rotate instructions*
IDIV

TIMING

Addressing	Encoding	Examples	88/86	286	386
reg,1	1101000w	sar bx,1	2	2	3
	11111,r/m				
mem,1	1101000w	sar value,1	23/15+EA	7	7
	mod,111,r/m				
	displacement				

Addressing	Encoding	Examples	88/86	286	386
reg,cl	1101001w 11111,r/m	sar bx,cl	8+4n	5+n	3
mem,cl	1101001w mod111,r/m displacement	sar value,cl	28/20+EA+4n	8n	7
reg,immed	1100000w 11111,r/m data	sar bx,4	-	5+n	3
mem,immed	1100000w mod,111,r/m data	sar value,10	-	8+n	3

EXAMPLE This routine divides a signed 32-bit number in DX , AX by 4. This could be done with a divide command; but for 8088 and 8086 processors, this is much faster.

```
mov   dx, 41h      . ; Put 41h in the high word
mov   ax, 1234h      ; Put 1234 in the low word
sar   dx,1           ; Divide by 2 leaving 2h
rcr   ax,1           ; Rotate will get the carry from
                     ; the previous shift 811Ah
sar   dx,1           ; Do it again to get a divide by 4
rcr   ax,1           ; dx = 1 ax = 408Dh
```

Shift Left   88/86   286   386
                                                        ▲   ▲   ▲

SHL

See SAL.

SHLD

SHLD

PURPOSE   To shift a double precision value left.

SYNTAX

SHLD	reg,reg,immed	*Shift two registers by the number of bits in the immediate value.*
SHLD	mem,reg,immed	*Shift a register into a memory value.*
SHLD	reg,reg,cl	*Shift two registers by the number of bits in cl.*
SHLD	mem,reg,cl	*Shift a register into a memory value.*

FLAGS

Overflow	Set if the sign bit changes
Sign	Matches the sign bit of the result
Zero	Set if the result is zero
Parity	Set if there are an even number of bits in the result
Carry	Matches the last bit sifted out
Aux. carry	Unpredictable

COMMENTS   When you use the 80386, this instruction can be very helpful when manipulating large values. It is also useful because bits can be shifted out of one register and into another. This could be used when examining a word one nibble at a time.

SEE ALSO

SHRD	*Shift right double*
SHL, SHR, SAL, SAR	*Other shift instructions*
ROL, ROR, RCL, RCR	*Rotate instructions*

TIMING

Addressing	Encoding	Example	88/86	286	386
reg,reg,immed	00001111 10100100 11,reg,r/m data	SHLD ax,bx,4	-	-	3
mem,reg,immed	00001111 10100100 mod,reg,r/m displacement data	SHLD value,cx,3	-	-	7

Addressing	Encoding	Example	88/86	286	386
reg,reg,cl	00001111	SHLD ax,bx,cl	-	-	3
	10100101				
	11,reg,r/m				
mem,reg,cl	00001111	SHLD value,ax,cl	-	-	7
	10100101				
	mod,reg,r/m				
	displacement				

EXAMPLE See the example for SHRD. Using SHLD instead of SHRD puts the digits in the correct order.

Shift Right   88/86   286   386
                                                              ▲   ▲   ▲

SHR

PURPOSE Use SHR to shift bits to the right. This is the same as dividing by two.

SYNTAX
SHR   reg/mem,cl   *Shift a register or memory value cl bits right.*
SHR   reg/mem,immed   *Shift a register or memory value an immediate*
                                    value bits right
                                      1 for 8088, 8086
                                      0-31 for 80286,80386.

FLAGS
Overflow	Set if the sign bit changes
Sign	Matches the sign bit of the result
Zero	Set if the result is zero
Parity	Set if there are an even number of bits in the result
Carry	Set if the low bit of the operand was set
Aux. carry	Unpredictable

COMMENTS The SHR instruction can be used to improve performance over the divide (DIV) instruction, when the program needs to do division by some power of two.

SEE ALSO
SHL,SAR,SAL   *Different shift instructions*
RCL,RCR,ROR,ROL   *Rotate instructions*
IDIV

SHR

TIMING

Addressing	Encoding	Examples	88/86	286	386
reg,1	1101000w 11101,r/m	shr bx,1	2	2	3
mem,1	1101000w mod,101,r/m displacement	shr value,1	23/15+EA	7	7
reg,cl	1101001w 11101,r/m	shr bx,cl	8+4n	5+n	3
mem,cl	1101001w mod,101,r/m displacement	shr value,cl	28/20+EA+4n	8n	7
reg,immed	1100000w 11101,r/m value	shr bx,4	-	5+n	3
mem,immed	1100000w mod,101,r/m value	shr value,10	-	8+n	3

EXAMPLE This routine divides a 32-bit number in DX , AX by 4. This could be done with a divide command; but for 8088 and 8086 processors, this is much faster.

```
mov  dx, 41h      ; Put 41h in the high word
mov  ax, 1234h    ; Put 1234 in the low word
shr  dx,1         ; Divide by 2 leaving 2h
rcr  ax,1         ; Rotate will get the carry from
                  ; the previous shift 811Ah
shr  dx,1         ; Do it again to get a divide by 4
rcr  ax,1         ; dx = 1 ax = 408Dh
```

Shift Right Double Precision   88/86   286   386
                                                        ▲   ▲   ▲

SHRD

PURPOSE To shift a double precision value right.

SYNTAX

SHRD	reg,reg,immed	*Shift two registers by the number of bits in the immediate value.*
SHRD	mem,reg,immed	*Shift a register into a memory value.*
SHRD	reg,reg,cl	*Shift two registers by the number of bits in cl.*
SHRD	mem,reg,cl	*Shift a register into a memory value.*

FLAGS

Overflow	Set if the sign bit changes
Sign	Matches the sign bit of the result
Zero	Set if the result is zero
Parity	Set if there are an even number of bits in the result
Carry	Matches the last bit sifted out
Aux. carry	Unpredictable

COMMENTS When you use the 80386, this instruction can be very helpful when manipulating large values. It is also useful because bits can be shifted out of one register and into another. This could be used when examining a word one nibble at a time.

SEE ALSO

SHLD	*Shift left double*
SHL, SHR, SAL, SAR	*Other shift instructions*
ROL, ROR, RCL, RCR	*Rotate instructions*

TIMING

Addressing	Encoding	Example	88/86	286	386
reg,reg,immed	00001111 10101100 11,reg,r/m data	SHRD ax,bx,4	-	-	3
mem,reg,immed	00001111 10101100 mod,reg,r/m displacement data	SHRD value,cx,3	-	-	7
reg,reg,cl	00001111 10101101	SHRD ax,bx,cl 11,reg,r/m	-	-	3
mem,reg,cl	00001111 10101101 mod,reg,r/m displacement	SHRD value,ax,cl	-	-	7

SHRD

EXAMPLE This routine prints the packed BCD number in BX in reverse order. It uses the SHRD instruction to get the digits out of BX.

```
        mov   cl, 4            ; The number of digits to print
Ploop:
        xor   dx, dx           ; Clear dx
        shrd  dx, bx, 4        ; Put a digit in dl
        or    dl, 30h          ; Make it ASCII
        mov   ah, 5            ; DOS print char function
        int   21h
        loop Ploop
```

Subtract with Borrow   88/86   286   386
                                                             ▲   ▲   ▲

SBB

PURPOSE To subtract one number from another, and then subtract the carry flag from the result.

SYNTAX

SBB	reg,reg	*Subtract a register from another register.*
SBB	reg,mem	*Subtract a memory value from a register.*
SBB	mem,reg	*Subtract a register from a memory value.*
SBB	reg,immed	*Subtract an immediate value from a register.*
SBB	mem,immed	*Subtract an immediate value from a memory value.*

FLAGS

Sign	Matches the sign bit of the result
Zero	Set if the result is zero
Parity	Set if there are an even number of bits in the result
Overflow	Set if the result of a sign subtraction is not in the valid range for the operands
Carry	Set if the value in the destination operand was less than the value in the source operand
Aux. carry	Set if there was a borrow in bit 3 or, if using 16-bit operands, into bit 7

COMMENTS The subtract with borrow instruction is usually used after a subtract instruction to subtract more significant bytes in a long number.

SEE ALSO

SUB	*The subtraction instruction*
ADD, ADC	*Addition commands*
NEG	*Twos complement instruction*

Addressing	Encoding	Example	88/86	286	386
reg,reg	0001100w 11,reg,r/m	SBB bx,cx	3	2	2
mem,reg	0001100w mod,reg,r/m displacement	SBB value,ax	24/16+EA	7	6
reg,mem	0001101w mod,reg,r/m displacement	SBB cx,value	13/9+EA	7	7
reg,immed	100000sw mod,reg,r/m data	SBB dx,5	4	3	2
mem,immed	100000sw mod,reg,r/m displacement data	SBB value,44	25/17+EA	7	7
acc,immed	0001110w data	SBB al,21	4	3	2

EXAMPLE   The size of a block of memory can be determined by subtracting the ending address of the memory from the starting address. If both addresses are in the same segment, you can use the SUB instruction; but if they are not, you need to calculate the 20-bit physical addresses and subtract them. You will need the SBB instruction to subtract correctly the upper four bits of each address.

   This function subtracts the far pointer in ES:DI from the far pointer in DS:SI.

```
mov   ax, ds          ; Get the segment of the
                      ; starting address
sub   bx, bx          ; Clear BX
shl   ax, 1           ; Times 16 gives the
rcl   bx, 1           ; physical address
shl   ax, 1
rcl   bx, 1
shl   ax, 1
rcl   bx, 1
shl   ax, 1
rcl   bx, 1
add   si, ax          ; Add it to the offset
```

```
adc   bx, 0            ; Add the high word
mov   ax, es           ; Get the ending segment
sub   cx, cx           ; Clear CX
shl   ax, 1            ; Times 16 for the physical
rcl   cx, 1            ; address
shl   ax, 1
rcl   cx, 1
shl   ax, 1
rcl   cx, 1
shl   ax, 1
rcl   cx, 1
add   di, ax           ; Add to the offset
sub   di, si           ; Subtract the starting
                       ; address from the ending
                       ; address
sbb   cx, dx           ; Subtract the high 4 bits
                       ; including any borrow
```

To find the amount of memory between 0452:0D03 and 2510:0003, place these addresses in DS:SI and ES:DI before entering this routine. The first half of the routine adjusts the starting address. After the SHL and RCL instructions, the AX register contains 4520h and the BX register contains 0. After adding these registers to the offset, the SI register contains 5223h and the BX register still contains 0. This is the physical address of the beginning of the memory block.

After doing the same procedure on the end address, the DI register contains 5103h (low word) and the CX register contains 0002h (high word). Subtracting the low words gives 0FEE0h and sets the carry flag. Using the SBB instruction on the high words puts 0001h in the CX register. The final result is 1FEE0h, or 130,784 bytes.

Scan a String   88/86   286   386
                                                          ▲   ▲   ▲

SCAS, SCASB, SCASW

PURPOSE   To compare the byte or word at ES:DI to AL or AX.

SYNTAX   SCAS   [seg:]operand
              SCASB
              SCASW

FLAGS   Sign   Matches the sign bit of the result
              Zero   Set if the result is zero

Parity	Set if there are an even number of bits in the result
Overflow	Set if the result of a sign subtraction is not in the valid range for the operands
Carry	Set if the value in the destination operand was less than the value in the source operand
Aux. carry	Set if there was a borrow in bit 3 or, if using 16-bit operands, into bit 7

COMMENTS The operand in the SCAS form of this instruction is only used to indicate the size of the data to use, and to specify a segment override register.

This instruction can be used with the REPNE prefix to find a byte or word in a block of data.

SEE ALSO

CMPS, CMPSB, CMPSW	*String compare*
LODS, LODSB, LODSW	*String load*
MOVS, MOVSR, MOVSW	*String move*
STOS, STOSB, STOSW	*String store*

TIMING

Addressing	Encoding	Example	88/86	286	386
immplied	10101011w	SCANSB	15/19	7	7

EXAMPLE See the example for CMPS.

Subtract   88/86 286 386
                                                              ▲   ▲   ▲

SUB

PURPOSE To subtract one number from another.

SYNTAX

SUB	reg,reg	*Subtract one register from another.*
SUB	reg,mem	*Subtract a memory value from a register.*
SUB	mem,reg	*Subtract a register from a memory value.*
SUB	reg,immed	*Subtract an immediate value from a register.*
SUB	mem,immed	*Subtract an immediate value from a memory value.*

FLAGS

Sign	Matches the sign bit of the result
Zero	Set if the result is zero
Parity	Set if there are an even number of bits in the result
Overflow	Set if the result of a sign subtraction is not in the valid range for the operands

SUB

Carry   Set if the value in the destination operand was less than the value in the source operand

Aux. carry   Set if there was a borrow in bit 3 or, if using 16-bit operands, into bit 7

COMMENTS   This version of the subtract instruction is used when the data fits into a byte or word. It is also used to subtract the least significant word in multi-word values.

SEE ALSO   SBB   *Subtract with borrow*

ADD, ADC   *The addition instructions*

TIMING

Addressing	Encoding	Example	88/86	286	386
reg,reg	0010101w 11,reg,r/m	SUB ax,bx	3	2	2
reg,mem	0010100w mod,reg,r/m displacement	SUB ax,value	13/9+EA	7	7
mem,reg	0010101w mod,reg,r/m displacement	SUB value,ax	24/16+EA	7	6
reg,immed	100000sw mod,reg,r/m data	SUB bx,5	4	3	2
mem,immed	100000sw mod,reg,r/m displacement data	SUB value,10	25/17+EA	7	7
acc,immed	0010110w data	SUB ax,17	4	3	2

EXAMPLE   When you use SHL instructions to multiply a number by 15, you must do three SHLs and three ADDs:

```
mov   bx, ax        ; BX = Number * 1
shl   bx, 1         ; BX = Number * 2
add   ax, bx        ; AX = Number * 3
shl   bx, 1         ; BX = Number * 4
add   ax, bx        ; AX = Number * 7
```

```
        shl   bx, 1              ; BX = Number * 8
        add   ax, bx             ; AX = Number * 15
```

This next example shows how to use the SUB instruction to reduce the total number of instructions:

```
        mov   bx, ax             ; BX = Number * 1
        shl   ax, 1              ; AX = Number * 2
        shl   ax, 1              ; AX = Number * 4
        shl   ax, 1              ; AX = Number * 8
        shl   ax, 1              ; AX = Number * 16
        sub   ax, bx             ; AX = Number * 15
```

If AX = 11, then the four shifts would make it 176. Subtracting 11 from this gives 165 or 15 * 11.

TEST bits   *88/86*   *286*   *386*
▲   ▲   ▲

TEST

PURPOSE   To test whether certain bits are on or off.

SYNTAX
TEST	reg,reg	*TEST two registers.*
TEST	mem,reg	*TEST a memory value against a register.*
TEST	reg,mem	*TEST a register against a memory value.*
TEST	reg,immed	*TEST a register against an immediate value.*
TEST	mem,immed	*TEST a memory value against an immediate value.*

FLAGS
Sign	Matches the sign bit of the result
Zero	Set if the result is zero
Parity	Set if there are an even number of bits in the result
Overflow	Cleared
Carry	Cleared
Aux. carry	Unpredictable result

Note that the actual result is thrown away, but the flags are set as if the actual result were used.

COMMENTS   The TEST instruction works by doing a Logical AND on the operands. The result of the AND is thrown away, but the flags are set. This instruction is often used to check the value of a flag bit.

TEST

SEE ALSO AND   *The AND instruction*
NOT, OR, XOR   *Other logical instructions*

TIMING

Addressing	Encoding	Example	88/86	286	386
reg,reg	1000011w 11,reg,r/m	TEST bx,ax	3	2	2
mem,reg*	1000011w mod,reg,r/m displacement	TEST value,ax	13/9+EA	6	5
reg,immed	1111011w mod,000,r/m data	TEST dx,4	5	3	2
mem,immed	1111011w mod,000,r/m displacement data	TEST value,5	11+EA	6	5
acc,immed	1010100w data	TEST ax,16	4	3	2

* There is no special encoding for reg,mem. Turbo Assembler will convert reg,mem to mem,reg, which gives the same result.

EXAMPLE This routine tests a range of bits in a word. The word is in the AX register. The CH register contains the bit position of the least significant bit to test. The CL register contains the number of bits to test.

```
mov   bx, 1        ; This will become the mask
shl   bx, cl       ; The move over enough for the mask
dec   bx           ; Now the right number of bits are
                   ; on
mov   cl, ch       ; Get the position
shl   bx, cl       ; Move the mask into position
test  ax, bx       ; Test the word with the mask
ret                ; if no bits in the field return
                   ; with the zero flag set
```

Consider the case where AX = 0110100111110000b, CH = 5, and CL = 6. The first two instructions put a one, followed by six *0s*, in BX (0000000001000000b).

When this is decremented, it becomes 0000000000111111b. This is the number of bits required for the mask. The next shift moves this mask to the required position (0000011111100000b). The TEST instruction does a "Logical-AND" between the mask and the value in AX for 0000000111100000b. The result is discarded, but the zero flag remains cleared.

Exclusive OR   88/86   286   386
                                                                    ▲   ▲   ▲

XOR

PURPOSE   To "Exclusive-OR" each of the bits in the operands together.

SYNTAX
XOR reg,reg	*XOR two registers.*
XOR mem,reg	*XOR a memory value with a register.*
XOR reg,mem	*XOR a register with a memory value.*
XOR reg,immed	*XOR a register with an immediate value.*
XOR mem,immed	*XOR a memory value with an immediate value.*

FLAGS
Sign	Matches the sign bit of the result
Zero	Set if the result is zero
Parity	Set if there are an even number of bits in the result
Overflow	Cleared
Carry	Cleared
Aux. carry	Unpredictable result

COMMENTS   Exclusive OR sets the bit in the result, if only one of the source bits is set. If both are set or none is set, then the result bit gets a 0. This can be used to invert certain bits because, if you "Exclusive-OR" with a one (1), the result will have the opposite of the bit being "Exclusive-ORed."

   If a value is "Exclusive-ORed" with itself, the result is 0. This is used as a quick way to clear a register. For example:

```
XOR   ax,ax    ; Clears ax with one byte and in 3
               ; cycles. A move would take 2 bytes
               ; and 4 cycles
```

SEE ALSO   AND, NOT, OR, TEST   *Other logical operators*

XOR

TIMING	Addressing	Encoding	Example	88/86	286	386
	reg,reg	0011001w 11,reg,r/m	XOR ax,ax	3	2	2
	mem,reg	0011001w mod,reg,r/m displacement	XOR value,ax	24/16+EA	7	6
	reg,mem	0011000w mod,reg,r/m displacement	XOR ax,value	13/9+EA	7	7
	reg,immed	100000sw mod,reg,r/m data	XOR bx,10	4	3	2
	mem,immed	100000sw mod,reg,r/m displacement, data	XOR value,17	25/17+EA	7	7
	acc,immed	0011010w data	XOR al,4	4	3	2

EXAMPLE Hash keys are used to index data. The data key is converted to a number that is used as in index into a table of pointers to the records. One way to make a hash key from a string is to "Exclusive-OR" each character, with the hash key rotating the key left after each character.

The following is a routine to make a hash key from the zero terminated string pointed to by the BX register. It puts the result in the CX register.

```
        xor  cx, cx              ; Clear the CX register
loop:
        cmp  byte ptr [bx], 0    ; Check for the end
        je   done
        xor  cl, byte ptr [bx]   ; XOR in a character
        shl  cx, 1               ; Shift the key left 1 bit
        inc  bx                  ; Point to next character
        jmp  short loop
done:
```

Chapter 6 Procedures, Loops, and Jumps

No program of any consequence moves from beginning to end in a straight line. A typical program calls subroutines, goes around in loops, and jumps from place to place. The path that a program takes can be either generally straight forward or extremely labyrinthine.

Most modern high level languages enforce some kind of structure on a program. However, this is not true in assembly language. You are free to code a flow of control just as complex as you can manage. This chapter not only shows you the assembly language instructions available for making this kind of "mess," but it also gives you some pointers for avoiding it altogether.

Jumping

By default, instructions are executed in the order that they appear in memory. Jumping is used to change the default and begin executing instructions at a new location. In 80x86 processors the address of the next instruction is in a special register called IP (Instruction Pointer). Jumping puts a different address value in this register.

The JMP Instruction

The JMP (JuMP) instruction loads a value into the IP register. The JMP instruction comes in two basic forms. In the first form, you give a label for the destination like this:

```
jmp   label
```

The assembler has three choices for how to translate this instruction into machine language. The differences concern how far away the destination is from the JMP instruction. You have the choice of letting the assembler decide or telling it exactly which one to use.

When the destination is within −128 to +127 bytes of the JMP instruction, the short format can be used. For example, to jump forward five bytes the assembler would generate these two bytes:

```
EDh  05h
```

The second byte is a signed value that is added to the IP register, and execution resumes at the resulting location. To force the assembler to use the short format, use the SHORT key word like this:

```
jmp  SHORT label
```

If the label is too far away for a short jump, you will get an error message when you try to assemble the program. You will have to remove the SHORT directive from the JMP instruction in order to get the program to assemble.

The next form of the JMP instruction is the NEAR jump. The NEAR jump works the same as the short jmp except that two bytes are used to show the destination. This increases the range to between −32,768 and +32,767 bytes. To jump backward 150 bytes, the assembler generates these three bytes:

```
E9h  6Ah  FFh
```

The last two bytes (0FF6Ah or −150) are the offset for the new address.

The last JMP instruction can go to any location in memory. It is called a FAR jump. The FAR jump uses four bytes to specify a new code segment and IP. When using 32-bit segments on an 80386 CPU, the FAR jump uses six bytes. The first four are the offset in the segment, and the last two are the segment selector. The assembler would generate the following codes for a jump to 0A1E:0100:

```
EAh  00h  01h  1Eh  0Ah
```

The last four bytes are the offset and segment to which the program jumps.

For the 8088 and 8086, the only performance difference between these instructions is the amount of memory they use. For the 80286 and 80386, there is a 5-cycle penalty for using FAR jumps.

Turbo Assembler lets you define a label as NEAR or FAR. When a program jumps to the label, whatever definition is used determines if the jump should be NEAR or FAR. (See Chapter 9 for more information on defining labels.)

Indirect Jumps

A common technique, used by command parsers for going to a function based on a command, is to use a table of function addresses. All the parser needs to do is calculate which function to jump to, and then jump to the address indicated.

To jump to a location specified by a table, you need some way to retrieve the destination from a register or memory. This is called an *indirect* jump. Table 6-1 shows the three different indirect jumps.

Table 6-1. *Indirect Jumps*

Addressing	Example	Explanation
Register	jmp cx	Jump to the address in the register. The 80386 can use 32-bit registers to jump around in 32-bit segments.
memory near	jmp WORD PTR	Jump to the near destination stored at the location indicated. All of the normal addressing modes are supported. The NEAR PTR directive tells the assembler to use the near jump by telling it to use two bytes.
memory far	jmp DWORD PTR	Jump to the far destination stored at the location indicated. The DWORD PTR directive tells the assembler to use the far jump by telling it to use four bytes.

Conditional Jumps

Programs need to do more than just jump around. They need to be able to make decisions based on numerous conditions. The way you do this on the 80x86 processors is to use *conditional* jumps. Conditional jumps use the state of the processor flags to decide whether to do a short jump, or to fall through to the next instruction. The 80386 can use near jumps instead of short jumps. The 18 conditions that can be tested are summarized in Table 6-2.

Table 6-2. *Conditional Jumps*

Unsigned Arithmetic Tests

Mnemonic	Description
JB/JNAE	If Below/Not Above or Equal (CF=1)
JAE/JNB	If Above or Equal/Not Below (CF=0)
JBE/JNA	If Below or Equal/Not Above (CF=1 ZF=1)
JA/JNBE	If Above/Not Below or Equal (CF=0 and ZF=0)

Signed Arithmetic Tests

Mnemonic	Description
JL/JNGE	If Less/Not Greater or Equal (SF<>OF)
JGE/JNL	If Greater or Equal/Not Less (SF=OF)
JLE/JNG	If Less or Equal/Not Greater (ZF=1 or SF<>OF)
JG/JNLE	If Greater/Not Less or Equal (ZF=0 or SF=OF)

Equality Tests

Mnemonic	Description
JE/JZ	If Equal/Zero (ZF=1)
JNE/JNZ	If Not Equal/Not Zero (ZF=0)

Sign Flag Tests

Mnemonic	Description
JS	If Sign is negative (SF=1)
JNS	If Sign is positive (SF=0)

Carry Flag Tests

Mnemonic	Description
JC	If Carry flag set
JNC	If Carry flag not set

Overflow Flag Tests

Mnemonic	Description
JO	If Overflow flag set
JNO	If Overflow flag cleared

Parity Flag Tests

Mnemonic	Description
JP/JPE	If Parity/Parity Even (PF=1)
JNP/JPO	If Not Parity/Parity Odd (PF=0)

To use a conditional jump, you must first set the flags. A common way to do this is to use the CMP instruction:

```
cmp   ax, bx    ; Compare ax to bx (Sets the flags as
                ; if the operands were subtracted)
je    match     ; Jump if ax = bx (ZF = 1)
```

Another instruction that is used before conditional jumps is TEST (to see if certain bits are set or not). In addition, all of the arithmetic and logical instructions set the flags. Conditional jumps can be used, for example, to see if an arithmetic instruction has overflowed:

```
add   ax, cx    ; Add two values
jc    unsigned  ; Use the carry with unsigned values
jo    signed    ; Use the overflow with signed values
```

The OR instruction can be used to set the sign, zero, and parity flags for the data in a register. "ORing" the register with itself will set the sign flag if the high bit is on, the zero flag if the data equals zero, and the parity flag if there is an even number of on bits in the data. The next example shows how to use the OR instruction to set the flags when reading a list of data:

```
            .DATA
Datalist    DB    "This is a list of bytes", 0

            .CODE
            mov   bx, OFFSET Datalist ; Get the address of the data
Dloop:
            mov   al, [bx]            ; Get a byte
            or    al, al             ; Set the flags
            jz    Done               ; Go to done when al = 0
            .                        ; Process the data
            .
            .
            inc   bx                 ; Point to the next byte
            jmp   Dloop              ; Another time around the loop
Done:
```

This routine puts the address of the data in the BX register. Then it copies the data at BX into the AL register. The MOV instruction does not set any flags, so this routine uses the OR instruction to set them. If the byte is zero, then the OR instruction will set the zero flag and the JZ instruction will jump to the label Done. If the byte is not zero, then the routine does any processing that is required before it jumps back to the top of the loop.

Using High Level Concepts in Assembly Language

High level languages provide commands to simplify the flow of control in the program. The while loop is used to loop through code until a certain condition is met. Decisions are made with if,then,else commands. The 80x86 processors do not directly implement these commands. It is up to the programmer to use jump and conditional jump instructions to implement these commands.

WHILE LOOP A while loop in a high level language evaluates a logical expression; and, if the expression is true, it executes the body of the loop. Making a loop with a simple expression is quite straightforward. The loop in the following expression runs until AL is equal to 0.

```
Loop1:
            or    al,al    ; Set the flags
            jz    Done
            .              ; This code must eventually set AL to
            .              ; 0 or the loop will never end
            .
            jmp   Loop1
Done:
```

Not all loops are so simple. The expression can have several tests combined by logical ANDs and ORs. In the next example the loop runs while the AL register is not 0, and the CX register is less than 10 or the BX register equals the DX register.

```
Loop2:
        or    al, al          ; Set the flags
        jz    Done            ; exit if 0
        cmp   cx, 10          ; otherwise see if CX < 10
        jb    Cxok
        cmp   bx, dx          ; or bx = dx
        jne   Done
Cxok:
        .
        .
        .
        jmp   Loop2
Done:
```

Notice that at any point in the expression there are three possible results. The first is that the expression must be false. Whenever the last term was false and the next logical operator is an AND, the expression must be false and the program jumps out of the loop. The next possible result is that the expression must be true. Whenever the last term was true and the next logical operator is an OR, the expression must be true and the program can jump into the body of the loop. The final possibility is that more of the expression must be evaluated. In the previous example, the conditional jumps were chosen so that, in this last case, the program simply falls through.

Things get tricky when the loop is so long that the short jumps used in conditional jumps cannot reach the exit label. One way to deal with this is to use the opposite conditional jump to jump over a JMP to the label.

```
Loop2:
        or    al,al
        jnz   Skip1           ; We really want to jump if zero but
        jmp   Done            ; done is too far away
Skip1:
        .
        .
        .
        jmp   Loop2
Done:
```

This is fine if there is only one thing to test, but it gets more complex and inefficient when there are several terms that must jump past the loop. One way around the problem is to put the test at the end of the loop. This puts the expression code closer to the end of the loop, so that short jumps can be used to exit. Since there is already a jump at the end of the loop, short jumps can jump to it when the expression is known to be true.

Using the same complex example as before, but putting the test at the end of the loop looks like this:

```
        jmp  Lptest            ; Jump to the test
Loop3:
        .
        .
        .
Lptest:
        or   al, al
        jz   Done              ; If al = 0 exit
        cmp  cx, 10
        jb   Cxok              ; If cx < 10 do the loop
        cmp  bx, dx
        jne  Done              ; If bx does not equal dx exit
Cxok:
        jmp  Loop3
Done:
```

With minor variations you can make do,until loops, for loops, and break instructions; or you can utilize other high level looping concepts.

IF, THEN, ELSE Decisions can be handled in high level languages with the if,then,else construction. In this construction an expression is evaluated so that if it is true, then the code following the then is executed; otherwise, the code following the else is executed. A simple example that tests for AL equal to 0 looks like this:

```
        or   al, al
        jnz  CElse       ; If not zero do "else"
        .                ; otherwise do "then"
        .
        .
        jmp  CEndif      ; When done skip the "else" part
CElse:
        .
        .
        .
CEndif:
```

Just as with the while loop, the if,then,else expression can be complicated. The next example uses the same expression that was used in the while loop example.

```
        or   al, al
        jnz  CElse             ; If al <> 0 do else
```

```
              cmp   cx, 10
              jb    CThen              ; If cx < 10 do then
              cmp   bx, dx
              jne   CElse
CThen:
                .
                .
                .

              jmp   CEndif
CElse:
                .
                .
                .

CEndif:
```

You will need to do some rearranging of the expression when the then code is too large to get around with short jumps. One thing to consider is reversing all the conditional jumps, and putting the else code first. If the else code is short enough, this could solve the problem.

ITERATING   Some loops just run a fixed number of times. The loop may read a given number of records from a file, or get data from a fixed-length buffer. This kind of loop uses a counter to keep track of how many times the loop should run. Each time through, the loop decrements the counter; and when the counter is zero, the loop is done.

The LOOP instruction uses the CX register as a counter for controlling a loop. The format is:

```
      loop destination
```

The LOOP instruction decrements the CX register; then, if the CX register is not 0, it does a short jump to destination. When CX equals zero, control goes to the instruction following LOOP. It works the same as the following code does:

```
          dec   cx              ; Decrement the CX register
          jnz   destination     ; Jump if not 0
```

The following example shows how to use the LOOP instruction to run a loop 12 times:

```
          mov   cx,12           ; Put the number of iterations in CX
Sloop:
            .                   ; whatever must be done
            .
            .
          loop Sloop            ; Decrement CX and jump if not 0
```

```
                                ; Continue with the rest of the program
                                ; when CX = 0
```

There is a variation on the LOOP instruction that uses the zero flag, in addition to the CX register, to determine when to exit the loop. The instruction comes in two varieties: LOOPZ (LOOP while Zero) and LOOPNZ (LOOP while Not Zero). The former instruction (LOOPZ) will jump if CX is not zero and the zero flag is set. The latter (LOOPNZ) will jump if CX is not zero and the zero flag is not set.

This form of the LOOP instruction can be used to go through a buffer until a condition is met, or the end of the buffer comes up. To do this, first put the length of the buffer in the CX register. Then loop through the bytes in the buffer. To exit the loop, set or reset the zero flag (depending on which LOOP instruction you use); and keep that setting until you get to the end of the loop.

The following example uses the LOOPNZ instruction to search a buffer for a 0. The buffer is 128 bytes long.

```
        mov   cx, 128                ; The length of the buffer
        mov   bx, OFFSET Buffer
Bloop:
        cmp   BYTE PTR [bx], 0       ; Look for a 0
        inc   bx
        loopnz Bloop
```

When this loop exits, it could be for one of two reasons: Either the end of the buffer came up, or else a 0 was found. There are two ways to know the difference. One is to use JZ or JNZ to test the state of the zero flag. The other is to use JCXZ (Jump if CX is Zero). This instruction does a short jump if CX is zero. It is just like the LOOP instruction, except that it does not decrement CX.

On the 80386 you can use the ECX register with the JCXZ instruction. To do this use JECXZ.

Subroutines

Subroutines can be used to save memory by allowing one piece of code to be used from several places in a program. They can also be used to make a program easier to understand by substituting a meaningful name for a sequence of instructions.

Some subroutines will be used by many different programs. These subroutines can save programming time. Instead of writing and debugging the code for each program, a subroutine from one program can be used in the next.

Calling and Returning from a Subroutine

The CALL instruction is used to call a subroutine. The format of the CALL instruction is:

```
call subroutine
```

For this instruction, subroutine is the label of the subroutine to call. As with the JMP instruction, labels can be NEAR or FAR. The difference between the JMP and CALL instructions is that the call instruction puts the address of the next instruction on the stack before jumping to the label. When the label is a FAR label, both the segment and the offset of the next instruction are pushed. For NEAR labels, only the offset is pushed.

When the subroutine is done, it must use the address on the stack to return to the calling routine. The RET instruction does this for you. This instruction needs to know whether the address on the stack is a NEAR or FAR address. There are two ways that the assembler can know which return to use. The first way is, of course, to *tell* it. The RETN and RETF instructions use NEAR and FAR addresses respectively. The other way is to let the assembler use the PROC directive at the beginning of the procedure to determine the type of return to use. (See Chapter 10 for more information on the PROC directive.)

The following code fragment shows a call to a function and the return in the function.

```
          .
          .
          .
          call AFunction
          .
          .
          .
AFunction PROC FAR        ; This is a far function
          .
          .
          .
          ret             ; Return to the calling program
AFunction ENDP            ; Tell the assembler this is the end of
                          ; the function
```

Stack Frames

The behavior of a subroutine can be changed by passing parameters to it. The subroutine can tell what happened by returning data. While the subroutine is running, it may require some memory to use for scratch values.

The calling routine can pass information in registers, and the results can be returned in registers. Any data space required can be set aside before the function is called.

This solution has some drawbacks. What if there are not enough registers? What happens if the subroutine calls itself? This is called *recursion*, and it is a common programming technique that requires each call to the subroutine to have its own data space. If each call uses the same data space, then each call to the subroutine will overwrite the data of the previous calls.

One way around these problems is to put the data on the stack. If more data must be passed, then use more stack. Local data can go on the stack each time the subroutine is called. This prevents one call from interfering with another. When the subroutine is done, the stack is cleared — freeing the memory for the next routine.

The passed parameters, return address, and local variables on the stack are called, collectively, the stack *frame*. Figure 6-1 shows a stack with several stack frames on it.

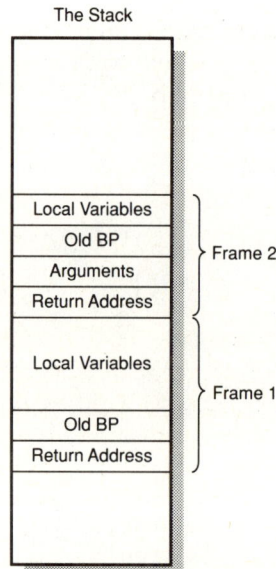

Figure 6-1. *The stack with stack frames on it.*

The following example shows a program that passes parameters to a subroutine on the stack. The subroutine makes some local variable space, and then sets up the BP register to reference the parameters and the local data.

When the subroutine is done, it clears up the local variables and then returns to the calling routine. Finally, the calling routine clears the passed parameters off the stack by adjusting the stack pointer.

```
            push bx             ; The second parameter
            mov  ax, 10
            push ax             ; The first parameter
            call MyFunc         ; Call the function
            add  sp, 4          ; Fix up the stack

MyFunc      PROC NEAR
            push bp             ; Save the old bp
            mov  bp, sp         ; The parameters are 4 bytes past
                                ; BP (2 bytes for the return
                                ; address and 2 more for the saved
                                ; BP)
            sub  sp, 10         ; Make 10 bytes of local storage
            mov  di, [bp+6]     ; Get the first parameter
            mov  cx, [bp+4]     ; Get the second parameter
            mov  [bp-10], cx    ; Save in local storage for use
                                ; later in the program
            mov  [bp-8], di     ; also in local storage
            .
            .
            .
            mov  sp,bp          ; Get rid of local storage
            pop  bp             ; Restore BP
            ret                 ; Go back to the calling routine
MyFunc      ENDP
```

If a subroutine is called many times, due to recursion for example, the instructions needed to adjust the stack can start to add up. It would be better if the subroutine itself could clear up the stack. The problem is that the return address is between the subroutine and the parameters. The 80x86 processor gets around this problem with a special form of the RET instruction. If the RET instruction is followed by a number, that number is added to the stack pointer after the return address is popped. This example shows how it works:

```
            .
            .
            .
            mov  ax, 50
            push ax             ; First parameter
            mov  ax, 21
            push ax             ; Second parameter
            call Func2          ; Call the function
```

```
Func2      PROC NEAR
           push bp                    ; Finish setting up the
           mov  bp, sp                ; Stack frame
           sub  sp, 4
           mov  ax, [bp+4]            ; The second parameter (21)
           add  ax, [bp+6]            ; The first parameter (50)
           .
           .
           .
           mov  sp, bp
           pop  bp
           ret  4                     ; Return and add 4 to SP
```

Notice that the order in which the parameters are pushed has been reversed. The first parameter for the function is the first one pushed. This order, and the fact that the subroutine fixes the stack, is sometimes called the *Pascal calling convention*. The first example is known as the *C calling convention*. The conventions are named after popular high level languages that use the convention.

The 80286 and 80386 provide two special instructions for dealing with stack frames. The ENTER instruction pushes BP, and copies the stack pointer to BP. Then it reserves space on the stack for local variables. This produces the same stack frame as in the previous example. The format of the instruction is:

```
ENTER     local, nesting level
```

The first parameter is the size of the local variable space. The second parameter is the nesting level, which allows data from calling routines to be available to the current routine. Setting the nesting level to 0 produces the same results as in the previous stack frame examples.

The LEAVE instruction is used at the end of the function to undo what the ENTER instruction did. It sets the stack pointer to BP and pops BP off the stack. You do not need to use any operands with the LEAVE instruction.

Interrupt Handling

Certain events that happen outside of the processor need to be handled right away. To get the processor's attention, a device sends an interrupt signal to the processor. Along with the interrupt signal, the hardware gives an interrupt number to the processor. The processor finishes the instruction that it was executing, and then gets an interrupt number from the device. This is an index into a list of addresses of the routines to execute for each interrupt number. This routine is called the *interrupt handler*. The processor pushes the flags, then the values in the CS and IP registers, and then jumps to the interrupt handler. When the interrupt handler is done, it uses a IRET instruction to get back to the interrupted program and restore the flags. Figure 6-2 shows how this process works.

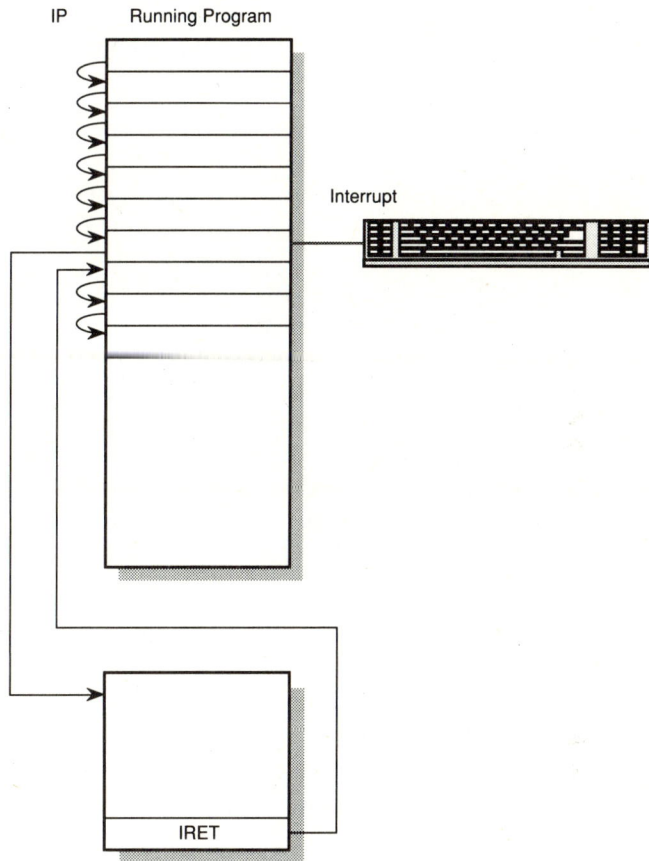

Figure 6-2. *Hardware interrupts.*

SOFTWARE INTERRUPTS A program can simulate an interrupt by using the INT instruction. The number following the INT instruction tells which interrupt handler to call. These software interrupts are often used by programs that must be accessed by other programs. Because the interrupt number can remain the same even when the interrupt handler moves, the calling program does not have to change when the called program moves. A good example of a program that is called in this way is MS-DOS.

MS-DOS provides many functions that can be used by programs. To use these functions, the program puts the function number in the AH register and gives an `INT 21h` command. For example, to print a character on-screen, put the character in the DL register, a 2 (the function number) in AH, and do the interrupt:

```
mov   dl, 'A'        ; Put the character in DL
mov   ah, 2          ; Put the function number in AH
int   21h            ; Call MS-DOS
```

SPECIAL CASE INTERRUPTS

Interrupt 3 is a special case. It is used by debugging programs for implementing break points. The opcode for the `INT 3` instruction is 0CCh. (An *opcode* is the code that the 80x86 executes.) Since it only takes one byte, it can be substituted for any instruction in the program being debugged. When the program gets to the replaced instruction, the `INT 3` calls the debugging program, which restores the instruction and lets the programmer examine registers and memory to see what the program has done.

Another special case interrupt instruction is the INTO instruction. This instruction looks at the overflow flag. If it is set, then it does software interrupt 4. This instruction can be used to test the results of an arithmetic operation and take special action in the case of an overflow. You should note that there is a lot of processor overhead in using interrupts. In the case of INTO, a processor would use fewer cycles to use the following:

```
      jno  Skip
      call Overrtn
Skip:
```

This would call `Overrtn` if the overflow flag is set, or `skip` it if not. On the 8086 chip, this would save nine clock cycles. More cycles are saved when it is time to return. An interrupt routine uses six more cycles than a regular `far` routine. This gives a total savings of 15 cycles every time the function is called. If speed is not a consideration, it should be noted that while INTO takes one byte, the alternative requires seven bytes.

SETTING INTERRUPT VECTORS

The 256 interrupt vectors are stored starting at location 0:0 in memory. Each four-byte entry consists of two bytes for the function offset, and two more for the segment. Before reading or writing an entry in this table, it is a good idea to turn off interrupts with the CLI instruction. After the entry has been changed, use the STI instruction to turn interrupts back on. The reason for this is that if you have only changed one part of the vector (offset or segment), when the interrupt occurs the processor will use the half-changed address. It is unlikely that this address will point to a routine that does you any good. The example to follow sets interrupt 0Bh to point to the function called `Func`.

```
        cli                             ; Turn off interrupts
        mov   ax, OFFSET Func           ; Get the address of the
        mov   bx, SEG Func              ; function to put in the table
        sub   cx, cx                    ; Put 0 in CX
        mov   es, cx                    ; Set segment 0
        mov   es:[1Ch], ax              ; Entry 1ch = 0bh * 4
        mov   es:[1Eh], bx
        sti                             ; Turn interrupts back on
```

When a program exits, MS-DOS is free to use the memory for something else. This is a problem if the program modified interrupt vectors to point to this memory space. When the interrupt occurs, the program will jump to a function that is no longer there. Most of the time this will cause the system to crash, but anything is possible. Just imagine what would happen if the next program loaded is able to format disks!

To prevent this problem, you should always restore the interrupt table to the way you found it before your program exits. MS-DOS provides two function calls that help when manipulating the interrupt vector table. They are function 35h to read an entry into the ES and BX registers, and function 25h to write an entry. The following example uses these functions to read the entry at interrupt vector 0Bh, then to replace it. Finally, when the program is finished, the original entry is restored.

```
; Program that uses interrupt 0bh

              .DATA
Old           DD   0                    ; Place for the old vector
              .CODE
Start:
        mov   ax, 350bh                 ; Read entry 0bh
        int   21h                       ; Call DOS
        mov   WORD PTR Old, bx          ; Save the old offset
        mov   WORD PTR Old+2, es        ; Save the old segment
        mov   bx, OFFSET Func           ; Get the address of
        mov   ax, SEG Func              ; The new function
        mov   es, ax
        mov   ax, 250bh                 ; Write entry 0bh
        int   21h                       ; Call DOS
        .                               ; The rest of the program
        .
        .

; Before exiting return the old interrupt vector

        les   bx, Old                   ; Get the old interrupt vector
        mov   ax, 250bh                 ; Write entry 0bh
        int   21h                       ; Call MS-DOS
```

```
; This is the function to be called when there is an int 0bh
Func    PROC    FAR
            .
            .
            .
        iret
Func    ENDP
        .STACK
END     Start
```

Summary

A program takes many twists and turns as it moves through memory. You must be careful that the path does not become so complex that you can no longer follow the logic of the program. The instructions for controlling the flow of control arc a doublc-cdgcd sword. Asscmbly language provides you with the freedom to jump from place to place almost at will. However, this kind of freedom can easily lead to a rat's nest of complex logic that may take heroic effort to maintain or debug.

With careful planning you can organize your program into while loops, if,then,else blocks, and subroutines. By sticking with these forms and avoiding capricious jumps, your programs will make much more sense when you come back to them, say, in six months in order to add a new feature.

BOUND

PURPOSE   To compare the index in the destination operand against the values in the source operand. If the destination is outside the two values in the source, the processor generates an interrupt number 5.

SYNTAX   BOUND   register, mem32

FLAGS   The flags are unaffected by this instruction.

COMMENTS   The destination register must be above the low word of the source operand and below the high word of the source operand. If these conditions are not met, then the processor will generate an interrupt number 5.

On IBM PCs and compatibles, interrupt 5 is used to print the screen. If you want to use the BOUND instruction, you will need to take over interrupt 5 to trap the out-of-bounds condition. This means that you will lose the print screen feature.

SEE ALSO   INT   *Software interrupt instruction*
INTO   *Interrupt on overflow*

TIMING

Addressing	Encoding	Example	88/86	286	386
reg, mem32	01100010 mod,reg,r/mdisplacement	Bound si, limits		23/13	37/10

EXAMPLE   This example takes over interrupt 5, checks the boundaries for an array, and then restore interrupt 5:

```
        .MODEL    SMALL
        .DATA
OldInt5 DD    ?                ; Place to store the old int
Array   DW    150 dup(0)       ; 150 byte array
Limits  DD    Array + (Array+150) * 65536
Inflag  DB    ?                ; 0 = in bounds, 1 = out

        .CODE
; Change the value in SI against the limits in Limits
; Set inflag based on the results of the test
```

BOUND

```
ChckArray PROC
          mov   ax, 3505h                ; MS-DOS get vector
          int   21h
          mov   WORD PTR OldInt5, bx     ; Save the old vector
          mov   WORD PTR OldInt5, es
          mov   ax, 2505h                ; MS-DOS set vector
          push  ds                       ; Save DS
          push  cs                       ; Copy CS
          pop   ds                       ; to DS
          mov   dx, OFFSET OutBounds
          int   21h                      ; Set Int 5h
          pop   ds                       ; Restore DS
          mov   Inflag, 0                ; Clear the flag
          bound si, Limits               ; Check the boundaries
          mov   ax, 2505h                ; Set the vector back
          push  ds
          lds   dx, OldInt5              ; Get the old interrupt
          int   21h
          pop   ds
          ret
ChckArray ENDP

; The interrupt routine to call if there is an error
OutBounds PROC FAR
          mov   Inflag, 1
          iret
OutBounds ENDP
```

Call a Procedure   88/86   286   386
                                                  ▲   ▲   ▲

CALL

PURPOSE   To transfer control to a procedure after pushing the address of the next instruction on the stack so the procedure can return.

SYNTAX   CALL Label
CALL FAR PTR Label
CALL register or memory location
CALL WORD PTR memory location
CALL DWORD PTR memory location

CALL

FLAGS   The flags are unaffected by this instruction.

COMMENTS   The CALL instruction is used to transfer control to a piece of code that will eventually return to the routine that called it. Since the routine can be called from several locations, the return address must be passed to the routine. This is done by having the call instruction push the return address onto the stack.

Because the offset range of a single code segment can only access 65536 bytes of memory, the CALL instruction has special forms for calling nearby routines or those that are beyond the limits of the current code segment. In the case where the destination of the call is a label, the definition of the label is used to determine if a NEAR or FAR call should be used. If the destination is a register location, then the size of the register or memory location is used. When the size or definition is wrong or ambiguous, the you can use NEAR, FAR, WORD PTR, and DWORD PTR modifiers to give the assembler a hint.

SEE ALSO   NEAR, FAR, PTR, WORD, DWORD   *Used to qualify the destination*

JA or JNBE, JAE or JNB, JB or   *Conditional jumps*
JNAE, JBE or JNA, JC, JE or JZ,
JG or JNLE, JGE or JNL, JL or
JNGE, JLE or JNG, JNC, JNE or
JNZ, JNO, JNP or JPO, JNS, JO,
JP or JPE, JS
JMP   *Unconditional jump*
RET   *Return from a procedure*

TIMING

Addressing	Encoding	Example	88/86	286	386
NEAR label	11101000	call func	23/19	7	7
	displacement (2 bytes)				
FAR label	10011010	call farfunc	36/28	13	17
	displacement (4 bytes)				
register	11111111	call si	20/16	7	7
	11,010,r/m				
word memory	11111111	call [bx]	29/21+EA11	10	
	mod,010,r/m				
dword memory	11111111	cail dword ptr [bx]	53/37+EA	16	22
	mod,011,r/m				

CALL

EXAMPLE   Procedures are used so that a program can do common operations with a single piece of code. Not only does this save memory, but it also means that the code only needs to be debugged once. This example shows a CALL to a routine that prints a string of characters at a given location on the screen. The location is passed in DH (row) and DL (column). The address of the string is in DS:BX.

```
; This code fragment sets up the registers for the call
; and calls the routine. The variables Curcol and Str have
; been defined elsewhere.
        .
        .
        .
        mov  dh, 24           ; The last row on the screen
        mov  dl, Curcol       ; Set the column to curcol
        mov  bx, OFFSET Str    ; Get the address of the
                              ; string

        call PrintAt
        .
        .
        .
```

```
; This is the subroutine. It calls the BIOS to position
; the cursor and then DOS to print the string. When it is
; done it returns to the calling routine.

PrintAt    PROC NEAR
           push bx            ; Save the address of the string
           mov  ah, 4         ; BIOS set cursor position function
           mov  bh, 0         ; Tell it to use the first page
           int  10h           ; Call BIOS video service
           pop  dx            ; Get the address of the string
           mov  ah, 9         ; MS-DOS print string function
           int  21h           ; Call MS-DOS
           ret                ; Return to the calling routine
PrintAt    ENDP
```

Make Stack Frame   88/86   286   386
                                                               ▲   ▲

ENTER

PURPOSE   To push the value in the BP register on to the stack, then set BP equal to the stack pointer, and finally move the stack pointer to provide space for local variable space.

ENTER

SYNTAX   ENTER   local_bytes, nesting_level

FLAGS   The flags are unaffected by this instruction.

COMMENTS   The stack frame is a convenient way to deal with the problem of passing data to a subroutine and providing local data storage. With all of the passed parameter and local data on the stack, the memory required can be used by the subroutine and then released when the subroutine is finished. Setting BP to point to this memory gives an easy way to address the memory.

The same effect can be achieved on the 8088 and 8086 with the following sequence of instructions:

```
push bp
mov  bp,sp
sub  sp, LocalBytes
```

SEE ALSO   CALL   To call a subroutine
LEAVE   To undo the ENTER when the subroutine is done
RET   To return from a subroutine

TIMING

Addressing	Encoding	Example	88/86	286	386
immed,0	11001000	enter 4,0		11	10
	data (2 bytes) data (1 byte)				
immed,1	11001000	enter 0,1		15	12
	data (2 bytes) data (1 byte)				
immed,immed	11001000	enter 6,2		12+4(n-1)	
	data (2 bytes) data (1 bytes)			15+4(n-1)	

EXAMPLE   This routine takes an address and a length as parameters. It loops through the characters at the address and counts the commas (,).

```
; This routine uses the C calling convention. The parameters
; are passed in the reverse order from which they appear in
; the C function call. It uses two words of local storage to
; keep track of what character is being checked and how many
; commas have been found.
; On exit the number of commas is put in AX, the stack is
; cleaned up and the function returns.
; To call from C use:
; commas = Cfunc(String, Len);
```

ENTER

```
                    .286                        ; Allow 80286 instruc-
                                                ; tions

                    .MODEL SMALL
                    .CODE
                    PUBLIC    Cfunc
_Cfunc              PROC
                    enter     4,0               ; Make a stack frame with
                                                ; 4 bytes of storage
                    mov       [bp-4], 0         ; Set count to 0
                    mov       [bp-2], 0         ; Set index to 0
                    mov       bx, [bp+4]        ; Get the string
Cloop:
                    mov       ax, [bp+6]        ; Get the length
                    cmp       [bp-2], ax        ; See if at the end of the
                                                ; string
                    jge       Done
                    cmp       BYTE PTR [bx], ',' ; Check for comma
                    jnz       NotComma
                    inc       WORD PTR [bp-4]   ; inc comma count
NotComma:
                    inc       WORD PTR [bp-2]   ; inc index
                    inc       bx                ; Point to next character
                    jmp       Cloop             ; Do it again
Done:
                    leave                       ; Put the stack back the way
                                                ; we found it
                    ret
_Cfunc              ENDP
```

Interrupt   88/86   286   386
                                                       ▲   ▲   ▲

INT

PURPOSE   To generate a software interrupt that simulates one of the 256 possible interrupts.

SYNTAX   INT   interrupt_number

FLAGS   The interrupt and trap flags are set to zero. All other flags are unaffected.

COMMENTS The INT instruction is like a far CALL except that, before it pushes the return address on the stack, it pushes the flags. Another difference is the way that the destination address is determined. The INT instruction specifies an interrupt number. This number is used as an index into the *interrupt vector table*. This table lists the addresses of all of the possible interrupts.

The function that is called can return to the calling routine by using an IRET instruction. This instruction pops the far return address off of the stack and then the flag register.

Software interrupts are used by programs that provide a function or group of functions for use by other programs. The reason interrupts are used instead of regular function calls is that, if the function is moved, only the interrupt vector table needs to be updated. The BIOS and MS-DOS are two well-known examples of this use of the software interrupt.

SEE ALSO

CALL, RET	*Used for regular procedures*
INTO	*Interrupt on overflow*
IRET	*Return from an interrupt routine*

TIMING

Addressing	Encoding	Example	88/86	286	386
immed	11001101 data	int 21h	71/51	23	37
3	11001100	int 3	72/52	23	33

EXAMPLE MS-DOS provides many functions through its software interrupt interface. The interrupt used is 21h. To use it, a function code is placed in the AH register. Any data required by the function goes in other registers. After the function is finished, it returns the results or error codes in registers.

This example shows how to use the MS-DOS functions to open and close a data file using file handles.

```
; Ask DOS to open a file
; After the processing is complete close the file

        mov   dx, OFFSET Filename   ; Get address of file name
        mov   ah, 3ch               ; DOS open function
        int   21h                   ; Call MS-DOS
        jnc   OpenOK                ; MS-DOS sets the carry flag
                                    ; if it could not open the
                                    ; file
        .                           ; Do something about not
        .                           ; being able to open the file
        .
```

```
OpenOK:
          mov  bx, ax              ; Put the handle in BX
            .                      ; Do file functions
            .
            .
          mov  ah, 3fh             ; MS-DOS close function
          int  21h                ; Close file
```

Interrupt on Overflow   88/86   286   386
                                                        ▲   ▲   ▲

INTO

PURPOSE   To generate a software interrupt 4 if the overflow flag is set.

SYNTAX   INTO

FLAGS   If the interrupt is taken, the interrupt and trap flags are set to 0. All other flags are unaffected by this instruction.

COMMENTS   DOS sets up interrupt 4 to point to an IRET instruction. This means that if you use the INTO instruction, the INTO instruction will push the flags, push the IP and CS registers, and then jump to the IRET instruction which returns without providing any service. You must set the interrupt vector to point to a function that will perform some useful operation when there is an overflow. The MS-DOS function 25h should be used to set interrupt vectors. Your program should also use the MS-DOS function 35h to read the old vector before changing the interrupt vector. This will allow the program to put the old vector back before it exits.

SEE ALSO   INT   *Generates software interrupts*
              IRET   *Return from an interrupt*

TIMING

Addressing	Encoding	Example	88/86	286	386
implied	11001110	into	73/53	24	35
			(4 noj)	(3 noj)	(3 noj)

EXAMPLE The first step in using the INTO instruction is to set the interrupt vector for Interrupt 4 to point to the routine that will handle the overflow condition. A program that sets an interrupt vector must be certain to restore the vector before the program exits. Failure to do this will leave the vector pointing to the middle of a program that is no longer in memory. Any future interrupts to that vector are at the mercy of whatever happens to end up at that location.

Use the INTO instruction after arithmetic operations that may have overflowed. In this example the routine prints a message when there is an overflow.

```
; Replace the interrupt 4 vector, do arithmetic, use the
; INTO instruction to print a message if there was an
; overflow.
            .MODEL    SMALL
            .DATA
OldInt   DD   0                    ; Place to save the old
                                   ; interrupt 4 vector
Overmsg  DB   "Overflow error",0ah, 0dh,"$"
            .CODE
Start    PROC
            mov  ax, SEG DGROUP
            mov  ds, ax
            mov  ax, 3504h         ; MS-DOS function to read int 4
            int  21h              ; Call MS-DOS
            mov  WORD PTR OldInt, bx   ; Save offset
            mov  WORD PTR OldInt+2, es ; Save segment
            push ds
            push cs                ; Copy the code segment
            pop  ds                ; to the extra segment
            mov  dx, OFFSET Overhand
            mov  ax, 2504h         ; MS-DOS function to write int 4
            int  21h
            mov  al, 30h           ; Set up for multiply
            mov  cl, 20h
            mul  cl                ; This will overflow
            into                   ; Call overflow handler
            push ds
            lds  dx, OldInt        ; Get the original int 4
            mov  ax, 2504h         ; MS-DOS function to write
                                   ; int 4
            int  21h               ; Call MS-DOS
            pop  ds
            mov  ah, 4ch           ; MS-DOS function to exit
                                   ; program
```

INTO

```
                    int  21h
         Start      ENDP

         ; This is the overflow handler. Any registers used must be
         ; saved on the stack, and restored before exiting.

         Overhand   PROC FAR               ; All interrupt handlers are
                                           ; FAR
                                           ; procedures
                    push ax                ; Save registers
                    push dx
                    push ds
                    mov  ax, SEG DGROUP     ; Get the data segment
                    mov  ds, ax            ; Put it in ds
                    mov  dx, OFFSET Overmsg
                    mov  ah, 9             ; MS-DOS function to print a
                                           ; message
                    int  21h               ; Call MS-DOS
                    pop  ds
                    pop  dx
                    pop  ax
         Overhand   ENDP
                    .STACK

                    END  Start
```

Interrupt Return   88/86   286   386
                                                            ▲   ▲   ▲

IRET/IRETD

PURPOSE   To return from a routine that was called via an interrupt. After the far return address is popped, the flags are popped also. Then control is returned to the return address found.

SYNTAX   IRET

IRETD   *Pops a double word to the flags on the 80386*

FLAGS   The flags are set to the values found on the stack.

COMMENTS   An interrupt can happen at any time. Because there is no way to know what might get interrupted, the interrupt routine must restore the processor to the exact state it was in when the interrupt occurred. Since the interrupt itself affected the flags, and the routine is likely to affect them further, the flags are pushed on the stack by the interrupt. When the routine returns, the flags must be restored from the stack. The IRET instruction does this.

SEE ALSO   CALL, RET   *Instructions used by regular subroutines*
               INT   *Do a software interrupt*

TIMING

Addressing	Encoding	Example	88/86	286	386
implied	11001111	iret	44/32	17	22

EXAMPLE   This routine is called when there is an interrupt from the serial I/O chip. It gets the data from the chip and places it in a *ring buffer*. Before returning, it resets the 8259 interrupt controller chip so more interrupts can get in.

```
; Read the UART on a serial chip interrupt
        .DATA
RingBuf DB   1024 dup(?)    ; Store serial data
Bptr    DW   0              ; Points to the next char to store

        .CODE
Serial  PROC FAR
        push ax             ; Save the registers used
        push bx
        push dx
        push ds
        mov  dx, 3f8h       ; Get serial port I/O address
        in   al, dx
        mov  ds, SEG DGROUP ; Get the segment of the data area
        mov  bx, Bptr       ; Get the ring buffer pointer
        mov  RingBuf[bx], al
        inc  bx
        and  bx, 1023       ; Don't let the pointer get past
                            ; the end of the buffer
        mov  Bptr, bx       ; Save the new pointer
        pop  ds             ; Restore the registers
        pop  dx
        pop  bx
        mov  al, 20h        ; Reset the interrupt controller
        out  20h, al
        pop  ax
        iret
Serial  ENDP
```

JA or JNBE

JA or JNBE, JAE or JNB, JB or JNAE, JBE or JNA, JC, JE or JZ, JG or JNLE, JGE or JNL, JL or JNGE, JLE or JNG, JNC, JNE or JNZ, JNO, JNP or JPO, JNS, JO, JP or JPE, JS

PURPOSE To test certain flags and do a short jump if the condition is met. Refer to Table 6-2 for what conditions can be tested with these instructions.

SYNTAX Jcondition   label

FLAGS The flags are unaffected by this instruction.

COMMENTS Conditional jumps are used to implement decisions in the logic of a program. They are usually proceeded by a CMP or TEST instruction that sets up the flags.

On the 80386 conditional jumps can do a near jump as well as the short jump that is used on the other processors. This increases the range of the jump from within –128 to +127 to within –32768 to +32767 bytes.

SEE ALSO
CMP   *Used to set the flags*
TEST   *Another way to set flags*
JMP   *The unconditional jump*

TIMING

Addressing	Encoding	Example	88/86	286	386
short label	0111cond displacement	jz dest	16 (4 noj)	7 (3 noj)	7 (3 noj)
near label	00001111 1000cond	jg ndest -	-		7 (3 noj)

See Table 6-3 for the values of cond.

Table 6-3. *Conditional Jump Instructions*

Instruction	Condition code
JA or JNBE	0111
JAE or JNB	0011
JB or JNAE	0010
JBE or JNA	0110
JC	0010
JE or JZ	0100
JG or JNLE	1111
JGE or JNL	1101
JL or JNGE	1100
JLE or JNG	1110
JNC	0011
JNE or JNZ	0101
JNO	0001
JNP or JPO	1011
JNS	1001
JO	0000
JP or JPE	1010
JS	1000

EXAMPLE   This routine tests the byte in AL to see if it is a numeric digit. If it is not a digit, AL is set to 0.

```
; Check for a digit in AL
        .CODE
IsDigit  PROC NEAR
        cmp   al, '0'       ; Check for zero
        jb    NotDigit      ; If AL < '0' then it's not a digit
        cmp   al, '9'       ; Check with nine
        ja    NotDigit      ; If AL > '9' then it's not a digit
        ret                 ; All OK return
NotDigit:
        xor   al, al        ; Set al to 0 for outside range
        ret
IsDigit  ENDP
```

JCXZ, JECXZ

JCXZ, JECXZ

PURPOSE   To check the CX register and do a short jump if it is equal to zero. On the 80386 the JECXZ instruction can be used to test the ECX register.

SYNTAX
```
JCXZ label
JECX label
```

FLAGS   The flags are unaffected by this instruction.

COMMENTS   The `LOOPCond` instruction and `REPCond` prefix can both exit before the CX register gets to zero. There are times when you need to know if the loop stopped because of the condition, or because CX is zero. Using this instruction is a convenient way to find out what happened.

SEE ALSO
CMPS	*String compare instruction*
SCAS	*String scan instruction*
REPE, REPNE	*Conditional repeat prefixes*
LOOPE, LOOPNE	*Conditional loop instructions*

TIMING

Addressing	Encoding	Example	88/86	286	386
label	11100011 displacement	jcxz notfound	18 (6 noj)	8 (4 noj)	9 (5 noj)

EXAMPLE   When searching a buffer for a character, you can use two tests. One is to check for the character, and the other is to check for the end of the buffer. This example searches a string for an open parentheses ['(']. The string is stored with the length in the first byte.

```
; Search a string for '(' The address of the string is in SI

        .DATA
FindParen PROC NEAR
        sub  cx, cx        ; Clear the CX register
        mov  cl, [si]      ; Get the length byte
        inc  si
```

```
            mov  al, '('          ; Set the character to
            repne scansb          ; Search for '('
            jcxz NotFound         ; if CX = 0 there was no '('
            ret                   ; Return with the address of
                                  ; the '(' in SI
NotFound:
            sub  si, si           ; Set SI to 0 to indicate not
                                  ; found

            ret
FindParen ENDP
```

Jump   88/86   286   386
                                                  ▲   ▲   ▲

JMP

PURPOSE   To jump to a specified location.

SYNTAX   JMP   Label

              JMP   SHORT Label

              JMP   FAR PTR Label

              JMP   register_or_memory

              JMP   WORD PTR memory

              JMP   DWORD PTR memory

FLAGS   The flags are unaffected by this instruction.

COMMENTS The jump instruction has three different forms, based on how far away the destination is. The short jump is for labels that are within –128 to +127 bytes from the jump instruction. The destination can be expressed in one (1) byte. To use this form, you must precede the label with the SHORT qualifier.

The near jump increases the range to within –32,768 to +32,767. This form requires two bytes for the destination. The assembler will use this form when the label is declared as a near label.

The far jump can go to any location in memory. The destination is four bytes, two for the segment and two for the offset. The assembler will use this form when the label is declared as a far label. The program can force the assembler to use a far jump by preceding the label with the FAR PTR qualifier.

JMP

Indirect jumps get the destination from a register or memory. All register jumps are near jumps to the address in the register. Indirect jumps using memory do near jumps, if the memory is a word; and far jumps, if the memory is a double word. You may use the WORD and DWORD qualifiers to override any assumptions that the assembler might make.

SEE ALSO

NEAR, FAR, PTR, SHORT, DWORD, WORD   *Qualifiers*

JA or JNBE, JAE or JNB, JB or   *Conditional jumps*
JNAE, JBE or JNA, JC, JE or JZ,
JG or JNLE, JGE or JNL, JL or
JNGE, JLE or JNG, JNC, JNE or JNZ,
JNO, JNP or JPO, JNS, JO, JP or
JPE, JS

TIMING

Addressing	Encoding	Example	88/86	286	386
short label	11101011 displacement	jmp SHORT lab	15	7	7
near label	11101001 displacement	jmp close	15	7	7
far label	11101010 displacement	jmp distant	15	11	12
register	11111111 11,100,r/m	jmp ax	11	7	7
memory near	11111111 mod,100,r/m displacement	jmp WORD [bx]	18+EA	11	10
memory	11111111 mod,101,r/m displacement	jmp DWORD [si]	24+EA	15	12

EXAMPLE

When you call MS-DOS via INT 21h, you use the AH register to pass a function number to MS-DOS. This is a common interface for many programs. To decode the function numbers, a table of function addresses is used. This example turns a function number into an index into a function table and jumps to the function indicated.

```
; Jump to a function in FuncTab based on the function number
; in AH
        .DATA
```

```
FuncTab    DD    Funct1, Funct2    ; Store the addresses of the
                                   ; functions here
           .CODE
DoFunc     PROC
           sub  bx, bx              ; Clear bx
           mov  bl, ah              ; Put the function number in
                                    ; BL
           shl  bx, 1               ; Multiply bx by four to get
           shl  bx, 1               ; the offset into the table
           jmp  DWORD FuncTab[bx]   ; Go to the function
DoFunc     ENDP
```

Leave a Procedure   88/86   286   386
                                                                ▲   ▲

LEAVE

PURPOSE   To undo the stack frame set up by the ENTER instruction.

SYNTAX   LEAVE

FLAGS   The flags are unaffected by this instruction.

COMMENTS   Stack frames are used to pass parameters to a subroutine, and to make room for local variables. On 80286 and 80386 processors, the ENTER and LEAVE instructions handle stack frames.

The LEAVE instruction sets the SP register to the value in the BP register. This step returns the space that was used for local variables. Next, the BP register is popped off the stack. This restores the BP register to the value it had before the function was called.

To get the same results on all 80x86 processors, the LEAVE instruction can be replaced by these instructions:

```
mov  sp, bp
pop  bp
```

SEE ALSO   CALL, RET   *To call and return from a subroutine*
               ENTER   *Makes the stack frame*

LEAVE

TIMING	Addressing	Encoding	Example	88/86	286	386
	implied	11001000	leave	-	5	4

EXAMPLE   See the example for ENTER.

Loop, Loop on a Condition   88/86   286   386
                                                               ▲   ▲   ▲

LOOP, LOOPE, LOOPNE

PURPOSE   To decrement the CX register and do a short jump if the CX register does not equal 0. The conditional loop instructions also test the zero flag before jumping.

SYNTAX
```
LOOP      label
LOOPE     label
LOOPNE    label
```

FLAGS   The flags are unaffected by this instruction.

COMMENTS   The LOOP instruction provides a way to make a loop that will run a given number of times. The LOOPE and LOOPNE instructions provide a way to get out of the loop when a certain condition is met.

The jump that the loop instruction takes is a short jump. This means that the label must be within −128 to +127 bytes of the loop instruction.

SEE ALSO
REP, REPE, REPNE	*Used for single instruction loops*
JMP	*To jump to a location*
JCXZ	*Jumps when CX is 0*

TIMING	Addressing	Encoding	Example	88/86	286	386
	LOOP	11100010	loop cloop	17	8	11
		displacement		(5 noj)	(4 noj)	
	LOOPE	11100001	loope again	18	8	11
		displacement		(6 noj)	(4 noj)	

LOOP, LOOPE, LOOPNE

Addressing	Encoding	Example	88/86	286	386
LOOPNE	11100000	loopne next	19	8	11
	displacement		(5 noj)	(4 noj)	

EXAMPLE   In this example the loop instruction is used to find the total length of a group of strings. The table ptrtab contains 10 pointers to strings. The strings end with a 0, and the length must be less than 80 bytes. Put the total length in DX.

```
; Calculate the total length of a group of strings
          .DATA
Str1      "This is the first string", 0
Str2      "This is the second string", 0
Str3      "This is the third string", 0
Str4      "This is the fourth string", 0
Str5      "This is the fifth string", 0
Str6      "This is the sixth string", 0
Str7      "This is the seventh string", 0
Str8      "This is the eighth string", 0
Str9      "This is the ninth string", 0
Str10     "This is the tenth string", 0

PtrTab    DW   Str1, Str2, Str3, Str4, Str5
          DW   Str6, Str7, Str8, Str9, Str10

          .CODE
GroupLen  PROC
          xor  dx, dx              ; Set the size to 0
          mov  bx, OFFSET PtrTab   ; Get the address of the table
          mov  cx, 10              ; The number of strings
OLoop:
          mov  si, [bx]            ; Get the address of the
                                   ; string
          inc  bx                  ; Point to the next entry
          inc  bx
          push cx                  ; Save the outer loop counter
          mov  cx, 80              ; Set cx to maximum string
                                   ; length
ILoop:
          mov  al, [si]            ; Get the byte
          inc  si                  ; Go to next byte
          or   al, al              ; Test for 0
          loopne ILoop             ; Do it again if no 0
          add  dx, 80              ; Add maximum length
```

LOOP, LOOPE, LOOPNE

```
        sub  dx, cx       ; Subtract bytes left
        pop  cx           ; Get the counter back
        loop OLoop        ; Do it again
        ret
GroupLen ENDP
```

Return from a Subroutine   88/86   286   386
                                                ▲   ▲   ▲

RET, RETN, RETF

PURPOSE   To pop a return address off of the stack and return control to the location indicated. One variation of the instruction adds the operand to the stack pointer after the return address has been popped.

SYNTAX   RET
             RET   parameters_size

FLAGS   The flags are unaffected by this instruction.

COMMENTS   A function may have been called with a far call or a near call. This affects the number of bytes in the return address on the stack. The assembler chooses which kind of return is required by looking at the type of procedure (NEAR or FAR) that the return is in. You may override this choice by using the RETN or RETF versions of the instruction.

When the stack is used to pass arguments to the function, something must be done to fix the stack. Since the return address is between the function and the arguments, it is not easy to just pop the arguments off the stack. The *RET n* format of the return instruction can be used in this case. It will add *n* to the stack pointer after the return address has been popped.

SEE ALSO   CALL   *To call a procedure*

RET, RETN, RETF

TIMING	Addressing	Encoding	Example	88/86	286	386
	RETN	11000011	retn	20/16	11	10
	RETN immed	11000010 data	ret 4	24/20	11	10
	RETF	11001011	retf	34/26	15	18
	RETF immed	11001010 data	retf 12	33/25	15	18

EXAMPLE   See the CALL instruction for an example of the RET instruction.

Chapter 7 Processor Control and Protected Mode Operation

The 80x86 processors have one or more registers for holding flags and other information about the state of the processor. Normally, you set or clear the flags as a side effect of arithmetic or logic instructions. To read the flags, you use the conditional jump instructions or the SET instructions. The first part of this chapter shows you several instructions that directly affect the flags.

One way to get more performance out of a computer is to add more processors. It makes sense that two processors working together on a problem can get the job done faster than one. With 80x86 systems, specialized processors called *co-processors* are often used to do certain tasks for the system. Special processor control instructions enable you to manage co-processors. The second part of this chapter describes the commands that control the processor and send commands to a co-processor.

Using more processors to boost power is fine, but what if all that power keeps going to waste while the computer waits for its user to press a key? This power can be recovered by instructing the system to do another task while it is waiting for that keystroke. So while you stare at a listing of your latest assembly language program, your computer can be recalculating a spread sheet. Dividing a computer's time among several tasks is called *multi-tasking*.

All of the 80x86 processors can be made to multi-task. With the 8088 and 8086 there are problems in keeping one task out of the way of another. The 80286 and 80386 have a special mode that keeps tasks out of each other's way. This is called *protected mode*. In addition, these later processors have special instructions for switching from one task to another. The last part of this chapter shows you how to use protected mode under MS-DOS.

Getting and Saving Flags

The 80x86 processor groups all the flags (overflow, carry, zero, and so forth) into one byte. You can move this byte into the AH register, and the AH register can be moved into it. The instructions to do this are LAHF (Load AH from Flags) and SAHF (Store AH to Flags). These instructions are useful when you want to save the state of the machine or restore it. For example, in a multi-tasking system, you want to save the state of one task (including all of the registers and the flags) and restore the state of the next task. Figure 7-1 shows where the flags are in the byte used by the LAHF and SAHF instructions.

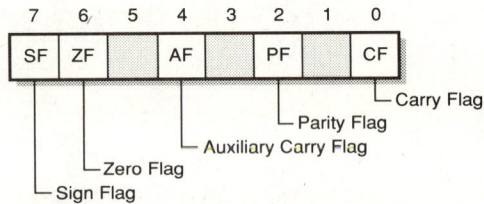

Figure 7-1. *The low byte of the flags register used in LAHF and SAHF.*

The 80286 and 80386 have another set of flags that control the mode of the processor. These flags are grouped into the Machine Status Word (MSW). Programs at the highest privilege level can move, load, and store this word from registers or memory. The instructions for this are LMSW (Load MSW) and SMSW (Store MSW). The format of these instructions is:

```
LMSW reg/mem
```

where `reg/mem` is a register or memory location. The LMSW instruction will load the MSW from the operand specified, and the SMSW will store the MSW in the operand. Figure 7-2 shows the format of the MSW.

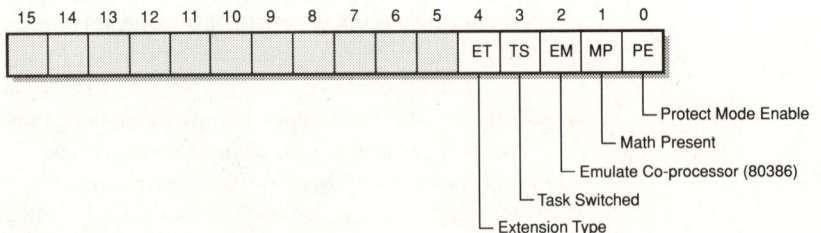

Figure 7-2. *The machine status word.*

Setting and Resetting the Flags

Several of the flags can be set or cleared using instructions specific to each flag. The examples of string routines in Chapter 4 used the CLD (CLear Direction flag) and STD (SeT Direction flag) to control the direction of string operations.

The carry flag can be controlled by several instructions whose only purpose is to control that flag. The instructions are STC (SeT the Carry), CMC (CoMplement the Carry), and CLC (CLear the Carry). They are used, respectively, to set the carry to 1, reverse the state of the carry, and reset the carry to 0.

The instructions STI (SeT the Interrupt flag) and CLI (CLear the Interrupt flag) are used to set and clear the interrupt flag. Hardware interrupts, such as for the keyboard or serial port, can only affect the processor when the interrupt flag is set. Routines that need to run as fast as possible can clear the interrupt flag, so that they can get the processor's full attention. You should remember to set the interrupt flag when the routine is finished. Failing to do this will leave your computer unable to respond to the keyboard or to any other interrupt-driven I/O device.

Processor Control

A computer system is more than just a CPU. It usually consists of serial ports, disks, memory, displays, keyboards, and perhaps more components. Each of these are subsystems that must work with the others in order to make the whole thing work. For example, if the memory chips are slower than the CPU, the memory circuits must add *wait states* to give the memory time to catch up.

Other devices have different ways of synchronizing with the rest of the system. There are five instructions that allow the processor to stop, wait, command, and block other devices.

Delays and Halts

When the processor must wait for a slower device, the simplest thing to do is *nothing* (for awhile). The NOP (No OPeration) instruction does nothing but use up a byte of memory and three clock cycles. The opcode that the assembler uses is actually an XCHG AX,AX instruction (90h). Both the facts that the NOP takes time and that it uses a single byte of memory can be useful.

While debugging you may find a bit of code that should not be there. To take it out, you will need to exit the debugger, edit the source, assemble the new source, and finally restart the debugger with the new program. An easier way to see what would happen if the code were gone is to cover it up with NOPs. Since the NOP only takes up space, the program will run as if the code were not there. When the new code is tested, you can go back to the source and make the necessary changes.

Another reason to use NOPs to fill space is to make the next instruction happen at an *even* address. Instructions on even addresses execute faster than if they are on odd addresses. Because the NOP itself takes time, you will only notice a speed improvement if you can get several instructions in a row on even addresses.

The NOP can be used to wait for a device to become ready. After a command is sent to a device, say, with an OUT instruction, it may take a short time for that device to be ready to reply or to receive another byte. One or more NOPs placed between the I/O instructions can provide this delay. If a slightly longer delay is required, you can use jmp $+2. This is a jump to the next instruction. It is similar to an NOP, but it uses two bytes and 15 cycles. One thing to remember when doing this kind of delay is that the length of a cycle is very different for different processor types. If precise delays are required, you should use the BIOS time of day interrupt (1Ah) or program the 8253 timer chip directly.

Another way to wait for a device is to stop the CPU. The HLT (HaLT) instruction does just that. Once halted, the CPU does nothing until an interrupt occurs. The interrupt will run and continue executing at the instruction following the HLT. This instruction does not get used very often. Not only is there usually something for the CPU to do, but the large number of interrupts (clock, keyboard, serial ports, network adapters, etc.) make sure that the computer does not stay halted for long.

Working with Co-processors

Co-processors are used to perform specialized tasks under the control of the main processor. The most common co-processors are the floating point processors from the 80x87 family. Other co-processors can handle video or data storage devices. By concentrating on one kind of operation, a co-processor can do a better job of that operation than the more general purpose 80x86 is able to do. Another benefit of using a co-processor is that, while the co-processor is doing its task, the main processor is free to do something else.

LOCKING THE BUS The bus is a group of wires or circuit traces that carry signals from one part of the computer to another. Microcomputer programs are very aware of buses, as the type of bus determines what optional devices can be added to the computer. The main processor and the co-processor can access data in memory via the memory bus. This can be a problem if both processors try to modify the same location at the same time. For example, suppose the main processor wants to increment a word in memory. It reads the word, then increments the value, and finally writes the word back to memory. What happens if, in the middle of the increment, the co-processor wants to modify the same word? If it reads the data after the main processor has read the data, it will modify the wrong value. If the co-processor gets the data first, then the main processor will increment the wrong value. In either case, whichever processor finishes first will have its work wiped out when the other processor writes on top of it.

To prevent this problem, you can use the LOCK prefix. This prevents any other processor from accessing the memory bus while the locked instruction is running. In the case of an increment instruction, the code looks like this:

```
lock inc [bx]
```

SYNCHRONIZING WITH A CO-PROCESSOR

Another way to prevent collisions between a co-processor and the main processor is to have the main processor wait until the co-processor has completed an instruction. The WAIT instruction does this. If your program is going to use data generated by the co-processor, it will need to wait for the co-processor to finish. Any attempt to read the data before the co-processor is finished will result in reading the wrong data.

The 8087 chip can only work on one instruction at a time. Therefore, you need to use a WAIT instruction before each floating point instruction. If you use the .8087 directive and the floating point mnemonics, Turbo Assembler will insert the WAIT instructions for you.

SENDING A COMMAND TO A CO-PROCESSOR

Co-processors are under the control of the main processor. In order to perform properly, the co-processor must be given instructions by the main processor. The ESC instruction is used to tell the co-processor what to do. An ESC instruction looks like this:

```
ESC  instruction, reg/mem
```

The instruction contains six bits of information that mean something to the co-processor. A register or memory location, indicated by reg/mem, is used as the data link to the co-processor. Normally, you do not need to use the ESC instruction, because the assembler provides a set of floating point mnemonics which it translates to the correct ESC instruction.

Protected Mode

Processors and co-processors need to be careful when accessing the same locations, so that they don't confuse each other. The same problem comes up when several tasks are running on the same processor in a multi-tasking system. If a task modifies memory, it must be careful that no other task is modifying the same memory at the same time. When the tasks know about each other, protocols can be used to handle this kind of problem. When a poorly written task starts modifying memory at random, it can easily crash the system.

After looking at this and other problems, Intel Corporation introduced *protected mode* on the 80286. In protected mode, tasks are protected from each other by allowing the CPU to control access to various resources. Tasks can only use resources that they have permission to use. Rogue tasks cannot get at other tasks' memories or I/O devices, and they can be shut down when they try.

The processor controls what a task can do by assigning each piece of code a *privilege level*. Programs at one privilege level can only use code at another privilege level under strictly controlled circumstances. Certain processor control instructions can only be used in programs at the highest privilege level. I/O instructions can only be used at the privilege level that has been set by a privileged task.

Getting into Protected Mode

When a computer using an 80286 or 80386 is turned on, it is in *real mode*. In real mode the processor works just like a fast 8088 or 8086 with more instructions. To take advantage of the protection and multi-tasking of these processors, you need to switch them to protected mode.

Once you have switched to protected mode, programs that do not use the protected mode memory segments will not run. MS-DOS and BIOS are examples of programs that will not run in protected mode. This means you cannot use these programs for I/O, or to handle any interrupts that occur.

One way to run in protected mode under MS-DOS is to turn off interrupts while in protected mode and not do any I/O. There are not many useful programs that fit in this category. Another way to do it is to write protected mode interrupt handlers for all of the hardware interrupts, and switch to real mode to do the software interrupts for BIOS and MS-DOS functions. This is the technique used by programming systems for protected mode called *DOS extenders*.

The following example shows how a program running on an 80386 can switch into protected mode, and then back into real mode. It handles the interrupt problem by turning off interrupts while in protected mode. Since this program does nothing but change modes, it does not need to call MS-DOS. However, you need to use the routines GoProtect and GoReal in the protected mode examples later in this chapter. Some of the data structures and terms used refer to protected mode concepts that are explained on pages to follow.

```
; Program to switch in and out of protected mode
; File PROTECT.ASM
        .MODEL    SMALL               ; Must match the model used in
                                      ; other modules
        .386P                         ; Allow 80386 protected mode
                                      ; instructions
        .DATA
EXECUT  EQU  10011010b                ; 16-bit code segment type
```

```
RDWRDATA    EQU   10010010b           ; Read/Write data segment type
STACKSEG    EQU   10010110b           ; Stack segment type
STATUS_PORT    EQU   64               ; Keyboard status port
A20_PORT    EQU   0d1
A20_ON      EQU   0df
A20_OFF     EQU   0ddh
KBD_PORT_A  EQU   60

; The following data definitions make up the Global Descriptor
; table.
GblDT       DW    0, 0, 0, 0          ; First descriptor (reserved)
            DW    0, 0, 0, 0          ; Data segment descriptor
            DW    0, 0, 0, 0          ; Code segment descriptor
            DW    0, 0, 0, 0          ; Stack segment descriptor

; This is the value to place in the Global Descriptor Table
; Register
GblDscTbl   DW    4 ^ 8 * 1           ; Segment limit
            DD    0

            .CODE
; This program starts in real mode. It sets up some data
; descriptors then calls GoProtect to switch to protected mode.
; After that it calls GoReal to return to real mode

Start       PROC
            mov   ax, SEG _DATA       ; Set up the data segment
            mov   ds, ax              ; register
            mov   si, OFFSET GblDT    ; Get the address of the GDT
            add   si, 8               ; The data descriptor
            mov   bx, 0FFFFh          ; The length of the segment
            mov   cx, RDWRDATA        ; The flags
            call  SetDscrpt           ; Set up the descriptor
            mov   ax, SEG _TEXT       ; Get the code segment
            add   si, 8               ; The code descriptor
            mov   bx, 0FFFFh          ; The length of the segment
            mov   cx, EXECUT          ; The flags
            call  SetDscrpt           ; Set up the descriptor
            mov   ax, SEG SSEG        ; Get the stack segment
            add   si, 8               ; The stack descriptor
            mov   bx, 0               ; The limit for the stack
            mov   cx, STACKSEG        ; The flags
            call  SetDscrpt           ; Set up the descriptor
            call  GoProtect           ; Enter protected mode
            call  GoReal
            mov   ah, 4Ch
            int   21h
```

```
Start      ENDP

; Set up a descriptor
; SI = Offset of the descriptor
; AX = Segment address for the selector
; BX = Length of the segment
; CX = Flags for the segment
SetDscrpt PROC
          mov   dl, ah             ; Get the high word of the
                                   ; segment address
          shl   ax, 4              ; AX * 16
          shr   dl, 4              ; High nibble in DL
          mov   WORD PTR [si], bx  ; Limit word
          mov   WORD PTR [si+2], ax ; Low word of base address
          mov   BYTE PTR [si+4], dl ; High byte of base address
          mov   WORD PTR [si+5], cx ; flags
          mov   BYTE PTR [si+7], 0  ; Misc.
          ret
SetDscrpt ENDP

; Enter protected mode
GoProtect PROC
          call  enable_a20
          mov   ax, SEG _DATA      ; Get the data segment address
          mov   dl, ah             ; and use it to calculate the
          shl   ax, 4              ; base address of the global
          shr   dl, 4              ; descriptor table
          sub   dh, dh
          add   ax, OFFSET GblDT   ; Add in the offset to the
                                   ; table
          adc   dl, 0
          mov   GblDscTbl+2, ax    ; Save the base address
          mov   GblDscTbl+4, dx
          lgdt  PWORD PTR GblDscTbl ; Load the GDTR
          cli                      ; Turn off interrupts
          smsw  ax                 ; Get the Machine Status Word
          and   ax, 1Fh            ; Don't use the paging bit
          or    ax, 1              ; Set PE bit
          lmsw  ax                 ; Set the Machine Status Word
          DB    0EAh               ; Far jmp
          DW    ClearPF            ; Offset
          DW    10h                ; Protected mode segment
ClearPF:
          mov   ax, 8              ; Data segment selector
          mov   ds, ax
          mov   ax, 18h            ; Stack segment selector
```

```
                mov   ss, ax
                ret
GoProtect  ENDP

; Return to real mode
GoReal     PROC
                mov   eax, CR0          ; Get the MSW
                and   eax, 07FFFFFFEh   ; Turn off the paging bit and
                                        ; the protect mode enable bit
                mov   CR0, eax          ; Put the new MSW back
                DB    0EAh              ; Far JMP
                DW    ClearPF2          ; Offset for the JMP
                DW    _TEXT             ; Real mode segment
ClearPF2:
                mov   ax, SEG DGROUP    ; Put back the real mode
                mov   ds, ax            ; segments
                mov   ax, SEG SSEG
                mov   ss, ax
                sti                     ; Turn on interrupts
                call disable_a20
                ret
GoReal     ENDP

PROC       enable_a20     NEAR
; Enables the a20 address line for virtual mode address space
                mov   al,A20_PORT
                out   STATUS_PORT,al
                mov   al,A20_ON
                out   KBD_PORT_A,al
                ret
ENDP       enable_a20

PROC       disable_a20    NEAR
; Disables the a20 address line
                mov   al,A20_PORT
                out   STATUS_PORT,al
                mov   al,A20_OFF
                out   KBD_PORT_A,al
                ret
ENDP       disable_a20

; Define a segment for the stack
SSEG SEGMENT   WORD STACK USE16 'STACK'
                DB    1024 DUP( ? )
SSEG ENDS
END
```

The data at `GblDT` is called the Global Descriptor Table (GDT). This table contains all the information the processor requires about segments in protected mode. The first part of the `Start` routine sets up the entries for each of the segments used in this program. (See the "Descriptor Tables" section in this chapter for a description of the fields in the GDT.)

After setting up the GDT, the `Start` routine calls `GoProtect` to enter protected mode. The first thing that `GoProtect` does is tell the processor the length and location of the descriptor table. It does this by calculating the location and putting it in memory at `GblDscTbl`. Then it uses the LGDT instruction to load the information from memory into the Global Descriptor Table Register (GDTR) in the processor. The next step is to shut off interrupts with the CLI instruction. Now the processor is ready to go into protected mode. To do this you need to set the PE (Protected mode Enable) bit in the MSW. There is no single instruction to do this, so you need to do all of the following: get the MSW into a register (with the LMSW instruction), change the bit, and send the changed word to the MSW (with the SMSW instruction).

Once in protected mode, you need to change the values in the segment registers from segment addresses to protected mode selectors. (See the "Using Selectors to Access Memory" section.) Each selector refers to one of the entries in the GDT. The selectors in this program are equal to the entry number times 8. The first segment register that the `GoProtect` routine sets up is the CS register. The only instruction that you can use to load this register is a FAR JMP. There are two problems with using a FAR JMP for this operation. The first is that Turbo Assembler will see a FAR JMP is not required and convert it to a SHORT JMP. The second problem is that the segment portion of a FAR label in a Turbo Assembler program is the address of the segment. In protected mode, the segment portion of a FAR label is a segment selector. To overcome these problems, the `GoProtect` routine pokes the opcode and operands for a FAR JMP with DB (Define Byte) and DW (Define Word) directives.

The `GoReal` function puts the 80386 back into real mode. To remain compatible with the 80286, the 80386 does not allow you to use the SMSW instruction to clear PE bit. On the 80386 you can also access the MSW with MOV instructions. The name used in MOV instructions for the MSW is `CR0`. The first three instructions in `GoReal` use this fact to clear the PE bit. Once the bit is clear, the processor is back in real mode. The first thing that must be done, once you are back in real mode, is to reload the segment registers with segment addresses.

Memory in Protected Mode

One resource that is used by all tasks is memory. Some memory is used for code and other memory is used for data. Protected mode classifies memory as to how it will be used. To use memory, the task must have permission to use the memory and must use it for the right purpose. A task may not modify a memory location that is *read only* or otherwise being used for code.

In addition to the protection it offers, protected mode also allows more memory to be used. The 80286 can address up to 16Mb of memory, compared to 1Mb on 8086 or 8088 systems, and the 80386 can address up to four gigabytes of memory. Not only can protected mode programs use more memory, but that memory does not even need to be installed. A memory segment that is not being used can be written to the disk and replaced by a memory segment that is being used.

DESCRIPTOR TABLES

A protected mode application never deals with physical addresses. Instead, the application uses selectors that reference descriptor tables containing the locations and lengths of all the memory segments. The descriptor tables are stored in memory, which means that there must be descriptors for the descriptor tables. Three descriptor tables can be loaded into the CPU. These tables are called the Global Descriptor Table (GDT), Local Descriptor Table (LDT), and Interrupt Descriptor Table (IDT).

The GDT contains descriptors that can be used by any task in the system (Figure 7-3). The descriptors here describe segments for all the descriptor tables, video memory, OS programmer interface code, and other common code or data areas. Programs running at the highest privilege level can get the location and length of the GDT by using the SGDT (Store GDT) instruction. The single argument to this instruction is a six-byte sized memory location. The first word is the number of descriptors in the table. The next two words are the base address of the table, which is the physical location of the GDT.

If you change the size or location of the GDT, you will have to tell the processor about the change. To do this, use the LGDT (Load GDT) instruction. This instruction uses the same format as the SGDT instruction; but instead of storing the address to memory, it loads the address into the processor's GDT register.

The IDT contains descriptors for all the segments that contain interrupt handlers. It is similar to, and replaces, the interrupt vector table used by real mode programs. The location of the IDT can be accessed in the same way as the GDT can be. The instructions to use are SIDT (Store IDT) and LIDT (Load IDT).

Each task may have its own LDT. The descriptors here are for memory that is specific to a particular task. Although only one LDT can be used at a time, several of them can be in memory. Multi-tasking systems switch LDTs when they switch tasks.

The location of the current LDT is accessed with the SLDT (Store LDT) and LLDT instructions. The argument to both of these instructions is a selector for a descriptor in the GDT.

USING SELECTORS TO ACCESS MEMORY

Protected mode processes use the same segment registers that are used in conventional programs. The difference is what is contained in the registers. In conventional programs the segment register is the address of a paragraph in memory. When a segment is combined with an offset, the result is a physical memory location. In protected mode the segment register contains a data selector. A selector consists of an index to a descriptor table, a table indicator, and a requested privilege level. Figure 7-4 shows how the selector is laid out.

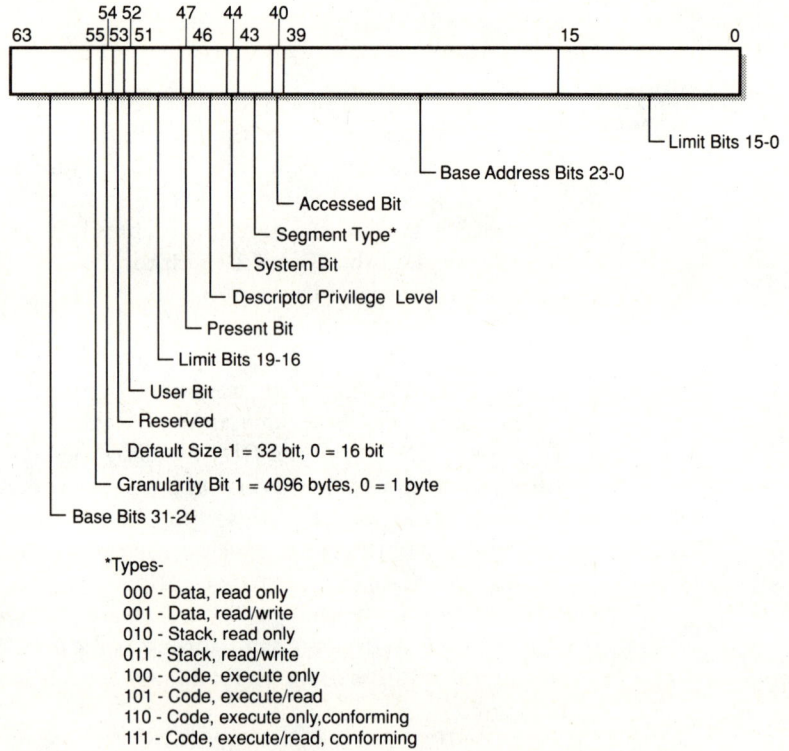

*Types-

```
000 - Data, read only
001 - Data, read/write
010 - Stack, read only
011 - Stack, read/write
100 - Code, execute only
101 - Code, execute/read
110 - Code, execute only,conforming
111 - Code, execute/read, conforming
```

Figure 7-3. *Format of a descriptor.*

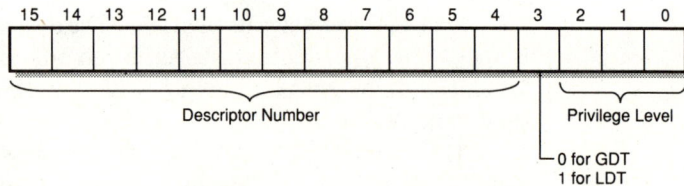

Figure 7-4. *Fields of a selector.*

To use a selector, you must be sure it is loaded into a segment register. Whenever a segment register is loaded, the value is checked to see if it is a valid selector, and if the task is at a high enough privilege level. If the register is DS, ES, FS, or GS, the segment must be readable. For the SS register, the segment must be readable and "writeable." The CS register requires an executable segment. If the selector is invalid, the 80386 will give a General Protection (GP) fault. The GP fault generates an interrupt (called an *exception* in protected mode). The exception handler can stop executing any program that causes a GP fault.

Another way to get a GP fault is to try and write to a read-only segment, or to read from a write-only segment. If there is some question about the permissions on a segment, there are three instructions that can be used. The first is the LAR (Load Access Rights) instruction. The LAR instruction checks a given selector to see if it is valid and, if it is, returns the access rights for the selector. The first operand for this instruction is a 16- or 32-bit register that will get the access rights of the selector specified by the second operand. If the selector is valid, the zero flag will be set; otherwise the zero flag is clear and the access rights are not copied. This is useful if you have a questionable selector, because you can see if it is correct before you put it in a segment register and cause a GP fault. The data returned gives you more information than you are likely to need. Table 7-1 describes the bits returned by LAR. If the destination register is 32 bits long, then all of the data is transferred. For 16-bit registers, only the lower 16 bits are used.

The following example shows how you can use the LAR instruction to determine if a selector is valid and can be used to read and write data:

```
; Check selector
; AX = selector to test
        lar   ebx, ax          ; Get the access rights for
                               ; the selector in AX
        jnz   BadSel            ; If no zero flag the selector
                               ; is bad
        and   ebx, 0E00h        ; Get the type bits
        cmp   ebx, 200h         ; See if it is data read/write
        jne   BadSel            ; If not it is bad
        .                      ; OK to use the selector here
        .
        .

BadSel:                        ; Come here to do something
        .                      ; about the bad selector
        .
        .
```

Table 7-1. *The Bits Returned by the LAR Instruction*

Bits	Description
31-24	Unused. Set to 0.
23	Granularity. When set the limit is in bytes, when cleared the limit is in 4096 byte blocks.
22	Default size. When set, operands are 32 bits by default; when cleared, operands are 16 bits.
21	Reserved.
20	Undefined.
19-16	Unused.
15	Present. When set, the segment is in physical memory; when clear, the segment is not in memory.
14-13	Privilege level. 0 is most privileged; 3 is least privileged.
12	System. When set, the segment is not a system segment; when clear, it is a system segment.
11-9	Type. The types are:
	000 Data, read only
	001 Data, read/write
	010 Stack, read only
	011 Stack, read/write
	100 Code, execute only
	101 Code, execute/read
	110 Code, execute only, conforming
	111 Code, execute/read, conforming.
8	Accessed. This bit is set if the segment has been read or written.
7-0	Unused. Set to 0.

The LAR instruction is cumbersome if all you want to know is whether a selector is valid and can be written to. In this case you can use VERW (VERify Writable) instead. This instruction uses one operand that is a selector. If the selector is valid and can be written to, the zero flag is set; otherwise, it is cleared.

A similar instruction lets you check if a selector is readable. The instruction is VERR (VERify Readable). It has the same format and results as the VERW instruction. By using the VERW and VERR instructions, the previous example becomes:

```
; Check the selector in AX for read/write permission
        verr ax                 ; See if readable
        jnz  BadSel             ; If no zero flag it is not
                                ; readable
        verw ax                 ; See if writeable
        jnz  BadSel             ; If no zero flag it is not
                                ; writeable
        .                       ; OK to use the selector here
        .
        .

BadSel:                         ; Come here to do something
        .                       ; about the bad selector
        .
        .
```

Segments in protected mode can be of different lengths. On the 80286 they can be from 1 to 65,536 bytes long. On the 80386 they can be up to four gigabytes long. If a program tries to read or write memory that is past the end of the segment, it results in a GP fault. To find out how long a segment is, you can use the LSL (Load Segment Limit) instruction. The format is:

```
lsl  reg16/32, regmem16/32
```

The first operand will be set to the length of the segment indicated by the selector in the second operand.

The last four instructions will tell you everything there is to know about a memory segment—except where it is. However, since a protected mode application does not need to know where memory segments are, this information should be adequate.

PRIVILEGE LEVELS

There are things that need to be done in protected mode that should not be done by just any program. For example, the GDT must be updated as the memory requirements of programs change. If any program could modify the GDT, it could wreak havoc on any location in memory.

Protected mode uses four different privilege levels to make sure that only certain programs can do certain things. The privilege level of a program affects what data it can access, what routines it can call, and even what instructions it can use.

Table 7-2 shows the instructions that can only be used by programs at the most privileged level (level 0). If a program with a higher privilege level number (less privileged) tries to use any of these instructions, it will cause a protection fault.

Table 7-2.   *Privileged Instructions*

ARPL	Adjust Requested Privilege Level
CLTS	CLear Task Switched flag
HLT	HaLT processor
LGDT, LIDT, LLDT	Load Descriptor Tables
LMSW	Load Machine Status Word
LTR	Load Task Register
MOV CRn/reg, reg/CRn	MOVe control registers
MOV DRn/reg, reg/DRn	MOVe debug registers
MOV TRn/reg, reg/TRn	MOVe test registers
SGDT, SIDT, SLDT	Store Descriptor Tables

The I/O and interrupt flag instructions can be executed by programs that are the same or more privileged than the I/O Privilege Level (IOPL) found in the extended flags register. This register includes the regular flags register, plus three new flags and two bits for the IOPL. Because the GoProtect routine sets the privilege level to 0 (highest level), it can use I/O instructions no matter what the IOPL is. If you want to control access to I/O, you should set the privilege level of the task to something other than 0, and make the IOPL less than the level used for the task. If the task tries to use an I/O instruction, it will generate an interrupt instead. If you have used GoProtect, or some other routine that does not allow interrupts, it will cause the processor to reset.

All memory segments have a privilege level. The Descriptor Privilege Level (DPL) field in the descriptor contains the privilege level for the segment. The privilege level of the segment that is running is called the Current Privilege Level (CPL). You can find the CPL by examining the low two bits of the CS register, like this:

```
mov   ax, cs    ; Get code selector
and   ax, 3     ; Mask for the low two bits
```

The CPL determines what you can do. A program can only access data segments that are at the same or less privileged levels. Only calls and jumps to code segments at the same privilege level are allowed. The stack being used must be at the same privilege level as the CPL.

This scheme means that an application running at level 3 cannot write on the GDT, which will most likely be at level 0. The program loader running at level 1 also cannot change the GDT, but it can load a new program into the level 3 application area.

The program loader running at level 1 not only cannot access the data for level 0, but it also cannot call or jump to routines in this area. It cannot even call or jump to the level 3 routine that it just loaded. Obviously, something must be done about this. It would be a fairly useless loader that could not execute the program it just loaded.

To get around the problem of not being able to code what is at another privilege level, you must use a call *gate*. This is a special descriptor that contains the selector and offset of the function to call. In this way an application program can only call a specific location in the program at a different privilege level.

The next example is a routine that changes a descriptor in the GDT into a call gate. You can add it to the program to change to protected mode. It should be called while setting up the other descriptors (before switching to protected mode). Remember to add extra space to the GblDT data for the call gate descriptor, and to change the limit at GblDscTbl.

```
; Make a call gate descriptor
; SI = Offset of the descriptor to change
; AL = Privilege level for calling functions
; BX = Offset of the function
; CX = Selector for the segment containing the function
MakeCG     PROC
           mov   WORD PTR [si], bx        ; The function offset
           mov   WORD PTR [si+2], cx      ; Selector
           mov   BYTE PTR [si+4], 0       ; Misc.
           shl   al, 5
           or    al, 10001100b            ; Set bits identifying
                                          ; this as a call gate

           sub   ah, ah
           mov   WORD PTR [si+5], AX
           mov   WORD PTR [si+7], 0
           ret
MakeCG     ENDP
```

Less privileged functions can use the call gate created by this function to call the more privileged function specified. The CALL instruction used must refer to the call gate descriptor:

```
call FAR PTR 0010:0000
```

The segment portion of the address (0010) refers to the call gate. The processor ignores the offset given here. Instead, it uses the offset from the call gate descriptor.

Some routines need to be available to programs at several different privilege levels. For example, the program loader, the program, and the memory swapper all need to access a routine that reads and writes to the disk. Instead of using a call gate to access the routine, you should use a conforming code segment. Conforming code segments run at the privilege level of the routine that called it. A segment is conforming if the descriptor says it is conforming in the type field.

Privileged programs can adjust the privilege level of a segment by modifying the DPL in the descriptor table. Other programs can only make a segment more privileged. The instruction for this is ARPL (Adjust Requested Privilege Level), and it looks like this:

```
arpl selector, reg
```

The *selector* can be a register or memory location indicating the segment to adjust. The register holds the privilege level to use. If the selector is less privileged, then it is changed to the new privilege level and the zero flag is set. Otherwise, the zero flag is cleared.

PAGING When running MS-DOS in an IBM-PC or compatible, the video RAM and the BIOS use memory locations from 0A0000h to 0FFFFFh. For systems with 8088 or 8086 CPUs, this is the end of addressable memory. In the larger address spaces of the 80286 and 80386, this MS-DOS screen and BIOS area fall right in the middle of the memory map. This means that programs need to make allowances for this hole in the middle of available memory.

The 80386 uses *paging* to overcome this problem. Paging divides up memory into pages that can be moved around the logical address space. Programs see memory as a sequential array of locations, but the physical memory can be scattered around. When a program references a memory location, the Memory Management Unit (MMU) in the 80386 looks up where that location is in physical memory and accesses that location.

If there is no physical memory holding the memory location that was requested, the MMU can call a program that can write a page of physical memory to the disk, read the required page, and translate the address. This is called *demand page virtual addressing*. What it means to the programmer is that a program can use the entire four-gigabyte address space of the 80386—

no matter how much or how little memory is actually installed. The only difference to the program is that it will slow down when it has to swap memory pages.

Paging is controlled by a table in memory and the values of the special registers in the 80386. However, the details of implementing a paging system are beyond the scope of this book. You can take advantage of paging by using one of several products that use the 80386 paging capabilities. With MS-DOS systems, the programmer can control paging by using a program that conforms to the Lotus, Intel Corporation, and Microsoft (LIM) standard.

Multi-tasking

The beginning of this chapter presented an example of how multi-tasking can be used to get more out of a computer, by enabling it to perform other tasks while waiting for input or output. When the computer switches from one task to another, it must store information about the task that was running, and load information about the task that is about to run. Such information includes the registers, the stack, the LDT, and the location of the instruction to execute next. This information is called the *context*.

SWITCHING TASKS   The first step in switching tasks is to save the context of the current task. Next, the context of the new task is read in. Finally, the new task is run. The 80386 uses a special descriptor that points to a Task State Segment (TSS) for each task. The TSS contains the context of the task with which it is associated. Another descriptor called a *task gate* is used to do the task switch. The task gate works in a way similar to the call gate.

A register called the Task Register (TR) tells the 80386 what TSS to use to save the current task's TSS. After the task switch, the TR gets set to the selector of the task that is about to run. The TR must be set to the TSS selector of the first task, before the first task switch occurs. To do this you can use the LTR (Load Task Register) instruction. The single operand for this instruction is a register or memory location, containing the selector for the current TSS. If you are interested in what TSS the current task is using, you can use the STR instruction. You cannot use the selector returned in order to access the data in the TSS, so this instruction is mostly ornamental.

The three functions in the following example prepare for multi-tasking, create a new task, and switch from one task to another. It assumes that the GDT contains a descriptor of a segment that can be used to hold task information. The selector for this segment is 28h; the next 64 descriptors must be reserved for possible tasks.

```
.MODEL    SMALL
PUBLIC    InitTask          ; Create the first task
PUBLIC    NewTask           ; Create a new task
PUBLIC    SwtchTask         ; Switch tasks
```

```
                .386
TaskSeg    SEGMENT   WORD PRIVATE USE16 'TASK'
TaskCnt    DW    0                                     ; The number of tasks
CurTask    DW    0                                     ; The task being executed
TskData    DB    104 * 64 dup(?)                       ; Room for task state data
TskJmp     DD    0
TaskSeg    ENDS
           .CODE
; Initialize the task switching mechanism
InitTask   PROC
           mov  ax, 8h                                 ; Selector for the GDT
           mov  ds, ax                                 ; put it in DS
           mov  si, 30h                                ; Offset for the first task
                                                       ; descriptor
           mov  ax, 103h                               ; TSS segment limit
           mov  WORD PTR [si], ax
           mov  ax, SEG TaskSeg                        ; Segment for the TSS
           mov  bl, ah
           shl  ax, 4
           shr  bl, 4
           add  ax, OFFSET TskData                     ; Add in the location of the
           adc  bl, 0                                  ; TSS
           mov  WORD PTR [si+2], ax
           mov  BYTE PTR [si+4], bl
           mov  WORD PTR [si+5], 011101001b            ; Set flags
           mov  BYTE PTR [si+7], 0
           mov  ax, 28h                                ; Selector for TaskSeg
           mov  ds, ax
           inc  TaskCnt
           mov  ax, 30h                                ; The first TSS descriptor
           ltr  ax                                     ; Load the task register
           ret
InitTask   ENDP

; Put a new task in the table
; AX = Offset of function for the task
; BX = Selector of the function
; CX = Selector for the stack
NewTask    PROC
           push ax                                     ; Save the parameters
           push bx
           push cx
           mov  ax, 8h                                 ; Selector for the GDT
           mov  ds, ax                                 ; put it in DS
```

```
            mov    si, TaskCnt               ; The number of the next task
            shl    si, 3                     ; times size of descriptor
            add    si, 30h                   ; Offset of first TSS
                                             ; descriptor
            mov    ax, 103h                  ; TSS segment limit
            mov    WORD PTR [si], ax
            mov    ax, SEG TaskSeg           ; Segment for the TSS
            mov    bl, ah
            shl    ax, 4
            shr    bl, 4
            mov    cx, TaskCnt
            shl    cx, 3
            add    cx, OFFSET TskData
            adc    bl, 0
            add    ax, cx                    ; Add in the location of the
            adc    bl, 0                     ; TSS
            mov    WORD PTR [si+2], ax
            mov    BYTE PTR [si+4], bl
            mov    WORD PTR [si+5], 011101001b ; Set flags
            mov    BYTE PTR [si+7], 0
            mov    ax, 28h                   ; Selector for TaskSeg
            mov    ds, ax
            mov    si, TaskCnt               ; Get the task number
            shl    si, 3
            mov    ax, si
            shl    si, 2
            add    ax, si
            shl    si, 1
            add    si, ax                    ; AX times 104
            add    si, OFFSET TskData
            sub    eax, eax                  ; Clear the high word
            pop    cx                        ; Restore parameters
            pop    bx
            pop    ax
            mov    [si+20h], eax             ; Save EIP
            mov    DWORD PTR [si+38h], 1024  ; Save ESP
            mov    [si+4Ch], ax
            mov    [si+50h], cx
            inc    TaskCnt
            ret
NewTask     ENDP

; Switch to the next task. This can be jumped to by an ISR for
; the clock interrupt or by a task that is ready to let another
; task have a chance
```

```
SwtchTask PROC
          mov   ax, 28h                      ; Selector for TaskSeg
          mov   ds, ax
          mov   ax, CurTask
          inc   ax                           ; Go to the next task
          cmp   ax, TskCnt                   ; See if we are past the end
          jb    Sk1                          ; of the list
          mov   ax, 1                        ; If so, go back to task 1
Sk1:
          mov   CurTask, ax
          shl   ax, 3                        ; Times 8
          add   ax, 30h                      ; The first selector
          mov   WORD PTR TskJmp+2, ax
          jmp   DWORD [TskJmp]               ; Do the next task
SwtchTask ENDP
```

TESTING FOR TASK SWITCHES

The purpose of saving and restoring contexts is to prevent a task from knowing about, or interfering with, other tasks in the computer. The program should not know that it is sharing the processor with other tasks. However, there are times when a program might want to know if other tasks are running. For example, a program that uses a common data segment knows that the data segment will be in the same state as long as no other task has run. There is a bit (bit 3) in the MSW register on the 80386 that is set whenever a task switch occurs. The CLTS (CLear Task Switched) instruction sets that bit to zero. The SMSW (see Chapter 4) can be used to get the MSW, so that the task switch bit can be tested. So a program that wants to see if it has been interrupted would look like this:

```
          clts               ; Clear the task switched bit
            .                ; Do processing
            .
            .
          smsw ax            ; Get the msw
          test ax,4          ; See if a task switch occurred
          jz   noswitch
            .                ; Make sure the other task did not
            .                ; mess us up
            .
noswitch:
            .                ; Continue processing
            .
            .
```

Summary

Co-processors and multi-tasking can be used to expand the power of a computer system. Multi-tasking enables you to use more of the main processor's power, and co-processors allow you to divide the load among more processors. The 80x86 processors provide ever-increasing capabilities in these areas.

With each new processor, microcomputers become more sophisticated. Protected mode provides features that were previously only available on mini- and mainframe computers. Paging allows memory configurations that once required extra circuitry (if such configurations were available at all) before the 80386 was developed.

For most programs co-processors, protected mode, and paging are only peripheral concerns. These programs can run unchanged on any of the processors in the 80x86 family. As the programs become more sophisticated, they are likely to benefit from some of the more advanced features of the newer processors.

ARPL

ARPL

PURPOSE To adjust the requested privilege level of a selector. If the requested privilege level of the selector is greater than the source register, adjust the privilege level to that of the source. If the privilege level of the source is the same or less than the source, leave it alone.

SYNTAX ARPL selector, reg　　*The selector is in a register or memory location. The second operand contains the privilege level for the selector.*

FLAGS If the selector is adjusted, then the zero flag is set. Otherwise it is cleared. All other flags are unaffected.

COMMENTS This instruction is often used by high privileged routines that are passed far pointers. In such a routine, the fact that it adjusts the privilege level is not as important as the fact that it tests the privilege level. If the selector was valid for the less privileged routine, it will be valid for the more privileged routine.

   A program can try to access memory that it is not supposed to access by asking the operating system to copy data to or from the protected memory. Since the operating system runs at the most privileged level, it can copy data from any selector to any other selector. This would defeat the memory protection, so it must be prevented. See the example to follow for a way in which the operating system can detect this.

SEE ALSO

LAR	*Load access rights*
LSL	*Load segment limit*
VERR/VERW	*Verify reading or writing*

TIMING

Addressing	Encoding	Example	88/86	286	386
reg,reg	01100011 11,reg,r/m	arpl ax,bx	-	10	20
memory,reg	01100011 mod,reg,r/m displacement	arpl select,ax	-	11	21

EXAMPLE This example shows how the operating system can use the ARPL instruction to detect an attempt at using a privileged segment. The privilege level of the calling function is in the CS that is on the stack. The called routine can access this data as [sp+2] for 16-bit segments on the 80286 and [sp+4] for 32-bit segments on the 80386.

```
; This function checks the privilege level of the calling
; routine against the privilege level of the selector passed
; in the BX register.
            .386p
            .CODE
CopyMem     PROC FAR
            arpl [sp+4], bx      ; Test the selector
            jz   error           ; Jump if CS needed to be adjusted
            .

            .
error:
            ret
CopyMem     ENDP
```

Clear Carry Flag   88/86   286   386
                                                        ▲   ▲   ▲

CLC

PURPOSE Set the carry flag equal to 0.

FLAGS The carry is cleared. All other flags are unchanged.

COMMENTS Normally, the carry is set or cleared as the result of arithmetic or logical operations. This instruction and the STC and CMC instructions let you control the carry flag directly. Many functions do this to tell the calling function if there was an error.

SEE ALSO CMC   *Complement the carry*
              STC   *Set the carry*

CLC

Addressing	Encoding	Example	88/86	286	386
implied	11111000	clc	2	2	2

TIMING

EXAMPLE This function calls MS-DOS to get the version number. If it is not version 3.x, then it returns with the carry set.

```
          .CODE
CheckVer  PROC
          mov  ah, 30h          ; MS-DOS get version function
          int  21h
          cmp  al, 3            ; Check major version number
          clc                  ; Clear the carry
          je   Done            ; If version 3 exit
          stc                  ; Set the carry (not ver. 3)
Done:
          ret
CheckVer  ENDP
```

Clear the Direction Flag   88/86   286   386
                                                      ▲   ▲   ▲

CLD

PURPOSE   To clear the direction flag.

SYNTAX   CLD   *Clear the direction flag.*

FLAGS   The direction flag is cleared.

COMMENTS When the direction flag is set, string operations will decrement the index registers. When it is clear, the index registers are incremented.

SEE ALSO STOS/MOVS/SCANS/INS/OUTS/CMPS   *String instructions*

              STD   *Set the direction flag*

TIMING	Addressing	Encoding	Example	88/86	286	386
	CLD	11111100	cld	2	2	2

EXAMPLE See the CMPS and SCANS instructions in Chapter 5.

Clear Interrupt Flag	88/86 ▲	286 ▲	386 ▲

CLI

PURPOSE To clear the interrupt flag.

SYNTAX CLI

COMMENTS Clearing the interrupt flag prevents the processor from being interrupted by any but the non-maskable, and by software interrupts. This is important when you are modifying the interrupt vector table or doing a time-critical routine. You should use the STI instruction to turn interrupts back on as soon as possible in order to prevent losing important interrupts.

SEE ALSO STI

TIMING	Addressing	Encoding	Example	88/86	286	386
	implied	11111010	cli	2	3	3

EXAMPLE An interrupt will push values onto the stack. If you need to change the stack, you do not want an interrupt to come along while you are in the middle of the operation. For most of the 80x86 processors, if you change the stack segment register, the processor will disable interrupts for the next instruction. Unfortunately, there are some versions of the 8088 for which this feature does not work. If your program may run on one of these processors, the safest procedure is to turn off interrupts yourself while changing the stack.

```
ASTACK    SEGMENT    STACK      'STACK'
          DB    1024 dup(?)              ; Allocate space for the stack
```

```
TOP        LABEL      BYTE              ; A pointer to the top of the
                                        ; stack
ASTACK     ENDS
           .CODE
NewStack   PROC
           cli                          ; Disable interrupts
           mov   ss, SEG ASTACK         ; Change the stack segment
           mov   sp, OFFSET TOP         ; and the stack pointer
           sti                          ; Turn interrupts back on
           ret
NewStack   ENDP
```

Clear Task Switched Flag   88/86   286   386
                                                            ▲   ▲

CLTS

PURPOSE To clear the task switched flag in the Machine Status Word (MSW).

SYNTAX clts

FLAGS The flags are unaffected by this instruction. The task switched flag is in a different register.

COMMENTS This instruction can only be used in privileged mode. It is the first half of a test to see if a task switch occurred between two points in the code. This tells the routine if any shared resources might have been changed.

SEE ALSO LMSW, SMSW   *Load and store the machine status word*

TIMING

Addressing	Encoding	Example	88/86	286	386
implied	00001111 00000110	clts	-	2	5

EXAMPLE The CLTS and LMSW instructions can be used to see if another had a chance to change parameters. The following code fragment shows how this is done.

```
; Clear the task flag, then set up parameters. Before the
; parameters ar used, check to see if the task switched flag
; is set.

              .386p
              .CODE
Funct         PROC FAR
setup:

              clts              ; Clear the task switched flag
              .                 ; Do set up
              .
              .
useit:
              lmsw ax           ; Get the MSW in ax
              test ax,8         ; Check the task switched flag
              jnz  setup        ; if set do the setup again
                                ; otherwise go ahead
              .
              .
Funct         ENDP
```

Complement the Carry   88/86   286   386
                                                ▲   ▲   ▲

CMC

PURPOSE To toggle the carry flag.

SYNTAX CMC

FLAGS The state of the carry flag is reversed.

COMMENTS The CMC instruction is useful when using the carry flag as an error indicator. Often the carry will be in the opposite state that is required for the error flag, so you can use the CMC instruction to fix it.

SEE ALSO CLC   *Clear the carry*
              STC   *Set the carry*

CMC

TIMING	Addressing	Encoding	Example	88/86	286	386
	implied	11110101	cmc	2	2	2

EXAMPLE   This example deletes all of the files named `fileXX.dat`, where XX is the numbers from 00 to 99. It also counts the number of files deleted.

```
            .MODEL    SMALL
            .DATA
DeleteCnt DW    0
FileName  DB    "FILE00.DAT", 0

            .CODE
DelFiles  PROC
            mov   dx, OFFSET FileName
            mov   ah, 41h
            int   21h                   ; Delete the file
            cmc                         ; Complement the carry
            adc   DeleteCnt, 0          ; Add the carry to the
                                        ; count
            mov   bx, OFFSET FileName + 5
            inc   BYTE PTR [bx]         ; Go to the next number
            cmp   BYTE PTR [bx], '9'    ; Compare to 9
            jle   DelFiles             ; Do the next file
            mov   BYTE PTR [bx], '0'    ; Back to zero
            dec   bx                  ; Go to the tens digit
            inc   BYTE PTR [bx]       ; Increment tens digit
            cmp   BYTE PTR [bx], '9'  ; Are we done?
            jle   DelFiles           ; Do the next file
            ret
DelFiles  ENDP
```

		88/86	286	386
Escape		▲	▲	▲

ESC

PURPOSE   To put an instruction and data on the data bus for use by the co-processor.

SYNTAX   ESC instruction, memory_or_register

FLAGS The flags are unaffected by this instruction.

COMMENTS Co-processors are used to do tasks to assist the main processors. The most common co-processors are the floating point processors. They are the 8087, 80287, and 80387. Although the ESC command can be used to communicate with these chips, it is not usually used because the assembler provides instruction mnemonics for the floating point instructions.

SEE ALSO WAIT, LOCK   *Other instructions used with Co-processors*

TIMING

Addressing	Encoding	Example	88/86	286	386
register	11011TTT 11,LLL,r/m	esc 5,al	2	9-20	various
memory	11011TTT mod,LLL,r/m	esc 29,[bx]	12/8+EA	9-20	various

Note:

TTT is the high six bits of the instruction; LLL is the low six bits.

EXAMPLE Using a floating point co-processor can speed up a program considerably. Any program that uses floating point math can make use of this co-processor. The performance gain comes not only from the fact that you don't need a lengthy subroutine, but also that the co-processor can be doing the calculation while the main processor continues with other operations.

The following code fragment uses the ESC instruction to add two floating point numbers.

```
            .MODEL      SMALL
            .DATA
real1       DQ    1.232
real2       DQ    4.5

            .CODE
; Add the floating point numbers at real1 and real2.
AddFloat    PROC
            wait                    ; Make sure the co-processor is
                                    ; ready
            esc    28h,real1        ; Send FLD instruction
            wait                    ; Let it finish the load
            esc    20h,real2        ; Send FADD
            wait                    ; Let it finish the add
            esc    2Ah,real1        ; Send FST
```

ESC

```
            ret
AddFloat    E
NDP
```

Halt   88/86   286   386
                                                    ▲   ▲   ▲

HLT

PURPOSE To halt the processor until an interrupt occurs.

SYNTAX hlt

FLAGS The flags are unaffected by this instruction.

COMMENTS This instruction is not used by many PC programs. There is usually something to do, even if only to check an I/O port periodically. Also, there are so many interrupts that the computer rarely stays halted for long.

In protected mode, the HLT instruction is a privileged instruction. It cannot be used in applications programs.

SEE ALSO WAIT   *Wait for the co-processor*

TIMING

Addressing	Encoding	Example	88/86	286	386
implied	11110100	hlt	2	2	5

EXAMPLE You could use HLT to stop the processor, while waiting for a key press. Since pressing a key generates an interrupt, processing would continue when the key is pressed. Not all keys are used when they are pressed (for example, the shift keys). Also, other devices are generating interrupts. So this routine tests for an actual key press after each interrupt.

```
; Halt while waiting for a key press

        .CODE
KeyIn   PROC FAR
        mov  ax, 40h      ; BIOS data area
        mov  es, ax
```

```
TestKey:
        mov   ax, es:[1ch]    ; Keyboard buffer tail
        cmp   es:[1ah], ax    ; Compare to buffer head
        jne   GotOne          ; If not equal there is a key
        hlt                   ; Halt while waiting
        jmp   TestKey         ; See if it was a key
GotOne:
        mov   bx, es:[1ah]    ; Get head in bx
        mov   ax, es:[bx]     ; Get key
        inc   bx              ; Add one to head
        cmp   bx, 34h         ; At the end ?
        jne   Skip
        mov   bx, 1eh         ; The start of the buffer
Skip:
        mov   es:[1ah], bx    ; Save the new head
        ret
KeyIn   ENDP
```

Load AH from the Flags Byte   88/86   286   386
                                               ▲   ▲   ▲

LAHF

PURPOSE   To read the low byte of the flags word into the AH register.

SYNTAX   LAHF

FLAGS   The flags are unaffected by this instruction.

COMMENTS   The flags that can be saved with this are: the sign flag, the zero flag, the auxiliary carry, the parity, and the carry flag.

SEE ALSO   SAHF   *Store the AH register to the flags*
               PUSHF, POPF   *Push and pop the flags*

TIMING

Addressing	Encoding	Example	88/86	286	386
implied	10011111	LAHF	4	2	2

LAHF

EXAMPLE   This routine reads the flags and store them at `OldFlags`.

```
              .MODEL    SMALL
              .DATA
OldFlags   DB   ?

              .CODE
Function   PROC
           lahf                    ; Read the flags into AH
           mov  OldFlags, ah       ; Save at OldFlags
           .                       ; Do code that may change the flags
           .
           .
           mov  ah, OldFlags       ; Get the flags back
           sahf
           ret
Function   ENDP
```

Load Access Rights   88/86   286   386
                                                                  ▲   ▲

LAR

PURPOSE   To find the access rights of a selector in protected mode.

SYNTAX   `LAR  register, selector`   *Selector is a register or memory location containing a selector. The register receives the access right flags.*

FLAGS   The zero flag is set if the selector is valid and visible at the current privilege level. All other flags are unaffected.

COMMENTS   This instruction can be used to find out several things about a selector. The following data is returned:

Granularity bit,

Default size bit,

Intel Corporation reserved bit,

User defined bit,

Present bit,

Descriptor Privilege Level,

System bit,

Descriptor Type Field, and

Accessed bit.

SEE ALSO VERR, VERW   *Verify read or write status*

TIMING

Addressing	Encoding	Example	88/86	286	386
reg,reg	00001111	lar ax,bx	-	14	15
	00000010	mod,reg,r/m			
reg,mem	00001111	lar ax,selector	-	16	16
	00000010	mod,reg,r/m displacement			

EXAMPLE   This routine checks the default size for data in the selector in the BX register.

```
lar  ax,bx       ; Get the access rights
test ax,200h     ; Test the size bit
jz   s16bit      ; if not set do 16-bit operations
 .               ; otherwise do 32-bit operations
 .
 .
s16bit:
```

Load Descriptor Table	88/86	286	386
		▲	▲

LGDT/LIDT/LLDT

PURPOSE   To load a descriptor table register.

SYNTAX   LGDT memory   *Load 6 bytes from memory into the Global Descriptor Table register.*

LIDT memory   *Load 6 bytes from memory into the Interrupt Descriptor Table register.*

LLDT register   *Load a 2-byte selector from a register to the Local Descriptor Table register.*

LGDT/LIDT/LLDT

LLDT memory   ***Load a 2-byte selector from memory to the Local Descriptor Table register.***

FLAGS The flags are unaffected by this instruction.

COMMENTS Descriptor tables are the foundation on which the protected mode memory mapped is based. These instructions are used by the operating system to update these tables.

SEE ALSO SGDT, SIDT, SLDT   ***Store descriptor tables in memory***

TIMING

Addressing	Encoding	Example	88/86	286	386
LGDT memory	00001111	lgdt desctab	-	11	11
	00000001	mod,010,r/m displacement			
LIDT memory	00001111	lidt intdesc	-	12	11
	00000001	mod,011,r/m displacement			
LLDT reg	00001111	lldt ax	-	17	20
	00000000	mod,010,r/m			
LLDT memory	00001111	lldt selector	-	19	24
	00000000	mod,010,r/m displacement			

EXAMPLE This routine sets the global descriptor table register to a table with one descriptor in it:

```
              .MODEL    SMALL
              .386P
              .DATA
Descript    STRUC                        ; Format of a descriptor
entry
      SegLimitLow    DW    0             ; Segment limit bits 0-15
      SegBaseLow     DW    0             ; Base address 0-15
      SegBaseMid     DB    0             ; Base address 16-23
      Access         DB    0             ; Access bits
      MiscBits       DB    0             ; Misc bits and limit
                                         ; 16-19
      SegBaseHi      DB    0             ; Base address bits 24-31
Descript    ENDS

; This descriptor covers the first megabyte of memory
GDTble    Descript   < 0FFFFh, 0, 0, 10010010b, 00001111b, 0 >
```

```
GDTLimit   DW    7                      ; Size of Descriptor
                                        ; table - 1
GDTBase    DD    ?

           .CODE
SetGDTR    PROC
           mov   ax, SEG DGROUP
           mov   bl, ah
           shl   ax, 4                  ; AX times 16
           shr   bl, 4                  ; and the high byte
           xor   bh, bh
           add   ax, OFFSET GDTble      ; Add in the location of
           adc   bx, 0                  ; the table
           mov   WORD PTR GDTBase, ax   ; Save the absolute
           mov   WORD PTR GDTBase+2, bx ; location of the table
           lgdt  GDTBase                ; Load the GDTR
           ret
SetGDTR    ENDP
```

Load Machine Status Word   88/86   286   386
                                                          ▲   ▲

LMSW

PURPOSE   To load a value from memory into the Machine Status Word.

SYNTAX   `LMSW reg/mem`   *Get the MSW from a register or memory location.*

FLAGS   The flags are unaffected by this instruction.

COMMENTS The Machine Status Word is a set of flags used in protected or real mode. The bits in the word are:

Protection enable,

Math chip present,

Emulate co-processor,

Task switched, and

Extension type.

SEE ALSO   `SMSW`   *Save machine status word*

LMSW

TIMING

Addressing	Encoding	Example	88/86	286	386
register	00001111	LMSW ax	-	3	10
	00000001	mod,110,r/m			
memory	00001111	LMSW flags	-	6	10
	00000001	mod,110,r/m displacement			

EXAMPLE The low bit in the MSW is the protected mode enable bit. This routine sets the bit to enter protected mode.

```
        .
        .
        .
   smsw ax              ; Get the MSW in AX
   or   ax, 1           ; Set the PE bit
   lmsw                 ; Set the new MSW
        .
        .
        .
```

Lock the Bus	88/86	286	386
	▲	▲	▲

LOCK

PURPOSE To lock out other processors while the next instruction is executing.

SYNTAX LOCK   instruction_to_lock

FLAGS The flags are unaffected by this instruction.

COMMENTS The LOCK prefix is usually used with instructions that read and write a memory location. If a co-processor writes to the memory location at the same time, the data found will not be what is expected.

SEE ALSO ESC   *To send instructions to the co-processor*
             WAIT   *Wait for the co-processor to finish*

LOCK

TIMING

Addressing	Encoding	Example	88/86	286	386
implied	11110000	lock inc numb	2	0	0

EXAMPLE The lock prefix can be used in a multi-processor environment when accessing shared memory. In this example, two processors use the byte at `EventCnt` to keep track of the number of times an event occurs.

```
; Count events lock the bus when changing the counter

        .CODE
CountEm  PROC FAR
         call isevent       ; See if there was an event
         test ax,eventflg    ; Test for an event
         jz   noevent        ; if no event don't count it
         lock inc  EventCnt  ; if there was an event count it
noevent:
         ret
CoutEm   ENDP
```

Load Segment Limit			88/86	286	386
				▲	▲

LSL

PURPOSE To load the length of a segment into a register.

SYNTAX lsl reg, selector   *Selector is a register or memory location that contains a selector. The segment limit is loaded into reg.*

FLAGS The zero flag is set if the selector is valid and visible at the current privilege level. The other flags are unaffected by this instruction.

COMMENTS This instruction is available in protected mode only. Due to the variable segment lengths available in protected mode, this instruction is provided to give the length of the segment.

SEE ALSO LAR   *Load access rights*

LSL

TIMING

Addressing	Encoding	Example	88/86	286	386
reg,reg	00001111	lsl ax,bx	-	14	20
	00000011	mod,reg,r/m			
reg,memory	00001111	lsl ax,selector	-	16	21
	00000011	mod,reg,r/m displacement			

EXAMPLE   This sets all of the bytes on the segment indicated by bx to zero.

```
        cld              ; Set the direction to forward
        movzx ebx, bx    ; Make the selector a 32-bit value for
                         ; the lsl instruction
        lsl   ecx, ebx
        mov   eax, 0     ; Get set to clear memory
        shr   ecx, 2     ; Divide the count by 4 bytes at a time
        mov   es, bx     ; Set up the segment
        xor   edi, edi   ; and offset
cloop:
        stosd            ; Store 4 bytes of zeros
        dec   ecx        ; Count down
        jnz   cloop
```

Load Task Register   88/86   286   386
                                                               ▲   ▲

LTR

PURPOSE   To load the contents of the task register.

SYNTAX   LTR   reg/memory   *Reg/memory contains the value to load*
                                         into the task register.

FLAGS   The flags are unaffected.

COMMENTS   The task register is used in protected mode to keep track of the task that should be switched out. All of the required bookkeeping is handled by the processor. The LTR instruction tells the processor about the first task.

SEE ALSO   STR

TIMING

Addressing	Encoding	Example	88/86	286	386
LTR reg	00001111	ltr ax	-	17	23
	00000000	mod,001,r/m			
LTR memory	00001111	ltr task	-	19	27
	00000000	mod,001,r/m displacement			

EXAMPLE The three functions in this example prepare for multi-tasking, create a new task, and switch from one task to another. It assumes that the GDT contains a descriptor of a segment that can be used to hold task information. The selector for this segment is 28h; the next 64 descriptors must be reserved for possible tasks.

```
        .MODEL   SMALL
        PUBLIC   InitTask               ; Create the first task
        PUBLIC   NewTask                ; Create a new task
        PUBLIC   SwtchTask              ; Switch tasks
        .386

TaskSeg SEGMENT  WORD PRIVATE USE16 'TASK'
TaskCnt DW  0                           ; The number of tasks
CurTask DW  0                           ; The task being executed
TskData DB  104 * 64 dup(?)             ; Room for task state data
TskJmp  DD  0
TaskSeg ENDS

        .CODE
; Initialize the task switching mechanism
InitTask PROC
        mov   ax, 8h                    ; Selector for the GDT
        mov   ds, ax                    ; put it in DS
        mov   si, 30h                   ; Offset for the first task
                                        ; descriptor
        mov   ax, 103h                  ; TSS segment limit
        mov   WORD PTR [si], ax
        mov   ax, SEG TaskSeg           ; Segment for the TSS
        mov   bl, ah
        shl   ax, 4
        shr   bl, 4
        add   ax, OFFSET TskData        ; Add in the location of the
        adc   bl, 0                     ; TSS
        mov   WORD PTR [si+2], ax
        mov   BYTE PTR [si+4], bl
```

```
                mov   WORD PTR [si+5], 011101001b  ; Set flags
                mov   BYTE PTR [si+7], 0
                mov   ax, 28h                    ; Selector for TaskSeg
                mov   ds, ax
                inc   TaskCnt
                mov   ax, 30h                    ; The first TSS descriptor
                ltr   ax                         ; Load the task register
                ret
InitTask   ENDP

; Put a new task in the table
; AX = Offset of function for the task
; BX = Selector of the function
; CX = Selector for the stack
NewTask    PROC
                push  ax                         ; Save the parameters
                push  bx
                push  cx
                mov   ax, 8h                     ; Selector for the GDT
                mov   ds, ax            .        ; put it in DS
                mov   si, TaskCnt                ; The number of the next task
                shl   si, 3                      ; times size of descriptor
                add   si, 30h                    ; Offset of first TSS
                                                 ; descriptor
                mov   ax, 103h                   ; TSS segment limit
                mov   WORD PTR [si], ax
                mov   ax, SEG TaskSeg            ; Segment for the TSS
                mov   bl, ah
                shl   ax, 4
                shr   bl, 4
                mov   cx, TaskCnt
                shl   cx, 3
                add   cx, OFFSET TskData
                adc   bl, 0
                add   ax, cx                     ; Add in the location of the
                adc   bl, 0                      ; TSS
                mov   WORD PTR [si+2], ax
                mov   BYTE PTR [si+4], bl
                mov   WORD PTR [si+5], 011101001b ; Set flags
                mov   BYTE PTR [si+7], 0
                mov   ax, 28h                    ; Selector for TaskSeg
                mov   ds, ax
                mov   si, TaskCnt                ; Get the task number
                shl   si, 3
                mov   ax, si
```

```
        shl   si, 2
        add   ax, si
        shl   si, 1
        add   si, ax              ; AX times 104
        add   si, OFFSET TskData
        sub   eax, eax            ; Clear the high word
        pop   cx                  ; Restore parameters
        pop   bx
        pop   ax
        mov   [si+20h], eax       ; Save EIP
        mov   DWORD PTR [si+38h], 1024  ; Save ESP
        mov   [si+4Ch], ax
        mov   [si+50h], cx
        inc   TaskCnt
        ret
NewTask ENDP

; Switch to the next task. This can be jumped to by an ISR for
; the clock interrupt or by a task that is ready to let another
; task have a chance
SwtchTask PROC
        mov   ax, 28h             ; Selector for TaskSeg
        mov   ds, ax
        mov   ax, CurTask
        inc   ax                  ; Go to the next task
        cmp   ax, TskCnt          ; See if we are past the end
        jb    Sk1                 ; of the list
        mov   ax, 1               ; If so, go back to task 1
Sk1:
        mov   CurTask, ax
        shl   ax, 3               ; Times 8
        add   ax, 30h             ; The first selector
        mov   WORD PTR TskJmp+2, ax
        jmp   DWORD [TskJmp]      ; Do the next task
SwtchTask ENDP
```

Store AH into the Flag Register   88/86   286   386
                                       ▲   ▲   ▲

SAHF

PURPOSE To set the flag register according to the byte in AH.

SAHF

SEE ALSO   LAHF   *Load the flags*

SYNTAX   SAHF

FLAGS   The sign, zero, auxiliary carry, parity, and carry flags are set from the AX register.

COMMENTS   The bits of the AX register are interpreted as follows:

```
LSB                                                              MSB

Carry, rsvd, Parity, rsvd, Auxiliary carry, rsvd, Zero, Sign
```

SEE ALSO   LAHF   *Load the flags*

TIMING

Addressing	Encoding	Example	88/86	286	386
implied	10011110	sahf	4	2	3

EXAMPLE   See the example for LAHF.

Store Descriptor Table	88/86	286	386
		▲	▲

SGDT/SIDT/SLDT

PURPOSE   To save the current descriptor table value in memory.

SYNTAX   SGDT memory   *Store the global descriptor table in memory.*

SIDT memory   *Store the interrupt descriptor table.*

SLDT register   *Store the selector for the local descriptor table in a register.*

SLDT memory   *Store the selector for the local descriptor table in memory.*

FLAGS   The flags are unaffected by this instruction.

COMMENTS   This instruction can be used in privileged mode to find out where the descriptor tables are. This is used by the operating system to modify the descriptors.

SEE ALSO LGDT, LIDT, LLDT *Load descriptor table registers*

TIMING

Addressing	Encoding	Example	88/86	286	386
SGDT	00001111	sgdt global	-	11	9
	00000001	mod,000,r/m displacement			
SIDT	00001111	sidt global	-	12	9
	00000001	mod,001,r/m displacement			
SLDT reg	00001111	sldt ax	-	2	2
	00000000	mod,000,r/m			
SLDT mem	00001111	sldt selector	-	3	2
	00000000	mod,000,r/m displacement			

EXAMPLE The operating system can use the SGDT instruction to locate the global descriptor table. There must be an entry in the GDT that covers all memory, and the data segment must indicate it.

```
; Get the offset and length of the global descriptor table.
; Put the address in EDI and the size in CX.

GDTable    PWORD      1 dup(?)              ; Make space for the GDT
EditGDT:
           sgdt GDTable                     ; Get the data
           mov  cx, WORD PTR GDTable        ; Extract the size
           mov  edi, DWORD PTR GDTable
           .
           .
           .
```

		88/86	286	386
Store the Machine Status Word			▲	▲

SMSW

PURPOSE To store the Machine Status Word in memory or a register.

SYNTAX SMSW register

SMSW memory

SMSW

FLAGS   The flags are unaffected by this instruction.

COMMENTS   The Machine Status Word is a collection of miscellaneous flags used by the 80286 and 80386. In order to inspect the flags, you must copy the Machine Status Word to memory or a register.

SEE ALSO   LMSW   *Load the MSW*

TIMING

Addressing	Encoding	Example	88/86	286	386
register	00001111	smsw ax	-	2	10
	00000001	mod,100,r/m			
memory	00001111	smsw machsw	-	3	3
	00000001	mod,100,r/m displacement			

EXAMPLE   See the example for LMSW.

Set the Direction Flag	88/86	286	386
	▲	▲	▲

STD

PURPOSE   To set the direction flag.

SYNTAX   STD   *Set the direction flag.*

FLAGS   The direction flag is set.

COMMENTS   When the direction flag is set, string operations will decrement the index registers. When it is clear, the index registers are incremented.

SEE ALSO   STOS/MOVS/SCANS/INS/OUTS/CMPS   *String instructions*

TIMING

Addressing	Encoding	Example	88/86	286	386
implied	11111101	std	2	2	2

EXAMPLE   See the CMPS and SCANS instructions in Chapter 5.

Set Interrupt Flag   88/86   286   386
                                                         ▲   ▲   ▲

STI

PURPOSE   To set the interrupts-enabled flag.

SYNTAX   STI   *Set the interrupts-enabled flag.*

FLAGS   The interrupt flag is set.

COMMENTS This instruction ensures that the processor will be able to respond to interrupts. If your program ever clears the interrupt flag, you should be sure to use
this instruction to re-enable interrupts. This will make sure that devices such
as the keyboard— which relies on interrupts—will work.

TIMING

Addressing	Encoding	Example	88/86	286	386
implied	11111011	sti	2	2	2

EXAMPLE   See the example for CLI.

Store Task Register   88/86   286   386
                                                                 ▲   ▲

STR

PURPOSE   To store the contents of the task register.

SYNTAX   STR   reg/memory   *Reg/memory contains the value to store.*

FLAGS   The flags are unaffected.

STR

COMMENTS The contents of the task register are useless to any program. It indicates a selector that cannot be read or written. This instruction is only provided as a complement to the LTR instruction.

SEE ALSO LTR   *Load task register*

TIMING

Addressing		Encoding	Example		88/86	286	386
STR	reg	00001111	str	bx	-	2	2
		00000000	mod,001,r/m				
STR	memory	00001111	str	task	-	3	2
		00000000	mod,001,r/m displacement				

EXAMPLE See the example for LTR.

Verify Read or Write Status	88/86	286	386
		▲	▲

VERR/VERW

PURPOSE To see if a protected mode segment is readable or writeable.

SYNTAX VERR selector   *Selector is a 16-bit register or memory value.*

VERW selector   *Selector is a 16-bit register or memory value.*

FLAGS The zero flag is set for VERR if the segment is readable. It is set for VERW if the segment is writeable. All other flags are unaffected by these instructions.

COMMENTS Protected mode segments have attributes that control how the segment will be used. Attempting to use a segment in the wrong way will cause a protection fault that will crash the program. These instructions can be used to avoid getting the fault by knowing what is allowed in a segment.

SEE ALSO LAR   *Load access rights*
LSL   *Load segment limit*

TIMING	Addressing	Encoding	Example	88/86	286	386
	VERR reg	00001111	verr ax	-	14	10
		00000000	11,100,r/m			
	VERR memory	00001111	verr selector	-	16	11
		00000000	mod,100,r/m			
	VERW reg	00001111	verw ax	-	14	15
		00000000	11,101,r/m			
	VERW memory	00001111	verw selector	-	16	16
		00000000	mod,101,r/m			

EXAMPLE Before writing to a segment, the program must be sure that it is writable. If the program is not sure, it should check

```
; Verify that a segment is writable before using it
    .386p              ; Allow protected mode instructions
    verw selector      ; Check write flag
    jnz  nowrite       ; if no 0 flag, it is unwriteable
    mov  es, selector  ; Put selector in a segment
                       ; register
    .                  ; Do further processing
    .
    .
nowrite:
```

Wait		88/86	826	836
		▲	▲	▲

WAIT

PURPOSE To wait for a hardware signal from a co-processor.

SYNTAX WAIT

FLAGS The flags are unaffected.

WAIT

COMMENTS   The 8087 and some other co-processors can only accept one instruction at a time. To make sure that the co-processor is ready for another instruction, you should use the WAIT instruction.

SEE ALSO   ESC

TIMING

Addressing	Encoding	Example	88/86	286	386
implied	10011011	wait	4	3	6

EXAMPLE   See the example for ESC.

III

TASM Directives and Operators

- ► Segment Declaration,

- ► Data Definition and Storage Allocation,

- ► Macros, Procedures, and Tools for Modular Programs,

- ► Code Generation, Error Handling, and Listings,

Chapter *8* *Segment Declaration*

Segments is one of the most complex aspects of programming the 80x86 processors. Even simple programs must at least insure that the segment registers have been initialized properly. For larger programs you must constantly be aware of the state of the segment registers, in order to get the program to do what you expect it to do. The traditional segment declaration directives do little to make segments clear. The first part of this chapter shows you what is going on with these directives, and gives examples of how you can use them in your programs.

In addition to the traditional segment directives, Turbo Assembler has several simplified segment directives. These directives take much of the pain out of programming segments by defining several segments for you. For many small programs you need only include a few lines at the beginning of the program to get a simple, sensible segment setup. The second part of this chapter describes the simplified segment directives and how to use them.

Understanding Segments

Different segment registers are used for different purposes. The CS register handles code references, the DS register is for data references, and the SS register is used with the stack. The ES register is an extra data segment and can be used when overriding the default data segment.

Older processors used *paging* to address larger memory spaces. Paging systems could choose pages from a large memory device. The CPU could only see 65536 bytes at a time, and the paging system kept the rest in reserve until a program asked for it. Since segmentation was replacing paging, it would also need to provide a way to address more memory.

The 8088 uses 20 bits to address one megabyte of memory. To use segmentation, the segment registers need to be 20 bits wide. Since the other registers are 16 bits wide, it would be difficult to load these odd-sized registers. The chosen solution was to load 16-bit values into the upper 16 bits of the segment register, and always set the lower four bits to zero. This meant that segments can now only start at addresses divisible by 16. Not perfect, but much better than a paging system.

To reference a physical memory address, the processor multiplies the value in the segment register by 16 and adds the offset. Figure 8-1 shows this addition.

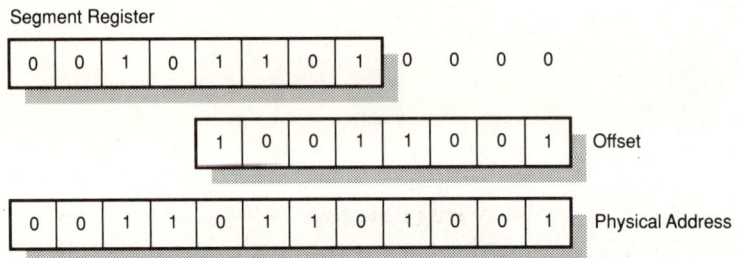

Segment Register

| 0 | 0 | 1 | 0 | 1 | 1 | 0 | 1 | 0 | 0 | 0 | 0 |

| | | | | 1 | 0 | 0 | 1 | 1 | 0 | 0 | 1 | Offset |

| 0 | 0 | 1 | 1 | 0 | 1 | 1 | 0 | 1 | 0 | 0 | 1 | Physical Address |

Figure 8-1. *Adding a segment register to an offset.*

Although a new segment starts every 16 bytes, each one is 65536 bytes long. This means that there can be more than one segment offset pair that addresses a given memory location. When the assembler calculates the offset for a label, it uses the segment in which the label is defined. You need to be sure that the value in the segment register you are using is the same as the assembler used in making the offset. For example, if you have two data segments in your program, you will need to switch the value in the data segment from one segment to the other, depending on what data item you are accessing.

Declaring Segments

Every segment in a Turbo Assembler program has a name. Any reference to the segment uses the name to identify the segment. Declaring a segment is the process of assigning a name to a given segment. When you declare a segment, you tell the assembler the name of the segment, how to place the segment in memory, and how to combine it with other segments.

Turbo Assembler provides directives to declare segments in two different ways. The first requires you to provide all of the information about the segment. The second lets you use several predefined segment types. The long version is presented first in the following paragraphs, so that you can learn the terminology of segment declarations. With this information you will be able to understand what the short forms of declarations do.

The SEGMENT Directive

Every segment has a SEGMENT directive that describes the segment. There are two forms of the SEGMENT directive, depending on whether you are using MASM or IDEAL mode. The formats are:

MASM mode:

```
name SEGMENT [alignment] [combine type] [segment size] ['class']
      .          ; code or data
      .
      .

[name] ENDS
```

IDEAL mode:

```
SEGMENT name [alignment] [combine type] [segment size] ['class']
      .          ; code or data
      .
      .

ENDS [name]
```

In both cases the segment begins with a SEGMENT directive that gives the name of the segment. The rest of these arguments are described later. Next comes the code or data that will be used in this segment. Finally, the ENDS directive marks the end of the segment.

There can be more than one segment declaration with the same name in a source file. In this case, the same named segments will be combined in the object file. Segments can also be *nested*, even though the 80x86 processor cannot use nested segments. The assembler will rearrange the segments so that they are not nested in the object file. This procedure is not recommended, as it can be quite confusing.

ALIGNING SEGMENTS

Because the lower four bits of the absolute memory address cannot be set by programs, each segment must begin on a 16-byte boundary, even though Turbo assembler lets you align a segment on other than 16-byte boundaries. When the program is assembled, the segment register is set to the nearest 16-byte boundary that is less than the actual segment location. Each of the offsets in the segment get adjusted to compensate for the difference in alignment. Figure 8-2 shows how this works.

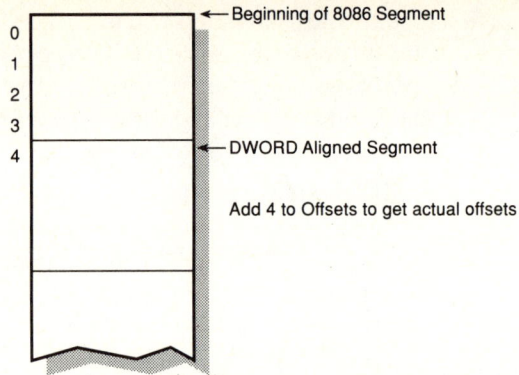

Figure 8-2. *Aligning segments on other than 16-byte boundaries.*

Table 8-1 shows the possible align types.

Table 8-1. *Align Types for Segments*

Type	Description
BYTE	Align to the next byte boundary
WORD	Align to the next word boundary
DWORD	Align to the next double word boundary
PARA	Align to the next paragraph (16-byte) boundary (Default)
PAGE	Align to the next page (256-byte) boundary

COMBINING SEGMENTS

The next field in the SEGMENT directive is the combine type. Segments with the same name are combined into a single segment. Combine types enable you to tell the assembler how to combine the pieces.

The first combine type does not really combine anything at all. As a matter of fact, it does not even create a segment in the object file. The *AT* combine type is used to make labels for specific areas in memory. The absolute segment address follows the AT to tell the assembler where the labels are. A segment with the AT combine type may not contain any code or data, only labels. The AT combine type can be used to reference the memory locations used by BIOS to store information about the system. The data segment will look something like this:

```
          IDEAL                       ; Use IDEAL mode format
SEGMENT BiosData BYTE AT 40h          ; Declare a byte aligned seg at
                                      ; 0040:0000
          org   10h                   ; Offset 0010h
LABEL     EquipLst   WORD             ; Use this label to access the
                                      ; equipment list word
          org   13h
LABEL     MemSize    WORD             ; How many K of memory are
                                      ; available
          org   17h
LABEL     KeyStatus  WORD             ; What shift keys are pressed
          org   1ah
LABEL     KeyHead    WORD             ; Head of the keyboard buffer
          org   1ch
LABEL     KeyTail    WORD             ; Tail of the keyboard buffer
          org   1eh
LABEL     KeyBuffer  WORD             ; First byte of the key buffer

ENDS BiosData
```

Once this segment is set up, the program can access the memory locations by referring to the labels in the segment. This code fragment reads the memory size from the BIOS data area:

```
          .
          .
          .
mov       ax, SEG BiosData    ; Get the segment
mov       ds, ax              ; Put it in the data
                              ; segment register
ASSUME    ds:BiosData         ; Tell the assembler DS
                              ; changed
mov       ax, MemSize         ; Read the memory size
          .
          .
          .
```

The next combine type is *COMMON*. Segments that have the same name and use the COMMON combine type all start at the same address. The length of the combined segment is the length of the longest segment used. Figure 8-3 shows several segments with the COMMON combine type.

There are times when different modules in a program need to look at a memory segment in two different ways. For example, one module may look at the block of memory as a group of records to be read and written to-and-from the disk. Another module may see the same data as a set of structures, while a third module sees it as a single block of bytes. With the COMMON combine type each of the modules can have it its own way. This is similar to unions in high level languages such as C.

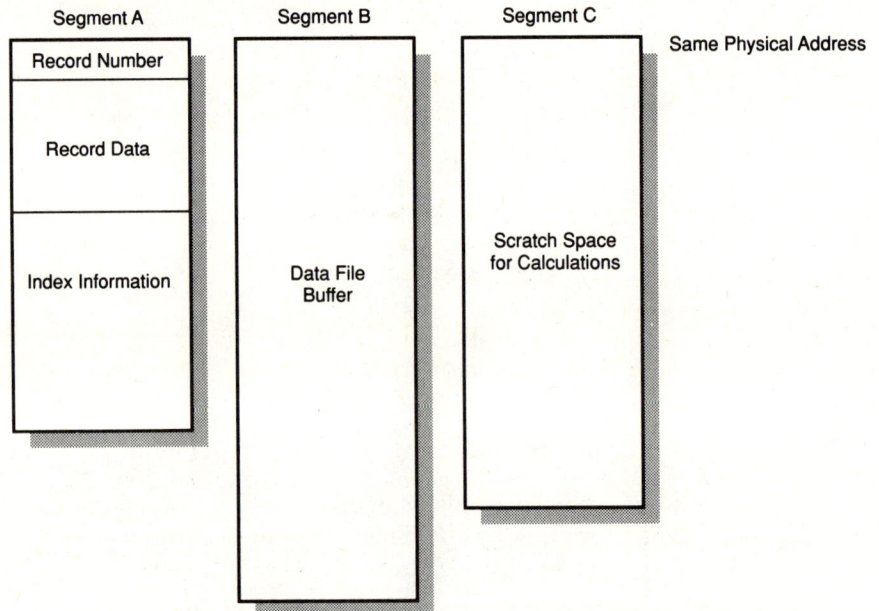

Figure 8-3.   *Segments with the COMMON combine type.*

Another use for segments with the COMMON combine type is to reuse memory. Some applications are too large for the available memory. In many cases the data used by one module does not need to be available while another module is running. For example, a sort routine may use a data segment to hold data about the progress of the sort. Once the records are sorted, the memory is no longer required and could be used by another routine for some other purpose. Since the two routines will likely use different variables, they will want to use different segment layouts. The COMMON combine type will allow both layouts to exist in the same block of memory.

The most common way to combine segments is to put them one after the other. The length of the combined segments is the total length of all of the segments used. Figure 8-4 shows this arrangement of segments. To combine segments in this way, you can use the *MEMORY* or *PUBLIC* combine types. These types are synonymous and will make all of the segments with the same name into one contiguous segment.

The *STACK* combine type is similar to the PUBLIC and MEMORY combine types. It will concatenate all of the segments with the same name, just as the PUBLIC and MEMORY types do. The difference is in how this will affect the initial state of the registers when the program is loaded. The SS register is set to the beginning of all the STACK segments. The SP register is set to the length of all the STACK segments. If you have at least one segment with a STACK combine type in your program, you do not have to write code to initialize the stack because the program loader will do it for you.

There are times when you don't want to combine segments at all. Several source files can use the same segment name for different segments that are used for similar purposes. To avoid having the assembler combine these segments you can use the *PRIVATE* combine type. If you do not use a combine type in a segment declaration, the PRIVATE type is used by default.

SEGMENT SIZE

One of the features of the 80386 is the ability to address up to four gigabytes of memory and use 32-bit registers. Another feature is that the 80386 remains compatible with the older processors. To provide both of these features in an efficient manner, the 80386 uses two different types of segments. The first type uses 16-bit data and address offsets just like the other 80x86 processors. The other uses 32-bit data and address offsets.

You can tell the assembler what kind of segment to use in the segment declaration. First you must tell the assembler to use 80386 protected mode instructions (use the .386P, P386, or P386N directives). Then you can follow the combine type with either the USE16 or USE32 segment types. Turbo assembler uses 16-bit segments by default.

This example shows how to define a 32-bit code segment:

```
            .386P                     ; Enable 80386 instructions
_CODE       SEGMENT   PUBLIC    USE32 'CODE'
_main       PROC      FAR
            mov       eax,4           ; Use a 32-bit register without an
                                      ; override
            add       bx, ax          ; This instruction requires an
                                      ; override
            ret
_CODE       ENDS
```

SEGMENT CLASSES

The last part of the SEGMENT directive defines the class of the segment. The class helps to determine how the segments will be arranged in memory. The linker will place all of the segments with the same class next to each other in the executable file. Note that the segments are not combined in any way; they are merely placed next to each other. The class field must be enclosed in double (") or single (') quotes. The class name may be anything: 'CODE' and 'DATA' and 'STACK' are commonly used.

Combining and Grouping Segments

The SEGMENT directive gives some control over the way that segments are arranged in memory. Setting the combine type puts segments with the same name in a single segment. The class field gives some control over the order of segments in the executable file. Turbo Assembler provides directives that give you more control over the grouping and ordering of segments.

GROUPS   The GROUP directive tells the assembler to put several segments together. This directive can be used in MASM or IDEAL mode. The formats are shown as follows.

MASM mode:

```
GroupName GROUP      SegmentName [, SegmentName]...
```

IDEAL mode:

```
GROUP     GroupName SegmentName [, SegmentName]...
```

The group name can be used in a program, just as a segment name can be. The segments specified will be concatenated into the group. Because a group can be used as a segment, the total size of all of the segments must be less than 65536 bytes.

Groups can be used to combine different kinds of segments. For example, COM files require that the code, data, and stack segments all be in the same 64K range. You can use the GROUP directive to set this up:

```
            ORG       100h
Program     GROUP     Cseg, Dseg
Cseg        SEGMENT   PARA PUBLIC 'CODE'
            ASSUME    cs:Program, ds:Program
Start       PROC FAR
            mov   dx, OFFSET Msg
            mov   ah, 9h
            int   21h
            mov   ah, 4ch
            int   21h
Start       ENDP
Cseg        ENDS

Dseg        SEGMENT    PARA PUBLIC 'DATA'
Msg         DB    "Hello, world", 0Dh, 0Ah, '$'
dseg        ENDS

END         start
```

SEGMENT SORTING

Normally, Turbo Assembler will place segments into the executable file in the order of the segments in the source. One way to change the order is to use classes in the segment directive. Another way is to use the .ALPHA, .SEQ, or DOSSEG directives. The .ALPHA directive will sort the segments into alphabetical order. To make sure that the segments will be in the order in which they are found in the source, you can use the .SEQ directive.

The DOSSEG directive uses the order found in high level languages. This directive should only be used in the source module that contains the starting address for the program. Using the DOSSEG directive puts all the segments with the class 'CODE' at the beginning of the program. Next come all the segments that do not have the class 'CODE' and are not in the group DGROUP. After that are the segments in DGROUP that have the class 'BEGDATA.' The next DGROUP segments are any that do not have the class 'BEGDATA' or 'BSS' or 'STACK.' The penultimate segments have the 'BSS' class. The final segments all have the 'STACK' class. Figure 8-4 shows the order of segments in memory.

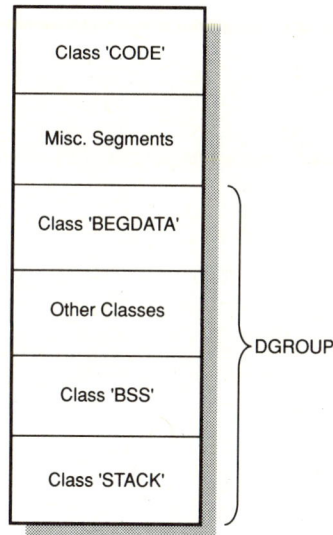

Figure 8-4. DOSSEG segment order.

Handling Segment Addresses and Offsets

When MS-DOS loads a program, it sets the segment registers. The CS register is set to the segment that contains the start address. The DS and ES registers point to the Program Segment Prefix (PSP). If there was a stack segment declared, the SS register points to this segment; otherwise, it points to one of the internal MS-DOS stacks.

The way MS-DOS sets the segments is not always the way your program wants them set. For example, most programs will use a different data segment; and before you can use this data segment, you must put the address of the data segment into the DS register. This example shows how to use the SEG operator to get the segment address of a segment:

```
mov   ax, SEG dseg      ; Get the segment address of dseg
mov   ds, ax            ; Put it in DS
```

Note that you cannot move immediate data into a segment register. The AX register is used to get the address and put it in the DS register. Another technique is to assemble commonly used segment addresses into the code segment and use direct addressing to put the value into the DS register.

```
mov   ds, cs:ptrdseg ; Read segment address from memory
      .
      .
      .
ptrdseg   DW   SEG dseg        ; Assemble the address in the code
                               ; segment
```

A memory location can be accessed from several different segments. If the segment register changes by one, and the offset changes by 16 in the opposite direction, then the segment:offset pair still points to the same location. By using the GROUP directive, you can make a value accessible from several different segments. The assembler calculates offsets by subtracting the absolute address indicated by the segment register from the absolute address of the label. Because the segment registers can be changed at run time, the assembler has no way of knowing what value is in a given segment register. You must use the ASSUME directive to tell the assembler what it needs to know. The format of the assume directive is:

```
ASSUME    sreg:segment [, sreg:segment]...
```

The assembler assumes that the segment register sreg indicates the segment specified in the last ASSUME statement.

Simplified Segment Declarations

As you use segments in your programs, you will find that you use the same segments over and over. You may always put data in a segment named dseg, and code in one named cseg. These segments will generally have the same combine types and groupings.

In high level languages, the programmer usually does not have control of the segments' names, but the compiler uses the same kinds of segments when it creates an object module.

If you know what the segments are that are used by the high level language, you can make your commonly used segments have the same names as the high level language. This will make it possible to link assembly language routines with routines in the high level language.

More and more languages are following the segment naming conventions of Microsoft languages. Turbo Assembler lets you use these naming conventions by providing simplified segment declarations for several commonly used segments. Using these declarations will not only make it possible to link in high level language routines, but they will also simplify the process of creating and using segments.

MEMORY MODELS

One factor that can change the way you arrange the segments is the amount of memory that the program will use. If the entire program will fit in 64K, then it makes sense to group everything into one segment. If the program is larger than 64K, the first step is to divide the data and the code into separate segments. If the code is greater than 64K, you will need more code segments; and if the data is greater than 64K, you will need more data segments.

The different ways of grouping segments are referred to as memory models. The .MODEL and MODEL (IDEAL mode) directive tells the assembler what memory model to use. The format of this directive is:

```
.MODEL    memory_model [,language]
```

Table 8-2 shows the possible memory models and their effect on the simplified segments. The optional *language* field tells the assembler what language standard to use (C or Pascal) when creating stack frames. (See Chapter 10 for more information on the language field.)

In addition to affecting the way segments are declared, the .MODEL directive sets the @CodeSize and @DataSize variables. These variables can be tested to determine what to do for different memory models. For example, in the MEDIUM, LARGE, and HUGE models, functions addresses require four bytes of storage, while in the other models they only need two bytes of storage. The @CodeSize variable can be used to reserve the correct amount of memory, as shown by the following:

```
IF    @CodeSize EQ 0      ; Assemble the following statement if
                          ; @CodeSize equals 0
FUNCPTR   DW    THEFUNC   ; Two bytes for near functions
ELSE                      ; Assemble the following statement if
                          ; @CodeSize does not equal 0
FUNCPTR   DD    THEFUNC   ; Four bytes for far functions
ENDIF
```

Table 8-2. *Memory Models*

Usual segment for the segment registers

Model	CS	DS	ES	SS
TINY	DGROUP	DGROUP	DGROUP	DGROUP
SMALL	_TEXT	DGROUP	DGROUP	DGROUP
MEDIUM	Name_TEXT	DGROUP	DGROUP	DGROUP
COMPACT	_TEXT	DGROUP	FAR_DATA	DGROUP
LARGE	Name_TEXT	DGROUP	FAR_DATA	DGROUP
HUGE	Name_TEXT	DGROUP	FAR_DATA	DGROUP

The Name portion of Name_TEXT is different for each source file in the program.

The FAR_DATA segment is PRIVATE, giving each source file its own FAR_DATA segment.

A SEGMENT FOR CODE

Turbo Assembler puts everything that follows the `.CODE` or `CODESEG` directives into a code segment.

The two directives are identical. In the MEDIUM, LARGE, or HUGE models, the name of the segment created is the name of the file followed by _TEXT. In all other models, the name is _TEXT. You do not need to know the name of the code segment in order to get the address of the code segment (_TEXT). Turbo Assembler provides the `@CODE` alias for the address. The `@CODE` alias can be used in expressions such as:

```
mov      ax, @CODE ; Put address of code segment in AX
mov      ds, ax    ; Then into DS
ASSUME   ds:@Code  ; Inform the assembler of the
                   ; change
```

Note that the `ASSUME` directive in the previous example is only needed because of the non-standard value in DS. When using the simplified segment directives, you do not need `ASSUME` directives if the segment registers contain the values shown in Table 8-2.

SEGMENTS FOR DATA

Data is divided into several segments, depending on how the data will be used. Four of the segments are put into a group called *DGROUP*. These segments are: _DATA for initialized data, _BSS for uninitialized data, CONST for constant data, and STACK for the stack. In the TINY model, the code segment is also included in the DGROUP. Turbo Assembler will make sure that the SS register points to this segment, but you must set the DS register before accessing any data. The `@Data` alias can be used to get the address of DGROUP.

```
mov  ax, @Data ; Get the address in AX
mov  ds, ax    ; then put it in DS
```

Two more segments, called *FAR_DATA* and *FAR_BSS*, are used in the LARGE data models. FAR_DATA is for initialized data, and FAR_BSS is for uninitialized data. These segments have a PRIVATE combine type, so each source file can have its own FAR DATA segments.

There are simplified segment declarations for each of the data segments. The `.DATA` or `DATASEG` directives are used to start the _DATA segment. Uninitialized data goes into the _BSS segment indicated by the `.DATA?` directive. Data that will not change, such as prompts and addresses used for indirect addressing, goes into the CONST segment. The `.CONST` or `CONST` directives mark the beginning of the CONST segment.

The last two segments used in the simplified segment declarations are the initialized and uninitialized FAR DATA segments. To start the initialized FAR DATA segment, use the `.FARDATA` or `FARDATA` directives. For the uninitialized FAR DATA segment, use `.FARDATA?`.

A SEGMENT FOR THE STACK All MS-DOS programs must provide a stack. The `.STACK` or `STACK` directive is all that is required to set up a stack for an assembly language program. It will set aside memory for the stack segment and insure that the SS and SP registers point to the stack when the program is run.

The `STACK` or `.STACK` directive by itself will create a stack segment 1024 bytes long. You can change the stack size by following the directive with the stack size to use. You should make sure that there is enough space in the stack to hold the return addresses and local variables for all the stack frames that can be active at once. Deeply nested function calls, such as those with recursive routines, can use up the reserved stack space and overwrite other areas of the program.

Telling the Program Where to Begin

Every MS-DOS program must indicate what function to execute first. Most high level languages handle this automatically, by either putting the first function in a specific location or giving it a specific name. Assembly language programs can start at any function, regardless of the name or location of the function. Oddly enough, you tell the program where to start by using the `END` directive. Every source file must have an `END` directive as its last line. The source file containing the first function to run should have that function's name following its `END` directive on the same line.

Summary

The standard segment directives enable you to create segments with any name, combine type, class, and so on. The SEGMENT directive tells the assembler just what kind of segment to use. The GROUP directive lets you put several segments together to make a single segment. The ASSUME directive lets you tell the assembler what segments you are using at any given point in the program.

With all of this control comes a certain amount of confusion. For most programs, several predefined segments are all that is required. Turbo Assembler has directives that set up the predefined segments used by high level languages. This not only makes declaring and using segments easier, but it also helps when combining object files from a high level language with object files from assembly language.

.ALPHA, DOSSEG, .SEQ

PURPOSE To determine the order of segments in the object file.

SYNTAX
.ALPHA	*Put segments in alphabetical order.*
DOSSEG	*Put segments in the order used by many high level languages.*
.SEQ	*Put the segments in the order they appear in the source.*

COMMENTS Normally, Turbo Assembler writes the segments in the same order as they are found in the source file. The /A option on the command line changes the default to alphabetical order. These directives will override any command line options and force the segments to be in the order specified.

   The DOSSEG directive is a little unusual in that it only needs to be in the source file that contains the starting address of the program. .ALPHA and .SEQ can be in each of the sources affected.

SEE ALSO .MODEL *This can affect the ordering of DOSSEG programs*

EXAMPLE This example will put the segments in alphabetical order even though they appear in random order.

```
        .ALPHA
Wseg SEGMENT    PUBLIC    'WCLASS'
        .
        .
        .

Wseg ENDS
Zseg SEGMENT    PUBLIC    'ZCLASS'
        .
        .
        .

Zseg ENDS
Aseg SEGMENT    PUBLIC    'ACLASS'
        .
        .
        .

Aseg ENDS
```

ASSUME

PURPOSE To tell Turbo Assembler what segment to associate with what segment register.

SYNTAX
```
ASSUME    segreg:segment [,register:segment]...
ASSUME    segreg:NOTHING
ASSUME    NOTHING
```

COMMENTS Because segments can overlap, a single location can be referred to by several `segment:offset` pairs. Turbo assembler needs to know what segment is being used to calculate the offset to use. The `ASSUME` directive lets you tell the assembler what to expect.

The `ASSUME` directive does not load the segment registers. You will need to make sure that the value in the register is the same as the value used in the `ASSUME` directive.

SEE ALSO SEGMENT

EXAMPLE This example shows a typical `ASSUME` directive for a program with separate code, data, and stack segments. DOS will set up the CS and SS registers when the program is loaded, but the DS register must be set by the program. Note that since the value of the ES register is unknown, it must be set to assume nothing.

```
ASSUME    CS:CODE, DS:DATA, SS:STACK, ES:NOTHING

mov  ax, SEG DATA   ; Put the segment address of DATA in AX
mov  ds, ax         ; then copy it to DS
     .
     .
     .
```

@Code

PURPOSE Alias for the address of the code segment (_TEXT).

SYNTAX @Code   *The address of the code segment.*

@Code

COMMENTS The @Code variable is a shorthand way to get the address of the _TEXT segment. It is equivalent to using the SEG operator with the name of the segment like this:

```
mov  ax, SEG _TEXT
```

SEE ALSO
```
.CODE, CODESEG
.DATA, DATASEG
.FARDATA, FARDATA
.FARDATA?, UFARDATA
```

EXAMPLE The most common use of the segment aliases is to get the address of the data segment into the DS register. The following code fragment can be used to do this.

```
.MODEL    SMALL
.DATA
                              ; Data declarations
.
.
.CODE
mov  ax, @Data               ; Get the address in AX
mov  ds, ax                  ; then move it to DS
.                            ; The rest of the program
.
.
.STACK    512
END
```

@CodeSize

PURPOSE To tell what memory model is in use.

SYNTAX `@CodeSize`   *Tells if NEAR or FAR procedures are being used.*

COMMENTS Different data models require different sized storage space for pointers and different strategies for using data. This predefined variable lets you write the code so that it behaves correctly in any memory model.

SEE ALSO `.MODEL`

@CodeSize

EXAMPLE A pointer requires four bytes in the large data models and two in the small data models. This code fragment checks the @DataSize variable to determine how much memory should be set aside.

```
            .MODEL SMALL
            .DATA
IF @DataSize EQ 0
DPTR DW    SmplData          ; Two bytes for small models
ELSE
DPTR DD    SmplData          ; Four bytes in large models
ENDIF
IF @CodeSize EQ 0
DPTR DW    SmplFunc          ; Two bytes for small models
ELSE
DPTR DD    SmplFunc          ; Four bytes in large models

ENDIF
```

.CODE, CODESEG

PURPOSE To start the code segment in programs that use the simplified segment declarations.

SYNTAX .CODE [name]

COMMENTS You must specify the memory model with the .MODEL directive before using .CODE or any of the simplified segment declarations. The name operand is used in the medium, large, and huge models to allow multiple code segments in a single source file. If the name is omitted, the name of the file will be used in these models.

SEE ALSO ASSUME, SEGMENT, ENDS
.DATA, .STACK, .FARDATA
.MODEL

EXAMPLE This example shows how the simplified segment declarations can be utilized to make using segments easier.

```
            .MODEL    SMALL      ; Make this small model
            .CONST               ; Make a segment for constant data
Mesg        DB   "Hello, World", 0dh, 0ah, '$'
            .DATA
```

```
LastDos    DB    0

           .CODE                    ; Make a segment for code
Start:
           mov   ax, @Data          ; Get the address of the data
                                     ; segment
           mov   ds, ax             ; And put it in DS
           mov   dx, OFFSET Mesg
           mov   ah, 9              ; MS-DOS print command
           mov   LastDos, ah        ; Save the command
           int   21h               ; Call MS-DOS
           mov   ah, 4ch            ; MS-DOS exit program command
           mov   LastDos, ah        ; Save the command
           int   21h               ; Call MS-DOS

           .STACK    512            ; Make a 512-byte stack

FND   Start
```

@CurSeg

PURPOSE Alias for the address of the current segment.
See @Code.

@Data

PURPOSE Alias for the address of the data segment (_DATA).
See @Code.

.DATA, .DATA?, DATASEG

PURPOSE To mark the beginning of the segments used for initialized (.DATA, DATASEG)
and uninitialized (.DATA?) data.

.DATA, .DATA?, DATASEG

SYNTAX .DATA
DATASEG
.DATA?

COMMENTS High level languages keep initialized and uninitialized data in separate segments. This is not important in MS-DOS, but it is done to be compatible with other operating systems that can make use of the distinction. If you access data via the DGROUP group, you will not need to be concerned with which segment contains the data to be used.

You must use the .MODEL directive to specify the memory model before using this or any other simplified segment declaration.

SEE ALSO .CODE, .CONST, .STACK
.MODEL
UDATASEG

EXAMPLE See the example for .CODE.

@DataSize

PURPOSE To tell what memory model is in use.

SYNTAX @DataSize *Tells if SMALL, LARGE, or HUGE data models are being used.*

COMMENTS Different data models require differently sized storage space for pointers and different strategies for using data. This predefined variable lets you write the code so that it behaves correctly in any memory model.

SEE ALSO .MODEL

EXAMPLE See the example for @CodeSize.

DOSSEG

See ALPHA.

END

PURPOSE To mark the end of the source file and optionally to set the starting point for the program.

SYNTAX `END  [Start_function]`

COMMENTS Every source file must have an `END` statement as the last line of the file. The source file that contains the entry point for the program should set the entry point in the `END` statement. Note that only one source file should have the entry point.

SEE ALSO `ENDS`
`ENDP`

EXAMPLE See the example for `.CODE`.

ENDS

PURPOSE To mark the end of a segment.

SYNTAX `MASM mode:`
`        segname ENDS`

`IDEAL mode:`
`        ENDS segname`

COMMENTS Every segment that is declared with the standard segment declarations must also end with an `ENDS`. Note that this is the same directive used to end structures. (See Chapter 9.)

SEE ALSO `END`
`ENDP`

EXAMPLE See the example for `GROUP`.

@FarData

PURPOSE   Alias for the address of the far data segment (FAR_DATA).
See @Code.

@FarData?

PURPOSE   Alias for the address of the uninitialized far data segment (FAR_DATA?).
See @Code.

.FARDATA, .FARDATA?, FARDATA

PURPOSE   To mark the beginning of far data segments for initialized (.FARDATA, FARDATA) and uninitialized (.FARDATA?) data. An optional name can be used to create more than one segment per source file.

SYNTAX
```
.FARDATA   [name]
FARDATA    [name]
.FARDATA?  [name]
```

COMMENTS   The far data segments are used to implement the large data memory models. Each of the segments has a PRIVATE combine type so that they make separate segments for each source file. This lets each source file define up to 64K of data.

The far data segment is separate from the other data segments. This means that you must load the segment address into a segment register before you can use the data in the segment. To access data in the same source file, you can use the @FarData alias to get the segment address. For data in other source files, you need a different scheme.

The CONST segment is often used to save the addresses of data items in the far data segment. The example shows how to set this up.

SEE ALSO   .CODE, .DATA, .STACK
.MODEL

.FARDATA, .FARDATA?, FARDATA

EXAMPLE   This example shows how to access far data that is defined in another source file.

```
; File: DATAFILE.ASM
; This file defines the data to be used in the code file
      .MODEL LARGE
      PUBLIC MesgStr          ; Make this visible to the other file
      .FARDATA
MesgStr   DB    "This is far data", 0Dh, 0Ah, '$'
END

; File: USEDATA.ASM
; This is the code that uses the data in the file above
         .MODEL LARGE
EXTRN MesgStr:BYTE           ; Indicate that this is in another
file
         .CONST
MSPtr DD MesgStr             ; Put the address of MesgStr here

         .CODE
Start:
         mov   ax, @Data     ; Get the data group in ax
         mov   ds, ax        ; Then copy it to DS
         lds   dx, MSPtr     ; Get the address of MesgStr in
                             ; DS:DX
         mov   ah, 9         ; MS-DOS print string command
         int   21h           ; Call MS-DOS
         mov   ah, 4ch       ; MS-DOS exit command
         int   21h           ; Call MS-DOS

         .STACK 512
END Start
```

Assemble both of these files and then link them with this command:

```
tlink usedata datafile
```

GROUP

PURPOSE   To combine one or more segments into a group that can be used like a single segment later in the program.

SYNTAX   MASM mode:
```
         groupname GROUP seg1 [,seg2]...
```

GROUP

```
IDEAL mode:
      GROUP groupname seg1 [,seg2]...
```

COMMENTS Groups are used to combine several different segments into a single group. This lets you access the data in any of the segments without needing to change the segment register for each segment.

Because a group is treated as a single segment, the total size of the segments in the group cannot exceed 64K.

SEE ALSO SEGMENT
ASSUME

EXAMPLE The simplified segment declarations combine several of the segments into a group called *DGROUP*. This example shows how to set this up with standard segment declarations.

```
_TEXT      SEGMENT    WORD PUBLIC 'CODE'
_TEXT      ENDS
FAR_DATA   SEGMENT    PARA PRIVATE 'FAR_DATA'
FAR_DATA   ENDS
FAR_BSS    SEGMENT    PARA PRIVATE 'FAR_BSS'
FAR_BSS    ENDS
_DATA      SEGMENT    WORD PUBLIC 'DATA'
_DATA      ENDS
CONST      SEGMENT    WORD PUBLIC 'CONST'
CONST      ENDS
_BSS       SEGMENT    WORD PUBLIC 'BSS'
_BSS       ENDS
STACK      SEGMENT    PARA STACK 'STACK'
STACK      ENDS

DGROUP     GROUP      _DATA, CONST, _BSS, STACK
```

.MODEL, MODEL

PURPOSE To set a memory model for use with the simplified segment declarations.

SYNTAX .MODEL memory_model [,language]
.MODEL TPASCAL

COMMENTS　The memory models that can be used are TINY, SMALL, MEDIUM, COMPACT, LARGE, and HUGE. In addition to modifying the segment declarations, the different models set the variables `@CodeSize` and `@DataSize`.

The language field tells the assembler what language conventions to use. The language can be C, Pascal, BASIC, FORTRAN, or Prolog. Each of the languages uses different entry and exit code for functions.

The TPASCAL form will make the assembler use the Turbo Pascal naming conventions.

SEE ALSO　`.CODE, .DATA, .STACK`

EXAMPLE　See the example for `.CODE`.

SEGMENT

PURPOSE　To define a segment.

SYNTAX
```
MASM mode:
      segname    SEGMENT [align] [combine] [use] ['class']
IDEAL mode:
      SEGMENT    segname [align] [combine] [use] ['class']
```

COMMENTS　The *align* type tells the assembler on what type of memory boundary to start the segment. Table 8-3 shows the possible align types.

Table 8-3.　*Align Types for Segments*

Type	Description
BYTE	Align to the next byte boundary
WORD	Align to the next word boundary
DWORD	Align to the next double word boundary
PARA	Align to the next paragraph (16-byte) boundary
PAGE	Align to the next page (256-byte) boundary

The *combine* type tells how this segment is to be combined with other segments having the same name. Table 8-4 shows the possible combine types.

SEGMENT

Table 8-4. *Combine Types for Segments*

Type	Description
AT address	The segment will be at a specific address.
COMMON	Put all segments with the same name at the same address.
MEMORY	Concatenate all segments with the same name.
PUBLIC	Same as MEMORY.
PRIVATE	Do not combine with any other segments.
STACK	Concatenate all segments with the same name and make the SS and SP registers point to the end of the segment when the program is loaded.

The *use* field is used in 80386 protected mode programs. It can be USE16 for segments that use 16-bit offsets or USE32 for segments that use 32-bit offsets.

The final field is the *class* field. The class must be enclosed in quotes. The class is used to control the order of segments in memory. All segments that have the same class will be placed next to each other.

SEE ALSO   ASSUME
ENDS

EXAMPLE   See the example for GROUP.

SEQ

See ALPHA.

.STACK, STACK

PURPOSE   To mark the beginning and specify the size of the stack segment.

SYNTAX   .STACK   [stack_size]

COMMENTS The stack size is the number of bytes to set aside for the stack. Be sure there is enough room for the most deeply nested function calls that are possible in the program. If you do not specify a stack size, the stack will be initialized to 1024 bytes.

The .STACK declaration will make sure that the SS and SP registers point to the end of the stack segment when the program is loaded.

SEE ALSO .CODE, .DATA, .CONST

EXAMPLE See the example for .CODE.

UDATASEG

See DATA?.

UFARDATA

See FARDATA?.

Chapter 9 Data Definition and Storage Allocation

In many programs the data that the program uses is at least as important as the code that manipulates the data. Graphical user interfaces use large amounts of data to store the elements of the display. Databases, word processors, and spreadsheets are all programs for manipulating data. The cornerstone of object-oriented programming is the fact that data controls the program. Turbo Assembler provides many powerful tools for dealing with data.

The data directives used in Turbo Assembler parallel the concepts found in some high level languages like Pascal or C. The idea behind the data directives is to provide a mechanism for the programmer to build complex data types from a small set of predefined data types. This technique lets you build whatever data type your program requires rather than trying to make do with predefined types. Another advantage is that you can see how a complex data type works by examining the definition. With predefined types, much of the information is hidden inside the compiler.

This chapter follows the form set by the data directives. The first part covers the basic data types used by the assembler. This section shows how to define data space and manipulate labels and other symbols. The next section shows the directives for building more complex data structures. Finally, there are some instructions for controlling where the data goes in memory.

Data Definition

Fundamentally, all data is just a series of one or more bytes. It is convenient to think of data at a slightly higher level of abstraction based on how the data is used. The basic data types used in Turbo Assembler are numeric, text, and pointers. These are the building blocks upon which the user-defined data types are built.

The numeric and text data types are, as you might expect, numbers and strings. Pointers are special numbers that point to a location in memory. Each of these types have variations. For example, numbers can use different numbers of bytes (typically 1, 2, or 4); strings can end with a zero or a dollar sign ($) or start with the length; and pointers can be near or far.

Data Definition Directives

To define data for your program, you must tell the assembler to set aside some memory for the data. Table 9-1 shows the directives that you can use to define differently sized data items.

Table 9-1. *Types of Data Definitions*

Directive	Description
DB	Defines byte sized pieces
DD	Defines double words (four bytes)
DF	Defines a pointer to data in a 80386 32-bit segment
	This directive uses an optional type field to indicate the type of data pointed to. The format is: [label] DF [type PTR] data [,data]...
DP	Same as DF
DQ	Defines a quadruple word (8 bytes)
DT	Defines a ten byte data area. The numbers used to initialize this data type are either packed binary coded decimal or high precision real numbers as used by the math co-processor
DW	Defines a word (2 bytes)

The data that you allocate with these directives cannot be used by your program unless the program knows where the data is. The way to get the location of the data is to attach a label to it. This example shows how to define data items with labels:

```
OneByte    DB    1          ; Make a 1 byte variable named
                            ; OneByte and put a 1 in it
MyWord     DW    ?          ; Make a word sized variable
```

```
                              ; named MyWord and do not put
                              ; a value in it
MWPoint    DD    MyWord       ; Make a double word sized
                              ; variable named MWPoint and
                              ; put the address of MyWord in
                              ; it
```

Turbo Assembler keeps track of the name, location, and size of each label that you define in this manner. When you use the name of the variable in the program (as in the definition of `MWPoint`), the assembler puts the location of the variable in the object file.

There are several variations that can be used with each of the data definition directives. For example, they can be used to define more than one item at a time:

```
WordLst   DW   10, 15, 21, 15     ; WordLst points to the first
                                  ; word in this list
```

The *DUP* operator lets you allocate arrays without typing a number for each element:

```
BigList   DB   128 DUP( 0 )       ; Make an array of 128 zeros
```

A question mark (?) in a data definition tells the assembler to allocate the memory, but does not put a value in it:

```
UnInit    DW   107 DUP( ? )       ; Make an uninitialized array
                                  ; of 107 words
```

There are other times when using a label to stand for a number is useful. For example, in a program that draws boxes on the screen, you will use the dimensions of the screen in several places. When you reassemble the program to run on a screen with different dimensions, you will need to find each of the locations and change them. It would be much easier if you could define labels that represent the dimensions of the screen. The `EQU` directive lets you do this. The label to the left of the directive represents the value on the right of the directive.

Another way to make a symbol that replaces data is very similar to the `EQU` directive. It uses the equals sign (=) to set a symbol equal to a numeric value. It cannot be used with strings, but it does have the feature of being able to redefine an already existing symbol. For example:

```
FieldSize = 20              ; All references to FieldSize will use 20
          .
          .
          .
```

```
FieldSize = 32            ; Now all references will use 32
          .
          .
          .

FieldSize = FieldSize + 10
```

The following example uses the EQU and data definition directives to draw a box on the screen:

```
; File BOX.ASM
; Program to draw a box around the screen
          .MODEL    SMALL
ScrnBase  EQU   0B800h              ; The address of screen memory
                                    ; (use 0B000h for monochrome)
TopLine   EQU   0                   ; Top line for the box
BotLine   EQU   24                  ; Bottom line for the box
LeftCol   EQU   0                   ; Left edge of the box
RightCol  EQU   79                  ; Right edge of the box
ScrnWid   EQU   80                  ; Width of the whole screen

UpLeft    EQU   0C9h                ; Character for upper left corner
UpRight   EQU   0BBh                ; Character for upper right corner
LowLeft   EQU   0C8h                ; Character for lower left corner
LowRight  EQU   0BCh                ; Character for lower right corner
Horz      EQU   0CDh                ; Horizontal character
Vert      EQU   0BAh                ; Vertical character

Attrib    EQU   07h                 ; Attribute to use

CallDOS   EQU   <int    21h>        ; Make a symbol for calling DOS
          .DATA
LeftAt    DW    0                   ; The begining of each line
          .CODE
Start:
          mov   ax, ScrnBase        ; Get the screen segment and
          mov   es, ax              ; put it in ES
          mov   ax, TopLine         ; Get the top line
          mov   bl, ScrnWid         ; Multiply by the width of the
          mul   bl                  ; screen
          add   ax, LeftCol         ; Add in left column
          shl   ax, 1               ; Times two for attrib byte
          mov   LeftAt, ax          ; and save location
          mov   di, ax              ; Put location in DI
          mov   al, UpLeft          ; Get the upper left char
          mov   ah, Attrib          ; Get attribute
          stosw                     ; Draw the corner
```

```
              mov   al, Horz          ; Get the horizontal bar
              mov   cx, RightCol      ; Get the right column
              sub   cx, LeftCol       ; Minus left equal width
              sub   cx, 2             ; Minus two for the edges
              rep   stosw             ; Draw the top line
              mov   al, UpRight       ; Get upper right corner and
              stosw                   ; draw it
              mov   cx, BotLine       ; Get the last line
              sub   cx, TopLine       ; Minus top equals height
              sub   cx, 2             ; Minus two for the top and bottom
SideLp:
              push  cx                ; Save it
              mov   di, ScrnWid       ; Get the width
              shl   di, 1             ; Times two
              add   di, LeftAt        ; Move to the next line
              mov   LeftAt, di        ; Save the new line
              mov   al, Vert          ; Get the vertical bar
              mov   ah, Attrib        ; Get attribute
              stosw                   ; Draw the corner
              mov   al, ' '           ; Put spaces inside
              mov   cx, RightCol      ; Get the right column
              sub   cx, LeftCol       ; Minus left equal width
              sub   cx, 2             ; Minus two for the edges
              rep   stosw             ; Draw the top line
              mov   al, Vert          ; Get vertical bar and
              stosw                   ; draw it
              pop   cx                ; Get line counter
              loop  SideLp            ; Do the next line

              mov   di, ScrnWid       ; Get the width
              shl   di, 1             ; Times two
              add   di, LeftAt        ; Move to the next line
              mov   al, LowLeft       ; Get the lower left char
              mov   ah, Attrib        ; Get attribute
              stosw                   ; Draw the corner
              mov   al, Horz          ; Get the horizontal bar
              mov   cx, RightCol      ; Get the right column
              sub   cx, LeftCol       ; Minus left equal width
              sub   cx, 2             ; Minus two for the edges
              rep   stosw             ; Draw the top line
              mov   al, LowRight      ; Get lower right corner and
              stosw                   ; draw it
              mov   ah, 4Ch           ; MS-DOS exit function
              CallDOS
              .STACK    512
END
```

To modify this routine to work on a 43-line EGA screen, all that is required is to change the label `BotLine` to 42. This is much easier than finding all the locations that use this value in the program and then changing them.

DEFINING NUMERIC DATA

In the box example, many of the numbers used are in hexadecimal format. This is indicated by the 'h' following the number. Numbers without the 'h' are assumed to be in decimal format. You can also use binary numbers ('b' suffix) or octal numbers ('o' suffix). The base used is called the *radix*. The default radix is 10, which is why decimal numbers do not require a suffix.

The `.RADIX` or `RADIX` directive can be used to change the default radix. The `.RADIX` directive takes an expression as its argument. The expression must evaluate to 2, 8, 10, or 16 for binary, octal, decimal, and hexadecimal, respectively. Any number that is in the radix specified does not need a character appended to it. Any other number still requires the character, including decimal numbers. Append the character 'd' to decimal numbers.

DEFINING TEXT DATA

A series of bytes used as ASCII values is known as *text*. The most common use of text is to print it on the screen. Text can also be used as labels for data, flags for conditional expressions, or data for files.

There are several ways to delimit text in Turbo Assembler programs. Which format you use depends on what you are going to do with the string. For example, when you store a string in memory, you can delimit it with single (') or double quotes ("). The `DB` directive can be used for storing a string like this:

```
MyStr    DB    "This is a text string",0
```

When the string is used with the `EQU` directive, it should be delimited with angle brackets (<string>). In the box example, the label `CallDOS` is equal to the string `int 21h`. Strings used in `EQU` statements are enclosed in angle brackets:

```
CallDOS   EQU   <int  21h>
```

DEFINING POINTERS

Pointers are a convenient way of dealing with large data items. For example, if a program wants to pass a string to a subroutine, it could copy the string to a memory location known to the subroutine; or it could simply pass a pointer to the string in a register or on the stack. You can do the same thing with pointers to arrays or pointers to structures.

If all of the items that use pointers are in the same segment, then a pointer only needs the offset portion of the address (NEAR pointer). If several segments are being used, then a pointer must include both the offset and the segment portions (FAR pointer).

To define a pointer, use the `DW` directive for NEAR pointers and the `DD` directive for FAR pointers. The data for either directive can be a label, a fixed value, or defined latter in the program. This example demonstrates how to define storage for pointers:

```
            .MODEL    SMALL
            .DATA
Array       DW   16 DUP(?)              ; An undefined array of 16
                                        ; words
Ptr1        DW   Array                  ; Put the offset of Array here
Ptr2        DD   0040001Eh              ; FAR pointer to the keyboard
                                        ; buffer
Ptr3        DW   ?                      ; Uninitialized pointer
            .CODE
Func1       PROC
            mov  ax, SEG DGROUP
            mov  ds, ax
            les  si, Ptr2               ; Load the pointer to the
                                        ; keyboard buffer in ES and SI
            mov  bx, Ptr1               ; Put the pointer to Array
                                        ; in BX
            mov  cx, 16                 ; The size of the array
CpLoop:
            mov  ax, es:[si]            ; Get a word
            mov  [bx], ax               ; Put it in Array
            add  bx, 2                  ; Move the pointers
            add  si, 2
            loop CpLoop
            mov  Ptr3, bx               ; Save the pointer to the end
                                        ; of Array at Ptr3
            ret

Func1       ENDP
```

Data Expressions

Expressions are a collection of one or more data items that are combined with operators such as the *addition* operator. Table 9-2 shows the operators that can be used in expressions. In general, you can use an expression anywhere that you would use a data item. For example, if you have a symbol NumRows that indicates how many rows there are on the screen and TopRow that gives the number of the top row on the screen; you can use the expression TopRow + NumRows - 1 to get the number of the last row on the screen. It is important to remember that these expressions are evaluated when the file is assembled— not while the program is running. Therefore, you cannot use memory values or registers in these expressions.

Table 9-2. *Expression Operators*
Precedence

Operator	MASM	IDEAL	Description
LENGTH	13	12	Return the length of a variable
MASK	13	12	Return a bit mask for a record
SIZE	13	12	Return the size of a data item
WIDTH	13	12	Return the width of a record field
.	12	2	Structure member selector
HIGH	11	11	Return the high part of an expression
LOW	11	11	Return the low part of an expression
+, -	10	10	Positive, negative number
:	9	3	Segment override
OFFSET	8	12	Return the offset of a pointer
PTR	8	1	Sets the size of an expression
SEG	8	12	Return the segment of a pointer
TYPE	8	NA	Return the type of a symbol
*, /	7	9	Multiply, divide
MOD	7	9	Modulus
SHL	7	9	Shift left
SHR	7	9	Shift right
+, -	6	8	Add, subtract
EQ	5	7	Check for equality
GE	5	7	Check for greater than or equal
GT	5	7	Check for greater than
LE	5	7	Check for less than or equal
LT	5	7	Check for less than
NE	5	7	Check for not equal
NOT	4	6	Bitwise invert
AND	3	5	Bitwise logical and
OR	2	4	Bitwise logical or
XOR	2	4	Bitwise logical exclusive or
LARGE	1	1	Convert an expression to 32 bits
SHORT	1	1	Make expression a short pointer
SMALL	1	1	Convert an expression to 16 bits

NUMERIC EXPRESSIONS

Numeric expressions are evaluated from left to right, except when there are parentheses or operators of unequal precedence. (See Table 9-2.) Operators with higher precedence will be executed first. Most of the operators, such as +, -, /, and *, will be familiar if you have used a high level language. Others, such as SHL, SHR, AND, XOR, etc., work the same way as the corresponding assembly language instruction. The comparison operators, such as GT (Greater Than), EQ (EQual to), LT (Less Than), etc., evaluate to 1 if the comparison is true and to 0 if the comparison is false.

TEXT EXPRESSIONS

The text operators are used to manipulate strings. Some of them are not strictly used in string expressions. For example, the SIZESTR directive takes a string argument but returns a numeric result (the length of the string):

```
StrLen    SIZESTR    <ABC>        ; StrLen = 3
```

Other text operators work exclusively with text. They are: CATSTR to concatenate strings, INSTR to find one string in another, and SUBSTR to extract a portion of the string.

Concatenating strings makes one string out of two by placing them one after the other. The resulting string can be used later in the program by referring to the label. The following example combines the strings <cats>, < and >, and <dogs>:

```
tmp       CATSTR     <cats>, < and > ; tmp = <cats and >
result    CATSTR     tmp, <dogs>     ; result = <cats and dogs>
```

SUBSTR extracts a portion of the string. To make SUBSTR work, you need to know the location of the string you want to extract. In some cases the INSTR directive can help. INSTR returns the location of one string in another. The following example uses these two directives to get the portion of a string called *fname* up to the substring <_FUNC>:

```
fname     EQU  <NEXT_FUNC>       ; Assign a string to fname
fpos      INSTR fname, <_FUNC>   ; Get the position of _FUNC
                                 ; (3)
result    SUBSTR fname, 0, fpos  ; Copy from the beginning to
                                 ; fpos (result = <NEXT>)
```

POINTER OPERATORS

Labels are pointers when used in expressions. The value of the label is the address of the data that goes with the label. You can use any of the numeric operators with labels in expressions. For example, to calculate the number of bytes between two labels, you can subtract the starting label from the ending label:

```
String1   DB   "This is a string", 0   ; Define a string
Length1   DW   Length1 - String1       ; Calculate the length of
                                        ; the string
```

When you use a label as an operand to an instruction, the assembler assumes that the instruction wants the data at the label. Many times you actually want to load the address of the data, not the data itself. To do this you can use the OFFSET and SEG directives.

```
          .MODEL    SMALL
          .FAR_DATA
Array     DB   1, 2, 3, 4, 5, 6
          .CODE
          .
          .
          .
          mov  ax, SEG Array
          mov  es, ax
          mov  ax, OFFSET Array
          .
          .
          .
```

Data Structures

Structures combine several data items of various types into a single new data item. Say, for example, your program uses pointers stored in memory. Figure 9-1 shows how the pointer is stored in a double word.

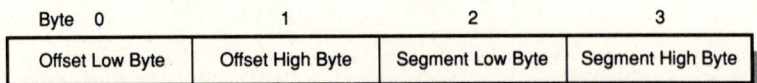

Byte 0	1	2	3
Offset Low Byte	Offset High Byte	Segment Low Byte	Segment High Byte

Figure 9-1. *Storing a pointer in memory.*

Instructions like LES and LDS can read the data defined as a double word. But how do you get just the segment or just the offset? One way is to use the PTR operator and some knowledge of the layout of the pointer to load the segment and offset:

```
mov  ax, WORD PTR ptr1   ; Get the offset
mov  bx, WORD PTR ptr1+2 ; Get the segment
```

The WORD PTR operator tells the assembler to ignore the fact that the ptr1 label defines a double word, and to act as if it defines a word.

This will work fine and many programs are written this way. The problem is that it is difficult to read. Not only that, but what happens when it needs to be converted to 32-bit segments on a 80386? You will need to go through the program and change all of the occurrences of ptr1+2 to ptr1+4. Structures provide a clearer way to code this and a smoother path for future changes.

Declaring and Defining Structures

To solve the problem with pointers, simply create a new type called *POINTER* that contains fields for the segment and the offset. The STRUC directive tells the assembler that the following data definitions are part of a structure. This example shows how to define the POINTER structure:

```
POINTER STRUC
PtrOff    DW    0          ; The offset portion of a pointer
                           ; (default = 0)
PtrSeg    DW    ?          ; The segment portion of a pointer
POINTER ENDS
```

This new data type can be used when declaring data similar to the way DB, or DW is used. Some typical declarations using the POINTER structure are:

```
Ptr1 POINTER    <OFFSET msg1, SEG msg1>   ; Store a pointer to msg1
Ptr2 POINTER    < , 0B800h>               ; Use the default offset
                                          ; and 0B800h for the
                                          ; segment
Ptr3 POINTER    10 dup(<0,0>)             ; Make array of ten
                                          ; pointers initialized to
                                          ; 0:0
```

In Ptr2 the offset field is left blank. This indicates that a default value should be used. The default comes from the definition. In this case the default value is 0.

Accessing Fields within a Structure

Once the structure is defined and the data declared, you need a way to access the data. This is done with the dot (.) operator. On the left side of the dot is the name of the variable, and on the right side is the name of the field. To load the offset of Ptr1 from the previous examples into the AX register and the segment in BX, use this:

```
mov   ax, Ptr1.PtrOff    ; Load the offset portion
mov   bx, Ptr1.PtrSeg    ; Load the segment portion
```

Turbo Assembler keeps all of the labels involved in a symbol table. It stores the address of the structure with the label Ptr1. The labels PtrOff and PtrSeg are set to the offsets of the labels into the segment. In this case PtrOff equals 0 and `PtrSeg` equals 2. The dot operator simply adds the address on the left to the offset on the right.

You can use the dot operator to add the offset to a base or index register, as well as to structure labels. This example shows how you can use this fact to read the fields from structures in an array:

```
            .MODEL      SMALL
            .DATA

POINTER STRUC
PtrOff     DW     0
PtrSeg     DW     0
POINTER STRUC
PtrArray   POINTER   10 dup(<>)      ; Make array of ten pointers

; Fix up the segments in the array. The BX register contains the
; number of pages that each of the segments in PtrArray were
; moved.
            .CODE
FixSegs    PROC
            mov  si, OFFSET PtrArray ; Get the address of the array

; The next line uses the SIZE operator to get the number of bytes
; in PtrArray. Then it uses the TYPE operator to get the number
; of bytes in the POINTER structure. The division give the number
; of elements in the array (in this case 10).
            mov  cx, ( SIZE PtrArray )/( TYPE POINTER )
PtrLoop:
            mov  ax, [si].PtrSeg     ; Get the segment in AX
            .
            .
            .

            add  si, TYPE POINTER    ; Point to the next item
            loop PtrLoop             ; Do the next one
```

UNIONS One problem with the POINTER type used in the previous examples is the verbose code required to initialize a pointer. It would be easier if you did not have to specify both the segment and the offset. The answer is to use unions. A *union* is just like a structure, except that each field in the union overlaps the other fields. This means that the same piece of memory can be referred to by several different symbols. What is important to this problem is that the different symbols can have different types. With unions a pointer definition and declaration looks like this:

```
POINTER UNION
            STRUC                    ; One version of a pointer is as
```

```
                     PtrOff DW Ø       ; an offset and
                     PtrSeg DW Ø       ; a segment
               ENDS
FarPtr     DD     Ø                     ; The other version is a double
                                        ; word

POINTER ENDS

Ptr1 POINTER    <?,Mesg>               ; This initializes the union. Note
                                        ; that you can only initialize one
                                        ; of the fields. The others must
                                        ; remain undefined.
```

The label `Ptr1`, in the example above, can be used as a double word pointer by using the expression `Ptr1.FarPtr`. The same four bytes can be used as two words with `Ptr1.PtrOff` and `Ptr1.PtrSeg`. `Ptr1` is initialized as if it were a structure. The difference is that instead of initializing all the fields, you only initialize one. In this example the first field, which is made up of the structure containing `PtrOff` and `PtrSeg`, is left undefined. The second field (the double word pointer at `FarPtr`) is set to the address in `Mesg`.

USING BIT FIELDS

Some variables never use all eight bits of a byte. The number of disk drives connected to a system rarely exceeds four. The number four can be encoded in three bits, or two if we assume at least one drive. When memory is tight, those other five or six bits can come in handy. Figure 9-2 shows how BIOS squeezes several numbers into a single word, so that it can return the equipment list in one register.

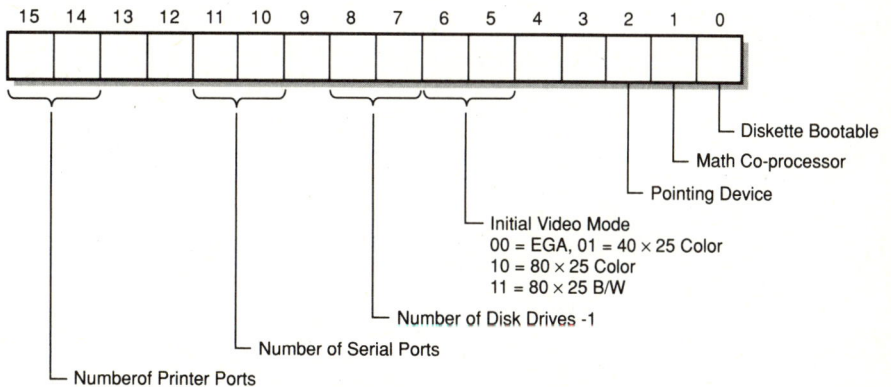

Figure 9-2. *Format of the BIOS equipment list word.*

The RECORD directive makes getting at the individual numbers easy. Records are like little structures that fit in a single byte or word. The RECORD directive is used to define a record. It looks like:

```
Name RECORD field:width[=expresion] [,field:width[=expression]]...
```

The label Name can be used to declare data that is in this record format. Record fields are like the fields of a structure: Instead of being the number of bytes from the beginning of the structure, these fields are the number of bits from the least significant bit. The width tells how many bits to use for this field, and expression is the default to use for the field. Making a variable for the equipment list looks like:

```
          .MODEL    SMALL
          .DATA
ELREC     RECORD    Printers:2, Resrv:2, Coms:3, Resrv2:1,
Drives:2, VidMode:2, Resrv3:1, Point:1, Math:1, Boot:1

EquipLst  ELREC     ?

          .CODE
GetComs   PROC
          mov   ax, 40h            ; BIOS Data segment
          mov   es, ax
          mov   ax, es:[10h]       ; Get the equipment list
          mov   EquipLst, ax       ; Put it in memory
          and   ax, MASK Coms      ; Mask the comport bits
          mov   cl, Coms           ; Get the shift count
          shr   ax, cl             ; Now AX contains the number
                                   ; of comports

          ret
GetComs   ENDP
END
```

This example uses the MASK operator to isolate the bits for the Coms field. In this case it makes a mask equal to 0000111000000000b, which covers the Coms field. Next, this routine shifts the result to the right to make AX equal to the value of the Coms field. The Coms label gives the number of bits to shift.

Positioning Data in Memory

Assembly language gives you more control than high level languages do in deciding what goes where in memory. By default, items within a segment are placed in memory in the order they are found in the source file. Figure 9-3 shows how code and data get placed in memory.

```
                                    Start   |      mov DS       |
                                            |  Low Byte DGROUP  |
    .CODE                                   |  High Byte DGROUP |
Start PROC                                  |    mov AX, DS     |
        mov DS, DGROUP
        mov AX, DS

        .
        .
        .

    .DATA                          DGROUP ANUM  |       10        |
ANUM DW 10, 20                                  |        0        |
Strng DB "This is a string", 0                  |       20        |
                                                |        0        |
                                                |       'T'       |
                                                |       'h'       |
                                                |       'i'       |
                                                |       's'       |
                                                |       ' '       |
                                                |       'i'       |
                                                |       's'       |
                                                |       ' '       |
                                                |       'a'       |
                                                |       ' '       |
                                                |       's'       |
                                                |       't'       |
                                                |       'r'       |
                                                |       'i'       |
                                                |       'n'       |
                                                |       'g'       |
                                                |        0        |
```

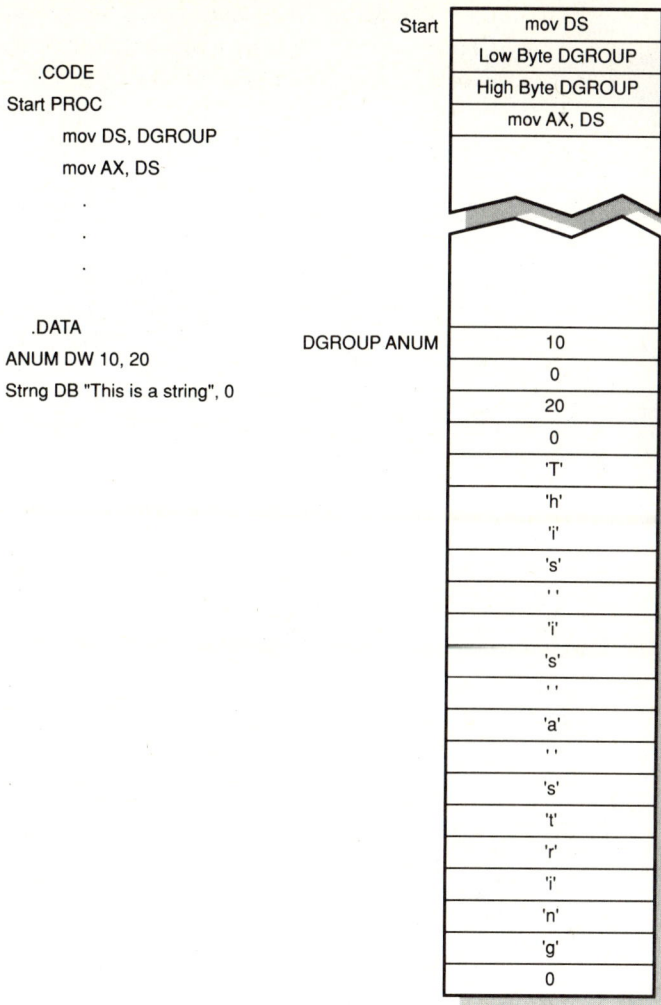

Figure 9-3.   *Placing code and data in memory.*

There are times when this default order is not what is wanted. For example, .COM programs must begin 256 bytes from the beginning of the code segment. Programs that will be placed in ROM may need to be at special locations and use specific alignments in memory. Turbo Assembler provides instructions that give you this kind of control.

Using the Location Counter

As Turbo Assembler assembles each line of an assembly language program, the resulting code or data is placed at the location indicated by a *location counter*. The location counter is then advanced past the item, ready for the next item. A program refers to the location counter by using a dollar sign ($) in an expression.

The location counter can be used to get the size of a piece of code or data. The difference between the end location of a piece of code or data and the beginning is the size of the item. This example shows how to use the location counter to make this calculation.

```
Begin       DB    "A test string"     ; This label is the address of
                                       ; the beginning of the item
Size        DW    $-Begin             ; The difference is the size
```

Setting the Location Counter

The location counter can be moved around the segment by using the ORG directive. The argument for the ORG directive is the new offset for the location counter. The argument can be an absolute address like 100h, or relative to the current location counter like $+14.

One use for the ORG directive is to move code and data for .COM files. Another is to place a label at a variable used by another program such as BIOS or MS-DOS. The following example shows both of these uses.

```
BIOS SEGMENT    AT 40h      ; Make a segment at segment
                            ; 40h
            ORG  17h        ; Make KeyStatus at 40:17
KeyStatus DB    ?
BIOS ENDS

COMSEG      SEGMENT PARA PUBLIC 'ALL'
            ASSUME    CS:COMSEG, DS:COMSEG, ES:NOTHING, SS:COMSEG
            ORG  100h       ; Offset for .COM files
Start:
            jmp  Begin      ; Jump over the data
Vars        DB   0          ; COM files put code and data in the
                            ; same segment
Begin:      .

            .

            .
COMSEG      ENDS
END Start
```

Aligning Data

The 8086 through 80286 processors access memory 16 bits at a time. When the processor reads a word that starts on an odd memory boundary, it must actually do two reads. The first read gets the word that contains the low byte, and the second gets the word that contains the high byte. This means that memory accesses are much faster if they begin on even memory addresses. The 80386 has a similar situation, except that it reads data four bytes at a time, so the fastest memory accesses begin on double word boundaries. Figure 9-4 shows how aligned data is placed in memory.

Addresses	Alignments
0	Byte, Word, DWORD, QWORD
1	Byte
2	Byte, Word
3	Byte
4	Byte, Word, DWORD
5	Byte
6	Byte,Word
7	Byte
8	Byte,Word, DWORD, QWORD
9	Byte
10	Byte, Word
11	Byte
12	Byte, Word, DWORD
13	Byte
14	Byte, Word
15	Byte
16	Byte, Word, DWORD, QWORD, PARAGRAPH
17	Byte
18	Byte, Word
19	Byte

Figure 9-4. *Different memory alignments.*

The EVEN directive moves the location counter to the next even address. If the counter is already at an even address, it will not be moved. The ALIGN directive is similar, but it is more flexible. The argument following the ALIGN directive is the boundary to be used. The boundary must be a power of two (2, 4, 8, 16, etc.). The next example shows the EVEN and ALIGN directives.

```
Var1      DB   0              ; Unknown alignment here
          EVEN
Var2      DW   ?              ; This will be at an even address
          ALIGN 256
Var3      DD   100            ; This will be at a 256-byte boundary
```

Alias Data Names

The LABEL directive defines a label at the current location without requiring any memory to be allocated. It takes a single argument that tells the type of the data at the label. The available types are NEAR, FAR, PROC, BYTE, WORD, DWORD, FWORD, PWORD, QWORD, TBYTE, or a structure name.

One use for the LABEL directive is to create Pascal strings. These are strings that begin with a byte containing the number of bytes in the string. The string itself follows the "length" byte. The problem with making a Pascal string in assembly language is that you need to know the length of the string before the string is defined. To solve this problem, you can create a label that follows the string, and then use the label in an expression that gives the length of the string:

```
          IDEAL                          ; Use ideal mode syntax
          DATASEG
PString   DB   PSEnd-PString, "This is the string"
PSEnd     LABEL BYTE
```

Summary

To write a significant program in assembly language, you may spend as much time working with the data as you do working with the code. Working with data can be made easier by making clear, modifiable symbols to represent the data.

Complex data types are built up from the basic data types. A strong grounding in DB, DW, DD, etc., along with strings and pointers, is the basis for moving on to structures and unions.

Structures can be used to define new data types and to group related data into a single block of data. Records extend the structure concept to fields that are only a few bits wide. Aliasing with unions and the LABEL directives enables you to use type checking in order to guard against errors.

AND

PURPOSE To perform Logical AND operation in expressions.

SYNTAX `expr1 AND expr2` *Do bitwise Logical AND on the results of the two expressions.*

COMMENTS This operator is used in expressions that will be evaluated when the program is assembled. These expressions can be used anywhere that a number would be appropriate.

SEE ALSO `MOD, SHL, SHR` *Other expression operators*
`NOT, OR, XOR` *Other logical operators*

EXAMPLE This example shows how the logical operators are used to manipulate masks.

```
        .MODEL    SMALL
Mask1   EQU 00001000b              ; Mask for a bit flag
Mask2   EQU 01000000b              ; Another flag mask
LowN    EQU 00001111b              ; Mask for the low nibble

        .DATA
FlagByte DB   ?                    ; The byte to test

        .CODE
; This function does not accomplish anything. It just
; fiddles with the flags.
DoFlags PROC
        and  FlagByte, NOT Mask1    ; Clear the flag bit
        test FlagByte, Mask1 OR Mask2 ; See if either flag is
                                      ; set
        or   FlagByte, Mask1 AND LowN ; Set the flag if it is
                                      ; in the low nibble
        and  FlagByte, (Mask1 AND LowN ) XOR LowN
                                    ; The instruction above
                                    ; clears all of the high
                                    ; nibbles and the flag if
                                    ; it is in the low
                                    ; nibble

        ret
DoFlags ENDP
```

ALIGN

ALIGN

PURPOSE　　To move the location counter to the next boundary address.

SYNTAX　　`ALIGN boundary`　　*The boundary must be a power of two (2, 4, 8, etc.).*

COMMENTS　　The different processors in the 80x86 family can get better performance by aligning data to boundaries that match the data bus size of the chip. Some high level languages align data on specific boundaries. The `ALIGN` directive can make the data compatible.

SEE ALSO　　`EVEN`　　*Align to even-numbered addresses*

EXAMPLE

```
        .MODEL   SMALL
        .DATA
data1   DB   1        ; Unaligned data
        ALIGN    4    ; Typical alignment on 80386 for
                      ; performance
data2   DW   ?        ; Aligned data
```

BYTE

PURPOSE　　To make an expression have the type BYTE.

SYNTAX　　`BYTE`　　*Make the expression result a byte.*

COMMENTS　　The type of an expression must be specified when there is no other way to get the type information. This can happen when using indirect addressing, or when using a label that will be defined later in the program.

SEE ALSO　　
`PTR`　　*Used to force expression to have a particular size*
`DWORD`　　*Make the expression result a double word*
`FAR`　　*Make the expression result a far code pointer*
`FWORD`　　*Make the expression result an 80386 32-bit segment far pointer*
`LARGE`　　*Make the expression result an 80386 32-bit segment near pointer*

NEAR   *Make the expression result a near code pointer*
PROC   *Make the expression result a near or far code pointer,*
               depending on the model in use
PWORD   *Same as FWORD*
QWORD   *Make the expression result a quad word*
SHORT   *Make the expression result a short pointer*
SMALL   *Make the expression result a 16-bit offset*
TBYTE   *Make the expression result a 10-byte value*
UNKNOWN   *Make the expression result have an unknown type*
WORD   *Make the expression result a word*

EXAMPLE When you MOV a constant to a memory location, the assembler needs to know if it should move a byte or a word. This example uses the BYTE directive to tell it which to use.

```
        .DATA
Table   DB    1024 dup(?)          ; Some storage space
RecNum  DW    ?                    ; The record number
RecSize DW    ?                    ; The size of a record

        .CODE
        .
        .
        .
        mov   ax, RecNum           ; Get the record number
        mov   bx, RecSize          ; and the record size
        mul   bx                   ; Product is record offset
        mov   bx, OFFSET Table     ; Get the location of the
                                   ; table
        add   bx, ax               ; Add in the offset
        mov   BYTE PTR [bx+10], 0  ; Store a byte at the location
                                   ; in BX
        .
        .
        .
```

CATSTR

PURPOSE To concatenate several strings into a single result.

SYNTAX name CATSTR string1 [,string2]...   *Combine strings and put the result in name.*

CATSTR

COMMENTS
The strings to be concatenated can be literal text enclosed in angle brackets (*<text>*), or a previously defined label that represents a string.

SEE ALSO   SUBSTR, INSTR, SIZESTR   *Other string operators*

EXAMPLE
```
; Define string variables
Str1 EQU <This is a sample string>
Str2 EQU <another string>

; Use them in expressions

pred INSTR Str1, <a sample String> ; Find the last part

Str3 SUBSTR Str1, 0, pred          ; Make a string that excludes
                                   ; the last part
Str4 CATSTR Str3, <another string> ; Makes "This is another
                                   ; string"
```

DB

PURPOSE   To allocate byte sized space for data and optionally assign labels to the location.

SYNTAX   [name]   DB   data [,data]...   *Create byte sized data items.*

COMMENTS   The DB directive can be initialized with numbers that will fit in a single byte. It can also be initialized with a string enclosed in quotation marks.

SEE ALSO   DUP   *Used in initializing data*
DD, DF, DP, DQ, DW

EXAMPLE
```
          .DATA
Msg       DB    "This is a string", 0    ; A series of bytes
Numb      DB    1, 2, 3, 255, -128       ; Numbers
Space     DB    1024     DUP(?)          ; Allocate 1024 bytes of
                                         ; space
```

DD

PURPOSE   To allocate double word sized space for data and optionally assign labels to the location.

SYNTAX   [name]   DD   data [,data]...   *Create double word sized data items.*

COMMENTS   The DD directive allocates memory eight bytes at a time. This lets you store unsigned numbers from 0 to 4,294,967,295 or signed numbers from –2,147,483,648 to 2,147,483,647. Another common use for double word data is to save far pointers.

SEE ALSO   DUP   *Used in initializing data*
DB, DF, DP, DQ, DT, DW

EXAMPLE
```
        .DATA
DataArea  DD    0, 4294967295, 0FF32h    ; Numbers
FarPoint  DD    DataArea                 ; A far pointer to
                                         ; DataArea
```

DF

PURPOSE   To allocate far pointer size (6 bytes) space for data and optionally assign labels to the location.

SYNTAX   [name]   DF   data [,data]...   *Create far pointers to 32 bit segments.*

COMMENTS   The 80386 can use segments that are up to four gigabytes long. To address the data in these segments, the offset portion of the address must be 32 bits wide. The DF directive provides storage for these long offsets plus the segment.

SEE ALSO   DUP   *Used in initializing data*
DB, DD, DQ, DT, DW

DF

EXAMPLE

```
            .386                      ; Allow 80386 instructions
            .DATA
DataArea    DW   0, 21, 0FF32h        ; Numbers
FarPoint    DF   DataArea             ; A far pointer to DataArea
```

DQ

PURPOSE   To allocate quad word sized (8 bytes) space for data and optionally assign labels to the location.

SYNTAX   [name]   DQ   data [,data]...   *Create quad word sized data items.*

COMMENTS   The DQ directive can be used to allocate space for the double precision real numbers used by math co-processors. A less common use is to allocate space for very large integers (up to 2^{64}).

SEE ALSO   DUP   *Used in initializing data*
DB, DD, DF, DT, DW

EXAMPLE

```
            .DATA
BigNum      DQ   0FFFF0000FFFF0000h   ; A huge number
RealNum     DQ   3.14159              ; A real numberDT
```

DT

PURPOSE   To allocate 10-byte sized space for data and optionally assign labels to the location.

SYNTAX   [name]   DT   data [,data]...   *Create ten byte sized data items.*

COMMENTS   This directive can be use to allocate space for 80-bit real numbers used by some math co-processors. When defined with other than real numbers, the assembler interprets the data as a packed BCD number.

SEE ALSO   DUP   *Used in initializing data*

EXAMPLE

```
BigBCD     DT 1234567890             ; Equivalent to the def below
BigBCD2    DB 1,2,3,4,5,6,7,8,9,0
Real       DT 1.5123                 ; 80-bit real number
```

DUP

PURPOSE To create an array of data items initialized to a single value, or create an uninitialized data space of a given size.

SYNTAX
```
count DUP(data)        Creates count instances of data.
count DUP(?)           Creates an uninitialized data area the
                       size of count items.
```

COMMENTS The DUP directive is used with the data definition directives (DB, DW, DQ, etc.). It makes an easy way to define large initialized or uninitialized data areas.

SEE ALSO DB, DD, DF, DP, DQ, DT, DW

EXAMPLE
```
array1    DW    20 dup(10)      ; Make 20 words with 10 in them
spaces    DB    80 dup( ' ' )   ; Make 80 spaces
buffer    DB    1024 dup(?)     ; Make 1024 byte buffer but don't
                                ; initialize it
```

DW

PURPOSE To allocate word sized space for data and optionally assign labels to the location.

SYNTAX
```
[name      DW    data [,data]...    Create word sized data items.
```

COMMENTS The DW directive is commonly used to define data that matches the 16-bit registers use in the 80x86 processors. The unsigned numbers that can be used range from 0 to 65,535 and signed numbers can range from –32,768 to 32,767. Another use for the DW directive is to define storage for NEAR pointers.

SEE ALSO
```
DUP                 Used in initializing data
DB, DD, DF, DQ, DT
```

EXAMPLE
```
          .DATA
Numbs     DW    -123, 41, 65535     ; Numbers
NearPoint DW    Numbs               ; A NEAR pointer to Numbs
```

DWORD

PURPOSE   To make an expression have a double word type.

SYNTAX   DWORD   *Make expression result a double word.*

COMMENTS   The type of an expression must be specified with one of these operators when there is no other way to get the type information. This can happen when using indirect addressing, or when using a label that will be defined later in the program.

SEE ALSO   PTR   *Used to force expression to have a particular size*

EXAMPLE   See the BYTE directive.

ENDS

PURPOSE   To mark the end of a structure or union.

SYNTAX   MASM mode:

[name] ENDS   *The end of a structure or union named* name.

IDEAL mode:

ENDS [name]   *The end of a structure or union named* name.

COMMENTS   This is the same directive that is used to mark the end of a segment. Turbo Assembler knows the difference by matching the names given. If no name is used then the ENDS goes with the most recent SEGMENT, STRUC, or UNION.

SEE ALSO   SEGMENT, STRUC, UNION

EXAMPLE   See the example for STRUC.

EVEN, EVENDATA

PURPOSE   To ensure that the location counter is at an even-numbered address.

SYNTAX   EVEN   *Used in code segments (inserts a NOP).*
EVENDATA   *Used in data segments (inserts a 0).*

COMMENTS   8086 and 80286 programs will run faster if data access can be done in a single 16-bit operation. The EVENDATA directive forces the next data item to be aligned for 16-bit operations.

SEE ALSO   ALIGN

EXAMPLE

```
unaligned db    0       ; This may or may not be aligned based on
                        ; what comes before it.
          EVENDATA
Aligned   dw    ?       ; This data is on an even numbered address
```

EQ

PURPOSE   To compare the results of two expressions and return TRUE if they are equal or FALSE if they are not.

SYNTAX   expr1 EQ expr2   *Returns true if expr1 equals expr2.*

COMMENTS   The expressions that use these operators are evaluated when the program is being assembled. To perform the same operations on program data at run time, you will need to write code to evaluate the expressions.

SEE ALSO   AND, NOT, OR, XOR   *Other expression operators*
GE, GT, LE, LT, NE

EXAMPLE   This example shows how you can use conditional assembly to make a program that can be modified by changing the symbols at the beginning.

```
    .MODEL   SMALL           ; This sets the predefined
                             ; symbols @DataSize and
                             ; @CodeSize
```

```
BUFSIZE   = 1024                      ; Describe the buffer to use
RECSIZE   = 415                       ; Describe the record to use
RECCNT    = 500
MEMSIZE   = 128000                    ; Amount of memory to use

IF RECSIZE * RECCNT GE MEMSIZE        ; See if enough memory for
                                      ; records
RECCNT    = MEMSIZE/RECSIZE           ; Set RECCNT to how many will
                                      ; fit

ENDIF

        .DATA
IF @DataSize EQ 0                     ; If using near data pointers
BuffPtr   DW  ?                       ; Allocate a word
ELSE                                  ; Otherwise
BuffPtr   DD  ?                       ; allocate a double word

        .CODE
IF RECSIZE LE BUFSIZE                 ; Compare record size to
                                      ; buffer size
        mov  cx, RECSIZE              ; Get the size of the record
ELSE
        mov  cx, BUFSIZE             ; The record is too big read
                                      ; buffer sized pieces

IF @DataSize NE 0                     ; If not, near data pointers
        les  bx, BuffPtr             ; and load the far pointer
ELSE                                  ; Otherwise
        push ds                       ; copy DS
        pop  es                       ; to ES
        mov  bx, BuffPtr             ; and get the NEAR pointer

ENDIF
```

FAR

PURPOSE To make an expression have the type FAR.

SYNTAX FAR   *Make expression result a far code pointer.*

COMMENTS The type of an expression must be specified when there is no other way to get the type information. This can happen when using indirect addressing, or when using a label that will be defined later in the program.

SEE ALSO

PTR	*Used to force the expression to have a particular size*
BYTE	*Make the expression result a byte*
DWORD	*Make the expression result a double word*
FWORD	*Make the expression result an 80386 32-bit segment far pointer*
LARGE	*Make the expression result an 80386 32-bit segment near pointer*
NEAR	*Make the expression result a near code pointer*
PROC	*Make the expression result a near or far code pointer, depending on the model in use*
PWORD	*Same as FWORD*
QWORD	*Make the expression result a quad word*
SHORT	*Make the expression result a short pointer*
SMALL	*Make the expression result a 16-bit offset*
TBYTE	*Make the expression result a 10-byte value*
UNKNOWN	*Make the expression result have an unknown type*
WORD	*Make the expression result a word*

EXAMPLE

```
        .
        .
        .
    call FAR func1      ; Forward reference requires size spec
        .
        .
        .
func1 proc far          ; The function to call
```

FWORD

PURPOSE   To make an expression have the far word type.

SYNTAX   FWORD   *Make expression result an 80386 32-bit segment far pointer.*

COMMENTS   The type of an expression must be specified when there is no other way to get the type information. This can happen when using indirect addressing, or when using a label that will be defined later in the program.

SEE ALSO

PTR	*Used to force the expression to have a particular size*
BYTE	*Make the expression result a byte*
DWORD	*Make the expression result a double word*

FWORD

FAR	*Make the expression result a far code pointer*
FWORD	*Make the expression result an 80386 32-bit segment far pointer*
LARGE	*Make the expression result an 80386 32-bit segment near pointer*
NEAR	*Make the expression result a near code pointer*
PROC	*Make the expression result a near or far code pointer depending on the model in use*
PWORD	*Same as FWORD*
QWORD	*Make the expression result a quad word*
SHORT	*Make the expression result a short pointer*
SMALL	*Make the expression result a 16-bit offset*
TBYTE	*Make the expression result a 10-byte value*
UNKNOWN	*Make the expression result have an unknown type*
WORD	*Make the expression result a word*

EXAMPLE   This example uses the FWORD directive to give the data at GDTSel the correct type for use with the LGDT directive.

```
        .MODEL    SMALL
        .386                    ; Allow 80386 instructions
        .DATA
GDTSel  DW   8 * 24 - 1         ; The limit field for the GDTR
        DD   0                  ; Base address for the GDT

        .CODE
        .
        .

        .
        lgdt FWORD GDTSel       ; Load the GDTR from memory
        .
        .

        .
```

GE

PURPOSE   To compare the results of two expressions and return TRUE if the first expression is greater than or equal to the second expression, or FALSE if it is not.

SYNTAX `expr1 GE expr2`   ***Returns true if expr1 greater than or equal to expr2.***

See `EQ`.

GT

PURPOSE To compare the results of two expressions and return TRUE if the first instruction is greater than the second, or FALSE if it is not.

SYNTAX `expr1 GT expr2`   ***Returns true if expr1 greater than expr2.***
See `EQ`.

HIGH

PURPOSE To get the most significant eight bits from an expression.

SYNTAX `HIGH expression`

IDEAL mode only:

`type HIGH expression`   ***Extract enough bits to fill type (BYTE, WORD, DWORD, etc.).***

COMMENTS Data can be defined that is too large to fit in a register (for example with `DD`, or `DQ`). The `HIGH` operator lets you break the high part of a number off so it can be dealt with by itself.

SEE ALSO `LOW`

EXAMPLE This example shows how to use the `HIGH` and `LOW` directives to extract the four bytes from a long integer.

```
         IDEAL
BigNum   EQU  12345678h                    ; A long
                                           ; integer
         .
         .
         .
```

```
        mov  al, BYTE LOW TooBig              ; Get the
lowest byte
        call SendData                         ; Send it
        mov  al, BYTE HIGH ( WORD LOW BigNum ) ; Get the next
        call SendData                         ; Send it
        mov  al, BYTE LOW ( WORD HIGH BigNum ) ; Get the next
        call SendData                         ; Send it
        mov  al, BYTE HIGH TooBig             ; Get the
highest byte
        call SendData                         ; Send it
        .
        .
        .
```

INSTR

PURPOSE   To find the position of one string in another.

SYNTAX   `name INSTR [start,]string1, string2`   *Find string2 in string1. Begin the search at the offsetin start.*

COMMENTS   The strings used in the `INSTR` can be text enclosed in angle brackets (*<text>*) or a symbol that refers to a string. The `INSTR` directive will be evaluated as the program is assembled. To manipulate strings at run time, you must write routines to handle them.

SEE ALSO   `CATSTR, SIZESTR, SUBSTR`

EXAMPLE   See example for `CATSTR`.

LABEL

PURPOSE   To make a label at the current location counter without advancing the location counter.

SYNTAX   MASM mode:

```
name LABEL type
```
Type can be NEAR, FAR, PROC, BYTE, WORD,
DWORD, FWORD, PWORD, QWORD, TBYTE.

IDEAL mode:

```
LABEL name type
```
Same types as in MASM mode.

COMMENTS   The `LABEL` directive is similar to unions. It can make a single location in the program accessible with different labels with different types.

SEE ALSO   `PROC`   *To make a procedure label*

EXAMPLE
```
BigPointer LABEL DWORD    ; To access the data as a double word
OffPtr     DW    ?        ; The same data as two words

SegPtr     DW    ?
```

LARGE

PURPOSE   To make an expression have the type LARGE.

SYNTAX   `LARGE`   *Make the expression result an 80386 32-bit segment*
near pointer.

COMMENTS   The `LARGE` directive makes the result of the expression suitable for use as a 32-bit offset.

SEE ALSO
`PTR`	*Used to force the expression to have a particular size*
`BYTE`	*Make the expression result a byte*
`DWORD`	*Make the expression result a double word*
`FAR`	*Make the expression result a far code pointer*
`FWORD`	*Make the expression result an 80386 32-bit segment far pointer*
`NEAR`	*Make the expression result a near code pointer*
`PROC`	*Make the expression result a near or far code pointer, depending on the model in use*
`PWORD`	*Same as FWORD*
`QWORD`	*Make the expression result a quad word*
`SHORT`	*Make the expression result a short pointer*
`SMALL`	*Make the expression result a 16-bit offset*
`TBYTE`	*Make the expression result a 10-byte value*

LARGE

UNKNOWN   *Make the expression result have an unknown type*
WORD   *Make the expression result a word*

EXAMPLE

```
        .MODEL    SMALL
        .386                         ; Allow 386 instructions
                                     ; Define a 32-bit segment
BigSeg  SEGMENT   PARA PUBLIC USE32 'DATA'
Numbs   DW   1234                    ; Make storage for a number
FarPoint DF   Numbs                  ; Make a far pointer to Numbs
BigSeg  ENDS

        .CODE
        .
        .
        .
        mov  ebx, LARGE FarPoint+2   ; Load the offset portion
        .
        .
        .
```

LE

PURPOSE   To compare the results of two expressions and return TRUE if the first expression is less than or equal to the second expression, or return FALSE if it is not.

SYNTAX   expr1 LE expr2   *Returns true if expr1 less than or equal to expr2.*
See EQ.

LENGTH

PURPOSE   To return the number of items duplicated at a label.

SYNTAX   LENGTH name   *Name is a symbol with DUPed data.*

COMMENTS The label must refer to data that was allocated with the DUP directive. The number returned is the number of items created by the DUP directive.

SEE ALSO SIZE, TYPE

EXAMPLE
```
; This program clears the data area at DataBlk to 0's
DataBlk    DW    411 DUP(?)          ; Define data with DUP

           sub  ax, ax               ; Clear AX
           mov  di, OFFSET DataBlk    ; Get the address of the block
           mov  cx, LENGTH DataBlk    ; The number of items
           rep  stosw                 ; Write to DataBlk
```

LOW

PURPOSE To get the most significant eight bits from an expression.

SYNTAX LOW expression

IDEAL mode only:

type LOW expression   *Extract enough bits to fill type (BYTE, WORD, DWORD, etc.).*

COMMENTS Data can be defined that is too large to fit in a register (for example with DD, or DQ). The HIGH operator lets you break the high part of a number off so it can be dealt with by itself.

SEE ALSO HIGH

EXAMPLE See HIGH.

LT

PURPOSE To compare the results of two expressions and return TRUE if the first expression is less than the second expression.

SYNTAX expr1 LT expr2   *Returns true if expr1 less than expr2.*
See EQ.

MASK

MASK

PURPOSE To create a mask that can be used to mask record fields.

SYNTAX MASK fieldname   *The mask covers the bits for the field.*
MASK record   *The mask covers all fields in the record.*

COMMENTS The MASK directive is helpful when manipulating the parts of records. If the MASK is ANDed with the byte or word containing the record, then only the field specified will be left in the byte or word. After it is isolated, the record can be shifted by the location of the field. These steps extract the field so that it can be used by itself.

SEE ALSO RECORD
WIDTH

EXAMPLE See the example for RECORD.

MOD

PURPOSE To return the remainder after dividing two expressions.

SYNTAX expr1 MOD expr2   *Give the remainder of dividing expr1 by expr2.*

COMMENTS This operator and the expressions that use it are evaluated as the program is assembled. To perform this operation on data at run time, you must write code to do it.

SEE ALSO AND, OR, NOT   *Other operators*
SHL, SHR   *Shift operators*

EXAMPLE
```
          .MODEL    SMALL
                              ; Clear a buffer
BufSize   = 1024              ; The number of bytes in the
                              ; buffer
          .DATA
Buffer    DB BufSize DUP(?)   ; The buffer to clear
```

```
            .CODE
ClearBuf    PROC
            mov   di, OFFSET Buffer    ; Get the address of the
                                       ; buffer
            sub   ax, ax               ; Clear AX
            mov   cx, BufSize SHR 1    ; Use the number of words to
                                       ; clear the buffer faster
            rep   stosw                ; Clear it
IF BufSize MOD 2                       ; See if the size is an odd
                                       ; number
            stosb                      ; Do the last byte
ENDIF
            ret

ClearBuf    ENDP
```

NE

PURPOSE To compare the results of two expressions and return TRUE if the first expression is not equal to the second expression, or return FALSE if it is.

SYNTAX expr1 NE expr2   *Returns true if expr1 not equal to expr2.*
See EQ.

NEAR

PURPOSE To make an expression have the type NEAR.

SYNTAX NEAR   *Make the expression result a near code pointer.*

COMMENTS The type of an expression must be specified when there is no other way to get the type information. This can happen when using indirect addressing, or when using a label that will be defined later in the program.

SEE ALSO PTR   *Used to force the expression to have a particular size*
            BYTE   *Make the expression result a byte*
            DWORD   *Make the expression result a double word*

NEAR

FAR	*Make the expression result a far code pointer*
FWORD	*Make the expression result an 80386 32-bit segment far pointer*
LARGE	*Make the expression result an 80386 32-bit segment near pointer*
PROC	*Make the expression result a near or far code pointer, depending on the model in use*
PWORD	*Same as FWORD*
QWORD	*Make the expression result a quad word*
SHORT	*Make the expression result a short pointer*
SMALL	*Make the expression result a 16-bit offset*
TBYTE	*Make the expression result a 10-byte value*
UNKNOWN	*Make the expression result have an unknown type*
WORD	*Make the expression result a word*

EXAMPLE This example uses the NEAR directive to tell the assembler to use a near CALL instruction.

```
        .MODEL    LARGE        ; Default calls are large
        .CODE
Proc1   PROC
        call NEAR SubFunc       ; Tell the assembler to use a
                                ; NEAR call

        ret
Proc1   ENDP

SubFunc   PROC NEAR             ; A near function
          .
          .
          .

SubFunc   ENDP
```

NOT

PURPOSE To perform logical operations in expressions.

SYNTAX NOT expr   *Do bitwise complement of the result of the expression.*

COMMENTS This operator is used in expressions that will be evaluated when the program is assembled. These expressions can be used anywhere that a number would be appropriate.

SEE ALSO   AND   *Logical AND*
           OR   *Logical OR*
           XOR   *Logical Exclusive OR*

EXAMPLE   See the AND directive.

OFFSET

PURPOSE   To get the offset of a label.

SYNTAX   OFFSET label

COMMENTS   Normally, using a label as an operand generates an instruction that reads the data at the label. Using the OFFSET operator generates an instruction that loads the address as immediate data.

SEE ALSO   SEG   *Get the segment of a label*

EXAMPLE
```
                .MODEL     SMALL
                .DATA
Msg             DB "This is a message$"
                .CODE
start:
        mov  ax, SEG DGROUP        ; Get the segment of DGROUP
        mov  ds, ax
        mov  dx, OFFSET Msg        ; Get the offset of Msg
        mov  ah, 9                 ; Print the message
        int  21h
        int  21h
        mov  ah, 4ch               ; Exit to DOS
        Int 21H
        .STACK     512
END start
```

OR

PURPOSE   To perform logical operations in expressions.

OR

COMMENTS This operator is used in expressions that will be evaluated when the program is assembled. These expressions can be used anywhere that a number would be appropriate.

SEE ALSO AND   *Logical AND*
          NOT   *Logical NOT*
          XOR   *Logical Exclusive OR*

EXAMPLE See the AND directive.

ORG

PURPOSE To change the location counter to a new value.

SYNTAX   ORG NewLocation   *NewLocation is the offset for the location counter.*

COMMENTS The ORG directive is used to place code or data at specific locations in the segment. For example, .COM programs must begin at offset 100h. The command ORG 100h accomplishes this. Another use for ORG is in accessing data in the BIOS data segment. Each data item in this segment is at a specific offset that you can get to with ORG.

SEE ALSO SEGMENT

EXAMPLE
```
; Make variables for the BIOS data segment
BIOSdata SEGMENT AT 40h
Com1Port  dw   ?          ; Com1 port address at offset 0
          ORG 17h
KeyStatus DW   ?          ; Keyboard status at offset 17h
          ORG 49h
VidMode   DB   ?          ; Video mode at offset 49h
BIOSdata ENDS
```

PROC

PURPOSE   To make an expression have the default type for procedures.

SYNTAX   PROC   *Make the expression result a near or far code pointer, depending on the model in use.*

COMMENTS   The type of an expression must be specified when there is no other way to get the type information. This can happen when using indirect addressing, or when using a label that will be defined later in the program. With the PROC operator, the actual type used depends on the model selected.

SEE ALSO

PTR	*Used to force the expression to have a particular size*
BYTE	*Make the expression result a byte*
DWORD	*Make the expression result a double word*
FAR	*Make the expression result a far code pointer*
FWORD	*Make the expression result an 80386 32-bit segment far pointer*
LARGE	*Make the expression result an 80386 32-bit segment near pointer*
NEAR	*Make the expression result a near code pointer*
PWORD	*Same as FWORD*
QWORD	*Make the expression result a quad word*
SHORT	*Make the expression result a short pointer*
SMALL	*Make the expression result a 16-bit offset*
TBYTE	*Make the expression result a 10-byte value*
UNKNOWN	*Make the expression result have an unknown type*
WORD	*Make the expression result a word*

EXAMPLE

```
        .MODEL    SMALL
        .CODE
Func1   PROC
        call PROC SubFunc   ; Forward reference requires size
                            ; spec
        ret
Func1   ENDP

SubFunc PROC               ; The function to call
        .
        .
        .
SubFunc ENDP
```

PTR

PURPOSE To make the data at an address have a particular size.

SYNTAX type PTR expression   *Type can be BYTE, WORD, DWORD, FWORD, PWORD, QWORD, TBYTE, PROC, NEAR, or FAR. The expression must be an address.*

COMMENTS The PTR directive is used when the size of the data is not known or wrong for the operation. Turbo Assembler cannot know the size of the data used in register indirect operations like mov [bx], 0. Adding a PTR directive (mov WORD PTR [bx],0) lets the assembler know the size of data to use. The assembler also does not know the size of labels that are defined later in the program. This is called a forward reference, and the PTR directive is required to tell the assembler how to use it.

SEE ALSO
BYTE
WORD
DWORD
FWORD
PWORD
QWORD
TBYTE
PROC
NEAR
FAR

EXAMPLE

```
; Another way to read large data items into registers
            .MODEL    LARGE
            .DATA
SampleData DD        1234
            .CODE
Start      PROC
           mov   ax, SEG DGROUP           ; Set up the DS
                                          ; register
           mov   ds, ax
           mov   ax, WORD PTR SampleData   ; Read the first word
                                           ; from SampleData
           mov   dx, WORD PTR SampleData+2 ; Read the second word
           call FAR PTR DoData             ; Use PTR for forward
                                           ; reference
```

```
        mov  BYTE PTR [bx], 0          ; Put a byte at bx
             .
             .
             .
Start        ENDP
DoData       PROC
             .
             .
             .
DoData       ENDP
             .STACK   1024
END Start
```

PWORD

See FWORD.

QWORD

PURPOSE   To make an expression have a particular type.

SYNTAX   QWORD   *Make the expression result a quad word.*

COMMENTS   The type of an expression must be specified when there is no other way to get the type information. This can happen when using indirect addressing, or when using a label that will be defined later in the program.

SEE ALSO
PTR	*Used to force the expression to have a particular size*
BYTE	*Make the expression result a byte*
DWORD	*Make the expression result a double word*
FAR	*Make the expression result a far code pointer*
FWORD	*Make the expression result an 80386 32-bit segment far pointer*
LARGE	*Make the expression result an 80386 32-bit segment near pointer*
NEAR	*Make the expression result a near code pointer*

QWORD

PROC	*Make the expression result a near or far code pointer, depending on the model in use*
PWORD	*Same as FWORD*
SHORT	*Make the expression result a short pointer*
SMALL	*Make the expression result a 16-bit offset*
TBYTE	*Make the expression result a 10-byte value*
UNKNOWN	*Make the expression result have an unknown type*
WORD	*Make the expression result a word*

EXAMPLE

```
                .MODEL
                .DATA
RealNumbs DQ    256  DUP(0)    ; Define an array of numbers

                .CODE
; Enter with an index to the array in AX
AddReal    PROC
           shl   ax, 1          ; Times 2
           shl   ax, 1          ; Times 4
           shl   ax, 1          ; Times 8
           mov   bx, OFFSET RealNumbs
           add   bx, ax
           fadd QWORD [bx]       ; Use the co-processor to add the
                                 ; number
           ret
AddReal    ENDP
```

.RADIX, RADIX

PURPOSE To set the default radix for numbers.

SYNTAX   `.RADIX    expression`   *The expression must evaluate to 2, 8, 10, or 16.*
            `RADIX    expression`

COMMENTS The default radix is base 10. Any number that does not have a letter appended to it which indicates its radix will be base 10. When the RADIX directive is used, then all of the numbers with unspecified radixes will be in the base given in the RADIX directive. If a constant is used in the RADIX directive, the constant must be base 10—no matter what the radix is or will be.

EXAMPLE
```
; All unspecified numbers are decimal by default
        DW    1234      ; A decimal number
```

```
        DB    15h        ; A hexadecimal number (h suffix)
.RADIX  8                ; Set radix to octal now unspecified
                         ; numbers are octal
        dw    1234       ; An octal number (= 668 decimal)
        dw    14d        ; A decimal number (d suffix)
```

RECORD

PURPOSE   To define a record that contains bit fields.

SYNTAX   MASM mode:

```
name RECORD field1:width[=expr] [,field2:width[=expr]]...
```

IDEAL mode:

```
RECORD name field1:width[=expr] [,field2:width[=expr]]...
```

COMMENTS   Records are like structures, except that the fields are portions of a byte or word. Each field gets width bits in the byte or word. The fields are allocated in the order given, from most significant bit to least. If the record is smaller than 8 or 16 bits, then all the fields will be shifted so that the last field includes the least significant bit. The optional expressions are default data to use when the record is declared.

The RECORD directive does not allocate any memory. Once the record is defined, its name can be used to declare memory the same way that a structure name can be used.

If the field name of a field in a record is used in an expression, it will give the number of bits to shift the record by in order to get the field to the least significant bit.

SEE ALSO   STRUC

EXAMPLE

```
        .MODEL    SMALL
        .DATA
ELREC   RECORD    Printers:2, Resrv:?, Coms:3, Resrv2:1,
Drives:2, VidMode:2, Resrv3:1, Point:1, Math:1, Boot:1

EquipLst ELREC    ?

        .CODE
GetComs PROC
        mov  ax, 40h              ; BIOS Data segment
```

```
        mov   es, ax
        mov   ax, es:[10h]        ; Get the equipment list
        mov   EquipLst, ax        ; Put it in memory
        and   ax, MASK Coms       ; Mask the comport bits
        mov   cl, Coms            ; Get the shift count
        shr   ax, cl              ; Now AX contains the number
                                  ; of comports

        ret
GetComs ENDP
END
```

SEG

PURPOSE   To return the segment portion of an address.

SYNTAX   `SEG expression`   *The expression must evaluate to an address.*

COMMENTS   Every label has some segment associated with it. For the labels that define data or code, the segment is the data or code segment containing the label. The `SEG` directive can also be used with segment or group names in order to give the address of the segment or group.

SEE ALSO   `OFFSET`

EXAMPLE   All programs must set up the DS register before using data. If the simplified segment directives are being used, then the DS register should point to the DGROUP group.

```
; General form of a typical program using simplified segments
        .MODEL    SMALL
        .DATA                     ; Define data in this
        .                         ; segment
        .
        .
        .CODE                     ; Put the code in this
Start   PROC                      ; segment
        mov   ax, SEG DGROUP      ; Get the segment of DGROUP
        mov   ds, ax              ; and put it in DS
        .
        .
        .
```

```
            ret
Start       ENDP                      ; End of the Start function
            .                         ; Other functions here
            .
            .
            .STACK     1024           ; Make a stack segment
END Start                             ; Tell the assembler to start
                                      ; the program at Start
```

SHL

PURPOSE To do an arithmetic shift left on an expression.

SYNTAX `expr1 SHL count` *Shift the value of expr1 left count times.*
See `MOD`.

SHORT

PURPOSE To make an expression have a particular type.

SYNTAX `SHORT` *Make the expression result a short pointer.*

COMMENTS The type of an expression must be specified when there is no other way to get the type information. This can happen when using indirect addressing, or when using a label that will be defined later in the program.

SEE ALSO
`PTR`	*Used to force the expression to have a particular size*
`BYTE`	*Make the expression result a byte*
`DWORD`	*Make the expression result a double word*
`FAR`	*Make the expression result a far code pointer*
`FWORD`	*Make the expression result an 80386 32-bit segment far pointer*
`LARGE`	*Make the expression result an 80386 32-bit segment near pointer*
`NEAR`	*Make the expression result a near code pointer*

SHORT

PROC	*Make the expression result a near or far code pointer, depending on the model in use*
PWORD	*Same as FWORD*
QWORD	*Make the expression result a quad word*
SMALL	*Make the expression result a 16-bit offset*
TBYTE	*Make the expression result a 10-byte value*
UNKNOWN	*Make the expression result have an unknown type*
WORD	*Make the expression result a word*

EXAMPLE

```
        .CODE
Func    PROC
        .
        .
        .
        jmp   SHORT FuncLbl        ; Tell the assembler to use a
        .                          ; short jump
        .                          ; There must be less than 127
        .                          ; bytes between the jmp and
                                   ; the label
FuncLbl:
```

SHR

PURPOSE To perform arithmetic operations on expressions.

SYNTAX expr1 SHR count   *Shift the value of expr1 right count times.*
See MOD.

SIZE

PURPOSE To return the size of a data item.

SYNTAX SIZE name   **name** *is a previously defined data item.*

COMMENTS The data item is one that has been declared with one of the data allocation directives (DB, DD, DW, etc.). The SIZE is the number of bytes allocated. If the DUP operator is used, the SIZE will be the number of bytes times the number used in the DUP.

In MASM mode the SIZE does not take into account multiple data items or nested DUP operators. In IDEAL mode, on the other hand, SIZE is the total number of bytes allocated with the label supplied.

SEE ALSO LENTGH, TYPE

EXAMPLE
```
IDEAL
        MODEL SMALL
        DATASEG
Strl    DB    "Hello\n", 0
        CODESEG
Start:
        mov  cx, SIZE Strl      ; In IDEAL mode this is 7 in
                                ; MASM mode it is 1

        .
        .
        .
        ret
        STACK     1024
END Start
```

SIZESTR

PURPOSE To return the number of characters in a string.

SYNTAX name SIZESTR string   *Put the length of string in name.*

COMMENTS The string for SIZESTR can be a literal string in angle brackets (*<text>*) or the result of one of the other string directives (EQU, CATSTR, SUBSTR). For strings declared with the DB directive, use SIZE in ideal mode.

SEE ALSO SUBSTR, CATSTR, INSTR
SIZE

EXAMPLE In Pascal programs a string has the length of the string followed by the string itself. The SIZESTR can be used when setting up literal strings for Pascal programs.

SIZESTR

```
; First, define symbols for the string and its length
StrDef    EQU      <This is the literal string>
StrLen    SIZESTR  StrDef

; Then declare a program variable that includes the size and the
; string
Str1      DB   StrLen, StrDef
```

SMALL

PURPOSE   To make an expression have the type SMALL.

SYNTAX   SMALL   *Make the expression result a 16-bit offset.*

COMMENTS   The type of an expression must be specified when there is no other way to get the type information. This can happen when using indirect addressing, or when using a label that will be defined later in the program.

SEE ALSO
PTR	*Used to force the expression to have a particular size*
BYTE	*Make the expression result a byte*
DWORD	*Make the expression result a double word*
FAR	*Make the expression result a far code pointer*
FWORD	*Make the expression result an 80386 32-bit segment far pointer*
LARGE	*Make the expression result an 80386 32-bit segment near pointer*
NEAR	*Make the expression result a near code pointer*
PROC	*Make the expression result a near or far code pointer, depending on the model in use*
PWORD	*Same as FWORD*
QWORD	*Make the expression result a quad word*
SHORT	*Make the expression result a short pointer*
TBYTE	*Make the expression result a 10-byte value*
UNKNOWN	*Make the expression result have an unknown type*
WORD	*Make the expression result a word*

EXAMPLE
```
          .MODEL    SMALL
          .386                           ; Allow 386 instructions
                                         ; Define a 16-bit segment
BigSeg    SEGMENT   PARA PUBLIC USE16 'DATA'
Numbs     DW   1234                      ; Make storage for a number
```

```
FarPoint   DD    Numbs              ; Make a far pointer to
                                    ; Numbs
BigSeg     ENDS
           .CODE
           .
           .
           .
       mov  bx, SMALL FarPoint+2  ; Load the offset portion
           .
           .
           .
```

STRUC

PURPOSE To begin the definition of a structure.

SYNTAX MASM mode:

name STRUC   *Define name as a structure made up of fields.*

[name] ENDS   *Data declarations, strucs, and unions.*

IDEAL mode:

STRUC name fields

ENDS [name]

COMMENTS Structures are a way of grouping related data items into a single symbol. The STRUC directive defines the way the related items are laid out, how they are named, and any default values for individual fields. Each field in the structure has a name that will be referenced when that field is used. It also has a type. The type depends on what data declaration is used (DB, DD, DW, etc.). Normally the data declaration for a field will use the question mark (?) symbol to indicate that the value of the field is undefined until the variables using the structure are defined. If actual data is used in declaring a field, then that data will be the default in any declarations of variables that use the structure.

SEE ALSO ENDS, UNION

EXAMPLE Structures are often used to represent data records in a database system. The structure lets the program treat the record as a single item when required.

STRUC

```
            .MODEL LARGE
            .DATA
; Define a structure for a name and address record
NameAddr STRUC
Name      DB   20 dup(?)          ; The person's name
Street    DB   20 dup(?)          ; His street address
City      DB   "Kirkland"         ; Default city is Kirkland
State     DB   "WA"               ; Default state is Washington
zip       DB   "980340000"        ; Use 9 digit Zip Codes
NameAddr STRUC

Rec1      NameAddr                ; Declare a record for names
FileHand  DW   ?                  ; File handle for the
                                  ; database
            .CODE
Start     PROC                    ; Initialized things
            mov  ax, SEG DGROUP
            mov  ds, ax
            .
            .
            .

Start     ENDP

PrintName PROC                    ; Print the name field
            mov  dx, OFFSET Rec1.Name ; Get address of name
            mov  ah, 9            ; MS-DOS command to print
            int  21h              ; a string
            ret

PrintName ENDP
WriteRec  PROC                    ; Write the record to a
                                  ; file
            mov  bx, FileHand     ; Get the file handle
            mov  cx, TYPE NameAddr ; Get the size of a
                                  ; record
            mov  dx, OFFSET Rec1  ; The address of the
                                  ; record
            mov  ah, 40h          ; MS-DOS command to write
            int  21h              ; a record
            ret
WriteRec  ENDP
END Start
```

SUBSTR

PURPOSE To extract a portion of a string and put it in another string.

SYNTAX `name SUBSTR string, position [,size]` *Puts the part of string at position and continuing for size bytes (or to the end of the string) into name.*

COMMENTS The string used in SUBSTR can be a literal string in angle brackets (*<text>*) or a previously defined string. The SUBSTR directive is evaluated as the program is being assembled. To operate on data strings, you will need to write your own string handling routines.

SEE ALSO CATSTR, INSTR, SIZESTR

EXAMPLE See the example for CATSTR.

TBYTE

PURPOSE To make an expression have the ten-byte type.

SYNTAX `TBYTE expression`

COMMENTS The type of an expression must be specified when there is no other way to get the type information. This can happen when using indirect addressing, or when using a label that will be defined later in the program.

SEE ALSO PTR *Used to force the expression to have a particular size*

EXAMPLE

```
          .MODEL    SMALL
          .DATA
TBArray   DT    100 DUP(?)

          .CODE
; Enter with index into array in AX
LongLoad  PROC
          mov  bx, OFFSET TBArray  ; Get the address of the array
          shl  ax, 1               ; Times 2
```

TBYTE

```
        add   bx, ax          ; Add to address
        shl   ax, 1            ; Times 4
        shl   ax, 1            ; Times 8
        add   bx, ax          ; Add to address
        fld   TBYTE [bx]      ; Tell the co-processor to
                              ; load the number
        ret
LongLoad ENDP
```

THIS

PURPOSE To make an operand that equals the current location counter.

SYNTAX THIS type   *Type is one of NEAR, FAR, PROC, BYTE, WORD, DWORD, FWORD, PWORD, QWORD, or TBYTE. It describes the type of data at the location.*

COMMENTS The THIS operator is similar to the dollar sign operator ($). The difference is that THIS defines a type for the data, which makes it useful in EQU or = operations where there is no other way to determine the type.

SEE ALSO EQU, LABEL

EXAMPLE Alabel   EQU   THIS DWORD   ; Make a label for this location
                                          ; that is a double word.

.TYPE, SYMTYPE

PURPOSE To return a byte describing a symbol.

SYNTAX .TYPE name   *Return the type of name.*
            SYMTYPE name   *Same operator. Use in IDEAL mode.*

COMMENTS The byte returned by .TYPE will have various bits set, depending on the type of symbol given. Table 9-3 shows the meanings of the bits.

Table 9-3. *Bits Returned by .TYPE*

Bit	Description
0	Program relative symbol
1	Data relative symbol
2	Constant
3	Direct addressing mode
4	Is a register
5	Symbol is defined
7	Symbol is external

SEE ALSO   TYPE

EXAMPLE   See TYPE.

TYPE

PURPOSE   To return a number indicating the type or size of a symbol.

SYNTAX   TYPE expression   *Returns the number of bytes that make up the type of expression. If the symbol is a NEAR function, the TYPE is -1. If the symbol is FAR, then the TYPE is -2.*

COMMENTS   The TYPE operator should be used instead of hard-coding the size of symbols into the program. If you need to change the data type in the future, you will not need to find where the size of the type is used. The TYPE operator will use the new size when the program is reassembled.

SEE ALSO   LENGTH, SIZE

EXAMPLE
```
            .MODEL    SMALL
            .DATA
Var1        DW    ?
            .CODE
Start:
            mov  ax, SEG DGROUP
            mov  ds, ax
```

TYPE

```
                        mov   es, ax
; Clear Var1 to zeros. No matter what the type of Var1 changes
; to, this code will work without modification.
                        sub   ax, ax          ; Clear the ax register
                        mov   cx, TYPE Var1   ; Get the size of Var1
                        mov   di, OFFSET Var1 ; Get the address of Var1
                        rep   stosb           ; Clear Var1
                        .STACK 512
END   Start
```

UNION

PURPOSE   To define a structure in which all the fields use the same memory locations.

SYNTAX   MASM mode:

```
name UNION
fields
[name] ENDS
```
Make a union named name.

IDEAL mode:

```
UNION name
fields
ENDS [name]
```

COMMENTS   Unions are defined, declared, and used just like a structure. The difference is that all of the fields in a union overlap each other. This feature can be used to access the same memory location in different ways that can include different data types.

SEE ALSO   STRUC, ENDS

EXAMPLE
```
              .MODEL
              .DATA
; Make a union to access pointers as a double word or
; as two single words
FarPtr    UNION
Big       DD    ?
          STRUC
PtrOff    dw    ?
```

```
          PtrSeg    dw    ?
          ENDS
FarPtr    ENDS

Msg1      db   "The pointer points here", 0
; Make a pointer to Msg1
Ptr1      FarPtr    < Msg1, ? >
          .CODE
          .
          .
          .
          mov  es, Ptr1.PtrSeg        ; Put the segment in ES
          mov  si, Ptr1.PtrOff        ; Put the offset in SI
          .
          .
          .
```

UNKNOWN

PURPOSE   To make an expression have a particular type.

SYNTAX   UNKNOWN   *Make the expression result have an unknown type.*

COMMENTS   This directive makes the expression have no type. See the example for how this can be used to make a label that can adapt to the situation in which it is used.

SEE ALSO

PTR	*Used to force the expression to have a particular size*
BYTE	*Make the expression result a byte*
DWORD	*Make the expression result a double word*
FAR	*Make the expression result a far code pointer*
FWORD	*Make the expression result an 80386 32-bit segment far pointer*
LARGE	*Make the expression result an 80386 32-bit segment near pointer*
NEAR	*Make the expression result a near code pointer*
PROC	*Make the expression result a near or far code pointer, depending on the model in use*
PWORD	*Same as FWORD*
QWORD	*Make the expression result a quad word*
SHORT	*Make the expression result a short pointer*
SMALL	*Make the expression result a 16-bit offset*

UNKNOWN

TBYTE	*Make the expression result a 10-byte value*
WORD	*Make the expression result a word*

EXAMPLE

```
        .MODEL
        .DATA
Buffer  DB  1024 DUP(0)         ; Make an array
BuffPtr EQU UNKNOWN Buffer      ; Make typeless symbol

        .CODE
Func1   PROC
        .
        .
        .
        mov  al, [BuffPtr]      ; Get the byte at Buffer
        mov  dx, [BuffPtr]      ; Get the word at Buffer
        .
        .
        .
Func1   ENDP
```

Note that without the UNKNOWN keyword, the second MOV directive would generate a type mismatch error.

WIDTH

PURPOSE To return the number of bits used in a RECORD or a RECORD field.

SYNTAX

WIDTH recordfield	*Gives the number of bits in the field.*
WIDTH record	*Gives the number of bits in the record.*

COMMENTS The WIDTH operator, along with the RECORD and MASK operators, gives you the information needed to write routines that make bit fields possible. The WIDTH operator can be used to create a mask or to calculate the range of numbers that will fit in a bit field.

SEE ALSO MASK, RECORD

EXAMPLE See the example for RECORD.

WORD

PURPOSE To make an expression have the type WORD.

SYNTAX WORD *Make the expression result a word.*

COMMENTS The type of an expression must be specified when there is no other way to get the type information. This can happen when using indirect addressing, or when using a label that will be defined later in the program.

SEE ALSO

PTR	*Used to force the expression to have a particular size*
BYTE	*Make the expression result a byte*
DWORD	*Make the expression result a double word*
FAR	*Make the expression result a far code pointer*
FWORD	*Make the expression result an 80386 32-bit segment far pointer*
LARGE	*Make the expression result an 80386 32-bit segment near pointer*
NEAR	*Make the expression result a near code pointer*
PROC	*Make the expression result a near or far code pointer, depending on the model in use*
PWORD	*Same as FWORD*
QWORD	*Make the expression result a quad word*
SHORT	*Make the expression result a short pointer*
SMALL	*Make the expression result a 16-bit offset*
TBYTE	*Make the expression result a 10-byte value*
UNKNOWN	*Make the expression result have an unknown type*

EXAMPLE The example uses the WORD directive to store a FAR pointer.

```
        .MODEL    SMALL
        .DATA
OldVect DD  ?                        ; Place to store the
                                     ; pointer

        .CODE
; Enter with AL set to the interrupt vector to get
GetVect PROC
        mov  ah, 35h                 ; MS-DOS get vector
                                     ; function
        int  21h                     ; Call MS-DOS
        mov  WORD PTR OldVect, bx    ; Save the low word
```

WORD

```
          mov  WORD PTR OldVect+2, es   ; Save the high word
          ret
GetVect   ENDP
```

XOR

PURPOSE To perform logical operations in expressions.

SYNTAX expr1 XOR expr2   *Do bitwise Exclusive OR on the results*
of the two expressions.

COMMENTS These operators are used in expressions that will be evaluated when the program is assembled. These expressions can be used anywhere that a number would be appropriate.

SEE ALSO AND   *Logical AND*
NOT   *Logical NOT*
OR   *Logical OR*

EXAMPLE See the AND directive.

10 Macros, Procedures, and Tools for Modular Programs

Trying to code and maintain a large program can be a daunting task, unless the program can be broken down into more manageable pieces. The computer treats a program as a series of bytes with an occasional jump or call disrupting the flow. There is no requirement that the order of the program parts make any more sense than it takes to get the job done. On the other hand, there is no requirement that the code be so complex that it cannot be understood by qualified programmers.

High level languages like C and Pascal help you write logical code by supporting structured programming techniques. The cornerstone of these techniques is the use of functions and procedures to break the program into more manageable pieces. In a well-designed program, each procedure can be written, tested, and maintained separately from the rest of the program.

To understand how a structured program works, you only need to understand the structure. The details of how a function or procedure does its specific job are not important to the overall program. When you are working on a single function or procedure, you only worry about that job—not the whole program.

Some structured techniques lead to the production of modules that can be used in other programs. For example, a module that contains routines that print on-screen has obvious uses in many programs. Code that can be reused in this way increases programming productivity. Whenever code can be reused, you save the time it would otherwise take to design and test the routines. Several useful modules may be collected together in libraries, which can then be used by the linker to add just the required modules to new programs.

Turbo Assembler allows you to apply structured techniques to assembly language programs. The program can be written in separate source files. In a structured Turbo Assembler program, each source file is a logical module in the program. The modules are further refined into procedures and macros. *Macros* are like procedures except that, instead of the processor calling the code, it is inserted into the program where it is used. The commands for creating procedures and macros let you strictly control the entry and exit points and data used in the procedure or macro. This is one of the keys to creating successful structured programs.

The use of data in a structured program is very important. A module should have as few side effects as possible. The commands in Turbo Assembler for exporting and importing data help to ensure that the side effects are limited to symbols that you specify.

A feature of structured programs is the ease with which they can be modified. When a change is required in a single module, the change can be made without affecting the rest of the program. You can exploit this feature of structured programs whenever you write programs that may have several different versions for different environments. In Turbo Assembler you can implement these different versions in the same source by using conditional assembly directives that tell the assembler what to assemble for various versions.

Dividing a Program into Modules

The first step to writing a structured program is to divide the program into modules. The choice of modules will have a large effect on the ease of writing, testing, and maintaining the final program. Each module should have some logical theme. The theme can be that all routines in the module perform similar operations, they all affect the same data, or they reflect the structure of the program. The theme should be chosen to limit the amount of interaction between modules, and to make it easy to see the structure of the program. For example, you may have a single module that handles the screen. This would limit module interactions by hiding all of the screen variables and providing a well-defined interface for displaying data. Another module might contain the functions used by one of the menus in the program. This would reflect the structure of the program.

Each module goes in a separate source file. Separate sources make it easy to see where the module begins and ends. This makes it easy for you to concentrate on one module at a time. The assembler lets you protect variables used in a module by limiting the scope of a variable to the file in which it is defined.

The scope of a symbol determines where in the program the symbol can be used. The scope of most symbols defined in a source file is the file itself. They can only be used in the file in which they are defined. One example of a symbol that has a wider scope is a segment with a PUBLIC *combine* type. These symbols are available in all files in the program.

A well-designed module can be used by other programs. A program needs only to conform to the interface requirements of the module in order to use it. Often several of these modules are combined into a library file, which can be created and maintained with the MS-DOS library manager LIB. When you link the program, you tell the linker what libraries to use. You can do this through linker commands or by using the INCLUDELIB directive. The format of the INCLUDELIB directive is:

```
INCLUDELIB     FileName
```

For this instruction, FileName is the name of the library to include. If you do not specify an extension, .LIB will be used. If you do not give a path, the assembler will search the directories specified in the /I command line option first, and then secondly in the current directory.

Sharing Symbols and Variables

Turbo Assembler can only use symbols that are defined in the source file being assembled. This prevents one source file from ever using the symbols in another source file. For structured programming that would seem to be ideal, the number of interactions between modules is zero. The flaw in this reasoning is that without some interaction, the code and data in the module can never be used by other modules. In that case it might as well not be there at all.

To get around this isolation, there are special definitions that can be used to define symbols that can be accessed in various modules. Making symbols available in more than one source file means that side effects can occur, but they will be limited to the symbols that the programmer has defined as available. This simplifies the debugging process by limiting the places that must be checked for adverse side effects.

PUBLIC SYMBOLS For a symbol in a module to be used by other modules, it must be made *public*. If a symbol is not public, it is safe from being used by any other module. The PUBLIC directive lets you control what symbols should be made available to other modules. The list of public symbols, separated by commas, follows the PUBLIC directive, like this:

```
PUBLIC    symbol1 [, symbol2]...
```

EXTERNAL SYMBOLS Once a module has made a symbol public, it can be used in another module. Before the symbol can be used, however, the module must tell the assembler to get the symbol from another module. In addition to indicating that the symbol is external, you must also tell the assembler the type of data the symbol represents. The EXTRN directive accomplishes both of these objectives. The format of the EXTERN directive is:

```
EXTRN      symbol1:type1 [,symbol2:type2]
```

The *types* can be: BYTE, WORD, DWORD, FWORD, PWORD, QWORD, TBYTE, NEAR, FAR, or PROC. The type is not checked against the module that made the symbol public, so it is up to you to ensure that the types match. The following example shows how two modules can share symbols.

```
; File MAIN.ASM
; This is the main file it uses a function in
; the other source file
        .MODEL    SMALL
        EXTRN     PrintMsg:PROC    ; This function is in the
                                   ; other file
        .DATA
        PUBLIC    Mesg1
Mesg1   DB    "Hello, world", 0Dh, 0Ah, '$'
        .CODE
Start:
        mov   ax, SEG DGROUP      ; Get the data segment
        mov   ds, ax              ; Put it in DS
        call  PrintMsg            ; Call the other module
        mov   ah, 4ch             ; MS-DOS exit function
        int   21h
        .STACK    512
END   Start
```

This program prints the message "Hello, world" on the screen. It does this by setting up some registers to point to the string to print, and then calling the routine PrintMsg to print the string. The EXTRN statement near the beginning of the example tells the assembler that the symbol PrintMsg is a procedure and that it is in some other source file.

This is the file containing PrintMsg:

```
; File PRINTMSG.ASM
; This module uses data from the first file
        .MODEL SMALL
        .DATA
        EXTRN     Mesg1:BYTE
        .CODE
        PUBLIC    PrintMsg

PrintMsg  PROC
        mov   dx, OFFSET Mesg1    ; Get the address of the data
                                 ; in the other file
        mov   ah, 9              ; DOS print function
```

```
                    int   21h
                    ret
PrintMsg   ENDP
END
```

This file uses the PUBLIC directive to indicate that the symbol PrintMsg should be made available to other modules. To use this program, you must assemble both source files and then combine them with the linker, like this:

```
tlink main printmsg
```

COMMON SYMBOLS

When using EXTRN and PUBLIC, you clearly define one module as the source of the data and another as the user of the data. Sometimes you do not need to have such a clear distinction between source and user. In other words, you may have modules that are both source and user. In this case you can use common variable symbols that are both public and external. The COMM directive is used to make common variables. The format of the COMM directive is:

```
COMM variable1:type[:size] [,variable2:type[:size]]
```

The *type* is the same as for the EXTRN directive. The optional *size* is the number of items the variable represents. If the size is omitted, then the default size is one item.

The EXTRN and PUBLIC directives can appear almost anywhere in the source file. (Note, however, that the EXTRN directive must precede any use of the symbol). The COMM directive, on the other hand, must appear in the segment that contains the common variables. The segment must be a public segment and must be the same for each of the modules that use the variable. With simplified segment directives, this is most often the .CODE segment.

Conditional Assembly

Conditional assembly is a technique that lets a single source file be used to create different versions of the program. To use conditional assembly, you define symbols that describe the program to assemble. The symbols are used in conditional expressions to tell the assembler what code or data to use in assembling the program.

A common example of conditional assembly is in modules that are written to be used by different programs with different memory modules. Different memory models use different sizes for pointers, and therefore must use different code to manipulate the pointers. The following example uses the predefined symbols DATASIZE and CODESIZE to determine the size of pointers required:

```
        .MODEL    SMALL     ; The code will work with other
                            ; models
```

```
                .DATA
IF DATASIZE
Ptr         DD    ?                    ; For large data use double
ELSE
Ptr         DW    ?                    ; Otherwise, just a word
ENDIF

                .CODE
                .
                .
                .
IF DATASIZE
            les   bx, Ptr              ; Get segment and offset
            mov   ax, ES:[bx]          ; Get the data at the pointer
ELSE
            mov   bx, Ptr              ; Just use the offset
            mov   ax, [bx]             ; Get the data at the pointer
ENDIF
                .
                .
                .
END
```

The code between the condition (IF) and the ENDIF is the conditional code. If the condition is true, then the code before the ELSE is used. If the condition is false, then the code between the ELSE and the ENDIF is used. You do not need to have an ELSE statement. In that case the code between the condition and the ENDIF will be used if the condition is true.

There are several other conditions that can be used instead of IF. There are also several variations on the ELSE statement that you can use. Table 10-1 shows all of the directives available for conditional assembly.

Table 10-1. *Conditional Assembly Directives*

Directive	Explanation
ELSE	Begins the second part of a conditional. The Code between the ELSE and the ENDIF will be used if the condition is false.

ELSE[cond]	Any of the IF directives can be combined to create a list of conditions. Only one of the parts will be used (the first one that is true).
	IF expression1
	   ... ; use if expression1 is true
	ELSEIF expression2
	   ... ; use if expression2 is true

Directive	Explanation
	ELSEIFDEF label
	... ; use if label is defined
	ENDIF
ENDIF	Marks the end of a conditional block.
IF expression	Use the following instructions if expression is true.
IF1	Use the following instructions if this is assembler pass 1.
IF2	Use the following instructions if this is assembler pass 2.
IFB arg	Use the following instructions if arg is blank.
IFDEF label	Use the following instructions if label is defined
IFDIF arg1,arg2	Use the following instructions if arg1 does not equal arg2
IFDIFI arg1,arg2	Same as IFDIF except arg1 and arg2 are compared without regard to case.
IFE expression	Use the following instructions if the expression evaluates to 0.
IFIDN arg1,arg2	Use the following instructions if arg1 matches arg2.
IFIDNI arg1,arg2	The same as IFIDN except arg1 and arg2 are compared without regard to case.
IFNB arg	Use the following instructions if arg is not blank.
IFNDEF label	Use the following instructions if label has not been defined.

Include Files

One of the steps in using conditional assembly to make several versions of a program from a single source is to define the flags that control the assembly. Often the same flags must be defined in several of the source files. When you must change the flags, you must do it in all of the source files. This is less than convenient and, fortunately, unnecessary.

The answer to this problem is to use *include files*. An include file is a source file that can be inserted in another file when it is assembled. Any portion of a source file can be placed in an include file and replaced with:

```
INCLUDE [PATH\]FILENAME[.EXT]
```

The filename names the file to include. If the path is omitted, Turbo Assembler will first search the directory in the /I command-line option and then the current directory. If the extension is omitted, then .ASM is assumed. Include files may also use the INCLUDE directive. This nesting may continue as deep as you want.

Include files are most useful when the instructions in the file are used in more than one module. Constants and literal strings, such as those created with EQU, are often used in this way. Another thing to consider putting in an include file are structure definitions. You can even put the declarations for *global data* in an include file.

The GLOBAL directive is designed to declare data in include files. It uses the same syntax as the COMM directive, but it does not have to be in the data segment. It accomplishes this task by requiring one of the source files that uses the include file to allocate space for the symbol. In the module that allocates space for the data, the GLOBAL directive works like the PUBLIC directive. In other modules the GLOBAL directive works like the EXTRN directive.

The following example uses the GLOBAL directive to declare global data. It uses conditional assembly to make sure that only one source file allocates space for the data:

```
            .MODEL    SMALL              ; Define the model here

GLOBAL Symbol1:BYTE
GLOBAL Aword:WORD
GLOBAL Mesg:BYTE
IFDEF MAIN
Symbol1    DB    ?
Aword      DW    1234h
Mesg       DB    "This is a string",0
ENDIF
```

To use this include file, one of the modules must define "main" before including the file:

```
MAIN       EQU 1                          ; The symbol MAIN must be
                                          ; declared in one of the files
                                          ; in the program. All other
                                          ; files should leave it
                                          ; undefined. Note that the
                                          ; actual value is not
                                          ; important, just that the
                                          ; symbol exists.

       INCLUDE DATADEFS.INC               ; The contents of the include
                                          ; file go here

            .CODE
```

```
        mov   ax, Aword            ; Get the data at Aword
        mov   Symbol1, al          ; Save the low byte at Symbol1
        .
        .
        .
```

Dividing Modules into Procedures

Once you have divided the program into modules, you need to consider what procedures to put into the module. The procedures should fit the theme of the module. For example, all functions in a module of screen routines should have something to do with the screen.

Some of the functions will be called from other modules. These functions should be referenced in a PUBLIC directive to make them visible. Other functions will be used only from within the module. In the example of a module of screen routines, the function to print a string on the screen would be one of the public functions. A function that keeps track of the current cursor location and screen attributes would be a private one.

Once you have written the module, you only need to concern yourself with the public procedures. The private procedures and other details of the module are not important to the rest of the program. This comes in handy when you want to use the module in another program. You may find that your new program requires the same screen routines. If the screen module is well-designed, all you need to print a string is to call the print string function. You do not need to know how it keeps track of the cursor or attributes.

Defining Procedures

The PROC directive marks the beginning of a procedure. In its simplest form, it tells the name of the function and whether you need a *near* or *far* call to call it. The format for this is:

MASM mode:

```
FuncName  PROC NEAR        ; Can be NEAR or FAR
```

IDEAL mode:

```
PROC FuncName NEAR        ; Can be NEAR or FAR
```

The following example shows a simple procedure for adding two long integers:

```
; Add the number in AX,BX to the number in CX, DX
AddLong   PROC NEAR
```

```
          add   bx, dx              ; Add the low words
          adc   ax, cx              ; Add the high words
          ret
AddLong   ENDP
```

As the previous example shows, following the PROC directive is the code for the procedure. Notice you need an ENDP directive at the end of the procedure. You can give the procedure name in the ENDP directive to eliminate any confusion about what ENDP goes with what procedure. In most cases the name is not needed. (Note that PROC and ENDP directives must be paired up. By giving the procedure name, you can guarantee what PROC goes with what ENDP.)

If the .MODEL directive appears at the beginning of the program, then you do not need to specify NEAR or FAR. For the MEDIUM, LARGE, and HUGE models, all procedures are FAR; and for SMALL and COMPACT models, they are NEAR. Specifying NEAR or FAR in a PROC directive overrides the model. This is handy for private procedures in the LARGE model. If all of the code in the module will fit in 64K of memory and only one code segment is used, then you can use NEAR for all of the private functions. This will save space and run faster, because the near call is two bytes shorter and six to 13 cycles faster than a far call. The public functions should be FAR in the MEDIUM, LARGE, or HUGE models, because the functions in other modules will reside in other segments, and so they require far jumps and calls.

SAVING REGISTERS   One of the principles of structured programming is that each function have as few side effects as possible. But in high level languages, side effects can show up in the global variables. In assembly language not only do you get side effects in global variables, but you can also get them in CPU registers. This problem is acute in the 80x86 processors due to the small number of registers.

To prevent register side effects, you can push the registers that the function will use on the stack. The following example shows how this works:

```
          EXTRN    Msg1:BYTE
Open      PROC     FAR
          push     ax              ; Save the ax register
          push     dx              ; Save the dx register
          .                        ; Do the function
          .
          .
          pop      dx              ; Restore the dx register
          pop      ax              ; Restore the ax register
          ret
Open      ENDP
```

You can get the assembler to save and restore the registers for you. The PROC directive can have a USES clause, in which you name all of the registers that the function will use. The previous example becomes:

```
         EXTRN     FileName:BYTE
         EXTRN     Handle:WORD
Open     PROC      FAR   USES ax dx
                              ; The assembler puts push
                              ; instructions here
              .               ; Do the function
              .
              .

                              ; The assembler puts pop
                              ; instructions here
         ret
Open     ENDP
```

Both of these examples generate the same code. With the second example you do not need to remember to pop all the registers that you pushed. The assembler makes sure that the correct things happen going in and going out of the function.

PASSING AND RETURNING VARIABLES

The function in the previous example is not very useful because it can only open FileName. To make it more versatile, it needs a way for the calling routine to tell it what file to open. Along with a way for the caller to specify the file, there should also be a way to get the handle back.

The stack frame idea that was presented in Chapter 6 can be used to pass a pointer to the function. This is the solution used in high level languages like Pascal and C. Some high level languages use the stack frame to return values to the caller, while others return values in the AX and DX registers. Figure 10-1 shows how different languages handle variables in the stack frame.

C Calling Convention

The Stack   Returning

4. Function makes local variables — Local Variables

3. Save BP — Base Pointer

2. Call function — Return Address

1. Push arguments — Argument / Last Argument

Calling

5. Remove local variables

6. Pop BP

7. Return to calling function

8. Calling function removes arguments

Pascal Calling Convention

Returning

4. Function makes local variables — Local Variables

3. Function saves BP — Base Pointer

2. Call function — Return Address

1. Push arguments — Argument / First Argument

Calling

5. Remove local variables

6. Pop BP

7. Remove arguments & return to calling function

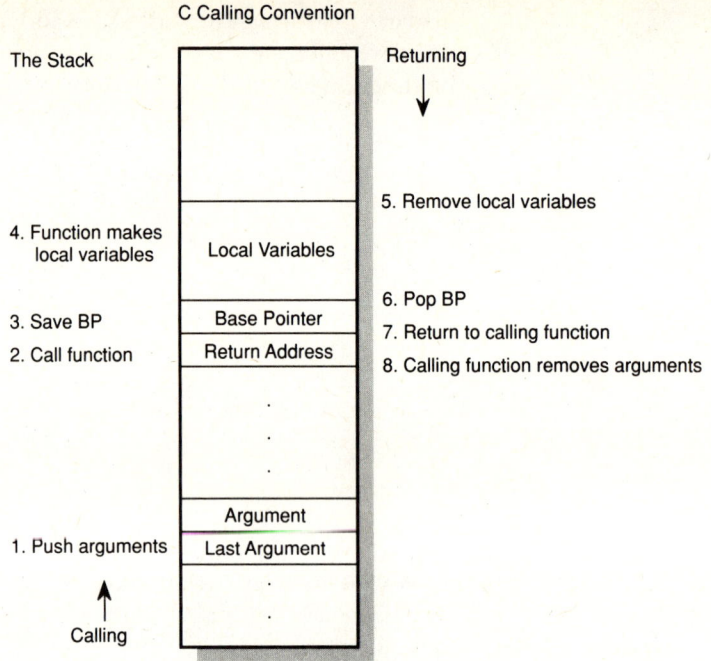

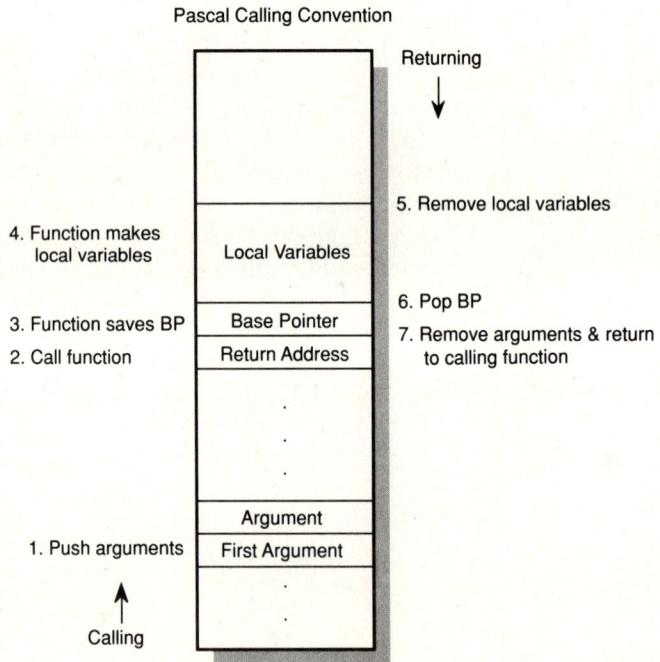

Figure 10-1. *The stack frame used in high level languages.*

The next example shows how to code functions that use the C-style stack frame to pass variables to the function.

```
              .
              .
              .
        mov       ax, 2
        push      ax                ; Pass mode
        mov       ax, OFFSET Msg1   ; Pass the address of the
        push      ax                ; string on the stack
        call      Open
        add       sp, 4             ; Fix the stack
        mov       Handle, ax        ; Save the handle
              .
              .
              .
Open    PROC      FAR
        push      bp
        mov       bp, sp
        mov       dx, [bp+6]        ; The file name
        mov       ah, 3Dh           ; DOS open file function
        mov       al, [bp+8]        ; Open for reading and writing
        int       21h               ; Calling DOS only changes
                                    ; the ax register
        jnc       NoErr
        mov       ax,-1             ; Use -1 to indicate an error
        pop       bp
        ret
Open    ENDP
```

The first part of this example shows how to push the arguments onto the stack, call the function, and return the stack pointer to its original location. The Open function shows how to use the arguments. The first step is to save the old BP, and then set it to the value of the stack pointer. This puts the first argument six bytes from BP (two for BP and four for the return address). The expression [bp+6] can be used to get this argument.

You can use the ARG directive to set up a stack frame for you. In addition, the ARG directive lets you give symbolic names to the arguments. Instead of using something like bp+6 to reference an argument, you can use its name. This makes the resulting program easier to understand. The open function with an ARG directive looks like this:

```
Open        PROC        FAR
; The next line sets up the stack frame
ARG         FileName:WORD, OpenMode:WORD
            push        bp
            mov         bp, sp
            mov         dx, [FileName] ; The file name
            mov         ah, 3Dh         ; MS-DOS open file function
            mov         al, [OpenMode] ; Open for reading and writing
            int         21h             ; Calling DOS only changes
                                        ; the ax register
            jnc         NoErr
            mov         ax,-1           ; Use -1 to indicate an error
            pop         bp
            ret
Open        ENDP
```

This example works the same way as the previous one. Instead of needing to remember the locations of the arguments on the stack, you can use the symbols FileName and OpenMode defined in the ARG statement.

The stack frame is also used for local variables. To put local variables in the stack frame, you need to adjust the stack pointer to make room for the variables. You access them with the BP register, as in the following example:

```
Func1       PROC
            push        bp
            mov         bp, sp
            sub         sp, 4           ; Make room for four bytes
            xor         ax, ax
            mov         [bp-2], ax      ; Set the first variable
            mov         [bp-4], ax      ; Set the second variable
            .
            .
            .
```

Turbo Assembler can do all of this for you if you use the LOCAL directive. The LOCAL directive looks like the ARGS directive. With LOCAL the example becomes:

```
Func1       PROC
LOCAL       VAR1:WORD, VAR2:WORD
            xor         ax, ax
            mov         [VAR1], ax      ; Clear VAR1
            mov         [VAR2], ax      ; Clear VAR2
            .
            .
            .
```

Macros

In Chapter 9 you saw how to make a symbol that stands for a string with the EQU directive. This kind of substitution is a simple form of *macro*. Macros can be used to stand for whole sections of code or data. Macros can have arguments and local variables just like functions.

Macros have many of the advantages of functions. They also have some advantages of their own. Macros are faster than the corresponding function, because they do not use a call or return. Using conditionals in a macro makes it possible to optimize a macro for each situation without adding code to the final program.

Each time you use a macro, it is expanded by the assembler to code or data. If a macro is used more than once, it will take more space than the corresponding function. You should weigh the performance against the memory requirements when deciding between using a macro or a function.

DEFINING A MACRO

The definition of a macro associates a *macro* name with the code or data to be substituted. For example, you can define a macro that calls DOS with an EXIT (function 4Ch) command like this:

```
DOSEXIT    MACRO                   ; Give the name of the macro
           mov      ah, 4Ch        ; Put command in AH
           int      21h            ; Call DOS
           ENDM                    ; Done with the definition
```

Notice that the ENDM directive is used to mark the end of the macro. Once the macro has been defined, using its name will make the assembler substitute the body of the macro in place of the name. The macro definition itself does not generate any code or data. The macro only affects the program when it is used. You can put the definitions for many commonly used macros into an include file for use in all of your programs. Only the ones that are actually used will take up space in the final program.

PASSING ARGUMENTS TO A MACRO

One of the macros that many programmers put in the include file is one that calls DOS. To call DOS, you must set up registers with the function number and any data the function requires. The macro that does this needs some way to know what values to put in the registers. The way to pass data to a macro is to include arguments in the macro definition, as follows:

```
CALLDOS    MACRO    FuncNumb, DXData  ; Macro arguments
           mov      ah, FuncNumb      ; Put function # in AX
           mov      dx, DXData        ; Put data in DX
           int      21h               ; Call DOS
           ENDM
```

When you use this macro, you give it the function number and data like this:

```
CALLDOS   41h, <OFFSET FileName>   ; Erase FileName
```

The angle brackets (<>) around the second argument are to prevent the assembler from trying to evaluate the argument before passing it to the macro. Table 10-2 shows this and other special macro operators.

Table 10-2.   *Special Macro Operators*

Operator	Description

&	Force an argument substitution. Used inside quotes and when the argument is right next to another symbol.
	
	With:
	
	`SUBMACRO    MACRO NUM, TEXT`
	`MSG&NUM     DB      '&TEXT'`
	`                    ENDM`
	
	`MAKEMSG     4, <Disk error>`
	Becomes:
	`MSG4                DB   'Disk error'`

<>	Literal string. Prevents the string from being evaluated before it is passed to the macro.
!	Quoted character operator. Prevents the next character from being used as an operator: `MAKEMSG       5, <A string with a !> in it >`
%	Expression evaluate operator. Evaluates an expression and passes the result to the macro: `MAKEMSG       %3+4, <This is MSG 7>` This example adds 3 to 4 and passes the result (7) as a single argument.

;;	Suppress comment. The comment will not be saved when the macro is used. This saves memory during assembly:
	
	`SUBMACRO    MACRO NUM, TEXT`
	`MSG&NUM     DB      '&TEXT'          ;; Don't save this comment`
	`                    ENDM`

LOCAL LABELS

Everywhere the macro name occurs, the assembler replaces it with the code in the macro. This is a problem if the macro contains a label. The second time you use the macro, the assembler will see the same label and generate an error. There are two ways that you can make a label *local* and avoid the multiple definition error.

The first way to make a local label is to use the LOCAL directive. This is the same directive that is used for local labels in procedures. The following example shows how to make a local label:

```
WAIT     MACRO     Delay
LOCAL    Tloop                          ; Tloop is a local label
         mov       ah, 0                ; Get clock count
         int       1Ah                  ; Call BIOS clock function
         add       ax, Delay            ; Figure time when done
         adc       dx, 0                ; Add any carry to high part
         mov       si, ax               ; Save the done time (low)
         mov       di, dx               ; Save the done time (high)
Tloop:
         mov       ah, 0                ; Keep checking the clock
         int       1Ah                  ; until done
         cmp       dx, di               ; Check the high part
         jb        Tloop                ; If high parts equal
         cmp       ax, si               ; then check the low part
         jb        Tloop                ; If not done loop
```

Another way to make a label local is to use the LOCALS directive and mark the label with a local prefix. The local prefix is @@ by default, but it can be changed with the LOCALS directive. If you want to turn off the use of local variables, you can use the NOLOCALS directive. With LOCALS, the WAIT macro looks like this:

```
LOCALS   $$                             ; Make local labels start with
                                        ; $$

WAIT     MACRO     Delay
         mov       ah, 0                ; Get clock count
         int       1Ah                  ; Call BIOS clock function
         add       ax, Delay            ; Figure time when done
         adc       dx, 0                ; Add any carry to high part
         mov       si, ax               ; Save the done time (low)
         mov       di, dx               ; Save the done time (high)
$$Tloop:
         mov       ah, 0                ; Keep checking the clock
         int       1Ah                  ; until done
         cmp       dx, di               ; Check the high part
         jb        Tloop                ; If high parts equal
```

```
        cmp     ax, si              ; then check the low part
        jb      Tloop               ; If not done loop
```

THE REPT LOOP   You can use loops in macros to define repetitive sequences of code or data.
There are three different types of loop in Turbo Assembler. The first type is the
REPT (repeat) loop. The argument for the repeat loop is the number of times
the loop will run. A common use for the REPT directive is to declare and initialize arrays of data. The next example shows how the REPT directive can be
used to make an array of a certain size containing a series of bytes. The bytes
will be initialized with a specific range of values, beginning with Start and ending
with Start + Size.

```
RANGE   MACRO   Start, Size
Value   =       Start               ; Make the initial Value
        REPT    Size                ; Do Size times
        DB      Value               ; Make a byte with Value in it
Value   =       Value+1             ; Increment the value
        ENDM                        ; End of the loop
        ENDM                        ; End of the macro
```

Note that the REPT directive uses the ENDM directive to end the loop. There
must be an ENDM directive for every loop or MACRO directive. The assembler ends
the last open loop or MACRO when it encounters an ENDM directive.

When you use this macro, it makes a list of DB statements, each with a
different value. Note that the equals sign (=) assignment is used instead of EQU.
This is because only the equals sign (=) assignment will allow the symbol to
be on both sides of the assignment. To use this macro, you would write
something like this:

```
LowAlpha   LABEL   BYTE              ; Make a label for the data
           RANGE   <'a'>, 26         ; Define 26 bytes starting at
                                     ; 'a'
UpAlpha    LABEL   BYTE              ; Now one for upper case
           RANGE   <'A'>, 26
```

THE IRP LOOP   The other two types of loops enable you to specify a list of data items that will
be used in the loop. The IRP directive repeats the code or data in the loop once
for each number in a list that you pass to it. You can use the IRP directive to
make code to evaluate a polynomial. The general form of a polynomial is:

$$C_1 x^n + C_2 x^{n-1} + \dots + C_{n+1} x^0$$

where C_1, C_2, etc., are coefficients and x is the number to plug into the equation.
Each term of the expression contains x raised to different powers. The

following example shows how to place all of the terms in order of the power of x, use a coefficient of 0 for each missing term, and specify the expression by listing the coefficients:

$$10x^4 + 5x^2 + 12x + 1$$

which can be specified by the list:

10, 0, 5, 12, 1

By using the IRP directive, you can make a macro that will evaluate polynomials:

```
; Macro to make code to evaluate a polynomial. Pass the variable
; to plug in the polynomial and the coefficients in reverse
; order. You cannot use AX, BX, CX, or DX for the variable.
POLY      MACRO      x, Coef    ; Give the variable and
                                ; cooefficients in
          mov        cx, 1      ; CX contains x to some power
                                ; Start with x to the 0th
          xor        bx, bx     ; The sum of the terms so far
          IRP        Trm, Coef  ; for each coefficient
          mov        ax, Trm    ; Get the Coef for this term
          imul       cx         ; Multiply by x to a power
          add        bx, ax     ; Add in this term
          mov        ax, x      ; Put x in AX
          imul       cx         ; Multiply it get x to the next
                                ; higher power
          mov        cx, ax
          ENDM                  ; End of the loop
          ENDM                  ; End of the macro
```

Note that the coefficients must be in reverse order from the standard polynomial form. This is because the loop raises x to different powers by successive multiplications. Also the macro uses the AX, BX, CX, and DX registers. If you do not want these registers changed, you can push them before the loop and pop them after. You cannot use AX, BX, CX, or DX for the first argument of this macro. This is because each of these registers is used in the loop. Failure to follow this requirement will cause a problem that is very difficult to debug. The comment at the beginning serves as a reminder not to use these registers. To use this macro to make code for the sample polynomial above, use this:

```
POLY          Var1, < 1, 12, 5, 0, 10>
```

THE IRPC LOOP

The `IRPC` directive is similar to the `IRP` directive except that the list is a list of characters instead of numbers. You can use the IRPC command to make a macro that looks up a character in a list of characters. This macro can be used to take a character that the user has input and see if it is in a list of commands.

```
; Find Char in Cmnds. Char must be an 8 bit register or memory
; value. On return BX is the number of the command or -1
; LOCALS must be on and the local prefix set to @@
PARSE      MACRO      Char, Cmnds
           xor        bx, bx          ; Set bx to 0
           IRPC       x, Cmnds        ; Loop through the possible
                                      ; commands
           cmp        Char, x         ; See if chars match
           je         @@Match         ; Exit loop when match found
           inc        bx              ; Increment index
           ENDM                       ; End of loop
@@Match:
           cmp        bx, SIZESTR     ; See if bx passed the end
           jb         @@Found         ; If BX less, then size jmp
           mov        bx, -1          ; otherwise set bx = -1
@@Found:
           ENDM
```

CONDITIONALS IN MACROS

The CALLDOS macro described earlier generates code to load the DX register even when it is not needed. The POLY macro generates code even when the coefficient is zero. Both of these macros work in these cases, but they are less efficient than they could be. You can use any of the conditional assembly directives to modify the macro for special cases. Thus, the CALLDOS macro becomes:

```
CALLDOS    MACRO      FuncNumb, DXData    ; Macro arguments
           mov        ah, FuncNumb        ; Put function # in AX
IFNB       <DXData>                       ; Check for blank
                                          ; argument
           mov        dx, DXData          ; Put data in DX
ENDIF
           int        21h                 ; Call DOS
           ENDM
```

In this example if you leave `DXData` blank, the macro will not include the line to load the DX register.

Also, the POLY example becomes:

```
; Macro to make code to evaluate a polynomial. Pass the variable
; to plug in the polynomial and the coefficients in reverse
; order. You cannot use AX, BX, CX, or DX for the variable.

POLY      MACRO      x, Coef    ; Give the variable and
                                ; coefficients in
          mov        cx, 1      ; CX contains x to some power
                                ; Start with x to the 0th
          xor        bx, bx     ; The sum of the terms so far
          IRP        Trm, Coef  ; for each coefficient
IF Trm                          ; See if Trm is not 0
          mov        ax, Trm    ; Get the Coef for this term
          imul       cx         ; Multiply by x to a power
          add        bx, ax     ; Add in this term
ENDIF
          mov        ax, x      ; Put x in AX
          mul        cx         ; Multiply it get x to the next
                                ; higher power
          mov        cx, ax
          ENDM                  ; End of the loop
          ENDM                  ; End of the macro
```

Since multiplying a number by 0 results in 0, there is no need to do the multiply for terms whose coefficient is 0. The conditional in this example leaves out the multiply and add instructions if the coefficient is 0.

Summary

Structured programming techniques can improve production, maintenance, and reusability of your programs. Separating programs into modules lets you think of the global picture of the program without getting bogged down in the details. Functions and macros are the next level of detail in a structured program. To use a well-defined function, all you need to know is what the function does. *How* the function does its job is actually the final level of detail.

The PUBLIC, EXTRN, COMM, and GLOBAL directives keep modules from having unexpected interactions. Only symbols that you want to use across modules can be used. This limits the side effects to those symbols only, thus simplifying the debugging process.

Functions need to have a well-defined interface to be properly structured. The PROC directive can be used to define the interface between functions. The interface can be modified to work with the several different interface techniques used in different high level languages.

Macros are another way to reduce a complex task to several shorter steps. The difference between a macro and a function is that a macro puts the code or data right where it is used, while a function makes the processor jump to the code and return. Macros can be used where the increased performance outweighs the increased memory requirements.

ARG

PURPOSE To specify the arguments for a procedure.

SYNTAX ARG ArgName[:[distance] [PTR] Type]

[,ArgName[:[distance] [PTR] Type]]... [= Size]

[RETURNS ArgName[:[distance] [PTR] Type]

[,ArgName[:[distance] [PTR] Type]]...]

ArgName	Is the symbol name to use.
distance	Is NEAR or FAR to indicate that the argument is a pointer.
PTR	Makes the assembler add debug information for Turbo debugger.
Type	Is the type of data for the argument. It can be WORD, DWORD, FWORD, PWORD, QWORD, TBYTE or a structure name.
Size	Is a symbol that is the size of the preceding arguments.
RETURNS	The arguments following this will not be popped off the stack when the function returns.

COMMENTS The ARG directive takes care of many of the details for passing arguments on the stack. It uses the language specified in the .MODEL directive to make sure that the function is compatible with a specific high level language. Each argument is at an offset on the stack relative to the BP register. Without the ARG directive, you would need to use expressions like bp+8 to refer to the arguments. Instead you can use the ArgName in the ARG directive.

Some high level languages, like C, push the arguments on the stack from right to left, while others, like Pascal, push the arguments from left to right. The ARG directive takes this into account so you should specify the arguments in the same order they would appear in the high level language.

SEE ALSO LOCAL
PROC
USES

EXAMPLE
```
; This function can be called from a C program with this line:
; Func(AnInt, AString, AChar);
;
        .MODEL    SMALL, C
```

ARG

```
          .CODE
_Func     PROC
ARG       AnInt:WORD, AString:PTR BYTE, AChar:BYTE
          mov       ax, [AnInt]    ; Get the first argument
                                   ;([bp-4])
          mov       di, [AString]  ; Second ([bp-6])
          mov       cl, [AChar]    ; Third ([bp-8])
          .
          .
          .

          ret
_Func     ENDP
```

COMM

PURPOSE   To define a variable that will be shared by several modules.

SYNTAX   COMM [distance] name:type [:count]

        [, [distance] name:type [:count]]...

distance	is NEAR or FAR depending on if the symbol is in DGROUP or not.
name	is the name of the variable.
type	is the type of data. It can be BYTE, WORD, DWORD, FWORD, PWORD, QWORD, TBYTE, or a structure name.
count	is the number of items in the symbol.

COMMENTS   The COMM directive tells the linker to allocate space for the variable. This means all of the modules that access it can use the same definition without having to use EXTRN and PUBLIC. This makes the COMM directive suitable for placement in an include file.

    You need to be sure that the COMM directive, or the include file that contains it, is in the correct data segment for the symbol. If it is not, the assembler will assume that the data can be reached with the DS register. This may or may not be true and may cause problems.

    Variables created with the COMM directive must be initialized by the program before they are used. See the GLOBAL directive for a way to make initialized communal variables.

SEE ALSO GLOBAL
EXTRN
PUBLIC

EXAMPLE Here is an include file with COMM variables:

```
; DATA.INC     a file of variables to include
COMM Name:BYTE:20        ; A 20 byte field for names
COMM Dscrpt:WORD         ; A file descriptor
COMM TRec:TransRec       ; A transaction file record (be sure
                         ; there is a structure definition
                         ; preceding this include file)
```

This module initializes the Dscpt variable:

```
            .MODEL    SMALL
            .DATA
INCLUDE     DATA.INC                     ; Put the include file here
FileName    DB        "TRANS.DAT",0
            .CODE
OpenFile    PROC
            mov       dx, OFFSET FileName
            mov       al, 2              ; Set up for read/write mode
            mov       ah, 3Dh            ; File open command
            int       21h                ; Call DOS
            jnc       OpenOK
            mov       ax, -1             ; If not open mark error
OpenOK:
            mov       Dscrpt, ax         ; Put AX in comm variable
            ret
OpenFile    ENDP
```

This file uses Dscrpt to read a record into TRec:

```
            .MODEL    SMALL
            .DATA
INCLUDE     DATA.INC
            .CODE
ReadRec     PROC
            mov       bx, Dscrpt         ; Get the file descriptor
                                         ; Put the size of a record in
                                         ; CX
            mov       cx, TYPE TransRec
                                         ; Put address of TRec in DS:DX
            mov       dx, OFFSET TRec
            mov       ah, 3Fh            ; DOS read file function
```

```
                int     21h              ; Call DOS
                ret
ReadRec  ENDP
```

ELSE

PURPOSE To mark the beginning of the alternative block in a conditional assembly block.

SYNTAX
```
IF condition
         .          Do this when condition is true
         .
         .
    ELSE
         .          Do this when condition is false
         .
         .
    ENDIF
```

COMMENTS The ELSE block is an option that is available with any of the IF conditionals. All of the statements between the ELSE and the ENDIF will be used if the condition is not true.

SEE ALSO
```
ENDIF
IF
IF1
IF2
IFB
IFDEF
IFDIF
IFDEFI
IFDIFI
IFE
IFIDN
IFIDNI
IFNB
IFNDEF
```

EXAMPLE See the example for IF.

ELSEIF, ELSEIF1, ELSEIF2, ELSEIFB, ELSEIFDEF, ELSEIFDIF, ELSEIFE, ELSEIFIDN, ELSEIFNB, ELSEIFNDEF

PURPOSE To mark the beginning of a nested conditional block.

SYNTAX

`ELSEIF expression`	*Do if expression is true.*
`ELSEIF1`	*Do if in assembler pass 1.*
`ELSEIF2`	*Do if in assembler pass 2.*
`ELSEIFB <arg>`	*Do if arg is blank.*
`ELSEIFDEF symbol`	*Do if symbol is defined.*
`ELSEIFDIF <arg1>,<arg2>`	*Do if arg1 and arg2 are different.*
`ELSEIFDIFI <arg1>,<arg2>`	*Do if arg1 and arg2 are different (ignore case).*
`ELSEIFE expression`	*Do if expression equals 0.*
`ELSEIFIDN <arg1>,<arg2>`	*Do if arg1 and arg2 are identical.*
`ELSEIFIDNI <arg1>,<arg2>`	*Do if arg1 and arg2 are identical (ignore case).*
`ELSEIFNB <arg>`	*Do if arg is not blank.*
`ELSEIFNDEF symbol`	*Do if symbol is not defined.*

COMMENTS Between the `IF` and the `ENDIF` there can be any number of `ELSEIF` directives. If the initial `IF` is false, then each `ELSEIF` will be evaluated until one of them is true. After doing the true block or if no true blocks can be found, the assembler goes to the `ENDIF`.

SEE ALSO
```
IF
IF1
IF2
IFB
IFDEF
IFDIF
IFDIFI
IFE
IFIDN
IFIDNI
IFNB
IFNDEF
ENDIF
```

EXAMPLE See the example for `IF`.

ENDIF

PURPOSE To mark the end of a conditional block.

SYNTAX IF condition

> .
> .
> .

[ELSE

> .
> .
> .]

ENDIF

COMMENTS There must be one ENDIF directive for every IF in a module. When an IF statement is false, the assembler goes to the matching ELSE or ENDIF statement. If the IF is true and the assembler comes to an ELSE, then it will go to the matching ENDIF before continuing the assembly. If the assembler sees an IF in a block that it is skipping over, it must see an ENDIF before it will start looking for the matching ELSE or ENDIF. This procedure lets you nest IF statements without ambiguities over what IF goes with what ELSE or ENDIF.

SEE ALSO IF
IF1
IF2
IFB
IFDEF
IFDIF
IFDIFI
IFE
IFIDN
IFIDNI
IFNB
IFNDEF
ELSE
ELSEIF
ELSEIF1
ELSEIF2
ELSEIFB
ELSEIFDEF
ELSEIFDIF
ELSEIFDIFI
ELSEIFE

```
ELSEIFIDN
ELSEIFIDNI
ELSEIFNB
ELSEIFNDEF
```

EXAMPLE   See the example for `IF`.

ENDM

PURPOSE   To mark the end of a macro or loop.

SYNTAX
```
name MACRO [args]
          .
          .
          .
          ENDM        Ends the macro
      REPT count
          .
          .
          .
          ENDM        Ends the loop
      IRP  var, <list>
          .
          .
          .
      ENDM             Ends the loop
      IRPC var, <string>
          .
          .
          .
      ENDM             Ends the loop
```

COMMENTS   Every macro and every loop must have an `ENDM` directive to mark the end of the macro or loop. When a loop is nested in a macro or another loop, the first `ENDM` goes with the innermost loop.

SEE ALSO
```
MACRO
REPT
IRP
IRPC
```

ENDM

EXAMPLE   See the example for MACRO.

ENDP

PURPOSE   To mark the end of a function that began with a PROC.

SYNTAX   MASM Mode:

```
name        PROC            The beginning of the function
                   .
                   .
                   .
[name]      ENDP
```

IDEAL Mode:

```
PROC        name
                   .
                   .
                   .
ENDP        [name]
```

COMMENTS   Every PROC must have an ENDP to mark the end of the procedure. The name may be omitted in the ENDP, in which case the name for the corresponding PROC statement will be used. PROC/ENDP blocks can be nested.

SEE ALSO   PROC

EXAMPLE   See the example for PROC.

EXITM

PURPOSE   To make the assembler ignore the rest of the macro or loop and continue assembling the rest of the program.

SYNTAX   EXITM

EXITM

COMMENTS   The EXITM is generally used with a conditional to exit from a macro or loop when certain conditions have been met. You can use this feature to skip the rest of a macro if it will not be needed, or to simulate a while loop with the repeat directive.

SEE ALSO   MACRO
REPT
IRP
IRPC

EXAMPLE

```
; This macro uses the EXITM directive to not use the last portion
; if it is not needed

AddNums    MACRO      arg1, arg2            ; Add the arguments macro
           mov        ax, WORD PTR arg1     ; Load the first argument
           add        ax, WORD PTR arg2     ; Add in the second
                                            ; argument
IF (TYPE arg1) LT 4                         ; See if the numbers are
           EXITM                            ; 1 word
ENDIF
           mov        dx, WORD PTR HIGH arg1
           adc        dx, WORD PTR HIGH arg2
           ENDM


; This loop uses the EXITM directive to simulate a while loop
MyMacro    MACRO      SizeData, Start
@@Size1    DB         ?                     ; Make room for size
Numb       =          Start
           REPT       SizeData              ; Loop up to size times
IF Numb GE 128                              ; Don't let the data get
           EXITM                            ; larger than 128
ENDIF
           DB         Numb                  ; Make a data item
Numb       =          Numb + 1
Last       =          $                     ; Remember this place
           ENDM
           ORG        @@Size1               ; Go back to the beginning
           DB         Numb - Start          ; Put the actual size there
           ORG        Last                  ; Go to the end of the data
           ENDM
```

EXTRN

PURPOSE To make a variable, which is defined in another module, available in the module containing the EXTRN statement.

SYNTAX EXTRN name:type[:count] [,name:type[:count]]...

name	is the name of the symbol.
type	the type of the variable NEAR, FAR, PROC, BYTE, WORD, DWORD, FWORD, PWORD, QWORD, TBYTE, or a structure name.
count	is the number of items in the variable.

COMMENTS The PUBLIC and EXTRN directives control what symbols can be used between modules. The EXTRN directive tells the assembler about symbols that are actually defined in other modules. The type and size information provided is the only information the assembler has about the variable. It is up to the programmer to make sure that the type and size match the type and size used in other modules.

The EXTRN directive can be inside or outside of a segment. If it is inside a segment, the assembler assumes that the variable is in that segment. If it is outside of a segment, then the assembler assumes that you will handle any segment overrides that will be required.

SEE ALSO PUBLIC
COMM
GLOBAL

EXAMPLE This file declares some symbols and makes them public:

```
            .MODEL    LARGE
            PUBLIC    AnInt, AString, ASPtr, Print, ClearScrn
            .DATA
AnInt       DW    10
AString     DB    "The string", 0Dh, 0Ah, '$'
CLSstr      DB    27, "[2J$"          ; ANSI clear screen command

            .CODE
; Print the string at DS:DX
Print       PROC
            mov   ah, 9              ; MS-DOS print string function
            int   21h                ; Call MS-DOS
            ret
```

```
Print     ENDP

; Use an ANSI escape sequence to clear the screen
ClearScrn PROC
          mov  ah, 9
          mov  dx, OFFSET CLSstr    ; Point to the clear screen
                                    ; string
          int  21h
          ret
ClearScrn ENDP
```

This file uses the symbols from the above file:

```
          .MODEL    LARGE
EXTRN     AnInt:WORD
EXTRN     AString:BYTE:12
EXTRN     Print:PROC
EXTRN     ClearScrn:PROC
          .DATA
ASPtr     DD   AString           ; Put the address of the
                                 ; string from the other file
                                 ; here

          .CODE
Start     PROC
          mov  ax, SEG DGROUP    ; Get the address for data
          mov  ds, ax            ; and put it in DS
          call ClearScrn         ; Call the function in the
                                 ; other source file

          mov  cx, AnInt         ; Get the number from the
                                 ; other file

BigLp:
          mov  dx, ASPtr         ; Get the address of the
                                 ; string

          call PrintStr          ; Print it
          loop BigLp             ; Repeat 10 times
          mov  ah, 4Ch           ; Put MS-DOS exit command in
                                 ; AH

          int  21h               ; Call MS-DOS
Start     ENDP
          .STACK    1024
END   Start
```

@FileName, ??FileName

PURPOSE To stand for the current file name.

SYNTAX
```
@FileName
??FileName
```

COMMENTS Each module is in its own file. The @FileName directive gives the name of the module. The name does not include the path or the extension. It will always be eight bytes long. If the name does not fill the eight bytes, it will be padded with spaces.

SEE ALSO   NAME   *Sets the name of the module*

EXAMPLE
```
; This program prints the name of the source file
           .MODEL     SMALL
           .DATA
FName:     DB              @FileName, 0Dh, 0Ah, "$"
           .CODE
Start:
           mov       ax, SEG DGROUP
           mov       ds, ax
           mov       dx, OFFSET FName      ; Get the address
           mov       ah, 9                 ; DOS Print
           int       21h                   ; Call DOS
           mov       ah, 4Ch               ; DOS Exit
           int       21h                   ; Call DOS
           .STACK    512
END Start
```

GLOBAL

PURPOSE To define a global symbol.

SYNTAX
```
GLOBAL     [distance] name:type [:count]
           [, [distance] name:type [:count]]...
```

       distance   is NEAR or FAR depending on if the symbol is in DGROUP or not.

name	is the name of the variable.
type	is the type of data. It can be BYTE, WORD, DWORD, FWORD, PWORD, QWORD, TBYTE, or a structure name.
count	is the number of items in the symbol.

COMMENTS

The GLOBAL directive is like a combination of the PUBLIC and EXTRN directives. In the module that defines the symbol, the GLOBAL directive is like a PUBLIC directive making the symbol visible to other modules. In the other modules, the GLOBAL directive is like an EXTRN directive.

The GLOBAL directive is often used in include files. Unlike the COMM directive, the GLOBAL directive can be used anywhere in the file before the variable is used. Since include files are often the first thing in a module, this works out well.

SEE ALSO

COMM
EXTRN
PUBLIC

EXAMPLE

Here is an include file with GLOBAL variables:

```
; DATA.INC    a file of variables to include
GLOBAL Name:BYTE:20     ; A 20 byte field for names
GLOBAL Dscrpt:WORD      ; A file descriptor
GLOBAL TRec:TransRec    ; A transaction file record (be sure
                        ; there is a structure definition
                        ; preceding this include file)
```

This module initializes the Dscpt variable:

```
INCLUDE    STRCDEFS.INC         ; Contains definitions for
                                ; structures
INCLUDE    DATA.INC             ; Put the include file here
           .MODEL    SMALL
           .DATA
FileName   DB        "TRANS.DAT",0
           .CODE
OpenFile   PROC
           mov       dx, OFFSET FileName
           mov       al, 2          ; Set up for read/write mode
           mov       ah, 3Dh        ; File open command
           int       21h            ; Call DOS
           jnc       OpenOK
           mov       ax, -1         ; If not open mark error
OpenOK:
```

```
            mov       Dscrpt, ax      ; Put AX in comm variable
            ret
OpenFile    ENDP
```

This file uses Dscrpt **to read a record into** TRec:

```
INCLUDE     STRCDEFS.INC
INCLUDE     DATA.INC
            .MODEL    SMALL
            .CODE
ReadRec     PROC
            mov       bx, Dscrpt      ; Get the file descriptor
                                      ; Put the size of a record in
                                      ; CX
            mov       cx, TYPE TransRec
                                      ; Put address of TRec in DS:DX
            mov       dx, OFFSET TRec
            mov       ah, 3Fh         ; DOS read file function
            int       21h             ; Call DOS
            ret
ReadRec     ENDP
```

IF, IF1, IF2, IFB, IFDEF, IFDIF, IFDIFI, IFE, IFIDN, IFIDNI, IFNB, IFNDEF

PURPOSE   To test a condition to see if the following block of code should be used.

SYNTAX
IF expression	*Do if expression is true.*
IF1	*Do if in assembler pass 1.*
EIF2	*Do if in assembler pass 2.*
IFB <arg>	*Do if arg is blank.*
IFDEF symbol	*Do if symbol is defined.*
IFDIF <arg1>,<arg2>	*Do if arg1 and arg2 are different.*
IFDIFI <arg1>,<arg2>	*Do if arg1 and arg2 are different (ignore case).*
IFE expression	*Do if expression equals 0.*
IFIDN <arg1>,<arg2>	*Do if arg1 and arg2 are identical.*
IFIDNI <arg1>,<arg2>	*Do if arg1 and arg2 are identical (ignore case).*

```
IFNB <arg>                      Do if arg is not blank.
IFNDEF symbol                   Do if symbol is not defined.
```

COMMENTS Conditionals are employed to use different code under different circumstances. They can be used to let the same source be used to create different versions of the program. In macros, they can make the macro use only code that is appropriate for the particular invocation of the macro.

The conditional block is all of the statements that come between the IF and the matching ENDIF. There can be an ELSE or a number of ELSEIF directives dividing the block into several blocks. Other IF statements can be nested in any of these blocks.

SEE ALSO
```
ELSE
ELSEIF
ENDIF
```

EXAMPLE
```
PrnErr    MACRO      Row, Col, Msg
IFB Row                                 ; If row is blank use
          mov        dh, 24             ; default
ELSEIF Row LE 24                        ; See if row is off screen
          mov        dh, Row
ELSE
IF1                                     ; Only print on pass 1
          DISPLAY "Invalid Row"
ENDIF
ENDIF

IFB Col                                 ; If col is blank use
          xor        dl, dl             ; default
ELSEIF (Col + (SIZESTR Msg) LE 79       ; See if string will fit
          mov        dl, Col
ELSE
IF1                                     ; Only print on pass 1
          DISPLAY "Invalid Column"
ENDIF
ENDIF
          xor        bh, bh             ; Set screen page 0
          mov        ah, 2              ; Move cursor function
          int        10h                ; Call BIOS
          mov        dx, OFFSET @@TMsg
          mov        ah, 9              ; Print function
          int        21h                ; Call DOS
          jmp        short @@Skip       ; Skip over the message
@@TMsg    DB         Msg                ; Store the Message here
```

```
                DB          '$'              ; Make sure string is
                                             ; terminated
    @@Skip:
                ENDM

    Func        PROC
                   .
                   .
                   .
    IFDEF       PrnErr                       ; Only use PrnErr if it has
                                             ; been defined
                PrnErr      10, 10, <Error #1>
    ELSE                                     ; Otherwise use the function
                mov         ax, ErrNumb1
                push        ax
                call        FPrnErr
                add         sp, 2
    ENDIF
```

INCLUDE

PURPOSE   To include the contents of a file in the file being assembled.

SYNTAX   `INCLUDE     FileName`

COMMENTS   Include files are used to define commonly used structures, macros, EQUates, and others. Putting this information in a single file keeps it from cluttering up the source files. It also means that if you need to change something in an include file, you do not need to hunt through all of the sources to make the change.

The `FileName` tells the assembler what file to load. If you leave off the extension, Turbo Assembler will use .INC. If you do not give a path, it will search the paths in the /I command line option and then in the current directory.

The contents of the include file will be loaded at the location of the include statement. This lets you place the contents wherever you want.

SEE ALSO   `INCLUDELIB`

EXAMPLE   See the example for `COMM`.

INCLUDELIB

PURPOSE To tell the linker to include a library file.

SYNTAX MASM mode:

```
INCLUDELIB filename
```

IDEAL mode:

```
INCLUDELIB "filename"
```

COMMENTS The file name is the name of the library to load. The default extension is .LIB. If you do not give a path, Turbo Assembler will search the paths in the /I command line option. If the file is not there, then Turbo Assembler will search the current directory.

The INCLUDELIB directive is an alternative to giving the library name as an option on the command line for the linker. If you use the INCLUDELIB directive, you should not use the command line option. This will cause multi-defined symbols.

SEE ALSO INCLUDE

EXAMPLE
```
INCLUDELIB EMU.LIB          ; Tell the linker to use EMU.LIB the
                            ; floating point emulator
```

IRP

PURPOSE To repeat a block of instructions using values from a list.

SYNTAX
```
IRP   variable, <arg [,arg]...>
      statements
ENDM
```

variable	the symbol that will be replaced by each of the args.
arg	the data to replace variable. Each time through the loop the next arg will be used.
statements	the statements that will be repeated.

IRP

COMMENTS   IRP loops are similar to REPT loops. The difference is that IRP loops let you use a list of items to place in the loop. This enables each iteration of the loop to do something slightly different. The items can be symbols, strings, or numbers.

SEE ALSO   IRPC
REPT

EXAMPLE
```
            .MODEL     SMALL
            .DATA
SaveM       DW   4 dup(?)
            .CODE
            .
            .
            .
Tmp         =     0                    ; A counter
IRP reg, <ax, bx, cx, dx>              ; Loop through a list of regs
            mov   SaveM+Tmp, reg       ; Save a register
Tmp         =     Tmp + 2              ; Go to the next offset
ENDP
            .
            .
            .
```

IRPC

PURPOSE   To repeat a block of statements using characters from a string.

SYNTAX   IRPC variable, string
        statements

ENDM

    variable   the symbol that will be replaced by each of the args.

    string   the characters to use. Each time through the loop the next character in the string will be used.

    statements   the statements that will be repeated.

COMMENTS   The IRPC directive is similar to the IRP directive. The difference is that instead of a list of arguments, the IRPC directive uses the characters in a string. The statement block will be repeated once for each letter. The letter will replace any instance of the variable in the body of the loop.

SEE ALSO   REPT
         IRP

EXAMPLE   ```
; Make a list of variables named Counter_a, Counter_e ...
IRPC letter, <aeiou>
Counter_&letter   DW   0
ENDM
```

---

# LOCAL

---

**PURPOSE**   To define local variables for procedures or macros.

**SYNTAX**   In macros:

```
LOCAL Symbol [,Symbol]
```

In procedures:

```
LOCAL name:type[:count] [,name:type[:count]]
```

Symbol	*Is the symbol that should be local in the macro.*
name	*The name of the local symbol in a procedure.*
type	*The type of symbol. One of BYTE, WORD, DWORD, FWORD, PWORD, QWORD, TBYTE, or structure name.*
count	*The number of items for this symbol.*

COMMENTS   In macros the LOCAL directive only makes the symbol local to the macro. You must define the symbol before it can be used.

In procedures the LOCAL directive does more than make the symbol local. It allocates space in the stack frame for the symbol. The assembler totals the size of all local symbols and adds an instruction to move the stack pointer below the local variable space.

Each of the symbols can be accessed by a base register indexed expression, using the BP register. For example, the first local variable might be at [bp-2]. If you use the local symbol name, the assembler will replace it with the correct expression.

SEE ALSO   PROC
         MACRO
         ARG
```

LOCAL

EXAMPLE
```
; Make a function that uses three local variables
MyFunc   PROC
LOCAL    AnInt:WORD, AnArray:WORD:14, AStr:PTR WORD
         xor     ax,ax
         mov     AnInt, ax        ; Set up the int
         mov     cx, 14
         lea     di, AnArray      ; Get the address of AnArray
         rep stosw                ; set it to 0's
         mov     cx, -1
         mov     si, AStr         ; Point to string
         rep     scansb           ; Look for a 0 byte
         not     cx               ; CX is the length of AStr
           .
           .
           .
MyFunc   PROC

; The symbols AnInt, AnArray, AStr are undefined outside of the
; procedure
```

LOCALS, NOLOCALS

PURPOSE   To enable or disable local symbols.

SYNTAX
```
LOCALS     [prefix]

NOLOCALS
```

prefix   *Two character sequence used as a prefix for local symbols. If the prefix is omitted, then @@ is the default prefix.*

COMMENTS   When you enable local symbols, then symbols that begin with the local prefix are local to the procedure, macro, union, or structure that contains the symbol. The prefix must be a valid start of a symbol. For example, "12" would not be a valid prefix.

The NOLOCALS directive turns off local symbols. If you specified a prefix in the LOCALS directive, it will be the default for the next LOCALS directive.

SEE ALSO
```
LOCAL
MACRO
PROC
```

EXAMPLE
```
         LOCALS                                      ; Turn on local variables
AFunc    PROC
                .
                .
                .
@@Start:                                             ; Local to AFunc
                .
                .
                .
AFunc    ENDP
BFunc    PROC
                .
                .
                .
@@Start:                                             ; Different from the other
                .                                    ; @@Start label
                .
                .
BFunc    ENDP
```

MACRO

PURPOSE   To mark the beginning of a macro definition.

SYNTAX   **MASM Mode:**

```
name MACRO [arg [,arg]...]
     statements

ENDM
```

IDEAL Mode:

```
MACRO name [arg [,arg]...]
     statements

ENDM
```

name	*Is the name of the macro being defined.*
arg	*Are argument names for the macro.*
statements	*Are the statements that will replace the name when the macro is used.*

MACRO

COMMENTS Whenever the macro name appears in the source file after the definition, the assembler will replace it with the statements in the definition. The statements can be any valid Turbo Assembler statements, including code, data directives, other directives, and even conditionals. Each MACRO definition must have an ENDM directive to mark the end of the definition.

You can pass arguments to the macro by following the name with the arguments to pass. The assembler replaces any occurrence of an argument name in the macro with the data passed for that argument.

SEE ALSO   ENDM
            PROC

EXAMPLE

```
; Define a macro that adds two arguments and puts the result in
; ax. To use the macro invoke it like this:
;         AddM      < 14, dx >      ; Add 14 to dx
AddM      MACRO     A, B
          mov       ax, A           ; Get the first argument into
                                    ; AX
          add       ax, B           ; Add in the second argument
          ENDM
```

PROC

PURPOSE To mark the beginning of a function.

SYNTAX MASM Mode:

```
name      PROC [distance] [uses reg [,reg]]
```

IDEAL Mode:

```
PROC      name [distance] [USES reg [,reg]]
```

name   *Is the name of the function.*

distance   *Is NEAR or FAR, depending on how the function will be called.*

reg   *Are the registers that should be put on the stack while the function is running.*

COMMENTS The PROC directive tells the assembler that the code that follows is a function. The distance argument tells the assembler what kind of return instruction to use. It also defines the size of the function name. Any reference to the name of the function, after the function has been defined, will use the size given.

If you use the USES clause, Turbo Assembler will insert code at the beginning of the function to save the registers named on the stack. It will also put code at end of the function to restore the registers from the stack. This code keeps the function from modifying registers that are being used in other parts of the program.

The statements between the PROC and ENDP directives can include local symbols. The local symbols must begin with the local symbols prefix. In addition, there must be a LOCALS keyword in the module before the function.

SEE ALSO
ARG
LOCAL
LOCALS
ENDP

EXAMPLE

```
        .MODEL    SMALL
; This function uses the SI and DI registers, and uses the
; function size indicated in the .MODEL directive.
Func1   PROC USES SI, DI
          .
          .
          .
        ret               ; Converted to RETN or RETF depending on
                          ; the memory model
Func1   ENDP

; This function does not save any registers and must be called
; with a far call.

Func2   PROC FAR
          .
          .
          .
        ret               ; Converted to RETF

Func2   ENDP

Main    PROC              ; Uses the default type set up in the
          .               ; MODEL directive
        call Func1        ; A NEAR call
        call Func2        ; A FAR call
        ret
Main    ENDP
```

PUBLIC

PURPOSE　To make a symbol visible to other modules.

SYNTAX　`PUBLIC symbol [,symbol]`

COMMENTS　Turbo Assembler gives the names of public symbols to the linker. Without this information the linker cannot resolve external references to the symbol. The `PUBLIC` directive makes a symbol public. The symbol can be a data variable, a label, or a function name.

　　　　The linker is not concerned about the type of the symbol. It is up to you to make sure that you use the same type for the symbol in each module. Failure to do this can result in errors that are very difficult to find.

SEE ALSO　`EXTRN`
　　　　`COMM`
　　　　`GLOBAL`

EXAMPLE　See the example for `EXTRN`.

PURGE

PURPOSE　To remove a macro definition.

SYNTAX　`PURGE macroname [,macroname]`

COMMENTS　Commonly used macro definitions can be collected together and put in an include file. One drawback to this technique is that a macro name in the include file may conflict with a symbol name in the program. If you change the include file, then it may not be correct for other programs. The answer is the `PURGE` directive, which removes the macro name from the assembler's symbol table. This leaves the name free for other uses.

SEE ALSO　`MACRO`

EXAMPLE　
```
INCLUDE MACROS.INC        ; Includes a macro named Print
PURGE Print               ; Remove Print from the symbol table
```

```
Print    PROC            ; OK to define a new symbol named Print
           .
           .
           .
```

REPT

PURPOSE   To repeat a block of statements.

SYNTAX
```
REPT expression
statements

ENDM
```

expression   *Evaluates to the number of times the loop will run.*

statements   *The statements that will be repeated.*

COMMENTS   The statements in a repeat block will be duplicated a given number of times. The number of times comes in the value of the expression. By replacing repetitive sequences with the REPT directive, you can make your program more concise and easier to read. You can use variables and conditionals inside of the loop for sequences that change.

SEE ALSO
```
IRP
IRPC
ENDM
```

EXAMPLE
```
; Define 10 bytes containing the numbers 1 through 10
Value    =        1            ; Make the initial Value
         REPT     10           ; Do 10 times
         DB       Value        ; Make a byte with Value in it
Value    =        Value+1      ; Increment the value
         ENDM                  ; End of the loop

; Make 4 shl instructions
         REPT     4
         shl      ax, 1
         ENDM
```

Chapter *11* *Code Generation, Error Handling, and Listings*

Turbo Assembler generates code for any of the processors in the 80x86 family. It can also generate instructions for any of the related math co-processors. You must tell the assembler what type of instructions to expect by using the directives presented in the first part of this chapter. In addition to the instruction set directives, the first part of this chapter gives you directives to tell the assembler how compatible it should be with Microsoft's MASM assembler.

Turbo Assembler can detect some types of errors as it is assembling the program. Some errors, like undefined symbols, must be corrected before the program can be assembled. Others, like using a line that is too long, give you a warning but permit the assembly to be completed. The second part of this chapter shows you how to control the handling of these errors and warnings.

Listing files show both the source code and what the assembler did with it. A *listing* is a valuable tool when it comes to debugging a program. The last part of this chapter shows you how to control the information that goes into a listing file.

The Personality of the Assembler

Turbo Assembler is really several assemblers in one. By default it is a MASM-compatible 8088/8086 assembler. But by using assembler directives, you can change its personality. Turbo Assembler can work with different processors, use MASM or Turbo directives, and include instructions for co-processors.

Different Processors

The Intel Corporation 80x86 family includes seven different microprocessors with five different instruction sets. The first of these processors are the 8088 and 8086. The instruction sets for these two processors are the same. By default the assembler assembles instructions for these processors. If your program includes an instruction that is only used by other processors in the family, the assembler will generate an error. To get Turbo Assembler to use the correct instruction set, you need to put the appropriate assembler directive at the beginning of the program. Table 11-1 shows these directives and what instruction set they represent. The directives that begin with a dot (.) can only be used in MASM mode. The directives beginning with a *P* can be used in MASM or IDEAL mode.

Table 11-1. *Directives for Processor-Specific Instructions*

Directive	Instructions allowed
.186, P186	All 80186/80188 instructions allowed.
.286, .286C, P286N	Non-priveleged 80286 instructions allowed.
.286P, P286	All 80286 instructions allowed.
.287, P287	All 80287 instructions allowed.
.386, .386C, P386N	Non-privileged 80386 instructions allowed.
.386P, P386	All 80386 instructions allowed.
.387, P387	All 80387 instructions allowed.
.8086, P8086	All 8086/8088 instructions allowed.
.8087, P8087	All 8087 instructions allowed.

Compatibility with MASM

Turbo Assembler is designed to be fully compatible with the MASM Assembler. You can write programs for Turbo Assembler that can be assembled by MASM. But you can also write programs for Turbo Assembler that use its own special features. These programs are no longer compatible with MASM.

There are some things that MASM does that are not used in Turbo Assembler. For example, MASM will let you use some commands that do not make sense, such as:

```
ABC   EQU  [BP+2]
      PUBLIC ABC      ;ABC does not refer to a memory location
```

Turbo Assembler gives a warning message for this kind of code. MASM can use its own format for floating point numbers. The MASM directive for this is .MSFLOAT. Turbo Assembler always uses the IEEE floating point format that is compatible with the math co-processors. Turbo Assembler does not accept the .MSFLOAT directive.

MASM MODE

The default mode for Turbo Assembler is the MASM-compatible mode. This means you can assemble a source file that was meant for MASM. Note that in this mode there are several directives that work only with Turbo Assembler. Therefore, while Turbo Assembler can assemble any MASM source, MASM cannot always assemble any Turbo Assembler source.

Turbo Assembler is compatible with versions 1 through 4 of MASM. To use some of the features of MASM 5.1, you must use the MASM51 directive. The features that can be used in this mode include SUBSTR, CATSTR, SIZESTR, and INSTR directives, and the backslash character (\) which indicates that the next line is a continuation of the current line.

The syntax for the LOCAL directive can be:

```
LOCAL name [[count]][:[distance] PTR] type]
```

If also in QUIRKS mode (which enables some quirky aspects of MASM):

- Local labels can use @F and @B for the prefix if the prefix is @@
- Variables can be redefined in PROCs
- C language PROCs are all PUBLIC and have a leading underscore.

Over the years several quirks have been found in the way MASM assembles programs. In some cases, programmers have taken advantage of these quirks in their programs. You can get Turbo Assembler to accept these quirks by using the QUIRKS directive. Effects of the QUIRKS directive are the following:

- No size checking for moving segment registers to memory. The code:

```
SEGVAL    DB    ?
          mov   SEGVAL, ds
```

is legal. In this case the byte following SEGVAL will be overwritten by the MOV.

- Ignore FAR PTR overrides on JMP instructions if the label is in the same segment as the JMP. (Note: Turbo Assembler 2.0 has this quirk enabled in the default mode.) The code:

```
        jmp   FAR PTR Next
Next:
```

becomes:

```
9Bh          ; 8 bit jmp
03h          ; Displacement to Next
90h, 90h, 90h   ; NOP's to cover the FAR
             ; displacement
```

- Lose type information in EQU or = statements. The code:

```
X    dw    0
Y    =     OFFSET X
     mov   ax, Y
```

will be assembled as MOV ax, [X] **instead of** mov ax, OFFSET X.

- Allow ALIGN directives to align on smaller boundaries than the segment containing the ALIGN. The ALIGN may be ignored since the linker can align the segment on different boundaries.

- Do not use sign-extend instructions on non-arithmetic instructions. All instructions that use immediate data can use a singlebyte to fill a 16-bit register if the number is between –128 and +127. The byte will be sign-extended by the processor. In QUIRKS mode this feature is used only for arithmetic instructions.

IDEAL MODE

Turbo Assembler has its own set of directives and syntax that is different from MASM, called *IDEAL* mode. The IDEAL directive tells the assembler to accept IDEAL mode syntax. If you want to switch back to MASM mode, you can use the MASM directive.

The syntax descriptions of the directives in this book include both the MASM and IDEAL mode versions of the directive. Other features of IDEAL mode are the following:

- 30% faster assembly.
- Structure member names can appear in more than one structure
- HIGH and LOW operators can extract different size portions
- EQU replacements are treated as strings
- Always gives data relative to the GROUP containing the data
- Square brackets surround the entire address expression
- SIZE operator gives the size of all items defined for a symbol
- Directives cannot begin with a dot (.).

The implications of IDEAL mode on using specific directives are discussed in the descriptions of those directives, following the summary at the end of this chapter.

Pseudo Instructions

Turbo Assembler can assemble instructions that are not really part of the instruction set being used. There are three types of pseudo instructions available. The first is the emulated floating point. Any floating point instructions following the EMUL directive, and preceding the NOEMUL directive, will generate code to use software floating point emulation instead of instructions to call a math co-processor. The EMUL directive is equivalent to the /e command line option. You must link in the emulation routines if you use the EMUL directive.

The second type of pseudo instruction involves conditional jumps. If you use the JUMPS directive, then you can use conditional jumps whose destinations are more than 128 to +127 bytes from the jump. Since there is no single instruction to do this on the 8088/86, the assembler actually generates two jump instructions. The first is a conditional jump that tests the opposite condition of the jump in the source. The destination of this jump is the instruction following the next jump. The next jump is an unconditional NEAR jump to the destination given in the source. For example:

```
        jc    nlabel    ; Jump if carry (nlabel is more than 128
                        ; bytes from this instruction)
```

becomes:

```
        jnc   @@a       ; Jump if no carry past the next jmp
        jmp   nlabel    ; If the carry set do near jump
@@a:
```

The last type of pseudo instruction is the *push immediate data* instruction. Normally you must put data into a register to push it on the stack. Turbo Assembler will let you push immediate data by substituting several instructions to do the job. For example:

```
push      21h                 ; Put 21h on the stack
```

becomes:

```
push      ax                  ; Make a space on the stack
push      bp                  ; Save the bp register
mov       bp, sp              ; Get the stack pointer
mov       [bp+2],21h          ; Put the data where AX is on the
                              ; stack
pop       bp                  ; Restore the bp register
```

Note that this is much more code than putting the data in AX and pushing AX. The reason for the extra code is the need to preserve all the registers involved.

Keeping Track of the Assembler

A single source file can be used to create many different versions of the program by modifying symbols that are used in *conditional assembly* statements. (See Chapter 10.) Creating a new version can lead to problems if the changes are not the ones you intended. One way to make sure that the right things are happening is to have the assembler print messages indicating what is going on. Turbo Assembler has several directives for doing this.

Printing Messages

The %OUT and DISPLAY directives print messages on the screen during the assembly. These directives are identical except that the string for DISPLAY must be enclosed in quotes. You can use these directives to indicate what options are being used for the assembly:

```
INCLUDE   config.inc                  ; Include symbols that
                                      ; configure the program

IF @CodeSize                          ; Test predefined symbol
%OUT Using small code model
ELSE
DISPLAY "Using large code model"
ENDIF
```

Errors and Warnings

Turbo Assembler informs you of errors and questionable code by displaying messages on the screen while it is assembling your program. If there are any errors in the program, Turbo Assembler will not generate an object file.

In addition to the regular errors, you can make your own error conditions. For example, you may want to make sure that an argument for a macro is not left out. You could define the macro like this:

```
MyMacro   MACRO arg1, arg2
.ERRB arg1                            ; Generate an error if arg1 is blank
Lab&arg1  db   arg2                   ; Make a symbol with arg1 in it
          ENDM
```

You can use the %OUT or DISPLAY directives with an error directive to give some information about the error. The previous example then becomes:

```
MyMacro    MACRO arg1, arg2
IFB arg1
.ERR
@OUT Missing argument for MyMacro
END
           ENDM
```

There are several different kinds of error conditions that you can use. Table 11-2 shows the possibilities. The directives that begin with a dot (.) are for MASM mode only. The others can be used in MASM mode or IDEAL mode.

Table 11-2.   *Error Directives*

Directive	Condition
.ERR, ERR	Unconditionally generate an error.
ERRIF expr	If expr is true generate an error.
.ERR1, ERRIF1	If pass 1 generate an error.
.ERR2, ERRIF2	If pass 2 generate an error.
.ERRB arg ERRB arg	If arg is blank generate an error.
.ERRDEF symbol ERRIFDEF symbol	If symbol is defined generate an error.
.ERRDIF arg1, arg2 ERRIFDIF arg1, arg2	If arg1 different from arg2 generate an error.
.ERRDIFI arg1, arg2 ERRIFDIFI arg1, arg2	Same as .ERRDIF except it ignores case.
.ERRE expr ERRIFE expr	If expr equals 0 generate an error.
.ERRIDN arg1, arg2 ERRIFIDN arg1, arg2	If arg1 and arg2 are identical generate an error.
.ERRIDNI arg1, arg2 ERRIFIDNI arg1, arg2	Same as .ERRIDN except it ignores case.
.ERRNB arg ERRIFNB arg	If arg is not blank generate an error.
.ERRNDEF symbol ERRNDEF symbol	If symbol not defined generate an error.
.ERRNZ expr ERRIFNZ expr	If expr is not 0 generate an error.

Comments

You have seen several examples of using a semicolon (;) to indicate that the text following is a comment. Each line that contains a comment must use the semicolon. You can make comments that include several lines by using the COMMENT directive. The argument for the comment directive is the character that marks the end of the comment. Note that the assembler ignores the entire line on which the comment termination delimiter occurs. This example shows how to use the COMMENT directive:

```
COMMENT ^  This is a comment
All of this text will be ignored by the assembler. The
assembler will begin assembling as soon as it sees
another circumflex.

^ This is the end of the comment. This line will also be ignored.
```

Listings

In addition to the object file, Turbo Assembler can generate a listing file that shows the source statements combined with information about what the assembler did with those statements. To get Turbo Assembler to generate a listing file, you must give a listing file name on the command line, as in this example:

```
c:\> tasm prnstr,,prnstr
```

The first name is the name of the file to assemble. The commas separate the different files that can be made. In this case there is no map file name, so the map file will not be generated. The last name is the name of the list file. Because there is no extension specified, the assembler will use .LST. Using this command will take this source file...

```
        %TABSIZE   4
        PAGE       50, 65
        %BIN       10
        %LINUM     0
        %PCNT      3
        %TEXT      45
        TITLE      Print Hello string

; Define constants
LF      EQU   0ah
CR      EQU   0dh
```

```
; Call DOS macro
CallOS    MACRO    cmnd
          mov      ah, cmnd
          int      21h
          ENDM

          .MODEL   Small
          .DATA

Msg       db       "Hello, World", LF, CR, '$'
          PAGE     ; Force a page break here
          .CODE
Start:
          mov      ax, SEG DGROUP      ; Set up the segment
          mov      ds, ax
          mov      dx, OFFSET Msg      ; Get the address
          CallOS   <9>                 ; DOS print function
          CallOS   <4ch>               ; DOS exit function

          .STACK
END       Start
```

...and make this listing file:

```
Turbo Assembler     Version 2.0      02/04/91 13:52:23
Page 1
PRNSTR.ASM
Print Hello string

; Define constants
   = 000A   LF     EQU   0ah
   = 000D   CR     EQU   0dh

; Call DOS macro
          CallOS   MACRO     cmnd
                   mov  ah, cmnd
                   int  21h
                   ENDM

  *00               .MODEL      Small
  *00               .DATA
  *00  48 65 6C     + Msg     db   "Hello, World",  +
       6C 6F 2C     + LF, CR, '$'
       20 57 6F     +
       72 6C 64     +
       0A 0D 24
```

```
  *0F                 .CODE
  *00        Start:
  *00  B8 0000s     mov   ax, SEG DGROUP    +
                 ; Set up the      segment
  *03  8E D8        mov   ds, ax
  *05  BA 0000r     mov   dx, OFFSET    Msg    +
; Get the address
                     CallOS       <9>            +
; DOS print function
1 *08  B4 09        mov   ah, 9
1 *0A  CD 21        int   21h
                     CallOS       <4ch>          +
; DOS exit function
1 *0C  B4 4C        mov   ah, 4ch
1 *0E  CD 21        int   21h

  *00                 .STACK
              END    Start
```

Symbol Name	Type	Value
??DATE	Text	"02/04/91"
??FILENAME	Text	"PRNSTR "
??TIME	Text	"13:52:22"
??VERSION	Number	0200
@CODE	Text	_TEXT
@CODESIZE	Text	0
@CPU	Text	0101H
@CURSEG	Text	_TEXT
@DATA	Text	DGROUP
@DATASIZE	Text	0
@FILENAME	Text	PRNSTR
@MODEL	Text	2
@WORDSIZE	Text	2
CR	Number	000D
LF	Number	000A
MSG	Byte	DGROUP:0000

```
START               Near   _TEXT:0000

Macro Name

CALLOS

Groups & Segments      Bit   Size Align  Combine Class

DGROUP                 Group
  STACK                16    0400 Para   Stack   STACK
  _DATA                16    000F Word   Public  DATA
_TEXT                  16    0010 Word   Public  CODE
```

The listing file can tell you many things about your program once you learn how to read it. Each page of the listing begins with a line indicating that it is a Turbo Assembler listing file, as well as the date and time it was assembled. The next line gives the page number. After that is the name of the file or subsection, and then the title for the file.

Each line from the source file appears in the listing file. To the left of the line is the value of the location counter and the code generated. Commands that do not generate code only show the location counter. The EQU or = directives show the value of the symbol defined that is preceded by an equal sign (=). When a macro is being expanded, the nesting level of the macro appears before the location counter.

The location of DGROUP cannot be determined until run time. The assembler puts zeros in the object file for this address and also puts a record in the object file that tells the linker to tell the program loader that such locations will need to be fixed up. The listing file shows this by placing an *s* in the listing of that location. The address of Msg also cannot be determined by the assembler. In this case it is the linker that will supply the correct value. The linker will add the offset of Msg in this module to the next available offset in the data segment. The assembler puts the offset of the symbol in the object file, and tells the assembler that this location will need to be fixed up. The listing file shows this by placing an *r* next to the address.

The last part of the listing file shows the symbol table which contains all of the symbols used in the module. The list shows the name, type, and value of each symbol defined. The list is sorted by name. Many of the symbols in the sample listing are automatically created by the assembler. Following the data symbols is a list of the macros defined. Finally, all the groups and segments used are listed. Group names are shown with the included segments indented below them. The list of segments shows the name, 16- or 32-bit flag, size in bytes, alignment, combine type, and class.

Formatting the Listing

Turbo Assembler does its best to format the listing file so it will be easy to read. For best results, you must tell it some things about how you will be looking at the file. In the previous example, the first directive is %TABSIZE. This tells the assembler how many columns each tab character uses. The default setting is 8. If the tab size does not match the tab size used on the output device, then the columns in the listing file will not line up.

The second directive is PAGE. This directive controls the size of the page. The first number is the number of lines, and the second number is the number of columns. The assembler will print up to the number of lines specified before starting a new page. If a line uses more than the given number of columns, the line will be truncated, or wrapped around, depending on the state of the %TRUNC flag. To make a new page, regardless of the number of lines, use the PAGE directive without any arguments.

The next five directives control the width of various fields in the listing file. These directives are useful in making a line short enough to fit on the page without wrapping. Table 11-3 shows these directives and the fields they control.

Table 11-3. *Directives for Controlling Field Width in Listings*

Directive	Default	Field
%BIN	20	Object code
%DEPTH	1	Macro nesting level
%LINUM	4	Line numbers
%PCNT	4 or 8	Location counter
%TEXT	NA	Source code

Controlling What Gets Printed

The listing file can become very large. The bigger it is, the more difficult it is to find the part that you need. You can shorten the listing file by telling it not to generate listings for part of the file. The .LIST and .XLIST directives turn on and off listings. This lets you keep any part of the program out of the listing. These directives are often used in *include* files to prevent the included information from cluttering up the listing.

You can tell the assembler to list only certain kinds of data in the listing. For example, the .LALL directive tells the assembler to include macro expansions in the listing. The .SALL directive tells the assembler not to include macro expansions in the listing file. You can eliminate statements that are in the false branch of a conditional with the .LFCOND directive. The %INCL directive includes the contents of include files in the listing, while %NOINCL prevents include files from being listed.

Listing Symbols

The symbol table at the end of the listing can be a useful debugging tool. It is an organized map of all of the data in the program. You can also use the .CREF directive to make the assembler output a cross-reference list of where each symbol is used.

If this is too much data for you, you can tell the assembler not to include any symbol table at all. The %NOSYMS directive prevents the generation of the symbol table. This directive can appear anywhere in the source file. There is a directive to enable the listing of symbols (%SYMS), but since this is the default state it is not required.

Cross-reference lists show all of the symbols in the program along with the line numbers for lines that use the symbol. If the .CREF directive is in the source file, then cross-reference information will be included in the symbol table listing. For the previous example, the cross-reference listing looks like this:

Symbol Name	Type	Value	Cref defined at #		
??DATE	Text	"02/04/91"			
??FILENAME	Text	"PRNSTR "			
??TIME	Text	"15:36:05"			
??VERSION	Number	0200			
@CODE	Text	_TEXT	#12	#12	#20
@CODESIZE	Text	0	#12		
@CPU	Text	0101H			
@CURSEG	Text	_TEXT	#13	#20	#36
@DATA	Text	DGROUP	#12		
@DATASIZE	Text	0	#12		
@FILENAME	Text	PRNSTR			
@MODEL	Text	2	#12		
@WORDSIZE	Text	2	#13	#20	#36
CR	Number	000D	#4	14	
LF	Number	000A	#3	14	
MSG	Byte	DGROUP:0000	#14	25	
START	Near	_TEXT:0000	#21	37	

Macro Name			Cref defined at #		
CALLOS			#7	27	31

Groups & Segments	Bits Size	Align Combine	Class	Cref defined at #		
DGROUP	Group			#12	12	22
STACK	16 0400	Para Stack	STACK	#36		
_DATA	16 000F	Word Public	DATA	#12	#13	
_TEXT	16 0010	Word Public	CODE	#12	12 #20	20

Line numbers that begin with an *octothorpe* (#) indicate lines that define the symbol. For example, the _DATA symbol is defined on lines 12 and 13. The other line numbers are the lines that use the symbol. Symbols without any line numbers are unreferenced symbols. You can restrict the symbol table to include only referenced symbols with the %CREFREF directive. The %CREFUREF directive will restrict the list to include only the unreferenced symbols.

Saving and Restoring Listing Controls

You can save the state of listing controls such as %INCL, %NOINCL, %CTRL, %NOCTRL so that you can temporarily change them. For example, if you have an include file that you do not want to put in the listing—but you do not know if the listing should continue after the include file is done—you could use the following:

```
%PUSHLCTL              ; Save the state of the listing controls
%NOLIST                ; Turn off the listing

        .

        .

        .

%POPLCTL               ; Restore the saved listing controls
```

The %PUSHLCTL and %POPLCTL directives save and restore the listing controls to a 16-level stack.

Summary

Turbo Assembler has several personalities. It can assemble instructions from all five different 80x86 instruction sets and all three math co-processors. You can use directives like .286 and .8087 to control what instruction set to use. In addition to the alternate instruction sets, Turbo Assembler can assemble directives for several different versions of MASM and its own IDEAL mode.

Keeping track of what the assembler is doing can simplify the process of assembling different versions of a program. The %OUT and DISPLAY directives print messages as the program is assembling. You can use the .ERR and related directives to tell the assembler and the operator that there is an error in the program.

Listing files tell you what the assembler has done with the source code. This is an important first step in debugging a program. Directives like PAGE and %TABSIZE let you control how the listing will be formatted. Other directives like .LIST and .LALL let you tell the assembler what to include in the listing file.

.186

PURPOSE To tell the assembler to allow instructions that are specific to the 80186 CPU.

SYNTAX .186

COMMENTS All instructions following this directive must be in the instruction set for the 80186 processor. The assembler only checks to see that the instructions are in the correct instruction set. You must insure that the program is run on a computer with the specified processor and co-processor.

SEE ALSO P186
P286
P286N
P207
P386
P386N
P387
P8086
P8087
PN087

EXAMPLE The 80186 and newer processors allow the PUSH instruction to push an immediate value:

```
.186                    ; Enable 80186 instructions
push 12                 ; Push the number 12 onto the stack
```

.286, .286C

PURPOSE To tell the assembler to allow real mode 80286 instructions.

SYNTAX .286
.286C

COMMENTS All instructions following this directive must be in the instruction set for the 80286 processor in real mode. The assembler only checks to see that the instructions in the source are in the correct instruction set. You must ensure that the program is run on a computer with the specified processor and co-processor.

.286, .286C

SEE ALSO   P186
P286
P286N
P287
P386
P386N
P387
P8086
P8087
PNO87

EXAMPLE

```
              .286                      ; Required to use the
                                        ; bound instruction
ArrayBnds DW   0, 99
Array     DB   100 DUP(?)
              .
              .
              .
          bound si, DWORD PTR ArrayBnds ; See if SI is in range
          mov  al, Arrary[si]           ; In bounds use SI
```

.286P

PURPOSE   To tell the assembler to allow 80286 protected mode instructions.

SYNTAX   .286P   *Allow all 80286 instructions.*

COMMENTS   Instructions following this directive can include 80286 protected mode instructions. Note that this instruction does not put the processor into protected mode nor does it verify that the processor used is an 80286.

SEE ALSO   P186
P286
P286N
P287
P386
P386N
P387
P8086
P8087
PNO87

EXAMPLE

```
        .286P              ; Allow protected mode
                           ; instructions
        lgdt ax            ; Protected mode instruction
                           ; to load the global
                           ; descriptor table
```

.287

PURPOSE To tell the assembler to allow instructions for the 80287 floating point co-processor.

SYNTAX .287   *Allow 80287 instructions.*

COMMENTS Instructions following this directive can include instructions for the 80287 co-processor. If you include the EMUL directive or use the /e command line option, the floating point instructions will be converted to calls to a floating point library. Otherwise, the assembler will generate ESC instructions to pass the floating point commands on to the co-processor.

SEE ALSO P186
P286
P286N
P287
P386
P386N
P387
P8086
P8087
PN087

EXAMPLE

```
.287                ; Allow floating point instructions
fsetpm              ; 80287 instruction
```

.386, .386C

PURPOSE To tell the assembler to allow 80386 real mode instructions.

.386, .386C

SYNTAX   .386
.386C

COMMENTS   All instructions following this directive must be in the instruction set for the 80386 processor in real mode. The assembler only checks to see that the instructions are in the correct instruction set. You must ensure that the program is run on a computer with the specified processor and co-processor.

SEE ALSO   P186
P286
P286N
P287
P386
P386N
P387
P8086
P8087
PN087

EXAMPLE   ```
; To use 32-bit registers you must enable 80386 instructions .

        .386   ; Enable 80386 instructions
        add   eax,14   ; Now you can use 32-bit registers
```

---

# .386P

**PURPOSE**   To tell the assembler to allow 80386 protected mode instructions.

**SYNTAX**   .386P

**COMMENTS**   All instructions following this directive must be in the instruction set for the 80386 processor's protected mode. This directive does not put the processor into protected mode nor does is determine if the processor is actually an 80386.

**SEE ALSO**   P186
P286
P286N
P287
P386
P386N
P387
```

```
P8086
P8087
PNO87
```

EXAMPLE   `.386P`   `; Enable protected mode`
                                       `; instructions`

```
mov  ax, TSS_Sel           ; Copy a task selector into AX
ltr  ax                    ; and put it in the task
                           ; register. (Protected mode
                           ; instruction)
```

.387

PURPOSE   To tell the assembler to allow 80387 instructions.

SYNTAX   `.387`

COMMENTS   Instructions following this directive can include instructions for the 80387 floating point co-processor. If you include the `EMUL` directive or use the /e command line option, the assembler will convert the floating point instructions to calls to a floating point library. Otherwise, the assembler will generate ESC instructions to pass the floating point instructions to the math co-processor.

SEE ALSO
```
P186
P286
P286N
P287
P386
P386N
P387
P8086
P8087
PNO87
```

EXAMPLE
```
.387           ; Allow 80387 instructions
fsin           ; An 80387 instruction
```

.8086

PURPOSE   To tell the assembler to only allow instructions for the 8088/86 and 8087 processors.

SYNTAX   .8086   *Allow 8086/8088 instructions.*

COMMENTS   All instructions following this directive must be in the instruction set for the 8088/86 processor. This instruction also enables instructions for the 8087 floating point co-processor. This is the default condition for the assembler.

SEE ALSO   P186
P286
P286N
P287
P386
P386N
P387
P8086
P8087
PN087

EXAMPLE   Normally you would not use this directive because this is the default state for the assembler. You can use it if you have a short section of code that is for one of the other processors and you want to shift back to 8088/86 mode after the code.

```
.386            ; Allow 80386 instructions
movsx eax, bx   ; Copy bx into eax with sign extension
.
.
.
.8086           ; Go back to 8086 instructions only
```

.8087

PURPOSE   To tell the assembler to allow instructions for the 8087 co-processor.

SYNTAX   .8087   *Allow 8087 instructions.*

.8087

COMMENTS Instructions following this directive can include instructions for the 8087 floating point co-processor. If you include the EMUL directive or assemble with the /e command line option, the assembler will generate calls to a floating point library. Otherwise, the assembler will generate ESC instructions to pass floating point commands on to the co-processor.

SEE ALSO P186
P286
P286N
P287
P386
P386N
P387
P8086
P8087
PNO87

EXAMPLE Normally you would not use this directive because the 8087 instructions are enabled by default. If you have a section of code that uses one of the other floating point co-processors you can use this directive to put the assembler back into 8087 mode.

```
.387            ; Allow 80387 instructions
fldpi           ; 80837 instruction

.8087           ; And back to 8087 mode
```

%BIN

PURPOSE To set the width of the object code field in listing files.

SYNTAX %BIN width
width   *is the number of columns to use for object code.*

COMMENTS The default width for object code in a listing file is 20 characters. If you intend to list the file on the screen, this represents one-fourth of the available space. This does not leave much room for other fields. You can use the %BIN directive to reduce the amount of space required for object code.

SEE ALSO %DEPTH
%LINUM
%PCNT
%TEXT

%BIN

EXAMPLE

```
%PAGESIZE 55, 75        ; Make a page with 55 lines and 75
                        ; columns
%BIN 10                 ; Shrink the object code field to
                        ; 10 columns
%DEPTH 2                ; Set the depth field to 2 columns
%LINUM 3                ; Set the line number field to 3
                        ; columns
%PCNT 3                 ; Set the location counter field to
                        ; 3 columns
%TEXT 50                ; Use 50 columns for source text
        .
        .
        .
```

%CONDS

PURPOSE   To tell the assembler to include lines in the false branch of a conditional block in the listing file.

SYNTAX   %CONDS   *Turn on listing for false branches in MASM or IDEAL mode.*

COMMENTS   Turbo Assembler will include the false branches of conditional blocks in the listing file. The %NOCONDS directive turns this feature off. You can use %CONDS to turn it back when you want to resume including false branches.

SEE ALSO   %MAC
%NOMAC
.LALL
.SALL
.XALL

EXAMPLE

```
%NOCONDS                ; Turn off listings for false branches
IFDEF SYM1              ; This will not be listed if SYM1 is
        .               ; undefined
        .
        .
ENDIF
%CONDS                  ; Turn on listings for false branches
IFIDN SYM1, <SAMPLE>    ; This will be listed no matter what
```

```
        .
        .
        .
ENDIF
```

.CREF, %CREF

PURPOSE   To control when cross reference information is to be included in the symbol table listing.

SYNTAX
.CREF   *Enable cross references in MASM mode.*
%CREF   *Enable cross references in MASM or IDEAL mode.*
.XCREF   *Disable cross references in MASM mode.*
%NOCREF   *Disable cross references in MASM or IDEAL mode.*

COMMENTS   Cross-reference information can be helpful in debugging a program by showing all of the locations that use a particular symbol. The .CREF or %CREF directives tell the assembler to put this information in the symbol table listing.

The .XCREF or %NOCREF directives disable cross-reference information. Since this is the default state you should not need to use these directives.

SEE ALSO   %CREFALL
%CREFREF
%CREFUREF

EXAMPLE

```
.CREF                     ; Enable cross-reference information
        .MODEL    SMALL
        .DATA             ; This line number will appear next to
                          ; the DGROUP and _DATA entries in the
                          ; symbol table listing
Var1    DW   1234         ; This line number will appear next to
                          ; Var1 in the symbol table listing
        .CODE             ; This line number will appear next to
                          ; the _TEXT entry in the symbol table
Start:                    ; This line number will appear next to
                          ; Start in the symbol table
        mov  Var1, ax     ; This line number will appear next to
                          ; Var1 in the symbol table listing
```

%CREFALL, %CREFREF, %CREFUREF

%CREFALL, %CREFREF, %CREFUREF

PURPOSE   To allow you to select what symbols to include in the cross-reference listing.

SYNTAX   %CREFALL   *Include all symbols.*
%CREFREF   *Include only referenced symbols.*
%CREFUREF   *Include only unreferenced symbols.*

COMMENTS   If cross-reference information is enabled, then Turbo Assembler will include all symbols in the listing. The %CREFREF and %CREFUREF directives limit the list to referenced or unreferenced symbols only. The assembler considers any symbol that has been defined but not used to be unreferenced.

The %CREFALL directive tells the assembler to include all symbols. Since this is the default state, you should not need to use this directive.

SEE ALSO   .CREF
%CREF
.XCREF
%NOCREF

EXAMPLE
```
.CREF                    ; Enable cross-reference information
%CREFREF                 ; Only include referenced symbols

        .MODEL    SMALL
        .DATA            ; This line number will appear next to
                         ; the DGROUP and _DATA entries in the
                         ; symbol table listing
Var1    DW   1234        ; This line number will appear next to
                         ; Var1 in the symbol table listing
        .CODE            ; This line number will appear next to
                         ; the _TEXT entry in the symbol table
Start:                   ; This line number will not appear
                         ; because the symbol is not referenced
        mov  Var1, ax    ; This line number will appear next to
                         ; Var1 in the symbol table listing
```

%CTLS

PURPOSE   To tell when listing control statements are to be included in the listing file.

SYNTAX   `%CTLS`   *Include listing control statements.*
             `%NOCTLS`   *Do not include listing control statements.*

COMMENTS   By default, Turbo Assembler does not include listing control statements like PAGE, %DEPTH, %BIN, etc., in the listing file. All listing control statements following the %CTLS directive will be included in the include file until a %NOCTLS directive is used.

SEE ALSO   `.LIST`
             `%LIST`
             `%NOLIST`
             `.XLIST`

EXAMPLE

```
PAGE 60, 120         ; This will not appear in the listing file
%CTLS                ; Include control statements in the listing
%BIN 5               ; This statement and all other listing
    .                ; controls will appear in the listing
    .
    .
%NOCTLS              ; Stop including control statements
%BIN 4               ; Now this statement will not appear in the
                     ; listing file
```

DISPLAY

PURPOSE   To display a string on the screen while the program is being assembled.

SYNTAX   `DISPLAY "text"`
             `text`   *The text to display.*

COMMENTS   You can use the display directive to track the progress of the assembly, and to indicate what conditional blocks are being used.

SEE ALSO   `%OUT`

EXAMPLE

```
INCLUDE CONFIG.INC          ; Get equates

IF @MODEL EQ 1              ; Display what model is being used
DISPLAY "TINY MODEL"
ELSEIF @MODEL EQ 2
DISPLAY "SMALL MODEL"
ELSEIF @MODEL EQ 3
```

DISPLAY

```
DISPLAY "MEDIUM MODEL"
ELSEIF @MODEL EQ 4
DISPLAY "COMPACT MODEL"
ELSEIF @MODEL EQ 5
DISPLAY "LARGE MODEL"
ELSEIF @MODEL EQ 6
DISPLAY "HUGE MODEL"
ENDIF
```

%DEPTH

PURPOSE   To set the width of the nesting depth field in listing files.

SYNTAX   `%DEPTH width`
`width`   *The number of columns to use.*

COMMENTS   The default width for the nesting depth field is one column. This is usually sufficient, but you may want to increase it to two columns for programs that use deeply nested macros.

SEE ALSO   `%PCNT`
`%BIN`
`%LINUM`
`%TEXT`

EXAMPLE   See the example for `%BIN`.

EMUL

PURPOSE   To tell the assembler to use emulated or co-processor floating point instructions.

SYNTAX   `EMUL`   *Use emulated instructions.*
`NOEMUL`   *Use co-processor instructions.*

COMMENTS   By default, Turbo Assembler converts floating point instructions into the proper ESC instructions to get the co-processor to do the instruction. The `EMUL` directive tells the assembler to call functions in a floating point emulation package. This is the same as using the /e command line option. The NOEMUL directive tells the assembler to resume using co-processor instructions.

If you use any emulated floating point instructions, you will need to link in a floating point library in order to link the program.

SEE ALSO
```
JUMPS
NOJUMPS
```

EXAMPLE
```
; Use emulated instructions if no co-processor available

          cmp  MathInst, 0    ; Check Math chip installed flag
          je   noMath
          NOEMUL              ; Don't emulate instructions
          fsave fbuf          ; Co-processor instruction
          jmp  done
noMath:
          EMUL                ; Emulate instructions
          fsave fbuf          ; Call library routine
done:
```

.ERR, .ERR1, .ERR2, .ERRB, .ERRDEF, .ERRDIF, .ERRDIFI, .ERRE, .ERRIDN, .ERRIDNI, .ERRNB, .ERRNDEF, .ERRNZ, ERR, ERRIF, ERRIF1, ERRIF2, ERRIFDEF, ERRIFDIF, ERRIFDIFI, ERRIFE, ERRIFIDN, ERRIFINDI, ERRIFNB, ERRIFNDEF

PURPOSE To generate an error.

SYNTAX MASM only:

.ERR	*Unconditional error.*
.ERR1	*Error if pass 1.*
.ERR2	*Error if pass 2.*
.ERRB arg	*Error if arg is blank.*
.ERRDEF sym	*Error if sym is defined.*
.ERRDIF arg1, arg2	*Error if arg1 different from arg2.*
.ERRDIFI arg1, arg2	*Same as ERRDIF except ignore case.*
.ERRE expr	*Error if expression is true.*
.ERRIDN arg1, arg2	*Error if arg1 identical to arg2.*

.ERR

.ERRIDNI	*Same as ERRIDN except ignore case.*
.ERRNB arg	*Error if arg is not blank.*
.ERRNDEF sym	*Error if sym is not defined.*
.ERRNZ expr	*Error if expr does not equal zero.*

MASM or IDEAL:

ERR	*Unconditional error.*
ERRIF expr	*Error if expr is true.*
ERRIF1	*Error if pass 1.*
ERRIF2	*Error if pass 2.*
ERRIFB arg	*Error if arg is blank.*
ERRIFDEF sym	*Error if sym is defined.*
ERRIFDIF arg1, arg2	*Error if arg1 different from arg2.*
ERRIFDIFI arg1, arg2	*Same as ERRDIF except ignore case.*
ERRIFE expr	*Error if expression is true.*
ERRIFIDN arg1, arg2	*Error if arg1 identical to arg2.*
ERRIFIDNI	*Same as ERRIDN except ignore case.*
ERRIFNB arg	*Error if arg is not blank.*
ERRIFNDEF sym	*Error if sym is not defined.*

COMMENTS   The error directives let you add your own errors to the list of errors used in Turbo Assembler. The types of things that you can make errors include macro arguments that are out-of-bounds, and incompatible *conditional assembly* flags.

Errors generated by the error directives have the same effect on the assembly that regular errors do. They cause an error message to be printed and increment the error count. The error message will include the line number and the fact that an error directive caused the error. If this message is not enough, you can use the %OUT or DISPLAY directives to give more information. Turbo Assembler will not generate an object file for a program with errors in it.

SEE ALSO   %OUT
DISPLAY

EXAMPLE
```
MyMacro   MACRO row, col
.ERRNZ row < 0 or row > 24    ; Give an error if row out of range
.ERRNZ col < 0 or col > 79    ; Give an error if col out of range
          .
          .
          .
          ENDM
```

IDEAL

PURPOSE To tell the assembler to use Ideal mode.

SYNTAX `IDEAL`

COMMENTS Turbo Assembler is compatible with Microsoft's MASM assembler. The `IDEAL` directive tells the assembler to use IDEAL mode directives and syntax. Programs in IDEAL mode are not compatible with MASM programs, but they can be assembled up to 30% faster.

SEE ALSO `MASM`

EXAMPLE

```
IDEAL
        MODEL      SMALL          ; Ideal mode model directive
        DATASEG                   ; Ideal mode data segment directive
        .
        .
        .
        CODESEG                   ; Ideal mode code segment directive
        PROC _main                ; Ideal mode syntax
        .
        .
        .
        ENDP _main                ; Ideal mode syntax
        .
        .
        .
```

%INCL

PURPOSE To determine if include files will be in the listing file.

SYNTAX `%INCL`   *Allow include files in the listing file.*
            `%NOINCL`   *Do not allow include files in the listing file.*

COMMENTS The default for Turbo Assembler is to put include files in the listing file. This can lead to large listing files containing information that is duplicated in the

%INCL

listing files of other modules. To prevent this you can use the `%NOINCL` directive to prevent the inclusion of include files in the listing file. The `%INCL` directive tells the assembler to resume putting include files in the listing.

SEE ALSO
```
.LALL
%MACS
%NOMACS
.SALL
.XALL
.LIST
%LIST
%NOLIST
.XLIST
```

EXAMPLE
```
%NOINCL
INCLUDE defs.inc        ; The contents of this file will not
                        ; appear in the listing file
```

JUMPS

PURPOSE To tell the assembler what to do with conditional jumps that are out of range.

SYNTAX
```
JUMPS           Generate code to emulate a conditional jump if the
                conditional jump is out of range.
NOJUMPS         Generate an error for conditional jumps that are
                out of range.
```

COMMENTS Conditional jumps can reach labels that are from −128 to +127 bytes away from the jump. Turbo Assembler can generate code that jumps farther by using a jump that tests the opposite condition to skip over a near or far jump to the label.

The default is to generate an error if the jump is out of range. The `JUMPS` directive tells the assembler to fix conditional jumps. The `NOJUMPS` directive returns the assembler to the default state.

EXAMPLE
```
        JUMPS           ; Allow long conditional jumps
        jnc  distant    ; The assembler turns this into:
                        ;       jc   @@a
                        ;       jmp  distant
                        ; @@a:
```

```
                              ; More than 128 bytes
              .
              .
              .
distant:
              .
              .
              .
```

.LALL

PURPOSE   To tell the assembler when to list macros.

SYNTAX   MASM mode only:

.LALL	*List macro expansions.*
.SALL	*Do not list macro expansions.*
.XALL	*List only macro expansions that result in code or data.*

MASM or IDEAL mode:

%MACS	*List macro expansions.*
%NOMACS	*Do not list macro expansions.*

COMMENTS   By default, Turbo Assembler puts each line of macros in the listing file every time the macro appears in the source. You can use .SALL or %NOMACS to shorten the listing file, by not putting macro expansions in the listing.

You can use .LALL or %MACS to resume showing macros in the listing. The .XALL directive includes only macros that make code or data. The conditionals and directives in the macro will not be included.

SEE ALSO   %INCL
%NOINCL

EXAMPLE
```
; Macro definitions go in the listing file
MyMacro    MACRO Arg1, Arg2
           push ax
           mov  ax, Arg2
           add  Arg2, ax
           pop  ax
           ENDM
```

.LALL

```
%NOINCL                         ; Do not include macros in listings
            .DATA
Result      DW    1234
            .CODE
            MyMacro <Result,44>  ; The expansion of this macro will
                                 ; not appear in the listing
%INCL                            ; Resume including macros
            MyMacro <cx,dx>      ; The expansion of this macro will
                                 ; appear in the listing file
```

.LFCOND

PURPOSE   To tell the assembler to include the false branch of a conditional block in the listing file.

SYNTAX   `.LFCONDS`   *Turn on listing for false branches in MASM mode.*

EXAMPLE   See `%CONDS`.

%LINUM

PURPOSE   To set the width of the line number field in listing files.

SYNTAX   `%LINUM    width`
`width`   *The number of columns to use for line numbers.*

COMMENTS   Listing files can include a line number for each line in the file. The default width for the line number field is four columns. If the listing files have more than 9999 lines, you will need to increase the width of the line number field. On the other hand, you may want to shorten the line number field to leave more room on a line for other fields.

SEE ALSO   `%BIN`
`%DEPTH`
`%PCNT`
`%TEXT`

EXAMPLE   See the example for `%BIN`.

.LIST, %LIST

PURPOSE To tell the assembler when to include or exclude lines from the listing file.

SYNTAX MASM mode only:

.LIST   *Begin including lines in the listing file.*
.XLIST   *Stop including lines in the listing file.*

MASM or IDEAL mode:

%LIST   *Begin including lines in the listing file.*
%NOLIST   *Stop including lines in the listing file.*

COMMENTS These directives let you trim uninteresting parts of a program from the listing file. A listing file that does not contain unwanted lines is easier to read.

SEE ALSO %MACS
%NOMACS
%INCL
%NOINCL

EXAMPLE

```
.XLIST                          ; Do not include the following
                                ; lines in listings.
            .MODEL    SMALL
INCLUDE   STRUCS.INC
            .DATA
              .
              .
              .
            .CODE
.LIST                           ; Now that the start-up stuff is
              .                 ; out of the way, begin putting
              .                 ; code in the listing
              .
.XLIST                          ; After the code, stop putting
                                ; things into the listing
            .STACK
END
```

%MACS

See .LALL.

MASM

PURPOSE   To tell the assembler to use MASM-compatible directives and syntax.

SYNTAX   MASM

COMMENTS   By default, Turbo Assembler is in MASM mode, which lets you assemble files for Microsoft's MASM assembler. Turbo Assembler also provides another mode that uses different directives and syntax. This mode is called IDEAL mode. Once you have switched to IDEAL mode, you can use the MASM directive to switch back to MASM mode.

SEE ALSO   IDEAL

EXAMPLE

```
IDEAL                           ; Switch to ideal mode
        MODEL SMALL
        DATASEG
          .
          .
          .
MASM                            ; Switch back to MASM mode
        .CODE                   ; Now you can use MASM mode
Start   PROC                    ; directives and syntax
```

MASM51

PURPOSE   To tell the assembler when to use commands from MASM 5.1.

SYNTAX   MASM51   *Allow MASM 5.1 directives.*
NOMASM51   *Disallow MASM 5.1 directives.*

COMMENTS Turbo Assembler is compatible with versions 1 through 4 of MASM. To use features from MASM 5.1, you must use the MASM51 directive. The features for MASM 5.1 are:

- SUBSTR, CATSTR, SIZESTR, and INSTR directives
- Lines may be continued with a backslash (\)
- Change syntax for the LOCAL directive to:

```
LOCAL Name [count] [:[distance] PTR [type]]
```

SEE ALSO QUIRKS

EXAMPLE
```
MASM51                              ; Enable 5.1 features
Str4 EQU <This is a string>
Str2 EQU < combined with another>
Str1 CATSTR Str4, Str2              ; This is a 5.1 directive.
                                    ; Without MASM51 you would get
                                    ; a syntax error
```

MULTERRS

PURPOSE To tell the assembler to report several or only one error for lines that contain multiple errors.

SYNTAX
MULTERRS   *Report all errors found on a line.*
NOMULTERRS   *Only report one error for each line with errors.*

COMMENTS The default is to print only the first error discovered on any given line. The assumption is that while you are fixing that error you will notice any others on the line. Some errors are more subtle. For example, you may use two memory reference arguments in a single instruction and one of them might use an undefined symbol. In this case it would be easy to fix either problem and miss the other one. The MULTERRS directive tells the assembler to print all the errors it finds on a line.

Printing multiple errors can lead to several error messages caused by the same root problem. This is known as *cascading errors*. It can happen when you use an undefined symbol in a definition. The assembler will report the first undefined symbol error, and then it will report an error when you use the symbol that should have been created.

SEE ALSO WARN
NOWARN

MULTERRS

EXAMPLE
```
MULTERRS                   ; Allow multiple error reporting
           mov  7, abc     ; Illegal operands and abc is undefined
```

NAME

PURPOSE   To set the module name in the object file.

SYNTAX
```
NAME modulename
modulename        is the name to use in the object file.
```

COMMENTS   Each object file contains a record that tells the linker what the module name is for that object file. This name is used by the linker when it prints an error message for the object file. By default, Turbo Assembler uses the name of the source file as the module name in the object file. You can use the `NAME` directive to change the module name.

You will only need to do this if you have some utility that requires the module name to be different. If you find that you need this feature, you should use IDEAL mode. In MASM mode the `NAME` directive does not do anything.

EXAMPLE
```
IDEAL            ; NAME only works in Ideal mode
NAME Module1     ; Set the module name
  .
  .
  .
```

%NEWPAGE

PURPOSE   To control pages in the lising file.

SYNTAX   `%NEWPAGE`   *Start a new page.*

COMMENTS   The `%NEWPAGE` directive can be used to make sure that a new part of the program always begins on a new page. When the listing is printed, this helps make the file more readable by clearly dividing the sections.

SEE ALSO
```
%BIN
%DEPTH
```

```
%LINUM
%PCNT
%TEXT
```

EXAMPLE   See `%PAGESIZE`.

%NOCONDS

See `%CONDS`.

%NOCREF

See `%CREF`.

%NOCTLS

See `%CTRLS`.

NOEMUL

See `EMUL`.

%NOINCL

See `%INCL`.

NOJUMPS

See JUMPS.

%NOLIST

See %LIST.

%NOMACS

See .LALL.

NOMASM51

See MASM51.

NOMULTERRS

See MULTERRS.

%NOSYMS

See %SYMS.

%NOTRUNC

See %TRUNC.

NOWARN

See WARN.

%OUT

PURPOSE To print a string while the program is being assembled.

SYNTAX %OUT text

    text   *The string to print.*

COMMENTS The %OUT directive prints the rest of the line on the screen. The text is printed as is, without any interpretation. You can use the %OUT directive to trace the progress of the assembly and verify that certain conditional blocks are being assembled.

      Both the %OUT and DISPLAY directives print messages on the screen during the assembly. These directives are identical except that the string for DISPLAY must be enclosed in quotes. You can use these directives to indicate what options are being used for the assembly.

SEE ALSO DISPLAY

EXAMPLE
```
INCLUDE CONFIG.INC              ; Get equates

IF @MODEL EQ 1                  ; Display what model is being used
DISPLAY "TINY MODEL"
ELSEIF @MODEL EQ 2
DISPLAY "SMALL MODEL"
ELSEIF @MODEL EQ 3
DISPLAY "MEDIUM MODEL"
ELSEIF @MODEL EQ 4
DISPLAY "COMPACT MODEL"
ELSEIF @MODEL EQ 5
```

```
DISPLAY "LARGE MODEL"
ELSEIF @MODEL EQ 6
DISPLAY "HUGE MODEL"
ENDIF
```

P186

IDEAL mode version of .186.

P286

IDEAL mode version of .286P.

P286N

IDEAL mode version of .286.

P287

IDEAL mode version of .287.

P386

IDEAL mode version of .386P.

P386N

IDEAL mode version of .386.

P387

IDEAL mode version of .387.

P8086

IDEAL mode version of .8086.

P8087

IDEAL mode version of .8087.

PN087

PURPOSE   To tell the assembler not to allow 8087 instructions.

SYNTAX   PN087   *Do not allow 8087 instructions.*

COMMENTS   The assembler will generate an error for each co-processor instruction following this directive. You can use this to make sure that there are no floating point instructions in a program that is not supposed to use them.

SEE ALSO   .186
.286
.286P

```
                        .287
                        .386
                        .386P
                        .387
                        .8086
                        .8087
```

EXAMPLE   This example uses *conditional assembly* to make a floating point co-processor version and an integer-only version. The PN087 directive ensures that there are no floating point instructions in the integer-only version:

```
IFDEF     Float                       ; See if symbol Float is
                                      ; defined (Defined by the
                                      ; programmer when the module
                                      ; is assembled)
          P8087                       ; Make sure floating point is
                                      ; OK
ELSE                                  ; Otherwise,
          PNO87                       ; don't allow 8087
                                      ; instructions
ENDIF

; Use the word at the top of the stack frame to determine
; the type of data to add. (1 = float, 2 = integer)
AddEm     PROC      NEAR
          push bp                     ; Save the BP register
          mov  bp, sp                 ; Set BP to the stack frame
          mov  ax, WORD [bp-4]        ; Get the data type in AX
IFDEF     Float                       ; If floating point allowed
          cmp  ax, 1                  ; See if the type is float
          jne  NotFloat
          fld  QWORD [bp-6]           ; Load the 1st number
          fadd QWORD [bp-14]          ; Add in the second number
          fsd  QWORD [bp-6]           ; Write the result back on the
                                      ; stack
NotFloat:
ENDIF
          cmp  ax, 2                  ; See if the type is integer
          jne  NotInt
          mov  ax, WORD [bp-8]        ; Get the second integer
          add  WORD [bp-6], ax        ; Add it to the first number
                                      ; on the stack
NotInt:
          pop  bp
          ret
AddEm     ENDP
```

PAGE

PURPOSE   To control pages in the lising file.

SYNTAX   MASM mode only:

```
PAGE                    Start a new page.
PAGE [rows][,cols]      Specify the number of rows and
                        columns on a page.
PAGE +                  Start a new section.
```

COMMENTS   A listing file can be anywhere from 59 to 255 columns wide. The wider the listing, the more information it can show and the easier it is to read. You should set the width to fit on the device you will use to display the listing file.

Each page will show the name of the file, the title and subtitle, page number, etc. The page will also contain a number of lines from the source file. You should select the total number of rows to get the best fit on the device you will use to display the file.

The PAGE directive can be used to make sure that a new part of the program always begins on a new page. When the listing is printed, this helps make the file more readable by clearly dividing the sections.

SEE ALSO
```
%BIN
%DEPTH
%LINUM
%PCNT
%TEXT
%NEWPAGE
%PAGESIZE
```

EXAMPLE
```
PAGE 50, 70          ; Make a 50 line by 70 column page
.MODEL    SMALL
.                    ; Structures and equates
.
.
PAGE                 ; Start a new page
.DATA                ; Do all data definitions
.
.
.
```

PAGE

```
PAGE                    ; Start a new page
.CODE                   ; Put code on the next page
.
.
.
```

%PAGESIZE

PURPOSE To set the size of a page in the listing file.

SYNTAX %PAGESIZE [rows][,cols]   *Specify the number of rows and columns on a page.*

COMMENTS A listing file can be anywhere from 59 to 255 columns wide. The wider the listing, the more information it can show and the easier it is to read. You should set the width to fit on the device you will use to display the listing file.

Each page will show the name of the file, the title and subtitle, page number, etc. The page will also contain a number of lines from the source file. You should select the total number of rows to get the best fit on the device you will use to display the file.

SEE ALSO
```
%BIN
%DEPTH
%LINUM
%PCNT
%TEXT
PAGE
%NEWPAGE
```

EXAMPLE
```
%PAGESIZE 50, 70       ; Make a 50 line by 70 column page
.MODEL    SMALL
.                      ; Structures and equates
.
.
%NEWPAGE               ; Start a new page
.DATA                  ; Do all data definitions
.
.
.
```

```
%NEWPAGE                ; Start a new page
.CODE                   ; Put code on the next page
.
.
.
```

%PCNT

PURPOSE   To set the width of the address field in the listing file.

SYNTAX   `%PCNT width`
`width`   *The number of columns to use for the address field.*

COMMENTS   The address field shows the segment and offset of each line in the file. By default, the width for this field is four columns for 16-bit segments and eight columns for 32-bit segments. This is enough to show the offset portion of the field. If you would like to see the segment for each line, you will need to increase the width by five columns. If you reduce the width of the field, the assembler will use as many of the least significant digits as will fit.

SEE ALSO   `%BIN`
`%DEPTH`
`%LINUM`
`%TEXT`

EXAMPLE   See the example for `%BIN`.

%POPLCTL

PURPOSE   To save and restore the state of the listing controls.

SYNTAX   `%POPLCTL`   *Pop the listing controls from the LCTL stack.*
`%PUSHLCTL`   *Push the listing controls onto the LCTL stack.*

COMMENTS   These directives can be used to save and restore certain listing controls. The controls that can be saved are all that can be enabled or disabled, such as `%MACS`, `%LIST`, `%INCL`, etc. You cannot save controls that take a value such as `%BIN` or `%PAGESIZE`.

%POPLCTL

You can use these directives in macros and include files that need to change controls and then go back to the original control settings. The LCTL stack can save up to 16 different settings.

SEE ALSO
```
%MACS
%LIST
%INCL
MULTERRS
JUMPS
%SYM
%CREF
```

EXAMPLE
```
; This is an include file.
%PUSHLCTL                       ; Save the controls from the file that
                                ; includes this file
%NOLIST                         ; Do not list the contents of this file
        .
        .
        .
%POPLCTL                        ; Restore controls. If the main file has
                                ; listing off, it will remain off. If
                                ; listing was on, it will resume listing.
```

%PUSHCTL

See %POPCTL.

QUIRKS

PURPOSE To ensure compatibility with MASM by allowing some of its more unusual aspects.

SYNTAX QUIRKS   *Allow full MASM compatibility.*

COMMENTS Programmers will find and use any trick that the assembler will allow, even when that trick is not intended to be part of the assembler. If you are faced with assembling one of these programs with Turbo Assembler, chances are that the QUIRKS directive will let the trick work in the way that the programmer intended.

SEE ALSO   MASM
                MASM51

EXAMPLE
```
        MASM51                          ; Enable MASM 5.1 compatibility
        QUIRKS                          ; Allow quirks
                .MODEL    SMALL, C
        SEGADDR    DB  ?                ; Notice that there is not enough
                                        ; room for a segment register here
        DUMMY      DW  ?
                .DATA
        DMBADDR    = OFFSET X
                .CODE
        Funct1     PROC                 ; Defines a public function named
                                        ; _Funct1
                   mov  SEGADDR,es      ; This is OK with QUIRKS on
                   jmp  FAR PTR lab1    ; This will be a near jump
                   mov  ax, DMBADDR     ; This loads the data at DUMMY
                                        ; not the address of DUMMY

                   .
                   .
                   .
        lab1       LABEL FAR
```

.SALL

See .LALL.

.SFCOND

PURPOSE   To control when lines in the false branch of a conditional block are to be placed in the listing file.

SYNTAX   .SFCOND   *Turn off listing for false branches in MASM mode.*

.SFCOND

EXAMPLE   See TFCOND.

SUBTTL, %SUBTTL

PURPOSE   To set the subtitle that will be used in listing files.

SYNTAX   MASM mode only:

SUBTTL text

MASM or IDEAL mode:

%SUBTTL "text"

COMMENTS   The listing file shows the title and subtitle at the beginning of each page. The SUBTTL or %SUBTTL directives set the subtitle that will be used on the next page heading.

SEE ALSO   TITLE
%TITLE

EXAMPLE   %PAGESIZE 50, 70
%SUBTTL   "A sample subtitle"
.
.
.

%SYMS

PURPOSE   To control if a symbol table will be included in the listing file.

SYNTAX   %SYMS   *Include the symbol table in the listing.*
%NOSYMS   *Do not include the symbol table in the listing.*

COMMENTS   The default for Turbo Assembler is to include symbols in the listing file. You can disable this feature by including the %NOSYMS directive in the source file. To re-enable the symbol table, use the %SYMS directive. You should not need to use the %SYMS directive unless you are unable to remove the %NOSYMS directive from the file for some reason.

SEE ALSO   `%CREF`
                `%NOCREF`

EXAMPLE   `%NOSYMS`   `; The symbol table will not appear in the`
                                       `; listing file.`

.
.
.

%TABSIZE

PURPOSE   To set the number of columns between tab stops in listing files.

SYNTAX   `%TABSIZE columns`
           `columns`   *The number of columns between tab stops.*

COMMENTS   The assembler uses TAB characters to line up the fields in the listing file. If the tabs are not the same size as for the display device, the listing file will not line up correctly. The default tab width is eight bytes.

SEE ALSO   `%BIN`
                `%DEPTH`
                `%LINUM`
                `%PAGE`
                `%PCNT`
                `%TEXT`

EXAMPLE   See the example for `%BIN`.

%TEXT

PURPOSE   To set the width for the source field in the listing file.

SYNTAX   `%TEXT width`
           `width`   *The width of the source field.*

COMMENTS   The last field on a line in the listing file is for source code. This field extends to the width of the page as set in the `PAGE` directive. At the end of the field, the rest of the text will be wrapped to the next line or truncated, based on the setting of the %TRUNC control.

The %TEXT directive lets you specify the width of the source field without using the PAGE directive. This gives you more direct control over this field, as the PAGE directive depends on the settings of the other fields in order to determine how many columns are available for the source.

SEE ALSO   PAGE
                  %PAGESIZE
                  %TRUNC
                  %NOTRUNC
                  %BIN
                  %DEPTH
                  %PCNT
                  %LINUM

.TFCOND

PURPOSE   To control when lines in the false branch of a conditional block are to be placed in the listing file.

SYNTAX   .TFCOND   *Toggle listing for false branches in MASM mode.*

COMMENTS   By default, Turbo Assembler will include the false branches of conditional blocks in the listing file. In MASM mode you can use .TFCOND to toggle the feature on and off.

SEE ALSO   %MAC
                  %NOMAC
                  .LALL
                  .SALL
                  .XALL
                  %CONDS
                  %NOCONDS
                  .SFCOND

EXAMPLE   .SFCOND   ; Turn off listings for false branches

                 IFDEF SYM1   ; This will not be listed if SYM1 is
                   .   ; undefined
                   .
                   .

```
ENDIF

.TFCOND                  ; Turn on listings for false branches
IFIDN SYM1, <SAMPLE>     ; This will be listed no matter what
          .
          .
          .
ENDIF
```

TITLE, %TITLE

PURPOSE   To set the title used in listing files.

SYNTAX   MASM mode only:

TITLE text   *Set the title to text.*

MASM or IDEAL mode:

%TITLE "text"   *Set the title to text.*

COMMENTS   The assembler prints the title at the top of each page in the listing file. The TITLE or %TITLE directives tell the assembler what title to use for the file. The title remains in effect for the entire file. You may not change it.

SEE ALSO   SUBTTL
%SUBTTL

EXAMPLE
```
%TITLE "This is a sample program"
%SUBTTL "The first section"
          .
          .
          .
```

%TRUNC

PURPOSE   To control what to do with lines that do not fit onto the page in listing files.

%TRUNC

SYNTAX

```
%TRUNC        Truncate long lines.
%NOTRUNC      Wrap long lines.
```

COMMENTS These directives give you control over what should be done with long lines. The default is to truncate long lines. The %NOTRUNC directive changes this action. With %NOTRUNC long lines will be split. The first part will have a plus sign (+) appended to it, and the rest of the line becomes a new line.

SEE ALSO

```
PAGE
%TEXT
```

EXAMPLE

```
%TRUNC                  ; Truncate long lines
          .DATA
Long      DB    "This line will be truncated in the listing file"
%NOTRUNC
Another   DB    "This line will be wrapped into two lines"
```

WARN

PURPOSE To enable or disable classes of warning messages.

SYNTAX

```
WARN [warnclass]      Enable a class of warning.
NOWARN [warnclass]    Disable a class of warning.
```

COMMENTS If you use WARN or NOWARN without a warning class, then all of the warnings will be enabled or disabled. Warning classes are the same as for the /W command line option. The possible warning classes are shown in Table 11-4.

Table 11-4. *Warning Classes*

Class	Warning
ASS	Assume segment is 16-bit
BRK	Brackets needed
ICG	Inefficient code generation
LCO	Location counter overflow
OPI	Open if conditional
OPP	Open procedure
OPS	Open segment

Class	Warning
OVF	Arithmetic overflow
PDC	Pass dependent construction
PRO	Write to memory in protected mode needs CS override

EXAMPLE

```
WARN      OPI        ; Enable open if warnings
IF    Enabled
          .
          .
          .
END                  ; Module ends before IF ends will give a
                     ; warning
```

.XALL

See .LALL.

.XCREF

See .CREF.

.XLIST

See .LIST.

IV

Techniques

► Writing Assembly Modules for High Level Languages,

► Using System Resources,

► Accessing and Controlling the Hardware,

► Video Control: Text and Graphics,

Chapter *12* *Writing Assembly Modules for High Level Languages*

Assembly Language is not the most efficient way to write a database application or a word processing program. It can be done, but the complexity of these applications begs for the abstraction of a high level language. This is one reason why most programmers will spend most of their time working in a high level language like C or Pascal.

Assembly Language must be used for the parts of a database or word processing application that need to interact with the hardware and run as efficiently as possible. All that is required to match the ease of high level language to the power of assembly language is a means of making calls and sharing data between the two. To do this, you need a way to combine the output of the assembler with the output of the compiler.

Most compilers and assemblers for MS-DOS machines generate object files that have the same format. This lets the linker put together pieces from many different sources. Unfortunately, the format does not specify everything that is needed to make the different pieces work together. You must deal with things like calling conventions, argument passing, and global data formats on your own.

Each high level language uses its own methods for communicating between modules. This chapter shows you some of the methods used by popular languages. It also tells you about other methods are available and how to use them. The documentation for your compiler should give you more information on using assembly language. You can also get the compiler itself to give you some hints about how to use assembly language routines. This is described later in the chapter.

Calling Between a High Level Language and Assembly Language

There are several ways to transfer control between high level languages and assembly language. One way is to use a software interrupt and function numbers, as do BIOS and MS-DOS. Most high level languages provide functions to be used with MS-DOS or BIOS calls. These can be adapted for use with other assembly language routines that use software interrupts for interfacing with other routines. The CPU registers are usually used to pass arguments for this kind of interface. The advantage of this technique is that the assembly language module can be loaded into memory and left there for use by many different programs. A good example of this technique is the mouse driver that uses interrupt 33h as an entry point for other programs to call it.

Another way to transfer control between a high level language and an assembly language program is to use subroutine calls and returns. In BASIC and FORTRAN, you do this with the *CALL* statement (CALL SUBNAME). In C language all functions are subroutines, so you need only give the name followed by parenthesis (SubName();). Pascal uses procedures for calling subroutines. To use a procedure, you only need the procedure name (SubName;). In assembly language the CALL command transfers control to another routine (call SubName).

In addition to the statement that actually does the call, each language needs statements to tell whether the function should be called with a NEAR or FAR call, whether the function takes arguments, and what return values the calling routine can expect. You must be sure that both the calling and the called module use the same calling conventions.

The MODEL Directive

The MODEL directive tells the assembler what kind of calling conventions to use. The specification of a memory model tells the assembler to use NEAR or FAR calls and returns. (See "Memory Models" in Chapter 8.) You can also use the language specifier to determine how to use the stack for passing arguments between functions. Most high level languages can be accommodated by using the C or Pascal calling conventions.

Stack Frames

Figure 12-1 shows the stack frame for C and Pascal calling conventions. The differences appear in the order that the arguments are arranged on the stack, and in which function is responsible for cleaning up the stack when the function exits. See Chapter 10 for more information on stack frames.

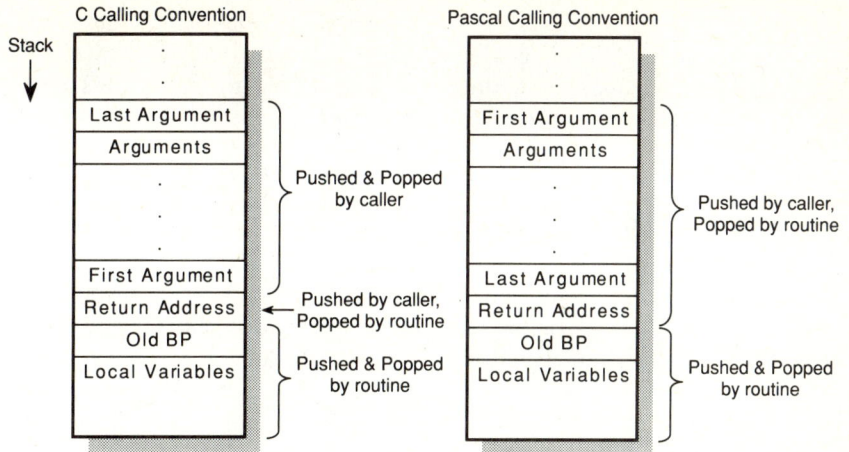

Figure 12-1. Stack frames for C and Pascal calling conventions.

THE C CALLING CONVENTION

Routines in C push the arguments in reverse order. This means that the first argument is on top of the stack. The reason for this is to allow functions, like the printf function in the C library, to have variable numbers of arguments. The first argument contains information about how many arguments to expect. If the arguments were pushed in order, then the function would need to know how many arguments to skip in order to get the argument that tells how many arguments there are. Figure 12-2 shows how this works.

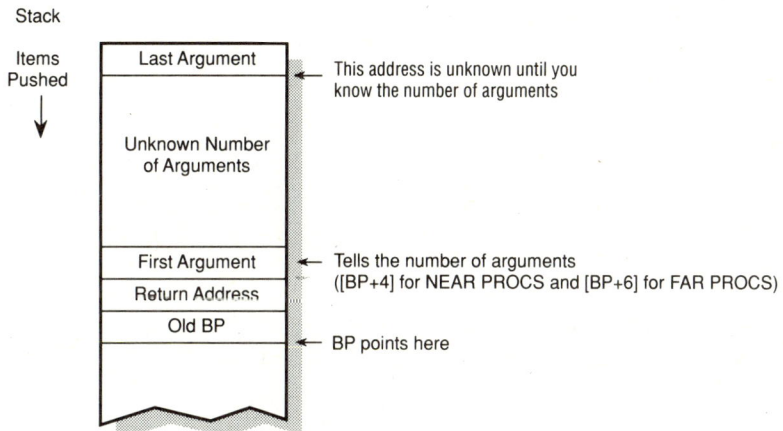

Figure 12-2. Variable numbers of arguments.

C requires the calling function to remove the arguments from the stack. This is also to allow functions to have variable numbers of arguments. The calling function knows how many arguments it pushed on the stack, while the called function must rely on the first argument containing the correct number of arguments.

THE PASCAL CALLING CONVENTION

Pascal does not allow functions to have variable numbers of arguments. This means that the arguments will be pushed on the stack in the same order as they appear. This also means that a function always uses the same amount of stack space for arguments, so it can clear the arguments off the stack. The 80x86 instruction RET n is an efficient way to do this. This procedure is so efficient that many C compilers allow the Pascal calling convention on programmer-selected functions. This is important to you as an assembly language programmer, because it means that even when you are writing functions for C programs, you may still need to use the Pascal calling convention.

THE ARG DIRECTIVE

When you specify a language in the MODEL directive, you tell the assembler about the order of arguments and what to do about removing arguments from the stack. If you use the ARG directive to label the arguments for a function, you do not need to worry about the argument order being used. The arguments in the ARG directive should always appear in the same order that the high level language uses. The assembler will sort out the order in which the arguments should appear on the stack.

USING TURBO ASSEMBLER TO HANDLE THE STACK

In older versions of Turbo Assembler, you had to push each of the arguments for a function in the correct order. However, a new feature of Turbo Assembler Version 2.0 allows it to handle pushing the arguments onto the stack when calling a function. To use these extended calls, simply tell the assembler what calling convention to use, and give it the memory or data items to pass with the call:

```
call MyFunc    C, ax, 0, Data4
```

The first argument tells the assembler to generate code to push the three arguments in the order used by C routines. You can also tell it to use Pascal conventions by making the first argument PASCAL.

RETURNING RESULTS

After the function does its job, it needs a way to send data back to the calling routine. There are three ways that this is done. The first is to modify the arguments on the stack and return control to the calling routine. When the calling routine removes the arguments from the stack, it gets the modified values. In the C calling convention, all of the arguments stay on the stack so that the calling function can do whatever it wants with them. For the Pascal calling convention, you must take special action to get a function to leave arguments on the stack. The RETURNS directive tells the assembler what arguments to leave when using the Pascal calling convention. This technique, which is not used very often, requires that the arguments be in a certain order.

A related and more common technique is to pass the address of a variable that is to be modified as an argument, instead of passing the variable itself. This kind of argument is said to be *passed by reference*, as opposed to arguments that are *passed by value*. The time function from the C standard library contains a good example of passing by reference. The function puts the number of seconds since midnight January 1, 1980, into a long integer. The long integer is passed by reference to the function:

```c
#include <time.h>

/* this function calls time to get the current time */
Func()
{
    time_t seconds;          /* declare a variable for the time */
                             /* time_t is defined in time.h it */
                             /* is usually a long integer (32 bits) */
    time( &seconds );        /* pass the address of seconds to time */
}
```

Note that in C the slash-and-asterisk (/* ... */) structures indicate comments. Semicolons have an entirely different meaning.

The time routine gets the time from the real-time clock and puts it in the long integer passed:

```
        .MODEL SMALL, C
        PUBLIC _time

_time   PROC
ARG     secs:PTR

        sub  ah, ah             ; AH = 0 is read clock
                                ; function
        int  1Ah                ; Call BIOS. Returns the
                                ; number of ticks since
                                ; midnight Jan 1, 1980 in CX
                                ; and DX
        push dx                 ; Convert ticks to seconds
                                ; (65536 ticks per hour)
        mov  ax, cx             ; Get the number of hours
        mov  cx, 3600           ; The number of seconds in an
                                ; hour
        imul cx                 ; Hours part converted
        mov  bx, [secs]         ; Get the argument
        mov  [bx], ax           ; Save the result in the long
```

12—Writing Assembly Modules for High Level Languages **493**

```
                mov  [bx+2], dx          ; passed
                pop  ax                  ; Get the 1/65536 of an hour
                imul cx                  ; Convert to seconds. DX
                                         ; contains whole seconds and
                                         ; AX contains 1/65536 of a
                                         ; second
                add  [bx], dx            ; Add these seconds to the
                adc  [bx+2], 0           ; converted hours
                ret
_time           ENDP
```

This function calls the BIOS time function (AH=0 interrupt 1Ah) to get the time. The time is reported in ticks (approximately 1/18th of a second) since midnight January 1, 1980. This value must be converted to time in seconds for the time function. After the value is converted, the address of the argument (at secs) is copied to BX. Then the routine copies the computed number of seconds to the location indicated by the BX register.

The third and final technique for returning data from a called function to the calling function is to put the data to return in the CPU registers. For this technique to work, the calling function and the called function need to agree on what registers to use. Most systems return 16-bit integers in AX, and 32-bit integers in DX and AX. Pointers can also be returned, but the registers used vary from compiler to compiler.

Some languages can return whole structures. For example, this pseudo code function loads the structure MyStru by calling the function StructFunc:

```
Begin function
    Define structure MyStru
            define integer IVar
            define character pointer Buffer
            define long integer Sample
    End of structure
    Set MyStru equal to the result of StructFunc
End of function
```

Since there are not enough registers to return any but the smallest of structures, something else must be going on. What happens in this case is that the function puts the structure in somewhere in its local memory area, and then returns a pointer to the structure. The calling routine copies the data from the function's local memory area to its own structure which is to receive the result. The assembly language version of the function above may look like this:

```
_Func       PROC
            call StructFunc          ; Call the function
            push ds                  ; Copy ds into es for copy
            pop  es
            mov  si, ax              ; Pointer in ax returned by the
```

```
                                       ; function
        lea  di, [bp-8]                ; Get the address of the structure
        mov  cx, 8                     ; The size of the structure
        rep  movsb                     ; Copy the structure
        ret
_Func   ENDP
```

Function Names

In the previous examples, you may have noticed that the names used in the
assembly language samples do not match the names in the C samples. This is
because C compilers prefix symbols with an underscore character (_). This
prevents the programmer from writing a routine that happens to have the same
name as an internal library function. Note that if you specify QUIRKS mode and
use the MODEL directive to specify C conventions, then Turbo Assembler will
prefix symbols with an underscore to all function names. In this case you do
not want to put an underscore in front of the function names. In cases where
the compiler requires underscores and you do not use them, however, the
linker will inform you that the symbol is undefined.

Sharing Global Data

You may need to share global data between assembly language routines and
high level languages. The module that defines the data needs to use the
equivalent of Turbo Assembler's PUBLIC directive. The module that uses the
data needs to use the equivalent of the EXTRN directive. These directives tell the
linker that the symbol names are to be shared. It is up to you to make sure that
the data is in the expected format and can be accessed from segments that are
available to the module.

Matching Data Types

The linker does not do any type checking when it allows one module to access
symbols in another module. If one module declares a 16-bit integer and
another uses it as if it were a 32-bit integer, the second function can overwrite
the data that it was not meant to use. This kind of problem is very difficult to
track down, so you should be careful to make sure the data types match.

Your compiler's documentation should tell you the format of various
data types. Most compilers use bytes for characters, words for integers, and
double words for long integers. Pointers are words or double words depending on the memory model. The issue becomes more complex when you work
with floating point numbers. The 80x86 has no built-in floating point format,
so compiler writers are on their own in this area. Many languages use a format

that matches the 80x87 math co-processor format. Other languages, like those from Microsoft, use their own floating point format. Figure 12-3 shows two floating point formats.

IEEE 4 Byte Range = 3.4E-38 to 3.4E+38

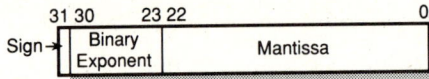

```
      31 30    23 22                        0
     ┌──┬──────┬─────────────────────────────┐
Sign→│  │Binary│                             │
     │  │Expo- │         Mantissa            │
     │  │nent  │                             │
     └──┴──────┴─────────────────────────────┘
```

IEEE 8 Byte Range = 1.7E-308 to1.7E+308

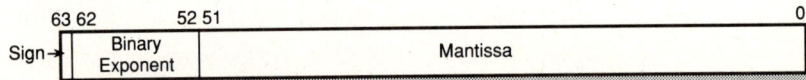

```
      63 62       52 51                                           0
     ┌──┬──────────┬─────────────────────────────────────────────┐
Sign→│  │Binary    │                                             │
     │  │Exponent  │              Mantissa                       │
     └──┴──────────┴─────────────────────────────────────────────┘
```

*Note the mantissas are normalized so that the high bit is always 1.
This bit is not stored with the rest of the mantissa.

Microsoft 10 Byte

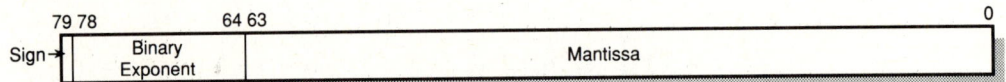

```
      79 78            64 63                                              0
     ┌──┬───────────────┬──────────────────────────────────────────────┐
Sign→│  │Binary         │                                              │
     │  │Exponent       │                Mantissa                      │
     └──┴───────────────┴──────────────────────────────────────────────┘
```

*Microsoft 10 byte floating point numbers normalize the mantissa, but
they do not drop the implied 1 bit.

Figure 12-3. *Floating point formats.*

You can use the STRUCT directive to make assembly language structures that match the structures used in high level languages. Because the commands for structures are different in different languages, you need to be careful when changing the format of a structure that you change it for *each* of the languages that use the structure.

Another problem that you need to be aware of is the type of alignment being used. Many high level languages align all structure items on even addresses. Some can use other sized alignments as well. Check your compiler's documentation and insert ALIGN directives as required in order to make the structures match.

Choosing Segments

The linker can give you access to any segment that a compiler might use, as long as you know the name of the segment. To access data, you need to know the name of the segment in which you can expect to find the data. It is also helpful to know what values you can expect to be found in the segment registers. Most modern compilers stick to the segment names recommended by Microsoft. Table 12-1 shows the segments and how they are used. These names are the same as those used in the simplified segment directives.

Table 12-1. *Commonly Used Segment Names*

Segment	Group	Purpose
_TEXT	*	All code goes in _TEXT for the small code models.
name_TEXT		Used for code. Each source file uses a different name.
FAR_DATA		Initialized far data. This segment has a private combine type so each module gets its own FAR_DATA segment.
FAR_BSS		Uninitialized far data. This segment also has a private combine type.
_DATA	DGROUP	NEAR initialized data.
CONST	DGROUP	Constant data. Often used to store the segment addresses of far data items.
_BSS	DGROUP	NEAR uninitialized data.
STACK	DGROUP	The stack.

* In the TINY model, the _TEXT segment is included in DGROUP.

The segment registers all have specific roles in this segment layout. The DS register and the SS register usually point to DGROUP. The CS register points to the current _TEXT segment and ES remains free to be used when accessing far data. (See Chapter 8 for more information on segments.)

Getting Help from the Compiler

The first place to look for information about interfacing assembly language routines with high level languages is the documentation for your compiler. The next place to look is the compiler itself. Many compilers have a command that makes them give assembly language output instead of object file output. You can use this feature to see how the compiler expects things to be laid out.

The first step is to write a routine in the high level language that does what the assembly language routine does. If this is not possible, you should write a routine that is as close as you can make it. The functions should have the names you intend to use. They should take the arguments and return the values that the assembly language routine does. If the assembly language routine uses structures and global variables, then the high level routine should use structures and global variables.

When the high level version of the function is as close to the assembly language version as it can be, use the compiler to make an assembly language version of the module. Now you have a *template* for the function in assembly language. All you need to do is replace the compiler code with the assembly code you want to use.

To see how this works, look at the following example. What is required is a function to draw circles on-screen as quickly as possible. The algorithm used is called *Bresenham's Algorithm*. It is very fast and does not require any floating point math.

To see how this algorithm works, refer to Figures 12-4 and 12-5. Figure 12-4 shows how you only need to calculate 1/8 of the points in the circle. The rest of the points are simple transformations of the points. Figure 12-5 shows the first 1/8 of the circle and how the points are calculated. Notice that as you move from left to right along the edge of the circle, the y value of each point is the same or one less than the y value for the previous point. Bresenham found a simple formula that tells when y should stay the same and when it should change. In this program the variable delta keeps track of when to change:

```c
/* draw circles */
#include <stdio.h>
#include <graph.h>

/* pass the x, y co-ords for the center, the radius, and the color */
void
circle( int cenx, int ceny, int radius, int colr )
{
    int x, y, delta;

    _setcolor( colr );
    y = radius;
    delta = 3 - 2 * radius;

    for( x=0; x<y; x++ )
    {
/* plot the point in all 8 sections */
        _setpixel( x+cenx, y+ceny );
        _setpixel( x+cenx, ceny-y );
        _setpixel( cenx-x, ceny-y );
```

```
                _setpixel( cenx-x, y+ceny );
                _setpixel( y+cenx, x+ceny );
                _setpixel( y+cenx, ceny-x );
                _setpixel( cenx-y, ceny-x );
                _setpixel( cenx-y, x+ceny );
/* see if y should change */
            if( delta < 0 )
                delta += 4 * x + 6;
            else
            {
                delta += 4 * ( x - y ) + 10;
                y--;
            }
        }
/* plot the last point */
    if( y )
    {
            _setpixel( y+cenx, y+ceny );
            _setpixel( y+cenx, ceny-y );
            _setpixel( cenx-y, ceny-y );
            _setpixel( cenx-y, y+ceny );
    }
}
```

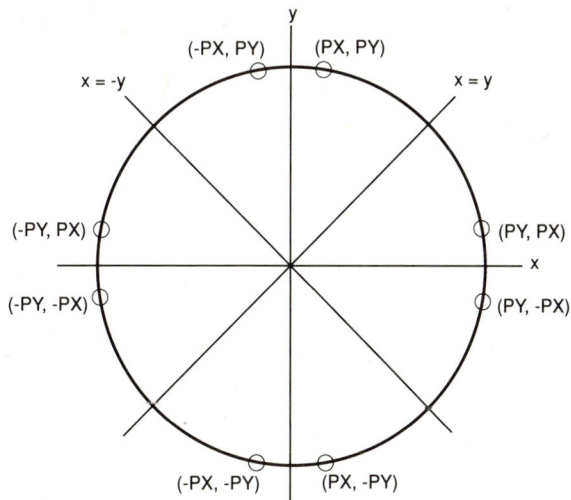

Figure 12-4. *Drawing a circle in eight segments.*

Delta = 3-2*Radius
Plot a point for each x

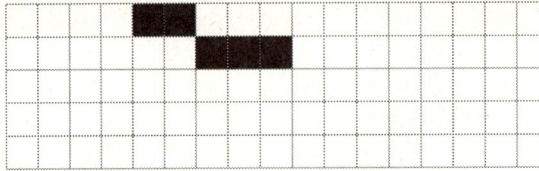

If Delta < 0, don't change y.
Change Delta to: Delta + 4*x + 6

If Delta ≥ 0, move down one pixel and
make Delta = Delta + 4*(x-y) + 6

Figure 12-5.   *Drawing an arc with Bresenham's Algorithm.*

The Microsoft C compiler will give an assembly language version of the circle routine, if you include "/Fa" on the command line when compiling. The result is the file that follows (but note, however, that different versions of Microsoft C may not compile these exact results):

```
;     Static Name Aliases
;
      TITLE    dcirc.c
      NAME     dcirc

      .8087
_TEXT     SEGMENT  WORD PUBLIC 'CODE'
_TEXT     ENDS
_DATA     SEGMENT  WORD PUBLIC 'DATA'
_DATA     ENDS
CONST     SEGMENT  WORD PUBLIC 'CONST'
CONST     ENDS
_BSS SEGMENT  WORD PUBLIC 'BSS'
_BSS ENDS
DGROUP    GROUP     CONST, _BSS, _DATA
      ASSUME  CS: _TEXT, DS: DGROUP, SS: DGROUP
EXTRN      __setpixel:FAR
EXTRN      __setcolor:FAR
_TEXT     SEGMENT
      ASSUME   CS: _TEXT
; Line 10
      PUBLIC   _circle
_circle   PROC NEAR
    push bp
    mov  bp,sp
    sub  sp,24
    push di
    push si
```

```
        push WORD PTR [bp+10]      ;colr
        call FAR PTR __setcolor
        add  sp,2
        mov  ax,WORD PTR [bp+8]  ;radius
        mov  WORD PTR [bp-4],ax   ;y
        shl  ax,1
        sub  ax,3
        neg  ax
        mov  WORD PTR [bp-6],ax   ;delta
        mov  WORD PTR [bp-2],0    ;x
        cmp  WORD PTR [bp-4],0    ;y
        jg   $JCC44
        jmp  $FB268
$JCC44:
        mov  WORD PTR [bp-8],6
        mov  di,WORD PTR [bp-4]   ;y
        mov  si,WORD PTR [bp-2]   ;x
$L20000:
        mov  ax,si
        add  ax,WORD PTR [bp+4]   ;cenx
        mov  WORD PTR [bp-10],ax
        mov  ax,di
        add  ax,WORD PTR [bp+6]   ;ceny
        mov  WORD PTR [bp-12],ax
        push ax
        push WORD PTR [bp-10]
        call FAR PTR __setpixel
        add  sp,4
        mov  ax,WORD PTR [bp+6]   ;ceny
        sub  ax,di
        mov  WORD PTR [bp-14],ax
        push ax
        push WORD PTR [bp-10]
        call FAR PTR __setpixel
        add  sp,4
        mov  ax,WORD PTR [bp+4]   ;cenx
        sub  ax,si
        mov  WORD PTR [bp-16],ax
        push WORD PTR [bp-14]
        push ax
        call FAR PTR __setpixel
        add  sp,4
        push WORD PTR [bp-12]
        push WORD PTR [bp-16]
```

```
        call FAR PTR __setpixel
        add  sp,4
        mov  ax,di
        add  ax,WORD PTR [bp+4]   ;cenx
        mov  WORD PTR [bp-18],ax
        mov  ax,si
        add  ax,WORD PTR [bp+6]   ;ceny
        mov  WORD PTR [bp-20],ax
        push ax
        push WORD PTR [bp-18]
        call FAR PTR __setpixel
        add  sp,4
        mov  ax,WORD PTR [bp+6]   ;ceny
        sub  ax,si
        mov  WORD PTR [bp-22],ax
        push ax
        push WORD PTR [bp-18]
        call FAR PTR __setpixel
        add  sp,4
        mov  ax,WORD PTR [bp+4]   ;cenx
        sub  ax,di
        mov  WORD PTR [bp-24],ax
        push WORD PTR [bp-22]
        push ax
        call FAR PTR __setpixel
        add  sp,4
        push WORD PTR [bp-20]
        push WORD PTR [bp-24]
        call FAR PTR __setpixel
        add  sp,4
        cmp  WORD PTR [bp-6],0    ;delta
        jge  $I269
        mov  ax,WORD PTR [bp-8]
        add  WORD PTR [bp-6],ax   ;delta
        jmp  SHORT $I270
$I269:
        mov  ax,si
        sub  ax,di
        shl  ax,1
        shl  ax,1
        add  ax,10
        add  WORD PTR [bp-6],ax   ;delta
        dec  di
$I270:
        add  WORD PTR [bp-8],4
```

```
        inc  si
        cmp  si,di
        jge  $JCC260
        jmp  $L20000
$JCC260:
        mov  WORD PTR [bp-4],di   ;y
        mov  WORD PTR [bp-2],si   ;x
$FB268:
        cmp  WORD PTR [bp-4],0    ;y
        je   $I271
        mov  si,WORD PTR [bp-4]   ;y
        add  si,WORD PTR [bp+4]   ;cenx
        mov  di,WORD PTR [bp-4]   ;y
        add  di,WORD PTR [bp+6]   ;ceny
        push di
        push si
        call FAR PTR __setpixel
        add  sp,4
        mov  ax,WORD PTR [bp+6]   ;ceny
        sub  ax,WORD PTR [bp-4]   ;y
        mov  WORD PTR [bp-24],ax
        push ax
        push si
        call FAR PTR __setpixel
        add  sp,4
        mov  si,WORD PTR [bp+4]   ;cenx
        sub  si,WORD PTR [bp-4]   ;y
        push WORD PTR [bp-24]
        push si
        call FAR PTR __setpixel
        add  sp,4
        push di
        push si
        call FAR PTR __setpixel
        add  sp,4
$I271:
        pop  si
        pop  di
        mov  sp,bp
        pop  bp
        ret
_circle  ENDP
_TEXT    ENDS
END
```

Note the comment that starts with the word "Line." This comment indicates what line from the source file goes with the following code. The compiler inserts comments like this to help you match up portions of the source with this listing.

There are a few places that can be optimized. The first is to put x and y into registers at the beginning of the program. In this case, x is in the SI register and y is in DI. Next, reduce the amount of things that happen to the stack. In the main loop, the only function that this function calls is _setpixel. You can save some time by allocating room for _setpixel's arguments on the stack, and then simply changing the values instead of pushing and popping them for every call. Since in most cases only one of the arguments changes, this technique gives better performance.

Perhaps even more speed could be squeezed out of this function by looking at _setpixel to see if the arguments could be passed in registers. However, since _setpixel is one of the Microsoft C library routines, such an examination is not practical here.

After optimization the module looks like this:

```
;      Static Name Aliases
;
       TITLE    dcirc.asm
       NAME     dcirc

       .8087
_TEXT      SEGMENT   WORD PUBLIC 'CODE'
_TEXT      ENDS
_DATA      SEGMENT   WORD PUBLIC 'DATA'
_DATA      ENDS
CONST      SEGMENT   WORD PUBLIC 'CONST'
CONST      ENDS
_BSS SEGMENT  WORD PUBLIC 'BSS'
_BSS ENDS
DGROUP     GROUP     CONST, _BSS, _DATA
       ASSUME  CS: _TEXT, DS: DGROUP, SS: DGROUP
EXTRN      __acrtused:ABS
EXTRN      __setpixel:FAR
EXTRN      __setcolor:FAR

_TEXT      SEGMENT
       ASSUME    CS: _TEXT
       PUBLIC    _circle
_circle    PROC NEAR
       push bp
       mov  bp,sp
       sub  sp,2                ; make room for delta
       push di
```

```
        push si
        sub   sp, 4                 ; make room for the _setpixel args
        push WORD PTR [bp+10]       ; colr
        call FAR PTR __setcolor
        add   sp,2
        mov   di,WORD PTR [bp+8]    ; y = radius
        mov   ax, di
        shl   ax,1                  ; radius * 2
        sub   ax,3                  ; - 3
        neg   ax                    ; change sign
        mov   WORD PTR [bp-2],ax    ; delta
        sub   si, si                ; clear x
$L20002:
        mov   ax,di
        add   ax,WORD PTR [bp+6]    ; y + ceny
        mov   WORD PTR [bp-8], ax   ; second arg
        mov   ax,si
        add   ax,WORD PTR [bp+4]    ; x + cenx
        mov   WORD PTR [bp-10], ax; first arg
        call FAR PTR __setpixel
        mov   dx,WORD PTR [bp+6]
        sub   ax,di                 ; ceny-y
        mov   WORD PTR [bp-8], ax
        call FAR PTR __setpixel
        mov   ax,WORD PTR [bp+4]    ; cenx - x
        sub   ax,si
        mov   WORD PTR [bp-10], ax
        call FAR PTR __setpixel
        mov   ax,WORD PTR [bp+6]
        add   ax, di                ; ceny + y
        mov   WORD PTR [bp-8], ax
        call FAR PTR __setpixel
        mov   ax, WORD PTR [bp+4]
        add   ax, di                ; cenx + y
        mov   WORD PTR [bp-10], ax
        mov   ax, WORD PTR [bp+6]
        add   ax, si                ; ceny + x
        mov   WORD PTR [bp-8], ax
        call FAR PTR __setpixel
        mov   ax, WORD PTR [bp+6]
        sub   ax,si                 ; ceny - x
        mov   WORD PTR [bp-8],ax
        call FAR PTR __setpixel
        mov   ax,WORD PTR [bp+4]
```

```
        sub  ax,di                  ; cenx - y
        mov  WORD PTR [bp-10],ax
        call FAR PTR __setpixel
        mov  ax, WORD PTR [bp+6]
        add  ax, si                 ; ceny + x
        mov  WORD PTR [bp-8], ax
        call FAR PTR __setpixel
        cmp  WORD PTR [bp-2], 0  ; delta
        jge  $I439
        mov  ax, si
        shl  ax, 1
        shl  ax, 1
        add  ax, 6
        add  WORD PTR [bp-2], ax
        jmp  SHORT $I440
$I439:
        mov  ax,si
        sub  ax,di
        shl  ax,1
        shl  ax,1
        add  ax,10
        add  WORD PTR [bp-2],ax  ; delta
        dec  di
$I440:
        inc  si
        cmp  si,di
        jge  $JCC928
        jmp  $L20002
$JCC928:
        or   di,di
        je   $I441
        mov  ax, WORD PTR [bp+4]
        add  ax, di                 ; cenx + y
        mov  WORD PTR [bp-10], ax; first arg
        mov  si, WORD PTR [bp+6]
        add  si, di                 ; ceny + y
        mov  WORD PTR [bp-8], si ; second arg
        call FAR PTR __setpixel
        mov  ax, WORD PTR [bp+6]
        sub  ax, di                 ; ceny - y
        mov  WORD PTR [bp-8], ax
        call FAR PTR __setpixel
        mov  ax, WORD PTR [bp+4]
        sub  ax, di
```

```
        mov  WORD PTR [bp-10], ax
        call FAR PTR __setpixel
        mov  WORD PTR [bp-8], si
        call FAR PTR __setpixel
$I441:
        add  sp, 4
        pop  si
        pop  di
        mov  sp,bp
        pop  bp
        ret
_circle    ENDP
_TEXT      ENDS
END
```

The modifications made include keeping *x* in the SI register and *y* in the DI register. The biggest modification is in the use of the stack frame. Just before calling __setcolor, this routine makes room on the stack for the two integers that will be passed to __setpixel. The label $L2002 marks the beginning of the calls to __setpixel. Instead of pushing the arguments over and over, this version of the _circle function modifies the arguments right in the stack frame.

Start-up Modules

When a program written in a high level language begins, it runs a routine that sets up the machine for the program. Some of the set-up, however, may not be required or desired for the specific program. For some languages this set-up may require as much as 50K of code. For applications that require as much memory as possible, you may want to replace the start-up routine with a shorter one that leaves out things that you do not need.

The next example shows a start-up routine for Microsoft C that does the absolute minimum number of things to get a C program started. Programs that need the features—such as the DOS version number or the heap—that have been removed can call routines to set them up. This lets you make programs that contain code for just what it needs, and nothing else.

```
; start up file for Microsoft C
        DOSSEG
        .MODEL   SMALL
extrn      _main:PROC

PUBLIC     __acrtused
__acrtused = 9876h
```

```
        .CODE
Start     PROC
        mov   ax, DGROUP                ; Set up the data segment
        mov   ds, ax
        assume      ds:DGROUP, ss:DGROUP
        call  _main                     ; Call the C program
        mov   ah,4ch                    ; Exit to DOS
        int   21h
Start     ENDP
        .STACK    1024
END   Start
```

An Example That Makes Sounds

When you want a routine that directly affects the hardware, assembly language may be the only way to go. This example shows how to use assembly language to make a routine that can be called by a high level language to make sounds on IBM PC-compatible computers. The routine programs the timer chips to create different notes of different durations.

There are three timers in IBM PCs and compatibles. The first timer is used by the BIOS time-of-day functions. It interrupts the system 18.2 times per second. The BIOS counts these interruptions and keeps the count in the four bytes beginning at 40:6C. The second timer can be set for a wide range of intervals. The output of this timer can be sent to the speaker to generate tones. The third timer is used to refresh RAM and is not used for making sounds.

The Play function gets a note and duration from a C program. The note tells it what frequency to send out to the speaker port, and the duration tells it how long to send it. The note argument can range from 0 to 13. A note of 0 means play no note. A note of one is middle C, two is C-sharp, three is D, and so on. The duration is given in ticks (65,536 ticks per hour or about 18.2 ticks per second). The following program uses Play to play a song:

```
struct {
    int note;
    int duration;
} Song[] =
{ {5, 9}, {3, 9}, {1, 9}, {3, 9}, {5, 9}, {5, 9}, {5, 9},
  {3, 9}, {3, 9}, {3, 9}, {5, 9}, {8, 9}, {8, 9}, {5, 9},
  {3, 9}, {1, 9}, {3, 9}, {5, 9}, {5, 9}, {5, 9}, {5, 9},
  {3, 9}, {3, 9}, {5, 9}, {3, 9}, {1, 18}, {-1, -1} };
```

```
main()
{
    for( i=0; Song[i].note != -1; i++ )
        Play( Song[i].note, Song[i].Duration );
}
```

The Play function, shown below, looks up the note in a table of timer intervals. Next, it sends the timer interval to the timer. After setting up the timer, it adds the duration to the tick count at 40:6C. This is the target tick count. The next step is to turn on the speaker. The speaker stays on until the tick count at 40:6C is greater than or equal to the previously computed target count. Finally, it turns off the speaker and returns to the calling program.

```
; Music program
; Call from a C program with:
;  Play( Note, Duration );
; Note=0 is a rest. Duration is in timer ticks (18.2 per second).

        .MODEL SMALL, C
        .DATA
; This are the timer counts for the notes middle C through high C
; each note is a half tone higher than the previous note
PUBLIC  _Play
NoteTab    DW  0, 4561, 4305, 4063, 3835, 3620, 3417, 3225, 3044
           DW  2873, 2712, 2560, 2416, 2280
        .CODE
_Play      PROC
ARG  Note:WORD, Duration:WORD
        mov   bx, [Note]                    ; Get the note
        shl   bx, 1                         ; Times 2 for words
        jz    Delay                         ; If 0 do not play a note
        mov   al, 0B6h
        out   43h, al                       ; Prepare the clock port
        mov   al, BYTE PTR NoteTab[bx]      ; Look up the low byte of
        out   42h, al                       ; the count
        mov   al, BYTE PTR NoteTab+1[bx]    ; Get the high byte
        out   42h, al
        in    al, 61h                       ; Get speaker mask
        or    al, 3                         ; Turn on speaker bits
        out   61h, al                       ; Send the new mask
Delay:
        push  ds                            ; Save the data segment
        mov   ax, 40h                       ; Set DS to the BIOS data area
        mov   ds, ax
        mov   bx, ds:[6Ch]                  ; Get the low word for timer
                                            ; ticks
```

```
        mov   cx, ds:[6Eh]              ; Get the high word
        add   bx, [Duration]            ; Add in the duration
        adc   cx, 0                     ; Add any carry to the high word
Ploop:                                  ; Wait for timer ticks to catch
        cmp   ds:[6Eh], cx              ; up with cx:bx
        jl    Ploop
        cmp   ds:[6Ch], bx
        jl    Ploop
        in    al, 61h                   ; Get the speaker mask
        and   al, 0FCh                  ; Turn off the speaker bits
        out   61h, al                   ; Send it
        pop   ds                        ; Restore DS
        ret                             ; Return to calling routine
_Play   ENDP
END
```

Summary

Each computer language has something that it does best. Assembly language is vital for writing programs that must access the hardware directly. It is also good for writing routines that run as fast as possible. High level languages are easier to use and understand. The best of both worlds is to use the appropriate language for the appropriate problem to be solved.

Turbo Assembler provides several commands that make this process easier. The .MODEL directive tells the assembler to use segments and calling conventions that work with several high level languages. Once you specify a language in the .MODEL directive, the assembler can generate code to pass arguments to subroutines. It also enables you to use the symbol names for those arguments in the subroutines.

The compiler itself is often the best source of information on how to link in assembly language routines. Many compilers can generate assembly language files from source code, and you can use these files to see how to work with those compilers.

Chapter *13* *Using System Resources*

IBM PCs and compatibles offer a number of resources that can be used by programs. These resources include memory, co-processors, disk drives, serial and parallel ports, sound, keyboard, mouse, and video. Programs can access these resources through special drivers, the BIOS, or MS-DOS.

Not all computers have all of these resources. Some may have others. In the case of disk drives and memory, different systems will have these resources in different amounts. The first part of this chapter shows you how to find out what resources are available.

There are some resources that a program must have, such as enough memory. Other resources, like a mouse, might be optional for a given program. In either case your program will need to have routines that work with the resources. The second part of this chapter shows you how to use memory, keyboard, video, serial and parallel ports, the mouse, and disk drives.

Identifying Resources

The first step in using the resources of a system is to determine what resources are available. Programs written for Turbo Assembler can be run on a wide range of computers. These computers can be configured in many different ways. This information is not all stored in easy-to-get-at locations. Your program will need to use a variety of techniques to get information about the computer configuration.

BIOS Services and Data Areas

The idea behind using a BIOS program in a microcomputer is to provide a standard interface with hardware across different machines. Part of this interface is to tell a program just what hardware is available. A program can access this information in two ways: the first is through the normal software interrupt interface, and the second is by looking at memory locations used by the BIOS.

BIOS FUNCTIONS   BIOS uses several different software interrupts in its interface. The interrupts used by BIOS range from 10h to 1Ah. Interrupt 5, which sends the text on the screen to the printer, is also part of the BIOS. Each interrupt has several functions that are selected by placing a function number in the AH register. Table 13-1 shows the BIOS functions that can be used in determining the configuration of the computer.

Table 13-1.   *BIOS Functions for Determining the System Configuration*

Interrupt	Function	Description
10h	0Fh	Get video mode
11h	N/A	Get equipment list
12h	N/A	Get base memory size
13h	15h	Get disk type
15h	88h	Get extended memory size
15h	0C0h	Get system configuration parameters

BIOS interrupt 10h provides a variety of video services. Function 0Fh gets the current video mode. You will need to use this function if your program writes directly to the video buffer in order to print text. There are two possible locations for the video buffer in text mode. If the video mode is 7, then the buffer starts at 0B000:0000. If it is 2 or 3 then the buffer starts at 0B800:0000. (See Chapter 14 for more information on using the video buffer.)

Interrupt 11h returns the equipment list in the AX register. The equipment list tells how many printers, disk drives, and serial ports are installed. It also indicates if a math co-processor, game adapter, or pointing device is installed. Figure 13-1 shows the format of the equipment list word.

Interrupt 12h returns the amount of base memory in the AX register. The number tells how many kilobytes are installed. On older PCs and compatibles, this number comes from the motherboard switch settings. Because some of these systems could add memory without changing the switches, this number can be inaccurate. The PC/AT, PS/2, and compatibles can also use extended memory. Interrupt 15h function 88h returns the amount of extended memory in the AX register.

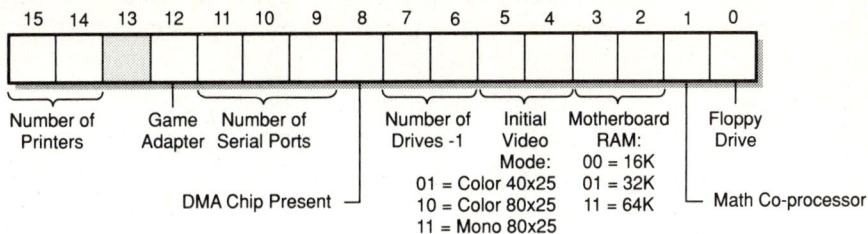

Figure 13-1. *The BIOS equipment list.*

Interrupt 13h functions 8h and 15h tell what kind of disk drive is installed. For each of these functions, you pass the drive ID in the DL register. The drive ID is the physical drive number. Drive numbers range from 0 through the number of drives minus one. Hard drives use drive numbers with the high bit on, and floppy drives have the high bit off. Function 8h returns the number of drives on the same controller, the number of heads, number of cylinders, and number of sectors per track. For PC/ATs and PS/2s, it also tells the type of diskette drive. Function 15h tells if the drive can tell when the diskette was changed and, for hard drives, the total number of sectors on the drive. Figure 13-2 shows how this information is arranged in the registers.

Interrupt 15h function 0C0h can be used with PC/ATs and PS/2s to give more information about the system. This function returns a pointer to the system configuration parameters in ES:BX. Figure 13-3 shows the format of these parameters.

BIOS DATA AREAS

Some of the information that you can get from BIOS functions can also be found in BIOS data areas. Other information that is not available through BIOS functions is also stored in these data areas. For example, the machine type and subtype from the system configuration parameters is located at F000:FFFE. At F000:FFF5 is the date that the BIOS was released.

Most of the useful data that BIOS has can be found in the BIOS data segment. To access this segment, you must load 40h into a segment register and use that register when accessing the data. Table 13-2 shows several interesting BIOS data segment locations.

Using Set-Up Information

Another place to look for information about how the computer is configured is in the set-up information. On PCs and PC/XTs, this is the setting of switches inside the computer. The PC/AT and PS/2 put set-up information into special nonvolatile RAM locations. This information includes how much memory is installed, what kind of display adapter to use, how many COM ports exist, and the disk drive type. Other information may also be included, depending on the particular make and model of the computer.

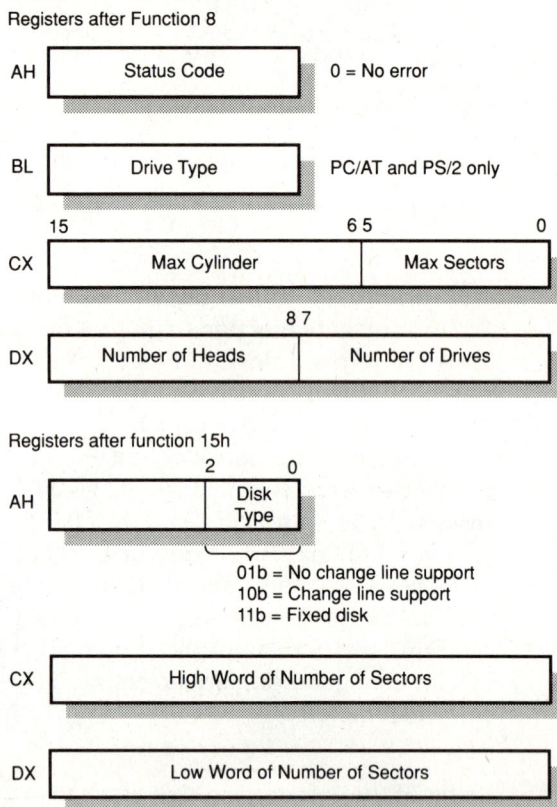

Registers after Function 8

| AH | Status Code | 0 = No error |

| BL | Drive Type | PC/AT and PS/2 only |

```
        15                      6 5              0
CX  |    Max Cylinder    |    Max Sectors    |
```

```
                            8 7
DX  |  Number of Heads   |  Number of Drives |
```

Registers after function 15h

```
                2       0
AH  |         |  Disk   |
    |         |  Type   |
```

01b = No change line support
10b = Change line support
11b = Fixed disk

| CX | High Word of Number of Sectors |

| DX | Low Word of Number of Sectors |

Figure 13-2. *Disk information returned by interrupt 13h functions 8 and 15h.*

To read the switch settings on the PC or PC/XT, use I/O ports 60h and 61h. The high bit of the byte at port 61h tells what you will find at port 60h. If the high bit is set, then the data at port 60h is from the keyboard controller. When it is not set, the data at port 60h reflects the state of the switches. To read the switches, you must clear this bit and then read the data at port 60h. Figure 13-4 shows the format of the data at port 60h.

For PC/ATs and PS/2s, the configuration information is contained in nonvolatile RAM contained in the Real Time Clock (RTC) chip. The RTC chip uses two I/O ports (70h and 71h) to pass information to and from the CPU. Port 70h is an index port that tells the RTC chip what data address to use. The data can be read or written from port 71h. The following example shows how to get the year from the RTC chip:

```
cli               ; Don't allow interrupts
mov  al, 9        ; Index for the year byte
out  70h, al      ; Send it to the index register
in   al, 71h      ; Read the data register. Year is in AL
sti               ; Turn interrupts back on
```

Figure 13-5 shows the information contained in the RTC RAM.

Table at ES:BX after INT 15h function C0h

Offset

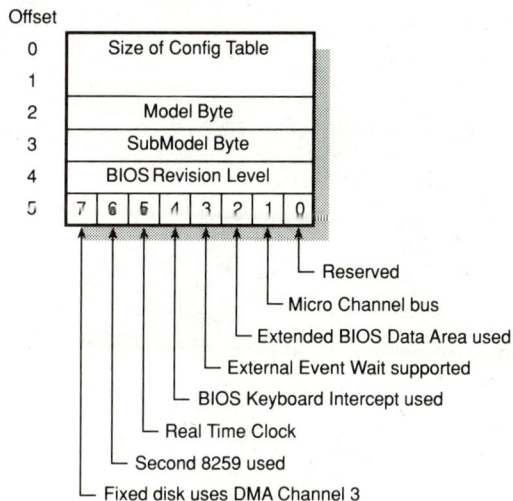

Figure 13-3. *System configuration parameters.*

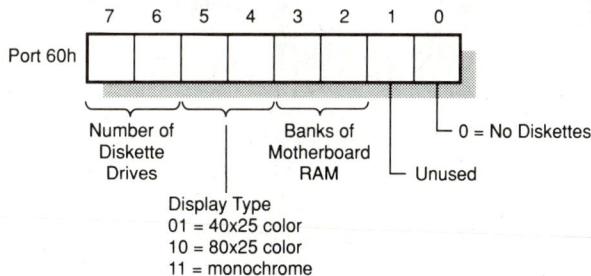

Figure 13-4. *Data at port 60h.*

CMOS Address	
0-9	Clock Data
10-13	Clock Status Registers
14-15	Diagnostic & Shutdown Information
16	Diskette Type
17-18	Fixed Disk Types
19	Reserved
20	Equipment List
21-22	Base Memory Size
23-24	Expansion Memory Size
25-26	Drive Types
27-45	Reserved
46-47	Checksum
48-49	Expansion Memory Size in Bytes
50	Century in BCD
51	Information Flag
52-63	Reserved

Figure 13-5. *Information in RTC RAM.*

Finding Resources with Programs

The only other way to find out about resources in the system is to write a program that will test for various resources. In many cases, however, this is the most reliable way to tell how a system is configured. None of the information from the BIOS data areas is guaranteed on any but actual IBM equipment. Compatible systems may or may not implement these things in the same way, if at all.

MEMORY Most programs stay within the memory that DOS allocates for them. Other programs may use all of the memory in the system. For example, a program that tests memory should test all memory locations.

Table 13-2. *The BIOS Data Segment*

Offset	Bytes	Description
0010h	2	Equipment list. The same data as returned by interrupt 11.
0013h	2	Memory size. The same data as returned by interrupt 12.
0049h	1	The current video mode. The same as interrupt 10h function 0Fh.
004Ch	2	Size of the video buffer.
0063h	2	Address of the CRT controller chip.
0087h	4	EGA configuration.

A program can determine what memory locations are usable by writing to the location and then reading the value back. If this works for several different values, then most likely there is RAM at that location. If the value read docs not match the value written, then the memory is either not there or it is a ROM.

Notice that this technique will destroy whatever is in the memory being tested. If you do not want to destroy the data at a memory location, you should read the location and put the data away while the location is being tested.

This function tests the memory pointed to by ES:BX to see if it is RAM:

```
isRAM     PROC
          mov   dx, es:[bx]      ; Read the data at es:bx
          mov   es:[bx],55h      ; Turn every other bit on
          cmp   es:[bx],55h      ; Check it
          jne   NotRAM
          mov   es:[bx],0AAh     ; Flip the bits
          cmp   es:[bx],0AAh
          je    RAM
NotRAM:
          sub   ax,ax            ; Indicate not ram
          jmp   SHORT Done
RAM:
          mov   ax, 1            ; Indicate RAM
Done:
          mov   es:[bx], dx      ; Put back the original value
          ret
isRAM     ENDP
```

SERIAL PORTS

The way to tell if a serial port is installed is to send some commands to the serial port chip and see if the results match what the chip should do. The next program checks for a serial port by putting the serial chip into loop-back mode and checking that a character sent is the same as the one received.

```
IsPort    PROC
          mov  dx, 3FCh  ; COM1 Modem control register
          in   al, dx    ; Get what is there
          mov  bl, al    ; Save it
          or   al, 10h   ; Set loop back bit
          out  dx, al    ; Send the command to the UART
          mov  dx, 3F8h  ; COM1 Data register
          mov  al, 55h
          out  dx, al    ; Send a byte
          mov  cx, 5000h ; Set up for a loop
          mov  dx, 3FDh  ; COM1 line status register
Wait1:
          in   al, dx    ; Get line status
          test al, 1     ; See if data received
          jnz  Readit    ; If set read the character
          loop Wait1
          jmp  SHORT Noport
Readit:
          mov  dx, 3F8h  ; COM1 Data port
          in   al, dx    ; Read the data
          cmp  al, 55h   ; Compare to the data sent
          clc            ; Indicate a port found
          je   PortOK    ; If it matches, this is a COM port
Noport:
          stc            ; Indicate no port found
PortOK:
          mov  dx, 3FCh  ; COM1 Modem control register
          mov  al, bl    ; Get the old state
          out  dx, al
          ret
IsPort    ENDP
```

The first part of this function puts COM1 into loop-back mode. In this mode any character sent should show up in the received data register of the port. In this case the character sent is 55h. The loop at Wait1 waits for the data to show up at the received data register. If the data shows up, the program goes to Readit where the data is read and compared with 55h. If the loop at Wait1 times out or the data does not match, the program goes to Noport where the carry is set. If the data matches, then the program clears the carry and jumps to PortOK. The last bit of code turns off loop-back mode and returns to the calling routine.

CPU TYPE   Each CPU in the 80x86 family is a little different from the other processors. A program can exploit these differences to determine what kind of processor is being used. For example the 8088 and 8086 will do a multi-bit shift for values of CL greater than or equal to 32. The 80188 and 80186 chips will not do this shift. With the 80286 a change was made in the way the `push sp` instruction works. Older processors push the undecremented stack pointer on the stack. The 80286 and 80386 push the decremented stack pointer. Another change that was made for the 80286 and newer chips is the use of interrupt 6 when the CPU tries to execute an illegal instruction. This lets you try an instruction that is only legal on the 80386. If it generates an interrupt 6, the CPU must be an 80286.

The following routine uses these differences to determine what kind of CPU is executing the program:

```
; Determine what kind of CPU is being used
        .MODEL SMALL
        .DATA
        .386                    ; Allow 80386 instructions
OldInt6 DD   ?
M88     DB   "This is an 8088/86", 0Dh, 0Ah, '$'
M186    DB   "This is an 80188/86", 0Dh, 0Ah, '$'
M286    DB   "This is an 80286',0Dh, 0Ah, '$'
M386    DB   "This is an 80386",0Dh, 0Ah, '$'

        .CODE
Start   PROC
        mov  ax, SEG DGROUP
        mov  ds, ax

; First see if it is an 8088/86 or an 80188/86

        mov  dx, sp             ; Save the stack pointer
        push sp
        pop  cx
        cmp  dx, cx             ; Only different if 8088/86 or
                                ; 80188/86

        je   Cpu1

; Check for 80186

        mov  ax, 1
        mov  cl, 32
        shl  ax, cl             ; See what happens for a 32-bit
                                ; shift
        jz   Not8088            ; Only the 80188/86 will attempt
                                ; this
        mov  dx, OFFSET M88
```

```
                 jmp  pexit
Not8088:
                 mov  dx, OFFSET M186
                 jmp  pexit

; See if it is an 80386

Cpu1:
                 mov  ax, 3506h        ; Get the address for int 6
                 int  21h
                 mov  WORD PTR OldInt6, bx
                 mov  WORD PTR OldInt6+2, es
                 push ds
                 push cs
                 pop  ds
                 mov  dx, OFFSET Not80386
                 mov  ax, 2506h
                 int  21h
                 pop  ds
                 inc  eax              ; Works with 80386 only
                 mov  dx, OFFSET M386
                 jmp  rexit            ; Fix int 6 print message and exit

Not80386:

; Couldn't do 32-bit operation it must be 80286

                 pop  ax               ; The only way to get here is by
                 pop  ax               ; an interrupt 6. These pops remove
                 pop  ax               ; the flags and return address from
                                       ; the stack
                 mov  dx, OFFSET M286

; Restore interrupt 6

rexit:
                 push dx
                 push ds
                 mov  dx, WORD PTR OldInt6
                 mov  ds, WORD PTR OldInt6+2
                 mov  ax, 2506h
                 int  21h
                 pop  ds
                 pop  dx
pexit:
                 mov  ah, 9            ; DOS print string function
```

```
           int  21h
           mov  ah, 4CH
           int  21h
Start      ENDP
           .STACK    1024
END Start
```

The first test checks if the CPU is an 8088, 8086, 80188, or 80186. The test for this uses the different way these chips handle the `push sp` instruction. The 8088, 8086, 80188, and 80186 change SP before pushing it, while all the other CPUs push it and then change it. The next test differentiates the 8088/86 from the 80188/86 CPUs. This test uses the fact that the 8088/86 CPUs will not do a shift of 32 bits or more. The last test checks if the CPU is an 80286 or 80386. This test uses the fact that these chips generate an interrupt 6 when it tries to execute an illegal instruction. The `inc eax` instruction is legal for the 80386 but illegal on the 80286. If an 80286 tries to execute this instruction, it does an interrupt 6 instead.

Accessing Resources

There are four ways to access resources on IBM PCs and compatibles. The first is to access the hardware directly. (Chapter 14 describes this technique in greater detail.) The other three are to use DOS, use BIOS, or to use a software driver program. The technique that should be used depends on the resource and what the application needs from it.

Memory

All programs need memory in which to run and store data. Figure 13-6 shows a typical memory layout for a PC. When DOS starts a program, it gives it all of the memory left in the Transient Program Area (TPA). When the program exits it frees all of its memory, making it available for other programs.

Programs that run other programs and Terminate but Stay Resident (TSR) programs must free a portion of the TPA to give room for other programs. There are four DOS functions that programs can use to change memory allocations. They are function 31h terminate but stay resident, 48h allocate memory block, 49h free memory block, and 4Ah resize memory block.

Function 31h lets a program exit without freeing up its memory. Before invoking this function, you must be sure that there is some way to get the program running again. Most TSR programs are restarted by some kind of interrupt. Perhaps when a certain key is pressed or after a number of timer interrupts or even a software interrupt from another program.

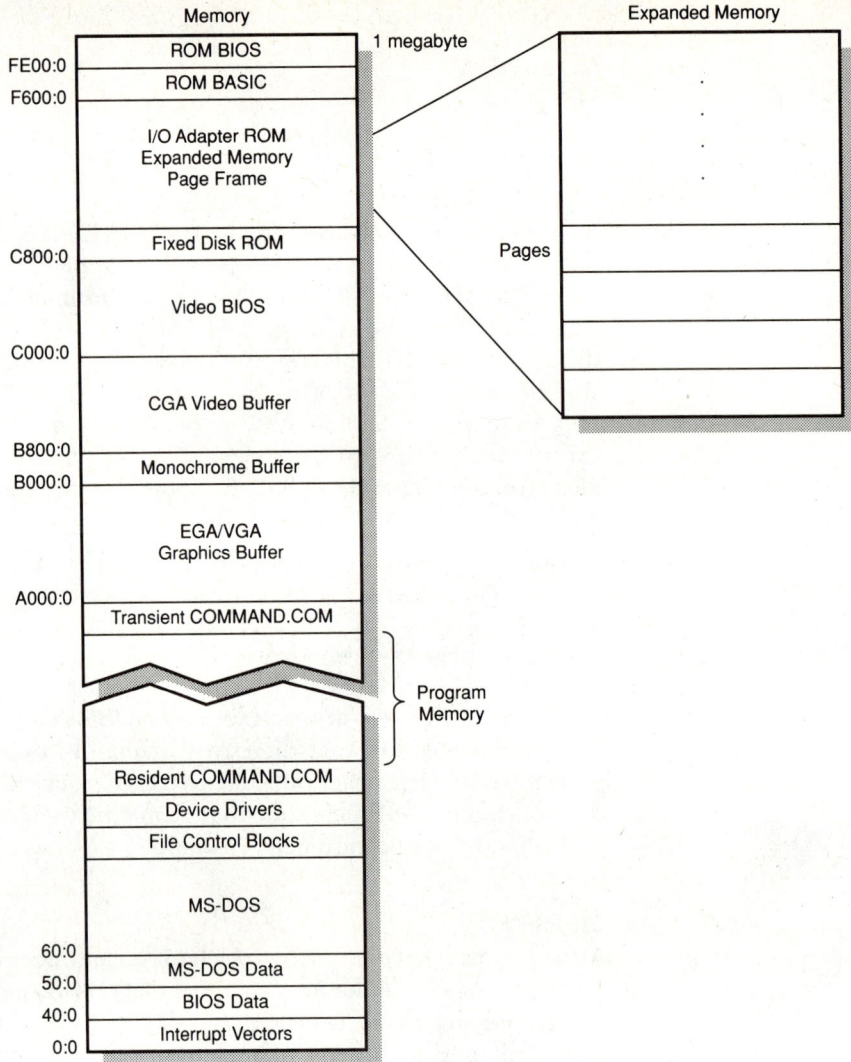

Figure 13-6. *Memory usage in PCs.*

To use function 31h, you put 31h in AH, a return code in AL, and the amount of memory to keep in DX. The amount of memory is in 16-byte paragraphs. This example shows how this can be done:

```
.MODEL SMALL
.CODE
    .
    .
    .
```

```
            mov   ax, 3100h        ; Get function number and return
                                   ; code
            mov   dx, SEG STACK    ; Get the location of the last
                                   ; segment
            sub   dx, SEG _TEXT    ; Minus the first segment give the
                                   ; size
            add   dx, 1024/16      ; Add in the size of the stack
                                   ; DX is the amount of memory to
                                   ; keep
            int   21h              ; Call MS-DOS
            .STACK   1024
END
```

Functions 48h, 49h, and 4Ah let you manipulate memory blocks. Since DOS allocates all available memory to a program when the program is loaded, the program must re-size its memory block before you can use any of these functions. The following example shows how to use function 4Ah to shrink the program's memory block to the minimum size:

```
            .MODEL SMALL
            .CODE
Start       PROC
            push ds                ; DS points to the memory block
                                   ; when the program is started
            pop   es               ; Put it in ES for the resize
                                   ; function
            mov   bx, SEG STACK    ; The location of the last segment
            sub   bx, SEG _TEXT    ; The location of the first segment
            add   bx, 1024/16      ; Plus the paragraphs in the stack
            mov   ah, 4Ah          ; DOS resize function
            int   21h
             .
             .
             .
Start       ENDP
            .STACK   1024
END         Start
```

Once you have reduced the program's memory block to the minimum size, you can use functions 48h and 49h to allocate and free memory blocks. To allocate a block, put the number of paragraphs required in BX and call function 48h. On return the AX register contains the segment address of the new block if the carry is clear, otherwise it contains an error code. To free the block, put the segment address of the block in the ES register and call function 49h.

If your program requires more memory than is available, you will get an error when trying to allocate a memory block. At this point you will have to find a way to reduce the memory requirements of the program or find more memory. One way to get more memory is to use the Lotus, Intel Corporation, or Microsoft (LIM) Expanded Memory System (EMS). If this memory is installed, your program can use it by issuing special commands to the LIM EMS driver.

The LIM EMS driver lets you use memory beyond the one-megabyte address limit of the 8086 chip. The same driver can be used with 80286 and 80386 systems that are in real mode. The way it works is by dividing the high memory into a number of 16K pages. The driver copies one or more of these pages into an area of low memory that has been set aside for this purpose. The driver also keeps track of which pages are being used by other programs. The next example shows how a simple program can use LIM EMS memory for saving data that will not fit in main memory:

```
; Example use of LIM memory
            .MODEL     SMALL
            .DATA

DevName   DB    "EMMXXXX0"            ; Name of the LIM EMS driver
EMMHand   DW    ?                     ; A handle to a EMS block
PageSeg   DW    ?                     ; Segment in low memory for
                                      ; EMS window
PageNumb  DW    0                     ; The first page in the window

            .CODE
            JUMPS                     ; Allow NEAR conditional jumps
LIMexam   PROC
            mov   ax, SEG DGROUP
            mov   ds, ax

; Check to see if LIM memory is installed

            sub   ax, ax
            mov   es, ax              ; Interrupt vector is in
                                      ; segment 0
            mov   bx, 19Ch            ; Offset for interrupt 67h
                                      ; (EMS driver)
            les   bx, DWORD PTR es:[bx]
            mov   cx, 8
            mov   di, 0Ah             ; Offset of device name
            mov   si, OFFSET DevName
            cld
            repe cmpsb                ; See if DevName matches
            jne   Exit                ; If not the same exit

; Find out if there are enough pages are available

            mov   ah, 42h            ; LIM get unallocated pages
            int   67h
```

```
            or   ah, ah              ; Check return status
            jnz  Exit
            cmp  bx, 10              ; See if more than ten pages
            jb   Exit

; Allocate pages

            mov  ah, 43h             ; LIM allocate pages
            mov  bx, 10              ; The number of pages
            int  67h
            or   ah, ah
            jnz  Exit
            mov  EMMHand, dx         ; Save the handle

; Get the page frame address

            mov  ah, 41h             ; Get the page frame address
            int  67h
            or   ah, ah              ; Check status
            jnz  Exit
            mov  PageSeg, bx         ; Save the page frame segment

; Copy data to the memory

            cld
loop1:
            mov  ah, 44h             ; Map an EMS page to a page frame
                                     ; page
            mov  al, 0               ; Map to page frame page zero
            mov  bx, PageNumb        ; Pick an EMS page
            mov  dx, EMMHand         ; Get the EMM handle
            int  67h
            or   ah, ah
            jnz  DeAlloc
            mov  cx, 3FFFh           ; The number of bytes in a page
            mov  es, PageSeg         ; Point to the page frame
            sub  di, di
            sub  al, al              ; Clear AL
loop2:                               ; Save numbers in the page
            stosb
            loop loop2
            inc  PageNumb            ; Go to the next page
            cmp  PageNumb, 10
            jb   loop1

; Unallocate pages

DeAlloc:
            mov  ah, 45h             ; EMM de-allocate
```

```
              mov    dx, EMMHand
              int    67h

; Return to DOS
Exit:
              mov    ah, 4Ch
              int    21h
LIMexam    ENDP
              .STACK    512
END  LIMexam
```

The first part of this function determines if the LIM EMS driver is installed. It does get the entry point for the function from the interrupt vector table, and looks at the memory 10 bytes past the entry point. If this memory contains "EMMXXXX0," then the driver is installed. The rest of the example shows the usual order for the function calls required to use LIM EMS. The first function (AH = 42h) tells how many unallocated pages are available. The next function (AH = 43h) allocates 10 pages of LIM EMS memory. After that, function 41h gets the address of the page frame. This is the location in low memory where you will find the selected LIM EMS pages. Function 44h puts the LIM EMS data in the page frame. The loops at loop1 and loop2 fill all of the pages with zeros. The last function (AH = 45h) de-allocates the pages used, so that they can be used by other programs. Your application will undoubtedly do more with the data in LIM memory than this example does, but it should give you some idea of how to use this memory.

Keyboard and Video

MS-DOS and BIOS have several functions that let you read the keyboard and write to the video screen. Table 13-3 shows some of the terminal I/O functions. (See Appendix C for more information on these functions.)

These functions have been used in many of the examples in this book. For a few more examples, see the example below for using the mouse.

MS-DOS can be extended by the use of device drivers. A device driver is a set of functions that MS-DOS can call when accessing a device. MS-DOS recognizes two kinds of devices, block and character. Block devices are things like disk drives that contain files. Each block device is referenced by a drive letter. Character devices are things that read or write one character at a time, like printers or modems. Each character device is referenced by the name of the device. MS-DOS refers to the keyboard and video screen as the CON: device.

Devices can be added or replaced by specifying a device file name in the CONFIG.SYS file. Several device drivers are included with MS-DOS. One of these drivers, ANSI.SYS replaces the built-in CON: driver. It looks at all the characters sent to the console device to find command strings. The command strings let you control many aspects of the screen. To use ANSI.SYS you must put this line into the CONFIG.SYS file and reboot:

```
device=c:\ansi.sys
```

Table 13-3. *PC Terminal I/O Functions*

Interrupt	Inputs	Outputs	Description
10h	AH=2 BH=display page DH=row DL=column	None	Set cursor position
10h	AH=6 AL=Lines BH=Fill attribute CH=Upper row CL=Left column DH=Lower row DL=Right column	None	Scroll window up
10h	AH=7 AL=Lines BH=Fill attribute CH=Upper row CL=Left column DH=Lower row DL=Right column	None	Scroll window down
10h	AH=9 AL=Character BH=Display page BL=Attribute CX=Repeat count	None	Write character and attribute
10h	AH=0Ah AL=Character BH=Display page BL=Color CX=Repeat count	None	Write character
10h	AH=0Eh AL=Character BH=Display Page BL=Color	None	Write character in teletype mode
16h	AH=0	AH=scan code AL=ASCII code	Read keyboard
16h	AH=1	ZF set if key available AH=scan code AL=ASCII code	Test keyboard

Table 13-3. *Continued*

Interrupt	Inputs	Outputs	Description
16h	AH=2	AL= bit 7 = Insert bit 6 = Caps lock bit 5 = Num lock bit 4 = Scroll lock bit 3 = Alt bit 2 = Ctrl bit 1 = Left shift bit 0 = Right shift	Get shift status
21h	AH=1	AL=Character	Input character and echo it
21h	AH=7	AL=Character	Direct input character without echo
21h	AH=8	AL=Character	Input character without echo
21h	AH=0Ah DS:DX=address of input buffer		Input a line
21h	AH=0Bh	AL=0FFh if key pressed AL=0 if no key pressed	Check keyboard
21h	AH=2 DL=character	Print a character	
21h	AH=9 DS:DX=string ending with '$'	Print a string	

Note that the ANSI.SYS file must be in the root directory for this to work. If it is in another directory, you should include the appropriate path.

With the ANSI.SYS driver loaded, programs can send it commands via the normal MS-DOS console output functions. Table 13-4 shows some of the command strings that you can use with ANSI.SYS loaded.

Table 13-4. *ANSI.SYS Functions*

In the sequences below, x is a number expressed in ASCII digits.

Sequence	Function
ESC[x;xH	Position the cursor. If no numbers are given go to the upper left corner
ESC[xA	Move cursor up x lines
ESC[xB	Move cursor down x lines
ESC[xC	Move cursor right x columns
ESC[xD	Move cursor left x columns
ESC[6n	Return a device status report
ESC[s	Save the cursor location
ESC[u	Restore cursor location
ESC[2J	Erase display
ESC[K	Erase line
ESC[x;...;xm	Set graphics rendition
	0 All attributes off
	1 Bold on
	2 Faint on
	3 Italic on
	5 Blink on
	6 Rapid blink on
	7 Reverse video on
	8 Concealed on
	30 Black
	31 Red
	32 Green
	33 Yellow
	34 Blue
	35 Magenta
	36 Cyan
	37 White
	40 Black

Table 13-4. *Continued*

Sequence	Function
	41 Red
	42 Green
	43 Yellow
	44 Blue
	45 Magenta
	46 Cyan
	47 White
	48 Subscript
	49 Superscript
ESC=xh	Set Mode
	0 40 X 25 Black and white
	1 40 X 25 Color
	2 80 X 25 Black and white
	3 80 X 25 Color
	4 320 X 200 Color
	5 320 X 200 Black and white
	6 640 X 200 Black and white
	7 Wraps at the end of each line

The following example shows how to use the ANSI.SYS driver to clear the screen and print a message in the center of the screen:

```
        .MODEL    SMALL
ESC     EQU  27h                    ; Define the escape character
        .DATA
MsgStr  DB   ESC, "[2J"             ; Clear the screen
        DB   ESC, "[12;34H"         ; Position the cursor
        DB   "Press any key$"       ; The message

        .CODE
Start   PROC
        mov  ax, OFFSET DGROUP
        mov  ds, ax
        mov  dx, OFFSET MsgStr      ; Get the address of the
                                    ; string
```

```
                  mov   ah, 9              ; MS-DOS print string
                  int   21h
                  mov   ah, 0
                  int   16h                ; Wait for a key
                  mov   ah, 4Ch
                  int   21h
Start      ENDP

           .STACK
END Start
```

Disk

MS-DOS has two sets of functions for reading and writing functions. The first involves the use of File Control Blocks (FCBs) to identify open files. These functions are included for compatibility with older operating systems. Because they are somewhat clumsy to use, they are not recommended. The other file functions use file handles to identify open files.

Before a file can be used, it must be opened. Opening a file instructs MS-DOS to look for a file with a given file name. When MS-DOS finds the file, it loads information about the file into a table in memory. Then MS-DOS returns a file handle that will be used by the program when referring to the file later. This example shows how to open a file:

```
           .MODEL    SMALL, C
           .CODE
; Open the file indicated by FName. FName is the location on the
; stack of a pointer to the name of the file. See Chapter 10 for
; information on the ARG directive.
OpenFile   PROC
ARG        FName:PTR
           mov   dx, FName      ; Get the address of the file name
           mov   ax, 3D02h      ; Open a file for reading and
                                ; writing
           int   21h
           jnc   Opdone         ; If no error return with handle in
                                ; AX
                                ; If the file cannot be opened it
                                ; is probably because it does not
                                ; exist. So create it.
           mov   dx, FName      ; Get the address of the file name
           mov   cx, 0
           mov   ah, 3Ch        ; Create a file
           int   21h
```

```
              jnc   Opdone         ; If no error return with handle in
                                   ; AX
              sub   ax, ax         ; Return 0 in AX for errors
Opdone:
              ret
OpenFile  ENDP
END
```

The first part of this procedure tries to open an existing file for reading or writing. DS:DX points to the file name and AL contains the file access code. Figure 13-7 shows the meanings of the bits in the file access code. If the file does not exist, the procedure calls the MS-DOS file create function. When creating a file, you must tell MS-DOS what kind of file to create. You do this by putting a file attribute word in CX. Figure 13-8 shows the possible file attributes.

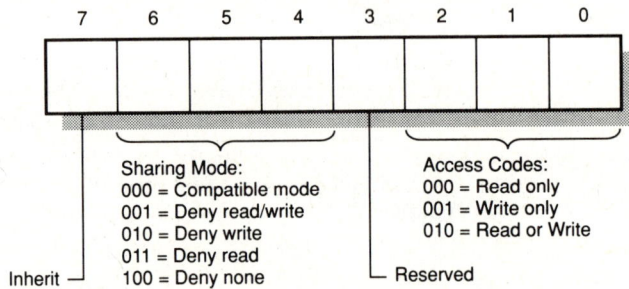

Figure 13-7. *File access codes.*

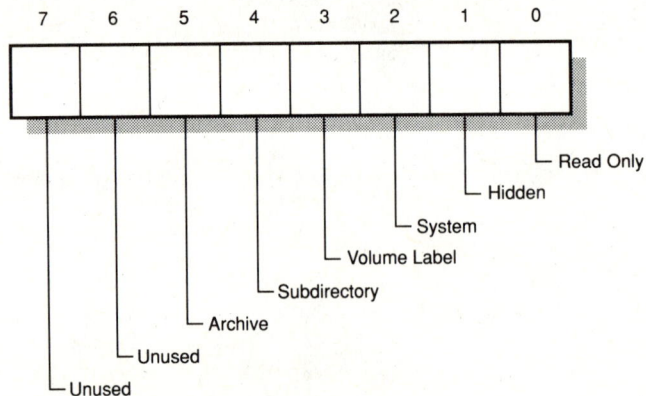

Figure 13-8. *File attributes.*

The file handle that was returned by the MS-DOS open function is used to refer to that file in the rest of the file functions. For example, to write to a file you would pass the data to write, the size of the data, and the file handle to DOS:

```
          .MODEL    SMALL, C
          .CODE
; Write the data at Buff to the file whose handle is at Hand. Cnt
; is the number of bytes to write. These variables are all
; locations in the stack frame (See Chapter 10).
WriteFile PROC
ARG       Hand:WORD, Buff:PTR, Cnt:WORD
          mov  ah, 40h        ; DOS write file function
          mov  bx, Hand        ; Put the file handle in BX
          mov  dx, Buff        ; Put the address of the data in
                               ; DS:DX
          mov  cx, Cnt         ; Put the number of bytes in CX
          int  21h             ; Call DOS
          ret
WriteFile ENDP
END
```

Reading works the same way, except that you use the read function number (3Fh) instead of the write function number:

```
          .MODEL    SMALL, C
          .CODE
; Read the data in the file whose handle is at Hand to Buff. Cnt
; is the number of bytes to write. These variables are all
; locations in the stack frame (See Chapter 10).
ReadFile  PROC
ARG       Hand:WORD, Buff:PTR, Cnt:WORD
          mov  ah, 3Fh        ; DOS read file function
          mov  bx, Hand        ; Put the file handle in BX
          mov  dx, Buff        ; Put the address of the data in
                               ; DS:DX
          mov  cx, Cnt         ; Put the number of bytes in CX
          int  21h             ; Call DOS
          ret
ReadFile  ENDP
END
```

Among the information that MS-DOS keeps on all open files is a file pointer location within the file. The file pointer identifies the point at which the next read or write will start. Each read or write moves the file pointer to the end of the data read or written. This works fine for files, such as text files that are read or written sequentially from beginning to end; but other files, such as databases, are often read in a more random order. You can use the MS-DOS move file pointer function (42h) to move the file pointer to any location in the file. The move file pointer function can move the pointer to any specific location in the file or to a location relative to the current location or relative to the end of the file. An assembly language function to move the file pointer might look like this:

```
        .MODEL    SMALL,C
        .CODE
; Move the file pointer of the file whose handle is Hand by Locat
; bytes. subfunc indicates where to begin the move from. See
; Chapter 10 for more information on the ARG directive.
lseek   PROC
ARG     Hand:WORD,Locat:DWORD,subfunc:BYTE
        mov  bx, Hand      ; Put the file handle in BX
        mov  cx, HIGH Locat ; Put the high word in CX
        mov  dx, LOW Locat  ; Put the low word in DX
        mov  al, subfunc   ; 0 - seek absolute location
                           ; 1 - seek relative to current
                           ; 2 - seek relative to end

        mov  ah, 42h
        int  21h
        ret
lseek   ENDP
```

When a program is finished with a file, it must close the file. This makes sure that any information about the file that may have changed gets written to the disk. Another reason for closing file is that MS-DOS only has a limited number of places to keep open file information. Closing the file frees the location to be used by another file. You can close the file by doing a close file function (3Eh) or by exiting the program. One of the steps performed by the exit to DOS function (4Ch) is to close any files that the program opened. You should close each file as soon as you are finished using it, and not rely on DOS to close the file when the program exits. The reason for this is that something may happen, such as the user turning the power off, before the program finishes. This may leave the file in an unusable state. The following function will close a file:

```
        .MODEL    SMALL, C
        .CODE
; Close the file whose handle is at Hand (See Chapter 10 for
; more information on the ARG directive).
Close   PROC
ARG     Hand:WORD
        mov  bx, Hand
```

```
            mov   ah, 3Eh          ; File close function
            int   21h
            ret
Close       ENDP
END
```

Serial and Parallel I/O Ports

MS-DOS includes built-in device drivers to handle the serial and parallel ports. For serial ports, the device names are COM1: and COM2:. The parallel port is called LPT1:. You can open these devices as if they were files. To send or receive data through these devices, you can use the read and write file functions. (Note that for most systems, the LPT1: driver is write-only).

There are some functions that you cannot access from DOS. For example, there is no DOS function to change the baud rate on the serial port. To perform these functions, you need to use BIOS functions. The serial port functions can be accessed through software Interrupt 14h, and the parallel port through Interrupt 17h.

The following program transfers data among the console, the serial port, and the parallel port. You can use this program to work with a modem or even to connect directly to another computer. This program requires a cable that is wired as shown in Figure 13-9. The BIOS routines may not be fast enough to keep up with serial data on your system. If this is the case, you will need to use the routines in Chapter 14 that work directly with the serial port chip.

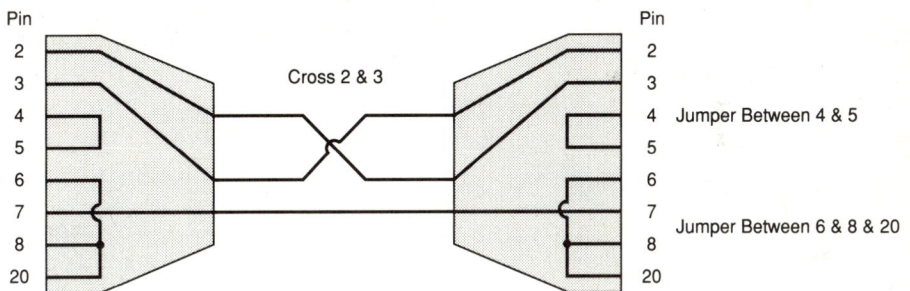

Figure 13-9. *PC to PC cable.*

```
; Copy data between the serial port, the console and the printer
; port
            .MODEL    SMALL
            .DATA
Prnname     DB    "LPT1:",0
```

```
Prnhand    DW    ?
Serdata    DB    ?
           .CODE
Start      PROC
           mov   ax, SEG DGROUP
           mov   ds, ax

; Initialize the serial port

           mov   ah, 0
           mov   al, 01000011b         ; Set 300 baud, no parity, 1
                                       ; stop bit and 8 data bits
           mov   dx, 0
           int   14h                   ; Call BIOS serial functions

; Initialize the printer port

           mov   ah, 3Dh               ; DOS open function
           mov   al, 1                 ; Open for writing only
           mov   dx, OFFSET Prnname
           int   21h
           mov   Prnhand, ax           ; Save the handle

; The main loop

mloop:

; Check for a key at the keyboard

           mov   ah, 1                 ; BIOS check for a key
           int   16h                   ; function
           jnz   NoKey
           mov   ah, 0                 ; Read the key
           int   16h

; Send the key character to the serial port

           mov   ah, 1                 ; BIOS send char to the serial
           mov   dx, 0                 ; port. Send the character in
           int   14h                   ; AL to the port in DX.
NoKey:

; Check for a character at the serial port

           mov   ah, 3                 ; BIOS get serial status
           mov   dx, 0
           int   14h
           test  al, 1                 ; Check data ready signal
           jz    NoSerial
           mov   ah, 2                 ; BIOS read serial port
```

```
            mov   dx, 0
            int   14h
            mov   Serdata, al        ; Save the character

; Print the character on the screen

            mov   dl, al             ; Put it in dl
            mov   ah, 2              ; DOS print char function
            int   21h

; Send the character to the printer

            mov   ah, 40h            ; DOS write function
            mov   dx, OFFSET Serdata ; The location of the data
            mov   cx, 1             ; Write 1 character
            int   21h
NoSerial:
            jmp   mloop
Start       ENDP
            .STACK    512
END   Start
```

The first part of this program initializes the serial and parallel ports. Then the loop, beginning at mloop, checks for data at the serial port or the keyboard. If there is data from the keyboard, it is sent out the serial port. If there is data from the serial port, it is sent to the screen and to the printer. This loop could continue forever.

Mouse

More and more systems are being equipped with mice. When used with properly designed software, the mouse makes using software easier. In MS-DOS computers, programs can get information from the mouse by sending commands to the mouse device driver. The mouse device driver is a program provided by the mouse manufacturer that keeps track of what the mouse is doing, and handles software interrupts from programs that use the mouse.

Different manufacturers have different ways to install the mouse driver, but once installed all mouse drivers provide the same software interface. To communicate with the mouse driver, the program loads commands into registers and executes software Interrupt 33h. This is similar to the way a program works with MS-DOS or BIOS. One difference is that while MS-DOS and BIOS are always available, the mouse driver may not be. Therefore, the first step in using the mouse driver is to see if it has been installed.

Checking to see if the mouse driver is installed is a simple process. All you need to do is to see if Interrupt 33h has been taken over. The address that an interrupt 33h jumps to is 0000:00CC (33h * 4). If the far pointer at this address is zero or if it points to an IRET instruction, the mouse driver is not loaded. Once you have verified that the driver is loaded, you can use the mouse.

The following program begins by checking to see if there is a mouse driver loaded. If it is, it will initialize the mouse and display a mouse cursor. Then it will process mouse events. If the user presses the left mouse button, the program will print an asterisk (*) at the mouse location. If the user presses the right button, the program will print a circumflex (^). As the user moves the mouse, the program will print the co-ordinates of the mouse cursor in the upper left-hand corner of the screen.

```
          .MODEL    SMALL
          .DATA
BStatus   DW    ?                      ; The button status
BXpos     DW    ?                      ; The mouse cursor column
BYpos     DW    ?                      ; The mouse cursor row

          .CODE
Mouse     PROC
          mov   ax, SEG DGROUP         ; Get the data segment
          mov   ds, ax

; Check to see if the mouse driver is loaded
          sub   ax, ax                 ; Set ax to 0
          mov   es, ax
          mov   bx, 0CCh               ; The location of int 33h
          mov   ax, WORD PTR es:[bx]
          or    ax, WORD PTR es:[bx+2]
          jz    Exit                   ; Vector is 0 then exit
          les   bx, DWORD PTR [bx]
          cmp   BYTE PTR es:[bx], 0CFh
          jnz   MouseOK                ; If not an iret then the
                                       ; Driver is installed
Exit:
          mov   ah, 4Ch                ; MS-DOS exit command
          int   21h
MouseOK:

; Initialize the mouse

          mov   ax, 0                  ; Mouse reset command
          int   33h                    ; Call mouse driver returns ah
                                       ; = 0FFh if the mouse is not
                                       ; installed
          inc   ah                     ; Check if mouse installed
          jz    Exit
          mov   ax, 10                 ; Mouse set text cursor
                                       ; command
          mov   bx, 0                  ; Use software cursor
          mov   cx, 0f000h             ; Set the mask
```

```
              mov   dx, 0704h            ; The cursor character
              int   33h

; Clear the screen

              mov   ah, 6               ; BIOS scroll command
              mov   al, 25              ; Line count
              mov   bh, 7               ; Use normal attribute
              mov   cx, 0               ; Upper left corner
              mov   dx, 184Ah           ; Lower right corner
              int   10h
MainLP:
              mov   ah, 1               ; BIOS test for a key
              int   16h
              jnz   NoKey
              mov   ah, 0               ; BIOS read key function
              int   16h                 ; Read the key
              mov   dh, 4Ch             ; and exit
              int   21h
NoKey:

; Get the mouse position and button status

              mov   ax, 3
              int   33h
              mov   BStatus, bx         ; Save the button status
              mov   BXpos, cx           ; Save the column
              mov   BYpos, dx           ; Save the row

; Check the left mouse button

              cmp   BStatus, 1
              jne   NotLeft
              mov   ah, 2               ; BIOS set cursor position
              sub   bh, bh              ; Video page 0
              mov   dh, dl              ; Put the row into DH
              mov   dl, cl              ; Put column in DL
              int   10h
              mov   ax, 2               ; Hide mouse cursor. This must
              int   33h                 ; be done whenever the screen
                                        ; is changed so that the mouse
                                        ; cursor does not get over
                                        ; written.
              mov   ah, 2               ; MS-DOS write a character
                                        ; function
              mov   dh, '*'
              int   21h
```

```
                mov   ax, 1               ; Turn mouse cursor back on
                int   33h

; Now check the right button

NotLeft:
                cmp   BStatus, 2
                jne   NotRight
                mov   ah, 2               ; BIOS set cursor position
                sub   bh, bh              ; Video page 0
                mov   dh, dl              ; Put the row into DH
                mov   dl, cl              ; Put column in DL
                int   10h
                mov   ax, 2               ; Hide mouse cursor. This must
                int   33h                 ; be done whenever the screen
                                          ; is changed so that the mouse
                                          ; cursor does not get over
                                          ; written.
                mov   ah, 2               ; MS-DOS write a character
                                          ; function
                mov   dh, '^'
                int   21h
                mov   ax, 1               ; Turn mouse cursor back on
                int   33h

; Print the location of the mouse cursor in the upper left corner

NotRight:
                mov   ah, 2               ; Position cursor
                sub   bh, bh
                sub   dx, dx
                int   10h
                mov   ax, BXpos           ; Get the column
                aam                       ; Convert to unpacked BCD
                push  ax                  ; Save the result
                mov   dh, ah              ; Get the high digit in DH
                add   dh, '0'             ; Convert it to ASCII
                mov   ah, 2               ; MS-DOS write a character
                                          ; function
                int   21h
                pop   ax                  ; Get back the number
                mov   dh, al              ; Put the low digit in DH
                add   dh, '0'             ; Convert to ASCII
                mov   ah, 2
                int   21h
                mov   ah, 2
```

```
            mov   dh, ','                ; Print a comma
            int   21h
            mov   ax, BYpos              ; Get the row
            aam                          ; Convert to unpacked BCD
            push  ax                     ; Save the result
            mov   dh, ah                 ; Get the high digit in DH
            add   dh, '0'                ; Convert it to ASCII
            mov   ah, 2                  ; MS-DOS write a character
                                         ; function
            int   21h
            pop   ax                     ; Get back the number
            mov   dh, al                 ; Put the low digit in dh
            add   dh, '0'                ; Convert to ASCII
            mov   ah, 2
            int   21h
            mov   ah, 2
            jmp   MainLP                 ; Do it all again
Mouse       ENDP
            .STACK    1024
END Mouse
```

The first part of this function verifies that the mouse device driver is installed and the mouse is connected. If the mouse is ready to go, it clears the screen and enters the loop beginning at MainLP. First, this loop checks for a keypress. If no key is pressed, it checks the mouse buttons and current mouse location. If a mouse button is pressed then the routine prints a "*" for the left button (just before NotLeft) or a "^" for the right button (just before NotRight). The code following NotRight prints the current mouse position and jumps back to MainLP.

Summary

There are many resources available to programs running on IBM PCs and compatibles. The first step to using these resources is to determine what resources are available. This can be done in several ways. The easiest is to ask BIOS. There are BIOS functions and memory locations that tell what devices BIOS knows about. Another thing to check is the setup information at port 60h or in the real-time clock registers. The last way to find out if a resource is available is to write a program that can detect the presence of the resource.

Once you know that the resource is available, you must know how to use it. DOS provides functions for most of the basic resources, like memory, the console, and disk drives. Other resources, like graphics screens and serial ports, can be accessed via BIOS functions. Some resources can be accessed via special programs provided by the manufacturer of the device. When these programs are loaded, you can access the resource in much the same way that you access DOS resources. Expanded memory and the mouse are examples of this kind of resource.

Chapter *14* *Accessing and Controlling the Hardware*

One reason for choosing assembly language is the fact that it can work directly with your hardware. There are two benefits of this: You can use features that you otherwise could not use, and you may often find that working with hardware directly is much faster than going through DOS or BIOS.

For one thing, most systems have video modes that cannot be used without special software. Yet in most cases where you need these features, you can assemble programs to use them. Also, changing the priorities of interrupts and reading key combinations (like ALT-SHIFT) are not generally possible with high level languages. This is because in order to control these things, you must be able to issue IN and OUT commands and turn the interrupts-enabled flag on and off. Most high level languages do not give you direct access to these instructions.

The first two sections of this chapter show you how to access directly the hardware that controls interrupts and the keyboard. You will see how to use unused key combinations to "pop up" a terminate-and-stay-resident (TSR) program.

Serial port drivers in BIOS were written to handle serial printers. When you use them to transfer large amounts of data at speeds above 2,400 baud, you often lose some of the data. This chapter also shows you how to write a different serial driver that can transfer data at speeds up to 115,200 baud. This driver also eliminates the need for the special cable described in Chapter 13.

The last section of this chapter shows you how to put everything together to make a TSR file transfer program. This program not only shows you how to access the hardware, but also how to avoid some of the pitfalls of writing pop-up programs.

Controlling Hardware Interrupts

Most of the time, the 80x86 processor goes from one instruction to the next in memory. Instructions such as JMP and CALL can change this to execute instructions from another area in memory. All of this is very orderly and predictable. If you know the state of the flags and the instruction being executed, you can predict what the next instruction will be.

Hardware interrupts add a little uncertainty to the order in which instructions are executed. Any time that the interrupts-enabled flag is set, an interrupt can come along and send the processor off executing some other piece of code. This code, called an Interrupt Service Routine (ISR), must respond to the event that caused the interrupt and return to the program that was interrupted with all of the flags and registers restored to the state they were in prior to the interrupt.

Interrupts originate in the various hardware devices that are on the motherboard or connected to the bus. Each of these devices attempts to get the attention of the processor by using interrupts. IBM PCs and compatibles use the 8259 interrupt controller chip to handle hardware interrupts. The job of the 8259 is to make sure that a low priority interrupt does not interrupt a higher priority interrupt, and that simultaneous interrupts do not cause one or the other interrupt to be ignored. It contains a table of hardware interrupts arranged by priority.

When an interrupt occurs, the 8259 blocks all lower priority interrupts until the interrupt routine sends a signal indicating that it is done. Table 14-1 shows the interrupts that the 8259 handles. When an interrupt occurs, the 8259 checks to see if there are any higher priority interrupts being serviced. If not, it passes the interrupt on to the CPU along with a number that identifies the interrupt, called the *interrupt number*. If the interrupts-enabled flag is set, the CPU finishes the current instruction and then calls the ISR for the interrupt. The address for the ISR comes from the Interrupt Vector Table (IVT) at memory address 0000:0000. The IVT has an entry for each of the 256 possible interrupt numbers. Each entry is the offset and segment of the ISR.

The 8259 needs to know when the ISR is finished so that it can pass on the next interrupt. It is the responsibilty of the ISR to send an End Of Interrupt (EOI) command to the 8259 at I/O port 20h (primary 8259) or 0A0h (secondary 8259). You do not need to wait until the actual end of the ISR to issue the EOI command. It can be sent any time the ISR is ready to allow more interrupts. The code to send an EOI looks like this:

```
mov  al, 20h      ; Put the EOI command in AL
out  20h, al      ; Send it to the primary 8259
```

Table 14-1.   *Interrupt Channels*

Channel	Description	Interrupt number
IRQ0	Timer	08h
IRQ1	Keyboard	09h
IRQ2	Cascade from second 8259 (AT only)	0Ah
IRQ8	Real time clock	70h
IRQ9	Redirect cascade	71h
IRQ10	Reserved	72h
IRQ11	Reserved	73h
IRQ12	Mouse	74h
IRQ13	Coprocessor exception	75h
IRQ14	Fixed disk	76h
IRQ15	Reserved	77h
IRQ3	Serial port 2	0Bh
IRQ4	Serial port 1	0Ch
IRQ5	Fixed disk	0Dh
IRQ6	Diskette	0Eh
IRQ7	Parallel port	0Fh

The 8259 keeps track of more than just the priorities and interrupt numbers of the interrupts that it handles. It also has a flag bit for each interrupt, called the *interrupt mask*, which can be set to indicate that the 8259 should ignore that interrupt. Part of the setup required for installing an ISR is to make sure that the mask bit is cleared so that the interrupt requests can get through. Figure 14-1 shows the bits in the interrupt mask.

Routines that need as much of the CPU's attention as possible can use these bits to allow only certain interrupts (for example, when the serial port is receiving data at 115,200 baud). Between the serial interrupts, clock interrupts, and disk interrupts, there may not be enough time to do it all. The code that follows prevents all interrupts except for the serial port. For most PCs this will leave enough time to handle the transfer.

```
mov  al, 11101111b      ; The 0 enables IRQ4 (COM1)
out  21, al             ; Send the mask to the 8259
```

Leaving your computer in this state is not recommended. With all other interrupts off, the keyboard, hard disk, system clock, and other devices will not work. Therefore, you should use this trick only for as short a period of time as possible. You can read port 21h, before modifying it, to get the value for restoring it when the time-critical routine is done:

```
          .DATA
OldMask   DB  ?                       ; A place to keep the mask
          .CODE
          in   al, 21h                ; Get the current interrupt mask
          mov  OldMask, al            ; Save it
          mov  al, 11101111b          ; Change the mask
          .                           ; Do time-critical stuff

          .

          .
          mov  al, OldMask            ; Get the old mask
          out  21h, al                ; Send it to the 8259
```

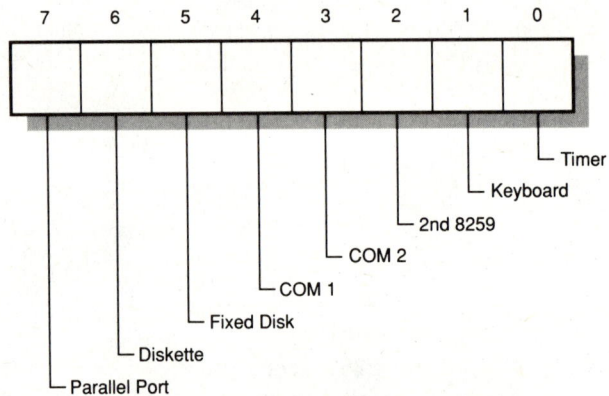

Figure 14-1.   *8259 interrupt mask bits.*

Accessing the Keyboard Controller

Whenever you press or release a key, the keyboard sends data to the chip in the computer called the *keyboard controller*. The keyboard controller generates interrupt number 09h to tell the CPU that there is keyboard data available. Normally, the entry in the Interrupt Vector Table points to an ISR in the BIOS ROM. This ISR reads the keyboard data from I/O port 60h. The lower seven bits of this number are the scan code for the key that was pressed or released. Figure 14-2 shows the scan codes for a typical keyboard. The BIOS keyboard ISR converts the keyboard activity into the shift status and regular key-presses. It puts any keys that it recognizes into the keyboard buffer in the BIOS data area. Other programs can get these keys by calling the BIOS software interrupt 16h functions.

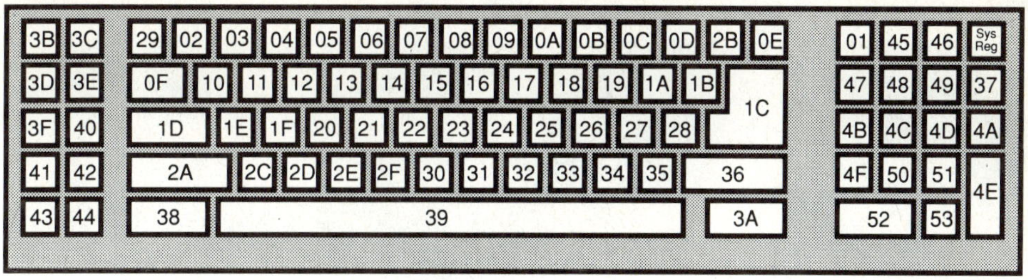

Figure 14-2. *Keyboard scan codes.*

You can take over the keyboard interrupt to allow your program to react to special key combinations. For example, to add a pop-up help system to your program, you can use a keyboard Interrupt Service Routine to pop-up a help screen whenever a certain key is pressed. The ISR for this appears as follows:

```
; File POPUP.ASM
            IDEAL                          ; Use IDEAL mode syntax
            MODEL    SMALL                 ; Any model will work (must
                                           ; match other modules)
            PUBLIC   OldKSR                ; Make these values available
            PUBLIC   KeyBrdISR             ; to other modules
            EXTRN    HelpStuff:PROC        ; The help routine to call

            DATASEG
KeyDown     EQU  03Bh                      ; Code for F1 key pressed

OldKSR           DD    ?                   ; Address of the replaced
                                           ; keyboard ISR

KeyFlag     DB   0                         ; Set to true when already in
                                           ; help


            CODESEG
PROC        KeyBrdISR FAR                  ; All ISRs are FAR
            push ax                        ; Save the AX register
            push ds                        ; Save the DS register
            mov   ax, DGROUP               ; and set it to the local data
            mov   ds, ax                   ; area
            in    al, 60h                  ; Read the keyboard data port
            cmp   al, KeyDown              ; Check for pop-up key pressed
            je    PopUp                    ; If it matches pop-up
DoDeflt:
            pushf                          ; Simulate an interrupt
            call [OldKSR]                  ; Go to the old keyboard ISR
            pop   ds                       ; Restore DS
            pop   ax                       ; Restore AX
```

```
                iret                      ; Return from this ISR
        PopUp:
                cmp   [KeyFlag], 1        ; See if help is already
                                          ; running
                je    DoDeflt             ; If so do the old ISR
                mov   [KeyFlag], 1        ; Say we are in
                sti                       ; Allow interrupts
                mov   al, 20h             ; Put EOI command in AL
                out   20h, al             ; Send it to the 8259
                call  HelpStuff           ; Do the pop-up routine
                mov   [KeyFlag], 0        ; Clear the flag so help can
                                          ; pop-up again
                pop   ds                  ; Restore the DX register
                pop   ax                  ; Restore the AX register
                iret
        ENDP  KeyBrdISR
        END
```

To use this routine, you need to assemble it and link it with a module that replaces the interrupt 09h vector with the address of this routine. It should also contain a routine named HelpStuff that brings up the help screen. Remember that the HelpStuff routine is part of the ISR. It needs to return all the registers that it uses to the values they had before the interrupt occurred. The following example shows how to set up the ISR and a simple HelpStuff routine.

```
; File LOADPOP.ASM
                IDEAL
                MODEL    SMALL                  ; Must match the other
                                                ; modules
                EXTRN    OldKSR:DWORD           ; The location of the old
                                                ; ISR
                EXTRN    KeyBrdISR:FAR          ; The ISR function
                PUBLIC   HelpStuff              ; Make this visible to
                                                ; other modules
                DATASEG
ScrSeg    DW    0B800h                          ; Segment of screen
                                                ; memory
HlpLine1  DB    "+==========================+", 0
HlpLine2  DB    "¦ This is the help screen ¦", 0
HlpLine3  DB    "+==========================+", 0
MainMsg   DB    "This is a message", 0Dh, 0AH, '$'

                CODESEG

; Set up the keyboard ISR and print a message
```

```
PROC      Start
          mov  ax, DGROUP                    ; Get the data segment
          mov  ds, ax                        ; Put it in DS
          mov  ax, 3509h                     ; Get the interrupt 9
                                             ; vector
          int  21h                           ; Call MS-DOS
          mov  [WORD PTR OldKSR], bx         ; Save the offset
          mov  [WORD PTR OldKSR+2], es       ; Save the segment
          push ds                            ; Save the data segment
          mov  ax, SEG KeyBrdISR
          mov  ds, ax                        ; Put the segment of the
                                             ; ISR
                                             ; in DS
          mov  dx, OFFSET KeyBrdISR
          mov  ax, 2509h                     ; Set interrupt 9
          int  21h                           ; Set the new vector
          pop  ds                            ; Restore the data segment
PrnLoop:
          mov  ah, 1                         ; BIOS test key function
          int  16h                           ; Call BIOS
          jnz  ExtLp                         ; If key pressed then
                                             ; exit
          mov  ah, 9                         ; MS-DOS print routine
          mov  dx, OFFSET MainMsg
          int  21h                           ; Call MS-DOS
          jmp  SHORT PrnLoop
ExtLp:
          mov  ah, 0                         ; BIOS Read key function
          int  16h                           ; Call BIOS
          mov  ax, 2509h                     ; Set interrupt 9
          lds  dx, [OldKSR]                  ; Get the old ISR address
          int  21h                           ; Call MS-DOS
          mov  ah, 4Ch                       ; MS-DOS exit function
          int  21h                           ; Call MS-DOS
ENDP      Start

; Do the help screen
PROC      HelpStuff
          push bx                            ; Save the registers
          push cx
          push dx
          push si
          push di
          push bp
          push es
```

```
                mov   es, [ScrSeg]              ; Get the screen memory
                                               ; segment
                cld
                mov   si, OFFSET HlpLine1       ; The line to print
                sub   di, di                   ; The location to print at
                call  PrnStr
                mov   dx, OFFSET HlpLine2
                mov   di, 160                  ; Line 2 column 1
                call  PrnStr
                mov   dx, OFFSET HlpLine3
                mov   di, 320                  ; Line 3 column 1
                call  PrnStr
                mov   ah, 0                    ; BIOS wait for a key
                                               ; function

                int   16h
                pop   es
                pop   bp                       ; Restore the registers
                pop   di
                pop   si
                pop   dx
                pop   cx
                pop   bx
                ret
        ENDP    HelpStuff

; Print a string without using MS-DOS
; SI = address of the string to print
; DI = Offset into screen memory for the string
; ES = Segment of screen memory

        PROC    PrnStr
PrLoop:
                lodsb                          ; Get a byte from the string
                or    al, al
                jz    Done
                stosb
                inc   di
                jmp   SHORT PrLoop
Done:
                ret

        ENDP    PrnStr

                STACK    1024
        END     Start
```

To assemble and link these modules into a program called LOADPOP, use the following commands:

```
tasm popup
tasm loadpop
tlink loadpop popup
```

Note the unusual way that the strings are printed in the function PrnStr. Instead of calling MS-DOS to print the strings, it writes them directly to screen memory. (See Chapter 15 for more information on this technique.) This must be done because of the problem associated with calling MS-DOS from an ISR. The problem is that the first thing MS-DOS does, when it is called, is switch to its own stack. If the keyboard interrupt occurs while MS-DOS has control, any call that it makes to MS-DOS will reset the stack that MS-DOS is using. When the keyboard ISR is finished, it returns control to the interrupted program (MS-DOS), but the damage has been done. The MS-DOS stack no longer contains the information required for MS-DOS to return. This is known as the *MS-DOS re-entrancy problem*, and it is one of the things that makes writing TSR programs so difficult.

The Serial Port

The serial port is one of the most versatile interfaces in the PC. It can be connected to terminals, printers, plotters, mice, modems, other computers, and even certain disk drives. In most IBM PC compatibles, the serial interface is controlled by an 8250 or equivalent chip. The CPU communicates with this chip via eight I/O ports. Figure 14-3 shows these ports.

BIOS software interrupt 14h provides routines that control the serial port. MS-DOS uses these routines to implement the COM1 and COM2 devices. These routines check the line status register to see if a character has been received, or if it is OK to send a character. This works fine at low speeds required by printers, but for high speed data communications it often loses data.

You can use interrupts to make sure that you do not lose any data. The first step is to set up the serial port to generate an interrupt when it receives a character. The Interrupt Service Routine needs to read the character from the serial port and save it in a buffer. This means that the main routine does not need to spend time checking for data at the serial port. It can do whatever processing is required, and get data from the buffer whenever it is ready.

Receiver Buffer Register (DLAB=0)
Transmitter Holding Register (DLAB=0)
Divisor Low Byte (DLAB=1)

7		0	COM1	COM2
	Data		3F8h	2F8h

Interrupt Enable Register (DLAB=0)
Divisor High Byte (DLAB=1)

7	4	3	2	1	0	COM1	COM2
Reserved		Modem Status	Receiving Data	Transmit Ready	Data Available	3F9h	2F9h

Interrupt Types

Interrupt ID Register

7	3	2	1	0	COM1	COM2
Reserved		Interrupt Type		No Interrupt	3FAh	2FAh

11b = Receiving Data
10b = Data Available
01b = Transmit Ready
00b = Modem Status

Line Control Register

7	6	5	4	3	2	1	0	COM1	COM2
DLAB	Send Break	Stick Parity	Even Parity	Parity Enable	Stop Bits	Character Size		3FBh	2FBh

00 = 5 bits

Modem Control Register

7	5	4	3	2	1	0	COM1	COM2
Reserved		Loop Back	OUT2	OUT1	RTS	DTR	3FCh	2FCh

Line Status Register

7	6	5	4	3	2	1	0	COM1	COM2
Reserved	Char. Sent	Trans-mitter	Break Detect	Framing Error	Parity Error	Overrun Error	Data Ready	3FDh	2FDh

Modem Status Register

7	6	5	4	3	2	1	0	COM1	COM2
Carrier Detect	Ring Indicator	Data Set Ready	Clr to Send	Delta CD	Ring Indicator	Delta DSR	Delta CTS	3FEh	2FEh

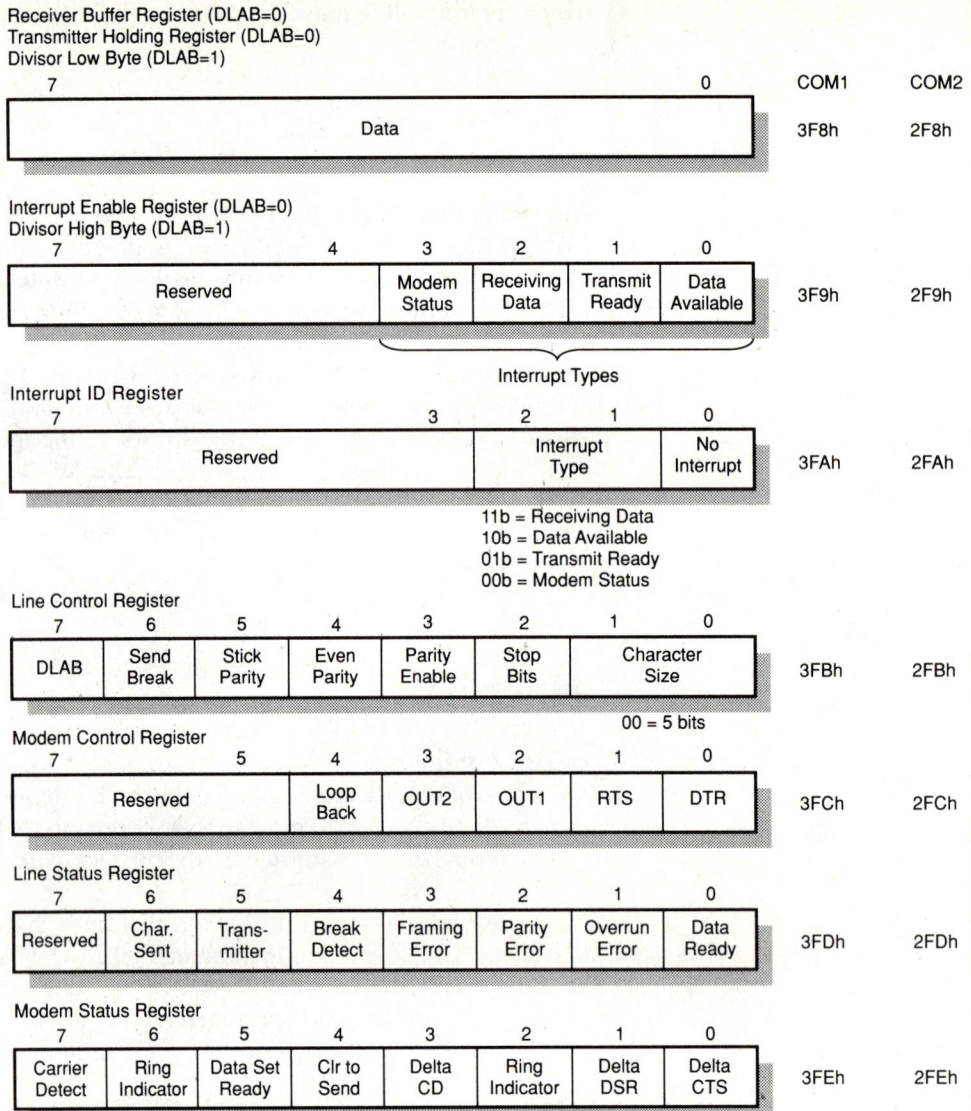

Figure 14-3. *The 8250 I/O ports.*

Initializing the Serial Port

There are two steps to initializing the serial port for data communications with interrupts. First, you must tell the 8250 about the kind of data that it should use, and then set up the Interrupt Service Routine. The following example is a routine that initializes the serial port:

```
; Initialize a serial port
; File SERINIT.ASM
            IDEAL                   ; Use IDEAL mode syntax
            MODEL SMALL             ; Must match other modules
            PUBLIC InitPort         ; Make this routine visible to
                                    ; other modules

            EXTRN SerISR:FAR        ; The address of the ISR

            DATASEG
; Baud rates    110    150    300    600    1200    2400    4800
Divisor    DW   0417h, 0300h, 0180h, 00C0h, 0060h, 0030h, 0018h
;               9600   19200  38400  115200
           DW   000Ch, 0006h, 0003h, 0001h
OldInt     DD   ?

            CODESEG
; Initialize COM1
; AX = line control parameters
; BX = Baud rate index (1=110, 2=150, 3=300...)
PROC        InitPort
            push ax                 ; Save the parameters
            mov  dx, 3FBh           ; Line control register
            in   al, dx             ; Get the current state
            or   al, 80h            ; Set up for baud rate
            out  dx, al
            mov  dx, 3F8h           ; Low byte of the divisor
            shl  bx, 1              ; Times two for a table of
                                    ; words
            mov  al, [BYTE PTR bx+Divisor]
            out  dx, al             ; Send the low byte
            inc  dx                 ; High byte of the divisor
            inc  bx
            mov  al, [BYTE PTR bx+Divisor]
            out  dx, al             ; Send the high byte
            pop  ax                 ; Get the parameters
            mov  dx, 3FBh           ; Line control register
            out  dx, al
            mov  dx, 3F8h           ; Read any pending character
; Set up for interrupts
            mov  ax, 350Bh          ; Get old interrupt vector
            int  21h
            mov  [WORD PTR OldInt], bx
            mov  [WORD PTR OldInt+2], es
            mov  dx, OFFSET SerISR  ; Get the offset of the ISR
```

```
            mov   ax, SEG SerISR      ; Get the segment of the ISR
            push  ds
            mov   ds, ax
            mov   ax, 250Bh           ; Set interrupt 0Bh
            int   21h
            pop   ds
            cli                       ; Don't allow interrupts yet
            mov   dx, 3FCh            ; Modem control register
            mov   al, 0Fh            ; Enable OUT2 interrupt
            out   dx, al
            sub   dx, 3               ; Serial interrupt enable
            mov   al, 1               ; Enable receiver interrupts
            out   dx, al
            in    al, 21h             ; Get the 8259 mask
            and   al, 0EFh            ; Enable COM1
            out   21h, al
            sti
            ret
ENDP        InitPort
END
```

The first part of this routine sets the data parameters. To see how this affects the data, look at Figure 14-4. Setting the divisor rate changes the frequency of the clock signal. The clock signal marks the beginning and the end of each bit. The number of times the clock goes up or down in a second is the baud rate. The baud rate of the serial port must match the baud rate of the data it receives from the CPU.

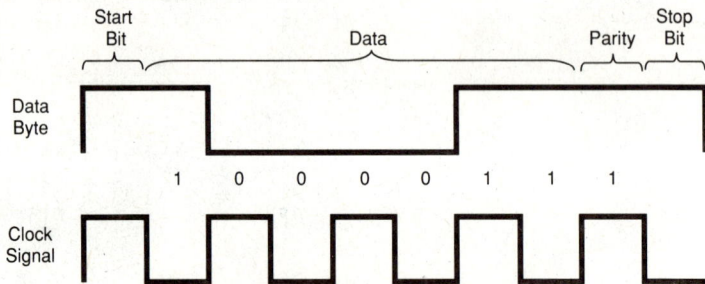

Figure 14-4.   *Serial data.*

The line control register in the 8250 describes the data that will be sent or received. Each part of the data signal is controlled by the line control register. (See Figures 14-3 and 14-4.) The data portion can be from five to eight bits long. Most data transfer programs use eight bits because this matches the size of a byte. Some text-only devices, like printers, use seven bits to match the size of an ASCII character.

After the data portion there may be a *parity bit*. The parity bit can be used to tell if the data portion is correct. Different devices use the parity bit in different ways. Some devices do not use it at all (no parity), others always set the parity bit (mark parity), and still others always clear the parity bit (space parity). If the number of one-bits in the data (including the parity bit) is even, then the data has even parity. If the number is odd, then the data has odd parity. When the parity that the receiver (any device with a serial interface) expects is different from the data received, then the receiver knows that the data is bad and should not be used.

The last part of a serial data byte is one or more stop bits. Most serial devices use a single *stop bit* to mark the end of the data. Some older devices may use two stop bits or 1.5 stop bits. After the stop bit, the signal drops to the low voltage and stays there until the next data byte is sent.

The second half of the initialization process is to set up the ISR and turn on serial interrupts. The first step is to make the entry for the serial port in the interrupt vector table point to the ISR. This must be done before any serial interrupts are possible, so that the processor will have some place to go when the interrupt occurs.

Next, you must tell the serial port to generate an interrupt when it receives data. To do this you must set the modem control register (see Figure 14-3) to enable the interrupt signal (OUT2). Then tell the interrupt-enable register what situations should generate an interrupt. In this case the 8250 will generate an interrupt when it has received a byte. The other three conditions are: ready to send a byte, data error detected, and modem status lines changed.

Finally, the 8259 must be told to allow interrupts from the serial port by clearing the bit for the serial interrupt in the interrupt mask register. Now the interrupts are all set up so you can set the interrupts-enabled bit with an STI instruction. Every time the serial port receives a character, it will call the ISR.

An Interrupt Service Routine for Serial Data

The following routine is an example of an ISR for serial data. It reads the serial port and puts the data into a buffer.

```
; File SERISR.ASM
        IDEAL                           ; Use ideal mode syntax
        MODEL    SMALL                  ; Must match the models used
                                        ; in other modules
        PUBLIC   Head, Tail, Buffer, SerISR

        DATASEG
Head    DW    0                         ; The next location to put
                                        ; data in the buffer
Tail    DW    0                         ; The next location to get
                                        ; data from the buffer
```

```
Buffer      DB   1024 DUP(0)
            CODESEG
PROC        SerISR    FAR              ; All ISRs are FAR
            push ax                    ; Save registers
            push dx
            push bx
            push ds
            mov  ax, DGROUP            ; Get the data segment
            mov  ds, ax                ; Put it in DS
            mov  dx, 3F8h              ; 8250 Data register port
            in   al, dx                ; Get the data
            mov  bx, [Head]            ; Get the place to put it
            mov  [Buffer+bx], al       ; Save the data
            inc  bx                    ; Go to the next location
            and  bx, 03FFh             ; Wrap at the end of the
                                       ; buffer
            mov  [Head], bx            ; Save the new location
            pop  ds                    ; Restore registers
            pop  bx
            pop  dx
            mov  al, 20h               ; Send EOI to 8259
            out  20h, al
            iret
ENDP        SerISR
END
```

The buffer used in this routine is called a *ring buffer* (also known as a *circular buffer*). The ring buffer allows new data to be added at one point and read at another point without moving the data in between. Figure 14-5 shows how this works.

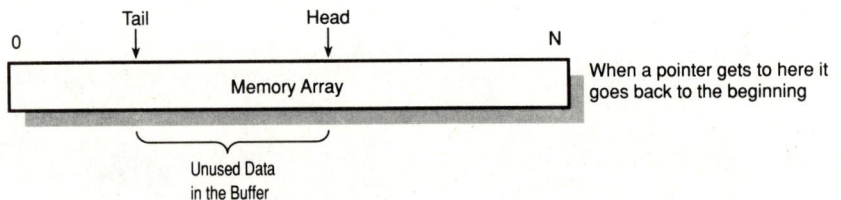

Figure 14-5. *A ring buffer.*

The word at Head is the offset into the buffer for the next character received. After storing the character, the ISR increments Head. If Head is larger than the size of the buffer, the ISR resets it to the beginning of the buffer. This makes the buffer into a ring.

Another routine (as follows) uses `Tail` to get data out of the buffer. When there is no data in the buffer, `Head` is equal to `Tail`. The `GetByte` function waits for the ISR to move `Head`. When `Head` moves, `GetByte` reads the data at `Tail` and moves `Tail` the same way that the ISR moves `Head`. Eventually `Tail` will catch up with `Head`, indicating that there is no data left:

```
                IDEAL                           ; Use IDEAL mode syntax
                MODEL      SMALL
EXTRN           Head:WORD, Tail:WORD, Buffer:BYTE
PUBLIC          TimeOut

                DATASEG
TimeOut         DW    5641                      ; Set timeout to 5 minutes

                CODESEG
; Get a byte from the serial port and return it in AL
; Set the carry if no data in 5 minutes
PROC            GetByte
                push es                         ; Save registers
                push cx
                push si
                mov   si, [Tail]                ; Get the end of the ring
                                                ; buffer
                mov   ax, 40h                   ; Set ES to the BIOS data
                                                ; area
                mov   es, ax
                mov   ax, [WORD PTR es:6Ch]     ; Get the time
                mov   cx, [WORD PTR es:6Eh]
                add   ax, [TimeOut]             ; Add in the time out
                                                ; interval
                adc   cx, 0
GBloop:
                cmp   si, [Head]                ; See if any characters in
                                                ; the buffer
                jne   GotOne                    ; Jump if there is a
                                                ; character
                cmp   cx, [WORD PTR es:6Eh]
                ja    GBloop                    ; If time left try again
                cmp   ax, [WORD PTR es:6Ch]
                ja    GBloop
                stc                             ; Indicate time out
                jmp   SHORT GBDone
GotOne:
                mov   al, [Buffer + si]         ; Get the character
                inc   si                        ; Increment tail
```

```
                   and   si, 3FFh              ; Tail Modulo 1024
                   mov   [Tail], si            ; Save the new pointer
                   clc                          ; Indicate good character
        GBDone:
                   pop   si                     ; Restore registers
                   pop   cx
                   pop   es
                   ret
        ENDP       GetByte
        END
```

Notice that the Tail behaves the same way as the Head does. This ensures that the data comes out of the buffer in the same order as it went in. When the tail catches up to the head, it means there is no more data available. Any routine that must wait for an external event, such as serial data arriving, must either be prepared to wait a long time or have some way of exiting after a given time interval. In this case the routine will exit if five minutes go by without any data. To indicate that the routine has timed out, it sets the carry flag.

Sending Serial Data

To send data out from the serial port, all you need to do is wait for the transmitter register in the 8250 to be empty, and then send the data. You can set the serial port to generate an interrupt when it is ready to send a character, or you can just look at the line status register to see if the transmitter-empty bit is cleared. If you use the interrupt and you also use the received data interrupt, you will need to modify your interrupt routine to check the 8250's interrupt ID register in order to see what kind of interrupt occurred.

Checking the line status register is the easiest way to send data. The following routine demonstrates this technique:

```
; Send the byte in AL to the serial port
SendByte   PROC
                   push ax                      ; Save the byte to send
                   mov   dx, 3FDh               ; The line status register
SBLoop:
                   in    al, dx
                   test al, 20h                 ; Check the transmitter
                                                ; holding register
                   jz    SBLoop                 ; If not ready, loop
                   pop   ax                     ; Get the byte to send
                   mov   dx, 3F8h               ; The data port
                   out   dx, al                 ; Send the byte
                   ret
          SendByte ENDP
```

At first, it might appear that SBLoop may wait a long time. This is not the case here, however, because the 8250 will always send the byte in the transmitter-holding register and clear this bit.

Receiving Files

One use for the serial routines presented in this chapter is to move files from one computer to another. You can do this by reading the file and using the SendByte procedure, previously shown, to send each byte. At the other end, use the ISR and the GetByte routine to receive the bytes, and then write them to a file. This would work except that serial data transfer is notoriously unreliable. There is no guarantee that the data at the receiving end is the same as the data that is being sent.

This next routine uses an error-free protocol, called *XMODEM*, to receive a file. This ensures that the file received is the same as the file transmitted:

```
; Program to do xmodem download
            .MODEL SMALL
PUBLIC    DwnLoad
EXTRN     SendByte:PROC
EXTRN     GetByte:PROC
EXTRN     TimeOut:WORD

SOH       EQU   1
STX       EQU   2
EOT       EQU   4
ACK       EQU   6
NAK       EQU   15h
CAN       EQU   18h

          .DATA
State     DB    0               ; State of the download
BlkNumb   DB    1               ; Number of the block being
                                ; received
ErrCnt    DB    0
jtab      DW    InitSt, GetBNmb
          DW    GetBlk, VerifyB
Buffer    DB    128 dup(0)
FHand     DW    ?
LineSt    DB    ?               ; The current line settings
          .CODE
; Call this function with DS:DX pointing to the name of the file
; to download
```

```
DwnLoad    PROC
           mov  ah, 3Ch              ; MS-DOS file create
           sub  cx, cx
           int  21h
           mov  FHand, ax            ; Save the file handle,
           mov  dx, 3FBh             ; Com1 line control port
           in   al, dx               ; Get the current settings
           mov  LineSt, al           ; Save them
           mov  al, 00000011b        ; Set 8N1
           out  dx, al
DLloop1:
           mov  bl, State            ; Use the current state
           sub  bh, bh               ; to decide what function in
           shl  bx, 1                ; jtab to use.
           call [jtab+bx]
           cmp  ErrCnt, 10
           jb   DLloop1              ; Loop if less than 10 errors
           mov  dx, 3FBh             ; Line status register
           mov  al, LineSt           ; Restore previous settings
           out  dx, al
           ret                       ; Return to calling routine
DwnLoad    ENDP

; Initialize the transfer
InitSt     PROC
           mov  al, NAK              ; Send a NAK to tell the
           call SendByte             ; sender that it is ready
           mov  TimeOut, 100         ; Set the time out < 6 secs
           call GetByte              ; Get the sender's response
           cmp  al, SOH              ; Is it an SOH?
           je   NS1                  ; Yes, go to next state
           inc  ErrCnt               ; No, log the error
           ret
NS1:
           inc  State                ; Go to the next state
           mov  ErrCnt, 0            ; Reset the error count
           ret
InitSt     ENDP

; Get the block number
GetBNmb    PROC
           mov  TimeOut, 50          ; Set the time out < 3 secs
           call GetByte              ; Get the block number
           jc   GBNErr               ; If time out, go to GBNErr
           push ax                   ; Save the block number
```

```
                call GetByte                 ; Get the check number
                pop  bx                      ; Recover the block number
                jc   GBNErr                  ; If time out, go to GBNErr
                not  al                      ; Invert check number
                cmp  al, bl                  ; If not the same, it's an
                                             ; error
                jne  GBNErr                  ; If not the same, go to
                                             ; GBNErr
                cmp  bl, BlkNumb             ; Compare to expected block
                                             ; number
                jne  GBNErr                  ; If not the same, go to
                                             ; GBNErr
                inc  State                   ; Otherwise, go to the next
                                             ; state
                ret
GBNErr:
                jmp  ErrFnd
GetBNmb   ENDP

; Get 128 bytes of data
GetBlk    PROC
                mov  TimeOut, 18             ; Set the time out to 1 sec
                mov  cx, 128                 ; The number of bytes to
                                             ; expect
                mov  di, OFFSET Buffer       ; Get the location of the
                                             ; buffer
                push ds                      ; Make ES = DS
                pop  es
                cld
GBLoop:
                call GetByte                 ; Get a byte of data
                jc   GBErr                   ; If time out go to GBErr
                stosb                        ; Save the byte
                loop GBLoop                  ; Get 128 bytes
                inc  State                   ; Go to verify data state
                ret
GBErr:
                jmp  ErrFnd
GetBlk    ENDP

; Verify the checksum
VerifyB   PROC
                mov  TimeOut, 50
                call GetByte                 ; Get the checksum byte
                jc   VerErr                  ; If time out go to VerErr
                sub  dl, dl                  ; Clear DL to begin checksum
```

```
                    mov     bx, OFFSET Buffer
                    mov     cx, 128                 ; The size of the buffer
        VerLoop:
                    add     dl, BYTE PTR [bx]       ; Add up the bytes
                    inc     bx
                    loop    VerLoop
                    cmp     al, dl
                    je      VerOK
        VerErr:
                    jmp     ErrFnd
        VerOK:
                    mov     ah, 40h                 ; Write to the file
                    mov     bx, FHand
                    mov     cx, 128
                    mov     dx, OFFSET Buffer
                    int     21h
                    mov     al, ACK                 ; Acknowledge the block
                    call    SendByte
                    call    GetByte                 ; See if there is another
                                                    ; block

                    jc      VerErr
                    inc     BlkNumb
                    cmp     al, EOT
                    jne     NxtBlk
                    mov     al, ACK                 ; Acknowledge the end of the
                                                    ; file

                    call    SendByte
                    mov     ErrCnt, 20              ; Bump up errors to exit
        NxtBlk:
                    mov     State, 1                ; Get the next block
                    ret
        VerifyB     ENDP

        ; report errors
        ErrFnd      PROC
                    mov     TimeOut, 10
        EF1:                                        ; Flush the buffer
                    call    GetByte
                    jnc     EF1                     ; by looping until time out
                    mov     TimeOut, 50
                    mov     al, NAK
                    call    SendByte
                    inc     ErrCnt
                    call    GetByte                 ; See if there is another
                                                    ; block
```

```
          mov   State, 1              ; Go back to get header state
          ret
ErrFnd    ENDP

END
```

The XMODEM protocol calls for the file to be divided into 128-byte pieces called *packets*. Figure 14-6 shows the format of an XMODEM packet. The transmitting computer sends each packet followed by a checksum. If the checksum computed by the receiving computer matches the checksum sent, then the receiving computer sends an acknowledgment. If the checksums do not match, then the receiving computer tells the sending computer to send the block again. When all of the blocks have been sent, the sending computer sends an End Of Transmission (EOT) character. The receiving computer acknowledges the EOT and closes the file.

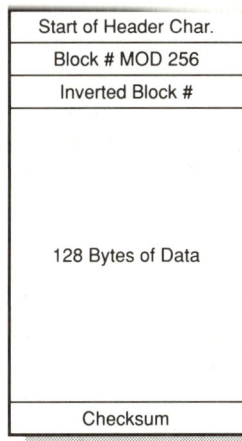

| Start of Header Char. |
| Block # MOD 256 |
| Inverted Block # |
| 128 Bytes of Data |
| Checksum |

Figure 14-6. *Format of an XMODEM data packet.*

Summary

Assembly language is often the best or only way to get your hardware to do what you want. Most high level languages do not provide the instructions required for using devices such as the 8259 interrupt controller. Other devices that require low level programming include the keyboard controller and the serial port.

The 8259 interrupt controller handles hardware interrupts. It tells the processor when an interrupt occurs and what device caused the interrupt. While the interrupt is being handled, the 8259 will not allow any other interrupts to get to the processor. Each ISR must send an EOI instruction to the 8259 when it is done, so that the 8259 can resume handling interrupts. Another feature of the 8259 is that you can program it to allow only specific interrupts. This gives you better control of where the CPU spends its time.

The keyboard controller can tell your program when any key is pressed or released. To find out the last key pressed or released, read port 60h. The keyboard controller also generates an interrupt when something happens on the keyboard. You can use this interrupt to bring up routines when you press certain keys.

The serial port can be connected to printers, plotters, modems, other computers, or a number of other devices. For slower devices you can use the routines in BIOS and MS-DOS to send data. For high speed applications, you need to use an ISR to receive data. This ensures that the processor is paying attention whenever there is data at the serial port.

Chapter *15* *Video Control: Text and Graphics*

Anyone who has ever tried to get an idea across knows that a good presentation is just as important as the good idea itself. This is also true in computer programs. The most sophisticated program is nothing without a "whiz-bang" interface to show it off.

You have already seen some simple examples of routines to access the display (for example, routines to draw a box in Chapter 9 and a circle in Chapter 12). The first part of this chapter goes into more detail about how those functions work, and you can learn how to adapt them for use with other display hardware.

The last part of this chapter gives you some details on how the graphics modes work. The first examples show how to draw pixels, which can then be combined into a line. The last example is an entertaining animation using lines.

Video Hardware

There are two parts to the display system hardware in IBM PCs and compatibles: the display adapter and the monitor. The *adapter* is an interface inside the PC. It contains the video control logic circuits and the video memory. The *monitor* is the screen that shows text and graphics. The adapter converts the information in the video memory into a series of dots, called *pixels*. It sends these dots to the monitor where they are displayed. Figure 15-1 illustrates these components.

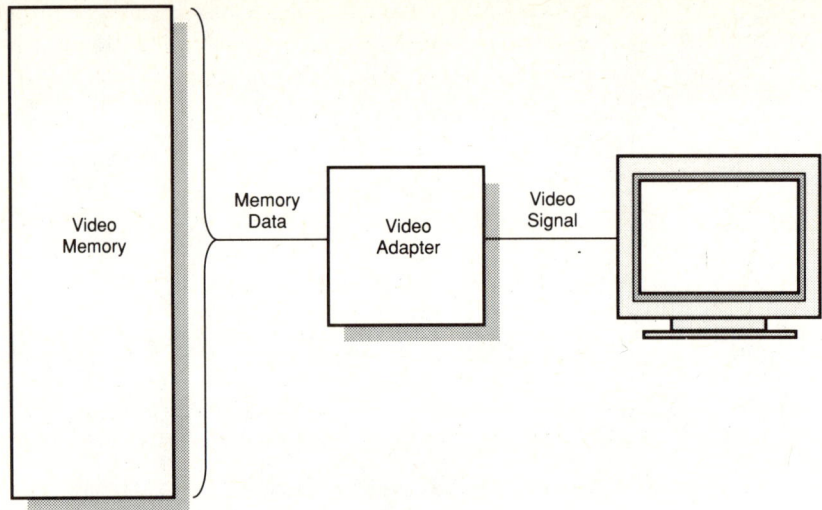

Figure 15-1. *Sending video to the monitor.*

Display Adapters

The display adapter is a circuit card that controls how to display the video memory on-screen. It can interpret the memory as text that must be converted to pixels, or as an array of pixels. It also controls the number of characters or pixels in a line, and how many lines go on the screen. IBM offers five major adapter types: the Monochrome Display Adapter (MDA), the Color Graphics Adapter (CGA), the Enhanced Graphics Adapter (EGA), Multi Color Graphics Array (MCGA), and the Video Graphics Array (VGA). Each of these adapters contains more colors and total pixels than the previous one.

The MDA is the simplest of all the display adapters. It can display text in just one color. The text appears on-screen in an 80x25 format. Each character can have one of several attributes that control such things as normal or inverse video, flashing, high intensity, or underlining. The next step up is the CGA card. This card can display text in either 80x25 or 40x25 format. Instead of attributes, the CGA card displays different colors. In addition to the text modes, the CGA offers two graphics modes: 320x200 pixels with four colors, and 640x200 with two colors. The EGA card adds four new graphics modes to the list: 320x200 with 16 colors, 640x200 with 16 colors, 640x350 monochrome, and 640x350 with four colors. Some EGA cards enable you to add extra memory, so that the highest resolution mode can have up to 16 colors. The MCGA adds one more graphics mode: 640x480 with two colors. Finally, the VGA adds yet two more: 640x480 with 16 colors, and 320x200 with 256 colors.

Other manufacturers offer adapters that are compatible with one or more of the IBM adapters. These adapters often have modes that give you still more colors or resolutions. The most common are the Hercules Graphics Card

(HGC), which offers graphics for monochrome monitors, and the Super-VGA, which uses more pixels to get higher resolutions. These modes are not standardized, so special drivers must be written for each one in order to take advantage of its extra features.

Video Monitors

The video monitor must be compatible with the display adapter being used. If the display adapter is an MDA, you must have a monochrome monitor; CGAs require a color monitor; VGAs require a higher resolution monitor; and so forth. There are two types of monitors that can be used with more than one adapter. The PS/2 monitors can tell an adapter whether they are black and white or color. The adapter then adjusts itself to use color or not. These monitors work with MCGA and VGA adapters that support this feature. Other manufacturers make monitors that detect the type of signal coming from the adapter and then adjust themselves to display it.

The type of monitor does not change the way you program the display adapter, but it does affect the colors (or lack of them) that you can see. It is a good idea to allow the program users to modify the colors used in your program. This gives them a chance to select colors that best display the fancy interface you have made.

Programming the Display Adapter

Many programs can get by with simply sending all output to the screen through DOS. A program to display a directory is a good example of this. You can use ANSI.SYS (see Chapter 13) to give you more control of the screen. With ANSI.SYS you can put the directory in a specific location on the screen, and use the cursor to select files. One drawback to this technique is that, by the time your print command has gone from your program to DOS to ANSI.SYS to the BIOS and finally to the screen, you have lost any chance for a high performance program.

At the lowest level, the display adapter can be programmed by reading and writing data at various I/O ports. Each type of adapter uses different types of ports and different addresses for the ports. Even adapters that are compatible at higher levels may use different I/O ports to control the adapter. To make the adapter useful to programmers, each one comes with its own BIOS on the card. The BIOS must provide functions that are compatible with those provided by IBM. If you program the adapter at this level, you should have no problem with compatibility.

The examples in this chapter show how to make high performance video routines. They combine BIOS routines with routines that directly access video memory. BIOS routines do the complex tasks like setting the mode and the color palette. Accessing video memory directly is the fastest way to get things on the screen.

Video Modes

There are 14 standard video modes supported by IBM display adapters. Each new adapter supports more modes than the previous one. Table 15-1 shows these modes and which adapters can use them.

Table 15-1. *Video Modes*

Mode	Adapter	Resolution	Type	Colors	Font size	Page	Buffer
0, 1	CGA	320x200	Text	16	8X8	8	B8000h
0, 1	EGA	320x350	Text	16	8X14	8	B8000h
0, 1	VGA	360x400	Text	16	9X16	8	B8000h
2, 3	CGA	640x200	Text	16	8X8	8	B8000h
2, 3	EGA	640x350	Text	16	8X14	8	B8000h
2, 3	VGA	720x400	Text	16	9X16	8	B8000h
4, 5	CGA	320x200	Graphic	4	8X8	1	B8000h
6	CGA	640x200	Graphic	2	8X8	1	B8000h
7	MDA	720x350	Text	MONO	9X14	8	B0000h
7	VGA*	720x400	Text	MONO	9X16	8	B0000h
13	EGA	320x200	Graphic	16	8X8	8	A0000h
14	EGA	640x200	Graphic	16	8X8	4	A0000h
15	EGA	640x350	Graphic	MONO	8X14	2	A0000h
16	EGA	640x350	Graphic	16	8X16	2	A0000h
17	VGA	640x480	Graphic	2	8X16	1	A0000h
18	VGA	640x480	Graphic	16	8X16	1	A0000h
19	VGA	320x200	Graphic	256	8X8	1	A0000h

Note that later adapters can use all earlier modes, except mode 7.

* The VGA adapter can use mode 7 if a monochrome monitor is attached.

The easiest way to select a video mode is to let BIOS do it for you. All of the BIOS video functions use interrupt 10h. The function to set the video mode is function 0. The section in this chapter on using graphics modes has an example of this.

Color Palettes

The VGA and EGA adapters can display a broad range of colors. The EGA can display 256 colors, and the VGA can display 262,144 colors. Neither of these adapters can display all the available colors at once, however. The EGA can display up to 16 colors at a time, and the VGA can display up to 256 colors at a time. When a program draws a pixel or character on the screen, it gives the adapter a color number (0-15 for EGA and 0-255 for VGA). The adapter looks at the *palette register* for that color to see what color to send to the monitor.

There are BIOS functions that let you change the palette registers, and thus the colors that appear on the screen. You can use this feature to create a simple animation. Figure 15-2 shows a spoked wheel. Each of the spokes is a different color. By shifting the colors in the palette registers, the wheel appears to spin. You can use the circle routine in Chapter 12 and the line drawing routine in this chapter to draw the wheel. The routine to shift the palette registers for VGA looks like this:

```
        .MODEL SMALL            ; Any model will work

        PUBLIC Animate          ; Make the function visible to
                                ; other modules

        .DATA
PBuff   DB    256 * 3 DUP ( ? ) ; Space for the palette
                                ; registers
Wrap    DB    3 DUP ( ? )       ; The color to move to the end
        .CODE
; This function assumes that video mode 13h and the picture is
; drawn
Animate PROC
        mov   ax, SEG DGROUP
        mov   ds, ax
        mov   es, ax            ; Set ES for BIOS function
        mov   dx, OFFSET PBuff   ; Point to the palette buffer
        sub   bx, bx            ; Starting color number
        mov   cx, 256           ; Number of colors
        mov   ax, 1017h         ; BIOS command to read palette
        int   10h
        cld                     ; Set direction = forward
AnLoop:
        mov   di, dx            ; Put the address in DI
        mov   si, di            ; Copy to the source
        lodsw                   ; Read 2 bytes
        mov   WORD PTR Wrap, ax  ; Save it for now
        lodsb                   ; Read 1 more byte
        mov   Wrap+2, al
        mov   cx, (254 * 3)/2   ; The number of words to move
        rep   movsw             ; Shift every color up 1
        mov   ax, WORD PTR Wrap  ; Get 2 bytes of last color
        stosw                   ; store them
        mov   al, Wrap+2        ; Get the last byte
        stosb                   ; store it
```

```
              sub  bx, bx                   ; First color to set
              mov  cx, 256                  ; Number of colors to set
              mov  ax, 1012h                ; BIOS command to write the
                                            ; palette
              mov  ah, 1                    ; BIOS check for key
              int  16h
              jnz  AnLoop                   ; If no key do it again
              mov  ah, 0                    ; Read the key
              int  16h
              ret
Animate       ENDP
              .STACK    1024
END
```

After you assemble this file, you will need to write a program to draw the circle and spokes. You can use the circle routine from Chapter 12 and the line drawing routine from later in this chapter. Once the picture is drawn, a call to `Animate` will put it in motion.

The first thing that `Animate` does is to call BIOS to read the palette registers (see Figure 15-2). It puts the data read into the array called `PBuff`. The job of the loop at `AnLoop` is to shift all of the palette values from one color to another and write this new palette to the palette registers. This creates the illusion of motion.

The EGA works in the same way except that it uses functions `1002h` and `1009h` to set and read the palette registers.

Determining the Adapter Type

Before you can use a display adapter, you need to know what kind it is. The type of adapter will tell you what modes you can use and where the video memory is located. The following example determines what kind of adapter is being used, and then sets up the `ScrBase` and `VidPage` variables that will be used by the text routines.

```
; Determine video type and memory location
              .MODEL    SMALL               ; Any model will work

              PUBLIC VideoType, VidType     ; Make these visible
              PUBLIC CurMode, ScrBase       ; to other modules
              PUBLIC VidPage

MDA           EQU  0
CGA           EQU  1
EGA           EQU  2
VGA           EQU  3

              .DATA
```

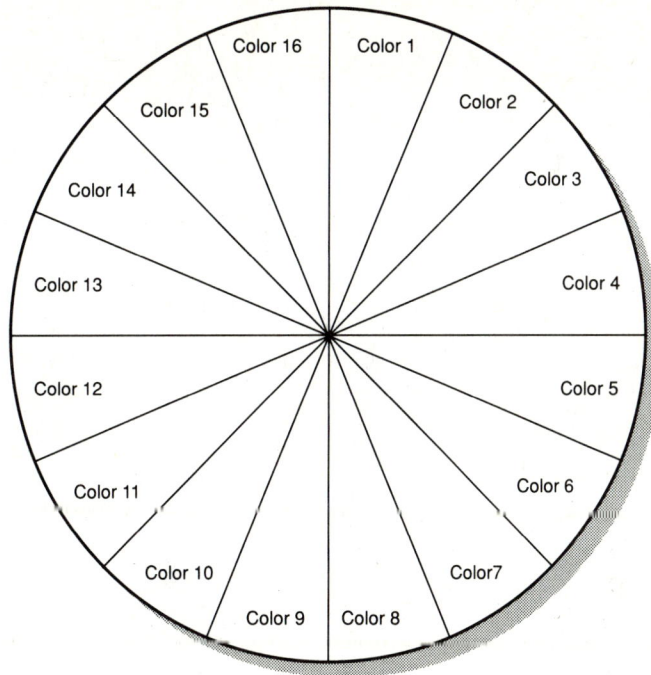

Figure 15-2. *Animation using the palette registers.*

```
VidType     DB    ?                    ; What kind of adapter
CurMode     DB    ?                    ; The current video mode
ScrBase     DW    0B800h               ; The segment for text
VidPage     DW    0                    ; The offset of the current
                                       ; video page

            .CODE
VideoType PROC
            mov   ah, 0Fh              ; Get video status from BIOS
            int   10h
            mov   CurMode, al          ; Save the current mode
            sub   bl, bl               ; Clear BL
            shl   bx, 1                ; Compute the video page
                                       ; address
            shl   bx, 1
            shl   bx, 1
            shl   bx, 1
            mov   VidPage, bx
            cmp   al, 7                ; Check for mode 7
            jne   NotMDA
```

```
                mov    ScrBase, 0B000h        ; Save the segment for MDA
                mov    VidType, MDA
                jmp    SHORT VTDone
NotMDA:
                mov    ax, 1B00h              ; See if this VGA only BIOS
                int    10h                    ; function works
                cmp    al, 1Bh
                jne    NotVGA
                mov    VidType, VGA
                jmp    SHORT VTDone
NotVGA:
                mov    ax, 40h                ; BIOS data segment
                mov    es, ax
                test   BYTE PTR es:[87h], 0FFh
                je     NotEGA
                mov    VidType, EGA
                jmp    VTDone
NotEGA:
                mov    VidType, CGA           ; It must be a CGA
VTDone:
                ret
VideoType ENDP
```

This example can be assembled and added to your library of useful modules. When you write a program that uses the video system, you can call this routine first to determine what type of adapter is being used.

The first thing that this routine does is to get the current video mode and memory page from BIOS. If the mode used is 7, then it must be an MDA (or a MCGA or VGA that is acting like an MDA). If it is not an MDA, the next test checks whether it is a VGA. The way it does this is to call a BIOS function that only works with a BIOS for a VGA. If it is not a VGA, then the routine tests for EGA. The test for EGA is to look at the byte at 0040:0087. This byte is the low byte of the video control state word. This byte is 0FFh for non-EGA adapters. If the card is not an EGA, then the only possibility left is a CGA.

Using Text Mode

Once you know the location of the video memory (ScrBase and VidPage), displaying characters on the screen is easy. Storing ASCII codes in even-numbered bytes in the video page is enough. You can also change the attribute or color of the character by writing to the odd-numbered bytes. Figure 15-3 shows you how memory locations are related to the location of the character on the screen.

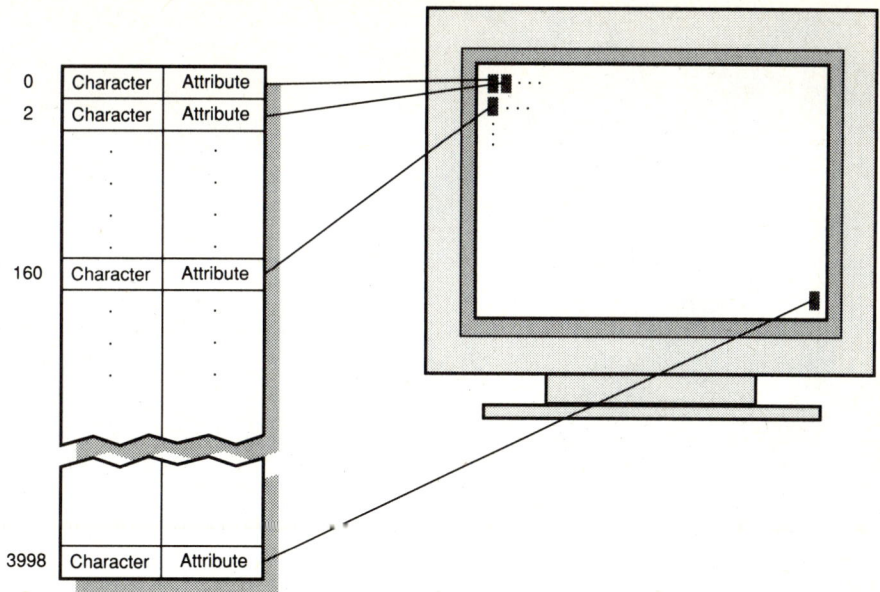

Figure 15-3. *Mapping memory to the screen.*

Characters and Attributes

Each character in video memory has an attribute byte. The MDA uses the attribute byte to set features such as underline, high intensity, and blinking for the character. All other adapters use the attribute byte to set the color of the character and the background. Figure 15-4 shows the format of the attribute byte.

The CGA and Snow

Video memory must be available to two processors at the same time. One is the CPU and the other is the video controller. Since a memory chip can only respond to one memory address at a time, the circuitry must make one device wait while the other is accessing memory. On some CGA cards, this delay appears as "snow" on the monitor screen. Other adapters use special circuits that automatically control snow.

To write on the CGA screen without snow, you must only write to video memory when the video controller is not accessing the video memory. Fortunately, this is the case during horizontal and vertical retraces. This is the time that the electron beam in the CRT is moving from left to right or from bottom to top. At these times the electron beam is turned off, and no snow can be created. The CGA status port at 3DAh has its low bit set during horizontal retrace. The following code can be used to ensure that you write data only at the beginning of a horizontal retrace:

```
        mov  dx, 3DAh               ; The CGA status port
RtrcOn:
        in   al, dx                 ; Get the status byte
        test al, 1                  ; Test retrace bit
        jnz  RtrcOn                 ; Wait for retrace to go off
RtrcOff:
        in   al, dx                 ; Wait for it to go back on
        test al, 1                  ; This ensures that there will
        jz   RtrcOff                ; be enough time to read or
                                    ; write
        .                           ; It is now safe to read or
        .                           ; write video memory
        .
```

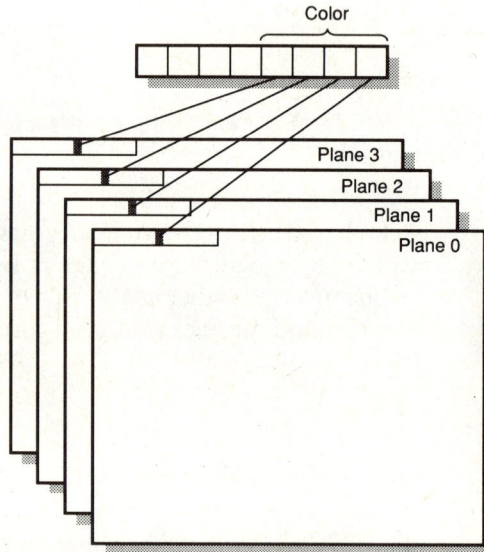

Figure 15-4. *EGA bit planes.*

Some Basic Text Routines

The VideoType routine, presented earlier, shows how to find the location of video memory. These next routines will use this information to put text on the screen.

PRINTING A CHARACTER

This routine prints the character in the DL register at the row in AH and the column in AL. It uses the attribute in the DH register:

```
; File PUTCHAR.ASM
            .MODEL   SMALL               ; Any model will work
            PUBLIC   PutChar             ; Make PutChar visible to
                                         ; other modules
EXTRN       VidType:BYTE
EXTRN       ScrBase:WORD
EXTRN       VidPage:WORD
CGA         EQU  1

            .CODE
PutChar     PROC
            mov  es, ScrBase             ; Load the base address
            sub  bh, bh                  ; Clear bh
            mov  bl, al                  ; Save the column in BX
            mov  al, ah                  ; Move the row to al
            mov  cl, 80                  ; Times 80 chars / row
            mul  cl
            add  bx, ax                  ; Add to the column
            shl  bx, 1                   ; Times 2 byte / character
            cmp  VidType, CGA            ; Check for snow
            jne  NoSnow
            push dx
            mov  dx, 3DAh                ; The CGA status port
RtrcOn:
            in   al, dx                  ; Get the status byte
            test al, 1                   ; Test retrace bit
            jnz  RtrcOn                  ; Wait for retrace to go off
RtrcOff:
            in   al, dx                  ; Wait for it to go back on
            test al, 1                   ; This insures that there will
            jz   RtrcOff                 ; be enough time to read or
                                         ; write
            pop  dx
NoSnow:
            mov  WORD PTR es:[bx+VidPage], dx
            ret
PutChar     ENDP
END
```

The first part of this routine calculates the address in video memory for the character. It uses the ScrBase variable that was determined with the VideoType routine. The first line puts the value at ScrBase into the ES register. After that, the routine puts the row into the AL register and multiplies it by 80 (the number of columns in each row). Next, it adds in the column number and multiplies the whole thing by two to get the word address for the character. The next step is to check for snow if this is a CGA card. Finally, the routine puts the character and attribute into video memory so the adapter will display it.

PRINTING A STRING OF CHARACTERS

One way to print a string of characters is to send each of the characters to the PutChar function. The disadvantage of this approach is that PutChar has to recalculate the address time it is called. The PrintStr function below prints the string at DS:SI on the screen at the row in AH and the column in AL. The string must end with a byte equal to 0. As with the PutChar function, the attribute is in the DH register.

```
; File PRNSTR.ASM
; Print a string
            .MODEL    SMALL              ; Any model will work
            PUBLIC    PrintStr
EXTRN     VidType:BYTE
EXTRN     ScrBase:WORD
EXTRN     VidPage:WORD
CGA       EQU  1

            .CODE
PrintStr  PROC
            mov   es, ScrBase            ; Load the base address
            sub   bh, bh                 ; Clear bh
            mov   bl, al                 ; Save the column in BX
            mov   al, ah                 ; Move the row to al
            mov   cl, 80                 ; Times 80 chars / row
            mul   cl
            add   bx, ax                 ; Add to the column
            shl   bx, 1                  ; Times 2 byte / character
            mov   di, OFFSET VidPage     ; Get the top of the page
            add   di, bx                 ; Add in the location for
                                         ; printing
            mov   ah, dh                 ; Put the attribute in AH
            cld
PSLoop:
            lodsb                        ; Read the next byte to print
            or    al, al                 ; Check for 0
            jz    PSDone
```

```
              push ax                   ; Save the char and attr
              cmp  VidType, CGA         ; Check for snow
              jne  NoSnow
              mov  dx, 3DAh             ; The CGA status port
RtrcOn:
              in   al, dx               ; Get the status byte
              test al, 1                ; Test retrace bit
              jnz  RtrcOn               ; Wait for retrace to go off
RtrcOff:
              in   al, dx               ; Wait for it to go back on
              test al, 1                ; This insures that there will
              jz   RtrcOff              ; be enough time to read or
                                        ; write
NoSnow:
              pop  ax                   ; Get back the char and attr
              stosw                     ; Save to the screen
              jmp  PSLoop
PSDone:
              ret
PrintStr  ENDP
END
```

The first part of this routine calculates the address in video memory for the string from `ScrBase` and `VidPage`. The code in `PSLoop` reads a character from the string, waits for the retrace, then writes the data to video memory. The `STOSW` instruction used to write the data to the screen also moves the location pointer in `ES:DI` to point to the next character location. `PSLoop` continues until it reads a zero from the string.

To see this routine work you will need to write a routine that sets up the variables and calls it. For example, the following routine uses `PrintStr` to display several strings:

```
; File     TEXTTEST.ASM
          .MODEL    SMALL          ; Must match the model for
                                   ; PrntStr

EXTRN     PrintStr:PROC
EXTRN     VideoType:PROC

          .DATA
String1   DB   "How many programmers does it take to replace"
          DB   " a light bulb?", 0
String2   DB   "None, that's a hardware problem!", 0

          .CODE
StrTest   PROC
```

```
                mov   ax, SEG DGROUP        ; Get the data segment
                mov   ds, ax
                mov   si, OFFSET String1    ; Get the offset of the first
                                            ; string
                mov   dh, 70h               ; Black letters on a white
                                            ; background
                mov   ax, 0A0Ah             ; Place it at (10, 10)
                call  PrintStr
                mov   ah, 0                 ; BIOS wait for a key
                int   16h                   ; BIOS keyboard service
                mov   si, OFFSET String2    ; Get the offset of the second
                                            ; string
                mov   dh, 17h               ; White letters on a blue
                                            ; background
                mov   ax, 0B0Ah             ; Place it at (11, 10)
                call  PrintStr
                mov   ah, 4Ch
                int   21h
StrTest     ENDP
END
```

CLEARING THE SCREEN

This next routine writes the character and attribute in DL and DH at the location in AL and AH. Then it moves forward one position and repeats the write. The CX register contains the number of times the character is printed. If you place 0 in AX (the top of the screen), 0720h in DX (spaces with a black attribute), and 2000 in CX (the number of characters on the screen), the screen will be cleared.

```
; File CLS.ASM
              .MODEL    SMALL              ; Any model will work

              PUBLIC    Fill
EXTRN     VidType:BYTE
EXTRN     ScrBase:WORD
EXTRN     VidPage:WORD
CGA       EQU  1

              .CODE

Fill      PROC
              mov   es, ScrBase            ; Load the base address
              sub   bh, bh                 ; Clear bh
              mov   bl, al                 ; Save the column in BX
              mov   al, ah                 ; Move the row to al
              push  cx                     ; Save the repeat count
```

```
        mov  cl, 80              ; Times 80 chars / row
        mul  cl
        add  bx, ax              ; Add to the column
        shl  bx, 1               ; Times 2 byte / character
        pop  cx                  ; Recover the repeat count
        mov  ax, dx              ; Put the char and attr in AX
FLoop:
        cmp  VidType, CGA        ; Check for snow
        jne  NoSnow
        push dx
        mov  dx, 3DAh            ; The CGA status port
RtrcOn:
        in   al, dx              ; Get the status byte
        test al, 1               ; Test retrace bit
        jnz  RtrcOn              ; Wait for retrace to go off
RtrcOff:
        in   al, dx              ; Wait for it to go back on
        test al, 1               ; This ensures that there will
        jz   RtrcOff             ; be enough time to read or
                                 ; write
        pop  dx
NoSnow:
        mov  WORD PTR es:[bx+VidPage], dx
        inc  bx
        inc  bx
        loop FLoop
        ret
Fill    ENDP
END
```

The first part of this routine is like the previous examples. It calculates the address in video memory to use. After that, the routine checks if it needs to check for snow. If so, it waits for a retrace before writing the character to video memory. The loop repeats until CX is 0.

Using Graphics Modes

The first step in using graphics modes is to select the mode to use. For the most part, this decision is based on the available video adapter. For each adapter, you need to choose between more pixels or more colors. Applications, like CAD/CAM, that require highly detailed drawings are better with more pixels. Other applications, like displaying photographs, are better with more colors. Once you have chosen the mode to use, you can select the routines that work best in that mode.

In graphics modes each byte represents one or more pixels. For black and white modes, a pixel only requires a single bit. As the number of colors increases, so does the number of bits required for each pixel. The four-color CGA modes use two bits per pixel, 16-color EGA modes use four bits per pixel, and the 256-color VGA mode uses eight bits per pixel.

Locating Video Memory

Video memory begins at location 0B8000h and ends at 0BFFFFh on the CGA card. The address of any given pixel depends on the mode being used. EGA and VGA modes require more than the 32,768 bytes of memory available at 0B8000h. To make room, the beginning address for EGA and VGA modes is 0A0000h. This increases the available memory from 32,768 bytes to 131,071 bytes.

There are two ways that memory can be arranged for graphics. One is to divide each byte into several pixels. For the CGA two-color modes, each byte is eight pixels; for four-color modes, it is four pixels, and so on.

PIXELS IN CGA MODES　　The CGA card has two graphics modes. One has 64,000 pixels and four colors, while the other has 128,000 pixels and only two colors. To draw a pixel on the screen, you must calculate the address of the byte that contains the pixel, and set the bits for the pixel. The formula for calculating the address of the byte to use is complicated by the way the memory is arranged. Every other line on the screen comes from the second half of video memory. This lets the CGA card use slower memory chips, by letting the chips for the next line get ready while the current line is being sent to the monitor. This technique is called *interlacing*.

If y is the line for the pixel and x is the column, the formula for calculating the byte offset in four-color mode is:

```
Offset = y * 80 + x / 4 + ( y AND 1 ) * 8192
```

Note that (y AND 1) * 8192 is 8192 only if y is odd. Otherwise, it is 0. Changing the constant for the number of pixels in a byte gives the formula for two-color mode:

```
Offset = y * 80 + x / 8 + ( y AND 1 ) * 8192
```

Once you know where the byte is, you need to calculate which bits make up the pixel and how to change them. You will need a mask byte to get rid of the pixels that are already there. Then you will need to shift the pixel into the correct position and OR it with the byte. To find the number of positions to shift, use these formulas:

```
2 color mode:

    Shift = x mod 8
```

4 color mode:

        Shift = (x mod 4) * 2

Using this information, a routine to write a pixel looks like the following:

```
; File CGAPIX.ASM
        .MODEL    SMALL
        .DATA
        PUBLIC    CGAPixel

ypos    DB    ?                       ; Temp y position
ScrBase DW    0B800h                  ; Segment for video memory
        .CODE
; Draw pixel at (AL, AH) use color in DL
CGAPixel PROC
        mov   es, ScrBase             ; The segment for video memory
        mov   cl, 3
        sub   bh, bh                  ; Clear the high byte of BX
        mov   bl, ah                  ; Now BX = y
        mov   ah, bh                  ; Clear high byte of AX
        mov   ypos, bl                ; Save the y coord
        and   bx, 0FEh                ; Lose the low bit
        shl   bx, cl                  ; bx = y times 8
        mov   cx, bx
        shl   bx, 1
        shl   bx, 1                   ; bx = y times 32
        add   bx, cx                  ; bx = y times 40
        mov   cx, ax                  ; Get x
        shr   cx, 1
        shr   cx, 1                   ; Divide x by 4
IFE  GMODE EQ 6                       ; If for graphics mode 6
        shr   cx, 1                   ; Divide x by 8
ENDIF
        add   bx, cx                  ; Add to the total
        test  ypos, 1                 ; See if y is odd
        jz    NotOdd
        add   bx, 8192                ; If y is odd, use second 8K
NotOdd:
IFE  GMODE EQ 6                       ; If for graphics mode 6
        and   ax, 7                   ; Use x to figure the number
        mov   cl, 7                   ; of bits to shift
        mov   ah, 0FEh                ; Make a mask
ELSE                                  ; If for mode 4 or 5
        and   ax, 3                   ; Use x to get the shift value
        shl   ax, 1                   ; Times 2 bits per pixel
```

```
                mov   cl, 6
                mov   ah, 0FCh            ; Make a mask
        ENDIF
                sub   cl, al
                mov   al, BYTE PTR es:[bx]
                rol   ah, cl              ; Move the mask into position
                and   al, ah              ; Mask out the old bits
                shl   dl, cl              ; Put the data in position
                or    al, dl              ; OR it into the byte
                mov   BYTE PTR es:[bx], al
                ret
        CGAPixel  ENDP
        END
```

The first part of this routine calculates the byte offset, using the formulas presented earlier. It uses *conditional assembly* statements to make different versions for modes 4 and 5 or mode 6. The first conditional block divides x by 8 instead of 4, if GMODE is set to 6.

The next part of the program, just above the label NotOdd, determines if the pixel is on an odd- or even-numbered line. If it is an odd-numbered line, 8192 is added to the address of the pixel.

The conditional block following the label NotOdd sets up the registers to calculate a mask to use for writing the pixel. The difference between CL and AL is the number of bits to shift the mask in AH. The next bit of code reads the byte that contains the pixel, calculates the mask to use, ANDs out the bits for the pixel, shifts the pixel into place, ORs the pixel into the byte, and writes the byte back to memory.

When you assemble this program, you will need to use a command line switch to tell the assembler the value for GMODE. For example, to assemble a version for mode 6, use this command line:

```
tasm /dGMODE=6 cgapix
```

PIXELS IN EGA MODES

Another way that memory can be arranged for graphics is to arrange memory in several layers or bit-planes. Each bit-plane is an array of pixels with one bit for each pixel. Imagine these bit-planes stacked on top of each other as shown in Figure 15-4. For any pixel, the color is determined by which bits are *on* in which bit-planes. The EGA card uses four bit-planes to get 16 different colors on the screen at a time.

One drawback to the bit-plane method is that to write a single pixel, you must access each of the bit-planes. For the EGA, this would mean eight memory accesses for each pixel (four to read the bytes, and four to write them back). The EGA adapter overcomes this problem by using a special hardware device called a *latch*. The latch can be programmed to hold a bit from each of the bit-planes. This makes reading and writing a pixel simple, because all you need to do is read or write a single byte through the latch. The latch can be programmed in other ways for different types of access, so the first step to drawing pixels with the EGA card is to make sure that the latch is in mode 2 (latch a single pixel mode). The following code sends the appropriate commands to the EGA card:

```
mov   dx, 3CEh              ; EGA index register
mov   ax, 0205h            ; Set up index number and data
out   dx, ax              ; to send. Use 16 bit output.
```

This code uses an interesting trick to access two adjacent I/O ports. The first port is an index register at 3CEh. Writing data to this port tells the adapter what kind of data to expect at the data port (3CFh). Each of these ports normally accepts a single byte. This code uses a word-size output instruction to write to both ports at once. Some hardware cannot accept data coming in like this, so check with the manufacturer before using this technique with devices other than the EGA adapter.

The next step is to calculate the address of the byte containing the pixel. Because the EGA adapter does not interlace lines, there is no need to test for odd and even lines. This simplifies the formula to:

```
For 320 pixels per line ( mode 13 ):
    Offset = y * 40 + x/8

For 640 pixels per line ( modes 14-16 ):
    Offset = y * 80 + x/8
```

Once you know what byte to address, you need to calculate what bit in the byte to look at. You can do this the same way you did for the CGA in two-color mode. Use the remainder, after dividing the column for the pixel by 8, to tell how many bits to shift the mask. You must send this mask to the latch before reading or writing video memory. The result is that whenever you read or write the byte containing the pixel, you will actually read or write the data in the latch—which is the color of the pixel. To allow the latch to work properly, you must always read a pixel before writing it. This lets the latch get the bits around the pixel, just as you did when you read a byte before modifying the pixel with the CGA.

The next routine draws a pixel on the EGA screen. When you call it, have the column in AX, the row in BX, and the color for the pixel in DL:

```
; File EGAPIX.ASM
          .MODEL    SMALL          ; Any model will work
PUBLIC    EGAPixel                 ; Make the entry visible to
                                   ; other modules

          .DATA
```

```
ScrBase    DW   0A000h                    ; Segment for video memory
           .CODE

; Draw pixel at (AX, BX) use color in DL
EGAPixel   PROC
           mov   es, ScrBase              ; The segment for video memory
IFE GMODE EQ 13                           ; For mode thirteen, multiply
           mov   cl, 3                     ; row by 40
ELSE                                      ; Otherwise, multiply it by 80
           mov   cl, 4
ENDIF
           shl   bx, cl                   ; bx = row times 8 or 16
           mov   cx, bx
           shl   bx, 1
           shl   bx, 1                     ; bx = row times 32 or 64
           add   bx, cx                    ; bx = row times 40 or 80
           mov   cx, ax                    ; Get the column
           shr   cx, 1
           shr   cx, 1
           shr   cx, 1                     ; Divide column by 8
           add   bx, cx                    ; Add to the total
           and   ax, 7                     ; Use column to figure the
           mov   cl, al                    ; number of bits to shift
           mov   ah, 80h                   ; Make a mask
           shr   ah, cl                    ; Move the mask into position
           mov   al, 8                     ; Index for EGA bit mask
           push  dx                        ; Save the color
           mov   dx, 3CEh
           out   dx, ax                    ; Send mask
           mov   al,BYTE PTR es:[bx]       ; Read data into the latch
           pop   dx
           and   dl, 0Fh
           mov   BYTE PTR es:[bx],dl       ; Send the color
           ret
EGAPixel   ENDP
END
```

The first part of this program uses one of the EGA formulas, presented earlier, to calculate the address of the byte containing the pixel. Note that it uses the GMODE symbol for conditional assembly, just like the CGA example. You must remember to define this symbol before you assemble the routine.

After calculating the address, the routine makes the mask to use. It does this by dividing the column number by 8 (the number of pixels in a byte) and shifting the mask byte (80h) to the right that number of bits. This mask is sent to the EGA adapter via the index and data ports at 3CEh.

The last step is to read the data from the previously calculated address in ES:BX to the latch registers. After that, the routine writes the color byte back to the same address. The latch logic will update the correct bit-planes, and the EGA adapter will display the pixel on the screen.

PIXELS IN VGA MODES

There are three new modes for the VGA card. The first two (modes 17 and 18) are similar to the EGA mode 16. As a matter of fact, the EGA pixel routine will work in mode 18 without modification. The only difference is that the range of acceptable values for the row number is increased from 0-349 to 0-479.

For mode 17 you can use most of the EGA routine. Replace the latch masking and pixel writing part with the masking and pixel writing from the CGA mode 6 code.

The last mode (mode 19) is one of the easiest to use. It has 320x200 pixels, and each pixel uses an entire byte. This means that you do not need to fool with masks or latches, just write the byte to memory. The formula for calculating the address of the pixel is:

```
Offset = 320 * y + x
```

The routine to draw the pixel is as follows:

```
; File VGAPIX.ASM
; Draw pixels in mode 13h
        .MODEL    SMALL
PUBLIC    VGAPixel

        .DATA
ScrBase   DW    0A000h          ; Segment for video memory

        .CODE
; AX = column, BX = row, DL = color
VGAPixel  PROC
        mov    es, ScrBase     ; Load the segment for video memory
        mov    cl, 6
        shl    bx, cl          ; BX = row times 64
        mov    cx, bx
        shl    bx, 1
        shl    bx, 1           ; BX = row times 256
        add    bx, cx          ; BX = row times 320
        add    bx, ax          ; Add the column to the total
                               ; Move the color byte to video
                               ; memory
        mov    BYTE PTR es:[bx], dl
        ret
VGAPixel  ENDP

END
```

The first part of this routine uses the formula above to calculate the address of the pixel in video memory. The calculation leaves the address in ES:BX. The last instruction, before the return, copies the color byte in DL to video memory so that the VGA card can display it.

Drawing a Line

Now that you know how to put pixels on the screen, you can use them to build up more interesting objects. The circle drawing program in Chapter 12 is one example. The next example shows how to draw a line. The algorithm used here is similar to the one used to draw a circle. It moves from one end-point to the other, using integer arithmetic to find the location of the next point. As a matter of fact, the line algorithm was discovered by Breshenham, the same man who discovered the circle algorithm. Figure 15-5 shows how the algorithm works.

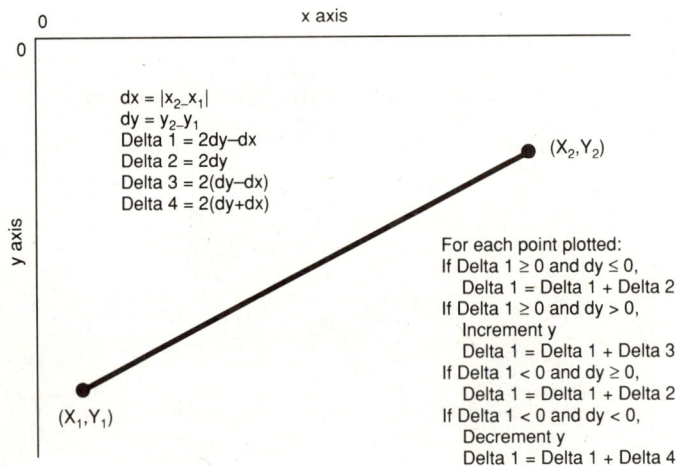

Figure 15-5. *Breshenham's line drawing algorithm.*

Note that the algorithm does not use any division, and the only multiplication is by a power of two. These things help make this a very fast way to draw a line. Another point of interest is the fact that the algorithm does not work for lines with a slope greater than one (more than 45-degrees from the x axis). To get around this, the program flips the x and y coordinates for the calculation, and then unflips them when plotting the point. Here is the routine to draw a line:

```
; File DRAWLINE.ASM
; Draw a line with Breshenham's Algorithm
```

```
          .MODEL SMALL              ; Any model will work. It must
                                    ; match the models used by the
                                    ; other routines.
PUBLIC    DrawLine                  ; Make this routine visible to
                                    ; other modules
EXTRN     CGAPixel:PROC             ; You can use any of the pixel
                                    ; drawing routines from this
                                    ; chapter

          .DATA
Color     DB    ?                   ; Place to save the line color
X1        DW    ?                   ; The starting point for the
Y1        DW    ?                   ; line
X2        DW    ?                   ; The ending point for the
Y2        DW    ?                   ; line
DiffX     DW    ?                   ; Difference between starting
DiffY     DW    ?                   ; point and ending point
Delt1     DW    ?                   ; Numbers used to keep track
Delt2     DW    ?                   ; of the line drawing
Delt3     DW    ?
Delt4     DW    ?
Flipped   DB    0                   ; True if x and y have been
                                    ; flipped

; Enter with:
;     AX = column of the starting point
;     BX = row of the starting point
;     SI = column of the ending point
;     DI = row of the ending point
;     DL = color of the line
          .CODE
DrawLine  PROC
          mov   Flipped, 0          ; Set to no flip state
          mov   Color, dl           ; Save color
          mov   X1, ax              ; Save starting column
          mov   Y1, bx              ; Save starting row
          sub   ax, si              ; Subtract ending column
          cwd                       ; Get absolute value
          xor   ax, dx
          sub   ax, dx
          mov   DiffX, ax           ; Save the difference
          mov   ax, bx
          sub   ax, di              ; Subtract row values
          cwd                       ; Get absolute value
          xor   ax, dx
```

```
                sub   ax, dx
                mov   DiffY, ax              ; Save the difference
                cmp   ax, DiffX             ; If slope < 1
                jle   NoFlip                ; don't flip column and row
                mov   Flipped, 1            ; Set flipped flag
                mov   DiffX, ax             ; Put DiffY in DiffX
                mov   ax, X1                ; Flip X1 and Y1
                mov   bx, Y1
                mov   X1, bx
                mov   Y1, ax

                mov   ax, si                ; Flip SI and DI
                mov   si, di
                mov   di, ax
NoFlip:
                mov   X2, si                ; Save the end point
                mov   Y2, di
                mov   ax, X1
                cmp   ax, X2                ; See if X1 > X2
                jle   NoFlip2               ; If not, don't flip ends
                mov   ax, Y2                ; Flip the y's
                mov   bx, Y1
                mov   Y1, ax
                mov   Y2, bx

                mov   ax, X2                ; Flip the x's
                mov   bx, X1
                mov   X2, bx
                mov   X1, ax
NoFlip2:
                mov   ax, Y2                ; Make signed DiffY
                sub   ax, Y1
                mov   DiffY, ax
                shl   ax, 1                 ; Delt2 = DiffY * 2
                mov   Delt2, ax
                sub   ax, DiffX            ; Delt1 = DiffY * 2 - DiffX
                mov   Delt1, ax
                mov   ax, DiffY            ; Delt3 = (DiffY - DiffX)*2
                sub   ax, DiffX
                shl   ax, 1
                mov   Delt3, ax
                mov   ax, DiffY            ; Delt4 = (DiffY + DiffX)*2
                add   ax, DiffX
                shl   ax, 1
                mov   Delt4, ax
LineLp:
```

```
                cmp     Flipped, 0          ; See if flipped
                jne     NoFlip3
                mov     ax, X1             ; Get the current point
                mov     bx, Y1
                jmp     SHORT DL1
NoFlip3:
                mov     ax, Y1
                mov     bx, X1
DL1:
                mov     dl, Color          ; Plot the point
                call    CGAPixel           ; Call the pixel routine. If
                                           ; you are using a different
                                           ; adapter, change this call to
                                           ; the appropriate pixel
                                           ; routine.
                mov     ax, X1             ; See if current point is
                cmp     ax, X2             ; past the end point
                jge     DLDone
                inc     X1                 ; Move to the next X pos
                cmp     Delt1, 0           ; Decide to change y or
                jge     DL2                ; not
                cmp     DiffY, 0           ; If Delt1 < 0
                jge     DL3                ; and DiffY < 0
                dec     Y1                 ; Move Y up one
                mov     ax, Delt4          ; and add Delt4 to Delt1
                jmp     SHORT DL4
DL2:                                       ; If Delt1 >= 0
                cmp     DiffY, 0           ; and DiffY >= 0
                jle     DL3
                inc     Y1                 ; Move Y down one
                mov     ax, Delt3          ; and add Delt3 to Delt1
                jmp     SHORT DL4
DL3:                                       ; If no change in Y, add Delt2
                mov     ax, Delt2          ; to Delt1
DL4:
                add     Delt1, ax
                jmp     SHORT LineLp
DLDone:
                ret
DrawLine        ENDP
END
```

The first thing that DrawLine does is to set up the variables that it will use. DiffX and DiffY are the numbers of pixels between the columns and rows of the end-points of the line. When the DiffY is greater than DiffX, then the slope is greater than one; so the column and row values must be swapped. The routine keeps track of this fact by setting the Flipped variable to one.

The two instructions after the label NoFlip save the row and column of the end-point in Y2 and X2. After that, the routine checks to see if the end-point is to the right of the starting point. If not, the routine swaps the ends around so that the rest of the program can have increasing column numbers.

The code after the label NoFlip2 calculates the values that will be used to determine when to change to the next row. These values are saved in the variables Delt1, Delt2, Delt3, and Delt4.

The label LineLp begins the loop that actually draws the line. The first step is to see if the rows and columns have been flipped. If so, they must be unflipped before drawing. The next step is to call the pixel drawing routine. Note that this example uses the CGA routine. You can substitute any of the other pixel routines here for other adapters. After it draws the point, DrawLine checks to see if it has drawn the last point, by comparing the current column to the column of the end-point.

If it is not past the end-point, DrawLine increments the current column number and calculates the next row value. The first test is to see if Delt1 is greater than 0. When both Delt1 and DiffY are negative, the current row is decremented and the code at DL4 adds Delt3 to Delt1. When they are both positive, then the current row is incremented and the code at DL4 adds Delt4 to Delt1. If the row does not need to be changed, then the code at DL3 adds Delt2 to Delt1. See the diagram in Figure 15-5 for more information about these calculations.

After the new point is calculated, the JMP instruction just before the DLDone label sends the processor back to the top of the loop to draw more points.

Playing with Lines

This next example shows how to use the line routine to make an animated display. It uses the line routine to draw a series of triangles that move around the screen in random directions. There is a queue that keeps track of all up to the last 32 triangles displayed. The queue is a ring buffer just like the one used in Chapter 14 for serial characters.

Each corner of the triangle has a vector that tells it where the corner for the next triangle goes. When a corner gets to the edge of the screen, the program changes the vector to some other random vector.

The random routine uses a principle called *relative primes* to make sure it gives numbers in a random sequence. This principle involves multiplying the last random number by a prime number (in this case 13) and dividing the result by a prime number larger than the largest random number required (in this case 257 is the prime number). The remainder of the division is the next prime number to use.

To prevent using the same sequence every time the program runs, the random number routine uses a *seed* value. The seed is the first number in the random sequence. The random number routine uses the clock tick value in the BIOS data area for its seed.

```
; File MOVELINE.ASM
            .MODEL SMALL
EXTRN       DrawLine:PROC           ; Use the DrawLine function
                                    ; from the previous example

            .DATA
QSTRU       STRUC                   ; This struct contains the
X1          DW    ?                 ; three points of the triangle
Y1          DW    ?
X2          DW    ?
Y2          DW    ?
X3          DW    ?
Y3          DW    ?
QSTRU       ENDS

Head DW     0                       ; The head of the queue
Tail DW     0                       ; The tail of the queue
QCnt DW     20                      ; The number of triangles in
                                    ; the queue
Cntr DW     50                      ; How long to wait before
                                    ; changing the queue size
seed DW     0                       ; Random number seed

Queue       QSTRU      32 DUP( <> )  ; Array of triangles

; These variables must be kept together
DeltX1      DB    ?                 ; Change in X for point 1
DeltY1      DB    ?                 ; Change in Y for point 1
DeltX2      DB    ?                 ; Change in X for point 2
DeltY2      DB    ?                 ; Change in Y for point 2
DeltX3      DB    ?                 ; Change in X for point 3
DeltY3      DB    ?                 ; Change in Y for point 3

            .CODE
Main        PROC
            mov   ax, SEG DGROUP
            mov   ds, ax
            mov   ax, GMODE         ; Set screen mode
            int   10h
            mov   bx, OFFSET Queue  ; Make the first triangle
            mov   [bx].X1, 159      ; Put it in the center
            mov   [bx].Y1, 99       ; of the screen
```

```
                mov   [bx].X2, 159
                mov   [bx].Y2, 99
                mov   [bx].X3, 159
                mov   [bx].Y3, 99
                mov   bx, OFFSET DeltX1
                mov   cx, 6
ILoop:                                    ; Set the initial directions
                call  Rand                ; Get a random number
                and   ax, 7               ; Between 0 and 7
                sub   ax, 3               ; Between -3 and 4
                shl   ax, 1               ; Between -6 and 8
                mov   [bx], al            ; Save it
                inc   bx
                loop  ILoop

BgLoop:
                dec   Cntr                ; Decrement the change counter
                jnz   BL1                 ; If not zero, no change
                call  Rand
                and   ax, 31              ; ax = 0 to 31
                and   ax, 25              ; ax = 25 to 56
                mov   Cntr, ax            ; Make new Cntr
                call  Rand
                mov   cl, 25
                div   cl                  ; AH = 0 to 24
                add   ah, 5               ; AH = 5 to 29
                mov   al, ah
                cbw
                mov   QCnt, ax            ; Set the new queue size
BL1:
                mov   bx, Head            ; Get the triangle number
                mov   dl, 3               ; Set the color
                call  DrawTri
                push  ds                  ; Prepare for copy
                pop   es
                mov   si, Head            ; Get the current triangle
                shl   si, 1               ; Times 12 (size of triangle
                shl   si, 1               ; structure)
                mov   ax, si
                shl   si, 1
                add   si, ax
                add   si, OFFSET Queue    ; Add in the location of the
                                          ; array
                mov   di, Head            ; Figure the address of the
                                          ; next triangle in the queue
```

```
            inc  di                    ; Increment
            and  di, 31                ; Wrap at the end of the array
            mov  Head, di              ; Save the new head
            shl  di, 1
            shl  di, 1
            mov  ax, di
            shl  di, 1
            add  di, ax
            add  di, OFFSET Queue
            mov  cx, 12                ; Copy 12 bytes
            cld
            rep  movsb
            sub  di, 12                ; Point at the new triangle
            mov  bx, di
            call Adjust                ; Add the vectors
Hdlp:
            mov  ax, Head              ; See if Head
            sub  ax, Tail              ; is the right distance
            jns  HdFirst               ; from Tail
            add  ax, 32                ; Take care of wrapped
                                       ; pointers
HdFirst:
            cmp  ax, QCnt              ; If difference is > QCnt
            jb   NoErase
            mov  bx, Tail              ; Go to the Tail
            mov  dl, 0                 ; Set the color to black
            call DrawTri               ; Undraw the triangle
            mov  ax, Tail              ; Move the tail
            inc  ax
            and  ax, 1Fh
            mov  Tail, ax
            jmp  SHORT Hdlp            ; Do until Tail is within QCnt
                                       ; of Head
NoErase:
            mov  ah, 1                 ; Test for keypressed
            int  16h
            jnz  TRDone                ; If a key pressed exit
            jmp  BgLoop                ; Keep going
TRDone:
            mov  ah, 0                 ; Read the keyboard
            int  16h
            mov  ax, 3                 ; Reset mode
            int  10h
            mov  ah, 4Ch               ; DOS exit function
```

```
                          int  21h
                    Main ENDP

                    ; Draw a triangle
                    DrawTri    PROC
                               shl  bx, 1              ; Multiply Triangle number
                               shl  bx, 1              ; by 12
                               mov  ax, bx
                               shl  bx, 1
                               add  bx, ax
                               mov  ax, [Queue+bx].X1  ; Get the first point
                               mov  cx, [Queue+bx].Y1
                               mov  si, [Queue+bx].X2  ; Get the second point
                               mov  di, [Queue+bx].Y2
                               push dx
                               push bx
                               mov  bx, cx
                               call DrawLine           ; Draw a line between them
                               pop  bx
                               pop  dx
                               mov  ax, [Queue+bx].X2  ; Get the second point
                               mov  cx, [Queue+bx].Y2
                               mov  si, [Queue+bx].X3  ; Get the third point
                               mov  di, [Queue+bx].Y3
                               push dx
                               push bx
                               mov  bx, cx
                               call DrawLine           ; Draw a line
                               pop  bx
                               pop  dx
                               mov  ax, [Queue+bx].X3  ; Get the third point
                               mov  cx, [Queue+bx].Y3
                               mov  si, [Queue+bx].X1  ; And the first point
                               mov  di, [Queue+bx].Y1
                               mov  bx, cx
                               call DrawLine           ; Draw the line
                               ret
                    DrawTri    ENDP

                        ; Return a random number in ax
                    Rand       PROC
                               push dx                 ; Save DX
                               push cx                 ; and CX
                               cmp  seed, 0            ; See if the seed needs
                               jne  SeedOK             ; to be initialized
```

```
                mov    ax, 40h              ; BIOS Data area
                mov    es, ax
                mov    ax, WORD PTR es:[6Ch]
                mov    seed, ax             ; Save the new seed
SeedOK:
                mov    ax, seed             ; Get the low word of seed
                mov    cl, 13               ; multiplier
                mul    cl
                sub    dx, dx               ; Clear DX
                mov    cx, 257              ; Large prime
                div    cx
                mov    seed, dx             ; Save the remainder
                mov    ax, dx
                pop    cx                   ; Restore CX
                pop    dx                   ; and DX
                ret
Rand      ENDP

; Adjust all of the points at BX with the changes at Delta
Adjust    PROC
                mov    si, OFFSET DeltX1    ; Line up on first delta
                mov    dx, 3                ; Number of points
ADLoop:
                mov    cx, [bx]             ; Get the word at bx
                mov    al, [si]             ; Get the Delta
                cbw
                add    cx, ax               ; The new point
                jns    BigEnough1
                mov    WORD PTR [bx], 0     ; Set x to zero
                call   FixDelt
                jmp    SHORT ADY
BigEnough1:
                cmp    cx, 319              ; Check for right edge
                jb     SmallEngh1
                mov    WORD PTR [bx], 319
                call   FixDelt
                jmp    SHORT ADY
SmallEngh1:
                mov    [bx], cx
ADY:
                mov    cx, [bx+2]           ; Get the word at bx
                mov    al, [si+1]           ; Get the Delta
                cbw
                add    cx, ax               ; The new point
                jns    BigEnough2
```

```
                mov   WORD PTR [bx+2], 0   ; Set y to zero
                call  FixDelt
                jmp   SHORT ADNext
BigEnough2:
                cmp   cx, 199               ; Check for right edge
                jb    SmallEngh2
                mov   WORD PTR [bx+2], 199
                call  FixDelt
                jmp   SHORT ADNext
SmallEngh2:
                mov   [bx+2], cx
ADNext:
                add   bx, 4                 ; Next point
                add   si, 2                 ; Next Delta
                dec   dx
                jnz   ADLoop
                ret
Adjust    ENDP

; Change the two deltas at SI to random values
FixDelt   PROC
                call  Rand                  ; Change the x Delta
                and   al, 7                 ; AL = 0 to 7
                sub   al, 4                 ; AL = -4 to 3
                js    FD1                   ; If positive
                inc   al                    ; AL = -4 to 4 but not 0
FD1:
                shl   al, 1                 ; AL = -8 to 8 but not 0
                mov   [si], al              ; Save the x delta
                call  Rand                  ; Change the y delta
                and   al, 7                 ; AL = 0 to 7
                sub   al, 4                 ; AL = -4 to 3
                js    FD2                   ; If positive
                inc   al                    ; AL = -4 to 4 but not 0
FD2:
                shl   al, 1                 ; AL = -8 to 8 but not 0
                mov   [si+1], al            ; Save the y delta
                ret
FixDelt   ENDP

                .STACK    1024
END Main
```

The code at the beginning of the program sets up the data segment, and then calls BIOS to set the mode. Note that it uses the GMODE symbol that was used in the CGA and EGA draw routines. You will need to define this symbol before you assemble the program. After setting the mode, the program sets the first triangle in the queue to a point near the middle of the screen. The code in ILoop sets the values that will be used to calculate the corners of the next triangle. It does this by calling the random number routine and scaling the result so that it is between −6 and 8.

The code in BigLoop is where all the action occurs. The first step is to check the variable Cntr to see if it is time to change the queue size. If it is, the program calls the random number routine twice to get a new value for Cntr and a new value for QCnt.

If the queue size does not need to be changed, the program jumps to BL1. This code calls the DrawTri routine to draw the next triangle. After drawing the triangle, the program copies the co-ordinates for the triangle into the next queue position. Then it calls the Adjust routine to change the co-ordinates based on the current delta values.

When the new triangle is computed, the main loop draws the triangle at the end of the queue using the color black. This has the effect of erasing the triangle. The last step in the loop is to see if a key has been pressed and, if not, to jump back to the top of the loop.

To use this program, you will need to assemble it and the line routine and the pixel drawing routine, and then link them all together. For example, to make a version for the VGA screen, use these commands:

```
tasm cgapix
tasm drawline
tasm /dGMODE=19 moveline
tlink moveline drawline vgapix
```

Summary

The first step to using the video system is to determine the type of adapter available and the mode or modes to use. This information tells you where to find the video memory and how it is arranged. The next step is to use BIOS to select the mode and begin putting text or pixels in video memory.

In text modes, every other byte of video memory is the ASCII value of the character to be displayed. The bytes in between indicate the attribute or color of the character. For most adapters you can write directly to the video memory at any time to change the screen. On some CGA adapters, this will cause "snow" on the screen during updates. To eliminate the snow, you must write only to the screen during the horizontal or vertical retrace periods.

Graphics modes are a little more complex, due to the number of them. Each mode uses a different arrangement of pixels, colors, and memory layout.

Of course, once you have routines to draw pixels in each of the modes, you can use standard graphics algorithms to draw lines and circles and other shapes.

The examples in this chapter are designed to work together and with other programs. The `moveline` program is a good example of how to use these routines. Some tips for using them are as follows:

- Include an EXTRN statement for each of the functions that you want to use at the beginning of your program.

- Match the memory model for your program to the memory model used in these modules.

- The DS register must be set to the DGROUP segment, and the other registers set to the data values required for each routine.

- Do not count on any register remaining the same after calling these routines. If you must save a register, PUSH it on the stack before calling and POP it off when the routine returns.

V

Appendixes

► TASM and TLink Command-Line Options,

► Debugger Commands,

► BIOS and DOS Interrupts and Functions,

► ASCII Conversions,

Appendix *A* **TASM and TLink Command-Line Options**

Table A-1. *Options for Turbo Assembler*

Option	Action taken
/A	Sort segments into alphabetical order before writing them to the object file.
/B	This option is recognized but no action is taken.
/C	Create a cross-reference file.
/D\<sym>[=val]	Define the symbol \<sym> and set it equal to val if specified.
/E	Generate calls to a floating point library for floating point instructions.
/H or /?	Show a list of available options.
/I\<pathname>	Get include files from the directory specified (\<pathname>).
/J\<directive>	Do \<directive> before assembling the source file.
/KH\<number>	Set maximum number of symbols allowed. The default is 8192. The maximum value that can be set with this option is 32768.
/KS\<number>	Set the size of the string space. Turbo Assembler can determine the correct size automatically in most cases. This option is for the occasional case where the assembler miscalculates.
/L	Generate a listing file.
/LA	Put code generated by high level language interface directives in the listing file.

Option	Action taken
/M<number>	Set the number of passes to use to resolve forward references. (TASM 2.0 only.)
/ML	Make case-sensitive symbols.
/MU	Make all symbols uppercase.
/MV<number>	Set the number of characters used to compare symbol names. (TASM 2.0 only.)
/MX	Make linker symbols case-sensitive.
/N	Do not include the symbol table in the listing file.
/P	Check for CS overrides in protected mode. Since only certain executable segments can include data, using a CS override may be an error.
/Q	Do not put copyright and file dependency records in the OBJ file. This option can reduce the size of the object file. (TASM 2.0 only.)
/R	Generate ESC instructions to call the math co-processor for floating point instructions.
/S	Place segments in the object file in the order that they appear in the source file.
/T	Do not print anything if there are no errors.
/U	This option is recognized but no action is taken.
/W−[class]	Do not print warning messages for class.
/W+[class]	Print warning messages for class.
ASS	Assuming segment is 16-bit.
BRK	Brackets needed.
ICG	Inefficient code generation.
LCO	Location counter overflow.
OPI	Open IF conditional.
OPP	Open procedure.
OPS	Open segment.
OVF	Arithmetic overflow.
PDC	Pass-dependent construction.
PRO	CS override used.
/X	Include false conditionals in listings.
/Z	Display source lines with error messages.
/ZD	Add line number records to the object file.
/ZI	Add debug information records to the object file.

[...] denotes optional items, <...> indicates required arguments.

Table A-2. *Options for the Linker*

Option	Action taken
/3	Enable 32-bit processing.
/C	Case-sensitive symbols.
/D	Give warning for duplicate symbols found in libraries.
/E	Ignore the extended dictionary.
/I	Initialize all segments.
/L	Include line numbers in the EXE file.
/M	Create a map file.
/N	Do not use default libraries.
/O	Overlay switch.
/S	Include detailed segment map in the map file.
/T	Create COM file.
/U	Include debugging information in the EXE file
/X	Do not create a map file.
/YE	Use expanded memory for work space.
/YX	Use extended memory for work space.

Table B-1. *Command Keys*

Key	Action
ALT-=	Define a keystroke macro.
ALT-	End macro recording.
ALT-1-9	Switch to the window specified.
ALT-B	Open Breakpoint menu.
ALT-D	Open Data menu.
ALT-F	Open File menu.
ALT-F1	Bring up the last help screen.
ALT-F2	Set a breakpoint at a given address.
ALT-F3	Close the current window.
ALT-F4	Un-do the last traced instruction.
ALT-F5	Show the output screen.
ALT-F6	Re-open the last closed window.
ALT-F7	Execute a single source instruction.
ALT-F8	Run until the return instruction for the current procedure is found.
ALT-F9	Run to a specified address.
ALT-F10	Bring up the local menu.
ALT-H	Open Help menu.
ALT-O	Open Options menu.
ALT-R	Open Run menu.
ALT-V	Open View menu.
ALT-W	Open Window menu.
ALT-X	Return to MS-DOS.
CTRL->	Shift starting address up one byte.
CTRL<-	Shift starting address down one byte.

(continued)

Option	Action
CTRL-A	Move to previous word.
CTRL-C	Scroll down one screen.
CTRL-D	Move right one column.
CTRL-E	Move up one line.
CTRL-F	Move to next word.
CTRL-F2	Reload the program.
CTRL-F4	Evaluate an expression.
CTRL-F5	Move or re-size a window.
CTRL-F7	Add a variable to the Watches window.
CTRL-F8	Toggle the breakpoint at the cursor.
CTRL-F9	Run the program.
CTRL-F10	Open the local menu.
CTRL-R	Scroll up one screen.
CTRL-S	Move left one column.
CTRL-X	Move down one line.
ESC	Back out of an inspector window or menu.
F1	Bring up a help screen.
F2	Set breakpoint at the cursor location.
F3	Select a module.
F4	Run to the cursor location.
F5	Zoom/unzoom the current window.
F6	Go to the next window.
F7	Execute a single source line.
F8	Execute a single source line but skip calls.
F9	Run program.
F10	Select the menu bar.
INS	Begin marking a text block.
SHIFT-F1	Bring up the help file index.
SHIFT-TAB	Move to previous window.
SHIFT-Arrow	Move cursor between panes.

Table B-2. *The System Menu*

Command	Action
Restore Standard	Restore the standard window layout.
Repaint Desktop	Redraw the entire debugger screen.
About	Display information about the debugger.

Table B-3. *The File Menu*

Command	Action
Open	Load a program for debugging.
Change Dir	Change the current directory.
Get Info	Display program information.
DOS Shell	Go to an MS-DOS command prompt.
Resident	Make Turbo Debugger into a terminate-and-stay-resident program.
Symbol Load	Load the symbol table from a program.
Table Relocate	Move the base address of the symbol table.
Quit	Exit Turbo Debugger.

Table B-4. *The View Menu*

Command	Action
Breakpoints	Open a window for breakpoints.
Stack	Open a window for stack frame information.
Log	Open a window for a log of events and data.
Watches	Open a window for variables to watch.
Variables	Open a window for global and local variables.
Module	Open a window for the source module.
File	Open a window for showing disk files.
CPU	Open a window for CPU information.
Dump	Open a window to display memory.
Registers	Open a window for CPU registers and flags.
Numeric Processor	Open a window for floating point information.
Execution History	Open a window for executed instructions.
Hierarchy	Open a window for object and class information.
Another	Open another window for:
Module	
Dump	
File	

Table B-5. *The Run Menu*

Command	Action
Run	Run the program.
Go to Cursor	Run up to the location of the cursor.
Trace Into	Execute the next source line.
Step Over	Trace, but skip over calls.
Execute To	Run to a specified address.
Until Return	Run until the return for the current procedure is found.
Animate	Trace the program without user intervention.
Back Trace	Undo the last instruction traced.
Instruction Trace	Execute one instruction.
Arguments	Set the command line arguments.
Program Reset	Reload the current program.

Table B-6. *The Breakpoints Menu*

Command	Action
Toggle	Toggle the breakpoint at the cursor location.
At	Set a breakpoint at a given location.
Changed Memory Global	Set a breakpoint for when the given memory locations change.
Expression True Global	Set a breakpoint for when an expression is true.
Delete All	Delete all breakpoints.

Table B-7. *The Data Menu*

Command	Action
Inspect	Inspect a data object.
Evaluate/Modify	Evaluate an expression.
Add Watch	Add a variable to the Watches window.
Function Return	Display the current procedures return value.

Table B-8. *The Options Menu*

Command	Action
Language	Set the language to use for evaluating expressions.
Macros	Open macro submenu:
Create	Begin recording a macro.
Stop Recording	End the macro recording.
Remove	Delete a macro.
Delete All	Delete all macros.
Display Options	Set the screen options.
Path for Source	Directory that contains the source files.
Save Options	Save the screen layout and macros to a file.
Restore Options	Load the options from a file.

Table B-9. *The Window Menu*

Command	Action
Zoom	Make a window full screen or return it to normal size.
Next	Make the next window active.
Next Pane	Make the next pane in a multi-pane window, such as the CPU window, active.
Size/Move	Move or re-size the window.
Iconize/Restore	Make the window very small or return it to normal size.
Close	Close the active window.
Undo Close	Re-open the last closed window.
Dump Pane to Log	Save the current pane in the log.
User Screen	Show the program output.
Open window list	Display list of windows that can be activated.
Window Pick	Display menu of displayed windows.

Table B-10. *The Help Menu*

Command	Action
Index	Show the help file index.
Previous Topic	Show the last help screen.
Help on Help	Describe how to use the help system.

Appendix C BIOS and DOS Interrupts and Functions

This appendix presents information about the interrupt scheme available for MS-DOS systems. The term interrupt refers to the procedure of interrupting the CPU while it is in the middle of processing one routine, saving its state, setting it to process another routine, then restoring the previous state so that it continues the first routine where it left off.

The CPU executes instructions in order, moving upward in memory sequentially, managing this upward progression by values in the CS:IP register pair. The CS register locates a segment base address in memory; the IP register locates an offset from the CS location. As the CPU executes each instruction, it increments IP by one or more bytes, depending on the size of the instruction being executed. Thus CS:IP always points to the next instruction to be executed.

The instruction used to interfere with this progression is the INT instruction, which is used with a 1-byte number. The INT instruction forces the CPU to save the flags, CS, and IP registers to the stack. The number refers to an entry at the base of memory in a structure called the Interrupt Vector Table (IVT). Each entry contains 4 bytes, which combine to form an address to be loaded into the CS:IP pair. At that address is the first instruction of a routine that is designed to handle a specific chore. This routine, called the Interrupt Service Routine (ISR), ends with a final instruction, the IRET instruction. The IRET instruction pops values from the stack to the IP, CS, and Flags registers, effectively restoring the former state of the CPU.

To summarize, the Interrupt Vector Table (IVT) at the base of memory contains up to 256 valid addresses of Interrupt Service Routines (ISR). To run any of these routines, execute the INT instruction followed by a number, for instance, the well-known INT 21h. The CPU saves the current Flags and CS:IP, loads the address stored at the IVT location (21h), and executes the instructions it finds there. When the CPU encounters an IRET instruction, it pops three words from the stack into IP, CS, and the Flags.

The 8088 family of CPU handles interrupts of several classes. One class is the *hardware interrupt*. A hardware interrupt is one which is triggered by the appearance of a voltage on either of two of the CPU pins, the NMI (Non-Maskable Interrupt) or the INTR (Interrupt) pins. Thus, there are two classes of hardware interrupt.

The NMI pin goes high only if the system hardware is dangerously faulty—if memory is bad. There is no way to test this case, so the ISR takes the best action to terminate all system activity immediately and avoid risk of further damage (for instance, writing damaged data in the defective area of memory into a file on disk, to mention only one evil scenario).

The INTR pin goes high as a result of a signal from the 8259 Peripheral Interface Controller (PIC) chip. If the Interrupt Flag (IF) is set, the CPU honors the request; if IF is cleared, the CPU ignores the request and continues executing the instructions of the current routine.

The other kinds of interrupts are called *software interrupts*. Software interrupts come in several classes. If the CPU is forced into a division of any value by zero, it issues an interrupt. If the Trap Flag (TF) is set, the CPU generates an interrupt after executing every instruction. Whenever the Overflow Flag (OF) is set, the CPU generates an interrupt.

You can use the INT instruction to generate any interrupt at all. This instruction gives you complete control over the machine, but some interrupts are best left alone. The following tables describe the various interrupts and whatever variations are peculiar to each.

BIOS Interrupts and Their Functions

The first sixteen interrupts, INT 0 to INT 0Fh, have special status. Intel documentation defines these for the CPU, which should ensure the inviolability of those definitions. However, IBM has redefined some of those interrupts for use in PC DOS (and hence, MS-DOS) systems. The following reference distinguishes between IBM and Intel definitions and treats the IBM definition as one to respect.

The next sixteen interrupts, INT 10h to INT 1Fh, are generally referred to as the BIOS interrupts proper, as distinct from those numbered below 10h and the "DOS" interrupts beginning at 20h and above (although when people refer to the BIOS interrupts, they usually mean interrupts 0 to 1Fh).

In general, use the functions that are part of the INT 21h *executive dispatcher*, if you can; their behavior is strictly defined. If you have to use services available only in the BIOS interrupt set, remember that the behavior of these functions is not as dependable from manufacturer to manufacturer. Also, where there is an equivalent INT 21h function, the BIOS functions generally offer no appreciable speed advantage. Unless you know exactly what you are up to, avoid any use of interrupts 0 to 0Fh.

INTERRUPT 00h Divide by Zero

This interrupt is generated by a division instruction that forces the CPU to divide a value by zero.

INTERRUPT 01h Single-Step Interrupt

This interrupt is generated by each instruction if the Trap Flag (TF) is set.

INTERRUPT 02h Nonmaskable Interrupt

This interrupt is triggered by the NMI (Non-Maskable Interrupt) pin, and signals a calamitous shut-down condition.

INTERRUPT 03h Breakpoint Interrupt

This interrupt is available for debugging use. Set an INT 03h instruction as a breakpoint in your code and design an ISR to report the state of the CPU, various address locations, and possibly other data, depending upon your application.

INTERRUPT 04h Overflow Interrupt

This interrupt is for use with the INTO instruction. If the Overflow Flag (OF) is set, and if an arithmetic instruction resets OF and the INTO instruction follows, the CPU acts as if you entered an INT 04h instruction.

INTERRUPT 05h Print Screen Interrupt

This interrupt is defined by Intel as the Array Bounds Exception, but in all MS-DOS systems, this interrupt is generated by the Shift-PrtSc key combination and results in printing the ASCII characters that are represented by the values of the screen.

INTERRUPT 06h Reserved

This interrupt is defined by Intel as the Unused Opcode Exception, generated by an instruction that does not invoke a logic routine in the CPU.

INTERRUPT 07h Reserved

This interrupt is defined by Intel as the Escape Opcode Exception, generated by an instruction for the math coprocessor in the case that the math coprocessor is not present.

INTERRUPT 08h System Timer

This interrupt is generated by the 8259 PIC IRQ0, which is the highest priority request of the eight possible 8259 IRQ possibilities. The Interrupt Service Routine (ISR) calls INT 1Ch, known as the "Timer Tick," which is initialized as an empty ISR (a single IRET instruction), but which many TSR and other time-dependent routines "capture" to install their own routines.

INTERRUPT 09h Keyboard Interrupt

Intel defines this as reserved. In an MS-DOS system, this interrupt is generated each time a key is pressed down or released.

INTERRUPT 0Ah (Various)

Intel defines this as DMA0 interrupt. For AT class machines, this interrupt adds service routines for additional hardware interrupt requests (8259 IRQ) for IRQ8 to IRQ15.

INTERRUPT 0Bh (Various)

Intel defines this as DMA1 interrupt. For AT class machines, the ISR for this interrupt provides a routine that services COM2 and COM4. For PC class machines, this interrupt provides service for COM1 and COM3. On PS/2 class machines, this interrupt is reserved (its purpose is not documented).

INTERRUPT 0Ch (Various)

Intel defines this as INTO Interrupt. For AT class machines, this interrupt provides service for COM1 and COM 3. For PC class machines, this services COM2 and COM 4. For PS/2 machines, this interrupt is reserved.

INTERRUPT 0Dh (Various)

Intel defines this as INT1 interrupt. On AT class machines, this provides service for LPT2. For PC class machines designed with hard disks (PC XT), this provides hard disk control. On PS/2 Model 30, this provides hard disk control; on other PS/2 machines, this interrupt is reserved.

INTERRUPT 0Eh Disk Controller

Intel defines this as INT2 interrupt. On MS-DOS machines, this interrupt provides service for the floppy disk controller, but its use is obsolete, due to improvements in other BIOS functions.

INTERRUPT 0Fh LPT1 Controller

Intel defines this as INT3 interrupt. On AT and PC machines, this interrupt provides service for the printer controller, although its use is now obsolete. On PS/2 machines, this interrupt is reserved.

INTERRUPT 10h Video

Interrupt 10h contains an elaborate set of functions and subfunctions. Each function is invoked by loading the appropriate value in the AH register. In the case in which a function hosts a set of subfunctions, invoke a subfunction by loading the appropriate value in the AL register. You may have to load other registers with appropriate values, for instance, the ASCII value for a character to be displayed, the address of a string, or a value specifying an attribute.

AH = 00h Set Video Mode

Use this function to set the display mode as well as clear the screen and select among several video adapters. Set the appropriate value in AL to enable a particular function. The entire family of subfunctions from AL = 00 to AL = 7Fh has a corresponding family from AL = 80h to AL = FFh; use these upper values to bypass the clear-screen function.

Entry: AH = 00h

The following values write to the video display memory area at segment 0B800h and activate CGA, EGA, MCGA, or VGA adapters:

AL = 00 or 80h, text, 40 × 25, monochrome
AL = 01 or 81h, text, 40 × 25, 16 colors
AL = 02 or 82h, text, 80 × 25, monochrome
AL = 03 or 83h, text, 80 × 25, 16 colors
AL = 04 or 84h, graphics, 320 × 200, 4 colors
AL = 05 or 85h, graphics, 320 × 200, monochrome
AL = 06 or 86h, graphics, 640 × 200, monochrome

The following value writes to 0B000h and activates the MDA, EGA, or VGA adapters:

AL = 07 or 87h, text, 80 × 25, monochrome

The following values write to segment 0B800h and activate the PCjr or Tandy 1000 built-in display circuitry:

AL = 08 or 88h, graphics, 160 × 200, 16 colors
AL = 09 or 89h, graphics, 320 × 200, 16 colors
AL = 0Ah or 8Ah, graphics, 640 × 200, 4 colors

The following values are reserved for internal use of the EGA BIOS:

AL = 0Bh or 8Bh, reserved
AL = 0Ch or 8Ch, reserved

The following values write to segment 0A000h and activate the EGA and VGA adapters:

AL = 0Dh or 8Dh, graphics, 320 × 200, 16 colors
AL = 0Eh or 8Eh, graphics, 640 × 200, 16 colors
AL = 0Fh or 8Fh, graphics, 640 × 350, 16 monochrome
AL = 10h or 90h, graphics, 640 × 350, 16 colors

The following value writes to segment 0A000h and activates the MCGA or VGA adapters:

AL = 11h or 91h, graphics, 640 × 480, monochrome

The following value writes to segment 0A000h and activates the VGA only:

AL = 12h or 92h, graphics, 640 × 480, 16 colors

The following value writes to segment 0A000h and activates the MCGA or VGA adapters:

AL = 13h or 93h, graphics, 320 × 200, 256 colors

AL values from 14h to 7Fh are not uniformly used. Manufacturers have chosen values to suit their needs. If you want to invoke the custom features of a video adapter, consult the documentation for the AL value and its corresponding mode.

Return: N/A

AH = 01h Set Cursor Type

Use this function in video text mode to determine the shape and blinking characteristics of the cursor.

Entry: AH = 01h

The CH and CL registers control the cursor size and blinking characteristics. In CH, bits 0 through 4 indicate the starting scan lines of the cursor, and bits 5 and 6 control the blinking characteristic (00 normal, 01 invisible, 10 slow, 11 fast). In CL, bits 0 through 4 indicate the ending scan lines. The cursor's shape depends on your choice of bit settings for CH and CL.

Return: N/A

AH = 02h Set Cursor Position

Use this function in video text mode to write the cursor to a position on the display.

Entry: AH = 02h

BH contains the page number, from 0 to 7, depending on the mode
DH and DL contain the row and column numbers

Return: N/A

AH = 03h Get Cursor Position and Characteristics

Use this function to inspect the current page, position, shape, and blinking characteristics of the cursor.

Entry: AH = 03h

Return: BH contains the page number, from 0 to 7
DH and DL contain the row and column numbers

CH contains the cursor blinking and start scan lines
CL contains the cursor ending scan lines

AH = 04h Read Light Pen Position

Use this function to inspect the current position of a light pen. This function is not valid on PS/2 machines.

Entry: AH = 04h

Return: DH and DL contain the current row and column numbers
CH or CX, depending on the mode, contains the pixel row
BX contains the pixel column
AH contains 1 or 0, indicating the light pen is triggered or not

AH = 05h Select Display Page

Use this function to select which page to display, from 0 to 7 depending on the mode (MDA allows one page only).

Entry: AH = 05h
AL = 0 to 7 for modes 00h, 01h, 07h, 0Dh: EGA, VGA
AL = 0 to 3 for modes 0Eh: EGA, VGA
AL = 0 to 1 for modes 0Fh, 10h: EGA, VGA
AL = 0 to 7 for modes 00h, 01h, 02h, 03h: MCGA
AL = 0 to 7 for modes 00h, 01h: CGA
AL = 0 to 3 for modes 02h, 03h: CGA

Other machines, such as the PCjr. and Cordata use other values in AL to perform other related tasks. Refer to the documentation of a particular machine or display adapter to exercise its unique features.

Return: N/A

AL = 06h Scroll Page Up

Use this function to scroll text upward a specified number of lines, adding blank lines to the bottom. You can specify values in CH,CL and DH,DL to identify a rectangular portion of the screen—a window—within which to scroll.

Entry: AH = 06h
AL contains the number of lines to scroll; if zero, the whole screen
BH contains values specifying the attributes for the blank lines
CH and CL contain the row and column of the upper left corner
DH and CL contain the row and column of the lower right corner

Return: N/A

Ah = 07h Scroll Page Down

This function works similarly to Function 6, but scrolls lines of text within a window down.

    Entry: AH = 07h
            AL contains number of lines to scroll; zero to blank the entire screen
            BH contains values specifying the attributes of the blank lines
            CH and CL contain the row and column of the upper left corner
            DH and DL contain the row and column of the lower right corner

AL = 08h Read Character and Attribute at Cursor

Use this function to inspect the character and its attributes that are at the cursor position.

    Entry: AH = 08h
            BH contains a value specifying the display page

    Return: AH contains a value specifying the attributes
            AL contains the ASCII value of the character

AH = 09h Write Character and Attribute at Cursor

Use this function to change the text character and its attributes that are at the cursor position.

    Entry: Ah = 09h
            AL contains the ASCII value for the character
            BH specifies the display page
            BL contains a value specifying the attributes of the new character
            CX specifies the number of times to duplicate the action

Note that if CX specifies additional writes, in text mode the function writes the identical character and attribute to subsequent character positions, wrapping down to the next line as necessary until done. In graphics mode, the function does not continue to the next lowest line. In either case, the cursor remains at its original position.

If BL contains its MSB set (value of 80h or greater), the function XORs the character with whatever occupies that position.

    Return: N/A

AH = 0Ah Write Character at Cursor

Use this function to write a character at the cursor position without changing the attribute characteristics of that location.

    Entry: AH = 0Ah
            AL contains the ASCII value for the character
            BH specifies the display page

BL specifies the color, if in graphics mode

CX specifies the number of times to duplicate the action

Return: N/A

Note that CX and BL values dictate similar operations as they do in Function 09h.

AH = 0Bh Set Color Palette

Use this function to specify which color palette is active or which color from that palette to display.

Entry: AH = 0Bh

BH contains palette color ID, 0 or 1

BL contains a value to be interpreted, depending on BH

If BH contains 0, the value in BL specifies background and border colors. If BH contains 1, the value in BL specifies which palette is to be selected.

Return: N/A

AH = 0Ch Write a Dot to a Pixel Location

Use this function to write a dot to a specified pixel position. Depending on the mode, you may be able to specify color.

Entry: AH = 0Ch

AL specifies the color of the dot, depending on the mode

BH specifies the video page number

DX specifies pixel row (0 to 199 or 349)

CX specifies pixel column (0 to 319 or 639, depending on the mode)

Return: N/A

AH = 0Dh Read Dot Color at a Pixel Location

Use this function to inspect the color at a specified pixel location.

Entry: AH = 0Dh

BH specifies the video page number

DX specifies the pixel row (0 to 199 or 349)

CX specifies the pixel column (0 to 319 or 639)

Return: AL contains a value that specifies the color

AH = 0Eh Write a Character in TTY Mode

Use this function to write an ASCII value to the display and increment the cursor position. Control characters behave according to their ASCII definitions and do not generate the associated graphics characters.

Entry: AH = 0Eh

> AL contains the ASCII value for a character
> BH must specify the current display page
> BL specifies the color, if in graphics mode

Return: N/A

AH = 0Fh Get Current Mode

Use this function to inspect the mode for the current video display page.

Entry: AH = 0Fh

Return: AH contains a value specifying the number of columns on the
> screen
> AL contains a value specifying the display mode
> BH contains a value identifying the current display page

AH = 10h Set Palette Registers

Use this function to control palette color information for EGA, VGA, PS/2, PCjr.,
and Tandy 1000 machines.

Entry: AH = 10h

> AL contains 0, 1, or 2 to specify palette, border, or all registers
> AL = 0, BL specifies palette register, BH specifies color value
> AL = 1, BH specifies color value
> AL = 2, ES:DX specifies address of a 17-byte list of colors
> AL = 3, for EGA, VGA, and MCGA, toggles intensity and blinking
> bits
> BL = 0 or 1 specifies intensity or blinking
> AL values 7 and above specify various read, write, or select
> functions, each of which require particular register combinations,
> some depending upon machine type

Return: N/A for AL = 0 to 3; various for other functions

AH = 11h to AH = 1Ch are specific to EGA, VGA, and later models of PC
and PS/2 machines. AH = 1Dh to FFh are reserved or are used in particular ways
depending upon an application or system configuration.

INTERRUPT 11h Get Equipment List

Use this interrupt to inspect which equipment is available as part of the system.

Entry: N/A

Return: AX contains a bit-wise word that specifies equipment (unless
> specified differently, a one value in the bit location indicates an
> installed device; zero indicates no device)

Bit	Meaning
0	Floppy disk drive
1	8087 math coprocessor
2, 3	11b indicates at least 64k motherboard RAM; PS/2: bit 2 indicates pointing device, bit 3 not used
4, 5	Initial video mode: 01b specifies 40 × 25 color; 10b specifies 80 × 25 color; 11b specifies 80 × 25 monochrome
6, 7	Number of disk drives (meaningless if bit 0 is zero): 00b specifies 1 drive; 01b specifies 2 drives; 10b specifies 3 drives; 11b specifies 4 drives
8	Not used (PCjr: specifies DMA present)
9–11	Number of serial cards
12	Game port (PS/2: not used)
13	Not used (PS/2: specifies internal modem)
14, 15	Number of printers

INTERRUPT 12h Memory Size

Use this interrupt to inspect the number of contiguous 1k memory blocks up to 640k.

Enter: N/A

Return: AX contains a value that reflects the memory available upon startup, not including EMS or extended memory

INTERRUPT 13h Floppy Disk

Use the functions of this interrupt to inspect and control various floppy disk drive functions. Functions AH = 00h to 05h work on all MS-DOS machines. Functions 06h and greater are defined differently depending upon machine type. Generally, AH is associated with the function or a status value; AL is associated with the number of sectors; CH is associated with the track number, CL with sector number; DH is associated with the head number (0 or 1) and DL with the drive number (00h to 7Fh specifies a floppy disk, 80h to FFh specifies a hard disk). ES:BX may specify the address of the current disk buffer.

AH = 00h Reset Floppy Disk Controller

Use this function to reset the floppy disk controller in the event of a disk I/O error.

Entry: AH = 00h
> DL specifies the drive; if the MSB is set, DL specifies a hard disk drive

Return: CF = 0 or 1, indicating success or failure
> AH contains a status byte (refer to AH = 01h)

AH = 01h Get Disk Status

Use this function to inspect the status of the most recent disk operation.

Enter: AH = 01h

Return: AH contains a status byte as follows:
> 00h = success
> 01h = bad command
> 02h = address mark not found: bad sector
> 03h = write attempt on write-protected disk
> 04h = sector not found
> 05h = hard disk reset failure
> 06h = diskette may have been changed
> 07h = hard disk parameter failure
> 08h = DMA overrun
> 09h = DMA across 64k boundary
> 0Ah = hard disk bad sector
> 0Bh = hard disk bad track
> 0Ch = invalid track
> 10h = CRC/ECC error
> 11h = corrected ECC
> 20h = controller failure
> 40h = seek failure
> 80h = time out, floppy drive not ready
> AAh = hard disk drive not ready
> BBh = hard disk undefined error

AH = 02h Read Floppy Disk Sectors

Use this function to read data from one or more sectors into memory.

Entry: AH = 02h
> AL contains the number of sectors to read (1 to 9)
> CH specifies the track number (0 to 39)
> CL specifies the starting sector number (1 to 9)
> DH specifies the head (0 or 1)
> DL specifies the drive number (0 to 3)
> ES:BX specifies the start address of the current disk buffer

Return: CF = 0 or 1, indicating success or failure

AH = 0 or status (per function AH = 01h)

AL = number of sectors read

AH = 03h Write Floppy Disk Sectors

Use this function to write data from a buffer in memory specified by ES:BX to sectors on the floppy disk drive as specified by AL, CH, CL, DH, and DL.

Entry: AH = 03h

AL specifies the number of sectors to write

CH specifies the track number (0 to 39)

CL specifies the sector number (1 to 9)

DH specifies the head (0 or 1)

DL specifies the drive number (0 to 3)

ES:BX specifies the start address of the current disk buffer

Return: CF = 0 or 1, indicating success or failure

AH contains the status byte

AL contains the number of sectors written

AH = 04h Verify Sectors

Use this function to compare the CRC (Cyclic Redundancy Check) value for a sector against the data contained within that sector. This is essentially a checksum method of data verification.

Entry: AH=04h; AL, CH, CL, DH, and DL indicate usual specifications

Return: CF = 0 or 1, indicating success or failure

AH contains the status code

AH = 05h Format a Track

This function formats tracks on an individual basis. Do not use this function unless you are absolutely certain of what you are doing, because you can easily destroy the FAT chaining scheme and thus lose the contents for all data on all subsequent tracks.

AH = 06h and above behave differently for different machines. Refer to the appropriate technical reference.

INTERRUPT 14h Serial I/O

Use the functions within this interrupt family to initialize, read, write, and inspect the serial port. Functions AH = 04h and above are specific to particular machines. Generally, the DX register specifies a particular port: 0, 1, 2, and 3 specify COM1, COM2, COM3, and COM4. The PC and older PC/XT machines support only COM1 and COM2.

AH = 00h Initialize a Serial Port

Use this function to initialize the serial port specified by the value in DX according to the parameter value in AL.

Entry: AH = 00h

DX specifies the port (COM1 or greater)

AL contains a bitwise byte that specifies parameters as follows

Bit	Meaning
0, 1	10b specifies a seven-bit word
	11b specifies an eight-bit word
2	0b or 1b specifies 1 or two stop bits
3, 4	00b or 10b specifies no parity, 01b or 11b specifies odd or even parity
5–7	from 000b to 111b specifies baudrates from 110, 150, 300, 600, 1200, 2400, 4800, and 9600

Return: AH contains a bitwise word indicating port status as follows

Bit	Meaning
0	Data ready
1	Overrun error
2	Parity error
3	Framing error
4	Break detection
5	Transmission buffer empty
6	Transmission shift register empty
7	Time out; all other bits invalid

AL contains a bitwise word indicating modem status

Bit	Meaning
0	Clear-To-Send (CTS) has changed
1	Data-Set-Ready (DSR) has changed
2	Trailing edge ring detection
3	Receive line signal has changed

Bit	Meaning
4	Clear-To-Send (CTS)
5	Data-Set-Ready (DSR)
6	Ring detection
7	Receive line signal detection

AH = 01h Write Character to Serial Port

Use this function to write a character to the serial port specified by DX.

Entry: AH = 01h
AL contains the byte to be transferred
DX specifies the port number

Return: AH indicates success or failure if the MSB (bit 7) is cleared or set;
if MSB = 1 (bit 7 is set), bits 0 to 6 indicate the cause of failure;
see port status bits in AH described for Function AH = 00h

AH = 02h Read Character from Serial Port

Use this function to read a character into AL from the serial port.

Entry: AH = 02h
DX specifies the port number

Return: AH indicates success or failure (MSB = 0 or 1), and in the event
of failure, bits 0 to 6 reflect cause (per port status description
described for AH = 00h)
AL contains the byte transferred from the port

AH = 03h Get Serial Port Status

Use this function to inspect the status of the serial port specified by DX. This
function works similarly to function AH = 00h, except that it does not initialize
or otherwise disturb the registers in the port.

AH = 04h and above are specific to various machines. Refer to the
technical reference for each machine for details.

INTERRUPT 15h Cassette Interface

The functions contained within the family of INT 15h are divided into various
categories. Functions AH = 00h to 03h are concerned with control of a cassette
storage device, now obsolete. Many more functions have been added to this
interrupt, but they are equally obscure, having to do with specific machines or
software products.

INTERRUPT 16h Keyboard

AH = 00h Read Character from Keyboard Buffer

Use this function to read the ASCII value and scan code of the key next entered into the keyboard buffer.

> Entry: AH = 00h

> Return: AH contains the keyboard scan code
> AL contains the ASCII value of the character

AH = 01h Get Keyboard Buffer Status

Use this function to check for an unprocessed keystroke in the keyboard buffer.

> Entry: AH = 01h

> Return: ZF = 0 or 1, indicating a keystroke ready or none waiting
> AH contains the scan code
> AL contains the ASCII value of the character

AH = 02h Get Keyboard Shift Byte

Use this function to inspect the keyboard shift status byte, a bitwise byte that reflects the current status of certain special keys.

> Entry: AH = 02h

> Return: AL contains the keyboard shift status byte, which indicates the following key conditions

Bit	Meaning
0	Right shift key is down
1	Left shift key is down
2	Control key is down
3	Alt key is down
4	Scroll lock is on
5	Num lock is on
6	Caps lock is on
7	Insert key is on

Functions AH = 04h and above are specific to particular machines. Check the documentation for the specific machine you are using.

INTERRUPT 17h Printer

Use the functions in this interrupt family to initialize, inspect, and send a character to the printer. Generally, the AL register contains the character to be printed, the DX register specifies the printer (0 to 2), and the printer status is returned as a bitwise byte in the AH register.

AH = 00h Write Character to Printer

Use this function to send a character to the printer.

> Entry: AH = 00h
> AL contains the character to be printed
> DX contains a value that specifies which printer to use (0 to 2)

> Return: AH contains a bitwise byte that reflects the status of the printer after the function executes, according to the following correspondence

Bit	Meaning
0	Timeout, printer not connected, not on, not working
1, 2	Not used
3	I/O error
4	Printer selected
5	Paper out
6	Acknowledge
7	Not busy

AH = 01h Initialize Printer

Use this function to initialize IBM or Epson and compatible printers with two bytes, 08h and 0Ch (some noncompatible printers may react adversely).

> Entry: AH = 01h
> DX contains a value that specifies which printer to use (0 to 2)

> Return: AH contains the printer status byte following execution of this function (see Function AH = 00h)

AH = 02h Get Printer Status

Use this function to inspect the status of the printer.

> Entry: AH = 02h
> DX specifies which printer to inspect (0 to 2)

> Return: AH contains the printer status byte (see Function AH = 00h)

INTERRUPT 18 ROM BASIC

Use this interrupt to transfer control from PC DOS to Tiny BASIC that resides in ROM on IBM machines.

INTERRUPT 19 Warm Book without Reset

Use this interrupt to reboot the machine by reading the contents of the boot sector into memory and continuing the boot process from that point on. Contents of RAM memory are otherwise not disturbed.

INTERRUPT 1A Clock

Use the functions in this interrupt family to read or set the time of day recorded in the system clock as the number of clock ticks past midnight (18.2065 ticks per second).

AH = 00h Read Time of Day

Use this function to inspect the time of day recorded in the system clock.

Entry: Ah = 00h

Return: AL contains a zero value if this function has executed within 24 hours of the previous midnight; passing midnight sets this "midnight flag"
CX and DX contain the high and low words of the clock count

AH = 01h Set Time of Day

Use this function to write into the system clock a new value that represents the number of clock ticks since the previous midnight.

Entry: AH = 01h
CX and DX contain the high and low words of the new clock count

Functions Ah = 02h and above are specific to particular machines. Check the documentation for the particular machine with which you are working.

INTERRUPT 1Bh Control-Break

To most users, the difference between Control-Break and Control-C is indistinguishable. In fact, this interrupt provides an important feature that distinguishes the Control-Break key from Control-C. When the user presses the Control-Break combination, the keyboard generates INT 1Bh immediately, thus interrupting whatever CPU activity is taking place. The nature of this interruption depends on the particular Interrupt Service Routine (ISR) to which vector 1Bh points.

When the user presses the Control-C combination, DOS receives it in the same way that it receives any other characters into the keyboard buffer. When DOS finally interprets the character, it sets a Control-C flag. DOS follows its normal keyboard-handling sequence, and in due course checks the Control-C flag and then activating whatever Control-C error-handling routine is installed.

The key difference is that the invocation of INT 1Bh allows immediate interruption of all system activity.

As a program designer, you have a choice of error handling. The Control-C choice allows DOS to complete any activities (for instance, writing to a file) before executing the error handler. The Control-Break choice lets you provide a more severe error-handling routine, but at the risk of disrupting DOS activities. It is sometimes a wise choice simply to install an IRET instruction as the INT 1Bh ISR, or you may want to install an ISR that simply sets the Control-C flag and lets the current process continue until DOS detects that warning in its proper course.

INTERRUPT 1Ch Clock Tick

This interrupt is triggered by INT 08h. Its default ISR is a simple IRET instruction. It is common practice for time-sensitive TSR applictions to "capture" this interrupt, installing a new vector that points to their ISR. As part of the technique of interrupt capture, it is important to record the original IVT address and provide control to that ISR, normally before your routine executes. In other words, when the captured interrupt is invoked, control is passed to your ISR. As one of your first jobs, you pass control to the original ISR, letting its IRET return control to you. Upon completion, your IRET returns control to the calling procedure.

Because the system default is an IRET, it may be tempting simply to let the IRET at the end of your ISR suffice instead of storing the original vector and return control to that ISR. In the case that another application has previously captured the INT 1Ch vector, your neglect will effectively bypass the ISR of the other application. The effect may be that the user notices that whenever your application is loaded, one or more other applications fail. If so, your reputation and that of your application may suffer. Always return control to the original ISR vector.

If you choose to install your own ISR for INT 1Ch, keep it short. INT 1Ch is triggered by INT 08h, which has the highest priority of all the hardware interrupts. If your ISR takes longer than 55 milliseconds, the system timer interrupts your ISR with INT 08h, which triggers INT 1Ch, which triggers your too-long ISR, and the result is that the system "hangs" there.

Keep it very short. Other ISRs may be installed along with yours, and the aggregate slow-down of several INT 1Ch ISRs may be annoying or even disruptive, depending upon the applications affected (communications or file I/O).

INTERRUPT 1Dh Video Initialization Tables

The vector at interrupt location 1Dh does not point to code. Rather, it points to a table that contains initialization values for the 6845 video controller. Do not execute an interrupt instruction for this location, because you would simply load the CS:IP registers with the first two word values in the table, with unpredictable results.

Do not play with these values. If the 6845 controller receives incorrect data, it can destroy the video display device almost instantly, much more quickly than you might be able to save it. Don't experiment with this at all.

INTERRUPT 1Eh Disk Initialization Table

The vector at interrupt location 1Eh does not point to code, but to a table of values that initialize the disk controller. As with INT 1Dh, similar warnings apply. Do not issue an interrupt instruction for this vector, and do not experiment with the values in this table; the results can be permanent loss of all data.

INTERRUPT 1Fh Graphics Character Set

The vector at interrupt location 1Fh does not point to code, but to a table of values that define the shapes of characters with ASCII values 128 to 255. Each character shape is defined by the bit settings in each of 8 bytes, the first byte defining the on/off state of pixels in the top row, the second byte defining pixels in the second row, and so on, with the eighth byte defining pixels in the eighth, or bottom, row. In other words, each character is a shape within an 8" by 8" pixel box.

This vector does not point to code, so don't issue an interrupt instruction for this vector. Also, experimenting with the values in this location alters the appearance of the high-valued characters. If you lose control, you have to reboot to restore graphic order.

The DOS Interrupt Family, INT 20h to INT 0FFh

The Interrupt Vector Table entries from INT 20h and above a defined by MS-DOS. They contain a variety of types. Some entries identify data structures, some contain CPU opcode, some are obsolete, some undocumented, and so on. Additionally, at any particular time, some interrupts may not work as advertised, depending on the system hardware manufacturer, operating system version, and other third-party software installed.

The following set of interrupt reference entries is accurate to the best of our abilities to ferret out information from IBM, Microsoft, third-party application vendors, and authors in The Waite Group extended family, as well as various programmers, consultants, and MS-DOS gossips we have encountered over the last ten years. Consider this information a guideline. MS-DOS implementations differ through versions and vendors. TSRs and other tricky software programs may alter any parts of the system. Especially view with skepticism those features which are officially "undocumented," "reserved," or "unused." If you use them or alter them in any way, be sure to experiment with them extensively on any and all systems on which your program may run before you release your program.

INTERRUPT 20h Program Terminate

This interrupt is for MS-DOS use only. Do not use INT 20h to terminate your program. Use DOS Function 4Ch for proper program termination.

Entry: CS = segment address of program's PSP

Return: None

INTERRUPT 21h Functions

Interrupt 21h, the Executive Function Dispatcher, or "DOS call," contains a set of nearly 100 functions that provide most services needed by an application program, including opening, closing, reading and writing files, reading keyboard input, writing to the display screen, getting and setting time and date, and a variety of control variables.

Briefly, the scheme works as follows. To call a DOS function, you have to load AH with the number of the function. You may have to load other registers, and you may also have to save any registers that will be changed.

When you have set up the CPU, issue INT 21h. The dispatch routine matches the value in AH to a table and executes the specified function. The function will succeed or fail, depending on your setup and also on the current state of the system. If it fails, it usually returns with the Carry Flag set and an error code in AX. It is good practice, therefore, to follow the INT 21h call with a JC and jump if CF is set to an error-handling routine.

Note: Unless otherwise noted, all functions check for Control-Break and Control-C. Upon detection, Interrupt 23h is executed.

Note: Some functions, notably those that move bytes from the console, do not work predictably if the device is redirected. Be particularly careful to avoid using these with routines that depend on detection of an End of File (EOF) marker or that may write beyond the capacity of a disk.

AH = 00h Program Terminate [All Versions]

This function is an older routine that terminates the current program. Do not use this; use Function 4Ch instead.

This function deallocates all memory belonging to the current program, flushing all file buffers (be sure to close FCBs properly if you call this function or you will lose whatever data you didn't save).

This function accesses the current PSP to restore vectors for INT 22h (program termination, PSP offset 0Ah), INT 23h (Control-Break, PSP offset 0Ch), and INT 24h (Critical-Break, PSP offset 0Fh). Control returns to the termination handler address specified at PSP offset 0Ah.

Entry: CS = segment address of program's PSP

Return: None

Related Functions: AH = 31h, AH = 4Ch

Related Interrupt: INT 20h

AH = 01h Input Character from Console with Echo [All Versions]

Use this function to read a character from the keyboard (STDIN). The routine polls the keyboard indefinitely until the user hits a key. The routine displays the character to the display (echo) and returns the ASCII code in the AL register. Normally, this routine detects Control-C.

If the user typed in a character from the extended character set, AL = 0. Therefore, always test AL for zero, and if true, call Function 1 a second time to read the value of the extended character.

If STDIN has been redirected, this function works somewhat unpredictably. It does not detect Control-C unless BREAK is ON, nor does it detect an EOF.

Entry: None

Return: If AL > 0 on first call, AL = standard ASCII character
If AL = 0 on first call, call Function 01h a second time to obtain extended ASCII character in AL

Related Functions: AH = 06h, AH = 07h, AH = 08h, AH = 3Fh

AH = 02h Output Character to Console [All Versions]

Use this function to write a character to the display (STDOUT). Load DL with the ASCII number for the character you wish to write (remember to convert binary numbers to their ASCII equivalents). The routine displays the value in DL.

Entry: DL = character to write to the display [version 1 only] or to StdOut [versions 2, 3, 4]

Return: None

Related Functions: AH = 06h, AH = 09h, AH = 40h

AH = 03h Input Character from Auxiliary Port [All Versions]

Use this function to read a character from the Standard Auxiliary Device (StdAux, default of which is COM1). This routine polls StdAux indefinitely until it receives a character. It returns the ASCII code for the character in the AL register. This routine responds to Control-C from the keyboard.

Generally, the StdAux device has no mechanism for storing characters and MS-DOS has no built-in routine to detect when a character is ready. This function offers no provision for polling the StdAux device. It is your job to write a routine to manage detection and transfer to memory. Because the requirements of many applications demand fast detection and data transfer, this function may not be suitable. Indeed, most commercial programs that control the serial port manage the job entirely, avoiding use of MS-DOS or BIOS calls. See Chapter 14 for further discussion.

Entry: None

Return: AL = character from first serial port [version 1 only] or from STDAUX [versions 2, 3, 4]

Related Function: AH = 3Fh

Related Interrupt: INT 14h

AH = 04h Output Character to Auxiliary Port [All Versions]

Use this function to write a character to StdAux (generally COM1). This routine polls the output device indefinitely until it (StdAux) is ready to receive a character. Load the DL register with the ASCII code of the character to send, load AH = 04h, then issue INT 21h. This routine responds to Control-C from the keyboard.

As with Function 3, this function does not allow you to determine the status of the output device; use of the function alone does not guarantee transmission. You must determine if this function is suitable.

Entry: DL = character to output to STDAUX

Return: None

Related Function: AH = 40h

Related Interrupt: INT 14h

AH = 05h Output Character to Printer [All Versions]

Use this function to send a character to the standard print device (LPT1 or PRN, generally the parallel port). This routine polls the output device indefinitely until it is not busy. Load DL with the ASCII code for the character, load AH with 05h, and issue INT 21h. This routine responds to Control-C from the keyboard.

As with Functions 3 and 4, this function does not provide a means to detect the status of the output device. Your program must somehow determine that the device will accept the character.

Entry: DL = character to output to STDPRN

Return: None

Related Function: AH = 40h

AH = 06h Direct Console I/O [All Versions]

Use this function to read and write any and all ASCII characters (i.e., the exact ASCII representation of the value of a byte, including control codes and the extended character set) from the console (both StdIn and StdOut, generally the display and keyboard). Naturally, this routine does not respond to Control-C from the keyboard.

The following description assumes that StdIn and StdOut have not been redirected. To read a character from StdIn, load DL with 0FFh; if the zero flag is clear (NZ), read the input character in the AL register. If the zero flag (ZR) is set, the input device has not sent a character. As with Function 1, AL = 00 indicates an extended character (assuming zero flag is clear), so issue the call a second time to retrieve it.

To write a character to StdOut, load DL with that character (not 0FFh), load AH with 06h, and issue INT 21h.

Entry: If DL <> 0FFh, output character in DL to STDOUT; otherwise perform direct console input

Return: None for direct console output; for direct console input; ZF = 1 if no character available, else AL = character

Related Functions: AH = 01h, AH = 02h, AH = 07h, AH = 08h, AH = 3Fh, AH = 40h

AH = 07h Direct Input Character from Console without Echo [All Versions]

Use this function to read a character from StdIn (the keyboard) without echoing it to StdOut (the display). This routine polls the input device indefinitely until it receives a character. Load AH with 07h, read the character in AL. As with Functions 1 and 6, if AL = 00, reissue the call to read an extended character. This routine does not respond to Control-C from the keyboard.

Entry: None

Return: AL = character from STDIN

Related Functions: AH = 01h, AH = 06h, AH = 08h, AH = 3Fh, AH = 40h

AH = 08h Input Character from Console without Echo [All Versions]

Use this function to read a character from StdIn (the keyboard) without echoing it to StdOut (the display). This routine polls the input device indefinitely until it receives a character. Load AH with 08h, issue INT 21h, read the character in AL. As with Functions 1, 6, and 7, if AL = 00, reissue the call to read an extended character. This routine responds to Control-C from the keyboard.

Entry: None

Return: AL = character from STDIN

Related Functions: AH = 01h, AH = 06h, AH = 08h, AH = 3Fh, AH = 40h

AH = 09h Output String to Console [All Versions]

Use this function to send a string of characters to StdOut (the display). First, be sure that the last character of the string is "$" (24h). The string may contain any ASCII characters from 00 to 0FFh (but this function ends transmission when it encounters the first "$", and the function does not transmit the "$").

Load DS:DX with the start address of the string, load AH with 09h, issue INT 21h, and the function will write the string. This function responds to Control-C from the keyboard.

Entry: DS:DX = pointer to string terminated by "$"

Return: None

Related Functions: AH = 02h, AH = 06h, AH = 40h

AH = 0Ah Input Buffered String from Console with Echo [All Versions]

Use this function to store a line of text from StdIn (the keyboard). This routine echoes characters to StdOut (the display). This routine polls StdIn indefinitely until it receives a carriage return (0Dh). It responds to Control-C from the keyboard.

Set DS:DX to the start address of the buffer area. Into the first byte of the buffer write a byte defining the size of the buffer. Load AH with 0Ah, issue INT 21h. This routine reads characters from the keyboard into the buffer, beginning at the third byte. The routine ends with the first carriage return (0Dh), writing the carriage return into the buffer and writing into the second byte of the buffer a value (0FDh or less) recording the number of characters in the buffer.

The routine writes up to one less number of characters in the buffer than you specify in the first byte. All subsequent characters are lost, and the routine sounds the bell to warn the user. Remember that the function polls the keyboard until the user enters a carriage return. Also, if your buffer is less than 0FDh, there is the possibility that the user will key in more characters than your buffer will store, in which case the last characters will be lost and the function will ring the bell. You may want to write a routine that handles that eventuality, if just to notify the user what happened.

Entry: DS:DX = pointer to input buffer

Return: None

Related Functions: AH = 01h, AH = 06h, AH = 07h, AH = 08h, AH = 3Fh, AH = 40h

AH = 0Bh Check Standard Input Status [All Versions]

Use this function to check the status of StdIn (the keyboard), i.e., check to see if the keyboard device has a character available. Load AH with 0Bh and issue INT 21h. The function returns 0FFh in the AL register if one or more characters is available; it returns 00 in AL if no character is available. This routine returns AH = 0FFh indefinitely until you retrieve the character with Functions 1, 6, 7, 8, 0Ah, or 3Fh. This routine responds to Control-C from the keyboard.

Entry: None

Return: AL = 0FFh if character available from STDIN; AL < > FFh if not

Related Functions: AH = 01h, AH = 06h, AH = 07h, AH = 08h, AH = 0Ah, AH = 3Fh, ax = 4406h

AH = 0Ch Clear Keyboard Buffer and Invoke Keyboard Function [All Versions]

Use this function to flush the current contents of the StdIn (keyboard) type-ahead buffer and then invoke Function 01h, 06h, 07h, 08h, or 0Ah to read new input. Load AH with 0Ch, load AL with the number of the function to invoke (1, 6, 7, 8, 0Ah), and issue INT 21h. Remember to set up the input buffer if you choose Function 0Ah. How this function returns values, and whether it responds to Control-C from the keyboard, depends upon the value you load into AL.

Entry: AL = INT 21h Function number (01h, 06h, 07h, 08h or 0Ah); other registers defined by function in AL; if AL contains a number other than those, the function flushes the input buffer and terminates

Return: AL = character (unless Function 0Ah was invoked); other registers defined by function in AL on entry

Related Functions: AH = 01h, AH = 06h, AH = 07h, AH = 08h, AH = 0Ah

AH = 0Dh Disk Reset [All Versions]

Use this function to write data from MS-DOS disk buffer areas to disk storage. This function does not close files, nor does it update the directory entries for any files. Use functions 10h or 3Eh to close files. DOS 3.3 provides a preferable function, AH = 68h, which automatically updates the directory and FAT. Because of its limited capabilities, use this only as a quick and dirty safety measure to be sure that code handling important or emergency situations will save any changes in memory to the files on disk. Include this call in your replacement Control-C interrupt handler, if you have written one.

Entry: None

Return: None

Related Functions: AH = 10h, AH = 3Eh, AH = 68h

Related Interrupts: INT 25h, INT 26h

AH = 0Eh Select Disk [All Versions]

Use this function to specify which disk drive is to be the default drive. Load DL with a number corresponding to the disk drive you wish to make current (0 = A:, 19h = Z:), load AH with 0Eh, and issue INT 21h. The function returns in AL a value equal to the number of disk drives in the system (minimum number is two); in the case of a single-floppy system, MS-DOS treats that drive as both A: and B:.

MS-DOS version 2.X allows up to 3Fh drives, MS-DOS 3.X allows up to 1Ah drives, MS-DOS 3.X and 4.X return a minimum of five logical drives unless the user overrides this with the LASTDRIVE command in the CONFIG.SYS file.

Entry: DL = drive number (0 = A:,..., 19h = Z:)

Return: AL = number of logical drives (0 = A:,..., 19h = Z:)

Related Function: AH = 19h

Related Interrupts: INT 25h, INT 26h

AH = 0Fh FCB Open File [All Versions]

This function provides limited utility for working with file-bound data under FCB (File Control Block) control. The preferred means of handling data is with respect to file handles rather than FCBs. The FCB is a data structure that exists to permit compatibility for running applications designed for the earliest versions of MS-DOS (versions 1.X), most of which are converted CP/M programs. (CP/M is an older operating system now declared obsolete by its manufacturer.)

The FCB data structure contains fields for the drive, file name, extension, size, time and date stamp, and other fields that identify data location and status in terms of records and blocks.

Use this function only to open an existing file that is not currently open and that exists in the current path specification of the current drive. If the file is already open or not in the current directory, the function fails, returning 0FFh in AL. If successful, the function fills in the fields for Current Block = 0, File Size, File Date, and File Time from directory information, and sets Current Record and Random Record both to 0.

Entry: DS:DX = pointer to unopened FCB

Return: AL = 00h if file was opened successfully; AL = 0FFh if not

Related Functions: AH = 10h through AH = 17h, AH = 21h through AH = 28h; the preferred alternate function is AH = 3Dh, Open Handle

AH = 10h FCB Close File [All Versions]

Set AH to 10h and DS:DX to the address of an opened FCB. INT 21h invokes a routine that searches the current disk for a file matching that named in the FCB. If successful, the routine updates directory entries to reflect the current FCB and returns 0 in AL. If unsuccessful, the routine returns 0FFh in AL. As a matter of good practice, design your programs to perform read and write operations in clusters, then close files as soon as possible to avoid inadvertent file corruption.

Entry: DS:DX = address of opened FCB

Return: AL = 00h if file was closed successfully; AL = 0FFh if not

Related Functions: AH = 10h through AH = 17h, and AH = 21h through AH = 28h; the preferred alternate function is AH = 3Dh, Open Handle

AH = 11h FCB Search for First Entry [All Versions]

This function searches the current drive and directory for a first match with the contents of an FCB for an unopened file. Specify this FCB by loading its address in DS:DX. If successful, this function creates a duplicate of the specified FCB located in the current Disk Transfer Area and returns AL = 0. If unsuccessful, this function returns AL = 0FFh. To search further, use Function AH = 12h, FCB Search Next Entry.

To use Function AH = 11h, first set up an FCB for an unopened file, setting the current drive, file name, and file extensions for your request. File names and extensions may contain wildcard characters. Initialize the remaining fields to zeros.

Use the extended FCB structure to work with hidden files, system files, and directories, setting the attribute byte to 02h, 04h, or 10h, respectively. The attribute is bitwise, so 06h passes searches for hidden and system files and 16h passes searches for directories. To search the volume label, set the attribute byte to 08h.

If you do not set up a Disk Transfer Area, this function uses the PSP, beginning at offset 80h. Use Function AH = 2Fh to get the address of the current DTA.

Entry: DS:DX = pointer to an unopened FCB

Return: AL = 00h if match was found; AL = 0FFh if not

Related Functions: AH = 10h through AH = 17h, AH = 21h through AH = 24h, AH = 26h through AH = 28h; the preferred alternate function is AH = 4Eh, Close Handle

AH = 12h FCB Search for Next Entry [All Versions]

Use this function after one invocation of Function AH = 11h. This function requires the same setup considerations as Function AH = 11h, that is, correct FCB fields and associated DTA. Load DS:DX with the address of the FCB and call this function. If successful, the function returns AL = 0 and initializes the current DTA, similarly to Function AH = 11h. If unsuccessful, the routine returns AL = 0FFh.

Your program must evaluate the file name in the current DTA to determine if a successful invocation has provided the file name you need. If not, call the function again until it delivers the needed file name or AL = 0FFh, indicating that it has exhausted all possibilities in the current directory.

Entry: DS:DX = pointer to FCB returned by previous search-first or search-next function call

Return: AL = 00h if match was found; AL = 0FFh if not

Related Functions: AH = 10h through AH = 17h, AH = 21h through AH = 24h, AH = 26h through AH = 28h; the preferred alternate function is AH = 4Fh, Find First File

AH = 13h FCB Delete File [All Versions]

Use this function to delete a file specified as the file name and extension of an FCB for an unopened file. If the file name or extension contain wildcard characters, the routine deletes all matching files. Set DS:DX to the desired FCB and invoke the function. If successful, the function returns AL = 0; if unsuccessful, the function returns AL = 0FFh to indicate it found no files in the current drive and directory that match the name in the FCB.

Entry: DS:DX = pointer to an unopened FCB

Return: AL = 00h if file was deleted; AL = 0FFh if not

Related Functions: AH = 10h through AH = 17h, AH = 21h through AH = 24h, AH = 26h through AH – 28h, the preferred alternate function is AH = 41h, Delete Directory Entry.

AH = 14h FCB Sequential Read [All Versions]

Use this function to read data from a file. Set DS:DX to the FCB of the opened file, then call this function. Data is read record by record. Records are stored together in blocks.

The function determines the byte size of the data record from the Record Size Field of the FCB. The assumption is that the file contains more than one record, and more than one block of records. The function determines which record to read from the values in the Current Block field and the Current Record field, and then increments the values in those fields.

If successful, the function reads a record into the current DTA and returns AL = 0. If the function has exhausted the file, it returns AL = 1, indicating that the DTA contains no new data. If the DTA does not provide correct storage (too small, crosses a segment boundary), the function returns AL = 02, indicating no read occurred. If the function encounters an End-Of-File (EOF) character (1Ah = Control-Z), it returns AL = 3 and stores the valid data in the DTA, followed by the EOF character, followed by as many zeros as are needed to fill the record.

Entry: DS:DX = pointer to an opened FCB

Return: AL = success/failure
                00h = read was successfully completed
                01h = no read attempted; already at end of file
                02h = read canceled; DTA too small
                03h = partial read completed; now at EOF

Related Functions: AH = 10h through AH = 17h, AH = 21h through AH = 24h, AH = 26h through AH = 28h; the preferred alternate function is AH = 3Fh, Read Handle

AH = 15h FCB Sequential Write [All Versions]

This function writes a record from the current DTA to the file specified in the FCB. Set DS:DX to the FCB of the opened file and invoke the function, which uses the same FCB control fields as Function AH = 14h, namely Record Size, Current Record, and Current Block. As part of its routine, the function increments the values in the Current Record and Current Block fields.

As with Function AH = 14h, this function returns values to indicate a successful or failed write, with AL = 0 indicating success, AL = 1 indicating disk too full, and AL = 2 a mismatch between the DTA and the file record specification. It is up to your program to test for success or failure and ensure data safety.

Entry: DS:DX =pointer to an opened FCB

Return: AL =success/failure
                00h = write was successfully completed
                01h = no write attempted; media is full
                02h = write canceled; DTA too small

Related Functions: AH =10h through AH = 17h, AH = 21h through AH = 24h, AH = 26h through AH = 28h; the preferred alternate function is AH = 3Dh, Open Handle

AH = 16h FCB Create File [All Versions]

To use this function, set DS:DX to point to an unopened FCB. The routine opens a file that matches the name in the Filename field, or creates a new file for an empty entry. Beware: if this routine finds an existing file, it resets its control values (for instance, length —> zero), destroying all contents without warning. You can create a hidden file or subdirectory by using an extended FCB.

Entry: DS:DX = pointer to an unopened FCB

Return: AL = 00h if file was created; AL = 0FFh if not

Related Functions: AH = 10h through AH = 17h, AH = 21h through AH = 24h, AH = 26h through AH = 28h; the preferred alternate function is: AH = 3Ch, Create Handle; AH = 5Ah, Create Temporary File; or AH = 5Bh, Create New File

AH = 17h FCB Rename File [All Versions]

To use this function, modify an FCB so that it contains two file names. The first file name is located at the expected offset within the FCB. The second file name is located immediately afterward, at offset 11h. (This function does not work with an extended FCB.) Upon invocation, the routine searches the current directory for a file with a name matching the first file name in the modified FCB. If successful, it substitutes the second file name in the modified FCB as the new directory name of the file. Upon completion, the function returns AL = 0 to indicate success or AL = 0FFh to indicate failure.

Entry: DS:DX = pointer to a modified FCB (new name starts in current block number field)

Return: AL = 00h if file was renamed; AL = 0FFh if not

Related Functions: AH = 10h through AH = 17h, AH = 21h through AH = 24h, AH = 26h through AH = 28h; the preferred alternate function is AH = 56h, Change Directory Entry

AH = 18h Undocumented

Not used by DOS (an outdated CP/M-compatible call).

AH = 19h Get Current Disk [All Versions]

Use this function to determine the current disk drive. The function returns a vALue in AL, from 0 to 19h for drives A to Z.

Entry: None

Return: AL = current drive number (0 = A:,...,25 = Z:)

AH = 1Ah Set Disk Transfer Address [All Versions]

Use this function to record the address of a buffer area in memory as the current DTA. Your program must set up the buffer so that it does not cross segment boundries. The function does not return a value indicating success or failure. Your warning comes when you try to read or write using the DTA. You may create a DTA of any size less than 64k, as long as it does not extend beyond or wrap around the segment area. You must set up FCB control values, such as Record Length and so on, to match the DTA size. A DTA that is too small to contain a file record generates read and write failures; one that is oversized offers no benefits but wastes memory. If you do not set up your own DTA, the system default uses the top 80h bytes of the PSP as the current DTA.

Entry: DS:DX = pointer to new DTA

Return: None

Related Functions: FCB Functions AH = 0Fh through AH = 17h, AH = 21h through AH = 24h, AH = 26h through AH = 28h

AH = 1Bh Get Default Drive Data [All Versions]

Use this function to obtain information about the current drive. You can determine the number of bytes per sector from the value in CX, the number of sectors per cluster from AL, and the number of clusters per drive from DX. The FAT ID byte tells you if the media is single- or double-sided with 8, 9, or 15 sectors per track, or if it is a fixed disk.

Entry: None

Return: DS:BX =pointer to byte containing FAT ID
        BX =0FFh DS, 8 sectors
            0FEh SS, 8 sectors
            0FDh DS, 9 sectors
            0FCh SS, 9 sectors
            0F9h DS, 15 sectors
            0F8h fixed disk
        DX =number of clusters per drive
        AL =number of sectors per cluster
        CX =number of bytes per sector

Related Functions: AH = 36h, Get Disk Free Space; AH = 1Ch, Get Drive Data

AH = 1Ch Get Drive Data [All Versions]

Use this function to obtain information about a disk in a drive specified in DL. This function works similarly to Function AH = 1Bh with the difference that you can specify any valid drive; Function AH = 1Bh returns information about the current default drive.

Entry: DL = drive number (0 = current drive, 1 = A:,...,26 = Z:)

Return: DS:BX = pointer to byte containing FAT ID
        DX = number of clusters per drive
        AL = number of sectors per cluster
        CX = number of bytes per sector

Related Functions: AH = 1Bh, AH = 36h,

Related Interrupt: INT 13h

AH = 1Dh Undocumented

Not used by DOS (an outdated CP/M-compatible call).

AH = 1Eh Undocumented

Not used by DOS (an outdated CP/M-compatible call).

AH = 1Fh Get Drive Parameter Block

This function is undocumented, which means it may vary between versions or between manufacturer's implementations of versions of MS-DOS. It returns in DS:DX the address of the DPB for the current drive.

Entry: DL = 0

Return: CF = 0, DS:DX contains address of DPB for current drive
CF = 1, AX contains error code

AH = 21h Random Read [All Versions]

Use this function to read a specified record from a file to the current DTA. Set DS:DX to the address of an opened FCB for the file, set up values in FCB fields for the Current Block, Record Size, Current Record, and Relative Record.

Entry: DS:DX = pointer to an opened FCB

Return: AL = return status
00h = read was successful
01h = end of file; no data read
02h = DTA is too small
03h = end of file; partial record read

Related Functions: AH = 10h through AH = 17h, AH = 21h through AH = 24h, AH = 26h through 28h, the preferred alternate function is AH = 3Fh, Read Handle

AH = 22h Random Write [All Versions]

Use this function to write a record from the DTA to a file controlled by an opened FCB. As with Function AH = 21h, you must set the appropriate values in the FCB, notably the Relative Record field.

Entry: DS:DX = pointer to an opened FCB

Return: AL = return status
00h = write was successful
01h = no write attempted; media full
02h = write canceled; DTA too small

Related Functions: AH = 10h through AH = 17h, AH = 21h through AH = 24h, AH = 26h through AH = 28h; the preferred alternate function is AH = 40h, Write Handle

AH = 23h Get File Size [All Versions]

Use this function to search the current directory for information on the size of a file specified in the unopened FCB located at DS:DX. Set the appropriate value in the Record Size field (0Eh). The function reads in the File Size field value (0Ch) and computes the value in the Relative Record field by dividing File Size by Record Size, rounding any division remainder up one integer.

Entry: DS:DX = pointer to an unopened FCB

Return: If AL = 00h, FCB random record field = records in file
If AL = 0FFh, file not found

Related Functions: AH = 10h through AH = 17h, AH = 21h through AH = 24h, AH = 26h through AH = 28h; the preferred alternate function is AH = 42h, Move File Pointer

AH = 24h Set Relative Record Field [All Versions]

Use this function to set the Relative Record Field of an opened FCB. Set DS:DX to point to the FCB. Set appropriate values in the fields for Current Block (0Ch) and Current Record (20h). Upon invocation, this routine calculates a new value in the Relative Record field based on the values in Current Block and Current Record.

Entry: DS:DX = pointer to an opened FCB

Return: None

Related Functions: AH = 10h through AH = 17h, AH = 21h through AH = 24h, AH = 26h through 28h; the preferred alternate function is AH = 42h, Move File Pointer

AH = 25h Set Interrupt Vector [All Versions]

Use this function to install the address of an Interrupt Service Routine (ISR) at a specified entry in the Interrupt Vector Table (IVT). Load AL with the IVT number entry (from 0 to 0FFh) and point DS:DX to the start address of your ISR. Warning: do not read or write directly to the IVT; MS-DOS tracks IVT values in various ways, and a direct write may cause unpredictable results.

Entry: AL = interrupt number to set
      DS:DX = pointer to new interrupt handling routine

Return: None

Related Function: AH = 35h

AH = 26h Create New Program Segment Prefix [All Versions]

This function creates a new PSP located at the segment address specified in DX. This function is obsolete. Use Function AH = 4Bh.

Entry: DX:0 = pointer to new PSP area

Return: None

Related Functions: AH = 10h through AH = 17h, AH = 21h through AH = 24h, AH = 26h through 28h; the preferred alternate function is ax = 4B00h, Load and Execute Program

AH = 27h Random Block Read [All Versions]

Use this function to read one or more records into the current DTA from a file specified in the FCB. Set DS:DX to point to the FCB and set a value in CX to specify the number of records to read. As the function performs multiple reads, it updates the Current Block, Current Record, and Relative Record fields. Be sure that the current DTA has the capacity to store the multiple records.

Entry: DS:DX = pointer to an opened FCB
           CX = number of records to read
Return: AL = return status
               00 = read was successful
               01 = end of file; no data read
               02 = DTA too small
               03 = end of file; partial record read
           CX = actual number of records read

Related Functions: AH = 10h through AH = 17h, AH = 21h through AH = 24h, AH = 26h through AH = 28h; the preferred alternate function is AH = 3Fh, Read Handle

AH = 28h Random Block Write [All Versions]

Use this function to write multiple records from the current DTA to a file specified in the FCB located at DS:DX. Load CX with the number of records to write. The function writes the first record to the disk file location specified by the Relative Record entry. Upon completion, the function returns CX loaded with the number of records actually written and AL with success or failure codes. Current Block, Current Record, and Relative Record fields are updated.

Entry: DS:DX = pointer to an opened FCB
           CX = number of records to be written

Return: AL = return status
               00h = write was successful
               01h = no write attempted; media full
               02h = write canceled; DTA too small
           CX = actual number of records written

Related Functions: AH = 10h through AH = 17h, AH = 21h through AH = 24h, AH = 26h through 28h; the preferred alternate function is AH = 40h, Write Handle

AH = 29h FCB Parse Filename [All Versions]

Use this function to parse a character string to detect the occurrence of a drive:filename.ext specification. Set DS:SI to the address of the string to parse and ES:DI to an uninitialized data area large enough to contain an FCB data structure. Set the least significant 4 bits in AL to values that control the parsing; the most significant 4 bits must be zero.

The function returns information about the use of wildcards or an invalid drive specification in AL. If the function is successful, DS:SI contains the address of the first byte past the valid filespec, and an unopened FCB structure for the specified file now exists in ES:DI.

Entry: DS:SI = pointer to a command line to parse
      ES:DI = pointer to FCB for parsed filename
      AL = parsing control

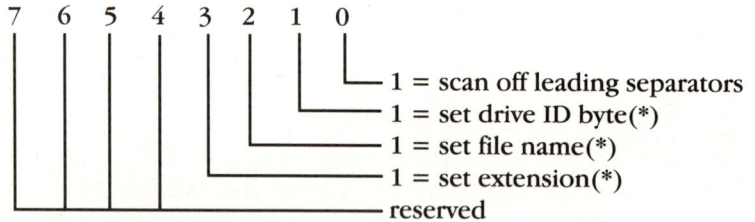

```
7   6   5   4   3   2   1   0
                        └──── 1 = scan off leading separators
                    └──────── 1 = set drive ID byte(*)
                └──────────── 1 = set file name(*)
            └──────────────── 1 = set extension(*)
└────────────────────────────── reserved
```

    (*) = only if specified on the command line

Return: DS:SI = pointer to first byte after parsed file name
      ES:DI = pointer to first byte of the formatted FCB
      AL = return status
          00h = no global characters encountered
          01h = global characters encountered
          0FFh = drive specified invalid

Related Functions: AH = 10h through AH = 17h, AH = 21h through AH =24h, AH = 26h through 28h

AH = 2Ah Get Date [All Versions]

Use this function to return the current system date.

Entry: None

Return: CX = year (1980 to 2099)
      DH = month (1 to 12)
      DL = day (1 to 31)
      AL = day of the week (0 = Sunday)

Related Functions: AH = 2Bh, AH = 2Ch, AH = 2Dh

Related Interrupt: INT 1Ah

AH = 2Bh Set Date [All Versions]

Use this function to reinitialize the system date settings.

Entry: CX = year (1980 to 2099)
      DH = month (1 to 12)
      DL = day (1 to 31)

Return: AL = 00h if date was valid; AL = 0FFh if not valid

Related Functions: AH = 2Ah, AH = 2Ch, AH = 2Dh

Related Interrupt: INT 1Ah

AH = 2Ch Get Time [All Versions]

Use this function to get the time of day. Do not depend on DL for accuracy. Some systems do not track hundredths of seconds; others generate approximate values depending on the strike of the INT 1Ch clock tick at 18.2 times per second.

Entry: None

Return: CH = hour (0 to 23)
       CL = minutes (0 to 59)
       DH = seconds (0 to 59)
       DL = hundredths (0 to 99)

Related Functions: AH = 2Ah, AH = 2Bh, AH = 2Dh

Related Interrupt: INT 1Ah

AH = 2Dh Set Time [All Versions]

Use this function to reinitialize the system time of day settings.

Entry: CH = hour (0 to 23)
      CL = minutes (0 to 59)
      DH = seconds (0 to 59)
      DL = hundredths (0 to 99)

Return: AL = 00h if time was valid; AL = 0FFh if not valid

Related Functions: AH = 2Ah, AH = 2Bh, AH = 2Ch

Related Interrupt: INT 1Ah

AH = 2Eh Set/Reset Verify Switch [All Versions]

Use this function to control verification of disk-write operations. Load AL with 0 to turn off verification, with 1 to turn verification on.

Entry: AL = 00h to set verify to off;
      AL = 01h to set verify to on

Return: None

Related Functions: AH = 15h, AH = 16h, AH = 22h, AH = 39h through AH = 3Ch, AH = 54h, ax = 5701h, AH = 5Ah, AH = 5Bh

Related Interrupts: INT 13h, INT 26h

AH = 2Fh Get Disk Transfer Address (DTA) [Versions 2, 3, 4]

This function returns the address of the current DTA in the ES:BX register pair. Call this routine before invoking FCB read or write operations.

Entry: None

Return: ES:BX = pointer to the current DTA

Related Functions: AH = 1Ah, also FCB read and write functions

AH = 30h Get MS-DOS Version Number [Versions 2, 3, 4]

This function returns the version number of the operating system, with the major version number in AL and the minor version number in AH. In addition, BH may return with the manufacturer's serial number, and BL:CX may return a 24-bit user serial number.

Entry: None

Return: AL = major version number (left of decimal)
            AH = minor version number (right of decimal)
            BX,CX = 0000

Note: AX = 0 if MS-DOS version 1.X

AH = 31h Terminate Process and Remain Resident [Versions 2, 3, 4]

This function lets you install resident code and release control to another program. You must devise a mechanism for later activation that allows for the system to be in an unpredictable state, possibly during a call to the INT 21h services, a disk read or write, or a critical error. There are three broad categories of program that use this function: replacement Interrupt Service Routines, "Hot-Key" programs, and background processors such as print spoolers. Each have their own advantages and disadvantages.

Generally you should design your program to be loaded as part of the boot-up process. As part of loading, your program should inspect the system, noting important MS-DOS structures as the address of the Critical-Break flag and Critical-Error handlers.

Immediately after load time, your program is the foreground program. At this time, MS-DOS recognizes its PSP, DTA, FCB, and other controls as the current data structures. When you invoke Function AH = 31h, you specify in DX how many paragraphs of memory above the PSP start address to keep.

The routine responds by returning control to the parent program, generally COMMAND.COM. Your PSP, code, and data are intact, but MS-DOS no longer recognizes your control structures as current. In effect, your program has joined the MS-DOS operating system memory area, reducing memory available for whatever program will be loaded as the new foreground program.

When your program later activates, it begins its new life blind. MS-DOS recognizes the current PSP, FCB, DTA, Job File Table, and other control structures as belonging to whatever program is the current ("foreground") program. Your program design must account for whatever is the state of the system in order not to corrupt or crash the system and the data of the foreground program.

Entry: AL = return code (batch ERRORLEVEL)
　　　　DX = number of memory paragraphs to stay resident

Return: None

Related Function: AH = 4Ch

Related Interrupt: INT 27h

AH = 32h Find Disk Parameter Block for Specified Drive
Undocumented (an obsolete CP/M style call).

This function behaves just as Function AH = 1Fh, with the addition of the ability to respond to a drive specification. Load DL with the drive spec number (0 is current, 1 is A:, 1Ah is Z) and issue the call.

Entry: DL = Disk Drive, (0 = current, 1 – 1A =A: – Z:)

Return: If CF = 0,
　　　　　AL = 00, valid drive
　　　　　AL = 0FFh, invalid drive
　　　　　DS:DX contains the start address of the DPB

Related Functions: AH = 1Fh, AH = 36h preferred

AH = 33h Get/Set Control-C (Control-Break) Check State
[Versions 2, 3, 4]
Use this function to get or set the state of Control-C checking. Load AL = 0 to return the existing state, load AL = 1 to enable or disable Control-C checking depending on DL = 0 or DL = 1. You may want to replace the default Control-C handler with your own; and be careful that you understand the effects of the currently installed Control-C handler, which may be installed or deinstalled without warning, depending on the program with which it works.

Entry: AL = 00h to get current state
　　　　AL = 01h to set Control-C check
　　　　DL = 00h to set Control-C to off
　　　　DL = 01h to set Control-C to on

Return: AL = 0FFh if error (AL neither 0 nor 1 at call)
　　　　　DL = 00h if Control-Break is off
　　　　　DL = 01h if on

Related Function: AH = 34h

Related Interrupts: INT 23h (don't issue directly), INT 24h

AH = 34h Get Critical Section Flag Address (Undocumented) [Version 3.X Known]

This function returns the address of the Critical Section (In-DOS) flag in ES:BX. The flag itself is a word set to zero if safe; set to any other value if not. This flag indicates that the INT 21h function dispatcher is working, which means that the system is in an unpredictable state. It is a good idea to incorporate a check for this flag as the first routine in a replacement ISR or TSR, especially if your program will use file I/O or INT 21h functions.

Warning: do not call Function AH = 34h from your ISR or TSR program. Call this function as part of your installation procedure to record the address before you abandon control. Upon reactivation, your routine need only inspect the value of the word at the address. It is important that you do not use INT 21h function calls if this flag is set, so it must be obvious that this warning includes this call (AH - 34h) as well.

Entry: None

Return: ES:BX contains the address of the Critical Section (In-DOS) flag

Related Function: AH = 33h

Related Interrupt: INT 24h

AH = 35h Get Interrupt Vector [Versions 2, 3, 4]

Use this function to inspect the address of the interrupt entry specified in AL. Do not read the address directly. This function returns the address in ES:BX.

Entry: AL = vector number

Return: ES:BX = pointer to the current interrupt handler

Related Function: AH = 25h

AH = 36h Get Disk Free Space [Versions 2, 3, 4]

This function returns in BX the number of clusters available on the specified drive, along with the number of sectors per cluster in AX, number of bytes per sector in CX, and clusters per drive in DX. To invoke this function, load the drive number in DL and call AH = 36h.

Entry: DL = drive number (0 = current drive, 1 = A:,...,26 = Z:)

Return: BX = number of available clusters
          DX = number of clusters on drive
          CX = number of bytes per sector
          If AX = 0FFFFh, drive is invalid
          If AX < > 0FFFFh, AX = number of sectors per cluster

AH = 37h Check or Change Switch Character (Undocumented)

Use this function to check or change the character that indicates an option switch on the command line. The default is the slash ("/") character. Load AL with 0 to get, 1 to set. DL contains the character.

Entry: AL = 0, read
AL = 1, load DL with new character

Return: If CF = 0
AL = 0, then DL contains current switch character
AL = 1, write
If CF = 1, check AX for error code

AH = 38h Get Current Country Information [Versions 2, 3, 4]

To use this function, load AL, BX, and DX with appropriate values. If DX contains 0FFFFh, the function sets the current country as your values dictate. If DX < 0FFFFh, the function returns information on the country request. If CF = 0, BX contains the country code. If CF = 1, AX contains an error code. The function returns additional information in a 34-byte data structure located at DS:DX.

Entry: AL = 00 to get current country information
AL = 01h through 0FFh for country codes < 255
AL = 0FFh for country codes > 255
BX = country code if AL = 0FFh
DS:DX = pointer to 34-byte country information buffer
DX = 0FFFFh to indicate "set country" [versions 3 and 4]

Return: If CF = 0, BX = country code
If CF = 1, AX = error code

Related Function: AH = 65h

3AH = 39h Create Subdirectory (MKDIR) [Versions 2, 3, 4]

To use this function, set DS:DX to the start address of an ASCIIZ pathname. If successful, the function returns CF = 0. If unsuccessful, CF = 1 and AX contains an error code. The function fails if the path specification is invalid, if the directory is not empty, or if the path specifies the root directory or the current directory.

Entry: DS:DX = pointer to ASCIIZ pathname

Return: If CF = 1
Errors: AX = 3, path not found
AX = 5, access denied

Related Functions: AH = 3Ah, AH = 3Bh

AH = 3Ah Remove Subdirectory (RMDIR) [Versions 2, 3, 4]

To use this function, set DS:DX to the address of an ASCIIZ string containing the path specification of the directory to be deleted. If successful, this function returns CF = 0. If unsuccessful, CF = 1 and AX contains an error code.

Entry: DS:DX = pointer to ASCIIZ pathname

Return: If CF = 1
        Errors: AX = 3, path not found
               AX = 5, access denied
               AX = 10h, path specifies current directory

Related Functions: AH = 39h, AH = 3Bh

AH = 3Bh Change Current Directory (CHDIR) [Versions 2, 3, 4]

Set DS:DX to the address of an ASCIIZ string that contains a valid path specification. The function returns CF = 0 if successful, CF = 1 and AX = 3 if not.

Entry: DS:DX = pointer to ASCIIZ pathname

Return: If CF = 1
        Errors: AX = 3, invalid path specification or path specifies a file, not a directory

Related Functions: AH = 39h, AH = 3Ah

AH = 3Ch Create a File Handle [Versions 2, 3, 4]

This function opens a new file in the drive and directory specified in the ASCIIZ path specification located at DS:DX. Load CX with a value to set the desired file attributes. If no drive or path is specified, the current drive and directory are used. This function does not check for the existence of a file with a matching name, and in the event of a match, the contents of the existing file are destroyed, unless that file has attribute settings more restrictive than that specified in this request. Upon success (blind to incidental file destruction), the function returns a new handle in AX and CF = 0. If unsuccessful, AX contains an error code and CF = 1.

Entry: DS:DX = pointer to ASCIIZ pathname
       CX = 00, normal attributes
           01, read-only
           02, hidden
           04, system
           08, volume ID name
           10h, subdirectory name
           20h, archive

Return: If CF = 0, AX = file's handle
       If CF = 1

AX = 3, invalid path specification
4, no available handles, too many open files
5, directory is full, a directory exists with the specified name, a matching file exists with restrictive attributes

Related Functions: AH = 3Dh, AH = 3Eh, AH = 3Fh, AH = 40h, AH = 4Eh

AH = 3Dh Open a File [Versions 2, 3, 4]

Use this function to open any file specified in an ASCIIZ string. Load DS:DX with the address of the string, and load AL with the appropriate access code, irrespective of attribute settings. Upon successful return, AX contains the handle for the file and CF = 0. Failure returns CF = 1 and an error code in AX.

Entry: DS:DX = pointer to an ASCIIZ pathname
AL = open mode:

```
7  6  5  4  3  2  1  0
                  └──┴──┴──── access mode: 000 = read-only
                                           001 = write-only
                                           010 = read/write
                  └────────── always 0
         └─────────────────── sharing mode: 000 = compatibility mode
                                             001 = deny read/write
                                             010 = deny write
                                             011 = deny read
                                             100 = deny none
└─────────────────────────── inheritance flag
```

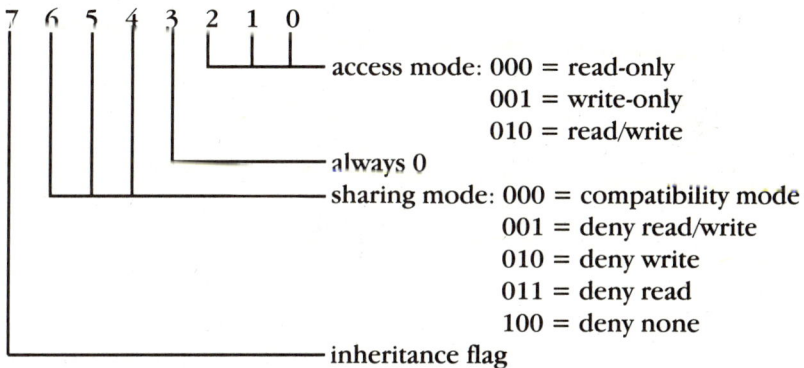

Return: If CF = 0, AX = file handle
If CF = 1
AX = 1, invalid function code
2, file not found
3, invalid path
4, no available handle—too many open files
5, access denied
0Ch, invalid access

Note: Opening of network files not available under DOS 2.X

Related Functions: AH = 3Ch, AH = 3Eh, AH = 3Fh, AH = 40h, AH = 4Eh

AH = 3Eh Close a File Handle [Versions 2, 3, 4]

Use this function to close a file, the handle of which is contained in BX. If successful, the function saves all related buffers to disk and returns CF = 0. If unsuccessful, the function returns CF = 1 and AX = 6, meaning invalid handle.

Entry: BX = file handle

Return: If CF = 1
         AX = 6, invalid handle

Related Functions: AH = 3Ch, AH = 3Dh, AH = 3Fh, AH = 40h, AH = 4Eh

AH = 3Fh Read from a File or Device [Versions 2, 3, 4]

Use this function to read a stream of bytes from a file or device, the handle of which is specified in BX. The CX register controls the number of bytes to be read. DS:DX points to a buffer area large enough to store the full read capacity. If successful, the function returns CF = 0 and the number of bytes read in AX. If unsuccessful, the function returns CF = 1 and an error code in AX.

Entry: BX = file handle
       CX = number of bytes to read
       DS:DX = pointer to read buffer

Return: If CF = 0, AX = number of bytes actually read
       If CF = 1
         AX = 5, read access denied
             6, invalid handle

Related Functions: AH = 3Ch, AH = 3Dh, AH = 3Eh, AH = 40h, AH = 4Eh

AH = 40h Write to a File or Device [Versions 2, 3, 4]

This function works similarly to Functions AH = 3Ch to AH = 3Fh. Load BX with the file handle, CF with the number of bytes to write to the file, and DS:DX with the address of the buffer containing the data. If successful, the function returns CF = 0 and AX contains the number of bytes written. If unsuccessful, the function returns CF = 1 and AX contains an error code. If CF = 0, AX should equal CX; if not, an error occurred, despite the CF = 0 indication.

Entry: BX = file handle
       CX = number of bytes to write
       DS:DX = pointer to write buffer

Return: If CF = 0, AX = number of bytes actually written
       If CF = 1
         AX = 5, file does not allow writing
             6, handle not open or invalid

Related Functions: AH = 3Ch to AH = 3Fh, AH = 4Eh, AH = 42h

AH = 41h Delete File from Specified Directory [Versions 2, 3, 4]

Use this function to delete the directory entry of a file specified in an ASCIIZ string at DS:DX. The filespec must name a file, not a subdirectory name, which is not set to read only. If successful, CF = 0. If unsuccessful, AX contains an error code.

Entry: DS:DX = pointer to an ASCIIZ file name

Return: If CF = 1
        AX = 2, invalid path or filespec (file not found)
            5, pathspec identifies a directory or read-only file

Related Function: AH = 43h

AH = 42h Move File Read/Write Pointer (LSEEK) [Versions 2, 3, 4]

The operating system maintains a 32-bit file pointer that it uses to reference the current position of read and write requests. Use this function to find the current location of the pointer or to change its position with respect to a file specified by a handle value in BX. Set AL to the appropriate control code and load CX:DX with the appropriate 32-bit offset from the beginning of the file. Upon successful return, CF = 0, and DX:AX contains the new position of the file pointer. If AL, CX, and DX all are set to 0, the function returns the current position of the file pointer in DX:AX. If unsuccessful, CF = 1 and AX contains an error code.

Entry: CX:DX = distance to move in bytes (offset)
      AL =origin of move:
           00 = beginning of file plus offset
           01 = current location plus offset
           02 = end of file plus offset
      BX = file's handle

Return: If CF = 0, DX:AX = new pointer location
      If CF = 1
           AX = 1, AL out of range
              6, handle not open

Related Function: AH = 40h

AH = 43h Change File Mode (CHMOD) [Versions 2, 3, 4]

Use this function to inspect or change the attributes of a file specified by an ASCIIZ string at DS:DX.

Entry: DS:DX = pointer to an ASCIIZ pathname
      AL = 00h to get attribute
      AL = 01h to set attribute
          CX =00, normal attributes
              01, read-only
              02, hidden
              04, system
              08, volume ID name
              10h, subdirectory name
              20h, archive

Return: If CF = 0 and AL = 00h
      CL = file's attributes
   If CF = 1
      AX = 1, AL out of range
           3, invalid path, file not found
           5, can't change attributes (directory or volume ID)

Related Function: AH = 41h

AH = 44h I/O Control for Devices (IOCTL)

This function consists of a set of subfunctions designed for control of a device specified by a handle in BX. Read and write functions are with respect to a buffer at DS:DX. If successful, CF = 0 and AX contains a report value. If not successful, CF = 1 and AX contains an error code. Device control is beyond the scope of this section. See the MS-DOS *Technical Reference Manual* for details on the specific IOCTL subfunctions.

    00h = get device information [versions 2, 3, 4]

    01h = set device information [versions 2, 3, 4]

    02h = read from character device [versions 2, 3, 4]

    03h = write to character device [versions 2, 3, 4]

    04h = read from block device [versions 2, 3, 4]

    05h = write to block device [versions 2, 3, 4]

    06h = get input status [versions 2, 3, 4]

    07h = get output status [versions 2, 3, 4]

    08h = is a particular block device changeable [versions 3 and 4]

    09h = is logical device local or remote [versions 3.1, 3.2, 3.3, 4]

    0Ah = is handle local or remote [versions 3.1, 3.2, 3.3, 4]

    0Bh = change sharing retry count [versions 3 and 4]

    0Ch = generic IOCTL handle request (code page switching) [versions 3.3 and 4]

    0Dh = block device generic IOCTL request [versions 3.2, 3.3, 4]

    0Eh = get logical device [versions 3.2, 3.3, 4]

    0Fh = set logical device [versions 3.2, 3.3, 4]

AH = 45h Duplicate a File Handle (DUP) [Versions 2, 3, 4]

Use this function to create a duplicate file handle for an open file specified by a handle in BX. If successful, CF = 0 and AX contains the new handle. From this point on, you can manipulate the file through either handle, and manipulation through one handle alters corresponding controls (file pointer) for the duplicate, the way dual pilot controls on a plane or automobile do. If unsuccessful, CF = 1 and AX contains an error code.

Entry: BX = existing file handle

Return: If CF = 0, AX = new duplicate file handle
If CF = 1
AX = 4, no available handle, too many open files
6, invalid handle or file not open

Related Functions: AH = 3Ch to 40h, AH = 42h, AH = 46h, AH = 4Eh

AH = 46h Force a Duplicate of a File Handle (FORCDUP) [Versions 2, 3, 4]

This function works the way Function AH = 45h does, except you load CX with a value you want to use as the duplicate handle.

Entry: BX = existing file handle
CX = desired duplicate file handle

Return: If CF = 1
AX = 4, no handle available (too many open files)
6, invalid handle or file not open

Related Functions: AH = 3Ch to AH = 40h, AH = 42h, AH = 45h, AH = 4Eh

AH = 47h Get Current Directory [Versions 2, 3, 4]

Use this function to get the current directory path specification. Set up a 64-byte buffer at DS:SI, load DL with the drive number (0 returns the current drive, 1 or greater specifies drive A: or above, in order). If the function succeeds, DS:SI contains the pathspec of the current directory and CF = 0. If not, CF = 1 and AX contains the error code 0Fh, invalid drive number.

Entry: DS:SI = pointer to a 64-byte user buffer
DL = drive number (0 = current drive, 1 = A:,...,26 = Z:)

Return: DS:SI = pointer to full pathname from root
If CF = 1
AX = 0Fh, invalid drive number
Note: Returned pathname does not include drive ID and leading "\"

Related Function: AH = 36h

AH = 48h Allocate Memory [Versions 2, 3, 4]

Use this function to allocate memory to the current process. Load BX with a number specifying the number of 16-byte paragraphs needed and call the function. If successful, CF = 0 and AX contains the segment address of the bottom of the memory block. If unsuccessful, CF = 1, BX contains the number of available paragraphs, and AX contains an error code.

Entry: BX = number of paragraphs of memory requested

Return: If CF = 0, AX:0 = pointer to allocated memory block
    If CF = 1
        AX = 7, damaged data in memory location (data changed by an unauthorized user program, memory control blocks damaged)
        8, insufficient available memory
    BX = size of the largest block of memory available in paragraphs

Related Functions: AH = 49h, AH = 4Ah, 4Bh

AH = 49h Free Allocated Memory [Versions 2, 3, 4]
Use this function to deallocate a block of memory that you obtained by using Function AH = 48h. Load ES with the segment address of the memory block and invoke the function. If successful, the function returns no indication, so be sure you have specified the memory block to abandon. If unsuccessful, CF = 1 and AX contains an error code.

Entry: ES = segment of allocated block to be freed

Return: IF CF = 1
        AX = 7, damaged memory or memory control blocks (see Function AH = 48h)
            8, ES points to a memory area not allocated by Function AH = 48h

Related Functions: AH = 48h, AH = 4Ah, 4Bh

AH = 4Ah Modify Allocated Memory Blocks (SETBLOCK) [Versions 2, 3, 4]
Use this function to increase or decrease the size of a block of memory allocated through Function AH = 48h. Load ES with the segment address and BX with the value of the new total number of paragraphs in the block. If successful, the function returns CF = 0. If unsuccessful, the function returns CF = 1, AX contains an error code, and BX contains the value of the total number of available paragraphs.

Entry: ES:0 = segment address of allocated block to be modified
    BX = new number paragraphs for block

Return: If CF = 1
        BX = maximum size possible for block
        AX = 7, damaged memory control blocks
            8, insufficient memory

9, ES does not specify a memory block allocated through Function AH = 48h

Related Functions: AH = 48h, AH = 49h, AH = 4Bh

AH = 4Bh Load and Execute a Program (EXEC) [Versions 2, 3, 4]

Use this function to load and execute another program. Upon invocation, this function loads the program and builds its PSP based on a parameter block that you provide. You must be sure that there is sufficient memory available to hold the program, including any data areas as well as MS-DOS control structures (PSP, FCBs, DTAs, memory control block, and so on).

Before you invoke this function, you must take care of the following setup details. DS:DX contains the address of an ASCIIZ string that specifies the file to be loaded. ES:BX points to a 14-byte parameter block. The parameter block contains four elements: a word containing the segment address of the environment, a doubleword specifying the address of the command line to install in the new program's PSP, and two doublewords pointing to each of two FCBs to be located in the new program's PSP.

If successful, CF = 0, the new program takes control, executes, then returns control to the instruction that follows the call to this function. If unsuccessful, this function returns CF = 1 and an error code in AX.

Entry: DS:DX = pointer to an ASCIIZ file specification
    AL = function value
        00h = load and execute the program
        03h = load an overlay
    ES:BX = pointer to parameter block:
        If AL = 00h

```
seg_env    dw    ?      ; segment of environment string
cmd_ptr    dd    ?      ; pointer to command line
fcb1_ptr   dd    ?      ; pointer to first FCB
fcb2_ptr   dd    ?      ; pointer to second FCB
```

        If AL = 03h

```
seg_load   dw    ?      ; segment at which to load file
rel_fact   dw    ?      ; relocation factor to be used
```

Return: If CF = 0, nothing
    If CF = 1
        AX = 7, damaged memory control blocks
            8, insufficient available memory
            9, ES specifies inaccessible memory area
        BX contains number of paragraphs available

Related Functions: AH = 48h through AH = 4Ah, AH = 4Ch

AH = 4Ch Terminate a Process (EXIT) [Versions 2, 3, 4]

This function is the approved means of returning control after your program has finished. The routine restores control to the program that called it, usually COMMAND.COM. As part of termination, you can load AL with a value that this routine passes back to the calling program. This AL value is tested by the IF command as part of the batch file facility.

Entry: AL = return code (batch ERRORLEVEL)

Return: None

Related Functions: AH = 31h, AH = 48h through 4Bh, AH = 4Dh

AH = 4Dh Get Return Code of Child Process [Versions 2, 3, 4]

Use this function to test termination of a child process. Upon return, check AH for return status and AL for any code you expect your program to return as part of its termination.

Entry: None

Return: AL = return code sent by subprocess
       AH = return status:
              00h = normal termination
              01h = Ctrl-Break termination
              02h = Critical-Error termination
              03h = stayed resident via INT 21h Function 31h

Related Functions: AH = 48h through AH = 4Ch

AH = 4Eh Find First Matching File (FINDFIRST) [Versions 2, 3, 4]

Use this function to search the specified directory for the first file with a name matching the filespec. Set DS:DX to the address of the ASCIIZ string that specifies the file and set CX to the appropriate attribute value. If CX = 0, this function recognizes normal files. If CX = 1, this function recognizes read-only and normal files; if CX = 2, it recognizes hidden files in addition, and so on.

If successful, the function returns CF = 0 and fills the current DTA with seven entries totaling 43 bytes. If unsuccessful, the function returns CF = 1 and AX contains an error code.

Entry: DS:DX = pointer to ASCIIZ file specification
       CX = attribute used during search

Return: If CF = 1
          AX = 2, file not found
               18, no more files

If CF = 0, the current DTA is filled as follows:

```
reserved   db 21 dup (?)  ; reserved
Attrib     db   ? ; file's attribute
Time       dw   ? ; file's time stamp
Date       dw   ? ; file's date stamp
Size       dd   ? ; file's size
Name       db 13 dup (?)   ; ASCIIZ file name
```

Related Function: AH = 4Fh

AH = 4Fh Find Next Matching File (FINDNEXT) [Versions 2, 3, 4]

Use this function to search the specified directory if Function AH = 4Eh returns AX = 2, indicating file not found. Upon success, this function fills the current DTA similarly to Function AH = 4Eh. Upon failure, CF = 1 and AX contains an error code.

Entry: DTA as returned from previous FINDFIRST or FINDNEXT call

Return: same as FINDFIRST function call

Related Function: AH = 4Eh

AH = 50h Set PSP (Undocumented)

This function accepts a value in BX as the segment address of the current PSP. Be careful that you have created a valid PSP at that address.

Entry: BX = address of new PSP

Return: CF = 0, success
CF = 1, big trouble

Related Functions: AH = 51h, AH = 55h

AH = 51h Get Current PSP (Undocumented)

Use this function to get the segment address of the current PSP in BX.

Entry: None

Return: BX contains segment address of current PSP

Related Functions: AH = 50h, AH = 55h

AH = 52h Get Address of Master List (Undocumented)

MS-DOS keeps a "list of lists," which tracks the critical data structures such as the System File Table (SFT), first Memory Control Block (MCB), pointers to device drivers, and so on. This function returns the start address of that master list in ES:BX.

Entry: None

Return: ES:BX contains address

AH = 53h Undocumented

AH = 54h Get Verify Setting [Versions 2, 3, 4]

Use this function to check whether or not disk verification is enabled for write operations. This function returns Al = 1 if so, AL = 0 if not.

Entry: None

Return: AL = 00h if verify is off; AL = 01h if verify is on

Related Function: AH = 2Eh

AH = 55h Create PSP (Undocumented)

This function creates a new PSP at a segment address specified in DX. This new data structure copies values from the current PSP at that location.

Entry: DX contains segment address for new PSP

Return: None

Related Functions: AH = 50, AH = 51

AH = 56h Respecify File Entry [Versions 2, 3, 4]

Use this function to change the specification of an entry in a directory specified by an ASCIIZ string at DS:DX. Set ES:DI to an ASCIIZ string containing the new specification. The drive specification must match.

Entry: DS:DX = pointer to old ASCIIZ [drive:path/file name]
ES:DI = pointer to new ASCIIZ [drive:path/file name]

Return: CF = 1
AX = 2, invalid path or file not found
5, access denied, DS:DX specifies directory, ES:DI specifies existing file, cannot open ES:DI file
17, mismatch drive spec

AX = 57h Get File's Date and Time [Versions 2, 3, 4]

Use this function to check or change the Date/Time stamp of a file specified by a handle in BX. To check the existing values, set AL = 0, invoke the function, and read date and time in DX and CX, respectively. To set the Date/Time stamp, load DX and CX with date and time values and invoke the function.

If successful, CF = 0; if not, CF = 1 and AX contains an error code.

Entry: BX = file's handle
    If AL = 0, get time, no other setup needed
    If AL = 1, set CX to time and DX to date

Return: If CF = 0, CX contains time and DX date
    If CF = 1
        AX = 1, AL contains incorrect value
            6, invalid handle or file not open

AH = 58h Get/Set Allocation Strategy

Use this function to direct the operating system to select a block of memory for your process based on the location (high or low) or size or to inspect the existing status of the current memory block allocated to your process. Set AL to check or set; set BX to specify changes to be made. If successful, the function returns CF = 0 and AX indicates the block type selected. If unsuccessful, CF − 1 and AX contains an error code.

Entry: AL = 0, get strategy
    AL = 1, set strategy
    BX = 0, first fit (lowest available block)
        1, best fit (smallest available block)
        2, last fit (highest available block)

Return: CF = 0, AL = 0, no return values
    CF = 0, AL = 1, AX contains the type (0, 1, 2)
    CF = 1, AX = 1, AL or BX out of range

AH = 59h Get Extended Error Information [Versions 3 and 4]

Use this function following an error indication to check for possible reasons and branch to likely solutions. Push all registers, then set BX to zero and call the function. Inspect BH, BL, and CH for information. Some indications are straightforward, for instance, BL = 5, terminate immediately without cleanup. Others require your program to respond or track details of hardware or system resources. Further exploration is beyond the scope of this appendix.

Entry: BX =0000h

Return: AX = extended error code
    BH − error class
        1, out of resource, storage
        2, temporary denial, retry
        3, not authorized
        4, process or system failure
        5, hardware failure
        6, operating system failure
        7, process failure

8, file not found
9, invalid format or type
10, file interlocked
11, disk media failure
12, other

BL = suggested action
1, retry, then notify user
2, retry later
3, get new keyboard input
4, terminate normally
5, terminate immediately
6, ignore error
7, request operator assistance

CH = locus
1, unknown
2, random-access block device
3, network
4, serial character device
5, random-access memory

CL, DX, SI, DI, ES and DS are destroyed

AH = 5Ah Create a Temporary File [Versions 3 and 4]

Use this function as a quick and dirty way to have the operating system create a file, avoiding the problem of duplicate file names. Set up DS:DX with the address of an ASCIIZ string containing a valid drive and path specification that ends with the backslash character ("\") followed by 13 bytes of additional memory. Set CX with the appropriate file attribute value.

If successful, this function returns CF = 0, the new handle in AX, and the new file name appended to the pathspec at DS:DX. Subsequent file handling, including reads, writes, and closes, must be managed by your process.

Entry: DS:DX = pointer to ASCIIZ string with drive and path followed by "\" and ending with a 13-byte buffer to hold the incoming file name
CX = file attributes

Return: If CF = 0, AX = file handle; DS:DX = pointer to ASCIIZ string complete with file name
If CF = 1
AX = 3, invalid pathspec
5, access denied

Related Function: AH = 5Bh

AH = 5Bh Create a New File [Versions 3 and 4]

Create a file with a name specified by an ASCIIZ string at DS:DX and attribute bits specified by the value in CX. If successful, the function returns CF = 0 and a handle in AX. If unsuccessful, CF = 1 and AX contains an error code.

Entry: DS:DX = pointer to ASCIIZ path/file name
CX = file attributes

Return: If CF = 0, AX = handle
If CF = 1
AX = 3, invalid path
4, no more files can be opened
5, access denied
80, file exists already

Related Function: AH = 5Ah

AH = 5Ch Lock/Unlock File Access [Versions 3 and 4]

Use this function if and only if the SHARE.EXE module has been loaded. This lets you lock or unlock a file region with an offset specified by CX:DX and a length specified by SI:DI. This function is appropriate in a network environment only.

Entry: AL = to lock file access; AL = 01h to unlock file access
BX = file handle
CX = high word of offset
DX = low word of offset
SI = high word of length
DI = low word of length

Return: If CF = 1, AX = error code

AH = 5Dh Undocumented

AX = 5E00h NETWORK: Get Machine Name [Versions 3.1, 3.2, 3.3, 4]

This function is usable only when running under Microsoft Networks. It returns the name the net uses for the local machine.

Entry: DS:DX = pointer to 16-byte buffer for ASCIIZ computer name

Return: If CF = 0, DS:DX = pointer to ASCIIZ computer name
If CF = 1, AX = error code
If CH = 0, name/number is undefined
If CH <> 0, name/number is defined; CL = NETBIOS name number

AX = 5E02h NETWORK: Set Printer Setup String
[Versions 3.1, 3.2, 3.3, 4]

Use this function to automate the creation of a file header to be included before file data is sent to a network printer. The file header contains control codes specific to that printer. This function is appropriate only when running Microsoft Networks.

Entry: BX = redirection list index
        CX = length of setup string (maximum length = 64 bytes)
        DS:SI = pointer to printer setup string

Return: If CF = 1, AX = error code

AX = 5E03h NETWORK: Get Printer Setup String
[Versions 3.1, 3.2, 3.3, 4]

This function retrieves the printer setup string, working similarly to AX = 5302h, appropriate only with Microsoft Networks.

Entry: BX = redirection list index
        ES:DI = pointer to 64-byte printer setup buffer

Return: If CF = 0, CX = length of returned data and ES:DI = pointer to printer setup string
        If CF = 1, AX = error code

AX = 5F02h NETWORK: Get Redirection List Entry
[Versions 3.1, 3.2, 3.3, 4]

Use this function to inspect which local logical names are associated with which network files in the network assign list. Use only with Microsoft Networks.

Entry: BX = redirection list index (zero-based)
        DS:SI = pointer to 128-byte buffer for local name
        ES:DI = pointer to 128-byte buffer for network name

Return: If CF = 0, BH = device status flag
                If Bit 0 = 0, device is valid
                If Bit 0 = 1, device is invalid
                BL = device type
                CX = stored parameter value
                DS:SI = ASCIIZ local name
                ES:DI = ASCIIZ network name
        If CF = 1, AX = error code

AX = 5F03h NETWORK: Redirect Device [Versions 3.1, 3.2, 3.3, 4]

Use this function to specify an association in the assign list between a local logical name and a network name. Use only with Microsoft Networks.

Entry: BL = device type:
        03 = Printer device
        04 = File device
    CX = 0000h
    DS:SI = pointer to ASCIIZ local name to redirect
    ES:DI = pointer to ASCIIZ network destination name

Return: If CF = 1, AX = error code

AH = 60h Undocumented

Ah = 61h Undocumented

AH = 62h Get Program Segment Prefix Address [Versions 3 and 4]

Use this function to return the address of the current Program Segment Prefix (PSP). Normally, the current PSP is located at CS:0000 of the foreground program, i.e., your process. You can, under the right conditions, call this function as part of an Interrupt Service Routine, an installed device driver, or TSR (terminate and stay resident) program. If the calling process is not the foreground program, it must take elaborate precautions to ensure system safety before making this or most other INT 21h calls.

Entry: None

Return: BX:0 = pointer to current PSP

AH = 63h Get DBCS Lead Byte Table

Available only with MS-DOS version 2.25.

AH = 64h Undocumented

AH = 65h Get Extended Country Information [Versions 3.3 and 4]

This function returns more detailed information, but of the same type as Function AH = 38h. See the MS-DOS technical reference for details.

Entry: AL = information ID
    BX = code page (–1 = global code page)
    DX = country ID (–1 = current country)
    CX = size
    ES:DI = pointer to country information buffer

Return: If CF = 0, CX = size of country information returned; ES:DI = pointer to country information
    If CF = 1, AX = error code

Related Functions: AH = 38h, AH = 66h

AH = 66h Get/Set Global Code Page [Versions 3.3 and 4]

Use this function to check or change the global code page from a file named COUNTRY.SYS.

> Entry: AL = 01h to get global code page; AL = 02h to set
> BX = code page (if AL = 02h)

> Return: If CF = 0, BX = active code page and DX = system code page
> If CF = 1, AX = error code

AH = 67h Set Handle Count [Versions 3.3 and 4]

Use this function to limit the number of files the calling process may have open simultaneously.

> Entry: BX = number of open handles allowed

> Return: If CF = 1, AX = error code

AH = 68h Commit File [Versions 3.3 and 4]

Use this function effectively to close a file specified by the handle value in BX, writing all buffers to disk, updating the Date/Time stamp if necessary, then reopening the file. This is nearly bulletproof, with the limitation that if the system must write buffers to a character rather than a block device, it returns CF = 0, but without writing.

> Entry: BX = file handle

> Return: CF = 1, AX = error code

AH = 69h—AH = 6Bh Undocumented

AH = 6Ch Extended Open/Create [Version 4]

Use this function to open, create, or replace a file identified by an ASCIIZ file specification at DS:SI. The difference between this and earlier functions pertains to the options available for controlling reads, writes, inheritance, buffer management, and other file features.

Entry: BX = open mode:

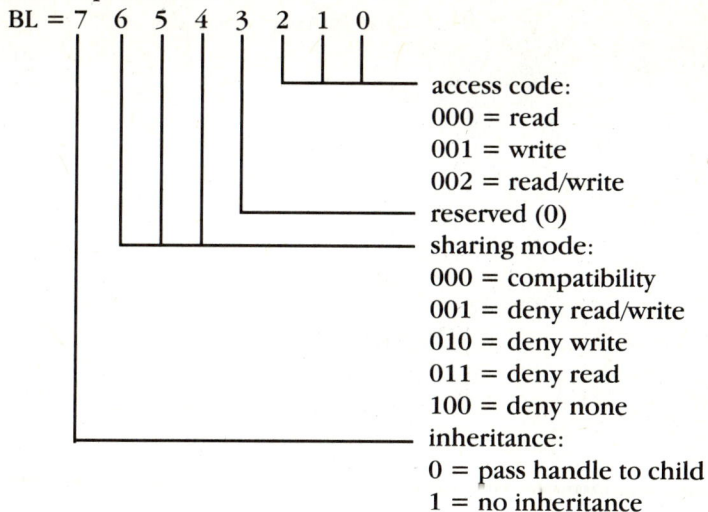

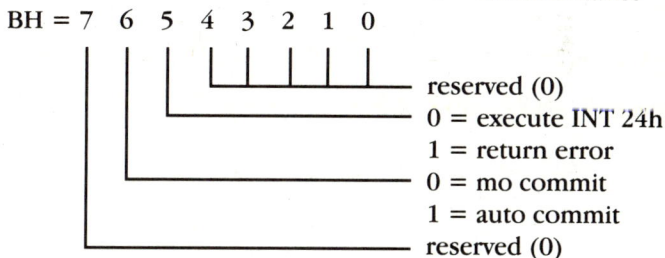

```
BL = 7  6  5  4  3  2  1  0
                     └──┴──┴──── access code:
                                 000 = read
                                 001 = write
                                 002 = read/write
                  └───────────── reserved (0)
         └──┴──┴──────────────── sharing mode:
                                 000 = compatibility
                                 001 = deny read/write
                                 010 = deny write
                                 011 = deny read
                                 100 = deny none
      └──────────────────────── inheritance:
                                 0 = pass handle to child
                                 1 = no inheritance

BH = 7  6  5  4  3  2  1  0
               └──┴──┴──┴──┴──── reserved (0)
            └──────────────────── 0 = execute INT 24h
                                  1 = return error
         └───────────────────── 0 = mo commit
                                 1 = auto commit
      └──────────────────────── reserved (0)
```

CX = new file attributes (ignored on file open)
DX = function control:

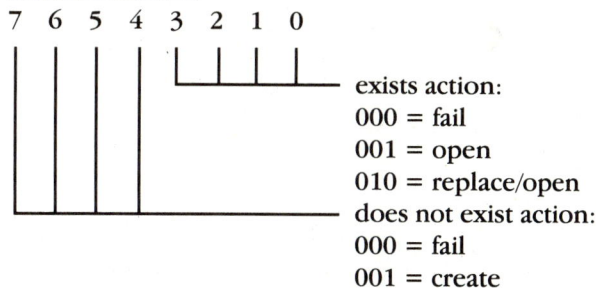

```
     7  6  5  4  3  2  1  0
                  └──┴──┴──── exists action:
                              000 = fail
                              001 = open
                              010 = replace/open
         └──┴──┴──────────── does not exist action:
                              000 = fail
                              001 = create
```

DS:SI = pointer to 64-byte ASCIIZ file specification

Return: If CF = 0, AX = file handle
                CX = action-taken code
                      1 = file opened
                      2 = file created/opened
                      3 = file replaced/opened
    If CF = 1, AX = error code

INTERRUPT 22h Terminate Address

The vector at this location points to the address of a routine that DOS uses when the current program returns control to DOS. As part of the loading process, the DOS loader copies the value at this location to offset address 0Ah in the PSP of the program being loaded.

Note: The routine located at this address is for DOS use only. Don't issue this interrupt directly. Also note that the first 2 bytes of the PSP are 0CDh 20h, which is the hex code for INT 20h. Assuming that the PSP resides in the first 256 bytes of the CS segment area, setting IP to zero executes this interrupt, terminating the program.

INTERRUPT 23h Control-C Exit Address

The vector at this location points to the address of the Control-C error handler; it is not an Interrupt Service Routine, and you should not issue an interrupt instruction for this vector.

As part of the normal housekeeping that DOS performs in executing most INT 21h function calls, DOS checks the status of the Control-C flag. If the flag is set, DOS executes a routine located at this address. It is common practice for designers of application programs to create custom routines to handle Control-C break requests according to the needs of their applications.

The Control-C mechanism differs from that of Control-Break in that DOS executes the Control-C routine as a result of executing most function calls. This allows proper completion of its operations and orderly system shut-down or whatever the current Control-C routine does. The Control-Break mechanism is a blind, immediate invocation of whatever routine is located at the address indicated by the vector for INT 1Bh (which similarly is not an ISR, but a routine that programmers frequently customize for the needs of their applications). This difference in design gives programmers a choice between error-handling routines that allow orderly DOS functionality and those that can interrupt and possibly rescue the system from more nearly catastrophic mishaps.

INTERRUPT 24h Critical Error Handler Address [Versions 3, 4]

DOS issues this interrupt upon detection of an unrecoverable I/O error. It defaults to print an "Abort, Retry, Ignore?" message in the resident portion of COMMAND.COM. Table C-1 lists the error codes and their names.

Entry: AH = bits

```
    7   6   5   4   3   2   1   0
                                └─ 0 read/1 write operation
                            ──── affected disk area:
                                 00 = DOS area; 01 FAT area;
                                 10 = directory; 11 = data area
                        ──────── FAIL allowed: 0 = no; 1 = yes
                    ──────────── RETRY allowed: 0 = no; 1 = yes
                ──────────────── IGNORE allowed: 0 = no; 1 = yes
            ──────────────────── (unused)
        ──────────────────────── 0 = disk error; 1 = other
```

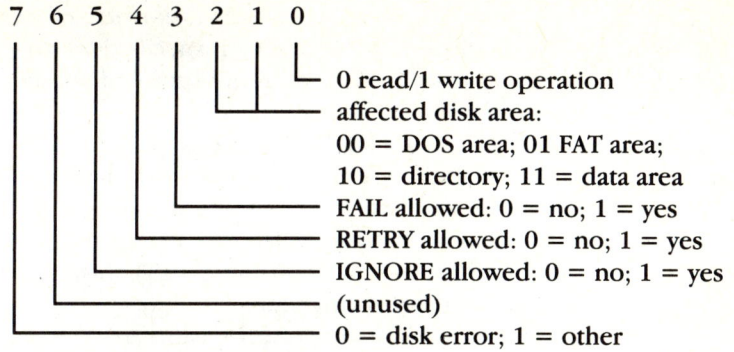

Entry: BP:SI = pointer to device header control block from which
        additional information can be retrieved
        DL = device error code, as follows:

Return: AL = 0, ignore the error
            1, retry the error
            2, terminate the program through INT 23h
            3, system failure: call in progress

Table C-1. *INT 24h Error Codes*

Error Code	Error Name
0	Attempt to write on write-protected disk
1	Unknown unit
2	Drive not ready
3	Unknown command
4	Data error (CRC)
5	Bad request structure length
6	Seek error
7	Unknown media type
8	Sector not found
9	Printer out of paper
A	Write fault
B	Read fault
C	General failure

INTERRUPT 25h Absolute Disk Read [All Versions]

This interrupt invokes a disk-read routine that begins reading from the current disk drive at a sector specified as an offset from sector zero up to 64k, transferring data from a specified number of subsequent sectors to a specified Data Transfer Area.

All MS-DOS versions provide this feature, but version 4 also provides an alternate entry format to accommodate disk-drive capacities greater than 32M. Note that MS-DOS up to version 3.3 provides an offset limit of 64k sectors and the alternate available in version 4 provides for up to 1G sectors. Be aware that the File Allocation Table (FAT) must be structured differently to accommodate the larger drive capacity.

Warning: use this with care. The routine reads data blindly from however many sectors you have specified into the DTA buffer. Be sure you have correctly calculated the number of bytes per sector to avoid DTA overflow.

= <32M:

    Entry: AL = drive number (0 = A, 1 = B, etc.)
          CX = number of sectors to read
          DX = relative sector number
          DS:BX = Disk Transfer Area

    Return: CF = 0, success
          CF = 1, failure
          AX = error code

>32M [version 4 only]:

    Entry: AL =drive number (0 = A, 1 = B, etc.)
          BX =pointer to 10-byte parameter list:
               32-bit dword specifies first sector to read
               16-bit word specifies number of sectors to read
               32-bit dword specifies DTA
          CX = –1 (indicates extended (>32M) format)

    Return: CF = 0, success
          CF = 1, failure
          AX contains error code

INTERRUPT 26h Absolute Write [All Versions]

This is the counterpart to INT 25h. Use this to write data from a specified Data Transfer Area to one or more sectors on the current disk drive. MS-DOS version 4 provides for writing to a disk drive with greater than 32M capacity.

Warning: As with INT 25h, this routine blindly transfers data from the specified memory address to the disk. Your only control is the specification of sectors in CX. Be sure to calculate the byte capacity of the sectors on the current disk drive, and be sure that the sectors to which you are writing are available for your use. If you miscalculate, you can overwrite other programs or data, even to the extent of overwriting the entire contents of the storage media.

= <32M:

    Entry: AL = drive number (0 = A, 1 = B, etc.)
           CX = number of sectors to write
           DX = beginning logical sector number
           DS:BX = Disk Transfer Area address

    Return: CF = 0 if successful transfer
            CF = 1 if unsuccessful transfer:
            AL = error code
            AH = 80h if attachment failed to respond
                  40h if SEEK operation failed
                  08h if bad CRC on disk read
                  04h if requested sector not found
                  03h if write attempt on write-protected diskette
                  02h if error other than types listed above
            AX = 0207h if failed to read/write extended format using conventional INT 25h/26h calls

INTERRUPT 27h Terminate and Stay Resident [All Versions]

This is a very early set of routines to let a program terminate foreground status, yet not deallocate its memory (hence, "terminate and stay resident"). Do not use this interrupt. Use DOS INT 21h Function AH = 31h instead.

    Entry: CS = segment address of program's PSP
           DX = bottom of available memory (your highest address + 1)

    Return: None

    Note: Does not close files

INTERRUPT 28h Keyboard Busy Loop (Background Dispatcher)

This interrupt is automatically invoked as part of the "get input from keyboard" routine (INT 21h, AH = 01h). When the ISR for this routine is active, MS-DOS is in a "safe" state, which means that the INT 21h stacks are predictable and disk access is safe.

    This is the preferred interrupt to use for background processing, and is used by the PRINT.COM utility and other TSRs. The procedure "captures" this interrupt by saving the IVT value in your routine, then writing the start address of the code for your routine in the IVT location 28h. When this interrupt is invoked, your routine becomes active. As with replacing any ISR, it is best that you first call the original ISR to activation, letting its IRET return control to your routine, which can then do its work. Be sure to push CS:IP and the flags before you call the original INT 28h ISR so that its final IRET will restore control properly.

INTERRUPT 29h Fast PUTCHAR (DOS Internal) [All Versions]

The INT 21h output routines call this interrupt to send output to a device (rather than to a file) if the device driver's attribute word has bit 3 set (04h). Do not call this directly.

INTERRUPT 2Ah Network Installation Check [Versions 3 and Above]

This interrupt contains several functions to check for presence of a network, determine the name of the network, check direct I/O, execute NETBIOS, get network resource information, and perform other undocumented network-related tasks. It is for Microsoft Networks.

INTERRUPT 2Bh–2Dh Undocumented

Reserved for MS-DOS.

INTERRUPT 2Eh Execute Command (Undocumented)

ES:SI contains the start address of a command string terminated with a carriage return. The earliest installed COMMAND.COM executes the command, destroying all registers. This is a hatchway means to execute a command from within memory. Be warned that the behavior of this routine is not predictable, so save all registers, including segment registers, and especially SS and SP.

INTERRUPT 2Fh Multiplex Interrupt Function Calls [Versions 3 and Above]

The documented purpose for this interrupt is to provide print spooler services (see AH entries below). In addition, this interrupt routine plays host to a variety of routines. As with other Interrupt Service Routines (ISRs), a particular member of the family is identified by a value in AH. Values 7Fh and below are reserved for printer management. Values 80h and above are available for the use of user-installable ISRs, providing an increased capacity for guest ISRs above the limit provided by capturing other allowable interrupt vectors.

The rules are limited. First, inspect to see if an AH entry value identifies a routine by setting AH to the value in question, AL to zero, and calling INT 2Fh. Inspect AL for 0 (not claimed), 1 (not available), or 0FFh (a routine is installed). As an example, you might call INT 2Fh with AH = 0C0h (the Microsoft approved lower limit for user-installable routines). If AL returns with zero, you can install your own ISR as a member of the family, number AH = 0C0h. Your ISR must respect the rules, so when another routine calls INT 2Fh, AH = 0Ch, you returns 0FFh in AL.

Table C-2 lists the error codes and their names.

Entry: AH = < 7Fh reserved for DOS
AH => 80h program ISR identifier
AL = function code
AX = 0100h Get PRINT Installed State

Return: AL = 0, PRINT not installed; OK to install
AL = 1, PRINT not installed; not OK to install
AL = FFh, PRINT is installed

Table C-2. *INT 2Fh Error Codes*

Error Code	Error Name
1	Invalid function
2	File not found
3	Path not found
4	Too many open files
5	Access denied
8	Queue full
9	Busy
C	Name too long
F	Invalid drive

AX = 0101h Submit File to PRINT

Entry: DS:DX = start address of submit packet
1 BYTE level (0)
1 DWORD pointer to ASCIIZ drive, path, and file name

Return: If CY = 1, AX = error code

AX = 0102h Cancel File in PRINT Queue

Entry: DS:DX = pointer to ASCIIZ drive, path, and file name to cancel

Return: If CY = 1, AX = error code

AX = 0103h Cancel All Files in PRINT Queue

Entry: None

Return: If CY = 1, AX = error code

AX = 0104h Pause and Return Status

Entry: None

Return: DX = error count
DS:SI = pointer to print queue consisting of file name entries 64 bytes long; last entry starts with null

AX = 0105h End of PRINT Status

Entry: None

Return: If CY = 1, AX = error code

AX = 0200h Get ASSIGN Installed State

Entry: None

Return: If AL = 0, ASSIGN not installed; OK to install
        If AL = 1, ASSIGN not installed; not OK to install
        If AL = FFh, ASSIGN is installed

AX = 1000h Get SHARE Installed State

Entry: None

Return: If AL = 0, SHARE not installed; OK to install
        If AL = 1, SHARE not installed; not OK to install
        If AL = FFh, SHARE is installed

AX = B700h Get APPEND Installed State

Entry: None

Return: If AL = 0, APPEND not installed; OK to install
        If AL = 1, APPEND not installed; not OK to install
        If AL = FFh, APPEND is installed

INTERRUPT 30h FAR JUMP Instruction

This interrupt works with INT 31h.

INTERRUPT 31h

This interrupt is the second part of INT 30h. INT 30h and INT 31h do not contain addresses of ISRs. They are an obsolete (CP/M-compatible) means of enabling FAR JUMPs.

INTERRUPT 32h

Not used.

INTERRUPT 33h

Microsoft Mouse.

INTERRUPT 34h—3Eh

Used for floating-point emulations in Microsoft C and Turbo C.

INTERRUPT 3Fh

Microsoft LINK.EXE overlay manager.

INTERRUPT 40h

A floppy disk handler (relocated by hard disk, original INT 13h), this IVT entry does not point to an ISR.

INTERRUPT 41h

This interrupt fixes disk parameters for XT, AT, XT2, XT286, PS, not ESDI disks. As with INT 40h, this IVT entry points to a data structure describing the parameters for the hard disk drive.

> 16-bit word specifies number of cylinders
>
> 8-bit byte specifies number of heads
>
> 8-bit byte contains value of zero
>
> 16-bit word specifies Write Pre-Comp
>
> 8-bit byte contains value of zero
>
> 8-bit byte contains value of zero
>
> 8-bit byte contains value of zero
>
> 8-bit byte contains value of zero
>
> 8-bit byte contains value of zero
>
> 16-bit word specifies landing zone
>
> 8-bit byte specifies sectors per track
>
> 8-bit byte contains value of zero

INTERRUPT 42h

Video handler for EGA, VGA, PS (original INT 10h).

INTERRUPT 43h

EGA initialization parameters for EGA, VGA, PS/2.

INTERRUPT 44h

Fonts for EGA, VGA, PC Convertible, PS/2.

INTERRUPT 45h Reserved

INTERRUPT 46h

Secondary fixed-disk parameters for AT, XT286, PS except ESDI.

INTERRUPT 47h Reserved

INTERRUPT 48h

PCjr Cordless Keyboard Translation Table.

INTERRUPT 49h

PCjr translation table for nonkeyboard scan code.

INTERRUPT 4AH
User alarm for AT, PC convertible, PS/2.

INTERRUPT 4Bh–4Fh Reserved

INTERRUPT 50h–57h
DesqView Interrupt Request 0–7.

INTERRUPT 58h Reserved

INTERRUPT 59h
GSS Computer Graphics Interface.

INTERRUPT 5Ah
Entry address for cluster adapter BIOS.

INTERRUPT 5Bh Reserved

INTERRUPT 5Ch NETBIOS Interface

Entry: ES:BX start address for Network Control Block

Return: AL = error code

INTERRUPT 5Dh–5Fh Reserved

INTERRUPT 60h–66h
User-available interrupt vectors.

INTERRUPT 67h Expanded Memory Manager (EMS)
See Memory section of Chapter 13.

INTERRUPT 68h–6Fh Unused

INTERRUPT 70h
Vectored hardware lines for AT, XT286, PS50, 60, 80 real-time clock.

INTERRUPT 71h
Vectored hardware lines for AT, XT286, PS50, 60, 80 LAN adapter 1.

INTERRUPT 72h
Vectored hardware lines for AT, XT286, PS50, 60, 80 Reserved.

INTERRUPT 73h
Vectored hardware lines for AT, XT286, PS50, 60, 80 Reserved.

INTERRUPT 74h

Vectored hardware lines for AT, XT286, PS50, 60, 80 PS50, 60, 80 mouse interrupt.

INTERRUPT 75h

Vectored hardware lines for AT, XT286, PS50, 60, 80 80287 error.

INTERRUPT 76h

Vectored hardware lines for AT, XT286, PS50, 60, 80 fixed disk.

INTERRUPT 77h

Vectored hardware lines for AT, XT286, PS50, 60, 80 Reserved.

INTERRUPT 78h–79h Unused

INTERRUPT 00F–85h

For use of BASIC interpreter.

INTERRUPT 86h

Transfer to ROM BASIC, relocated INT 18h.

INTERRUPT 87h–F0h

For use of BASIC interpreter.

INTERRUPT F1h–FDh

Publicly available interrupt.

INTERRUPT FEh–FFh Unusable

Appendix **D ASCII Conversions**

Table D-1 cross-references terminal keys with their decimal (base 10), hexadecimal (base 16), octal (base 8), and ASCII (American Standard Code for Information Interchange) assignments. The key sequences that consist of Ctrl-are typed by simultaneously pressing the Control key and the key indicated. These sequences are based on those defined for most standard terminals, such as the Diablo 1640 keyboard and the Televideo series of terminals, and may be defined differently on other keyboards.

Table D-1. _ASCII Cross-Reference_

DEC X_{10}	HEX X_{16}	OCT X_{8}	ASCII	IBM Graphics Character	Terminal Key*
0	00	00	NUL		\<Ctrl-@\>
1	01	01	SOH	☺	\<Ctrl-A\>
2	02	02	STX	☻	\<Ctrl-B\>
3	03	03	ETX	♥	\<Ctrl-C\>
4	04	04	EOT	♦	\<Ctrl-D\>
5	05	05	ENQ	♣	\<Ctrl-E\>
6	06	06	ACK	♠	\<Ctrl-F\>
7	07	07	BEL	●	\<Ctrl-G\>
8	08	10	BS	▣	\<Ctrl-H\>
9	09	11	HT	○	\<Ctrl-I\>
10	0A	12	LF	■	\<Ctrl-J\>

DEC X_{10}	HEX X_{16}	OCT X_8	ASCII	IBM Graphics Character	Terminal Key*
11	0B	13	VT	♂	<Ctrl-K>
12	0C	14	FF	♀	<Ctrl-L>
13	0D	15	CR	♪	<Ctrl-M>
14	0E	16	SO	♫	<Ctrl-N>
15	0F	17	SI	☼	<Ctrl-O>
16	10	20	DLE	▶	<Ctrl-P>
17	11	21	DC1	◀	<Ctrl-Q>
18	12	22	DC2	↕	<Ctrl-R>
19	13	23	DC3	‼	<Ctrl-S>
20	14	24	DC4	¶	<Ctrl-T>
21	15	25	NAK	§	<Ctrl-U>
22	16	26	SYN	▬	<Ctrl-V>
23	17	27	ETB	↨	<Ctrl-W>
24	18	30	CAN	↑	<Ctrl-X>
25	19	31	EM	↓	<Ctrl-Y>
26	1A	32	SUB	→	<Ctrl-Z>
27	1B	33	ESC	←	<Esc>
28	1C	34	FS	∟	<Ctrl-\>
29	1D	35	GS	↔	<Ctrl-'>
30	1E	36	RS	▲	<Ctrl-=>
31	1F	37	US	▼	<Ctrl-->
32	20	40	SP		(Space) <SPACE BAR>
33	21	41	!	!	!(Exclamation mark)
34	22	42	"	"	"(Quotation mark)
35	23	43	#	#	#(Number sign or octothorpe)
36	24	44	$	$	$(Dollar sign)

DEC X_{10}	HEX X_{16}	OCT X_8	ASCII	IBM Graphics Character	Terminal Key*
37	25	45	%	%	%(Percent)
38	26	46	&	&	&(Ampersand)
39	27	47	'	'	'(Apostrophe or acute accent)
40	28	50	(	(	((Opening parenthesis)
41	29	51	)	)	)(Closing parenthesis)
42	2A	52	*	*	*(Asterisk)
43	2B	53	+	+	+(Plus)
44	2C	54	,	,	,(Comma)
45	2D	55	-	-	-(Hyphen, dash, or minus)
46	2E	56	.	.	.(Period)
47	2F	57	/	/	/(Forward slant)
48	30	60	0	0	0
49	31	61	1	1	1
50	32	62	2	2	2
51	33	63	3	3	3
52	34	64	4	4	4
53	35	65	5	5	5
54	36	66	6	6	6
55	37	67	7	7	7
56	38	70	8	8	8
57	39	71	9	9	9
58	3A	72	:	:	:(Colon)
59	3B	73	;	;	;(Semicolon)
60	3C	74	<	<	<(Less than)
61	3D	75	=	=	=(Equals)

DEC X_{10}	HEX X_{16}	OCT X_8	ASCII	IBM Graphics Character	Terminal Key*
62	3E	76	>	>	>(Greater than)
63	3F	77	?	?	?(Question mark)
64	40	100	@	@	@(Commercial at)
65	41	101	A	A	A
66	42	102	B	B	B
67	43	103	C	C	C
68	44	104	D	D	D
69	45	105	E	E	E
70	46	106	F	F	F
71	47	107	G	G	G
72	48	110	H	H	H
73	49	111	I	I	I
74	4A	112	J	J	J
75	4B	113	K	K	K
76	4C	114	L	L	L
77	4D	115	M	M	M
78	4E	116	N	N	N
79	4F	117	O	O	O
80	50	120	P	P	P
81	51	121	Q	Q	Q
82	52	122	R	R	R
83	53	123	S	S	S
84	54	124	T	T	T
85	55	125	U	U	U
86	56	126	V	V	V
87	57	127	W	W	W
88	58	130	X	X	X
89	59	131	Y	Y	Y

DEC X_{10}	HEX X_{16}	OCT X_8	ASCII	IBM Graphics Character	Terminal Key*
90	5A	132	Z	Z	Z
91	5B	133	[	[	[(Opening bracket)
92	5C	134	\	\	\(Reverse slant)
93	5D	135	]	]	](Closing bracket)
94	5E	136	^	^	^(Caret or circumflex)
95	5F	137	_	_	_(Underscore or underline)
96	60	140	`	`	`(Grave accent)
97	61	141	a	a	a
98	62	142	b	b	b
99	63	143	c	c	c
100	64	144	d	d	d
101	65	145	e	e	e
102	66	146	f	f	f
103	67	147	g	g	g
104	68	150	h	h	h
105	69	151	i	i	i
106	6A	152	j	j	j
107	6B	153	k	k	k
108	6C	154	l	l	l
109	6D	155	m	m	m
110	6E	156	n	n	n
111	6F	157	o	o	o
112	70	160	p	p	p
113	71	161	q	q	q
114	72	162	r	r	r
115	73	163	s	s	s

DEC X_{10}	HEX X_{16}	OCT X_8	ASCII	IBM Graphics Character	Terminal Key*
116	74	164	t	t	t
117	75	165	u	u	u
118	76	166	v	v	v
119	77	167	w	w	w
120	78	170	x	x	x
121	79	171	y	y	y
122	7A	172	z	z	z
123	7B	173	{	{	{(Opening brace)
124	7C	174	:	:	:(Vertical bar; logical OR)
125	7D	175	}	}	}(Closing brace)
126	7E	176	~	~	~(Tilde)
127	7F	177	DEL	DEL	>Del<

*Those key sequences consisting of <Ctrl-> are typed in by pressing the Ctrl key, and while it is held down, pressing the key indicated. These sequences are based on those defined for the IBM Personal Computer series keyboards. The key sequences may be defined differently on other keyboards. IBM Extended ASCII characters can be displayed by pressing the <Alt> key and then typing the decimal code of the character on the keypad.

Abbreviations:

DEC = Decimal (Base 10)
HEC = Hexadecimal (Base 16)
OCT   = Octal (Base 8)
ASCII = American Standard Code for Information Interchange

Nonprintable ASCII Character Definitions

ACK (ACKNOWLEDGMENT) A communication control character that serves as a general "yes" answer to various queries but also sometimes indicates "I received your last transmission and I'm ready for your next."

BELL (BELL) A general-purpose control character that activates a bell, beeper, or other audible alarm on the device to which it was sent.

BS (BACKSPACE) A format effector control character that moves the carriage, print head, or cursor back one space or position.

CAN (CANCEL) A general-purpose control character that indicates that the material in the previous transmission is to be disregarded. The amount of material is decided by the user.

CR (CARRIAGE RETURN OR RETURN) A format effector control character that moves the carriage, print head, or cursor on a terminal back to the beginning of the line. On most terminals, the Return key causes both a CR and an LF (line feed).

DC1-DC4 (DEVICE CONTROLS) General-purpose control characters that control the user's terminal or similar devices. No standard functions are assigned, except that DC4 frequently means *stop*. The CCITT (Comité Consultatif International Télégraphe et Téléphone [International Telegraph and Telephone Consultative Committee]) suggests a number of possible assignments. In general, CCITT prefers using the first two controls for *on*, and the last two for *off*, and DC2 and DC4 to refer to the more important device. In some systems, these codes are labeled XON, TAPE, XOFF, and NO TAPE, respectively. X means *transmitter*, and TAPE and NO TAPE mean *tape on* and *tape off*. These labels are found on the keytops of some terminals.

DEL (DELETE) A general-purpose control character that deletes a character. Called RUBOUT on some terminals, DEL is not strictly a control character because it is not grouped with the other ASCII control characters. The DEL function has a binary all-ones bit pattern (1111 1111, base 2). The reason is historic: The only way to erase a bit pattern punched into paper tape was to punch out all the holes so that the resulting pattern was equivalent to a null. ASCII still considers DEL equivalent to a null, although many operating systems use DEL to erase the preceding character.

DLE (DATA LINK ESCAPE) A communications control character that uses a special type of escape sequence specifically for controlling the data line and transmission facilities.

EM (END OF MEDIUM) A general-purpose control character that indicates the end of paper tape (or other storage medium) or is the end of the material on the medium.

ENQ (ENQUIRY) A communications control character that usually is used for requesting identification or status information. In some systems, this code is WRU (who are you?).

EOT (END OF TRANSMISSION) A communications control character that marks the end of a transmission after one or more messages.

ESC (ESCAPE) A general-purpose character that marks the beginning of an escape sequence. An escape sequence consists of a series of codes, which as a group have a special meaning, usually a control function. On some terminals, ESC is called ALT MODE.

ETB (END OF TRANSMISSION BLOCK) A communications control character that is used when you want to break up a long message into blocks. ETB marks block boundaries. The blocks usually have nothing to do with the format of the message being transmitted.

EXT (END OF TEXT) A communications control character that marks the end of a text. *See* SOH. This code was originally called EOM (end of message) and may be labeled as such on some terminals.

FF (FORM FEED) A format effector character that causes the carriage, print wheel, or cursor to advance to the top of the next page.

FS, GS, RS, US (FILE, GROUP, RECORD, AND UNIT SEPARATOR) A set of information separator control characters that delimit portions of information. No standard usage exists, except that FS is expected to refer to the largest division and US to the smallest.

HT (HORIZONTAL TAB) A format effector control character that tabs the carriage, print wheel, or cursor to the next predetermined stop on the same line. The user usually decides where the horizontal tab stops are positioned.

LF (LINE FEED) A format effector control character that moves the carriage, print head, or cursor down one line. Most systems combine CR (carriage return) with LF, and the new line is called NL (new line).

NAK (NEGATIVE ACKNOWLEDGMENT) A communications control character that indicates no in answer to various queries. Sometimes it is defined as "I received your last transmission, but it had errors and I'm waiting for a retransmission."

NUL (NULL) A general-purpose control character that mainly is used as a space filler. *See also* SYN.

SI (SHIFT IN) A general-purpose control character that is used after an SO code to indicate that codes revert to normal ASCII meaning.

SO (SHIFT OUT) A general-purpose control character that indicates the following bit patterns have meanings outside the standard ASCII set and will continue to do so until SI is entered.

SOH (START OF HEADING) A communications control character that marks the beginning of a heading when headings are used in messages along with text. Headings usually state the name and location of an addressee. This code was originally called SOM (start of message).

STX (START OF TEXT) A communications control character that is used as a marker of the beginning of text and end of heading (if used). This code was originally called EOA (end of address).

SUB (SUBSTITUTE) A general-purpose control character indicating a character that is to take the place of a character known to be wrong.

SYN (SYNCHRONOUS IDLE) A communications control character used by some high-speed data communications systems that use synchronized clocks at the transmitter and receiver ends. During idle periods, when there are no bit patterns to enable the receiver's clock to track the transmitter's, the receiver may drift out of sync. Every transmission following an idle period therefore is replaced by three or four SYN characters. The SYN code has a bit pattern that enables the receiver not only to lock onto the transmitter's clock but also to determine the beginning and end points of each character. SYN characters may also be used to fill short idle periods to maintain synchronization, hence the name.

VT (VERTICAL TAB) A format effector control character that tabs the carriage, print head, or cursor to the next predetermined stop (usually a line).

Hexadecimal to Decimal Conversion

Figure D-1 shows how the hexadecimal number 5F9D is converted to its decimal equivalent.

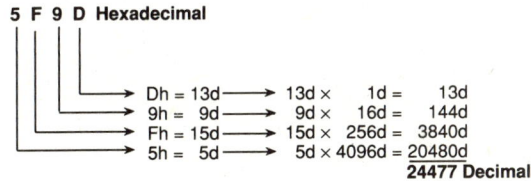

```
5 F 9 D  Hexadecimal

        Dh = 13d  ———→  13d ×     1d =      13d
        9h =  9d  ———→   9d ×    16d =     144d
        Fh = 15d  ———→  15d ×   256d =    3840d
        5h =  5d  ———→   5d × 4096d =   20480d
                                        24477 Decimal
```

Figure D-1. *Conversion of hexadecimal number 5F9D to its decimal equivalent.*

Each hexadecimal digit is always 16 times greater than the digit immediately to the right.

Decimal to Hexadecimal Conversion

The conversion process is reversed when converting decimal numbers to hexadecimal. Start by selecting the leftmost digit and determine its significance in the number (thousands, hundreds, etc.). The decimal is then divided by the hexadecimal value of the first digit's relative position. If, for example, the first digit is in the thousands position, divide by 4,096 (decimal equivalent of 1,000 hexadecimal). The result is the first hexadecimal digit. The remainder is divided by the hexadecimal value of the next digit's relative position (that is, divide the hundreds digit by 256 because 256 is the hexadecimal equivalent of 100 decimal). Figure D-2 shows how the decimal number derived in the previous example is converted back to hexadecimal.

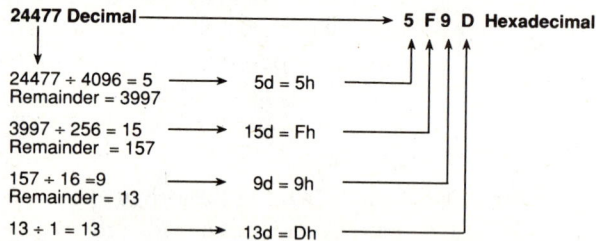

Figure D-2. *Decimal number 24477 converted back to its hexadecimal equivalent.*

Table D-2. *IBM Extended Cross-Reference*

Binary X_2	OCT X_8	DEC X_{10}	HEX X_{16}	Ext. ASCII
1000 0000	200	128	80	Ç
1000 0001	201	129	81	ü
1000 0010	202	130	82	é
1000 0011	203	131	83	â
1000 0100	204	132	84	ä
1000 0101	205	133	85	à
1000 0110	206	134	86	å
1000 0111	207	135	87	ç
1000 1000	210	136	88	ê
1000 1001	211	137	89	ë
1000 1010	212	138	8A	è
1000 1011	213	139	8B	ï
1000 1100	214	140	8C	î
1000 1101	215	141	8D	ì
1000 1110	216	142	8E	Ä
1000 1111	217	143	8F	Å

Binary X_2	OCT X_8	DEC X_{10}	HEX X_{16}	Ext. ASCII
1001 0000	220	144	90	É
1001 0001	221	145	91	æ
1001 0010	222	146	92	Æ
1001 0011	223	147	93	ô
1001 0100	224	148	94	ö
1001 0101	225	149	95	ò
1001 0110	226	150	96	û
1001 0111	227	151	97	ù
1001 1000	230	152	98	y
1001 1001	231	153	99	Ö
1001 1010	232	154	9A	Ü
1001 1011	233	155	9B	¢
1001 1100	234	156	9C	£
1001 1101	235	157	9D	¥
1001 1110	236	158	9E	P₁
1001 1111	237	159	9F	*f*
1010 0000	240	160	A0	á
1010 0001	241	161	A1	í
1010 0010	242	162	A2	ó
1010 0011	243	163	A3	ú
1010 0100	244	164	A4	ñ
1010 0101	245	165	A5	Ñ
1010 0110	246	166	A6	a̱
1010 0111	247	167	A7	o̱
1010 1000	250	168	A8	¿
1010 1001	251	169	A9	⌐
1010 1010	252	170	AA	¬
1010 1011	253	171	AB	$^1/_2$
1010 1100	254	172	AC	$^1/_4$

Binary X_2	OCT X_8	DEC X_{10}	HEX X_{16}	Ext. ASCII
1010 1101	255	173	AD	i
1010 1110	256	174	AE	«
1010 1111	257	175	AF	»
1011 0000	260	176	B0	▒
1011 0001	261	177	B1	▓
1011 0010	262	178	B2	▓
1011 0011	263	179	B3	│
1011 0100	264	180	B4	┤
1011 0101	265	181	B5	╡
1011 0110	266	182	B6	╢
1011 0111	267	183	B7	╖
1011 1000	270	184	B8	╕
1011 1001	271	185	B9	╣
1011 1010	272	186	BA	║
1011 1011	273	187	BB	╗
1011 1100	274	188	BC	╝
1011 1101	275	189	BD	╜
1011 1110	276	190	BE	╛
1011 1111	277	191	BF	┐
1100 0000	300	192	C0	└
1100 0001	301	193	C1	┴
1100 0010	302	194	C2	┬
1100 0011	303	195	C3	├
1100 0100	304	196	C4	─
1100 0101	305	197	C5	┼
1100 0110	306	198	C6	╞
1100 0111	307	199	C7	╟
1100 1000	310	200	C8	╚
1100 1001	311	201	C9	╔

Binary X_2	OCT X_8	DEC X_{10}	HEX X_{16}	Ext. ASCII
1100 1010	312	202	CA	⊥
1100 1011	313	203	CB	⊤
1100 1100	314	204	CC	⊢
1100 1101	315	205	CD	=
1100 1110	316	206	CE	╬
1100 1111	317	207	CF	⊥
1101 0000	320	208	D0	⊥
1101 0001	321	209	D1	⊤
1101 0010	322	210	D2	π
1101 0010	323	211	D3	⊔
1101 0100	324	212	D4	⊢
1101 0101	325	213	D5	⊨
1101 0110	326	214	D6	⊓
1101 0111	327	215	D7	╫
1101 1000	330	216	D8	╪
1101 1001	331	217	D9	⌐
1101 1010	332	218	DA	⌐
1101 1011	333	219	DB	■
1101 1100	334	220	DC	■
1101 1101	335	221	DD	▌
1101 1110	336	222	DE	▐
1101 1111	337	223	DF	■
1110 0000	340	224	E0	∝
1110 0001	341	225	E1	ß
1110 0010	342	226	E2	Γ
1110 0011	343	227	E3	π
1110 0100	344	228	E4	Σ
1110 0101	345	229	E5	σ
1110 0110	346	230	E6	μ

Binary X_2	OCT X_8	DEC X_{10}	HEX X_{16}	Ext. ASCII
1110 0111	347	231	E7	⊤
1110 1000	350	232	E8	Φ
1110 1001	351	233	E9	θ
1110 1010	352	234	EA	Ω
1110 1011	353	235	EB	δ
1110 1100	354	236	EC	∞
1110 1101	355	237	ED	∅
1110 1110	356	238	EE	∈
1110 1111	357	239	EF	∩
1110 0000	360	240	F0	≡
1111 0001	361	241	F1	±
1111 0010	362	242	F2	≥
1111 0011	363	243	F3	≤
1111 0100	364	244	F4	⌠
1111 0101	365	245	F5	⌡
1111 0110	366	246	F6	÷
1111 0111	367	247	F7	≈
1111 1000	370	248	F8	°
1111 1001	371	249	F9	•
1111 1010	372	250	FA	·
1111 1011	373	251	FB	√
1111 1100	374	252	FC	η
1111 1101	375	253	FD	^{2}
1111 1110	376	254	FE	■
1111 1111	377	255	FF	

Index

Symbols

%OUT directive, 438
.TYPE directive, 378-379
@Code alias, 312-313
@CodeSize alias, 313-314
@CurSeg alias, 315
@Data alias, 315-316
@DataSize alias, 316
00h Divide by Zero Interrupt, 613
01h Single-Step Interrupt, 613
02h Nonmaskable Interrupt, 613
03h Breakpoint Interrupt, 613
04h Overflow Interrupt, 613
05h Print Screen Interrupt, 613
06h Reserved Interrupt, 613
07h Reserved Interrupt, 613
08h System Timer Interrupt, 613
09h Keyboard Interrupt, 614
0Ah (Various) Interrupt, 614
0Bh (Various) Interrupt, 614
0Ch (Various) Interrupt, 614
0Dh (Various) Interrupt, 614
0Eh Disk Controller Interrupt, 614
0Fh LPT1 Controller Interrupt, 614
10h Video Interrupt, 512, 614
   00h Set Video Mode, 615, 616

01h Set Cursor Type, 616
02h Set Cursor Position, 616
03h Get Cursor Position and Characteristics, 616
04h Read Light Pen Position, 617
05h Select Display Page, 617
06h Scroll Page Up, 617
07h Scroll Page Down, 618
08h Read Character and Attribute at Cursor, 618
09h Write Character and Attribute at Cursor, 618
0Ah Write Character at Cursor, 618
0Bh Set Color Palette, 619
0Ch Write a Dot to a Pixel Location, 619
0Dh Read Dot Color at a Pixel Location, 619
0Eh Write a Character in TTY Mode, 619
0Fh Get Current Mode, 620
10h Set Palette Registers, 620
11h BIOS interrupt, 512
11h Get Equipment List Interrupt, 620-621
12h Memory Size Interrupt, 512, 621
13h Floppy Disk Interrupt, 512, 621
   00h Reset Floppy Disk Controller, 621
   01h Get Disk Status, 622
   02h Read Floppy Disk Sectors, 622-623

03h Write Floppy Disk Sectors, 623
04h Verify Sectors, 623
05h Format a Track, 623
14h Serial I/O Interrupt, 623
00h Initialize a Serial Port, 624-625
01h Write Character to Serial Port, 625
02h Read Character from Serial Port, 625
03h Get Serial Port Status, 625
15h Cassette Interface Interrupt, 625
16h Keyboard Interrupt, 626
00h Read Character from Keyboard
Buffer, 626
01h Get Keyboard Buffer Status, 626
02h Get Keyboard Shift Byte, 626
17h Printer Interrupt, 627
00h Write Character to Printer, 627
01h Initialize Printer, 627
02h Get Printer Status, 627
18 ROM BASIC Interrupt, 628
.186 directive, 447
19 Warm Boot without Reset Interrupt, 628
1A Clock Interrupt, 628
00h Read Time of Day, 628
01h Set Time of Day, 628
1Bh Control-Break Interrupt, 628-629
1Ch Clock Tick Interrupt, 629
1Dh Video Initialization Tables Interrupt,
629
1Eh Disk Initialization Table Interrupt, 630
1Fh Graphics Character Set Interrupt, 630
20h Program Terminate Interrupt, 631
21h Functions Interrupt, 631
339h Create Subdirectory (MKDIR), 651
00h Program Terminate, 631
01h Input Character from Console with
Echo, 632
02h Output Character to Console, 632
03h Input Character from Auxiliary Port,
632-633
04h Output Character to Auxiliary Port,
633
05h Output Character to Printer, 633
06h Direct Console I/O, 633-634

07h Direct Input Character from Console,
634
08h Input Character from Console
without Echo, 634
09h Output String to Console, 634-635
0Ah Input Buffered String from Console
with Echo, 635
0Bh Check Standard Input Status,
635-636
0Ch Clear Keyboard Buffer and Invoke
Keyboard, 636
0Dh Disk Reset, 636
0Eh Select Disk, 636-637
0Fh FCB Open File, 637
10h FCB Close File, 637-638
11h FCB Search for First Entry, 638
12h FCB Search for Next Entry, 638-639
13h FCB Delete File, 639
14h FCB Sequential Read, 639-640
15h FCB Sequential Write, 640
16h FCB Create File, 640
17h FCB Rename File, 640-641
18h Undocumented, 641
19h Get Current Disk, 641
1Ah Set Disk Transfer Address, 641
1Bh Get Default Drive Data, 641-642
1Ch Get Drive Data, 642
1Dh Undocumented, 642
1Eh Undocumented, 642
1Fh Get Drive Parameter Block, 642
21h Random Read, 643
22h Random Write, 643
23h Get File Size, 643-644
24h Set Relative Record Field, 644
25h Set Interrupt Vector, 644
26h Create New Program Segment Prefix,
644
27h Random Block Read, 644-645
28h Random Block Write, 645
29h FCB Parse Filename, 645-646
2Ah Get Date, 646
2Bh Set Date, 646-647
2Ch Get Time, 647
2Dh Set Time, 647

2Eh Set/Reset Verify Switch, 647

2Fh Get Disk Transfer Address (DTA), 648

30h Get MS-DOS Version Number, 648

31h Terminate Process and Remain Resident, 648-649

32h Find Disk Parameter Block for Specified D, 649

33h Get/Set Control-C (Control-Break) Che, 649-650

34h Get Critical Section Flag Address, 650

35h Get Interrupt Vector, 650

36h Get Disk Free Space, 650

37h Check or Change Switch Character, 651

38h Get Current Country Information, 651

3Ah Remove Subdirectory (RMDIR), 652

3Bh Change Current Directory (CHDIR), 652

3Ch Create a File Handle, 652-653

3Dh Open a File, 653

3Eh Close a File Handle, 653, 654

3Fh Read from a File or Device, 654

40h Write to a File or Device, 654

41h Delete File from Specified Directory, 654-655

42h Move File Read/Write Pointer (LSEEK), 655

43h Change File Mode (CHMOD), 655-656

44h I/O Control for Devices (IOCTL), 656

45h Duplicate a File Handle (DUP), 656, 657

46h Force a Duplicate of a File Handle (FORCD), 657

47h Get Current Directory, 657

48h Allocate Memory, 657-658

49h Free Allocated Memory, 658

4Ah Modify Allocated Memory Blocks (SETBLOCK), 658-659

4Bh Load and Execute a Program (EXEC), 659-660

4Ch Terminate a Process (EXIT), 660

4Dh Get Return Code of Child Process, 660

4Eh Find First Matching File (FINDFIRST), 660-661

4Fh Find Next Matching File (FINDNEXT), 661

50h Set PSP, 661

51h Get Current PSP, 661

52h Get Address of Master List, 661

53h Undocumented, 662

54h Get Verify Setting, 662

55h Create PSP, 662

56h Respecify File Entry, 662

57h Get File's Date and Time, 662-663

58h Get/Set Allocation Strategy, 663

59h Get Extended Error Information, 663-664

5Ah Create a Temporary File, 664

5Bh Create a New File, 665

5Ch Lock/Unlock File Access, 665

5Dh Undocumented, 665

5E00h NETWORK: Get Machine Name, 665

5E02h NETWORK: Set Printer Setup String, 666

5E03h NETWORK: Get Printer Setup String, 666

5F02h NETWORK: Get Redirection List Entry, 666

5F03h NETWORK: Redirect Device, 666-667

60h Undocumented, 667

Ah = 61h Undocumented, 667

62h Get Program Segment Prefix Address, 667

63h Get DBCS Lead Byte Table, 667

64h Undocumented, 667

65h Get Extended Country Information, 667

66h Get/Set Global Code Page, 668

67h Set Handle Count, 668

68h Commit File, 668

69h–6Bh Undocumented, 668
6Ch Extended Open/Create, 668-669
22h Terminate Address Interrupt, 670
23h Control-C Exit Address Interrupt, 670
24h Critical Error Handler Address Interrupt, 670-671
25h Absolute Disk Read Interrupt, 672
26h Absolute Write Interrupt, 672-673
27h Terminate and Stay Resident Interrupt, 673
.286 directive, 447-448
.286C directive, 447-448
.286P directive, 448-449
.287 directive, 449
28h Keyboard Busy Loop Interrupt, 673
29h Fast PUTCHAR Interrupt, 674
2Ah Network Installation Check Interrupt, 674
2Bh–2Dh Undocumented Interrupts, 674
2Eh Execute Command Interrupt, 674
2Fh Multiplex Interrupt Function Calls Interrupt, 674-675
　0101h Submit File to PRINT, 675
　0102h Cancel File in PRINT Queue, 675
　0103h Cancel All Files in PRINT Queue, 675
　0104h Pause and Return Status, 675
　0105h End of PRINT Status, 675-676
　0200h Get ASSIGN Installed State, 676
　1000h Get SHARE Installed State, 676
　B700h Get APPEND Installed State, 676
30h FAR JUMP Instruction Interrupt, 676
31h Interrupt, 676
32h Interrupt, 676
33h Interrupt, 676
34h–3Eh Interrupt, 676
.386 directive, 449-450
.386C directive, 449-450
.386P directive, 450-451
.387 directive, 451
3Fh Interrupt, 676
40h Interrupt, 677
41h Interrupt, 677
42h Interrupt, 677

43h Interrupt, 677
44h Interrupt, 677
45h Reserved Interrupt, 677
46h Interrupt, 677
47h Reserved Interrupt, 677
48h Interrupt, 677
49h Interrupt, 677
4Ah Interrupt, 678
4Bh–4Fh Reserved Interrupt, 678
4Ch Terminate a Process (EXIT) function, 660
50h–57h Interrupt, 678
58h Reserved Interrupt, 678
59h Interrupt, 678
5Ah Interrupt, 678
5Bh Reserved Interrupt, 678
5Ch NETBIOS Interface Interrupt, 678
5Dh–5Fh Reserved Interrupt, 678
60h–66h Interrupt, 678
68h–6Fh Unused Interrupt, 678
70h Interrupt, 678
71h Interrupt, 678
72h Interrupt, 678
73h Interrupt, 678
74h Interrupt, 679
75h Interrupt, 679
76h Interrupt, 679
77h Interrupt, 679
78h–79h Unused Interrupt, 679
80286 microprocessors
　ENTER instruction, 218
　protected mode, 245
80386 microprocessors
　ENTER instruction, 218
　protected mode, 245
　SET instruction, 73, 74
.8086 directive, 452
.8087 directive, 452-453
80h–85h Interrupt, 679
80x86 microprocessors, 4
　interrupts, 8-9
　memory, 4-5
　　registers, 5-7
　　stack, 7-8

8250 serial chip, 551
8259 interrupt controller chip, 544-545
86h Interrupt, 679
87h–F0h Interrupt, 679

A

AAA instruction, 128, 147-148
AAD instruction, 128, 148-149
AAM instruction, 128, 149-150
AAS instruction, 128, 150-151
accessing fields with structures, 335-336
ADC instruction, 151-153
ADD instruction, 119, 153-154
addition, 119
addressing memory
    addressing modes
        base, 45-48, 67-68
        base direct, 48
        base indexed, 45 48, 67
        direct, 45-47, 67-68
        direct base, 45, 67
        direct indexed, 45, 67
        direct scaled index, 46, 68
        effective address
        immediate, 44, 47, 66
        implied, 44, 47, 66
        indexed, 45, 47
        segment overrides, 69-70
        storing in registers, 68-69
    segments and offsets, 305-306
aliases, 342
    @Code, 312-313
    @CodeSize, 313-314
    @CurSeg, 315
    @Data, 315-316
    @DataSize, 316
ALIGN directive, 341, 344
aligning
    data, 341-342
    segments, 299
        BYTE align type, 300
        DWORD align type, 300
        PAGE align type, 300
        PARA align type, 300
        WORD align type, 300
.ALPHA directive, 305, 311
AND instruction, 135, 154-155, 343
animated lines, 590-597
ANSI.SYS device driver, 526, 530-531
    ESC functions, 529-531
ARG directive, 397-398, 407-408, 492
arithmetic instructions, 43
    BCD (Binary Coded Decimal) numbers,
        127-129
    comparing numbers, 121
    decrementing, 120-121
    destination operand, 115
    displaying numbers, 116-119
    division, 122-123
    incrementing, 120-121
    multiplication, 122
    sign extending, 125-126
    signed arithmetic, 124-125
    signed division, 126
    signed multiplication, 126
    source operand, 115
    status flags, 126-127
    syntax, 115-116
ARPL instruction, 260, 268-269
arrays
    checking boundaries, 80-81
assembling source files, 25
ASSUME directive, 38-39, 306, 312
AT segment combine type, 300-301
auxiliary carry flag, 127
AX register, 6

B

B700h Get APPEND Installed State function,
    676
base addressing mode, 45-48, 67-68
base direct addressing mode, 48
base indexed addressing mode, 45, 48, 67
BCD (Binary Coded Decimal) numbers,
    127-129
BCT instruction, 157-159

%BIN directive, 453-454
Binary Coded Decimal (BCD) numbers
  see BCD numbers
BIOS data areas, 513, 517
BIOS Interrupts, 512-515
  00h Divide by Zero, 613
  01h Single-Step, 613
  02h Nonmaskable, 613
  03h Breakpoint, 613
  04h Overflow, 613
  05h Print Screen, 613
  06h Reserved, 613
  07h Reserved, 613
  08h System Timer, 613
  09h Keyboard, 614
  0Ah (Various), 614
  0Bh (Various), 614
  0Ch (Various), 614
  0Dh (Various), 614
  0Eh Disk Controller, 614
  0Fh LPT1 Controller, 614
  10h Video, 512, 614-620
  11h Get Equipment List, 512, 620-621
  12h Memory Size, 512, 621
  13h Floppy Disk, 512, 621-623
  14h Serial I/O, 623-625
  15h Cassette Interface, 625
  16h Keyboard, 626
  17h Printer, 627
  18 ROM BASIC, 628
  19 Warm Book without Reset, 628
  1A Clock, 628
  1Bh Control-Break, 628-629
  1Ch Clock Tick, 629
  1Dh Video Initialization Tables, 629
  1Eh Disk Initialization Table, 630
  1Fh Graphics Character Set, 630
  20h Program Terminate, 631
  21h Functions, 631-669
  22h Terminate Address, 670
  23h Control-C Exit Address, 670
  24h Critical Error Handler Address,
    670-671
  25h Absolute Disk Read, 672

  26h Absolute Write, 672-673
  27h Terminate and Stay Resident, 673
  28h Keyboard Busy Loop, 673
  29h Fast PUTCHAR, 674
  2Ah Network Installation Check, 674
  2Bh–2Dh Undocumented, 674
  2Eh Execute Command, 674
  2Fh Multiplex Interrupt Function Calls,
    674-676
  30h FAR JUMP Instruction, 676
  31h, 676
  32h, 676
  33h, 676
  34h–3Eh, 676
  3Fh, 676
  40h, 677
  41h, 677
  42h, 677
  43h, 677
  44h, 677
  45h Reserved, 677
  46h, 677
  47h Reserved, 677
  48h, 677
  49h, 677
  4Ah, 678
  4Bh–4Fh Reserved, 678
  50h–57h, 678
  58h Reserved, 678
  59h, 678
  5Ah, 678
  5Bh Reserved, 678
  5Ch NETBIOS Interface, 678
  5Dh–5Fh Reserved, 678
  60h–66h, 678
  67h Expanded Memory Manager (EMS),
    678
  68h–6Fh Unused, 678
  70h, 678
  71h, 678
  72h, 678
  73h, 678
  74h, 679
  75h, 679

76h, 679
77h, 679
78h–79h Unused, 679
80F–85h, 679
86h, 679
87h–F0h, 679
F1h–FDh, 679
FEh–FFh Unused, 679
controlling memory, 521-526
equipment list, 512
mouse, 537-541
parallel ports, 535-537
serial ports, 535-537
terminal I/O functions, 526-531
bit fields, 337-338
bit-shift instructions, 138-139, 157-160,
    188-196
  rotating bits, 139-140
  shift operations, 140-143
  squeezing out unused bits, 143-145
Boolean logic operations
  AND instruction, 135
  NOT instruction (inclusive OR), 137-138
  OR instruction (inclusive OR), 135-136
  XOR instruction (inclusive OR), 136-137
BOUND instruction, 80-81, 223-224
BP register, 6, 69-70
Bresenham's Algorithm, 498-507
BSF instruction, 156-157
BSR instruction, 156-157
BT instruction, 157-159
BTR instruction, 157-159
BTS instruction, 157-159
bus, locking, 248-249
BX register, 6
BYTE directive, 344-345
BYTE segment align type, 300

C

C calling convention, 218, 491-492
  returning results, 492-495
call gates, 261-262
CALL instruction, 215, 224-226

calling routines/subroutines, 215
  calling between high level and assembly
      languages, 490, 492-495
    compilers, 497-507
    sharing global data, 495-496
    start-up modules, 507-508
  C calling convention, 218, 491-492
  PASCAL calling convention, 218, 492
  stack frames, 215-218
CATSTR string operator, 345-346
CBW instruction, 125, 160
CDQ instruction, 125, 160-161
CDW instruction, 164-165
checking array boundaries, 80-81
classes of segments, 303
CLC instruction, 6, 247, 269-270
CLD instruction, 6, 247, 270-271
clearing
  flags, 247
  screen, 578-579
CLI instruction, 6, 220, 247, 271-272
clock, 514-516
CLTS instruction, 260, 266, 272-273
CMC instruction, 6, 247, 273-274
CMP instruction, 121, 161-163
CMPS instruction, 163-164
CMPSB instruction, 163-164
CMPSW instruction, 163-164
.CODE directive, 33-34, 308, 314-315
@Code alias, 312-313
code segments, 308
CODESEG directive, 308, 314-315
@CodeSize alias, 313-314
Color Graphics Adapter (CGA), 566
  graphics modes, 580-582
  snow, 573-574
color palettes, 568-571
combining segments, 300-303
  AT combine type, 300-301
  COMMON combine type, 301-302
  MEMORY combine type, 302
  PRIVATE combine type, 303
  PUBLIC combine type, 302
  STACK combine type, 302

COMM directive, 389, 408-410
command-line options
TLINK, 603
Turbo Assembler, 601-602
commands
entering in Turbo Debugger, 53-54
function keys, 54
menus, 54-55
COMMENT directive, 440
comments, 440
COMMON segment combine type, 301-302
common symbols, 389
COMPACT memory model, 308
comparing numbers, 121
co-processors, 245
locking the bus, 248-249
sending commands to, 249
compatibility with MASM, 434-436
conditional
assembly, 37, 41, 42, 389-391
jumps, 207-210, 437
statements in macros, 404-405
%CONDS directive, 454-455
controlling
macro operations, 387-388
memory with BIOS interrupts, 521-526
CPU type, finding with programs, 519-521
.CREF directive, 455
%CREFALL directive, 456
%CREFREF directive, 456
%CREFUREF directive, 456
cross-reference listing file, 28
CS register, 4, 6
%CTLS directive, 456-457
Current Privilege Level (CPL), 260-261
@CurSeg alias, 315
CWD instruction, 125
CWDE instruction, 125, 165-166
CX register, 6

D

DAA instruction, 127-128, 166-167
DAS instruction, 128, 167-168

@Data alias, 315-316
data
aligning, 341-342
definitions, 326-330
numeric, 330
pointer, 330-331
text, 330
expressions, 331-332
numeric expressions, 332-333
operators, 332
text expressions, 333
returning from procedures, 492-495
data segments, 308-309
.DATA directive, 33
DB directive, 346
DD directives, 347
debugging programs, 55-62
DEC instruction, 120-121, 168-169
declaring
segments, 298-303
nested segments, 299
structures, 335
decrementing counters, 120-121
defining
macros, 399
numeric data, 330
pointer data, 330-331
procedures, 393-394
structures, 335
text data, 330
delaying microprocessors, 247-248
demand page virtual addressing, 262-263
%DEPTH directive, 458
Descriptor Privilege Level (DPL), 260
descriptor tables, 255-256
Global Descriptor Table (GDT), 254-255
Interrupt Descriptor Table (IDT), 255
Local Descriptor Table (LDT), 255
destination operand, 115
determining video adapter type, 570-572
device drivers, 11, 13-14
ANSI.SYS, 526, 530-531
ESC functions, 529-531
mouse drivers, 537-541

DF directive, 347-348
DI register, 6
direct addressing mode, 45-47, 67-68
direct base addressing mode, 45, 67
direct indexed addressing mode, 45, 67
direct scaled index addressing mode,
    46, 68
directives, 33
  .186, 447
  .286, 447-448
  .286C, 447-448
  .286P, 448-449
  .287, 449
  .386, 449-450
  .386C, 449-450
  .386P, 450-451
  .387, 451
  .8086, 452
  .8087, 452-453
  ALIGN, 341, 344
  .ALPHA, 305, 311
  ARG, 397-398, 407-408, 492
  ASSUME, 38-39, 306, 312
  %BIN, 453-454
  BYTE, 344-345
  .CODE, 33-34, 308, 314-315
  CODESEG, 308, 314-315
  COMM, 389, 408-410
  COMMENT, 440
  conditional assembly, 37, 41-42
  %CONDS, 454-455
  .CREF, 455
  %CREFALL, 456
  %CREFREF, 456
  %CREFUREF, 456
  %CTLS, 456-457
  .DATA, 33
  DB, 346
  DD, 347
  %DEPTH, 458
  DF, 347-348
  DISPLAY, 438, 457-458
  .DOSSEG, 311
  DOSSEG, 316

DQ, 348
DUP, 349
DW, 349-350
EMUL, 437, 458-459
END, 317
ENDM, 399, 413-414
ENDP, 414
ENDS, 38, 317, 350
EQ, 351-352
EQU, 327-330
ERR, 459-460
ERR1, 459-460
ERR2, 459-460
ERRB, 459-460
ERRDEF, 459-460
ERRDIF, 459-460
ERRDIFI, 459-460
ERRE, 459-460
ERRIDN, 459-460
ERRIDNI, 459-460
ERRIF, 459-460
ERRIF1, 459-460
ERRIF2, 459-460
ERRIFDEF, 459-460
ERRIFDIF, 459-460
ERRIFDIFI, 459-460
ERRIFE, 459-460
ERRIFIDN, 459-460
ERRIFINDI, 459-460
ERRIFNB, 459-460
ERRIFNDEF, 459-460
ERRNB, 459-460
ERRNDEF, 459-460
ERRNZ, 459-460
EVEN, 341, 351
EVENDATA, 351
EXITM, 414-415
expressions, 36, 39
EXTERN, 387-389
EXTRN, 416-417
FAR, 352-353
FWORD, 353-354
GE, 354-355
GLOBAL, 392-393, 418-420

GROUP, 304, 319-320
GT, 355
HIGH, 355-356
IDEAL, 436-437, 461
%INCL, 461-462
INCLUDE, 392, 422
INCLUDELIB, 387, 423
INSTR, 356
IRP, 402-403, 423-424
IRPC, 404, 424-425
JUMPS, 437, 462-463
LABEL, 342, 356-357
.LALL, 463-464
LARGE, 357-358
LE, 358
LENGTH, 358-359
.LFCOND, 464
LIST, 465-466
LOCAL, 398, 425-426
LOCALS, 401-402, 426-427
LOW, 359
LT, 359
MACRO, 427-428
macros, 36, 39-41
MASK, 360
MASM, 466
MASM51, 466-467
MOD, 360-361
.MODEL, 307, 320-321
MODEL, 490
MULTERRS, 467-468
NAME, 468
NE, 361
NEAR, 361-362
%NEWPAGE, 468-469
NOEMUL, 437, 458-459
NOJUMPS, 462-463
NOLOCALS, 426-427
NOT, 362-363
OFFSET, 334, 363
OR, 363-364
ORG, 340, 364
%OUT, 438, 471-472
P186, 472

P286, 472
P286N, 472
P287, 472
P386, 472
P386N, 473
P387, 473
P8086, 473
P8087, 473
PAGE, 475-476
%PAGESIZE, 476-477
%PCNT, 477
PNO87, 473-474
%POPLCTL, 477-478
PROC, 365, 393-395, 397-398, 428-429
procedures, 36, 39-41
processor control, 37
PTR, 366-367
PUBLIC, 387, 430-431
QUIRKS, 478-479
QWORD, 367-368
RADIX, 368-369
RECORD, 369-370
REPT, 402, 431
RETURNS, 492-495
SEG, 334, 370-371
SEGMENT, 38, 299-303, 321-322
.SEQ, 305, 311
SFCOND, 479-480
SHL, 371-372
SHR, 372-373
SIZE, 373
SIZESTR, 373-374
SMALL, 374-375
.STACK, 322-323
STRUC, 375-376
STRUCT, 335
SUBSTR, 377
SUBTTL, 480
symbols, 36, 39
%SYMS, 480-481
SYMTYPE, 378-379
%TABSIZE, 481
TBYTE, 377-378
%TEXT, 481-482

TFCOND, 482-483
TITLE, 483
.TYPE, 378-379
TYPE, 379-380
UNION, 380-381
UNKNOWN, 381-382
WARN, 484-485
WIDTH, 382-384
XOR, 384
display adapters, 566-567
DISPLAY directive, 438, 457-458
displaying numbers, 116-119
DIV instruction, 122-123, 170-171
division, 122-123
DOS extenders, 250-254
.DOSSEG directive, 305, 311
DOSSEG directive, 316
DQ directive, 348
drawing lines, 586-590
    animated lines, 590-597
DS register, 4, 6, 69-70
DUP directive, 349
DW directive, 349-350
DWORD segment align type, 300
DX register, 6

E

effective addresses, 66-68
    segment overrides, 69-70
    storing in registers, 68-69
ELSE conditional assembly directive,
    390, 410
ELSEIF conditional assembly directive, 411
ELSEIF1 conditional assembly directive, 411
ELSEIF2 conditional assembly directive, 411
ELSEIFB conditional assembly directive,
    411
ELSEIFDEF conditional assembly directive,
    411
ELSEIFDIF conditional assembly directive,
    411
ELSEIFE conditional assembly directive, 411

ELSEIFIDN conditional assembly directive,
    411
ELSEIFNB conditional assembly directive,
    411
ELSEIFNDEF conditional assembly direc-
    tive, 411
EMUL directive, 437, 458-459
emulated floating point instructions, 437
END directive, 317
ENDIF conditional assembly directive, 391,
    412-413
ENDM directive, 399, 413-414
ENDP directive, 414
ENDS directive, 38, 317, 350
Enhanced Graphics Adapter (EGA), 566
    graphics modes, 582-584
ENTER instruction, 218, 226-228
entering commands in Turbo Debugger,
    53-54
    function keys, 54
    menus, 54-55
EQ directive, 351-352
EQU directive, 327-330
equipment list (BIOS interrupt), 512
ERR directive, 459-460
ERR1 directive, 459-460
ERR2 directive, 459-460
ERRB directive, 459-460
ERRDEF directive, 459-460
ERRDIF directive, 459-460
ERRDIFI directive, 459-460
ERRE directive, 459-460
ERRIDN directive, 459-460
ERRIDNI directive, 459-460
ERRIF directive, 459-460
ERRIF1 directive, 459-460
ERRIF2 directive, 459-460
ERRIFDEF directive, 459-460
ERRIFDIF directive, 459-460
ERRIFDIFI directive, 459-460
ERRIFE directive, 459-460
ERRIFIDN directive, 459-460
ERRIFINDI directive, 459-460
ERRIFNB directive, 459-460

ERRIFNDEF directive, 459-460
ERRNB directive, 459-460
ERRNDEF directive, 459-460
ERRNZ directive, 459-460
error conditions, 438-439
ES register, 4, 6
ESC functions (ANSI.SYS device driver),
    529-531
ESC instruction, 249, 274-276
EVEN directive, 341, 351
EVENDATA directives, 351
exclusive OR instructions, 136-137
EXITM directives, 414-415
expression operators, 332
expressions directives, 36, 39
EXTERN directive, 387-389, 416-417
external symbols, 387-389

F

FAR directive, 352-353
FAR jumps, 206
far pointers, 70-71
faults, General Protection (GP), 257
fields, bit, 337-338
File Control Blocks (FCBs), 531-535
files
    cross-reference listing, 28
    File Control Blocks (FCB), 531-535
    handles, 531-535
    include files, 391-393
    linking, 25, 28-30
    listing, 28
    MAKE.EXE, 30-33
    object, 25, 28
    reading, 531-535
    source, 22-24
    TASM.CFG, 26
    writing, 531-535
flags
    auxiliary carry, 127
    clearing, 247
    getting, 246
    overflow, 126

parity, 127
saving, 246
setting, 247
sign, 126
status, 126-127
zero, 126
flags register, 5-7
formatting listing files, 443-444
function keys for Turbo Debugger com-
    mands, 54
functions
    see procedures
FWORD directive, 353-354

G

GE directive, 354-355
General Protection (GP) faults, 257
getting flags, 246
Global Descriptor Table (GDT), 254-255
GLOBAL directive, 392-393, 418-420
graphics modes
    line drawing, 586-590
        animated lines, 590-597
    pixels in CGA, 580-582
    pixels in EGA, 582-584
    pixels in VGA, 585
GROUP directive, 304, 319-320
grouping segments, 304
GT directive, 355

H

halting microprocessors, 248
handles (file handles), 531-535
hardware interrupts, 544-546
    8259 interrupt controller chip, 544-545
    interrupt masks, 545-546
    Interrupt Service Routine (ISR), 544
    Interrupt Vector Table (IVT), 544-545
    keyboard controller, 546-551
HIGH directive, 355-356
HLT instruction, 248, 260, 276-277
HUGE memory model, 308

I

I/O operations, 81-83
I/O ports, set-up information, 513-516
IDEAL directive, 436-437, 461
IDEAL mode, 37, 436-437
IDIV instruction, 122-123, 171-172
IF conditional assembly directive, 391, 420-422
IF, THEN, ELSE loops, 212-213
IF1 conditional assembly directive, 391, 420-422
IF2 conditional assembly directive, 391, 420-422
IFB conditional assembly directive, 420-422
IFB conditional assembly directives, 391
IFDEF conditional assembly directive, 420-422
IFDEF conditional assembly directives, 391
IFDIF conditional assembly directive, 391, 420-422
IFDIFI conditional assembly directive, 391, 420-422
IFE conditional assembly directive, 391, 420-422
IFIDN conditional assembly directive, 391, 420-422
IFIDNI conditional assembly directive, 391, 420-422
IFNB conditional assembly directive, 391, 420-422
IFNDEF conditional assembly directive, 391, 420-422
immediate addressing mode, 44, 47, 66
implied addressing mode, 44, 47, 66
IMUL instruction, 122
IN instruction, 81-82, 84
INC instruction, 120-121, 175-176
%INCL directive, 461-462
INCLUDE directive, 392, 422
include files, 391-393
INCLUDELIB directive, 387, 423
inclusive OR instructions, 135-136
incrementing counters, 120-121

indexed addressing mode, 45, 47
indirect jumps, 206-207
    memory far jumps, 207
    memory near jump, 207
    register, 207
initializing serial ports, 552-555
INS instruction, 82-83, 85
INSB instruction, 85
INSD instruction, 85
installing Turbo Assembler, 21-22
INSTR directive, 356
instructions, 43
    AAA, 128, 147-148
    AAD, 128, 148-149
    AAM, 128, 149-150
    AAS, 128, 150-151
    ADC, 151-153
    ADD, 119, 153-154
    AND, 135, 154-155
    arithmetic, 43, 115-116
    ARPL, 260, 268-269
    BCT, 157-159
    bit-shift, 43, 138-139
    BOUND, 80-81, 223-224
    BSR, 156-157
    BT, 157-159
    BTR, 157-159
    BTS, 157-159
    CALL, 215, 224-226
    CBW, 125, 160
    CDQ, 125, 160-161
    CLC, 6, 247, 269-270
    CLD, 6, 247, 270-271
    CLI, 6, 220, 247, 271-272
    CLTS, 260, 266, 272-273
    CMC, 6, 247, 273-274
    CMP, 121, 161-163
    CMPS, 163-164
    CMPSB, 163-164
    CMPSW, 163-164
    CWD, 125, 164-165
    CWDE, 125, 165-166
    DAA, 127-128, 166-167
    DAS, 128, 167-168

data movement, 43, 65-66
DEC, 120-121, 168-169
DIV, 122-123, 170-171
ENTER, 218, 226-228
ESC, 249, 274-276
HLT, 248, 260, 276-277
IDIV, 122-123, 171-172
IMUL, 122, 173-175
IN, 81-82, 84
INC, 120-121, 175-176
INS, 82-83, 85
INSB, 85
INSD, 85
INSW, 85
INT, 219, 228-230
INTO, 220, 230-232
IRET, 219, 232-233
IRETD, 232-233
JA, 234-235
JAE, 234-235
JB, 234-235
JBE, 234-235
JC, 234-235
JCXZ, 214, 236-237
JE, 234-235
JECXZ, 236-237
JG, 234-235
JGE, 234-235
JL, 234-235
JLE, 234-235
JMP, 205-206, 237-239
JNA, 234-235
JNAE, 234-235
JNB, 234-235
JNBE, 234-235
JNC, 234-235
JNE, 234-235
JNG, 234-235
JNGE, 234-235
JNL, 234-235
JNLE, 234-235
JNO, 234-235
JNP, 234-235
JNS, 234-235

JNZ, 234-235
JO, 234-235
JP, 234-235
JPE, 234-235
JPO, 234-235
JS, 234-235
jumps, 43
JZ, 234-235
LAHF, 6, 246, 277-278
LAR, 257-258, 278-279
LDS, 71, 86-87
LEA, 68-69, 88-89
LEAVE, 218, 239-240
LES, 70, 87
LFS, 71, 88
LGDT, 255, 260, 279-281
LGS, 71, 88
LIDT, 255, 260, 279-281
LLDT, 255, 260, 279-281
LMSW, 246, 260, 281-282
LOCK, 282-283
LODS, 79-80, 90-91
logic, 43, 134
LOOP, 213-214, 240-242
loop, 43
LOOPE, 240-242
LOOPNE, 240-242
LOOPNZ, 214
LOOPZ, 214
LSL, 259, 283-284
LSS, 71, 88
LTR, 260, 284-287
MOV, 65-66, 71, 91-93, 260
MOVS, 93-95
MOVSX, 72, 96-97
MOVZX, 72, 97
MUL, 122, 176-178
NEG, 124-125, 178-179
NOP, 247-248
NOT, 137-138, 179-180
OR, 135-136, 180-181
OUT, 81-82, 98-99
OUTS, 82-83, 99-100
POP, 75-76, 100-102

POPA, 76, 102-104
POPAD, 76, 102-104
POPF, 6, 103-104
POPFD, 103-104
procedures, 43
processor control, 44
processor-specific, 433-434
pseudo, 437-438
PUSH, 75-76, 104-105
PUSHA, 76, 105-106
PUSHAD, 76, 105-106
PUSHF, 6, 76, 107-108
PUSHFD, 76, 107-108
RCL, 139-140, 182-183
RCR, 139-140, 183-186
RET, 215, 217, 242-243
RETF, 215, 242-243
RETN, 215, 242-243
ROL, 139-140
ROR, 139-140, 186-188
SAHF, 6, 246, 288
SAL, 140-143, 188-189
SAR, 140-143, 190-191
SBB, 119-120, 196-198
SCAS, 198-199
SCASB, 198-199
SCASW, 198-199
SET, 73-74, 109-111
SGDT, 260, 288-289
SHL, 140-143, 191
SHLD, 192-193
SHR, 140-143, 193-194
SHRD, 143, 194-196
SIDT, 255, 260, 288-289
SLDT, 255, 260, 288-289
SMSW, 246, 289-290
STC, 6, 247
STD, 6, 247, 290-291
STI, 6, 247, 291
STOS, 79-80, 111-112
STR, 291-292
SUB, 119-120, 199, 200-201
TEST, 138, 201-203
VERR, 259, 292-293

VERW, 259, 292-293
WAIT, 249, 293-294
XCHG, 71, 112-113
XLAT, 71-72, 113-114
XLATB, 113-114
XOR, 136-137, 203-204
INSW instruction, 85
INT instruction, 219, 228-230
Interrupt Descriptor Table (IDT), 255
Interrupt Service Routine (ISR), 544
Interrupt Vector Table (IVT), 544-545
interrupts, 8-9
    see also BIOS interrupts and hardware
        interrupts
    accessing assembly language from high-
        level languages, 490
    interrupt handler routines, 218-222
    interrupt masks, 545-546
    interrupt vector table, 8
    interrupt vectors, 220-221
INTO instruction, 220, 230-232
IP register, 5, 205-206
IRET instruction, 219, 232-233
IRETD instruction, 232-233
IRP directive, 402-403, 423-424
IRPC directive, 404, 424-425
iterating loops, 213-214

J

JA instruction, 234-235
JAE instructions, 234-235
JB instruction, 234-235
JBE instruction, 234-235
JC instruction, 234-235
JCXZ instruction, 214, 236-237
JE instruction, 234-235
JECXZ, 236-237
JG instruction, 234-235
JGE instruction, 234-235
JL instruction, 234-235
JLE instruction, 234-235
JMP instruction, 205-206, 237-239
JNA instruction, 234-235

JNAE instruction, 234-235
JNB instruction, 234-235
JNBE instruction, 234-235
JNC instruction, 234-235
JNE instruction, 234-235
JNG instruction, 234-235
JNGE instruction, 234-235
JNL instruction, 234-235
JNLE instruction, 234-235
JNO instruction, 234-235
JNP instruction, 234-235
JNS instruction, 234-235
JNZ instruction, 234-235
JO instruction, 234-235
JP instruction, 234-235
JPE instruction, 234-235
JPO instruction, 234-235
JS instruction, 234-235
jump instructions, 43
jumping
    conditional jumps, 207-210, 437
    FAR jumps, 206
    indirect jumps, 206-207
    IP register, 205-206
    NEAR jumps, 206
    SHORT jumps, 206
JUMPS directive, 437, 462-463
JZ instruction, 234-235

K-L

keyboard controller, 546-551
LABEL directive, 342, 356-357
LAHF instruction, 6, 246, 277-278
.LALL directive, 463-464
LAR instruction, 257-258, 278-279
LARGE directive, 357-358
LARGE memory model, 308
LDS instruction, 71, 86-87
LE directives, 358
LEA instruction, 68-69, 88-89
LEAVE instruction, 218, 239-240
LENGTH directive, 358-359
LES instruction, 70, 87

.LFCOND directive, 464
LFS instruction, 71, 88
LGDT instruction, 260, 279-281
LGDT instructions, 255
LGS instruction, 71, 88
LIDT instruction, 255, 260, 279-281
LIM EMS memory, 524-526
lines
    drawing, 586-590
        animated lines, 590-597
linking files, 25, 28-30
LIST directive, 465-466
listing files, 28, 440-443
    controlling entries, 444
    controls, 446
    formatting, 443-444
    symbol table, 445-446
LLDT instruction, 255, 260, 279-281
LMSW instruction, 246, 260, 281-282
Local Descriptor Table (LDT), 255
LOCAL directive, 398, 425-426
local labels in macros, 401-402
LOCALS directive, 401-402, 426-427
location counter, 340
    setting, 340
LOCK instruction, 282-283
LOCK prefix, 249
locking the bus, 248-249
LODS instruction, 79-80, 90-91
logic instructions, 43, 134
    AND, 135, 154-155
    NOT, 137-138, 179-180
    OR, 135-136, 180-181
    TEST, 138, 201-203
    testing bits, 138
    XOR, 136-137, 203-204
LOOP instruction, 213-214, 240-242
LOOPE instruction, 240-242
LOOPNE instruction, 240-242
LOOPNZ instruction, 214
loops
    IF, THEN, ELSE, 212-213
    in macros, 402-404
    IRP directive, 402-403

IRPC directive, 404
iterating, 213-214
loop instructions, 43
REPT directive, 402
WHILE, 210-212
LOOPZ instruction, 214
LOW directive, 359
LSL instruction, 259, 283-284
LSS instruction, 71, 88
LT directive, 359
LTR instruction, 260, 284-287

M

Machine Status Word (MSW), 246
MACRO directive, 427-428
macros
    conditional statements, 404-405
    defining, 399
    directives, 36, 39-41
    local labels, 401-402
    loops, 402-404
    passing arguments to, 399-400
        operators, 400
MAKE utility, 30-33
MASK directive, 360
MASM (Microsoft Assembler), 37
    Turbo Assembler compatibility, 434-436
MASM directive, 466
MASM mode, 435-436
MASM51 directive, 466-467
MEDIUM memory model, 308
memory
    addressing segments and offsets, 305-306
    aligning data, 341-342
    bit fields, 337-338
    controlling with BIOS interrupts, 521-526
    finding with programs, 516-517
    LIM EMS, 524-526
    loading far pointers, 70-71
    location counter, 340
        setting, 340
    MS-DOS, 16-17
    paging, 262-263

protected mode, 254-255
    selectors, 255-259
registers, 5-7
segmented, 4-5
stack, 7-8
TSRs, 521-523
memory far jumps, 207
Memory Management Units (MMU),
    262-263
memory models, 307
memory near jumps, 207
MEMORY segment combine types, 302
menus, Turbo Debugger commands, 54-55
microprocessors
    80386, 73-74
    80x86, 4
        interrupts, 8-9
        memory, 4-8
    co-processors, 245
    delays, 247-248
    finding CPU type with programs, 519-521
    halting, 248
    processor-specific instructions, 433-434
MOD directive, 360-361
.MODEL directive, 307, 320-321
MODEL directive, 490
modes
    addresssing, 66-68
    IDEAL, 37, 436-437
    MASM, 435-436
modular programming, 389-391
    calling between high-level and assembly
        languages, 490, 492-495
    common symbols, 389
    compilers for high-level languages,
        497-507
    conditional statements
        macros, 404-405
    external symbols, 387-389
    include files, 391-393
    macros
        defining, 399
        local labels, 401-402
        loops, 402-404
        passing arguments to, 399-400

procedures, 393
   defining, 393-394
   passing variables, 395, 397-398
   returning variables, 395, 397-398
   saving registers, 394-395
  public symbols, 387
  sharing data between high-level and
   assembly languages, 495-496
  start-up modules for high-level languages,
   507-508
monitors, 567
Monochrome Display Adapter (MDA), 566
mouse, 537-541
MOV instruction, 65-66, 71, 91-93, 260
moving data, 65-66
  addressing modes, 66-68
  effective addresses
   segment overrides, 69-70
   storing in registers, 68-69
  exchanging values, 71
  loading far pointers, 70-71
  stack frames, 76-77
  string operations, 77-80
MOVS instruction, 93-95
MOVSX instruction, 72, 96-97
MOVZX instruction, 72, 97
MS-DOS
  device drivers, 11, 13-14
  file system, 9-11
  memory management, 16-17
  peripherals, 18-19
  program execution, 14-16
MUL instruction, 122, 176-178
MULTERRS directive, 467-468
Multi Color Graphics Array (MCGA), 566
multiplication, 122
multitasking, 245
  task gate, 263
  Task Register (TR), 263
  Task State Segment (TSS), 263
  task switching, 263-266
  testing for task switches, 266

N

NAME directive, 468
NE directives, 361
NEAR directive, 361-362
NEAR jumps, 206
near pointers, 70-71
NEG instruction, 124-125, 178-179
nested segments, 299
%NEWPAGE directive, 468-469
NOEMUL directive, 437, 458-459
NOJUMPS directive, 462-463
NOLOCALS directive, 426-427
NOP instruction, 247-248
NOT directive, 362-363
NOT instruction, 137-138, 179-180
numbers
  BCD (Binary Coded Decimal), 127-129
  comparing, 121
  displaying, 116-119
numeric data, defining, 330
numeric expressions, 332-333

O

object files, 25, 28
OFFSET directive, 334, 363
offsets (segments), 305-306
operators
  AND, 343
  CATSTR, 345-346
  expression operators, 332
  pointer, 333-334
OR directive, 363-364
OR instruction, 135-136, 180-181
ORG directive, 340, 364
%OUT directive, 471-472
OUT instruction, 81-82, 98-99
OUTS instruction, 82-83, 99-100
overflow flag, 126

P

P186 directive, 472
P286 directive, 472
P286N directive, 472
P287 directive, 472
P386 directive, 472
P386N directive, 473
P387 directive, 473
P8086 directive, 473
P8087 directive, 473
PAGE directive, 475-476
PAGE segment align type, 300
%PAGESIZE directive, 476-477
paging memory, 262-263
  demand page virtual addressing, 262-263
palettes (color), 568-571
PARA segment align type, 300
parallel ports, 535-537
parity bit, 555
parity flag, 127
PASCAL calling convention, 218, 492
passing
  arguments to macros, 399-400
    operators, 400
  variables to procedures, 395, 397-398
%PCNT directive, 477
peripherals, 18-19
PNO87 directive, 473-474
pointers
  defining, 330-331
  far, 70-71
  near, 70-71
  pointer operators, 333-334
POP instruction, 75-76, 100-102
POPA instruction, 76, 102-104
POPAD instruction, 76, 102-104
POPF instruction, 6, 103-104
POPFD instruction, 103-104
%POPLCTL directive, 477-478
popping data off the stack, 75-76
ports
  parallel, 535-537
  serial, 535-537

initializing, 552-555
  reading from, 555-558
  writing to, 558-563
prefixes
  LOCK, 249
  REP, 78-79
printing characters to screen, 574-578
PRIVATE segment combine type, 303
privilege levels
  call gates, 261-262
  Current Privilege Level (CPL), 260-261
  Descriptor Privilege Level (DPL), 260
  in protected mode, 260-262
PROC directive, 365, 393-395, 397-398, 428-429
procedures, 393
  defining, 393-394
  directives, 36, 39-41
  instructions, 43
  passing variables to, 395, 397-398
  returning data from, 492-495
  returning variables, 395, 397-398
  saving registers, 394-395
processor control directives, 37
processor control instructions, 44
processor-specific instructions, 433-434
Program Segment Prefix (PSP), 15, 305
programs
  debugging, 55-62
  structure, 23-24
protected mode, 245, 249-250
  descriptor tables, 254-256
  DOS extenders, 250-254
  memory, 254-255
    selectors, 255-259
  privilege levels, 260-262
  switching into, 250-254
  versions of Turbo Debugger, 52
pseudo instructions, 437-438
PSP (Program Segment Prefix), 15
PTR directive, 366-367
PUBLIC directive, 387, 430-431
PUBLIC segment combine type, 302
public symbols, 387

push immediate data instructions, 437-438
PUSH instruction, 75-76, 104-105
PUSHA instruction, 76, 105-106
PUSHAD instruction, 76, 105-106
PUSHF instruction, 6, 76, 107-108
PUSHFD instruction, 76, 107-108
pushing data on the stack, 75-76

Q-R

QUIRKS directive, 478-479
QWORD directive, 367-368
RADIX directive, 368
RCL instruction, 139-140, 182-183
RCR instruction, 139-140, 183-186
reading files, 531-535
reading from serial ports, 555-558
Real Time Clock (RTC) chip, 514-516
RECORD directive, 369-370
recursion, 216
register indirect jump, 207
registers, 5-7
  AX, 6
  BP, 6, 69-70
  BX, 6
  CS, 4, 6
  CX, 6
  DI, 6
  DS, 4, 6, 69-70
  DX, 6
  ES, 4, 6
  flags, 5-7
  IP, 5, 205-206
  saving, 394-395
  SI, 6
  SP, 6-7
  SS, 4, 6-7, 69-70
  storing effective addresses, 68-69
REP prefix, 78-79
REPT directive, 402, 431
restoring listing file controls, 446
RET instruction, 215, 217, 242-243
RETF instruction, 215, 242-243

RETN instruction, 215, 242-243
returning
  data from procedures, 492-495
  from subroutines, 215
  variables from procedures, 395, 397-398
RETURNS directive, 492-495
ROL instruction, 139-140
ROR instruction, 139-140, 186-188
rotating bits, 139-140

S

SAHF instruction, 6, 246, 288
SAL instruction, 140-143, 188-189
SAR instruction, 140-143, 190-191
saving
  flags, 246
  listing files controls, 446
  registers, 394-395
SBB instruction, 119-120, 196-198
SCAS instruction, 198-199
SCASB instruction, 198-199
SCASW instruction, 198-199
SEG directive, 334, 370-371
SEGMENT directive, 38, 299-303, 321-322
segments, 37-39
  aligning, 299
  classes, 303
  code, 308
  combining, 300-303
  data, 308-309
  declaring, 298-303
  grouping, 304
  memory models, 307
  offsets, 305-306
  overrides, 69-70
  Program Segment Prefix (PSP), 305
  size, 303
  sorting, 305
  stack, 309
sending commands to co-processors, 249
.SEQ directive, 305, 311

serial ports, 535-537, 551-552
  finding with programs, 518
  initializing, 552-555
  reading from, 555-558
  writing to, 558-563
  XMODEM protocol, 559-563
SET instruction, 73-74, 109-111
set-up information, I/O ports, 513-516
setting
  flags, 247
  location counter, 340
SFCOND directive, 479-480
SGDT instruction, 260
SGDT instructions, 288-289
shift operations, 140-143
SHL directive, 371-372
SHL instruction, 140-143, 191
SHLD instruction, 192-193
SHLD instructions, 143
SHORT jumps, 206
SHR directive, 373
SHR instruction, 140-143, 193-194
SHRD instruction, 143, 194-196
SI register, 6
SIDT instruction, 255, 260, 288-289
sign flag, 126
signed arithmetic, 124
  changing signs, 124-125
  division, 126
  multiplication, 126
  sign extending, 125-126
SIZE directive, 373
size of segments, 303
SIZESTR directive, 373-374
SLDT instruction, 255, 260, 288-289
SMALL directive, 374-375
SMALL memory model, 308
SMSW instruction, 246, 289-290
snow on CGA, 573-574
sorting segments, 305
source files
  assembling, 25
  creating, 22-24
  listing files, 440-443, 445-446

source operand, 115
SP register, 6-7
squeezing out unused bits with bit-shift
    instructions, 143-145
SS register, 4, 6-7, 69-70
.STACK directive, 322-323
stack, 7-8
  handling arguments in Turbo Assembler,
    492
  popping data, 75-76
  pushing data, 75-76
  segment, 309
  stack frames, 76-77, 126-127, 490-491
    C calling convention, 491-492
    PASCAL calling convention, 492
    subroutines, 215-218
  stack pointer, 74-75
STACK segment combine type, 302
start-up modules for high-level languages,
    507-508
status flags, 126-127
  auxiliary carry, 127
  overflow flag, 126
  parity flag, 127
  sign flag, 126
  zero flag, 126
STC instruction, 6, 247
STD instruction, 6, 247
STD instructions, 290-291
STI instruction, 6, 247, 291
stop bit, 555
STOS instruction, 79-80, 111-112
STR instruction, 291-292
string operations, 77-79
  loading data, 79-80
  storing data, 79-80
STRUC directive, 375-376
STRUCT directive, 335
structure of programs, 23-24
structures
  accessing fields, 335-336
  declaring, 335
  defining, 335

SUB instruction, 119-120, 199-201
subroutines, 214
    calling, 215
    recursion, 216
    returning from, 215
    stack frames, 215-218
SUBSTR directive, 377
subtraction, 119-120
SUBTTL directive, 480
switching into protected mode, 250-254
switching tasks, 263-266
    testing for task switching, 266
symbol directives, 36, 39
symbol tables in listing files, 445-446
symbols
    common, 389
    external, 387-389
    public, 387
%SYMS directive, 480-481
SYMTYPE directive, 378-379
system clock, 514-516
system resources
    CPU type, 519-521
    memory, 516-517
    serial ports, 518

T

%TABSIZE directive, 481
task gate, 263
Task Register (TR), 263
Task State Segment (TSS), 263
task switching, 263-266
    testing for task switches, 266
TASM.CFG file, 26
TBYTE directive, 377-378
terminal I/O functions, 526-531
    ANSI.SYS device driver, 526, 529-531
TEST instruction, 138, 201-203
testing bits (logic instructions), 138
testing for task switches, 266
%TEXT directive, 481-482

text expressions, 333
text mode (video adapters), 572
TFCOND directive, 482-483
THIS operator, 378
TINY memory model, 308
TITLE directive, 483
TLINK command-line options, 603
TSRs, 521-523
Turbo Assembler
    command-line options, 601-602
    cross-reference listing, 28
    installing, 21-22
    linking files, 28-30
    listing file, 28
    MASM compatibility, 434-436
    object files, 28
    program structure, 23-24
    TASM command
        switches, 27
    TASM.CFG file, 26
Turbo Debugger, 51-52
    commands/command keys, 605-607,
        608-610
    debugging programs, 55-62
    entering commands, 53-54
        function keys, 54
        menus, 54-55
    protected mode versions, 52
    screen components, 52-53
TYPE directive, 379-380

U

UNION directive, 380-381
unions, 336-337
UNKNOWN directive, 381-382

V

values, exchanging, 71
VERR instruction, 259, 292-293
VERW instruction, 259, 292-293

video
    clearing screen, 578-579
    Color Graphics Adapter (CGA)
        graphics modes, 580-582
        snow, 573-574
    color palettes, 568-571
    determining adapter type, 570-572
    drawing lines, 586-597
    Enhanced Graphics Adapter, 566
        graphics modes, 582-584
    hardware, 566-567
    printing characters to screen, 574-578
    text mode, 572
    Video Graphics Array, 566
        graphics modes, 585
        video modes, 568
Virtual Graphics Array (VGA)
    graphics modes, 585

W

WAIT instruction, 249, 293-294
WARN directive, 484-485
WHILE loop, 210-212
WIDTH directive, 382-384
WORD segment align type, 300
writing
    characters to screen, 574-578
    to files, 531-535
    to serial ports, 558-563

X-Z

XCHG instruction, 71, 112-113
XLAT instruction, 71-72, 113-114
XLATB instruction, 113-114
XMODEM telecommunications protocol, 559-563
XOR directive, 384
XOR instruction, 136-137, 203-204
zero flag, 126

The Waite Group

100 Shoreline Highway, Suite 285   Mill Valley, CA 94941   (415) 331-0575

Compuserve: 75146,3515   usenet:hplabs!well!mitch   AppleLink: D2097

Dear Reader:

Thank you for considering the purchase of our book. Readers have come to know products from **The Waite Group** for the care and quality we put into them. Let me tell you a little about our group and how we make our books.

It started in 1976 when I could not find a computer book that really taught me anything. The books that were available talked down to people, lacked illustrations and examples, were poorly laid out, and were written as if you already understood all the terminology. So I set out to write a good book about microcomputers. This was to be a special book—very graphic, with a friendly and casual style, and filled with examples. The result was an instant best-seller.

Over the years, I developed this approach into a "formula" (nothing really secret here, just a lot of hard work—I am a crazy man about technical accuracy and high-quality illustrations). I began to find writers who wanted to write books in this way. This lead to coauthoring and then to multiple-author books and many more titles (over seventy titles currently on the market). As The Waite Group author base grew, I trained a group of editors to manage our products. We now have a team devoted to putting together the best possible book package and maintaining the high standard of our existing books.

We greatly appreciate and use any advice our readers send us (and you send us a lot). We have discovered that our readers are detail nuts: you want indexes that really work, tables of contents that dig deeply into the subject, illustrations, tons of examples, reference cards, and more.

The Waite Group's Turbo Assembler Bible is an example of how even a reference book can be fun to read and use. It is the sixth entry in our popular "Bible" series, and readers keep asking for more! This Bible answers the requests of many programmers who have outgrown tutorial books on TASM and the Microsoft Macro Assembler and are in need of a complete reference guide to processor instructions, TASM directives, and macros. This book features concise tutorials and complete reference entries including compatibility boxes, clear syntax statements, real-world examples, comments, cross-references, details on flags, timing, undocumented features, and little-known facts.

If you also use the Microsoft Macro Assembler, you might want to explore our companion book, *The Waite Group's Microsoft Macro Assembler Bible*. If you're a C programmer learning assembly language, you may be interested in *The Waite Group's Microsoft C Bible* or *The Waite Group's Turbo C++ Bible*. If you'd like to extend your knowledge of C and C++ programming, you'll want to take a look at some of our other titles, including *The Waite Group's C Programming Using Turbo C++* and *The Waite Group's Microsoft C Programming for the PC*, two best-selling tutorial books. If you are interested in learning C using the computer as a teacher, you'll want to order our new software product *Master C*, explained in the back of this book. A list of all our titles follows this letter. In fact, let us know which topics you've been unable to find, and we'll try to write about them.

Thanks again for considering the purchase of this title. If you care to tell me anything you like (or don't like) about the book, please write or send email to the addresses on this letterhead.

Sincerely,

Mitchell Waite
The Waite Group

★★ # The Waite Group Library

If you enjoyed this book, you may be interested in these additional subjects and titles from The Waite Group and SAMS. Reader level is as follows: ★ = introductory, ★★ = intermediate, ★★★ = advanced, Δ = all levels. You can order these books by calling 1-800-628-7360.

Level	Title	Catalog #	Price	
	━━━━━ C and C++ Programming Language ━━━━━			
Tutorial, UNIX & ANSI				
★	The New C Primer Plus, Waite and Prata	22687	$29.95	
★	C: Step-by-Step, Waite and Prata	22651	$29.95	
★★	C++ Programming, Berry	22619	$24.95	
Tutorial, Product Specific				
★	Microsoft C Programming for the PC, Second Edition, Lafore	22738	$29.95	NEW
★	Turbo C Programming for the PC, Revised Edition, Lafore	22660	$29.95	
★	C Programming Using Turbo C++, Lafore	22737	$29.95	
Reference, Product Specific				
★★	Microsoft C Bible, 2nd Edition, Barkakati	22736	$29.95	NEW
★★	QuickC Bible, Barkakati	22632	$29.95	
★★	Turbo C Bible, Barkakati	22631	$29.95	
★★	Turbo C++ Bible, Second Edition, Barkakati	22742	$29.95	NEW
	━━━━━ DOS ━━━━━			
Tutorial, General Users				
★	Discovering MS-DOS, O'Day	22407	$19.95	
★	Understanding MS-DOS, Second Edition, The Waite Group	27298	$19.95	
Tutorial/Reference, General Users				
★★	MS-DOS Bible, Third Edition, Simrin	22693	$24.95	
Tutorial/Reference, Power Users				
★★	Tricks of the MS-DOS Masters, Second Edition, The Waite Group	22717	$29.95	
★★★	MS-DOS Developer's Guide, Second Edition, The Waite Group	22630	$29.95	NEW
	━━━━━ UNIX Operating System ━━━━━			
Tutorial, General Users				
★	UNIX System V Primer, Revised Edition, Waite, Prata, and Martin	22570	$29.95	
★★	UNIX System V Bible, Prata and Martin	22562	$29.95	
★	UNIX Primer Plus, Second Edition, Waite, Prata, Martin	22729	$29.95	
★★	UNIX Communications, Second Edition, Henderson, Anderson, Costales	22773	$29.95	
Tutorial/Reference, Power Users and Programmers				
★★	Tricks of the UNIX Masters, Sage	22449	$29.95	
	━━━━━ Assembly Language ━━━━━			
Tutorial/Reference, General Users				
★★	Microsoft Macro Assembler Bible, Barkakati	22659	$29.95	

Processor Instructions and Turbo Assembler Directives Arranged by Subject

---

NOTE: (286) means instruction is available in 80286 and 80386 only. (386) marks instructions that are 80386-specific. Unmarked instructions are available on all 80x86 processors.

Processor Instructions

Data Movement

IN, *84*
INS (286), *85*
LDS, *86*
LEA, *88*
LES, *87*
LFS (386), *88*
LGS (386), *88*
LODS, *90*
LSS (386), *88*
MOV, *91*
MOVS, *93*
MOVSX (386), *96*
MOVZX (386), *97*
OUT, *98*
OUTS (286), *99*
POP, *100*
POPA (286), *102*
POPF, *103*
PUSH, *104*
PUSHA (286), *105*
PUSHF, *107*
REP, *109*
REPE or REPZ, *109*
REPNE or REPNZ, *109*
STOS, *111*
XCHG, *112*
XLAT or XLATB, *113*

Arithmetic, Logical, and Bit Shift Operations

AAA, *147*
AAD, *148*
AAM, *149*
AAS, *150*
ADC, *151*
ADD, *153*
AND, *343*
[...] (386), *156*
[...], *156*
[...] *57*
[...] *60*
[...]

CWDE (386), *165*
DAA, *166*
DAS, *167*
DEC, *168*
DIV, *170*
IDIV, *171*
IMUL, *173*
INC, *175*
MUL, *176*
NEG, *178*
NOT, *179*
OR, *180*
RCL, *182*
RCR, *183*
ROL, *185*
ROR, *186*
SAL or SHL, *191*
SAR, *190*
SBB, *196*
SCAS, *198*
SETA or SETNBE (386), *109*
SETAE or SETNB (386), *109*
SETB or SETNAE (386), *109*
SETBE or SETNA (386), *109*
SETC (386), *109*
SETE or SETZ (386), *109*
SETG or SETNLE (386), *109*
SETGE or SETNL (386), *109*
SETL or SETNGE (386), *109*
SETLE or SETNG (386), *109*
SETNC (386), *109*
SETNE or SETNZ (386), *109*
SETNO (386), *109*
SETNP or SETPO (386), *109*
SETNS (386), *109*
SETO (386), *109*
SETP or SETPE (386), *109*
SETS (386), *109*
SHLD (386), *192*
SHR, *193*
SHRD (386), *194*
SUB, *199*
TEST, *201*
XOR, *203*

Procedures, Loops, and Jumps

BOUND (286), *223*
CALL, *224*
ENTER (286), *226*
INT, *228*
INTO, *230*
IRET, *232*
JA or JNBE, *234*

JAE or JNB, *234*
JB or JNAE, *234*
JBE or JNA, *234*
JC, *234*
JCXZ or JECXZ, *236*
JE or JZ, *234*
JG or JNLE, *234*
JGE or JNL, *234*
JL or JNGE, *234*
JLE or JNZ, *234*
JMP, *237*
JNC, *234*
JNE or JNG, *234*
JNO, *234*
JNP or JPO, *234*
JNS, *234*
JO, *234*
JP or JPE, *234*
JS, *234*
LEAVE (286), *239*
LOOP, *240*
LOOPE or LOOPZ, *240*
LOOPNE or LOOPNZ, *240*
RET, *242*
RETF, *242*
RETN, *242*

Processor Control and Protected Mode Operation

ARPL (286), *268*
CLC, *269*
CLD, *270*
CLI, *271*
CLTS (286), *272*
CMC, *273*
ESC, *274*
HLT, *276*
LAHF, *277*
LAR (286), *278*
LGDT (286), *279*
LIDT (286), *279*
LLDT (286), *279*
LMSW (286), *281*
LOCK, *282*
LSL (286), *283*
LTR (286), *284*
NOP, *247*
SAHF, *288*
SGDT (286), *288*
SIDT(286), *288*
SLDT (286), *288*
SMSW (286), *289*
STC, *269*

Waite Group Reader Feedback Card **SAMS**

Help Us Make A Better Book

To better serve our readers, we would like your opinion on the contents and quality of this book. Please fill out this card and return it to *The Waite Group*, 100 Shoreline Hwy., Suite A-285, Mill Valley, CA, 94941 (415) 331-0575.

Name _____

Company _____

Address _____

City _____

State _____ ZIP _____ Phone _____

1. How would you rate the content of this book?

- ☐ Excellent
- ☐ Very Good
- ☐ Good
- ☐ Fair
- ☐ Below Average
- ☐ Poor

2. What were the things you liked *most* about this book?

- ☐ Content
- ☐ Pace
- ☐ Writing Style
- ☐ Accuracy
- ☐ Compat. Boxes
- ☐ Listings
- ☐ Reference
- ☐ Format
- ☐ Examples
- ☐ Index
- ☐ Jump Table
- ☐ Cover
- ☐ Price
- ☐ Illustrations
- ☐ Construction

3. Please explain the one thing you liked *most* about this book.
_____
_____
_____

4. What were the things you liked *least* about this book?

- ☐ Content
- ☐ Pace
- ☐ Writing Style
- ☐ Accuracy
- ☐ Compat. Boxes
- ☐ Listings
- ☐ Reference
- ☐ Format
- ☐ Examples
- ☐ Index
- ☐ Jump Table
- ☐ Cover
- ☐ Price
- ☐ Illustrations
- ☐ Construction

5. Please explain the one thing you liked *least* about this book.
_____
_____
_____

6. How do you use this book? For work, recreation, look-up, self-training, classroom, etc?
_____
_____
_____
_____
_____

7. How would you rate your assembly language programming skills?

- ☐ Beginning
- ☐ Advanced
- ☐ Intermediate
- ☐ Professional

8. Where did you purchase this particular book?

- ☐ Book Chain
- ☐ Small Book Store
- ☐ Computer Store
- ☐ Other: _____
- ☐ Direct Mail
- ☐ Book Club
- ☐ School Book Store

_____

9. Can you name another similar book you like better than this one, or one that is as good, and tell us why?
_____
_____

10. How many Waite Group books do you own? _____

11. What are your favorite Waite Group books?
_____
_____

12. What topics or specific titles would you like to see The Waite Group develop?
_____
_____
_____

13. What version of Turbo Assembler are you using?
_____

14. What other programming languages do you know?
_____

15. Any other comments you have about this book or other Waite Group titles?
_____
_____
_____
_____

16. ☐ Check here to receive a free Waite Group catalog.